Documents of the American Revolution

Volume I

Calendar
1770–1771

DOCUMENTS
OF THE
AMERICAN REVOLUTION

1770–1783

(Colonial Office Series)

Volume I

CALENDAR
1770–1771

Edited by
K. G. DAVIES

IRISH UNIVERSITY PRESS
Shannon   Ireland

CONTENTS

ACKNOWLEDGEMENTS

The editor gratefully acknowledges help received from Dr R. F. Hunnisett, Miss Daphne Gifford, and Mr L. G. Seed, all of the staff of the Public Record Office; and from the typists of the Irish University Press, in particular Mrs Valerie Barrett and Miss Teresa Hall. The copy-editing was done by Miss Clare Craven also of the Irish University Press.

INTRODUCTION

The Colonial Office records at the Public Record Office, London, supply the principal documentation of the British administration of North America and—from the British point of view—of the revolution which ended it.[1] Formed by the archives of the Secretary of State and the Board of Trade, they are records of administrative action: to evaluate them it is necessary to know a little of these two branches of British government and of their relationship to one another.[2]

In the first half of the eighteenth century colonial business was the responsibility of one of the two 'ancient' Secretaries of State, the Secretary for the Southern Department, to whom the colonies were assigned as an additional burden on top of his diplomatic duties. Thomas Pelham-Holles, Duke of Newcastle, who held the post from 1724 to 1754, carried this burden lightly, giving no very high priority to colonial matters. By the middle of the eighteenth century, after nearly thirty years of Newcastle, Britain had an extensive, burgeoning Atlantic empire but central institutions inadequate to govern it. Much of the work which Newcastle did not do fell to the Lords Commissioners for Trade and Plantations, commonly called the Board of Trade. This body, created in 1696 to investigate and advise the government on commercial and colonial affairs, was endowed with little or no executive authority; yet by Newcastle's default, it was left to conduct a great deal of the necessary correspondence with the American and West Indian colonies.[3] Since the Board could not act, and the Secretary of State would not, an atmosphere of cheerful *laissez-faire* prevailed in the administration of America in which the colonists established useful precedents for independence.

The French wars in mid-eighteenth century shocked the British government into greater awareness of American problems and into the contemplation of change. Two approaches to reform were tried at the

---

1　The most easily available descriptions of and guides to the Colonial Office records are *Guide to the Contents of the Public Record Office* (London, H.M.S.O., 1963), Vol. II, p. 52; Ralph B. Pugh, *The Records of the Colonial and Dominion Offices*, Public Record Office Handbooks No. 3 (London, H.M.S.O., 1964); *Public Record Office, Lists and Indexes*, No. XXXVI (London, H.M.S.O., 1911; New York, Kraus Reprint, 1963); Charles M. Andrews, *Guide to the Materials for American History to 1783, in the Public Record Office of Great Britain*, Vol. I, The State Papers (Washington, D.C., Carnegie Institution of Washington, 1912; New York, Kraus Reprint, 1965).

2　Margaret M. Spector, *The American Department of the British Government, 1768–1782* (New York, Columbia University Press, 1940); Arthur H. Basye, *The Lords Commissioners of Trade and Plantations* (New Haven, Yale University Press, 1925).

3　In the year 1738, for example, the Secretary of State for the Southern Department received about eighty letters on American and West Indian business but originated only twelve. The Board of Trade originated eighty-two letters and its secretary fifty-five. *Calendar of State Papers, America and West Indies*, Vol. XLIV, 1738 (London, H.M.S.O., 1969).

centre. The first, which lasted from 1752 to 1761, was an experiment in governing America by means of the Board of Trade, which under an ambitious President, George Montagu Dunk, Earl of Halifax, was given a share of colonial patronage and a near-monopoly of correspondence with colonial governors, only the most important and most secret matters being reserved for the Secretary of State's attention. These arrangements were not deemed a success, virtually ending with Halifax's resignation in 1761 and completely given up in the next few years. By 1770 the Board of Trade had not only been stripped of the authority Halifax had won for it but had suffered a decline of prestige from which it was never to recover.

The second approach to reform also owed something to Halifax, who aspired to occupy a third Secretaryship of State with responsibility for the colonies. He did not succeed; but in 1768 the third Secretaryship, for the American Department, was instituted and Wills Hill, 1st Earl of Hillsborough, appointed to it. By this time all possibility of rivalry between Secretary and Board (if such had ever seriously existed) had disappeared. The new Secretary, if not accorded all the respect due to the 'ancient' Secretaries, was a leading minister specializing in colonial business, the member of the Board little more than his creatures. Hillsborough himself was President of the Board, attending many of, if not all, its meetings and signing most of, if not all, its letters. His senior under-secretary, John Pownall, was the Board's secretary, the interlocking of the two offices being such that it is not always easy to tell in which capacity Pownall was acting. Although the two establishments remained separate, the distinction between Secretary of State and Board of Trade by 1770 is of importance chiefly in explaining the archives kept by each, which have merged to form the present-day Colonial Office records.

Records of the Secretary of State

The Secretary of State's regular correspondents in North America were:

(i) the governors or acting governors of the eighteen British colonies;

(ii) the commander-in-chief of British land-forces in North America, in 1770 Lieutenant-General Thomas Gage;

(iii) the two Superintendants of Indian Affairs, Sir William Johnson for the Northern District, and Captain John Stuart for the Southern District;

(iv) the officials engaged upon the general survey of North America, Captain Samuel Holland and William Gerard De Brahm.

These letters, originals from America, drafts from Whitehall, form the core of the Colonial Office records before the Revolution. Hillsborough occasionally received dispatches from other Crown servants in America and usually replied to them; but apart from John Wentworth, who was Surveyor of the King's Woods as well as Governor of New Hampshire, and John Duport, Chief Justice of the new colony in the Island of St John, he did not have regular correspondence with them. It was not unknown for him to write to private petitioners in America, such as Lieutenant George McDougall whose claim to Hog Island, Detroit, was something of an embarrassment to government in 1770; but such miscellaneous correspondence formed only a small fraction of the letters passing in and out of his office.

The distribution of Hillsborough's American correspondence in 1770–1771 is as follows:

	IN LETTERS		OUT LETTERS	
	1770	1771	1770	1771
(i) *Governors*				
Connecticut	2	1	3	1
East Florida	11	12	9	8
Georgia	13	14	6	4
Maryland	4	2	5	2
Massachusetts	35	24	15	9
Newfoundland	3	7	1	4
New Hampshire	8	3	3	—
New Jersey	4	13	6	5
New York	19	26	8	10
North Carolina	16	31	5	5
Nova Scotia	15	15	9	11
Pennsylvania	3	5	4	2
Quebec	10	13	6	6
Rhode Island	—	3	2	2
St John, Island of	4	7	1	3
South Carolina	23	17	9	5
Virginia	25	23	10	7
West Florida	34	35	3	4
Circulars	—	—	3	4
(ii) *Commander-in-chief*				
Gage	23	13	16	12
(iii) *Superintendants*				
Johnson	4	2	3	2
Stuart	12	9	6	4
(iv) *Surveyors*				
Holland	3	—	2	1
De Brahm	5	4	2	1
(v) *Others*	19	16	4	5

A very general correlation can here be seen between the volume of the Secretary of State's American correspondence and the number and magnitude of the problems facing him and his correspondents. 1770 was undoubtedly a more trying year than 1771: Hillsborough's 138 out-letters for 1770 and 111 for 1771 reflect this. Thirty-five letters from the governor of Massachusetts in 1770, compared to twenty-four in 1771, indicate the additional correspondence brought about by the events in Boston of 5 March 1770, the occupation of Castle William by British troops and the trial of Captain Thomas Preston, just as the campaign of 1771 against the Regulators in North Carolina is marked by the near-doubling of letters from that colony.

The correlation is not, however, a very precise one. In the first place, governors of proprietary and charter-colonies (Connecticut, Maryland, Pennsylvania and Rhode Island) wrote to the Secretary of State, as they had always done, as rarely and as briefly as possible. Thus Philadelphia's proceedings on the subject of non-importation, though they appear in the Secretary of State's correspondence for 1770, are by no means adequately represented there. There may be, one thinks, something a little disingenuous in Governor John Penn's apology for having forgotten to mention that the merchants of his city had joined an association not to import British goods.[4]

Secondly, the number of letters credited to each governor is affected by the different styles of correspondence in use. Some governors wrote a letter to the Secretary of State merely to acknowledge receipt of his last dispatch, putting their own news into another letter. Some governors addressed to Pownall, the under-secretary, or to the Board of Trade, letters which others sent to Hillsborough. Such habits raise or lower the annual totals without necessarily denoting a rise or fall in the number of problems facing a colony.

Thirdly, the arrival of a new governor was often the signal for a burst of correspondence in which the new man made all kinds of suggestions for improving his command. West Florida got a new acting governor, Durnford, early in 1770 and a new governor, Chester, later in the same year, both of whom had much to say. This helps to explain West Florida's position at the top of the table of Hillsborough's correspondents in 1770–1771, though it is also the case that a good deal was going on in this interesting province in the fields of new settlement, Indian affairs and Anglo-Spanish relations, all of which needed to be reported to the Secretary of State.

The Secretary of State for the American Department also corresponded with other departments of state in London: Treasury, Admiralty, War Office, Board of Ordnance, Post Office etc. and with the two other Secretaries of State whose principal responsibility was for foreign affairs. This domestic correspondence covered financial matters such as the disposal of colonial quitrents, which Hillsborough had to refer to the Treasury; military matters, such as the plan for fortifying St John's, Newfoundland, put forward by the Board of Ordnance; naval and postal matters; and matters arising in North America—for example, Spanish fishing on and off the coast of East Florida—which required the attention of the Secretary of State for the Southern Department.

Hillsborough's departmental correspondence in 1770–1771 was distributed as follows:

4 Below, Vol. I, No. 350; Vol. II, No. XLIV.

	IN LETTERS		OUT LETTERS	
	1770	1771	1770	1771
Admiralty	9	11	15	5
Law Officers	3	1	4	1
Lord Chamberlain	—	2	5	1
Ordnance	9	3	6	2
Post Office	—	1	3	1
Secretaries of State	2	2	4	6
Treasury	—	—	9	3
Treasurer of Household	—	—	1	—
War Office	2	1	1	2

This table is by no means an accurate reflection of the volume of business carried on by the American Department with other departments, much of which was conducted at under-secretary level.

The correspondence of the under-secretaries, John Pownall (from 1768) and William Knox (from 1770) is of course comprehended within the Colonial Office records. No doubt these two officials drafted many of the dispatches to America which Hillsborough signed, but they did not themselves sign letters of importance to the colonies. Pownall wrote letters notifying governors of the annual estimates, distributed revised forms of prayer for the royal family, and circulated information on how tar was made in Sweden. He also received from the colonies letters covering papers such as Acts, Minutes of Council and lists of land grants, destined for the Board of Trade. Most of this was formal business. When Hillsborough was on holiday in August-September 1770 and in August-October 1771, the flow of letters from Whitehall to America dried up to a trickle of bare acknowledgements signed by Pownall. When a dispatch of prime importance, Governor Tryon's announcement of his victory over the Regulators on 16 May 1771, reached Whitehall a few days after Hillsborough had set off for his Irish estates, Lord Rochford, one of the 'ancient' Secretaries of State, was brought in to sign the letter of congratulation and to convey the King's thanks to the North Carolina militia.[5] This was exceptional: while Hillsborough was in Ireland, the administration of America from Whitehall virtually came to a stop. Unofficially, the under-secretaries corresponded extensively with the colonies, but these were private letters which do not normally appear in the Colonial Office records.[6]

In inter-departmental business, however, the under-secretaries came into their own, Pownall in particular signing many letters to his opposite number in other offices: Robinson and Cooper at the Treasury, Stephens at the Admiralty, Todd at the Post Office, Boddington at the Board of Ordnance, and Sutton and Wood, under-secretaries in the departments of the other Secretaries of State. Pownall's departmental correspondence in 1770–1771 was distributed as follows, with the proviso that probably not all of it has survived:

5   Below, Vol. I, No. 1435.
6   Spector, *American Department*, p. 119. Below, Vol. I, No. 93 for what may be an example of a private letter strayed into the public records, and Nos. 1460 and 1462 for private letters purposely preserved.

	IN LETTERS		OUT LETTERS	
	1770	1771	1770	1771
Admiralty	1	5	3	1
Law Officers	—	—	3	—
Lord Chancellor	—	1	1	1
Ordnance	1	1	—	2
Post Office	3	9	17	4
Privy Council	—	—	9	5
Secretaries of State	—	1	1	1
Treasury	20	19	12	13

The importance of these permanent officials in keeping government business in motion is apparent from the Colonial Office records. Their contribution to policy making is more elusive but not seriously to be doubted. Long service, if nothing else, lent authority to some of them. All Pownall's working life was spent in colonial administration: in 1770 he had been under-secretary for only two years, but before that had served twenty-five years as clerk and secretary in the Board of Trade.[7]

Hillsborough's was not of course the only British department of state to correspond with the colonies. The Admiralty corresponded with the commodore, R.N., on the North American station, and with captains of H.M. ships in American waters, passing to the Secretary of State news or complaints (such as the bad state of the Halifax light-house) with which he was expected to deal.[8] Constitutionally, the Admiralty had to be informed of certain royal decisions by one of the Secretaries of State: an example is the instruction by Hillsborough (below, No. 626) to prepare ships for sea in view of the crisis in Anglo-Spanish relations in late 1770 over the Falkland Islands incident. Such orders went, however, from Hillsborough to the Admiralty, not from Hillsborough directly to America. There is no series of letters between the Secretary of State for the American Department and the commodore, R.N., at Halifax, Nova Scotia, parallel to that between Hillsborough and the commander-in-chief of British land-forces, General Gage at New York. Lord Barrington, Secretary at War, also corresponded with Gage,[9] but this did not stop Hillsborough from giving detailed orders respecting British troops in America. Constitutionally, his authority to do so depended on the primacy of the Secretaries of State over other royal officials in naval and military matters. As William

7 Spector, *American Department*, Chapter VII.
8 Principal Admiralty correspondence in the Public Record Office dealing with North America 1770–1783: Admirals Dispatches, Adm. 1/483–489; Orders and Instructions from Lords of Admiralty, Adm. 2/95–108; and Secret Orders and Letters, Adm. 3/1333–1336. The series known as Captains Letters, Adm. 1/1435–2738, is arranged by date and initial letter of name of correspondent, not by station. See *Public Record Office, Lists and Indexes*, No. XVIII (London, H.M.S.O., 1904; New York, Kraus Reprint, 1963).
9 Gage's letters to Barrington are in Public Record Office, W.O.1/2 and W.O.1/9. These volumes together with W.O.1/10–13 contain the dispatches of the Commander-in-chief, North America, to the Secretary at War for the period 1770–1783. The Secretary at War's out-letters are in W.O.4/273–275. For other material, see *Public Record Office, Lists and Indexes*, No. XXVIII (London, H.M.S.O., 1908; New York, Kraus Reprint, 1963).

Knox explained, 'Everyone who is at all acquainted with the constitution of this Government must know that all warlike preparations, every military operation, and every naval equipment must be directed by a Secretary of State.'[10] Barrington was not 'one of His Majesty's Principal Secretaries of State'; Hillsborough was. Whether the Secretary could have established a direct authority over naval affairs in America similar to that which he wielded in the military sphere is not clear. Hillsborough did not try, and this difference is reflected throughout the Colonial Office records. On the whole, the arrangement was a fortunate one. Politically the presence of the British army in the colonies raised much thornier issues than the Navy's use of American ports. The willingness or otherwise of Assemblies, such as those of New Jersey and New York, to contribute to the subsistence of these troops was one such issue. The anxiety of governors of colonies of recent foundation (East and West Florida, the Island of St John) to attract troops to their provinces to help with public works and to stimulate trade by spending their pay, was another. If all matters like these had had to reach Hillsborough through the War Office, decision-making would have been prolonged and complicated. Happily they did not, and the interdepartmental friction that might have arisen from this situation was perhaps reduced by good personal relations between Hillsborough and Barrington and between Hillsborough and Gage.[11]

The Post Office and Treasury likewise corresponded directly with their own men in America and with the governors.[12] Hillsborough naturally liked to be informed of these transactions. 'In one of the visits I had the honour of making to your lordship before I left England' wrote Governor Chester from Pensacola 'I remember that you mentioned to me the inconvenience that often attended your not being acquainted with the correspondence that sometimes happened between His Majesty's governors and the Public Boards in England.'[13] Very likely Hillsborough mentioned this inconvenience to all governors on appointment, and several examples can be found in the records of 1770–1771 of their heeding his wishes and sending him copies of their letters to other departments. It is, however, unlikely that they did so in every instance.

The Commissioners of Customs at Boston, established in 1767, reported not to Hillsborough but to the Treasury;[14] which explains why Customs officers in America generally appear in the Colonial Office records not so much as men doing a job of work but as victims of private violence carrying grievances to government or as the subject of

10 Quoted in Spector, *The American Department*, p. 79.
11 John Shy, *Towards Lexington: the Role of the British Army in the Coming of the American Revolution* (Princeton, N.J., Princeton University Press, 1965), p. 291.
12 For Treasury, see Andrews, *Guide to the Materials . . . in the Public Record Office*, Vol. II, p. 136; for Post Office, see Charles M. Andrews, *Guide to the Manuscript Materials for the History of the United States to 1783, in the British Museum, in Minor London Archives, and in the Libraries of Oxford and Cambridge* (Washington, D.C., Carnegie Institution of Washington, 1908), p. 273.
13 Public Record Office, C.O.5/588, p. 143.
14 Dora M. Clark, 'The American Board of Customs, 1767–1783' in *American Historical Review*, Vol. XLV, No. 4 (1940).

complaints from outraged governors who felt that their authority over Customs matters had slipped away from them. Jealousy between Commissioners and governors is suggested by Governor Carleton's bitter letter of 4 July 1770,[15] one piece of evidence among others that the British administration in and of North America was something less than a monolith.

Records of the Commissioners for Trade and Plantations (Board of Trade)

In 1770 the Board of Trade still corresponded with governors of colonies, though far less frequently than in the early eighteenth century. In two years, 1770–1771, it wrote as a Board only ten letters to America, twenty-one being written to it in the same period. In fact its business with the governors was rather more than these figures suggest, some of the letters addressed to Pownall being intended for him, as secretary, to place before the Board. Even so, the aggregate of its correspondence with North America by this date was small: much of it was of a fairly formal kind, and the remainder referred to laws enacted by colonial legislatures and sent to the Board for scrutiny. In 1770 and 1771 the Board was corresponding, in a fact-finding way, with the governor of Virginia on the subject of the proposed grant of land on the Ohio to Thomas Walpole, Benjamin Franklin and others, which the British Treasury was disposed to encourage but which Hillsborough actively disliked. Correspondence of this kind, however, seldom now came the Board's way.

With one or two minor exceptions, the Board's business reached it by formal reference from the Privy Council or the Privy Council's Committee for Plantation Affairs, or by informal reference from the Secretary of State. Its reports, on these matters put to it, were made to the King (ninety in 1770–1771) and the Committee for Plantation Affairs (twenty-three in 1770–1771).

The Privy Council, constitutionally the supreme authority in colonial administration, appointed to governorships and to certain other offices including seats in colonial Councils (the King's Councils in the colonies), issued formal instructions to governors, and upheld or disallowed colonial laws. These were the matters on which the Board of Trade tendered advice, most Orders in Council respecting the colonies being founded on its reports. Usually the Board proposed action as well as reporting facts; sometimes it reported facts only, 'submitting' the necessary action to the King's wisdom. In matters of highest moment the Board's advice might not be sought, the Privy Council acting on the recommendation of its own Committee for Plantation Affairs. An Order in Council of 6 July 1770 furnishes an example: this directed that in consequence of disorders in Massachusetts the *rendezvous* of H.M. ships in America should be changed from Halifax to Boston and that Castle William should be garrisoned by the King's troops.[16]

15 Below, Vol. II, No. LXI.
16 Below, Vol. II, No. LXII.

References to the Board of Trade were chiefly of two kinds. First, the Board's opinion was sought on the validity of colonial laws, which it in turn referred to its legal adviser. From 1770 this was Richard ('Omniscient') Jackson, a former secretary of George Grenville, whose function, as explained to him in a letter from John Pownall of 30 April 1770, was to be the Board's consultant 'on all matters of law which they do not conceive to be of the importance to require the opinion of His Majesty's Attorney and Solicitor-General'.[17] Jackson's reports to the Board of Trade (fifty-one of them from his appointment to the end of 1771) are a useful source for the history of colonial law making on the eve of the American Revolution.

Jackson's reports normally deal with the conformity or otherwise of colonial laws to the laws of Great Britain, sometimes in rather general terms. He was not, however, shy of pointing out objections other than legal, as can be seen from his treatment of the Act passed in Virginia in 1769 laying an additional duty on slaves imported into the colony. The purpose of the law was, and was recognized to be, not the raising of revenue but the hindering of the slave trade for fear of the growing imbalance between white and black population. Jackson admitted that the Act was not objectionable in point of law and that the presence of two blacks to every white in the colony was disquieting, but submitted to the Board the question of how far the Act was expedient in point of commercial policy. The Board, having received petitions against the Act from the merchants of Liverpool and Lancaster, decided that it was not expedient and recommended disallowance to the King, which was duly performed by Order in Council.[18]

In most cases the Board of Trade founded its own reports on colonial laws on Jackson's advice, but not always. On 18 July 1770, for example, Jackson recommended that an Act passed in New Hampshire to restrain the taking of excessive usury should be disallowed on grounds of its small utility and its requirement of oaths to be taken by debtors and creditors: 'such an encouragement to perjury (a crime so subversive of all government) ought nowhere to subsist'.[19] The Board thought otherwise and recommended that the Act should be allowed to stand, though informing the King of Jackson's opinion. The Act was allowed. Now and again Jackson was asked to give his views on matters other than colonial legislation, two examples from 1771 being worthy of notice. On 16 April he reported his opinion that the King had the power to confer baronetcies on French Canadians; and on 5 June he gave the opinion that, as British law then stood, white pine trees standing on private property in Massachusetts were protected, but added the interesting rider that the same law deprived the trees of another protection, the self-interest of the owner.[20]

The second main business of the Board of Trade at this time was to examine and report to the King or to the Committee of Council for Plantation Affairs on petitions referred to it, which ranged from routine

17 C.O.324/18, p. 368.
18 Below, Vol. I, Nos. 508, 742, 805–806.
19 C.O.5/930, fos. 86–87d.
20 Below, Vol. I, Nos. 1127, 1239, 1281.

requests by ex-servicemen for grants of land in America to petitions raising important political issues. An example of the latter is the reference to the Board of a petition by Charles Garth, agent for South Carolina, praying for the rescinding of the King's additional instruction of 14 April 1770 to the governor of that colony which was intended to deprive the Commons House of Assembly of the power to vote money without concurrence of Governor and Council. To this was added the radical demand that the Governor should inform the Commons House of all representations he made to the King or his ministers on the subject of its proceedings. On this matter the Board had, earlier in 1770, presented the Committee of Council for Plantation Affairs with a nineteen-page report on the constitutional history of South Carolina: not much more work could have been needed in order to be able to recommend the dismissal of Garth's petition, which the Board proposed on 27 March 1771 and the Privy Council ordered on 7 June.[21]

Besides the scrutiny of colonial laws and the consideration of petitions, the Board was responsible for drafting commissions and instructions to colonial governors at first appointment, and of somewhat more importance the additional instructions to governors which formed the Crown's customary response to new political or constitutional situations created by American ingenuity. The nearest approach to patronage now left to the Board was its recommendation to the King of persons fit to be appointed members of Councils in the colonies; but here it may be truer to say that the Board endorsed nominations on which the Secretary of State had already decided.

A large part of the records of the Board of Trade after the curtailment of its authority in 1761 and 1766 consists of papers sent to it for information, and of these the greatest number are signed duplicates of dispatches from colonial governors to the Secretary of State. These records derived from the practice followed by governors of sending home duplicates of their letters, by separate conveyance, the purpose of course being to ensure the safe arrival of at least one. In fact both usually arrived, and the duplicate was disposed of by passing it, for information, to the Board of Trade. Owing to the vagaries of the mail, the duplicate not infrequently arrived before the 'original': then, endorsed 'Original not recd.', it became the record preserved in the Secretary of State's files. When the original turned up later, as it nearly always did, it became the Board's record and continues to-day to be part of the Board's archives. Thus the signed duplicate was accorded the same credence as the 'original', though in fact minor discrepancies between duplicates and 'originals' can be found, and an occasional variation in postscript.

Hillsborough's American correspondents, other than governors, seem also to have sent duplicates of their dispatches as a matter of routine, but few of them have survived amongst the records of the Board of Trade. Gage's duplicates are conspicuously absent: in all probability they were not passed to the Board. A few of Stuart's (Indian affairs) and a few of Holland's (Surveys) will be found in the Board's

21 Below, Vol. I, Nos. 145, 804, 1072, 1292.

Plantations General section, but none of Johnson's (Indian affairs) for the period covered by this volume. Entry-books of the Board's out-letters had been kept for years before 1770, and in many instances drafts also have survived; but the Board did not keep entry-books of in-letters, let alone of papers sent to it for information, so that there is no way of knowing for certain which reached it and which did not.

Publication of the Colonial Office Records

During the past 150 years, but more especially between 1850 and 1900, many of the Colonial Office documents from the beginning of the colonial period down to the Revolution were edited for state governments and state historical societies in the U.S.A.[22] Briefly, the purpose of each editor was to publish material relating to his own colony and no more, a natural enough approach considering that the sponsors were usually the states themselves. Local patriotism and local resources in this way were harnessed to record-publication: the products were the great monuments of scholarship and industry edited by E.B. O'Callaghan (New York), W. L. Saunders (North Carolina), A. D. Candler (Georgia) and others.

Nothing will or can replace these editions; it is no disparagement, more than a century after they started to appear, to raise the question whether this approach, colony by colony, to the publication of the officials records of British administration was the only one possible or the best. For one thing, editorial methods were bound to be different from editor to editor and from colony to colony: the result, it has been authoritatively stated, is 'enormous variation among the states in the character and quality of their publications'.[23] This variation is to be seen not merely in editorial techniques but also in the selection of what to print. Leonard W. Labaree, forty years ago, summed up the achievements of the state publishing programmes and concluded that much had been left undone: not all the gaps have since been filled.[24]

Secondly, the choice of a single colony as the unit of record-publication does justice to certain themes in the history of that colony but

22   An easily accessible list of publications, colony by colony, is in Oscar Handlin and others, *Harvard Guide to American History* (Cambridge, Mass., Harvard University Press, 1954), pp. 125–139. There is a useful summary of what was and what was not achieved in the nineteenth century in Adelaide R. Hasse, 'Materials for a Bibliography of the Public Archives of the Thirteen Original States' in the *Annual Report of the American Historical Association for 1906*, Vol. II (Washington, D.C., 1908). Amongst more recent publications, special mention must be made of C. E. Carter, *Correspondence of Thomas Gage*, 2 vols. (New Haven, Yale University Press, 1931–1933); and *Letters and Papers of Cadwallader Colden*, New York Historical Society Collections, Vols. L–LVI, LXVII–LXVIII (New York, 1918–1937). A calendar of the Colonial Office material regarding Quebec, Nova Scotia and the Island of St John/Prince Edward Island, was published in the annual *Report on Canadian Archives* for 1890, 1894 and 1895 (Ottawa, 1891, 1895 and 1896). The principal British contributions have been *Acts of the Privy Council, Colonial Series*, 6 vols. (London, H.M.S.O., 1908–1912) and *Journals of the Commissioners for Trade and Plantations*, 14 vols. (London, H.M.S.O., 1920–1938). The *Calendar of State Papers, Colonial Series*, 44 volumes (London, H.M.S.O., 1860–1969) brings the Colonial Office records of North America into a proper relationship with one another, and is the only major series to do so; but progress has been slow and bridgehead is only at 1738.
23   *Harvard Guide*, p. 126.
24   *Royal Government in America* (New Haven, Yale University Press, 1930), pp. 454–459.

less than justice to others. The tussles between the royal governor and the elected Assembly of a colony such as South Carolina can be studied from the provincial correspondence and from the journals of the Commons House and Council. The same convenience does not extend to historical problems transcending the geographical limits of a colony. Although many Americans on the eve of the Revolution were almost fatally preoccupied with the affairs of their own province, it is at the same time true that continental problems were multiplying and clamouring for attention. Prominent among them were the westward expansion of settlement towards and into the Mississippi Valley; the disturbances to Indian trade and Indians relations caused by this expansion; and the disposition of British army units and posts to assist, retard or control the westward movement. To none of these problems can the state publishing programmes of Colonial Office records be said to have done full justice.

Thirdly, the nineteenth-century approach to publication has given, in some instances, less than a complete picture of the processes by which administrative decisions were reached in London. Official records, whether letters, minutes, accounts, commissions, warrants or other instruments, were not created for the benefit of historians but were the outcome of acts of administration which, to be correctly construed, need to be placed in context of and in relation to other acts by the same authority and other acts by different but connected authorities. The Colonial Office records are the evidence of *British* administration: properly to evaluate them, London must be regarded as well as Boston and New York; Whitehall as well as Westminster; Treasury, Admiralty and War Office as well as Colonial Office. The logical extension of an inclusive approach to record-publication would of course be to incorporate the archives of these departments and perhaps of Parliament in a single series with those of the Colonial Office. That unfortunately is not at present possible, though something on these lines may be attempted in the future. Meanwhile, the case for joining the correspondence of the Secretary of State with other departments to his American correspondence is a strong one.

Purpose and Scope of this Publication

The purpose of this publication is, by comprehension instead of selection, to restore to the Colonial Office correspondence as much as possible of the relationship which each part had to the sum at the moment of its creation. No competition is intended with the style and purpose of the state editions of the nineteenth century. As to style, they were published when printing was cheap and will never be matched for lavishness. As to purpose, they were concerned with colonies as the embryos of states; this deals with an empire, how it was run, and how it responded or failed to respond to stress.

The Colonial Office records consisting of a good deal more than the correspondence relating to North America, the scope of this publication must be defined, first, by listing the categories and types of records of the period 1770–1783 which have *not* been brought within it, vizt. records of the British West Indian colonies, Gibraltar and

Senegambia; legislatives Acts of Assemblies; Sessional Papers (Minutes of Councils and Journals of Assemblies, except where these have been preserved in the form of enclosures to correspondence); Minutes of the Commissioners for Trade and Plantations (the Board of Trade); and a small number of private papers which, through interception of the mails, capture or accident, have become attached to the Colonial Office records though having no administrative relationship to them. Some of these omissions, especially the first, have been made with regret. The historical connexions between the British West Indies and North America are close. In peace they were linked by trade in lumber, provisions, slaves, rum and molasses; and in the War of Independence naval actions between British and French in the Caribbean shaped the course and outcome of the continental struggle. Archivally and administratively, the Colonial Office records respecting Jamaica and Barbados are as nearly related to those of New York and Massachusetts as are those of Nova Scotia. It is moreover a fact to be regretted that very few of the records of the British West Indian colonies in the later eighteenth century have as yet found their way into print. These are compelling arguments for bringing the Caribbean material within the scope of the series; that they have had to be set aside is solely owing to considerations of cost and time.

With these exceptions the intention has been and is to draw within this series the surviving Colonial Office correspondence respecting North America, including those colonies which are now parts of Canada, for the period of the American Revolution, beginning in 1770 and ending in 1783: some 570 manuscript volumes and bundles of records. This design denotes the assembling of documents which, although classified as belonging to different colonies or to no colony, have kinship with one another, both administratively and as to subject-matter, and which archivally derive unity from the fact that they arrived on the desk of the Secretary of State for the American Department or his undersecretaries in Whitehall and were available in their files when they voiced an opinion or recommended a course of action. The aim of the publication might be expressed as the recreation of the situation in which the administrator in Whitehall was placed.

Editorial Methods

Over 500 manuscript volumes and bundles form the corpus of records on which this publication will be based. These volumes vary in size, the average being about 200 folios, suggesting a grand total of perhaps 120,000 folios for the years 1770 to 1783. The aggregate number of documents will not be known until completion: the years 1770 and 1771 have together furnished (without defining a document too precisely) a total of 1761 principal items with 1223 enclosures, 2984 documents in all. This number may well be exceeded towards 1775, and thereafter will certainly decline as colonies break away and cease correspondence. The decline will be partly but not wholly compensated by greater activity in those colonies which remained under British rule and on the part of departments in London concerned with fighting the war in America.

The reduction of this mass of material to order necessitates regimentation and a good deal of compression. Transcription of every surviving document is, it need hardly be said, out of the question; nor in every case would it be of much value, for the Colonial Office records—like all official and most private archives—contain some matter of a formal kind (Orders in Council, instructions to governors etc.), as well as matter which in its original form is scarcely printable (accounts, Naval Officers' returns), and matter which there would be general agreement is of a repetitious nature and of only limited historical interest. All such records invite abridgement. On the other hand, there are many dispatches and some other documents which no historian would be satisfied to receive in any but their original form.

The editorial solution to this problem has been and will be to include a summary description of every surviving document, arranged in chronological sequence, in volumes of *Calendars* of which this is the first. From these documents have been selected those which, in the editor's opinion, are of sufficient historical importance (whether previously published or not) to justify transcription *in extenso :* these will appear in volumes of *Transcripts,* the first two of which will be published simultaneously with, or soon after, this first volume of *Calendar.* Thus Volume I in the series is the *Calendar* for 1770–1771; Volume II the *Transcripts* for 1770; and Volume III the *Transcripts* for 1771. Volume IV will be the *Calendar* for 1772–1773; Volume V the *Transcripts* for 1772; and Volume VI the *Transcripts* for 1773 etc.

Documents in a *Calendar* volume which have been selected to appear in the appropriate volume of *Transcripts* are identified by an asterisk (*) placed in front of the document. An explanation of the principles of selection will be found in the Introduction to Volume II of the series.

The Calendar

The *Calendar* is intended to serve as a *catalogue raisonné* of all documents comprehended within the scheme of publication. Its purposes are, first, to facilitate reference to the documents in the Public Record Office, to the transcripts of some of them which are kept at the Library of Congress, and to the photographic copies of some or all of them which are held by libraries in the United States and elsewhere; secondly, to place each document in the context supplied by other documents in the Colonial Office group to which it is related; and, thirdly, to supply by means of the index an epitomized guide to the principal persons, places and subjects mentioned in these records.

The information given in a *Calendar* entry comprises : date, place of origin, names of originator and addressee; summary of principal subject-matter; language of document, if not English; status of document (draft, copy etc.); its length; endorsements, if any; the official (Public Record Office) reference; and the status and reference of other versions of the document surviving in the Colonial Office group.

(i) *Date, place of origin, originator and addressee.* Undated documents have in most instances been assigned a date by the editor, derived either from the date of receipt noted on the dorse or from some other source: these assigned dates have been placed in square brackets e.g. [January 15]. Where no date can confidently be suggested, documents have been placed at the end of the month, year or volume, whichever has seemed most appropriate. Where the name of originator or addressee is not supplied by the document but can be confidently inferred, it has been placed in square brackets, e.g. John Pownall to [Governor Thomas Hutchinson]. If the suggestion is tentative a query has been added.

(ii) *Subject-matter*. The *Calendar* is intended to aid, not obviate, reference to the manuscripts, to printed versions thereof, and to the *Transcripts*. The summary of subject-matter gives only a general indication of the principal contents of a document. It is not claimed that every person, place or topic mentioned in every document is reported in a *Calendar* entry. Summaries of subject-matter are given in a compressed form: they are intended to be read in conjunction with the index, which supplies cross-references, and with the corresponding volume of *Transcripts* and its index, which provide extended accounts of the major topics indicated in the *Calendar*.

In the case of formal commissions and instruction to governors, inventories of military stores, lists of land grants, minutes of Councils which have survived as enclosures to correspondence, and some other similar documents, their presence and official reference have been noted in the *Calendar* but no attempt made to summarize their contents in detail.

(iii) *Language*. A number of documents in this volume are in French, and a few in Spanish. The original language is indicated in the *Calendar* but the summary is given in English.   . .

(iv) *Status of Document*. For the purpose of the *Calendar*, six categories of document have been recognized: signed originals, signed duplicates, drafts, entries, copies and prints.

(a) Signed originals. A letter has been deemed to be a signed original if signed by its originator and not otherwise described by him or by the recipient. Designation: *Signed*.

(b) Signed duplicates. The circumstances under which duplicates of dispatches from governors have survived in the Board of Trade's records have already been described (above, p. 10). For the purpose of the *Calendar* a document has been deemed to be a duplicate if described as such and signed by its originator. A few correspondents used the term 'copy' to denote a signed duplicate. Designation: *Duplicate*.

(c) Drafts. Versions of out-letters retained by the Secretary of State, the under-secretaries or the Board of Trade, are deemed to be drafts. Most are fair drafts, corresponding exactly (at least in intention) to the letter sent. Some (mainly of the Board of Trade) are foul or rough drafts with manuscript corrections. Both kinds are normally written on only one (vertical) half of the paper. Designation: *Draft*.

(d) Entries. By the 1760's the retention in the Secretary's office of the draft of an outgoing letter and the preservation of an incoming letter were no longer considered adequate to ensure ready reference to the archives. Entry-books began to be kept. Nearly all the Secretary's letters, in and out, and many of the letters of the under-secretaries were copied into these entry-books, as were the out-letters (but not the in-letters) of the Board of Trade. Comparison of originals and drafts with entries suggest many minor inaccuracies in copying. Designation: *Entry*.

(e) Copies. Most enclosures to principal documents were copies, some being certified as authentic copies, some not. Where the duplicate of an incoming dispatch has survived, it will often be found that the governor or other originator has not sent second copies of the enclosures which went with his original, or has sent second copies of some but not of all of them. Moreover, enclosures to incoming letters were not copied into the Secretary of State's entry-books, though their existence was usually noted. Consequently, and paradoxically, enclosures are often unique documents, at least within the Colonial Office group. Designation: *Copy*.

(f) Prints. Little use of printing was made at this time by British departments of state for the internal dissemination of information. There is an instance in the period 1770–1771, the reprinting at Hillsborough's direction of a pamphlet describing methods used in Sweden for the manufacture of tar and pitch, copies of which were sent to colonies with an interest in naval stores; but this was unusual. Several colonies in America printed their Acts and proceedings of Assembly; some printed proclamations have survived; and governors of several colonies (Massachusetts, New York, South Carolina and Georgia) sent copies of colonial *Gazettes* and newspapers as enclosures to their dispatches to Hillsborough. A number of printed documents and papers have thus found their way into the Colonial Office records. Designation: *Printed*.

A few documents fall into none of the above categories, e.g. some petitions which appear to be 'originals' but which bear no signature.

(v) *Length of Document*. The length of a *Calendar* entry bears no necessary relation to the length of the document being described: it may rather reflect the number of distinct subjects with which that document deals. The number of pages or parts of pages occupied by the document has therefore been given immediately after the definition of the status of that document, e.g. *Signed*. 2 pp.; *Copy*. 7½ pp. etc. The use of unusually large or small sheets of paper has also been noted.

(vi) *Endorsements*. Most original documents, duplicates and drafts, and some copies, carry endorsements, made in most cases by a person other than the originator. These endorsements, by the recipient or filing-clerk, may be summaries of the contents of the document, made for ease of reference and containing only information which has already been provided by the *Calendar* entry: such have been disregarded. On the other hand, there are endorsements which supply fresh information such as the date on which a letter was received or the action taken upon it. These have been recorded in the *Calendar*.

Original letters received at the office of the Secretary of State generally bear an endorsement recording date of receipt, e.g. 'R, 29 April'. The endorsement 'R, do.' denotes that the document was received on the same day as that on which it was written.

Letters received by the Board of Trade were usually endorsed with the date of receipt and the date on which the document was placed before a meeting of the Board, e.g. 'Recd. 29 April, Read 8 May 1770'. It would, however, be well not to take seriously all the Board of Trade's endorsements: those written on documents which were sent to it for action are no doubt genuine, but those on some of the papers sent to it for information appear to be fictitious.

(vii) *Official Reference*. The official (Public Record Office) reference is given in square brackets at the end of each *Calendar* entry. Where there is a covering letter and one or more enclosures immediately following, a single reference to all those documents has been given.

Some confusion has been introduced into styles of reference to the Colonial Office records by variations in practice on the part of the Public Record Office over a number of years. Apart from the complete change of system of numbering volumes and bundles which began to be introduced in 1907,[25] there are rich possibilities of confusion within volumes. Most volumes which were made up, either in the eighteenth century or in modern times, from loose papers, i.e. drafts and originals, have been given folio references: these have been adopted in the *Calendar* wherever they exist. In a few volumes rival systems of foliation will be found, one stamped, the other a pencilled number enclosed in a diamond (denoting that the volume has passed through the Repairs Department of the Public Record Office); here, for the sake of uniformity, the stamped folio number has been used for all citations in the *Calendar*. A small number of volumes of original correspondence, e.g. those for West Florida, have been paginated instead of foliated.

The Colonial Office entry-books were in most cases paginated in the eighteenth century; in all such cases page references have been given in the *Calendar*.

(viii) *Other Versions of the Document*. From the preceding explanations, it will have become apparent that two or sometimes three versions of a document may have survived in the Colonial Office records, e.g. original letter, duplicate and entry. In such cases the location of these other versions has been stated immediately after the official reference to the document described in the *Calendar* entry. Significant variations from one version to another, such as postscripts and endorsements, have in many instances been noted; but no guarantee is given that every such variation has been observed.

Maps

Maps, sketches, plans of fortifications etc. which were enclosed with dispatches from America have for the most part become detached from their parent document. Some were removed on arrival in the Secretary

---

25   The effect of which was to render obsolete all references given in editions of Colonial Office records published in U.S.A. until that time. See Andrews, *Guide*, Vol. I, p. iv and pp. 279–307 for key to the change.

of State's office; others have been transferred by officials of the Public Record Office during the twentieth century to form a separate map collection. Brief descriptions of maps, together with their present official references, have been given in the *Calendar*; but it is the hope of the editor and publishers to include in this series a volume devoted to maps, in which fuller descriptions will be provided.

The Calendar : Volume I

The choice of the year 1770 to open the series requires little comment. The 'natural' beginning of any study in depth of the period of the American Revolution is 1763; but this would have set too daunting a task for both editor and publisher. The selection of 1770 means that the series plunges *in medias res*, but the same objection could probably be made with equal force against any year later than 1765. Expediency mainly has dictated the choice of 1770 but, as the year in which Lord North became 1st Commissioner of the Treasury and the year of the Boston Massacre, it is as good as most and better than some.

The records from which this volume has been compiled are as follows:

(1) Secretary of State's Correspondence with Home Departments etc.
    C.O.5/119   C.O.5/138   C.O.5/154   C.O.5/250
    C.O.5/133–134   C.O.5/145   C.O.5/247   see also under (2)

(2) Secretary of State's Correspondence with Superintendants of Indian Affairs, Surveyors in North America, etc.
    C.O.5/71–73   C.O.5/227–228   C.O.5/243
    (These volumes contain some correspondence with
                    Home Departments)

(3) Secretary of State's Correspondence with Commander-in-chief, North America,
    C.O.5/88–90   C.O.5/234–235   C.O.5/241

(4) Miscellaneous
    C.O.5/26–27   sealed originals and some copies of Orders in
                        Council
    C.O.5/43   correspondence mainly concerning Canada
                        Reconnoissances
    C.O.5/114   petitions, mostly undated, mostly to
                        Hillsborough
    C.O.5/203–205   commissions etc.
    C.O.5/246   private letters to and from Hillsborough

(5) Correspondence of Secretary of State and Board of Trade with Colonies

N. Carolina	C.O.5/301–302	C.O.5/313–315	C.O.5/328–329
	C.O.5/305	C.O.5/320	C.O.5/332
	C.O.5/307	C.O.5/325–326	
S. Carolina	C.O.5/379–381	C.O.5/399	C.O.5/408–409
	C.O.5/393–394	C.O.5/404	

E. Florida	C.O.5/544–545	C.O.5/563	
	C.O.5/551–552	C.O.5/566–567	
W. Florida	C.O.5/577–578	C.O.5/600	C.O.5/612–613
	C.O.5/587–589	C.O.5/605–606	C.O.5/619–621
Georgia	C.O.5/651–652	C.O.5/674	
	C.O.5/660–661	C.O.5/677–678	
Massachusetts	C.O.5/754	C.O.5/765	C.O.5/893–894
	C.O.5/759–761	C.O.5/768	C.O.5/897
New Hampshire	C.O.5/896	C.O.5/937	C.O.5/945
	C.O.5/930	C.O.5/943	C.O.5/947
New Jersey	C.O.5/979	C.O.5/999	C.O.5/1003
	C.O.5/990–991	C.O.5/1001	
New York	C.O.5/1074–75	C.O.5/1101–03	C.O.5/1138
	C.O.5/1080	C.O.5/1131	C.O.5/1141

Proprietaries
(Connecticut

(Connecticut	C.O.5/1277–78	C.O.5/1296	
Maryland	C.O.5/1283–84	C.O.5/1300–01	
Pennsylvania			
Rhode Island)			
Virginia	C.O.5/1332–34	C.O.5/1348–49	C.O.5/1372
	C.O.5/1336	C.O.5/1369	C.O.5/1375
Quebec	C.O.42/7–8	C.O.42/87	C.O.43/8
	C.O.42/30–31	C.O.43/2	C.O.43/12–13
Newfoundland	C.O.194/18	C.O.195/10	C.O.195/15
	C.O.194/29–30	C.O.195/12	
Nova Scotia	C.O.217/25–26	C.O.218/7	C.O.218/25
	C.O.217/34	C.O.218/17–18	
I. of St John	C.O.226/1	C.O.227/1–2	
	C.O.226/4–5		

(6) General Correspondence etc. of Board of Trade

	C.O.323/27–28	C.O.324/42	C.O.324/54
	C.O.324/18	C.O.324/51	C.O.324/60

Index

The index being an integral part of the volume, the user is invited to consult the note (below, p. 462) where the principles of compilation have been explained.

Corrigenda

The editor will be pleased to receive and will acknowledge notification of errors. They should be sent to him care of the publishers at 81 Merrion Square, Dublin, 2, Ireland.

PRINCIPAL ROYAL OFFICERS IN NORTH AMERICA
1770–1771

Commander-in-chief

Lieut.-General Thomas Gage.

Governors and Acting Governors

East Florida: Governor James Grant to 9 May 1771, when he went home; Lieut.-Governor John Moultrie became acting Governor.

Georgia: Governor James Wright to 10 July 1771, when he went home; President James Habersham became acting Governor.

Massachusetts: Lieut.-Governor Thomas Hutchinson. His commission as Governor was sent from Whitehall on 7 December 1770.

Newfoundland: visiting Governor, Captain John Byron, R.N.

New Hampshire: Governor John Wentworth.

New Jersey: Governor William Franklin.

New York: Lieut.-Governor Cadwallader Colden was acting Governor to 18 October 1770, when Governor Earl of Dunmore arrived. Dunmore left the colony after the arrival of Governor William Tryon on 7 July 1771.

North Carolina: Governor William Tryon to 30 June 1771, when he left for New York. President James Hasell was acting Governor to 11 August 1771, when Governor Josiah Martin arrived.

Nova Scotia: Governor Lord William Campbell to 17 October 1771, when he went on leave for recovery of health; President Benjamin Green became acting Governor.

Quebec: Governor Guy Carleton until his return to England; President Hector Theophilus Cramahé became acting Governor on 9 August 1770; his commission as Lieut.-Governor was sent from Whitehall on 3 July 1771.

St John, Island of: Walter Patterson, first Governor, arrived 30 August 1770.

South Carolina: Lieut.-Governor William Bull was acting Governor until return of Governor Lord Charles Montagu on 16 September 1771.

Virginia: Governor Viscount Botetourt died 15 October 1770. President William Nelson was acting Governor until arrival from New York of Governor Earl of Dunmore on 25 September 1771.

West Florida: Lieut.-Governor Elias Durnford was acting Governor until arrival of Governor Peter Chester on 10 August 1770.

Superintendents of Indian Affairs

Northern District: Sir William Johnson, Bt.

Southern District: Captain John Stuart, in South Carolina until 28 April 1771 when he left for West Florida, arriving on or before 1 August and remaining there for rest of the year.

General Surveyors

Northern District: Captain Samuel Holland.

Southern District: William Gerard De Brahm, called home by letter from Whitehall dated 3 May 1771 to answer complaints.

Surveyor-General of Woods

John Wentworth.

CALENDAR 1770-1771

* denotes that document appears in appropriate volume of *Transcripts*

1

1 January, Brunswick

Governor William Tryon to Earl of Hillsborough (No. 44), sending Minutes of Council of North Carolina, 6 May to present. Attorney-General Marmaduke Jones, Chief Justice Howard and Samuel Cornell, recommended to be of the Council. Thomas Lloyd, formerly proposed, is now unwilling; Samuel Swann is now too old; Eustace McCulloch is appointed agent; Mr Heron and Mr Strudwick, absent, are expected to return. Plans I have already sent for reform in collection of quitrents will require time for accomplishment. *Duplicate. Signed. 3 pp. Endorsed*, R, 4 April, original not received. [C.O.5, 313, fos. 27–28d; signed original, dated 6 January, endorsed duplicate, in C.O.5, 301, fos. 118–119d; extract, referring to membership of Council, endorsed Read 30 April 1770, in C.O.5, 301, fos. 88–89d; entry, dated 1 January, in C.O.5, 328, pp. 172–175]

2

1 January, Brunswick

* Same to same (No. 45), acknowledging duplicate of No. 27; original of this and No. 26 not yet to hand. I agree that colonies should provide for their own security. Assembly of North Carolina refused to provide for defence. Objection to Tonnage Bill is from unwillingness to tax vessels owned in the country. Extreme want of circulating medium. When new emission of bills is authorized, present heavily counterfeited currency should cease to be legal tender. *Duplicate. Signed. 2 pp. Endorsed*, R, 4 April, original not recd. [C.O.5, 313, fos. 29–30d; signed original, dated 6 January 1770, endorsed duplicate, in C.O.5, 301, fos. 120–121d; entry in C.O.5, 328, pp. 175–177]

3

1 January, Boston

Lieut.-Governor Thomas Hutchinson to Earl of Hillsborough (No. 1), sending confession of Thomas Austin, prisoner for piracy, who has been sent to Lords of Admiralty in *Paoli*, Captain Hall. Last newspaper from New York sent. *Signed. 1 p. Endorsed*, R, 6 February. [C.O.5, 759, fos. 19–20d; entry in C.O.5, 768, p. 69]

4

2 January, Whitehall

John Pownall to Anthony Todd. South Carolina and West Indies packet-boat to be detained. *Entry.* ½ p. [C.O.5, 241, p. 241]

5

4 January, New York

Lieut.-Governor Cadwallader Colden to Earl of Hillsborough (No. 7), enclosing following. Settlement of country west of Connecticut River is retarded by controversy between New Hampshire proprietors and this government. Those proprietors were formerly willing to take new grants from New York at reduced fees, but Governor Sir H. Moore insisted on full fees. *Signed.* 3½ pp. *Endorsed*, R, 7 February 1770. *Enclosed:*

    i. Petition of persons named in No. iii to Lieut.-Governor Colden. Connecticut River is eastern boundary of New York, but government of New Hampshire granted vast number of townships west of that river. Petitioners were entitled to land for war service and applied for grants in area between Hudson River, Wood Creek, Lake Champlain and headwaters of Connecticut River and Green Mountains. Government of New York is restrained by H.M.'s instruction from making grants there. 2¼ pp.

    ii. New York, 10 December 1769. Resolution of meeting of persons claiming land for war service, appointing John Small, brigade-major to General Gage, to represent their case to Lieut.-Governor Colden. *Copy.* ½ p.

    iii. Schedule of persons concerned in No. i. Captains are entitled to 3000 acres, lieutenants, ensigns, surgeons and apothecaries' mates to 2000, N.C.O.s to 200, privates to 50. Names of 99 claimants. 2¾ pp. [C.O.5, 1101, fos. 14–20d; entry of covering letter in C.O.5, 1138, pp. 123–127]

6

5 January, St James's

Order of King in Council, approving draft commission for Peter Chester to be Governor of West Florida. *Copy.* 1 p. *Endorsed*, Recd. 12 December, Read 21 December 1772. [C.O.5, 579, pp. 147–150; sealed original in C.O.5, 26, fos. 66–67d]

7

5 January, St James's

Same, approving draft of instructions to proprietors of Pennsylvania on John Penn's becoming Deputy Governor. *Copy.* 1¾ pp. *Endorsed*, Recd. 12 December, Read 21 December 1772. [C.O.5, 1278, fos. 102–103d; copy of instructions in C.O.5, 203, fos. 30–55d; sealed original of Order in C.O.5, 26, fos. 68–69d]

8

5 January, St James's

Same, appointing John Stuart to be of the Councils in the several provinces in his department during continuance of his superintendancy; but not to act in judicial capacity in civil cases nor take on administration of government. *Copy.* 2 pp. *Endorsed,* Recd. 12 December, Read 21 December 1772. [C.O.323, 27, pp. 297–300; sealed original in C.O.5, 26, fos. 70–71d; warrants in C.O.324, 42, pp. 159–162]

9

5 January, St James's

Same, authorizing Governor of New Hampshire, as Chancellor, to apply for powers to issue commissions for custody of idiots. *Copy.* 2½ pp. *Endorsed,* Recd. 12 December, Read 21 December 1772. [C.O.5, 930, fos. 154–155d]

10

6 January, New York

* Maj.-General Thomas Gage to Earl of Hillsborough (No. 39), acknowledging No. 23. The 9th regiment should by now be in Ireland. Embarkation and disembarkation at St Augustine should be in small craft. Report on Fort Chartres. Inhabitants of Detroit appear to have no claim to Hog Island—granted by H.M. to Lieut. Macdougal— beyond title of sixty years possession. Report on Six Nations: we appear to have alternative of permitting or encouraging the Indians to go to war with each other or of uniting them to our own danger. Mr Stuart reports meeting at Augusta with Upper Creeks and Cherokees, at which they complained of irregularities in trade. *Signed.* 6¼ pp. *Endorsed,* R, 7 February. *Enclosed :*

  i. Johnson Hall, 8 December 1769. Sir W. Johnson to Maj.-General Gage, reporting renewal of treaty between Six Nations and Chero- kees. Possibility of war between them and Western Indians; they want meeting with Indians of Canada this winter. Unless engaged in something of that kind, the Six Nations may be drawn into more dangerous designs. *Copy.* 3 pp. [C.O.5, 88, fos. 26–31d; entry in C.O.5, 234, pp. 28–40]

11

6 January, New York

Lieut.-Governor Cadwallader Colden to Commissioners for Trade and Plantations. Yesterday I passed bill for granting £2000 for troops; and, with advice of Council, bill for emitting £120,000 in bills of credit, which is similar to that transmitted by Sir H. Moore. Copies sent, with copy of Act explaining duty of loan-officers. Other Acts to follow. *Signed.* 2½ pp. *Endorsed,* Recd. 7 February, Read 8 February 1770. [C.O.5, 1074, fos. 204–205d]

12

6 January, New York

★ Same to Earl of Hillsborough (No. 8), acknowledging No. 34.
Enclosed were at time of opposition to bill for supplying troops here.
Opposition party was disappointed at small numbers at meetings of
Sons of Liberty. Bill for supplying troops was passed only by com-
promise and by expectations of assent to bill for emitting bills of credit.
Council advised assent to latter, copy sent to Board of Trade. No
public business could have been carried on without it. *Signed.* 4½ pp.
Endorsed, R, 7 February 1770. *Enclosed :*

> i. New York, 16 December 1769. Address by a Son of Liberty *To
> the Betrayed Inhabitants of City and Colony of New York,* opposing
> troops and charging De Lancey family with betrayal of liberties.
> *Printed.* 1¾ pp.

> ii. New York, 20 December 1769. Proclamation by Lieut.-Governor
> Colden declaring condemnation of No. i by Assembly of New York.
> Reward of £100 for discovery of author. *Printed.* 1 p.

> iii. New York, 20 December 1769. Same, of printed paper *To the
> Public,* calling meeting of opponents of troops. Reward of £50 for
> discovery of author. *Printed.* 1 p.

> iv. New York, 23 December 1769. *Answer to Citizen's Address to the
> Public,* by A Plebeian, exhorting Sons of Liberty to stand firm.
> *Printed.* 2¾ pp. [C.O.5, 1101, fos. 21–28d; entry of covering letter in
> C.O.5, 1138, pp. 127–132; extract of covering letter, endorsed Recd.,
> Read 8 February 1770, in C.O.5, 1074, fos. 206–208d]

13

6 January, Charleston

Lieut.-Governor William Bull to Commissioners for Trade and
Plantations, sending journals of Council to end of last year and journal
of Assembly to beginning of present session. *Signed.* ¾ p. *Endorsed,*
Recd., Read 7 February 1770. [C.O.5, 379, fos. 95–96d]

14

8 January, Whitehall

Earl of Hillsborough to Lord Chamberlain, asking for customary
allowance of plate to Peter Chester, appointed Governor of West
Florida. *Entry.* ½ p. [C.O.5, 619, p. 29]

15

8 January, Whitehall

Same to Lords of Admiralty, asking for usual powers to be granted to
Peter Chester, appointed Governor of West Florida. *Entry.* ½ p.
[C.O.5, 619, p. 29]

16

8 January, Brunswick

Governor William Tryon to Earl of Hillsborough (No. 46). My No. 32
presumed lost, duplicate sent. My sensibility wounded by last Assembly.
Governor's house at New Bern expected to be completed by end of year.
When this is settled, I wish year's leave unless my services are acceptable
as Governor of New York. *Duplicate. Signed.* 3½ pp. *Endorsed,* R, 4
April, original not recd. [C.O.5, 313, fos. 31–32d; signed original,
endorsed duplicate, in C.O.5, 301, fos. 122–123d; entry in C.O.5, 328,
pp. 177–180]

17

8 January, Boston

Lieut.-Governor Thomas Hutchinson to Earl of Hillsborough (No. 2),
acknowledging No. 29. On 4 January I issued proclamation proroguing
the Court to second Wednesday in March, having first informed the
Council. The public clamour much less than I expected. *Signed.* 1 p.
Endorsed, R, 20 February 1770. *Enclosed:*

 i. Boston, 4 January 1770. Proclamation as above. *Printed.* 1 p.
 [C.O.5, 759, fos. 31–33d; entry of covering letter in C.O.5, 768,
 pp. 70–71]

18

8 January, Charleston

Lieut.-Governor William Bull to Earl of Hillsborough (No. 22),
acknowledging No. 29. *Signed.* 1 p. *Endorsed,* R, 7 February 1770.
[C.O.5, 393, fos. 16–17d; signed duplicate in C.O.5, 379, fos. 105–106d;
entry in C.O.5, 409, p. 91]

19

9 January, Treasury

Thomas Bradshaw to John Pownall, sending memorial of John Ellis,
agent for West Florida, and inquiring if payment should be made of
sums requested, expended on Indian affairs. *Signed.* 1 p. *Endorsed,* R,
10 January. Memorial returned to Treasury. [C.O.5, 587, pp. 1–4]

20

9 January, Treasury

Same to same, enclosing following, and inquiring if payment should be
made of bills drawn by Lieut.-Governor Browne for £150 10s. for
Mr Westropp's salary while deputy-superintendant of Indian affairs
at Mobile. *Signed.* 1 p. *Endorsed,* R, 10 January. *Enclosed:*

 i. Pensacola, 5 October 1769. Lieut.-Governor Montfort Browne to
 Lords of Treasury. Mr Westropp's salary is due from 26 September

1768 to 23 July 1769 when he was superseded by Charles Stuart. *Signed.* 2 pp. *Endorsed,* R, 18 December, Read 20 December 1769. [C.O.5, 587, pp. 5–12]

21

10 January, St James's

Commission to Peter Chester to be Governor of West Florida. *Entry.* 24 pp. [C.O.5, 619, pp. 30–53]

22

11 January, Whitehall

John Pownall to Anthony Todd. Packet-boats to be detained to Thursday for Lord Hillsborough's dispatches for America. *Entry.* ½ p. [C.O.5, 241, p. 241]

23

12 January, Treasury

Thomas Bradshaw to John Pownall. General Gage has been directed to pay sum due to artificers employed at Oswego in last war. *Signed.* 1 p. *Endorsed,* R, do. [C.O.5, 1283, fos. 98–99d; entry in C.O.5, 1300, p. 22]

24

12 January, Treasury

Same to same. Lords of Treasury have no objection to remission of fines on two poor women in Virginia as proposed by Governor Lord Botetourt. *Signed.* ¾ p. *Endorsed,* R, do. [C.O.5, 1348, fos. 21–22d]

25

12 January, Halifax

Governor Lord William Campbell to Earl of Hillsborough (No. 56), acknowledging No. 32 and explaining transactions at isles of St Peter and Miquelon. Bills drawn in favour of Mrs Lockman, widow. *Signed.* 2 pp. *Endorsed,* R, 2 April. [C.O.217, 47, fos. 19–20d; signed duplicate, not so described, in C.O.217, 26, fos. 20–21d; entry in C.O.218, 17, pp. 231–232]

26

12 January, Charleston

Lieut.-Governor William Bull to Earl of Hillsborough (No. 23). 240 lbs. raw silk sent to London, first to receive bounty. *Signed.* ¾ p. *Endorsed,* R, 20 February. [C.O.5, 393, fos. 20–21d; entry in C.O.5, 409, p. 92]

27

[*12 January*]

Memorial of Gilbert Ross and James Mill of London, merchants, to Commissioners for Trade and Plantations, praying for confirmation of Act passed in South Carolina in 1769 for incorporating the Fellowship Society. *Signed*, Charles Palmer, agent. 1 p. *Endorsed*, Recd. 12 January, Read 25 January 1770. [C.O.5, 379, fos. 67–68d]

28

13 January, Treasury

Grey Cooper to John Pownall, enclosing following and requesting information respecting quitrents. *Signed.* ¾ p. *Endorsed*, Recd. 13 January, Read 17 January 1770. *Enclosed:*

    i. Treasury Minute, 4 January 1770. Mr Walpole, Mr Sarjant, Dr Franklin and Mr Wharton attended and offered £10,460 7s. 3d. for land sold to H.M. by Six Nations at Fort Stanwix, and quitrent of 2s. for every 100 acres of cultivable land. If other departments approve application, Treasury approve of purchase price but postpone matter of quitrents for further information. *Copy.* 1¾ pp. *Endorsed*, Read 17 January 1770. [C.O.5, 1332, fos. 148–151d]

29

15 January, Whitehall

John Pownall to Anthony Todd. Packet-boats to be detained to Thursday. *Entry.* ½ p. [C.O.5, 241, p. 242]

30

16 January, St Augustine

* Governor James Grant to Earl of Hillsborough (No. 34), acknowledging No. 24. Our planters think themselves entitled to premiums on indigo: crop of nearly ten thousandweight to be sent to London. Negroes arrived from Africa. Five companies of 31st regiment are under orders for West Florida, leaving 21st regiment and two companies of 31st here. *Signed. Endorsed*, R, 31 March. [C.O.5, 551, fos. 15–16d; signed duplicate in C.O.5, 544, fos. 167–168d; entry in C.O.5, 567, pp. 139–141]

31

17 January, Treasury

Thomas Bradshaw to John Pownall, enclosing following. Lords of Treasury are of opinion that fine should be remitted. *Signed.* ¾ p. *Addressed. Endorsed*, R, 18th. *Enclosed:*

    i. Charleston, 12 August 1769. Lieut.-Governor William Bull to Lords of Treasury, asking for remission of fine of £11 15s. sterling imposed on John Fulmer and three others, poor German settlers, for attempted rescue. They were sentenced to three months imprisonment and have served two months over. *Copy*. 1¼ pp. [C.O.5, 393, fos. 7–10d; entry of covering letter in C.O.5, 409, pp. 84–85]

32

18 January, Whitehall

* Earl of Hillsborough to Lieut.-Governor Cadwallader Colden (No. 36), acknowledging No. 5 and blaming him for declaring to Assembly of New York that late duties would without distinction probably be taken off in next session of Parliament, and for allowing Assembly to frame new bill respecting paper currency while H.M. was considering former one. New Assembly's concurrence in resolves of Virginia Assembly not a favourable omen. King's speech to Parliament of 9th inst., addresses of both Houses and H.M.'s reply enclosed. Great Seal given to Charles Yorke. *Draft*. 3¼ pp. [C.O.5, 1101, fos. 8–9d; entry in C.O.5, 1141, pp. 109–111]

33

18 January, Whitehall

Same to Maj.-General Thomas Gage (No. 25). Your conduct concerning 9th and 21st regiments approved. Policy of making St Augustine a principal military station very doubtful. General O'Reilly's forbidding import of foreign goods to Louisiana and Englishmen residing at New Orleans is rigorous but warranted by treaty. Defence of Quebec to be considered. Security of posts in the interior merits attention. King's speech and addresses of both Houses of Parliament, sent, show resolution to discountenance associations against importation from Great Britain. Reinforce Lieut.-Colonel Dalrymple if necessary. Hopes New York and New Jersey will make usual provision for troops quartered there. Great Seal given to Charles Yorke. *Draft*. 3½ pp. [C.O.5, 88, fos. 17–19d; entry in C.O.5, 241, pp. 242–246]

34

18 January, Whitehall

* Same to Lieut.-Governor Thomas Hutchinson (No. 31). Enclosed King's speech to Parliament of 9th inst. and addresses of both Houses show that measures will be taken to suppress associations formed to obstruct Britain's trade with colonies. Sitting of Assembly not to be postponed. In view of insults to troops at Boston, Maj.-General Gage has been ordered to reinforce Colonel Dalrymple if necessary. Great Seal given to Charles Yorke. *Entry*. 3 pp. [C.O.5, 765, pp. 71–74; draft in C.O.5, 759, fos. 21–22d]

35

18 January, Whitehall

* Same to Governor William Tryon (No. 30), acknowledging No. 39.
H.M. is concerned at conduct of North Carolina, hitherto decent and
moderate. Writs for new Assembly to be issued; be cautious in your
speech to them to say no more than necessary. King's speech to Parliament and addresses of both Houses, sent. Great Seal given to Charles
Yorke. *Draft.* 2¾ pp. [C.O.5, 313, fos. 1–2d; entry in C.O.5, 332,
pp. 42–44]

36

18 January, Whitehall

Same to Governor Lord William Campbell (No. 34), acknowledging
Nos. 51–54. No expectation that your proposition relative to roads
will be adopted. If Mr Goold quits military employment and if you
recommend him to Register's office, I will take King's pleasure thereon.
King's speech to Parliament, addresses of both Houses and H.M.'s
reply sent. Great Seal given to Charles Yorke. *Draft.* 1½ pp. [C.O.217,
47, fos. 1–2d; entry in C.O.218, 25, pp. 65–67]

37

18 January, Whitehall

Same to Governor Lord Botetourt (No. 29), acknowledging Nos. 20–21
and enclosures. It is to be wished that your speech to Assembly on 7
November had been confined to spirit of form sent you in my No. 26.
Your Nos. 18–19 and 22 acknowledged. Sole right of vending map of
Virginia you wish for Mr Henry was granted long since. King's speech
to Parliament on 9th inst., addresses of both Houses and H.M.'s
answers, sent. Great Seal delivered to Charles Yorke. *Draft.* 2 pp.
[C.O.5, 1348, fos. 23–24d; entry in C.O.5, 1375, pp. 88–90]

38

18 January, Whitehall

Same to Governor Guy Carleton (No. 30), acknowledging Nos. 24–27
and papers by Mr Morgan. Mr Maseres's leave of absence lamented
but you could not refuse; appointment of Mr Kneller as Attorney-
General *pro tem.* approved. Mr Vialers has no authority to speak in my
name. King's speech to Parliament of 9th inst., addresses of both
Houses and King's answers, sent. Great Seal given to Charles Yorke.
Draft. 2½ pp. [C.O.42, 30, fos. 1–2d; entry in C.O.43, 8, pp. 78–80]

39

18 January, Whitehall

Same to Governor John Wentworth (No. 27), sending Order in
Council containing H.M.'s final decision on provision for custody of

idiots; letter from Treasury by which you will see their sense of your merit as Surveyor of Woods; and H.M.'s speech to Parliament on 9th inst., etc. Great Seal given to Charles Yorke. *Draft.* 1¼ pp. [C.O.5, 937, fos. 1–2d; entry, with Order, dated 5 January 1770, in C.O.5, 947, pp. 40–44]

40

18 January, Whitehall

Same to Deputy Governor John Penn (No. 21), acknowledging duplicates of Nos. 17–20 but no originals. It would have redounded to honour of merchants of Philadelphia, had they kept to resolution of declining association against importation. I learned of this from public prints. King's speech to Parliament of 9th inst. etc. sent. Great Seal delivered to Charles Yorke. *Draft.* 1½ pp. [C.O.5, 1283, fos. 1–2d; entry in C.O.5, 1301, pp. 123–124]

41

18 January, Whitehall

Same to Governor William Franklin (No. 22), sending King's speech to Parliament of 9th inst. etc. It is Stephen, not Courtlandt, Skinner who is made member of Council of New Jersey. Great Seal given to Charles Yorke. *Draft.* 1 p. [C.O.5, 990, fos. 1–2d; entry in C.O.5, 1003, p. 26]

42

18 January, Whitehall

Same to Governor and Company of Connecticut (No. 17) and Governor and Company of Rhode Island (No. 19), sending King's speech to Parliament of 9th inst. etc. Great Seal given to Charles Yorke. *Draft.* ¼ p. [C.O.5, 1283, fos. 68–69d; entry (Connecticut) in C.O.5, 1301, p. 269; entry (Rhode Island) in C.O.5, 1301, p. 442]

43

18 January, Whitehall

Same to Deputy Governor Robert Eden (No. 16), sending King's speech to Parliament of 9th inst. etc. Great Seal delivered to Charles Yorke. *Entry.* ½ p. [C.O.5, 1301, p. 8]

44

18 January, Whitehall

Same to Governors of Maryland, South Carolina, Georgia, East Florida, West Florida, Bahamas, and to Sir William Johnson and John Stuart, sending King's speech to Parliament on 9th inst., addresses of both Houses and H.M.'s answers. Great Seal given to Charles Yorke.

Draft. 1 p. [C.O.5, 71, Pt. 1, fos. 5–8d; entries in C.O.5, 408, p. 29 (S.C.), C.O.5, 677, p. 38 (Ga.), C.O.5, 566, p. 26 (E. Fla.), C.O.5, 619, p. 54 (W. Fla.), C.O.5, 241, p. 247 (Johnson, Stuart)]

45

18 January

John Pownall to Anthony Todd, sending packets for North America and West Indies, to be dispatched forthwith. *Entry.* ½ p. [C.O.5, 241, p. 248]

46

19 January, Whitehall

John Pownall to Grey Cooper, acknowledging letter of 13 January and Treasury minute on memorial of Mr Walpole and others; and enclosing following. *Entry.* 1 p. *Enclosed:*

i. Account of quitrents reserved on grants of land in colonies nearest to lands proposed to be purchased by Mr Walpole and others: Virginia, Maryland, Pennsylvania, New York. *Entry.* 2½ pp. [C.O.5, 1369, pp. 10–13; draft in C.O.5, 1336, fos. 155–157d]

47

20 January, Brunswick

Governor William Tryon to Earl of Hillsborough (No. 47), enclosing list of patents granted in land-office at Brunswick in December last. *Signed.* ½ p. *Endorsed,* R, 4 April. *Enclosed:*

i. 16 January 1770. List of patents granted in North Carolina at December Court of Claims by Governor Tryon. *Certified,* by John London, deputy secretary. 14 pp. *Endorsed,* In Governor's letter No. 47. [Covering letter in C.O.5, 313, fos. 33–34d; signed duplicate in C.O.5, 301, fos. 125–126d; entry in C.O.5, 328, pp. 180–181. Enclosure in C.O.5, 320, fos. 98–105d]

48

20 January, Savannah

Governor James Wright to Earl of Hillsborough (No. 39), acknowledging letter of 2 November and leave of absence. I shall fortify and prepare Mr Habersham before my departure. *Duplicate. Signed.* PS. No resolutions for non-importation have taken effect here. 2 small pp. *Endorsed,* R, 3 April. [C.O.5, 660, fos. 82–83d; signed original, but endorsed duplicate, in C.O.5, 651, fos. 16–17d; entry in C.O.5, 678, pp. 172–173]

49

20 January, Pensacola

Lieut.-Governor Elias Durnford to Earl of Hillsborough (No. 1), reporting arrival in West Florida and making allegations against Montfort Browne, his predecessor. *Signed.* ¾ p. [C.O.5, 577, pp. 205–208]

50

20 January, Charleston

John Stuart to Earl of Hillsborough (No. 18), enclosing papers concerning proposed extension of Virginia's boundaries. Dr Walker and Colonel Lewis are greatly interested. Trouble is likely from repeated applications to the savages for lands. *Signed.* 2 pp. *Endorsed*, R, 31 March. *Enclosed:*

i. Williamsburg, 18 December 1769. Governor Lord Botetourt to John Stuart, enclosing following. I beg your assistance towards completing this great work. *Copy.* 1 p.

ii. Address of House of Burgesses of Virginia to Governor Lord Botetourt, concerning extension of colony's boundaries. *Copy.* 1 p.

iii. Memorial of same to same on same subject, with remarks thereon. *Copy.* 5 pp.

iv. Charleston, 13 January 1770. John Stuart to Governor Lord Botetourt, resisting proposed extension of boundary. Reasons why Indians will not give up lands. *Copy.* 4 pp.

v. 29 July 1769. Abstract of talk by Cherokees to John Stuart, complaining of encroachments by Virginia. *Copy. Signatories,* Oucconastotah, Attakullakulla, Otacite, Willanawaw, Skotteloske; John Watts, interpreter. 1 p.

vi. Williamsburg, 20 December 1768. David Ross to Alexander Cameron. Plans for acquisition of Indian lands. *Copy.* 2½ pp. [C.O.5, 71, Pt. 1, fos. 52–66d; entry of covering letter in C.O.5, 227, pp. 223–224; signed duplicate of covering letter, copies of enclosures i-v, and a copy of Lord Botetourt's speech to Council and Burgesses of Virginia, dated 21 December 1769, in C.O.323, 27, pp. 7–42]

51

[21 January]

Petition of Edward Montagu, agent for Virginia, to Commissioners for Trade and Plantations, praying for advices of application for lands which, if approved, would sever large part of Virginia and affect rights of many. *Signed.* 1½ pp. *Endorsed*, Recd., Read 21 January 1770. [C.O.5, 1332, fos. 154–155d]

52

22 January, Treasury

Thomas Bradshaw to John Pownall, inquiring what would be suitable bounty for Captain Carver, whose plans etc. made during his expedition into interior of North America have been delivered to Commissioners for Trade and Plantations. *Signed.* ¾ p. *Addressed. Endorsed,* Recd., Read 25 January. [C.O.323, 28, pp. 303–306]

53

23 January, Whitehall

Earl of Hillsborough to Viscount Weymouth, sending extract of letter from Lieut.-Governor Browne complaining of General O'Reilly's obstructing free navigation of Mississippi, and papers on which that complaint appears to be based. *Draft.* ¾ p. [C.O.5, 587, pp. 61–64; entry in C.O.5, 619, pp. 54–55]

54

24 January, Whitehall

John Pownall to Thomas Bradshaw, acknowledging two letters of 9 January, concerning West Florida. Payment should be suspended and more particular account required of appointments for which sums are demanded. *Draft.* 1½ pp. [C.O.5, 587, pp. 65–68; entry in C.O.5, 619, pp. 55–57]

55

24 January, Williamsburg

Governor Lord Botetourt to Earl of Hillsborough (No. 27), enclosing following. I shall have very little weight in this country if seat of government is to be so distressed. *Duplicate. Signed.* ¾ p. *Endorsed,* R, 9 March, original not recd. *Enclosed :*

  i. Williamsburg, 28 January 1770. Governor Lord Botetourt to Commissioners of Customs at Boston, enclosing following. I entreat you to take no step until you hear from England. *Signed Copy.* ½ p.

  ii. Address and Memorial of City of Williamsburg to Governor Lord Botetourt, opposing scheme for removing Custom-house for Upper District of James River from Williamsburg to Bermuda Hundred. *Copy. Signatory,* John Blair, jnr., Mayor. 3¾ pp. [C.O.5, 1348, fos. 53–58d; signed original of covering letter, and copies of enclosures, in C.O.5, 1333, fos. 20–22d, 25, 25d; entry of covering letter in C.O.5, 1372, pp. 100–101]

56

24 January, Boston

* Lieut.-Governor Thomas Hutchinson to Earl of Hillsborough (No. 3), reporting meeting last week in Boston of those concerned in non-importation of goods from Great Britain. Two of my sons, who were of the merchants who had sold, were constrained to comply with the agreement of the meeting. The meeting was not tumultuous, but much of the proceedings were illiberal and puerile. I warned the moderator that violence from inferior people would involve them all in high treason. I dare say non-importation cannot hold another year; nevertheless they obstinately persist. There were J.P.s, lawyers, inhabitants of property and three Representatives at the meeting, together with a mixed multitude persuaded that they were struggling for liberties of America. Had the Council been with me, this meeting might have been prevented. *Signed.* 3 pp. *Endorsed*, R, 7 March. *Enclosed*:

i. Extract of minutes of Council of Massachusetts, 18, 19, 20, 22, 23 January 1770. *Copy*, certified by John Cotton, deputy secretary. 5½ pp.

ii. 22 January 1770. Declaration sworn by William Jackson, trader, that William Molineaux with a great number of people came to his shop in Boston on 17 January and tried to get him to let them in. *Copy*, certified by John Cotton. 1 p.

iii. Boston, 23 January 1770. Lieut.-Governor Hutchinson to people assembled at Faneuil Hall, calling on meeting to disperse and warning of consequences of going from house to house, demanding property. *Copy*. 1 p.

iv. Boston, 23 January 1770. Same to William Phillips, covering No. iii. *Copy*. ½ p.

v. Message to Sheriff Greenleaf. The lieut.-governor's address has been read at this meeting. It is the unanimous opinion of the body that this meeting is warranted by law. *Copy*, certified by John Cotton. ½ p. [C.O.5, 759, fos. 36–45d; entry of covering letter and of Nos. ii–v in C.O.5, 768, pp. 71–78; signed duplicate of covering letter and copies of enclosures i, iii–v, in C.O.5, 894, pp. 11–26]

57

24 January

Petition of Arthur Lee, agent for certain inhabitants of Great Britain, Virginia and Maryland, to Commissioners for Trade and Plantations, praying that lands they have previously petitioned for be not granted to others. *Signed.* 1 p. *Endorsed*, (illegible, damaged). [C.O.5, 1332, fos. 152–153d]

58

26 January, Williamsburg

Governor Lord Botetourt to Earl of Hillsborough (No. 28), asking for directions in enclosed case. *Signed.* ½ p. *Endorsed,* R, 26 March. *Enclosed:*

i. Williamsburg, 25 January 1770. John Randolph, Judge of Vice-Admiralty Court, to Governor Lord Botetourt. David Ferguson is to be tried for murder of negro boy. He is also accused of murdering three mariners on the high seas, for which he cannot be tried here for want of commission. *Signed.* 1 small p. [C.O.5, 1348, fos. 61–64d; signed duplicate of covering letter, and copy of enclosure, in C.O.5, 1333, fos. 23–24A dorse; entry in C.O.5, 1372, pp. 101–102]

59

27 January, Pensacola

Lieut.-Governor Elias Durnford to Earl of Hillsborough (No. 2), reporting irregularities by Lieut.-Governor Montfort Browne, leading to resignations from Council of West Florida. Council now restored: recommendations to fill future vacancies. *Duplicate. Unsigned.* 7 pp. *Endorsed,* R, 21 April, original not received. *Enclosed:*

i. Address of inhabitants of Pensacola to Lieut.-Governor Durnford. *Copy,* of No. 312vi. 1½ pp. [C.O.5, 587, pp. 85–96; signed original of covering letter in C.O.5, 577, pp. 209–216; entry of covering letter in C.O.5, 620, pp. 204–213]

60

27 January, Charleston

John Stuart to Earl of Hillsborough (No. 19). Indian reluctance to part with lands, particularly Creeks. Seminolies are separated from Creeks and live near St Augustine; if they could be reunited, I should be able to obtain cession of land in East Florida. Provinces should pass laws respecting their boundaries. *Signed.* 2 pp. *Endorsed,* R, 10 April. [C.O.5, 71, Pt. 1, fos. 69–70d; entry in C.O.5, 227, pp. 228–230; signed duplicate in C.O.323, 27, pp. 43–46]

61

28 January, Williamsburg

Governor Lord Botetourt to Earl of Hillsborough (No. 29). Proposal to remove Custom-house from Williamsburg is stimulated by proprietors and neighbourhood of Bermuda Hundred who want seat of government there. Enclosed proves regard to H.M.'s interest paid in this colony. *Signed.* ¾ p. *Endorsed,* R, 2 April. *Enclosed:*

i. Newspaper cutting listing sheriffs who have failed to settle accounts or pay balances. *Printed.* 1 p. [C.O.5, 1348, fos. 69–70A dorse; entry of covering letter in C.O.5, 1372, pp. 104–105]

62

29 January, Whitehall

John Pownall to Grey Cooper, sending copies of petitions of Colonel
Mercer for grant of lands on Ohio River and of Arthur Lee for grant
of 2½ million acres of land ceded by Indians at Treaty of Fort Stanwix,
with copies of memorials from each on being informed of Mr Walpole's
petition for part of these lands. *Entry.* 1½ pp. [C.O.5, 1369, pp. 14–15;
draft in C.O.5, 1336, fos. 158–159d]

63

29 January, Whitehall

Same to Thomas Bradshaw. Commissioners for Trade and Plantations
are at a loss to form opinion on bounty to be paid Mr Carver. Copy of
their report to Committee of Council on Mr Carver's petition, sent.
Entry. 1¼ pp. Mem: £1129 15s. 3d. recommended by Lords of Council
to Treasury, to be paid Captain Carver. [C.O.324, 18, pp. 365–366]

64

29 January, Whitehall

Same to Richard Cumberland, agent for Nova Scotia, requesting
attendance on subject of civil establishment for 1770 and statement of
balance remaining. *Entry.* ½ p. Like letters sent to William Knox, agent
for East Florida; J. Campbell, agent for Georgia; John Ellis, agent for
West Florida. [C.O.324, 18, p. 366]

65

[29 January]

Memorial of Charles Garth, agent for South Carolina, to Commissioners for Trade and Plantations, praying for continuation of bounty on
indigo. *Signed.* 1¾ pp. *Endorsed,* Recd. 29 January, Read 8 February
1770. [C.O.5, 379, fos. 73–74d]

66

31 January, Boston

Lieut.-Governor Thomas Hutchinson to John Pownall, enclosing
the following very extraordinary vote of Council. This is done to avoid
charge of sitting as Council without Governor. *Signed.* 1 small p.
Endorsed, R, 15 March. *Enclosed:*

   i. Extracts of minutes of Council of Massachusetts, 14 July 1769,
   ordering members to be a committee fully authorized, in the recess
   of General Court, to instruct William Bollan, their agent. *Copy,*
   certified by John Cotton, deputy secretary. 1 small p.

ii. Cutting [from New York newspaper], inscribed 12 January, reporting public suspicions of the soldiers. *Printed.* 1 small p. [C.O.5, 759, fos. 47–51d; entry of covering letter and No. i in C.O.5, 768, pp. 79–80]

67

31 January, Williamsburg

Governor Lord Botetourt to Earl of Hillsborough (No. 26), sending Acts of Virginia, resolves of Assembly and printed journals of House of Burgesses and Council, and two letters from Treasurer Nicholas on the Acts. Written copy of journal of Burgesses will be sent by next ship. My power of serving H.M. here will greatly depend on answers to desires of Assembly. *Triplicate. Signed.* 1 p. *Endorsed,* Sent in box by Captain Nix. R, 9 March, original and duplicate not recd. [C.O.5, 1348, fos. 51–52; signed original, with PS covering enclosure of set of Virginia laws, in C.O.5, 1333, fos. 14–14A dorse; signed duplicate, with PS giving text of speech of adjournment to Assembly, in C.O.5, 1333, fos. 15–15A dorse; entry in C.O.5, 1372, pp. 99–100]

68

1 February, Savannah

Governor James Wright to Earl of Hillsborough (No. 40), notifying appointment of James Hume as acting Attorney-General of Georgia in succession to Mr Greene, resigned. *Duplicate. Signed.* 1 small p. *Endorsed,* R, 3 April. [C.O.5, 660, fos. 84–85d; signed original, endorsed duplicate, in C.O.5, 651, fos. 18–19d; entry in C.O.5, 678, p. 174]

69

1 February, Tower of London

Report on magazines and ordnance storehouses in West Florida and also those built by the contingency of General Gage. *Signed,* Arthur Neil. 2¾ pp. *Endorsed,* Delivered by Colonel Chester, 7 February. [C.O.5, 587, pp. 69–72]

70

3 February, Pensacola

* Lieut.-Governor Elias Durnford to Earl of Hillsborough (No. 3). Fort Bute should be re-established and town laid out there, which will attract the most opulent French inhabitants. Town should be established on east side of Mobile Bay below Red Cliffs. Old fort at Mobile is decayed; materials might be used for barracks. Traders on the Illinois should be obliged to give bond to send furs to Fort Bute. *Unsigned.* 5½ pp. *Endorsed,* R, 21 April. [C.O.5, 587, pp. 97–104; signed duplicate in C.O.5, 577, pp. 217–224; entry in C.O.5, 620, pp. 213–219]

71

5 February, Boston

Lieut.-Governor Thomas Hutchinson to John Pownall, notifying progress of paper-mills and slit-mill at Milton, belonging to James Boyes. In paper he may succeed; in nails I think he cannot. We never yet could make any nails less than a deck-nail so cheap as we import them from England. *Signed.* 1 small p. *Endorsed*, R, 15 March. [C.O.5, 759, fo. 52, 52d; entry in C.O.5, 768, pp. 80–81]

72

5 February, London

Petition of John Greeve of Lurgan, Ireland, to Commissioners for Trade and Plantations, praying for grant of 20,000 acres of land in Nova Scotia. *Signed.* ¾ p. *Endorsed*, Recd. 6, Read 7 February 1770. [C.O.217, 25, fos. 194–195d]

73

[7 February]

Petition of Edward Wildman to Commissioners for Trade and Plantations, for 5000 acres of land in West Florida. 1 p. *Endorsed*, Recd., Read 7 February 1770. [C.O.5, 577, pp. 165–168]

74

7 February, Whitehall

Commissioners for Trade and Plantations to the King, recommending grant of 10,000 acres of land in Nova Scotia (half of what was prayed for) to John Greeve of Lurgan. *Entry. Signatories*, Hillsborough, George Rice, Thomas Robinson, Lisburne. 3 pp. [C.O.218, 7, pp. 273–275]

75

7 February, Whitehall

Same to same, recommending grant of 10,000 acres of land in East Florida to Godfrey Thornton, of London, merchant. *Entry. Signatories*, Hillsborough, George Rice, Thomas Robinson, Lisburne. 3 pp. [C.O.5, 563, pp. 271–273]

76

7 February, Whitehall

Same to same, recommending grant of 10,000 acres of land in East Florida to John Cornwall of London, merchant. *Entry. Signatories*, as preceding. 2½ pp. [C.O.5, 563, pp. 274–276]

77

7 February, Whitehall

Same to same, recommending that petition of Edward Wildman, who is going with Governor Chester, for 5,000 acres of land in West Florida, be granted. *Entry. Signatories*, Hillsborough, Soame Jenyns, George Rice, William Fitzherbert. 2½ pp. [C.O.5, 600, pp. 29–31]

78

7 February, Whitehall

John Pownall to Anthony Todd. Packet-boats to be detained to Saturday. *Entry.* ½ p. [C.O.5, 241, p. 248]

79

7 February, Ordnance Office

John Boddington to John Pownall, reporting on supply of ordnance and progress of works at and in: Antigua; Halifax; St John's, Newfoundland; Grenada; St Vincent; Dominica. *Signed.* 2½ pp. *Endorsed,* R, 7 February. [C.O.5, 71, Pt. 1, fos. 14–15d; entry in C.O.5, 227, pp. 219–221]

80

7 February, Pensacola

Lieut.-Governor Elias Durnford to Earl of Hillsborough (No. 4), enclosing papers. *Signed.* ½ p. *Endorsed,* R, 21 April. *Enclosed :*

i. Pensacola, 7 February 1770. Lieut.-Governor Durnford to General Gage, sending copy of No. ii. Rum from Mr Bradley's store and jealousy of traders may have contributed to this incident. Re-establishment of Fort Bute and appointment of commissaries to Indians absolutely essential. Orders by General O'Reilly enclosed. *Copy.* 1½ pp.

ii. New Orleans, 1 February 1770. John Bradley to Lieut.-Governor Durnford. Abandonment by troops and ruinous state of fort puts us in dangerous situation in Natchez. My store was plundered by eighteen Choctaws on 18 January: we killed two and retired to Manchack. There are about 2000 Choctaws from Fort Panmure to Grand Gulf. General O'Reilly assists us. Disappointment of presents appears to have induced Indians to act thus. *Copy.* 7 pp.

iii. New Orleans, 27 January 1770. Translation of orders by General O'Reilly, Governor of Louisiana, to commanders, for harmony with British officers and subjects. *Copy.* 1½ pp.

iv. Account given by Mr Fergy to Governor in Council in West Florida of Indian attack at the Natchez. *Copy.* 2½ pp. [C.O.5, 587, pp. 105–128; signed duplicate of covering letter, dated 6 February

1770, copy of enclosure i, dated 6 February, and copies of enclosures ii–iv, all in C.O.5, 577, pp. 229–252; entry of covering letter in C.O.5, 620, p. 220]

81

8 February, Whitehall

Commissioners for Trade and Plantations to the King, recommending disallowance of bill passed in New York similar to that passed in 1769 for emitting £120,000 in bills of credit. It is submitted whether Lieut.-Governor Colden was justified in assenting to this bill without suspending clause, contrary to instruction of 1766. *Entry. Signatories,* Hillsborough, George Rice, William Fitzherbert, Lisburne. 3½ pp. [C.O.5, 1131, pp. 42–45; draft in C.O.5, 1080, pp. 335–342]

82

8 February, Whitehall

Same to same, proposing Rev. James Horrocks to be of the Council in Virginia in room of Presley Thornton, deceased. *Entry. Signatories,* as preceding. 1 p. [C.O.5, 1369, pp. 15–16; draft in C.O.5, 1336, fos. 160–160A dorse]

83

9 February, St James's

Order of King in Council, appointing Rev. James Horrocks to be of the Council in Virginia in room of Presley Thornton, deceased. *Copy.* ¾ p. *Endorsed,* Recd. 12 December, Read 21 December 1772. [C.O.5, 1334, fos. 6–6A dorse; entry of warrant, dated 14th February, in C.O.324, 42, p. 167; sealed original of Order in C.O.5, 26, fos. 72–73d]

84

9 February, St James's

Same, disallowing Act passed in New York in 1769 for emitting £120,000 in bills of credit. *Copy.* 1 p. *Endorsed,* Recd. 12 December, Read 21 December 1772. [C.O.5, 1076, fos. 188–189d]

85

9 February, Whitehall

John Pownall to Attorney- and Solicitor-General, sending Tax Act passed in Massachusetts in July 1769, and other papers, for opinion whether Commissioners and other officers of Customs in America are liable to be taxed in this way for salaries paid out of money not granted by General Court of that colony. *Entry.* 1½ pp. [C.O.5, 920, pp. 276–277; draft in C.O.5, 897, fos. 267–268]

86

9 February, Whitehall

Same to Clerk of Council in Waiting, sending copy of letter from lieut.-governor of South Carolina to be laid before Privy Council as containing matters of high importance. *Entry.* ½ p. [C.O.5, 408, p. 29]

87

9 February, Johnson Hall

Sir William Johnson to Earl of Hillsborough (private). Major Gorham is continued as deputy agent for Nova Scotia. Lieutenant Benjamin Roberts recommended. *Signed.* 1 p. *Endorsed*, R, 12 April. [C.O.5, 71, Pt. 1, fos. 71–72d; entry in C.O.5, 227, pp. 230–231; extract, commending Roberts, endorsed Read 10 May 1771, in C.O.323, 27, pp. 93–96]

88

10 February, Whitehall

Order of Committee of Council for Plantation Affairs, referring following to Commissioners for Trade and Plantations. *Seal. Signed,* Stephen Cottrell. 1 p. *Endorsed*, Recd. 26 February 1770. *Enclosed :*

　i. Memorial of Edward Bell to the King, praying for grants of 100,000 and 20,000 acres of land in back-lands of Virginia on Ohio and elsewhere. *Copy.* 2½ pp.

　ii. Case of Edward Bell, setting out services as storekeeper at Bremen and evidence of character. *Copy.* 2¾ pp. [C.O.5, 1332, fos. 167–172d]

89

10 February, Whitehall

Earl of Hillsborough to Board of Ordnance, requesting account of ordnance supplied to American colonies since 1763, and of ordnance-establishments. *Draft.* ½ p. [C.O.5, 71, Pt. 1, fos. 16–17d; entry in C.O.5, 241, p. 249]

90

10 February, Whitehall

Same to same, sending copies of letters from lieut.-governor of West Florida requesting ordnance stores and repairs to magazines and storehouses, and other papers. *Draft.* 1 p. [C.O.5, 587, pp. 73–76; entry in C.O.5, 619, pp. 57–58]

91

10 February, Whitehall

Same to Lords of Admiralty, inquiring what is practice in respect of collection of Greenwich Hospital duty in Massachusetts. *Entry.* ¾ p. [C.O.5, 765, pp. 71–74; draft in C.O.5, 759, fos. 23–24d]

92

10 February, Whitehall

John Pownall to Clerk of Council in Waiting, enclosing following. *Draft.* ½ p. *Enclosed:*

i. Hertford, 11 December 1769. Commissioners for settling boundary between New York and New Jersey to Earl of Hillsborough, enclosing following. *Copy. Signatories,* C. Andrew Elliott, Andrew Oliver, Charles Morris, Jared Ingersoll. 1 p. *Endorsed,* R, 7 February 1770.

ii. Hertford, 8, 9, 11 December 1769. Proceedings of above commissioners. Adjourned to 4 July through want of quorum. *Copy. Signatories,* as No. i. 8¼ pp.

iii. 7 October 1767. Commission for settling New York-New Jersey boundary. *Copy.* 7 pp. [C.O.5, 1101, fos. 29–41d; entry of covering letter in C.O.5, 1141, p. 112]

93

10 February, Pensacola

William Clifton to John Pownall. I shall comply with whatever terms you make on Mr Buel's behalf. Mr Durnford's appointment gives general satisfaction. Seat of government of this province should be removed: known sterility of Pensacola causes general prejudice. *Signed.* 2 small pp. *Endorsed,* R, 21 April. [C.O.5, 587, pp. 231–234; entry in C.O.5, 620, pp. 242–243]

94

10 February, Johnson Hall

* Sir William Johnson to Earl of Hillsborough (No. 12), reporting congress of Cherokees and Six Nations at Onondaga and meeting with them here. They are disposed to unite and attack other tribes. Further congress with chiefs urgently desired. It is disagreeable that we must either let them cut each other's throats or risk their discharging their fury on our traders and frontiers. *Signed.* 3 pp. *Endorsed,* R, 12 April. [C.O.5, 71, Pt. 1, fos. 73–74d; entry in C.O.5, 227, pp. 231–234]

95

12 February, Burlington

Governor William Franklin to Earl of Hillsborough, sending Acts passed in New Jersey last session and Minutes of Council. Act for striking £100,000 in bills of credit does not make the money legal tender in all payments. Assembly was persuaded not to tack supply for troops onto this Act. Act supplementary to Act for dividing Bergen Common may be opposed by William Bayard; refer to Council minutes of 16 November for reasons why Council advised assent to it. *Signed.* 4 pp. *Endorsed,* R, 3 April. [C.O.5, 990, fos. 9–11d; extract, endorsed Read 4 April 1770, in C.O.5, 979, fos. 13–14d; another extract, endorsed Read 9 April 1770, in C.O.5, 979, fos. 15–16d; entry in C.O.5, 1001, pp. 109–114]

96

[*12 February*]

Memorial of rice-planters and landowners in East Florida to Earl of Hillsborough, praying for same freedom to export rice to Europe south of Cape Finisterre enjoyed by South Carolina and Georgia. *Signed,* Gilbert Ross and thirty-six others. 2¼ pp. *Endorsed,* R, 12 February 1770. Copy transmitted to Treasury, 23 February 1770. [C.O.5, 551, fos. 9–10d]

97

[*12 February*]

Memorial of landowners in East Florida and merchants of London trading there, to Earl of Hillsborough, praying that St Mary's River be made port of entry. St Augustine harbour is dangerous and has little water-communication with rest of province. *Signed,* Peter Taylor and thirty others. 3 pp. *Endorsed,* R, 12 February. Copy transmitted to Treasury, 23 February 1770. [C.O.5, 551, fos. 11–12d]

98

13 February, Whitehall

Order of Committee of Council for Plantation Affairs referring following to Commissioners for Trade and Plantations. *Seal. Signed,* Stephen Cottrell. 1 p. *Endorsed,* Recd. 16 February, Read 19 February 1770. *Enclosed:*

i. Charleston, 12 December 1769. Lieut.-Governor William Bull to Earl of Hillsborough, reporting vote of Commons House of Assembly of South Carolina on 8 December, ordering Treasurer to advance £10,500 currency for remitting to Great Britain for support of rights and liberties. It is probably for supporters of Bill of Rights in London. *Copy.* 4½ pp. [C.O.5, 379, fos. 75–80d]

99

13 February

Case laid before Attorney-General relating to order by Commons House of Assembly of South Carolina on 8 December 1769 for issuing money, with his opinion thereon. The payment is not legal, though the practice is of a few years, irregularly introduced. It would be hard to make the Treasurer liable to legal consequences of wrong payment. *Copy. Signatory,* William de Gray. 18 pp. *Endorsed,* Read 19 February 1770. [C.O.5, 379, fos. 81–90d]

100

13 February, Ordnance Office

Board of Ordnance to Earl of Hillsborough. We are of opinion that batteries at Halifax, if repaired, can be of little defence to town or dockyard. Reports enclosed. *Signed,* H. S. Conway, Charles Frederick, A. Wilkinson, Charles Cocks. 1½ pp. *Endorsed,* R, 16 February. *Enclosed :*

i. Greenwich, 31 January 1770. Chief Engineer W. Skinner to Board of Ordnance, reporting as in covering letter. *Copy.* 1½ pp.

ii. London, 9 January 1770. Captain John Brewse to Board of Ordnance, to same effect. *Copy.* 3¼ pp. [C.O.217, 47, fos. 7–12d; entry of covering letter in C.O.218, 7, pp. 229–230]

101

14 February, St James's

Order of King in Council, disallowing Act passed in New York in 1770 for emitting £120,000 in bills of credit. *Copy.* 1½ pp. *Endorsed,* Recd. 12 December, Read 21 December 1772. [C.O.5, 1076, fos. 190–191d]

102

14 February, Pensacola

Lieut.-Governor Elias Durnford to John Pownall, complaining of Montfort Browne. Engineer Campbell will probably complain concerning land improperly granted to him by Mr Browne. *Signed.* 3 pp. *Endorsed,* R, 21 April. [C.O.5, 587, pp. 191–194; entry in C.O.5, 620, pp. 231–233]

103

15 February, Whitehall

Earl of Hillsborough to Lords of Admiralty. Governor Chester is to have passage for himself, family and baggage, in one of H.M. ships, by way of Jamaica to West Florida. *Draft.* ½ p. [C.O.5, 587, pp. 77–80; entry in C.O.5, 619, p. 58]

104

15 February, Whitehall

Commissioners for Trade and Plantations to the King, enclosing the following. *Signed,* Soame Jenyns, George Rice, Thomas Robinson, William Fitzherbert. 3 pp. *Enclosed:*

i. 13 February 1770. Opinion of Attorney- and Solicitor-General, sent to Commissioners for Trade and Plantations. We have considered the Tax Act passed in Massachusetts in July 1769 and are of opinion that the salaries of Commissioners and other officers of Customs in America are liable to be taxed where they reside. *Copy. Signatories,* William de Grey, J. Dunning, 2½ pp. [C.O.5, 759, fos. 25–28d; entry of covering letter and opinion in C.O.5, 765, pp. 77–80; entry of covering letter in C.O.5, 920, pp. 278–280; draft of same in C.O.5, 897, fos. 269–270d]

105

15 February, Whitehall

Same to same, enclosing following. No material alteration from instructions to late governor except that we have inserted articles 14 and 17 restraining governor from assenting to Acts for public or private lotteries without H.M.'s directions or from establishing any regulations relative to Assembly inconsistent with his instructions. 26th article relating to Surveyor-General of Customs in North America omitted, that office being abolished. *Entry. Signatories,* Hillsborough, Soame Jenyns, William Fitzherbert, George Rice. 2 pp. *Enclosed:*

i. Draft of instructions for Peter Chester, Captain-General and Governor-in-Chief of West Florida; St James's, 2 March 1770. *Entry.* 107 pp.

ii. Draft of instructions in pursuance of laws relating to trade and navigation, for same. *Entry.* 67 pp. [C.O.5, 600, pp. 33–208]

106

15 February, Whitehall

Same to Committee of Council for Plantation Affairs, recommending grant of 5000 acres of land in Georgia to Henry Yonge, Surveyor-General of Georgia. *Entry. Signatories,* George Rice, William Fitzherbert, Soame Jenyns. 2 pp. [C.O.5, 674, pp. 344–345]

107

15 February, Whitehall

John Pownall to Anthony Todd. American packet-boats to be detained to Saturday. *Entry.* ¼ p. [C.O.5, 241, p. 249]

108

15 February, Whitehall

Same to Grey Cooper, sending copy of petition of agent of Virginia, seeking advice of application to Treasury for grant of land which, if completed, will sever large part of that dominion and affect rights of individuals. *Entry.* 1 p. [C.O.5, 1369, pp. 16–17; draft in C.O.5, 1336, fos. 161–161A dorse]

109

15 February, Pensacola

Lieut.-Governor Elias Durnford to Earl of Hillsborough, complaining of Montfort Browne, particularly for seeking to reduce fees of office of Surveyor-General. *Signed.* 3½ pp. *Endorsed*, R, 21 April. [C.O.5, 587, pp. 129–132; entry in C.O.5, 620, pp. 221–225]

110

15 February, Pensacola

Same to John Pownall. Chief Justice Clifton will give directions on affair you mentioned to me in England. *Signed.* 1½ pp. *Endorsed*, R, 21 April. [C.O.5, 587, pp. 195–198; entry in C.O.5, 620, pp. 233–234]

111

15 February

Petition of Captain Allan MacDonald, eldest captain in 59th regiment, to Commissioners for Trade and Plantations, praying for grant of 1200 acres of land and 10,000 more, in Cape Breton, petitioned for in 1769. ½ p. *Endorsed*, Read 21 September 1770. [C.O.217, 25, fos. 196–197d]

112

[15 February]

Memorials of Thomas and Richard Penn to Commissioners for Trade and Plantations, asking for papers relative to application by Mr Wharton and others for grant of large tract of land lately ceded to H.M. by Indians; and, if affected, to be heard against it by counsel. 1 p. *Endorsed*, Read 15 February 1770. [C.O.5, 1277, pp. 555–558]

113

16 February, Pensacola

Lieut.-Governor Elias Durnford to Earl of Hillsborough (No. 4), making charges against late lieut.-governor, Montfort Browne, and enclosing papers. *Signed.* 5 pp. *Endorsed*, R, 21 April. Perhaps 5. *Enclosed:*

i. Pensacola, 14 February 1770. State of provincial accounts of West Florida. *Copy. Signatory,* Montfort Browne. 1 large p.

ii. *Isabella,* Monday morning. Undated letter from Montfort Browne to Elias Durnford. I have taken the King's instructions with me; copy at secretary's office. I shall make all possible dispatch back. Act for me during my absence as for a brother. Ride out to see what they are doing at my plantation. Adieu. Compliments to everybody. *Copy.* 1 p.

iii. Undated letter from Elias Durnford to Montfort Browne, requesting immediate return as confusion seems likely. I have prorogued Assembly. You have it in your power to check imprudent behaviour on their part, if you will return. *Copy.* 1½ pp.

iv. Undated statement by Elias Durnford on his former friendship with Montfort Browne and on charges against Browne concerning provincial funds and inquiry thereinto; including letter from Browne to Durnford of 12 May 1769 and reply of same date. 8½ pp.

v. Pensacola, 26 December 1769. Lieut.-Governor Durnford to Montfort Browne, notifying arrival and requesting his presence. *Copy.* ½ p.

vi. New Grove, 9 January 1770. Montfort Browne to Lieut.-Governor Durnford. Government-house will be cleared and public papers and seal given to you. *Copy.* 1¼ pp.

vii. Pensacola, 13 January 1770. Lieut.-Governor Durnford to Montfort Browne, asking for H.M.'s instructions and other papers, and that no payment be made to Daniel Hicky, Indian commissary. *Copy.* ½ p.

viii. Pensacola, 13 January 1770. Same to same, asking why Francis Poussett was dismissed from post of deputy secretary of West Florida. *Copy.* ½ p.

ix. Pensacola, 15 January 1770. Montfort Browne to Lieut.-Governor Durnford. Persons were dismissed with sufficient reason. I protest against your proceedings both before and since Governor Eliot's death. *Copy.* 1 p.

x. Pensacola, 18 January 1770. Same to same, requesting minutes of Council of his administration to copy and take home to England. *Copy.* ½ p.

xi. Pensacola, 19 January 1770. Lieut.-Governor Elias Durnford to Montfort Browne, refusing above request. I shall send copy of minutes to England, and will supply copy to you if you think this insufficient. Copy of your private account enclosed. Mr Hicky not to be paid until his accounts are passed; Mr Hartley not to be paid. *Copy.* 1½ pp.

xii. Pensacola, 20 January 1770. Montfort Browne to Lieut.-Governor Durnford, further protesting. As dissimulation is not my talent,

I cannot therefore subscribe myself your most obliged humble servant. *Copy.* $1\frac{1}{2}$ pp.

xiii. Pensacola, 1 February 1770. Lieut.-Governor Durnford to Montfort Browne, requesting contingent and Indian accounts and that Hicky and Hartley be not paid. *Copy.* $\frac{1}{2}$ p.

xiv. Pensacola, 1 February 1770. J. Crawford to Lieut.-Governor Durnford. Mr Browne will produce accounts requested but desires no unnecessary correspondence or intercourse. *Copy.* $\frac{1}{2}$ p.

xv. Pensacola, 2 February 1770. Lieut.-Governor Durnford to Montfort Browne. Every kind of correspondence from me to you is disagreeable. Archives of French inhabitants and other papers requested. *Copy.* $\frac{1}{2}$ p.

xvi. Pensacola, 5 February 1770. Montfort Browne to Lieut.-Governor Durnford, demanding immediate justice before he sails in eight or ten days time. *Copy.* $\frac{1}{2}$ p.

xvii. Pensacola, 5 February 1770. Lieut.-Governor Durnford to Montfort Browne. I have asked Attorney-General for opinion on your request. *Copy.* $\frac{1}{2}$ p.

xviii. Pensacola, 5 February 1770. Lieut.-Governor Durnford to Attorney-General Wegg, requesting opinion on Mr Browne's demand. *Copy.* $\frac{1}{2}$ p.

xix. Pensacola, 6 February 1770. Montfort Browne to Lieut.-Governor Durnford, protesting at soldiers with fixed bayonets at his door. I am even refused to go to the bog-house. *Copy.* 1 p.

xx. Pensacola, 6 February 1770. Attorney-General Wegg to Lieut.-Governor Durnford. In Mr Jones's present state, nothing can be done. If he were dead or out of danger, special commission of oyer and terminer might be made out. *Copy.* $\frac{1}{2}$ p.

xxi. Pensacola, 6 February 1770. Lieut.-Governor Durnford to Montfort Browne, enclosing opinion of Attorney-General. *Copy.* $\frac{1}{2}$ p.

xxii. Pensacola, 9 February 1770. Same to same, requesting public accounts of province, invoices of Indian goods sent here, and Mr Hicky's copies of issues. *Copy.* $\frac{1}{2}$ p.

xxiii. Pensacola, 9 February 1770. Montfort Browne to Lieut.-Governor Durnford. A day approaches when neither villainy nor craft dare look me in the face; this supports me against the black confederacy formed against my honour and innocence. It hurts me even to subscribe to you. *Copy.* $\frac{1}{2}$ p.

xxiv. Pensacola, 14 February 1770. Lieut.-Governor Durnford to Montfort Browne, requesting vouchers which make up general account of provincial and Indian contingencies. *Copy.* $\frac{3}{4}$ p. [Covering letter with enclosures i-iv, vii-xxiii, in C.O.5, 587, pp. 133–190; signed duplicate of covering letter, but dated 15 February, with enclosures v-xvi and xix-xxiv, in C.O.5, 577, pp. 253–332, with some differences of dating by one day; entry of covering letter in C.O.5, 620, pp. 225–230]

114

[*16 February*]

Memorial of Phineas Lyman, maj.-general of Connecticut militia in war of 1756–1763, to Commissioners for Trade and Plantations, praying for 150,000 acres of land in Natchez country, West Florida, in recognition of services. *Signed.* 7 small pp. *Endorsed,* Recd. 16 February, Read 19 February 1770. [C.O.5, 577, pp. 169–176]

115

17 February, Whitehall

Earl of Hillsborough to Maj.-General Thomas Gage (No. 26), acknowledging Nos. 38 and 39. Forts on Providence Island to be supplied with ordnance when repairs are completed. H.M. ships to undertake, if possible, transport of troops between Bahamas and St Augustine; one company will be sufficient. New York's Act for raising half the money for quartering troops is repealed. 9th regiment is safe in Ireland. St Augustine is not proper as station for troops. Illinois country should either be abandoned or held on some other plan. Possession of Hog Island for sixty years by French settlers seems just title. News of Indian affairs expected from Sir W. Johnson. Great Seal in commission, Lord North made 1st Commissioner of Treasury. *Draft.* 5¼ pp. [C.O.5, 88, fos. 32–35d; entry in C.O.5, 241, pp. 250–255]

116

17 February, Whitehall

Same to same. Separate and secret. Orders have lately been placed in London for arms and accoutrements said to be for regiment of light horse of New York militia. There may be no cause for alarm, but inquire secretly into it. *Draft.* 2 pp. *Enclosed:*

 * i. Secretary's Office, 10 February 1770. Information from Mr Rawle, giving grounds for above apprehensions, and reporting inquiry for arms from Boston. *Copy.* 2½ small pp. [C.O.5, 88, fos. 36–39d; entry of covering letter in C.O.5, 241, pp. 256–257]

117

17 February, Whitehall

 * Same to Lieut.-Governor Cadwallader Colden (No. 37), acknowledging Nos. 6–8. Your consenting to bill for emitting bills of credit disapproved. Bill for that purpose sent by Sir H. Moore and bill you sent, both disallowed; Orders in Council sent. However, Parliament will be moved to pass Act enabling New York to have desired bill. Petition concerning lands west of Connecticut River appears just; referred to Commissioners for Trade and Plantations. Great Seal put in commission, Lord North made 1st Commissioner of Treasury. *Draft.* 4 pp. [C.O.5, 1101, fos. 42–44d; entry, with Orders in Council of 9 and 14 February 1770 disallowing said Acts, in C.O.5, 1141, pp. 113–122]

118

17 February, Whitehall

Same to Governor Lord Botetourt (No. 30), acknowledging Nos. 23–25. Mr Horrocks's mandamus for seat in Council in Virginia goes by this packet. Papers concerning extension of boundary sent to Board of Trade. Proposal concerning copper coin and augmenting salaries of Councillors needs consideration: final decision would be with Treasury. Request for liberty to import salt directly from Europe referred to Board of Trade. Great Seal put in commission; Lord North made 1st Commissioner of Treasury. *Draft.* 3 pp. [C.O.5, 1348, fos. 49–50d; entry in C.O.5, 1375, pp. 91–93]

119

17 February, Whitehall

Same to Governor Lord William Campbell (No. 35), acknowledging No. 55. Officers responsible for furnishing copies of Journals of Assembly and laws of Nova Scotia have been negligent. Copy of No. 100 and enclosures, sent. Great Seal put in commission; Lord North made 1st Commissioner of Treasury. *Draft.* 2 pp. [C.O.217, 47, fos. 13–14d; entry in C.O.218, 25, pp. 67–69]

120

17 February, Whitehall

Same to same (separate). Mr Crawley's grant is not to be voided for non-settlement for further period of four years. *Draft.* ¾ p. *Enclosed:*

i. Memorial of Edward Crawley, one of Council of Nova Scotia, to Earl of Hillsborough, praying for further period of four years in which to settle land granted to him in Nova Scotia in 1765. *Entry.* 1½ pp. [Covering letter in C.O.217, 47, fos. 15–16d; entry in C.O.218, 25, pp. 69–70; enclosure in C.O.218, 25, pp. 70–72]

121

17 February, Whitehall

Same to Governor Guy Carleton (No. 31), acknowledging letter of 22 November last. Application by Abbé Joncaire to return to Canada will not be encouraged. Great Seal put in commission; Lord North made 1st Commissioner of Treasury. *Draft.* ½ p. [C.O.42, 30, fos. 5–6d; entry in C.O.43, 8, pp. 80–81]

122

17 February, Whitehall

Same to Governor James Wright (No. 29), acknowledging No. 38. H.M. hopes that Lower House of Assembly may be prevented from taking further notice of letter from Speaker of House of Burgesses of

Virginia. From what you said in No. 38, I had no doubt that associations for non-importation had taken place in Georgia. Great Seal has been put in commission, Lord North made 1st Commissioner of Treasury. *Draft.* 1½ pp. [C.O.5, 660, fos. 78–79d; entry in C.O.5, 677, pp. 39–40]

123

17 February, Whitehall

Same to Governor James Grant (No. 26), acknowledging Nos. 31–33. Great Seal put in commission; Lord North made 1st Commissioner of Treasury. *Draft.* 1 p. [C.O.5, 551, fos. 7–8d; entry in C.O.5, 566, p. 27]

124

17 February, Whitehall

Same to Governor William Tryon (No. 31), acknowledging Nos. 40–43. Board of Trade's recommendation about allowances proposed for members of Council of North Carolina may have met with difficulty at Treasury. Great Seal in commission; Lord North made 1st Commissioner of Treasury. *Draft.* 1½ pp. [C.O.5, 313, fos. 22–23d; entry in C.O.5, 332, pp. 44–46]

125

17 February, Whitehall

* Same to Lieut.-Governor William Bull (No. 33), acknowledging Nos. 19–22. Resolution of Commons House of Assembly of South Carolina of 8 December last was unwarranted, disrespectful and of great concern to H.M. Instruction thereon should reach you mid-May. Your conduct approved. Great Seal in commission; Lord North made 1st Commissioner of Treasury. *Draft.* 2¾ pp. [C.O.5, 393, fos. 18–19d; entry in C.O.5, 408, pp. 30–32]

126

17 February, Whitehall

Same to Lieut.-Governor Thomas Hutchinson (No. 32), acknowledging Nos. 11 and 13, letter of 1 January, and paper on associations for non-importation. Customs officers to be supported consistent with justice. Opinion of Law Officers sent on taxation of Customs Officers. Petition concerning Seamen's Sixpences sent to Admiralty. Great Seal put in commission; Lord North made 1st Commissioner of Treasury. *Entry.* 2 pp. [C.O.5, 765, pp. 75–76; draft in C.O.5, 759, fos. 29–30d]

127

17 February, Whitehall

Same to Governor Jonathan Trumbull (No. 18), acknowledging Nos. 12, 14–16. You are to transmit journals of Assembly of Connecticut and copies of laws; none received later than 1768. *Draft.* 1¼ pp. [C.O.5, 1283, fos. 78–79d; entry in C.O.5, 1301, pp. 269–270]

128

17 February, Whitehall

Same to Governor and Company of Rhode Island (No. 20), requesting journal of Assembly and copies of laws; none received later than 7 Geo. III. *Draft.* ¾ p. [C.O.5, 1283, fos. 100–101d; entry in C.O.5, 1301, p. 443]

129

17 February, Whitehall

Same to Deputy Governor John Penn (No. 22). Great Seal put in commission, Lord North made 1st Commissioner of Treasury. *Entry.* ½ p. [C.O.5, 1301, p. 125]

130

17 February, Whitehall

Same to Deputy Governor Robert Eden (No. 17), acknowledging dispatch of 23 November. Temper and moderation of Assembly of Maryland carry pleasing appearance. Your conduct approved. You are to transmit journals and proceedings of Assembly and copies of laws; none received later than 1763. Great Seal put in commission; Lord North made 1st Commissioner of Treasury. *Draft.* 2 pp. [C.O.5, 1283, fos. 15–16d; entry in C.O.5, 1301, pp. 9–10]

131

17 February, Whitehall

Same to Governors of New Hampshire, New Jersey, Pennsylvania and Bermuda. Great Seal placed in commission; Lord North made 1st Commissioner of Treasury. *Draft.* ½ p. [C.O.5, 71, Pt. 1, fos. 20–21d; entry of letter to Governor Wentworth (No. 28) in C.O.5, 947, p. 44; entry of letter to Governor Franklin (No. 23) in C.O.5, 1003, p. 27]

132

17 February, Whitehall

Same to John Stuart (No. 14), acknowledging No. 17. Warrants for your admission as member extraordinary of Councils in your district have been prepared. Reports wanted on Choctaw Indians and on case of deputy superintendent for Indian affairs appointed by Lieut.-Governor Browne, whom you refused to pay. *Draft.* 2 pp. [C.O.5, 71, Pt. 1, fos. 18–19d; entry in C.O.5, 241, pp. 258–259]

133

17 February, Whitehall

John Pownall to Anthony Todd, sending dispatches to go forthwith by New York and North Carolina packets. West India packets to be detained till further orders. *Entry.* ½ p. [C.O.5, 241, p. 250]

134

17 February, Pensacola

Lieut.-Governor Elias Durnford to Earl of Hillsborough (No. 6), enclosing following. Choctaws claim lands in Mississippi quarter of this province, and expect congress as right. If land is not ceded to us by Lower Creeks in the treaty, congress should be called to get it from them. I will mark out boundary with Choctaws on Mobile and Tombigbee rivers, but wish to let that on Mississippi rest. Withdrawing commissaries was a loss to the nation. *Unsigned.* 2½ pp. *Endorsed*, R, 21 April. *Enclosed :*

    i. Charleston, 4 January 1770. John Stuart to Lieut.-Governor Durnford. Boundaries with Choctaws are fixed by Treaty of Mobile of 1765; they did not claim lands on Mississippi. Upper Creeks are delicate on subject of land. Our limits from Pensacola Bay to Apalachicola were fully described in Treaty of Augusta of 1768. I cannot negotiate for additional cessions without orders from home. Since commissaries were withdrawn, traders have returned to their former abuses, and we can no longer learn Indians' true intentions. Regiment is ordered to your province from St Augustine. *Copy.* 4 pp.

    * ii. Some Thoughts on Indian Trade by Lieut.-Governor Durnford. Regulations needed: each province to send traders only into parts nearest to it; tariff with each Indian tribe to be same; rum to be rationed and one commissary or more allowed to each province to check irregularities; little or no credit to be given to Indians. West Florida needs congress with Lower Creeks to get more land, and one with tribes on or near Mississippi. 2¼ pp. [Covering letter and enclosure i in C.O.5, 587, pp. 199–210; signed duplicate of covering letter, dated 18 February, and copies of enclosures i-ii, in C.O.5, 577, pp. 333–346; entry of covering letter in C.O.5, 620, pp. 234–237]

135

18 February, N.H.

* Governor John Wentworth to Earl of Hillsborough (No. 29), acknowledging No. 25. General Assembly voted to petition H.M. for £6000, proportion of Parliamentary grant to colonies for aid in last war. Annexing to New Hampshire district west of Connecticut River was mentioned but deferred. Assembly hope for royal allowance of County Act. No new manufactures set up since my residence here; nail-making tried at Portsmouth but given over. No non-importation committees

or associations in this province. Inhabitants on lands west of Connecticut River are importunate; Council of New Hampshire resolved to form a state of the case. Much confusion there. *Signed.* 9 pp. *Endorsed,* R, 7 May. [C.O.5, 937, fos. 3–8d; extract relating to lands on Connecticut River, endorsed Recd., Read 13 July 1770, in C.O.5, 930, fos. 84–85d; signed duplicate in C.O.5, 930, fos. 88–94d; entry in C.O.5, 945, pp. 143–149]

136

18 February, Pensacola

Lieut.-Governor Elias Durnford to Earl of Hillsborough (No. 7), enclosing minutes of Council of West Florida, relating to Mr Browne's being released. *Signed.* ½ p. *Endorsed,* R, 21 April. *Enclosed :*

i. 17 February 1770. Proceedings of Council of West Florida. *Copy,* certified by Francis Poussett. 3½ pp. [C.O.5, 587, pp. 211–218; signed duplicate of covering letter, dated 19 February, in C.O.5, 577, pp. 347–350; entry of covering letter in C.O.5, 620, pp. 237–238]

137

18 February, Pensacola

Same to [John Pownall], setting forth circumstances of following. The governor cannot grant more than 1000 acres over and above family-right. *Unsigned.* 3¼ pp. *Endorsed,* R, 21 April. *Enclosed :*

i. 18 February 1770. Minutes of Council of West Florida, recording grant of land in 1769 to John Campbell and Edward Crofton. *Copy,* sworn before E. R. Wegg. 1¼ pp. [C.O.5, 587, pp. 219–226; entry of covering letter in C.O.5, 620, pp. 238–242]

138

20 February, Brunswick

Governor William Tryon to Earl of Hillsborough (No. 48), enclosing paper by Attorney-General of Virginia, from which, with other papers, materials may be drawn for reform of quitrents. *Duplicate. Signed.* 1 p. *Endorsed,* R, 11 April, original not recd. *Enclosed :*

i. 26 September 1769. John Randolph to Governor Tryon, enclosing following. *Copy.* 1 p.

ii. A few observations pointing out method for fixing the payment of H.M.'s quitrents in North Carolina. *Copy.* 3½ pp.

iii. Specimen register for above. 2 pp. [C.O.5, 313, fos. 35–42d; signed original, endorsed duplicate, with copies of enclosures, in C.O.5, 301, fos. 127–135d; entry of covering letter and enclosures i–ii in C.O.5, 328, pp. 181–189]

139

21 February, New York

Maj.-General Thomas Gage to Earl of Hillsborough (No. 40), acknowledging No. 24. There are at present twelve companies of troops in
East Florida; more can be spared for West Florida. I shall send 16th
regiment from here to Pensacola. Forts in West Florida will be repaired.
Ownership of Hog Island will probably be determined by Council.
Barracks proposed for St Augustine will be better built at Pensacola.
Sir W. Johnson's difficulties in holding congress the Six Nations want
are because of expense. There was opposition in Assembly here to
paying for quartering of troops. Copy of indictment by grand jury at
Boston enclosed. *Signed.* 6 pp. *Endorsed,* R, 2 April. *Enclosed :*

* i. Philadelphia, 1 January 1770. George Croghan, deputy agent
for Indian affairs, to General Gage, reporting apprehension of
Indian designs for rupture in the spring. There was a meeting in the
fall of Ohio, Seneca, Shawnese and Delawares, with Hurons,
Chipawas, Ottawa and Potawotomis, at which complaint was made
of the Six Nations. Mr McKee goes to Fort Pitt this week, I hope he
will find out what the Indians intend. *Copy.* 3 pp.

ii. Court of Assize, Boston, 21 November 1769. Presentment by
grand jury of Thomas Gage for letter written by him to Earl of
Hillsborough in which he slandered and vilified people of Boston.
True bill. *Copy.* 1 p. [C.O.5, 88, fos. 40–47d; entry in C.O.5, 234,
pp. 40–52]

140

21 February, New York

* Lieut.-Governor Cadwallader Colden to Earl of Hillsborough (No. 9),
acknowledging No. 35. Consenting to bill for emitting bills of credit
defended. Assembly passed Act declaring Judges of Supreme Court
incapable of being members of Assembly, copy enclosed, and refused
to admit Mr Livingston. Assembly also passed Act enabling H.M.'s
subjects by birth or naturalization to inherit, notwithstanding defect of
purchase before naturalization; to which I assented, with suspending
clause. Agreement with General Gage enclosed. Act passed appointing
commissioners to meet those of neighbouring colonies to regulate
Indian trade. Affray between townspeople of New York and soldiers was
narrowly averted by interposition of magistrates. Persons who appear
on these occasions are of inferior rank but directed by persons of distinction and encouraged by persons of note in England. Opponents of
government mainly Dissenters, friends are Church of England,
Lutheran, Old Dutch Congregation, with several Presbyterians.
Alexander McDougal in gaol awaiting trial for writing and publishing
To the Betrayed Inhabitants. Signed. 8½ pp. *Endorsed,* R, 2 April.
Enclosed :

i. Act declaring certain persons incapable of sitting in General Assembly of New York. *Copy,* certified by G. Banyar, deputy secretary. 1¼ pp.

ii. New York, 15 January 1770. Agreement between General Gage and Lieut.-Governor Colden for applying the £2000 granted by New York for supply of troops. *Copy.* 2½ pp. [C.O.5, 1101, fos. 45–53d; signed duplicate of covering letter, and copy of No. ii, in C.O.5, 1074, fos. 219–224d; entry of covering letter in C.O.5, 1138, pp. 132–142; extract of covering letter, endorsed Read 4 April, in C.O.5, 1074, fos. 209–210d; copy of Act declaring certain persons incapable of being members of Assembly of New York, endorsed Read 4 April 1770, in C.O.5, 1074, fos. 211–212d]

141

21 February, New York

Same to Commissioners for Trade and Plantations, sending journal of Assembly 21 November 1769–27 January 1770; Acts to follow. Acts for emitting £120,000 in bills of credit, rendering judges incapable of being members of Assembly, and to confirm titles to real estate notwithstanding defect of purchase before naturalization, are all that deserve particular attention. Council rejected some bills in favour of Dissenters; and I withheld assent from bill for regulating militia. Great good humour and agreement prevailed between several branches of legislature; peaceable disposition among the people, notwithstanding endeavours to create disturbances. *Signed.* 2 pp. *Endorsed,* Recd., Read 2 April 1770. [C.O.5, 1074, fos. 213–214d]

142

21 February, Annapolis

* Deputy Governor Robert Eden to Earl of Hillsborough (No. 5), reporting affair of *Good Intent,* William Errington, chartered by John Buchanan, merchant in London, with goods to sundry merchants here. Commissioners from interested counties met here: resolves are in *Gazette* of 15th inst. My attempts to convince them of impropriety of their conduct failed. The brig sails tomorrow. Mr Buchanan signed City address, which gave great offence here. *Signed.* 4 pp. *Endorsed,* R, 26 April. *Enclosed:*

i. *Maryland Gazette,* 25 January 1770, containing notice that *Good Intent* is expected and calling meeting. *Printed.* 2 pp.

ii. *Maryland Gazette,* 15 February 1770, reporting proceedings concerning *Good Intent. Printed.* 4 pp. [C.O.5, 1283, fos. 23–27d; signed duplicate of covering letter, and copy of No. i, in C.O.5, 1278, fos. 25–28d; entry of covering letter in C.O.5, 1300, pp. 236–239]

143

22 February, Whitehall

John Pownall to Thomas Bradshaw, sending copy of letter from Commissioners of Customs at Boston to Lieut.-Governor Hutchinson, and opinion of Law Officers [No. 104i] on case stated in this letter. *Entry.* ¾ p. [C.O.5, 765, p. 81; draft in C.O.5, 759, fos. 34–35d]

144

22 February, Williamsburg

Governor Lord Botetourt to Earl of Hillsborough (private), enclosing following. I wish Colonel Tryon may succeed to New York: he and General Carleton are best governors on the continent. Sir William Draper commended. Duplicates of papers sent with my No. 26 and Naval Officer's accounts, sent. *Signed.* ¾ small p. *Endorsed,* R, 8 April. *Enclosed :*

* i. Charleston, 13 January 1770. John Stuart to Governor Lord Botetourt. *Copy,* of No. 50 iv. 2¾ pp.

ii. Williamsburg, 8 February 1770. Governor Lord Botetourt to John Stuart. No land proposed to be taken without consent of those entitled to part with it. Until H.M.'s orders shall be received, adventurers from this colony will be restrained from settling beyond the line. *Signed Copy.* ¾ p.

iii. Toquah, 29 July 1769. Talk from Cherokees to John Stuart. *Copy,* of No. 50 v. 1 p.

* iv. Winchester, 9 February 1770. Colonel Adam Stephen to Governor Lord Botetourt, reporting inquiry into Indian Stephen's death. *Copy.* 1½ pp. [C.O.5, 1348, fos. 73–82d; list of enclosures in C.O.5, 1372, p. 108]

145

23 February, Whitehall

Commissioners for Trade and Plantations to Committee of Council for Plantation Affairs. We have considered Lieut.-Governor Bull's letter relating to vote of 8 December by Assembly of South Carolina for payment of money. Until 1731 no appropriated money was paid out of Treasury of South Carolina except by order concurred in by Governor, Council and Commons House. About 1732 mode of granting supplies was changed, though the practice of orders by Assembly alone did not begin for several years afterwards. We concur with Attorney-General's opinion, in answer to Lord Hillsborough's questions, that the vote was unconstitutional and not warranted by the modern practice of few years. *Entry. Signatories,* George Rice, John Roberts, William Fitzherbert, Lisburne. 19 pp. [C.O.5, 404, pp. 406–424]

146

23 February, Whitehall

John Pownall to Anthony Todd, sending dispatches for West Indies to go forthwith. *Entry.* ¼ p. [C.O.5, 241, p. 260]

147

23 February, Whitehall

Same to Thomas Bradshaw, sending copies of memorials [Nos. 96 and 97] regarding East Florida for Treasury's consideration. *Draft.* ¾ p. [C.O.5, 551, fos. 13–14d; entry in C.O.5, 566, p. 28]

148

24 February, Treasury

Thomas Bradshaw to John Pownall, enclosing following for opinion of Commissioners for Trade and Plantations. *Signed.* 1 p. *Endorsed,* Recd., Read 26 February. *Enclosed:*

    i. London, 4 December 1769. Memorial of John Ellis, agent for West Florida, to Lords of Treasury, concerning payment of fees to Attorney-General Edmund Rush Wegg, which Lieut.-Governor Browne disputes. *Signed.* 1 p. *Endorsed,* 6 December 1769. No objection by Commissioners for Trade and Plantations to presentation to Treasury, but no approbation of contents.

    ii. Fees of Attorney-General Wegg, 1765–1769. Balance due, £93 15s. 5d., for which he received bills from Lieut.-Governor Browne, 24 July 1769. 9 pp. *Endorsed,* Recd. 15 December, Read 19 December 1769. Postponed that part of memorial relating to payment of fees. [C.O.5, 577, pp. 177–192]

149

26 February, St James's

Order of King in Council, approving draft instructions for Peter Chester, Governor of West Florida. *Copy.* 1½ pp. *Endorsed,* Recd. 12 December, Read 21 December 1772. [C.O.5, 579, pp. 151–154; copy of instructions and instructions in pursuance of laws relating to trade and navigation in C.O.5, 203, fos. 56–94d; sealed original of Order in C.O.5, 26, fos. 76–77d]

150

26 February, Whitehall

Commissioners for Trade and Plantations to the King, recommending disallowance of Act passed in New York in January last to explain duty of loan officers. *Entry. Signatories,* Hillsborough, Soame Jenyns, John Roberts, William Fitzherbert. 1 p. [C.O.5, 1131, p. 46; draft in C.O.5, 1080, pp. 343–346]

151

26 February

Commission to Joseph Gorham to be Lieut.-Governor of Placentia, Newfoundland. *Entry.* 1 p. [C.O.324, 42, p. 170]

152

26 February, Princeton

Richard Stockton to Earl of Hillsborough, enclosing following. *Signed.* 3 small pp. *Endorsed,* R, 10 April. *Enclosed:*

   i. Princeton, 27 January 1770. Report of Richard Stockton that governor of New Jersey is authorized to hold courts of equity and sit as judge. *Signed.* 13 large pp. [C.O.5, 990, fos. 62–70d]

153

27 February

Ordinance of Georgia reappointing Benjamin Franklin agent of the province. *Entry.* 3 pp. [C.O.324, 60, pp. 332–334]

154

28 February, Whitehall

Order of Committee of Council for Plantation Affairs, referring following to Commissioners for Trade and Plantations, for report. *Seal. Signed,* Stephen Cottrell. ¾ p. *Endorsed,* Recd. 1 March, Read 9 March 1770. *Enclosed:*

   i. List of nineteen Acts passed in Pennsylvania in 1769. 2½ pp. [C.O.5, 1277, pp. 563–570]

155

28 February, Boston

* Lieut.-Governor Thomas Hutchinson to Earl of Hillsborough (No. 4), acknowledging No. 30. I have prorogued General Court to Cambridge. If I were to refuse all Councillors concerned in or favourers of combinations, I should have no Council. Disorders continue in Boston with pageants outside doors of those who continue to sell imported goods. One lad was shot, another wounded, by a person who says he was in danger of the crowd: the funeral was perhaps the largest ever known in America. Council would not agree to proclamation against disorders. In other matters than those concerning repeal of Revenue etc. Acts, government of the province retains its vigour. *Duplicate. Signed.* 2 pp. *Endorsed,* R, 21 April 1770, original not recd. [C.O.5, 759, fos. 57–58d; entry in C.O.5, 768, pp. 82–85]

156

1 March, Savannah

Governor James Wright to Earl of Hillsborough (No. 41), acknowledging No. 27. I have removed Mr Bryan from Council: he now holds no office other than being in commission of peace. Undoubtedly combinations against importing are ungrateful and illegal: attempts to promote them in this province have proved ineffectual. *Signed.* 1½ small pp. *Endorsed*, R, 20 April. [C.O.5, 660, fos. 88–89d; signed duplicate in C.O.5, 651, fos. 20–21d; entry in C.O.5, 678, pp. 174–175]

157

2 March, Whitehall

Earl of Hillsborough to Treasurer of Household, sending paper to be delivered to House of Commons in pursuance of their address to H.M. of 21 February. *Entry.* 1 p. *Enclosed:*

i. Account of Associations in American colonies not to import certain goods from Great Britain, such as have been sent to Earl of Hillsborough since 1 August 1768. [Title of paper only] *Entry.* ¼ p. [C.O.5, 241, pp. 260–261]

158

2 March

Warrant to Governor Peter Chester to admit Jacob Blackwell to Council in West Florida. *Entry.* ½ p. [C.O.324, 42, pp. 176–177]

159

[3 March]

Proposals for better peopling, cultivating and securing West Florida, delivered by Colonel Chester to Earl of Hillsborough. Two regiments needed, with artillery; coastal defences; a strong fort in the Natchez. No special advantage in Fort Bute unless Iberville River is made navigable. Foreign Protestants should be transported at government's expense, and given food, tools and seed. Roads should be built; premiums given for agricultural developments. Commissary for Indian affairs should be appointed in the province: part of the £3000 a year Mr Stuart is allowed for presents to Indians should be applied to West Florida's use. Definition needed of relations between governor and commanding officer of troops. Present fort at Pensacola should be destroyed; there should be built barracks and ordnance buildings, and two or three forts or blockhouses on heights at back of town. Wishes to know if confirmatory grants should be given to French inhabitants and those who bought from French. 2¾ pp. *Endorsed*, R, 3 March 1770. [C.O.5, 587, pp. 81–84]

160

[*3 March*]

Memorial of George Walker of Nova Scotia to Commissioners for Trade and Plantations, praying for appointment of person in nature of sub-governor over coast from Bay of Vert to Bay of Chaleurs, with power to regulate fishery and stop illicit trade of French with settlers. 4 large pp. *Endorsed,* Recd. 3 March, Read 9 March 1770. [C.O.217, 25, fos. 198–200d]

161

6 March, Halifax

Governor Lord William Campbell to Earl of Hillsborough (No. 57), acknowledging No. 33. Rev. Moreau, missionary to French Protestants at Lunenburg, dead; memorial enclosed. *Signed.* 2 pp. *Endorsed,* R, 3 May. *Enclosed:*

i. Memorial of Mrs Moreau, widow of John Baptist Moreau, to Governor Lord William Campbell, praying for allowance. *Copy.* 1½ pp. [C.O.217, 47, fos. 23–26d; signed duplicate of covering letter, and copy of enclosure, in C.O.217, 26, fos. 22–25d; entry of covering letter in C.O.218, 17, pp. 232–233]

162

6 March, Charleston

* Lieut.-Governor William Bull to Earl of Hillsborough (No. 23), acknowledging Nos. 30 and 31 and duplicate of 29. Enclosures forwarded. Case of person sentenced to death recommended to clemency. Commerce greatly interrupted by Associators but no violence yet. All members of Council but one and almost all H.M.'s servants have refused to subscribe. Vines imported for French colony; olives next year. Assembly recommended to put grammar-school on better establishment and endow college. Mr Hammerer has quitted plans for civilizing Indians. *Signed.* 3½ pp. *Endorsed,* R, 11 April. *Enclosed:*

i. Report of committee of Assembly of South Carolina with proposals about education. *Copy.* 1½ pp. [C.O.5, 393, fos. 22–25d; signed duplicate of covering letter in C.O.5, 379, fos. 107–109d; entry of covering letter in C.O.5, 409, pp. 92–97]

163

[*6 March*]

Memorial of Richard Gracraft, agent-solicitor for Mohican Indians, to Commissioners for Trade and Plantations, asking for copy of papers in complaint in 1703 of Mohicans against Connecticut. 1 p. *Endorsed,* Recd. 6 March, Read 9 March 1770. [C.O.5, 1277, pp. 559–562]

164

7 March, Whitehall

Earl of Hillsborough to Lieut.-Governor Thomas Hutchinson (No. 33), acknowledging letters of 8 and 24 January. It was right to communicate to Council of Massachusetts the Order proroguing Assembly, and satisfactory that it will not be attended with public inconvenience. North American mail goes to-night; will write by next. *Entry.* ¾ p. [C.O.5, 765, pp. 81–82; draft in C.O.5, 759, fo. 46]

165

7 March, Whitehall

John Pownall to Lieut.-Governor Elias Durnford, sending copy of estimate on which vote of £4800 for civil establishment of West Florida for midsummer 1769 to midsummer 1770 is grounded. Principal items: Governor's salary, £1200; contingencies, £1000; Indian presents, £1000; Chief Justice's salary, £500; agent's salary £200. *Entry.* 1 p. [C.O.5, 619, p. 59; another entry of estimates, dated 7 February, in C.O.5, 600, p. 32]

166

7 March, Whitehall

Same to Governor Lord William Campbell, enclosing following. *Entry.* ½ p. *Enclosed:*

i. Estimate of civil establishment for Nova Scotia for 1770. Total, £4239 0s. 5d. Principal items: salary of Governor (£500), of Chief Justice (£500), stipends etc. for ministers and schoolmasters (£440), orphan-house (£384 1s. 5d.), allowances to Surveyors of Lands (£321 15s.), allowance for priest to Micmac Indians (£100), destitute persons (£175). *Entry.* 1½ pp. [C.O.218, 25, pp. 72–74; another entry of enclosure in C.O.218, 7, pp. 276–278]

167

7 March, Whitehall

Same to Governor James Grant, enclosing following. *Entry.* ¼ p. *Enclosed:*

i. Estimate of civil establishment of East Florida, 24 June 1769–24 June 1770. Total, £4750. Principal items: salary of Governor, £1200; presents to Indians, £1000; salary of Chief Justice, contingencies, and encouragement of vines, silk etc., £500 each; salary of agent £200. *Entry.* ¾ p. [C.O.5, 566, p. 29; another entry of estimate in C.O.5, 563, p. 277]

168

7 March, Whitehall

Same to Governor James Wright, enclosing estimate on which House of Commons vote for civil establishment of Georgia for 1769–1770 is based. *Entry.* ½ p. *Enclosed:*

i. Estimate, as above. Total: £3,086. Principal items: salaries of Governor (£1000), Chief Justice (£500), agent (£200), Surveyor of Lands (£150), Attorney-General (£150); contingent expenses (£500). *Entry.* 1 p. [C.O.5, 677, pp. 40–41; entry of estimate, dated 7 February, in C.O.5, 674, p. 376]

169

7 March, Whitehall

Letters from same to Samuel Holland and William de Brahm, sending estimate on which vote by House of Commons of £1885 4s. for general surveys in America in 1770 is based. *Entry.* 1½ pp. [C.O.5, 241, pp. 261–262; entry of estimate in C.O.324, 18, p. 367]

170

7 March, Charleston

★ Lieut.-Governor William Bull to Earl of Hillsborough (No. 24). Assembly have agreed on building court-houses and gaols. It is difficult to recommend names of persons to be Associate Judges. Men in London might be prevailed on to accept such offices. *Signed.* 3 pp. *Endorsed,* R, 11 April. [C.O.5, 393, fos. 26–27d; signed duplicate in C.O.5, 379, fos. 110–111d; entry in C.O.5, 409, pp. 97–101]

171

[7 March]

Memorial of Phineas Lyman to Commissioners for Trade and Plantations for 20,000 acres of land in West Florida, without fees, in recognition of services. *Signed.* 2 small pp. *Endorsed,* Recd. 7 March, Read 9 March. [C.O.5, 577, pp. 193–196]

172

8 March, Paris

Extract of letter from Paul Veron to Andrew De Visme & Co., in London, regarding payment of coupons on Canada Reconnoissances. *French. Copy.* 1 p. *Addressed,* To Committee for Canada Reconnoissances. [C.O.5, 43, fos. 318–319d]

173

9 March, Ordnance Office

Board of Ordnance to Earl of Hillsborough, enclosing account of ordnance supplied to American colonies since 1763 and of ordnance-establishments. *Signed,* H. S. Conway, Charles Frederick, A. Wilkinson, W. K. Earle, Charles Cocks. 1 p. *Endorsed,* R, 14th, with seven enclosures. *Enclosed :*

    i. East Florida: ordnance, stores etc. supplied since 1763. 4½ pp.

    ii. West Florida: same. 6½ pp.

    iii. New York: same. 4 pp.

    iv. Quebec: same. 1½ pp.

    v. Grenada, Dominica, Tobago: same. 8½ pp.

    vi. Account of ordnance-establishments (personnel) in West Florida, East Florida, Quebec, Grenada, St Vincent's, Tobago. 2 pp. [C.O.5, 71, Pt. 1, fos. 22–51d; entry of covering letter in C.O.5, 227, pp. 222–223]

174

9 March, Parsons Green, [near London]

Charles Pryce, Attorney-General of Georgia, to [John Pownall], asking for extension of leave of absence until August next because of financial misfortune. *Signed.* 2½ small pp. [C.O.5, 660, fos. 80–81d]

175

10 March, Whitehall

Commissioners for Trade and Plantations to the King, proposing Arthur Neil and Philip Comyns to be of Council in West Florida. *Entry. Signatories,* Hillsborough, Soame Jenyns, George Rice, William Fitzherbert. 1 p. [C.O.5, 600, p. 209]

176

Before 12 March

Undated statement by Richard Palms of Boston. Between nine and ten o'clock last Monday evening the 5th inst. I heard one of the bells ring, which I thought was for fire. I went towards where I thought it was, and was told that the soldiers were murdering the inhabitants. I asked where the soldiers were, and was answered in King Street and that there was a rumpus at the Custom-house door. As soon as I got there I saw Captain Preston at the head of six or seven soldiers; the soldiers had their guns breasthigh with their bayonets fixed. I went immediately to Captain Preston and asked him if the soldiers' guns were loaded; his answer was they were loaded with powder and ball. I then asked him if he intended they should fire on the inhabitants; his answer to me was by no means. I did not hear him speak to them. I saw a piece of ice fall among the soldiers, immediately upon this the soldier upon his right hand fired his gun. That instant I heard the word 'fire', but by whom I know not. The soldier at his left hand fired next and the others one after another as fast as they could. I turned myself to my left and saw one man dead, upon which I struck at the soldier who first fired the gun and hit his left arm or hand which made his gun fall. I then struck at Captain Preston and thought I hit his head, but he says I hit his arm. On my making the stroke at him, I fell on my right knee. I saw the soldier that fired the first fire going to push his bayonet at me, after which I threw my stick at his head; he gave back and gave me an opportunity to jump out of the way, or must [have] been run through the body. I directly passed through Exchange Lane and so up the next by Mr Kent's office, and saw three people on the ground and saw Mr Gridley with several other persons carrying Mr Morton's apprentice up to the prison-house. I followed him and saw he had a ball-shot through his breast. At my return [I] found the soldiers were gone to the main guard. *Copy.* 2¼ small pp. [C.O.5, 759, fos. 86–87d]

177

12 March, Boston

★ Lieut.-Governor Thomas Hutchinson to Earl of Hillsborough (No. 5), reporting firing of troops on crowd on 5 March, and arrest of Captain Preston and seven or eight privates. Four were killed, two more said to be mortally wounded, others less dangerously wounded. After consideration, and with unanimous advice of Council and many others, I asked Lieut.-Colonel Dalrymple to remove both 14th and 29th regiments from Boston to barracks at castle. *Signed.* 4 pp. *Endorsed,* R, 21 April 1770. *Enclosed:*

★ i. Boston, 6 March 1770. Lieut.-Governor Hutchinson to General Gage, reporting the shooting and removal of both regiments from town. *Copy.* 2¾ pp.

ii. Boston, 6 March 1770. Extract of minutes of Council of Massachusetts, relating to above events. *Copy,* certified by John Cotton, deputy secretary. 3½ pp. [C.O.5, 759, fos. 59–65d; entry of covering letter and No. i in C.O.5, 768, pp. 85–97; signed duplicate of covering letter, and copy of No. i, in C.O.5, 894, pp. 27–38]

178

13 March, Boston

Certificate by Lieut.-Governor Thomas Hutchinson that Foster Hutchinson is Justice of the Peace for Suffolk County, Massachusetts. *Seal. Signed,* John Cotton, deputy secretary. 1 p. *Enclosed:*

★ i. Andrew Oliver's sworn account of proceedings in Council of Massachusetts on 6 and 7 March 1770, at which Council advised lieut.-governor to ask Lieut.-Colonel Dalrymple to remove 14th and

29th regiment from Boston to the castle to avoid bloodshed and overpowering of troops by inhabitants. *Signed. Attested,* by Foster Hutchinson. 3¼ pp. [C.O.5, 759, fos. 113–116d]

179

13 March, Boston

* Lieut.-Colonel William Dalrymple to Earl of Hillsborough, enclosing the following. *Signed.* 2 small pp. *Endorsed,* R, 2, April 1770. *Enclosed:*

* i. Narrative of the late transactions at Boston. A brief account of events leading up to the shooting on 5 March, and an account of events at the Council meeting on 6 March at which the lieut.-governor asked the commanding officer of the troops to remove both regiments from Boston. 7 pp.

* ii. Case of Captain Thomas Preston, 29th regiment, describing events of 5 March and his part therein, his arrest next day, and false witnesses against him. *Signed,* Thomas Preston. 6¼ pp. [C.O.5, 759, fos. 117–126d; entry of covering letter in C.O.5, 768, pp. 98–99]

180

13 March

Statement by Samuel Bliss. On 5 March between 9 a.m. and 10 p.m., sentry outside Custom-house, Boston, loaded his musket and swore to fire if molested, which occasioned numbers to gather around him, some of whom told him to fire and be damned. Captain Preston's guard came out with fixed bayonets and, forming a half-circle, began without provocation to push their bayonets at people. Deponent heard Captain Preston say guns were loaded but would not be fired. He saw a cake of ice or snowball strike a grenadier, who fired. He heard the word 'fire' several times, and supposed they were uttered by the soldiers. He saw Michael Johnson dead on the ground. Sentries then retired to main guard. *Copy.* 2¼ small pp. [C.O.5, 759, fos. 103–104d]

181

13 March, Boston

Affidavit sworn before James Murray, J.P., by Captain Samuel Leslie, 14th regiment. After the bell rang about 9.30 p.m. on 5 March, the mob abused and provoked the soldiers till firing took place. *Signed,* James Murray. ½ p. [C.O.5, 759, fo. 67]

182

13 March, Boston

Same, by Thomas Lochead, soldier, 14th regiment, testifying to insulting behaviour of townspeople in King Street, Boston, on evening of 5 March. *Signed,* James Murray. 2¼ small pp. [C.O.5, 759, fos. 68–69d]

183

13 March, Boston

Same, by John Weir, surgeon, 14th regiment. He was in a back parlour of house in Cornhill and saw behaviour of crowd. *Signed*, James Murray. 2 small pp. [C.O.5, 759, fos. 70–71d]

184

13 March, Boston

Same, by Hugh Dickson, lieutenant, and David St Clair, ensign, 29th regiment. They were in Smith's barracks at 9 p.m. on 5 March and testify to violence of mob which assembled outside. They believe there was a premeditated design to attack the soldiers. It has of late been unsafe for officer or soldier to walk the streets of Boston at night. *Signed*, James Murray. 2½ small pp. [C.O.5, 759, fos. 72–73d]

185

13 March, Boston

Same, by Capt./Lieutenant John Goldfinch, 14th regiment. About 9 p.m. on 5 March he saw fighting between many townspeople and a few soldiers of 29th regiment outside their barracks. The soldiers were got into their barracks. He was surrounded by armed crowd in the streets, got away, was knocked senseless by another party but relieved by arrival of three officers' servants. *Signed*, James Murray. 3¼ small pp. [C.O.5, 759, fos. 80–81d]

186

13 March, Boston

Same, by Lieutenant Paul Minchin, 29th regiment. There was fighting outside barracks on 5 March and townspeople tried to break in. *Signed*, James Murray. 1½ pp. [C.O.5, 759, fos. 82–83d]

187

13 March, Boston

Same, by Lieutenant Thomas Buckley and Ensign Thomas Steele, 29th regiment, to same effect as preceding. They believe there was a formed design on part of townspeople to attack the soldiers. *Signed*, James Murray. 1½ pp. [C.O.5, 759, fos. 84–85d]

188

13 March, Boston

Same, by William Napier, ensign, 14th regiment. On 5 March between 9 p.m. and 10 p.m. he and other officers on their way to join their regiment after the drum beat to arms were attacked and insulted by townspeople. *Signed*, James Murray. 1 p. [C.O.5, 759, fo. 88, 88d]

189

13 March, Boston

Same, by Lieutenant Daniel Mattear, 14th regiment, to same effect as preceding. *Signed,* James Murray. 2 small pp. [C.O.5, 759, fos. 89–90d]

190

13 March, Boston

Same, by Andrew Laurie, ensign, 14th regiment, to same effect as preceding. *Signed,* James Murray. 1¼ small pp. [C.O.5, 759, fos. 91–92d]

191

14 March, Boston

Same, by Lieutenant James Vibart, 29th regiment. He has many times been insulted in Boston, and on 12 March at 8 p.m. was knocked senseless by a person unknown. *Signed,* James Murray. 1 small p. [C.O.5, 759, fos. 95–96d]

192

13 March, Boston

Same, by Lieutenant Alexander Ross, 14th regiment. On his way from barracks to join his regiment on 5 March after the drum beat to arms, he was attacked in Quaker Lane. *Signed,* James Murray. 1½ small pp. [C.O.5, 759, fos. 97–98d]

193

13 March, Boston

Same, by William Davies, sgt.-major, 14th regiment. About 8 p.m. on 5 March he saw a large crowd with firearms, cutlasses and bludgeons. About 9 p.m. near the market-place, he saw the mob divide into three, one going to main-guard, one to Smith's barracks, one to Ropewalk. *Signed,* James Murray. 2½ small pp. [C.O.5, 759, fos. 99–100d]

194

13 March, Boston

Same, by Thomas Greenwood, inhabitant. When he heard bells about 9 p.m. on 5 March, he assisted in bringing fire-engine towards King Street. Here he was told that there was no fire but that soldiers and inhabitants were fighting. He saw crowd provoke sentry outside Custom-house. The guard was called out and provoked in the same manner. Crowd called 'Damn you, you rascals, fire. You dare not fire. Fire and be damn'd. Why don't you fire?' The officer warned the crowd that if they continued to attack he would be obliged to fire. Then a grenadier at the right of the party was struck, staggered, recovered and, with the soldier next to him, fired. Soon after, five or six more fired. Deponent saw several people drop. *Signed,* James Murray. 1½ pp. [C.O.5, 759, fo. 102, 102d]

195

13 March, Boston

Same, by Henry Haltwood, ensign, 14th regiment. After drum beat to arms between 9 and 10 p.m. on 5 March, he was insulted, threatened and knocked down, going from barracks to his regiment. *Signed,* James Murray. 2½ small pp. [C.O.5, 759, fos. 105–106d]

196

13 March, Boston

Same, by Lieutenant James Barford, 29th regiment. He was officer of main guard on 5 March. He and Captain Preston were told by a number of inhabitants that sentry at Custom-house would certainly be murdered if not relieved. Captain Preston went with twelve men to relieve sentry. *Signed,* James Murray. 1½ small pp. [C.O.5, 759, fos. 107–108d]

197

13 March, Boston

Same, by Lieutenant William Brown, jnr., 14th regiment. After drum beat to arms between 9 and 10 p.m. on 5 March, going from his quarters to join his regiment he was attacked and struck in Quaker Lane. *Signed,* James Murray, 1 small p. [C.O.5, 759, fos. 109–110d]

198

14 March, Boston

Same, by Alexander Mall, ensign, 14th regiment. He was in Smith's barracks on night of 5 March and testifies to same effect as Lieutenant Hugh Dickson. *Signed,* James Murray. 2 small pp. [C.O.5, 759, fos. 74–75d]

199

14 March, Boston

Same, by Captain Edmund Mason, 14th regiment. He was in his house in Court Square, Boston, at 9.20 p.m. on 5 March and saw and heard mob. He heard people crying 'Damn you, fire, fire, why don't you fire? We dare you to fire. Hack them down, murder them all.' He saw flash and heard report of three pieces fired, and immediately after twice more. *Signed,* James Murray. 2½ small pp. [C.O.5, 759, fos. 76–77d]

200

14 March, Boston

Same, by John Gillespie. About 7 p.m. on 5 March in south end of Boston, he met forty or fifty parties of up to six in each, armed with clubs. He saw crowd in King Street and heard shots fired. There were people there who urged crowd to let the soldiers alone as well as those who urged attacking them. *Copy.* 2¼ pp. [C.O.5, 759, fos. 78–79d]

201

14 March, Boston

Same, by Henry Dougan, acting surgeon, 29th regiment, to same effect as his affidavit of 25 July 1770. [*See* No. 709lxx.] *Signed,* James Murray. ½ p. [C.O.5, 759, fos. 93–94d]

202

14 March, St James's

Order of King in Council, on report of Committee for Plantation Affairs, dismissing petition of House of Representatives of Massachusetts against Sir Francis Bernard as groundless, vexatious and scandalous. *Entry.* 6¼ pp. [C.O.5, 765, pp. 85–91]

203

14 March, St James's

Same, disallowing Act passed in New York in 1770 to explain duty of loan-officers. *Copy.* 1¼ pp. *Endorsed,* Recd. 12 December, Read 21 December 1772. [C.O.5, 1076, fos. 192–193d]

204

14 March, Whitehall

Earl of Hillsborough to Lords of Treasury, sending copy of Lord Botetourt's letter of 24 January and enclosures relative to removal of Custom-house from Williamsburg to Bermuda Hundred. *Draft.* 1 p. [C.O.5, 1348, fos. 59–60d; entry in C.O.5, 1375, p. 94]

205

15 March, Boston

Affidavit sworn before James Murray, J.P. by Edward Hill, late servant to George Spooner, merchant, of Boston. On 5 March he saw Captain Preston with party of men go towards Custom-house and heard two shots and then three more. He saw Captain Preston stop a soldier from firing. He saw officers of 14th regiment pursued by people crying 'Knock them down, sons of bitches'. He himself was knocked down and run through his jacket by a sword. *Copy.* 2 pp. [C.O.5, 759, fos. 111–112d]

206

16 March, Whitehall

Order of Committee of Council for Plantation Affairs, referring following to Commissioners for Trade and Plantations. *Seal. Signed,* W. Blair. ¾ p. *Endorsed,* Recd. 19 March, Read 26 March 1770. *Enclosed:*

i. Petition of William Baillie, late captain, 17th regiment of dragoons, to the King, praying for grant of 10,000 acres of land in Nova Scotia. *Copy.* 1 p. [C.O.217, 25, fos. 201–204d]

207

16 March, Whitehall

Earl of Hillsborough to Lords of Admiralty, requesting passage to New York for Earl of Dunmore on one of H.M. ships. *Entry.* ½ p. [C.O.5, 1141, p. 122]

208

16 March, Whitehall

* Commissioners for Trade and Plantations to Governor Lord Botetourt, requesting account of lands granted by Virginia beyond line of settlement prescribed by H.M.'s proclamation of October 1763, which will be of much use in consideration of disposition of lands ceded by Indians at Fort Stanwix. *Entry. Signatories,* Soame Jenyns, George Rice, William Fitzherbert, Lisburne. 3½ pp. [C.O.5, 1369, pp. 22–25; draft in C.O.5, 1336, fos. 162–163d]

209

16 March, Whitehall

Same to the King, recommending that petition of Phineas Lyman for 20,000 acres of land in West Florida, without fees, be granted. *Entry. Signatories,* Hillsborough, Soame Jenyns, George Rice, William Fitzherbert, Lisburne. 2 pp. [C.O.5, 600, pp. 210–211]

210

20 March, Williamsburg

Governor Lord Botetourt to Earl of Hillsborough (No. 30), acknowledging No. 28, warrant for addition to Attorney-General's salary, and remission of fines on Mary Dalton and Sarah Gibbs. Directions requested for marking boundary between Virginia and Pennsylvania. *Signed.* 1 p. *Endorsed,* R, 23 April. *Enclosed:*

i. 30 November 1769. Resolution of House of Burgesses of Virginia thanking Lord Botetourt for proposal to send four mad people to Philadelphia Hospital; House to pay expenses. *Copy.* ½ p.

ii. Williamsburg, 20 March 1770. Governor Lord Botetourt to Governor Penn. John Ingman, who has confessed to murder of Indian Stephen, is sent to you with papers. *Signed Copy.* 1 p.

iii. Williamsburg, 20 March 1770. Same to Mr Willing, sending four mad people to Philadelphia Hospital. *Signed Copy.* ½ small p. [C.O.5, 1348, fos. 89–96d; entry of covering letter in C.O.5, 1372, pp. 108–109]

211

[*20 March*]

Petition of William Bayard of New York to Commissioners for Trade and Plantations, praying for recommendation of disallowance of Act passed in New Jersey last session supplementary to Act for appointing commissioners for settling rights to common lands of Bergen. 2½ pp. *Endorsed,* Recd. 20 March, Read 26 March 1770. [C.O.5, 979, fos. 11–12d]

212

[*20 March*]

Petition of Henry Muilman, President, and Joseph Mico, Vice-President and Treasurer of West New Jersey Society, to Commissioners for Trade and Plantations, praying for copy of report of Attorney-General in 1699 on claim of Daniel Coxe to lands in North America. *Signed.* 2½ large pp. *Endorsed,* Recd. 20 March, Read 26 March 1770. [C.O.323, 28, pp. 307–310]

213

22 March, Charleston

Lieut.-Governor William Bull to Earl of Hillsborough (No. 25). On 28 April last in Court of Admiralty Mathew Turner was sentenced to death for murder in Bay of Honduras, but recommended for mercy. H.M.'s pleasure requested. *Signed.* 1 p. *Endorsed,* R, 4 June. *Enclosed :*

i. Charleston, 5 May 1769. Warrant for reprieve of Mathew Turner. *Copy,* signed by Thomas Skottowe, secretary. 1 large p. [C.O.5, 393, fos. 34–36d; signed duplicate of covering letter and copy of enclosure in C.O.5, 379, fos. 112–114d; entry of covering letter in C.O.5, 409, pp. 101–102]

214

24 March, Whitehall

Earl of Hillsborough to Lieut.-Governor Thomas Hutchinson (No. 34). Your caution in avoiding use of military at Boston in January approved. Order in Council acquitting Sir Francis Bernard sent; he has resigned his government. Remonstrance, address and petition to the King with H.M.'s answer are in enclosed *Gazette. Entry.* 2 pp. [C.O.5, 765, pp. 82–84; draft in C.O.5, 759, fos. 53–54d]

215

24 March, Whitehall

Same to Governor of Nova Scotia (No. 37) and Governor of New Hampshire (No. 29), sending *Gazette* of 17th inst. containing remonstrance to H.M. with answer, and proceedings of Parliament in consequence thereof. These will inform you of dangerous views of those who seek to disturb peace and of firmness with which legislature has resisted. *Draft.* 1 p. [C.O.217, 47, fos. 17–18d; entry in C.O.218, 25, p. 75; another entry in C.O.5, 947, p. 45]

216

25 March, Pensacola

Lieut.-Governor Elias Durnford to Earl of Hillsborough (No. 8), enclosing estimate of cost of establishing post at Iberville River. Fifty men would make a show of our intentions of settling that quarter. Road would be necessary about eleven miles along the Iberville. I have urged General Gage to build new barracks here: I hope barracks intended for St Augustine will be fixed here. Since arrival of Major McKenzie and 31st regiment (two companies excepted), I have undertaken with him a ferry at River Perdido and also to open the road to Mobile. I have considered moving troops to east side of Mobile Bay. *Signed.* 4 pp. *Endorsed,* R, 23 July. *Enclosed:*

i. Estimates for posts in West Florida. Fort Bute, on Mississippi near the Iberville: £333 6s. 8d. to build, £327 5s. a year to maintain. Post on the lakes to stop illicit trade by inhabitants of New Orleans: £215 13s. 4d. to build, £149 5s. a year to maintain. Post on Mobile River, to protect settlers: £86 to build, £20 a year to maintain. 6 pp. [C.O.5, 587, pp. 247–264; entry of covering letter in C.O.5, 620, pp. 246–249]

217

25 March, Pensacola

Same to same (No. 9), enclosing following, copy sent to Board of Ordnance. *Signed.* ½ p. *Endorsed,* R, 23 July. *Enclosed:*

i. Pensacola, 22 March 1770. Demand of ordnance stores for West Florida for 1770. *Signed,* Francis Downman, Lieutenant, R.A.; John Watkins, acting storekeeper; Benjamin Gower; William Wilton for Joseph Smith. 6½ pp. [C.O.5, 587, pp. 265–276; entry of covering letter in C.O.5, 620, pp. 249–250]

218

27 March, Boston

* Lieut.-Governor Thomas Hutchinson to Earl of Hillsborough (No. 6). House of Representatives till yesterday refused to do business except at Boston; they have now appointed committee of grievances.

In Boston they have printed depositions concerning the late unfortunate action, and intend to publish them in England. The town's committee presses for trial of officer and soldiers. Grand jury has found bills against three or four persons, one a Customs waiter, for firing when the soldiers fired. Commissioners of Customs will be received at Castle William in case of danger. There is no authority in the government which would support either Commissioners or Revenue Acts. Asks to be relieved by person of superior body and mind. *Signed.* 3½ small pp. *Endorsed,* R, 14 May. *Enclosed:*

i. Proceedings of House of Representatives and Council at Cambridge, Massachusetts, 15–23 March 1770. *Copy.* 8 pp.

ii. Cutting from *New Hampshire* [*Gazette*], Friday, 23 March 17[70], containing article criticizing soldiers in Massachusetts and opposing standing army without consent of the subject. *Printed.* 1 p.

iii. Cutting from unidentified newspaper, March 1770, concerning place of meeting of Massachusetts Assembly. *Printed.* 1 p. [C.O.5, 759, fos. 143–151d; entry of covering letter in C.O.5, 768, pp. 108–111]

219

27 March, St Augustine

Governor James Grant to Earl of Hillsborough (No. 35). Indigo samples sent, and bottle of salop thought equal to East India salop. Spaniards fish on southern coast; they give presents to Indians, a few of whom have been to Havana. But sole Spanish object is to fish. 16th regiment going to Pensacola is severe disappointment. With one-tenth the help Nova Scotia had, the province would soon make a figure. *Signed.* 3 pp. *Endorsed,* R, 7 June. [C.O.5, 551, fos. 21–22d; signed duplicate in C.O.5, 544, fos. 169–170d; entry in C.O.5, 567, pp. 143–147]

220

28 March, Treasury

Sir Ferdinando Poole to John Pownall. Lords of Treasury have directed that no steps be taken for removal of Custom-house from Williamsburg till they have been acquainted with reasons. *Signed.* 1 p. *Addressed. Endorsed,* R, 29th. [C.O.5, 1348, fos. 65–66d; entry in C.O.5, 1372, p. 104]

221

28 March, Quebec

* Governor Guy Carleton to Earl of Hillsborough (No. 28), enclosing following. Protestants in commissions of peace have repaired their fortunes at expense of the people; outcry is general. J.P.s should be reduced to power they have in England, and part of ancient mode of

justice revived. By present plan, King's judges paid by Crown may chiefly take cognizance of matters of property. *Signed*. 5 pp. *Endorsed,* R, 4 June. *Enclosed :*

i. Quebec, 28 March 1770. Certificate that following is true copy. *Signed,* Guy Carleton, George Allsopp, deputy secretary. 1 p.

ii. Ordinance for more effectual administration of justice and for regulating courts of law in Quebec. *Copy.* 27 pp.

iii. Yamaska, 3 July 1769. A captain of militia to Governor Carleton, complaining of injustices; with copy of blank summons used by J.P.s and bailiffs to excite people to litigation. *French. Copy.* 4 pp. [C.O.42, 30, fos. 7–26d; entry of covering letter in C.O.43, 12, pp. 248–253; signed duplicate of covering letter, endorsed Read 12 September 1770, and copy of No. iii, in C.O.42, 7, fos. 131–138d]

222

29 March, Whitehall

Commissioners for Trade and Plantations to the King, recommending grant of 10,000 acres of land in Nova Scotia to William Baillie, late captain, 17th regiment of dragoons. *Entry. Signatories,* Hillsborough, Soame Jenyns, George Rice, William Fitzherbert. 3 pp. [C.O.218, 7, pp. 279–281]

223

29 March, Whitehall

John Pownall to Mr Nuthall, asking for copies of certain commissions under Great Seal for laying before Parliament. *Entry.* ¾ p. [C.O.5, 241, p. 263]

224

29 March, Quebec

Governor Guy Carleton to Earl of Hillsborough (No. 29), acknowledging No. 28 and leave of absence. I shall review troops before I leave. *Signed.* 1½ pp. *Endorsed,* R, 4 June. [C.O.42, 30, fos. 27–28d; entry in C.O.43, 12, pp. 253–254; signed duplicate in C.O.42, 7, fos. 155–156d]

225

30 March, Brunswick

Governor William Tryon to Earl of Hillsborough (No. 49), acknowledging No. 26 and instruction. How are private lotteries to be prevented? *Signed.* 1 p. *Endorsed,* R, 12 June. [C.O.5, 313, fos. 50–51d; signed duplicate in C.O.5, 301, fos. 136–137d; entry in C.O.5, 328, pp. 189–190]

226

31 March, Whitehall

Earl of Hillsborough to Attorney-General, sending copy of Lord Botetourt's letter [No. 58] and enclosure. Report your opinion how case of murder of mariners on high seas is to be tried. *Draft.* 1½ pp. [C.O.5, 1348, fos. 67–68d; entry in C.O.5, 1375, pp. 95–96]

227

31 March, London

Memorial of Messrs. Bridgen & Waller and Messrs. Hindley & Needham, merchants trading to North Carolina and importers of naval stores, to Earl of Hillsborough, suggesting law which might be passed in North Carolina for regulating manufacture and improving quality of pitch, tar and turpentine. Naval stores from North Carolina have been adulterated and bad. *Signed.* 6½ pp. *Endorsed,* Copy transmitted to Governor Tryon, 14 April 1770. [C.O.5, 313, fos. 24–26A dorse]

228

[March?]

Undated statement by John Inman. On night of 5 March, he saw the soldiers place themselves by Custom-house, Boston, and heard them charging their guns. The people called to the soldiers to fire. *Copy.* ¾ small p. [C.O.5, 759, fo. 101, 101d]

229

2 April, Whitehall

John Pownall to [Robert] Wood, sending petition of Mr Bayard to be laid before Viscount Weymouth. *Entry.* ½ p. [C.O.5, 1141, p. 123]

230

2 April, Whitehall

Same to Anthony Todd. New York and South Carolina mails to be detained to Saturday. *Entry.* ¼ p. [C.O.5, 241, p. 265]

231

2 April

List of eleven papers laid before House of Commons respecting royal commissions to commanders-in-chief of H.M.'s troops in America. *Entry.* 1¾ pp. [C.O.5, 241, pp. 264–265]

232

[*2 April*]

Memorial of Charles Garth, agent of South Carolina, to Commissioners for Trade and Plantations, praying for settling of boundary between North and South Carolina on line stated. *Signed.* 8 pp. *Endorsed,* Recd. 2 April, Read 11 April 1770. [C.O.5, 380, fos. 9–13d]

233

[*2 April*]

Memorial of Joseph Martin, late lieutenant, 68th regiment, to Commissioners for Trade and Plantations, praying for grant of land in New York with remission of quitrent and fees. *Copy.* 1 p. *Endorsed,* Recd. 2 April, Read 10 May 1770. [C.O.5, 1074, fos. 215–216d]

234

3 April, Whitehall

Order of Committee of Council for Plantation Affairs, directing Commissioners for Trade and Plantations to prepare draft of additional instruction to governor of South Carolina to prevent Assembly from ordering public money to be issued in illegal manner. *Seal. Signed,* Stephen Cottrell. 1½ pp. *Endorsed,* Recd., Read 4 April 1770. [C.O.5, 379, fos. 91–92d]

235

4 April, Whitehall

Commissioners for Trade and Plantations to the King, recommending grant of 2000 acres of land in New York to John Thomson, late lieutenant, 108th Regiment. *Entry. Signatories,* Hillsborough, Soame Jenyns, George Rice, William Fitzherbert. 1 p. [C.O.5, 1131, p. 47; draft in C.O.5, 1080, pp. 347–350]

236

4 April, Whitehall

Same to Committee of Council for Plantation Affairs, enclosing following. *Entry. Signatories,* as preceding. 1 p. *Enclosed :*

    i. Draft additional instruction to Governor Lord Charles Montagu, or in his absence to lieut.-governor of South Carolina [*See* No. 268]. *Entry.* 5½ pp. [C.O.5, 404, pp. 425–431]

237

5 April, St James's

Order of King in Council, appointing Arthur Neil and Philip Comyns to be of the Council in West Florida. *Copy.* 1 p. *Endorsed,* Recd. 12

December, Read 21 December 1772. [C.O.5, 579, pp. 155–158; entries of warrants for Neil, dated 13 April, and Comyns, dated 14 April, in C.O.324, 42, p.177; sealed original of Order in C.O.5, 26, fos. 101–102d]

238

5 April, St James's

Same, approving draft of additional instruction to Governor of South Carolina to prevent Assembly from ordering illegal issue of money. *Copy.* ¾ p. *Endorsed,* Recd. 12 December, Read 21 December 1772. [C.O.5, 380, fos. 78–79d; sealed original in C.O.5, 26, fos. 80–81d]

239

5 April, St James's

Same, on report of Committee for Plantation Affairs of this day concerning vote of Assembly of South Carolina of 8 December 1769 for payment by Treasurer of £10,500 currency. Approved draft of additional instruction to governor to prevent Assembly from ordering illegal issue of money; ordered that Attorney-General of South Carolina prosecute the Treasurer. *Copy.* 9 pp. *Endorsed,* Recd. 12 December, Read 21 December 1772. [C.O.5, 380, fos. 72–77d; copy in C.O.5, 26, fos. 82–87d]

240

5 April, St James's

Viscount Weymouth to Earl of Hillsborough, enclosing following. *Signed.* 1 p. *Endorsed,* R, do. *Enclosed :*

 i. Memorial on fishery of Terre-Neuve in 1769, presented by French ambassador. French complain (1) of being forbidden inner harbour of Bonavista; (2) of growth of English shore-establishments; (3) that French were prevented from fishing on Sundays and feastdays; (4) that English claim to restrict French to harbour where a ship makes first establishment; (5) that whale found dead at sea was confiscated by English. *French. Copy.* 14½ pp. [C.O.194, 29, fos. 3–12d; entry of covering letter in C.O.195, 12, pp. 86–87; another copy of No. i, endorsed Read 9 April, in C.O.194, 18, fos. 50–56d]

241

5 April

Attorney-General William de Gray to Earl of Hillsborough. If master of vessel is acquitted of murder for which he is to be tried in Virginia, he may be tried in England for murders committed on high seas. *Signed.* 1½ pp. [C.O.5, 1348, fos. 71–72d; entry in C.O.5, 1372, pp. 105–107]

242

6 April, Treasury

Grey Cooper to John Pownall. Lords of Treasury have directed that St Mary's River be made member of port of St Augustine; removal of Custom-house there under consideration by Commissioners of Customs at Boston. *Signed.* 1½ pp. *Addressed. Endorsed,* R, 8th. [C.O.5, 551, fos. 17–18d; entry in C.O.5, 567, pp. 141–143]

243

6 April, Charleston

Lieut.-Governor William Bull to Earl of Hillsborough. I received packet from Governor Sherley few days ago. Letters for Governor Bruere and Mr Stuart have been forwarded. *Signed.* 1 p. *Endorsed,* R, 4 June. [C.O.5, 393, fos. 37–38d; entry in C.O.5, 409, pp. 102–103]

244

10 April, New York

* Lieut.-General Thomas Gage to Earl of Hillsborough (No. 41), reporting events in Boston and firing on the mob by a guard under Captain Preston. Four or five killed, more wounded. Captain Preston and party were committed to prison, unlikely to get a fair trial. Troops have been removed from Boston to Island of Castle William. *Signed.* 7½ pp. *Endorsed,* R, 4 June. [C.O.5, 88, fos. 55–59d; entry in C.O.5, 234, pp. 52–56]

245

10 April, Quebec

Governor Guy Carleton to Earl of Hillsborough (No. 30), enclosing following, in which additional clause is inserted to prevent traders delivering belts or messages affecting the King's interests. *Signed.* ¾ p. *Endorsed,* R, 18 June. *Enclosed:*

i. Specimen of bonds entered into by Indian traders. *English* and *French.* 2 pp.

ii. Specimen of licences granted to Indian traders. *English* and *French.* 2 pp. [C.O.42, 30, fos. 31–34d; entry of covering letter in C.O.43, 12, pp. 254–255; signed duplicate of covering letter and copies of enclosures, in C.O.42, 7, fos. 157–160d]

246

10 April, Quebec

Same to same (No. 31), enclosing following. *Signed.* ½ p. *Endorsed,* R, 18 June. *Enclosed:*

i. Minutes of Council of Quebec, 10 January–15 February 1770. *Copy,* certified by George Allsopp, deputy clerk. *Countersigned,* Guy Carleton. 11 pp. [C.O.42, 30, fos. 35–42d; entry of covering letter in C.O.43, 12, p. 255; signed duplicate of covering letter in C.O.42, 7, fo. 161, 161d]

247

10 April, Brunswick

Governor William Tryon to Earl of Hillsborough (No. 50). Assembly showed no beneficence towards injuries by storm of 7 September last. *Signed.* 1 p. *Endorsed,* R, 12 June. [C.O.5, 313, fos. 52–53d; signed duplicate in C.O.5, 301, fos. 138–139d; entry in C.O.5, 328, pp. 190–191]

248

11 April, Whitehall

Commissioners for Trade and Plantations to the King, recommending disallowance of Act passed in New York in 1770 declaring certain persons incapable of being members of General Assembly. *Entry. Signatories,* Hillsborough, Edward Eliot, William Fitzherbert, John Roberts. 1¼ pp. [C.O.5, 1131, pp. 48–49; draft in C.O.5, 1080, pp. 351–354]

249

11 April, Whitehall

Same to same, recommending for disallowance Act passed in New Jersey in 1769 supplementary to Act for settling claims to common lands of Bergen. *Entry. Signatories,* Hillsborough, Soame Jenyns, William Fitzherbert, Edward Eliot. 5½ pp. [C.O.5, 999, pp. 218–224]

250

11 April, Whitehall

Same to same, reporting that in Act passed in New Jersey in 1769 for striking £100,000 in bills of credit there is clause in substance same with clause in Act passed in New York laid before H.M. on 8 February last. *Entry. Signatories,* Hillsborough, Soame Jenyns, George Rice, William Fitzherbert. 1½ pp. [C.O.5, 999, pp. 217–218]

251

11 April, Whitehall

Same to same, enclosing following, which is conformable to commission to the last governor. *Entry. Signatories,* as preceding. 1 p. *Enclosed:*

i. Draft of commission for Thomas Hutchinson to be Governor of Massachusetts. *Entry.* 21 pp. [C.O.5, 920, pp. 281–303; draft of covering letter in C.O.5, 897, fos. 271–272d]

252

11 April, Whitehall

Earl of Hillsborough to Governor Lord William Campbell (No. 38), acknowledging No. 56. Article for contingent services in estimates for Nova Scotia has been for some time discontinued: no fund for service you mention. *Draft.* ¾ p. [C.O.217, 47, fos. 21–22d; entry in C.O.218, 25, p. 76]

253

11 April, Whitehall

John Pownall to Anthony Todd. Lord Hillsborough's dispatches for southern colonies and islands going by private ships, he leaves it to Postmaster's discretion to fix time of departure of *Nottingham* and *Duncannon* packet-boats. Mail for New York to be detained to Saturday. *Entry.* ½ p. [C.O.5, 241, p. 266]

254

11 April, Brunswick

Governor William Tryon to Earl of Hillsborough (No. 51), acknowledging No. 30. Writs for new Assembly were issued in February; Council advise meeting in November. Your directions at opening of Assembly will be observed. *Signed.* 1½ pp. *Endorsed,* R, 12 June. [C.O.5, 313, fos. 54–55d; signed duplicate in C.O.5, 301, fos. 140–141d; entry in C.O.5, 328, pp. 191–192]

255

12 April, N.H.

* Governor John Wentworth to Earl of Hillsborough (No. 30). Assembly resolved to forward petition for relief from Revenue Act, which has lain on table for two years. Five men killed at Boston has spread flame through all the continent. Attempts made to lead people into violence against Commissioners of Customs. Good order maintained. Paul Wentworth recommended to succeed Theodore Atkinson, dead, in Council. *Signed.* 5 small pp. *Endorsed,* R, 18 June. [C.O.5, 937, fos. 11–14d; extract regarding Paul Wentworth, endorsed Recd., Read 13 July, in C.O.5, 930, fos. 82–83; entry in C.O.5, 945, pp. 149–153]

256

12 April, Savannah

Governor James Wright to Earl of Hillsborough (No. 42), acknowledging No. 28. *Signed.* 1 small p. *Endorsed,* R, 12 June. [C.O.5, 660, fos. 90–91d; signed duplicate in C.O.5, 651, fos. 22–23d; entry in C.O.5, 678, p. 176]

257

12 April, Brunswick

Governor William Tryon to Earl of Hillsborough (No. 52), enclosing minutes of Council of North Carolina. Inhabitants of Rowan, Anson and Orange Counties continue in state of disobedience, partly occasioned by Lord Granville's land-office being shut for five years. Many settlers from northern colonies have occupied vacant land but, having no security, are unwilling to pay for government. *Signed.* 1½ pp. *Endorsed,* R, 12 June. *Enclosed:*

    i. Minutes of Council of North Carolina, 5 April–9 April 1770. *Copy,* certified by John London, deputy secretary. 6 pp. [C.O.5, 313, fos. 56–61d; signed duplicate of covering letter in C.O.5, 301, fos. 142–143d; entry of covering letter in C.O.5, 328, pp. 192–194]

258

13 April, Brunswick

Same to same (No. 53), enclosing following, which certify irregularity in present mode of collecting quitrents. *Duplicate. Signed.* 1 p. *Endorsed,* R, 12 June. *Enclosed:*

    i. 9 April 1770. Receiver-General John Rutherford to Governor Tryon, enclosing following, with comments. *Copy.* 1½ pp.

    ii. Receiver-General's accounts of quitrents in North Carolina, 25 March 1766–25 March 1770, with account of suits brought on behalf of the Crown. 19 pp. [*These accounts have been repaired and re-assembled in incorrect sequence.*] [C.O.5, 313, fos. 62–76d; entry of covering letter in C.O.5, 328, pp. 194–195]

259

13 April, St James's

Warrant to Attorney- and Solicitor-General to prepare commission for Thomas Hutchinson to be Captain-General and Governor-in-Chief of Massachusetts. *Entry.* 18 pp. [C.O.5, 765, pp. 96–114]

260

14 April, Whitehall

Earl of Hillsborough to Earl of Rochford, enclosing following and requesting information from Sweden. *Draft.* ½ p. *Enclosed:*

    i. London, 27 March 1770. Messrs. Bridgen & Waller and Hindley & Needham to Earl of Hillsborough. American tar is not good enough for cordage for H.M. ships. Difference must be in the making. *Signed.* 1¼ pp. *Addressed.* [C.O.5, 71, Pt. 1, fos. 85–88d; entry of covering letter in C.O.5, 241, p. 283; draft of covering letter in C.O.5, 313, fos. 46–47d]

261

14 April, Whitehall

* Same to Maj.-General Thomas Gage (No. 27), acknowledging No. 40. Sending 9th regiment to Pensacola and building barracks there instead of St Augustine, approved. Uniting the Indians may abstractly be founded on justice and humanity; good policy points out different system of conduct. Your conduct regarding quartering of troops approved. Indictment of you by grand jury at Boston exposes itself to contempt; H.M. has referred it to law officers. *Draft.* 3½ pp. [C.O.5, 88, fos. 48–50d; entry in C.O.5, 241, pp. 266–271]

262

14 April, Whitehall

Same to same (No. 28), sending copy of letter from Sir W. Johnson, with reply. Enable Sir William to pay extra cost of congress with Northern confederacy. *Draft.* ½ p. [C.O.5, 88, fos. 51–52d; entry in C.O.5, 241, p. 271]

263

14 April, Whitehall

Same to Governor Lord Botetourt (No. 31), acknowledging Nos. 27–29 and papers referred to in No. 26. Mr Stuart's arguments in respect to extension of Virginia boundary appear very forcible. Copy of Nos. 220 and 241 on removal of Custom-house and case of Captain Ferguson, sent. Ralph Wormeley is to solicit your recommendation to be of the Council. *Draft.* 2¼ pp. [C.O.5, 1348, fos. 87–88d; entry in C.O.5, 1375, pp. 96–99]

264

14 April, Whitehall

* Same to Lieut.-Governor Cadwallader Colden (No. 38), acknowledging No. 9. Order in Council disallowing Act for explaining duty of loan-officers sent. Your assenting to paper currency bill and to bill disqualifying judges from sitting in Assembly, disapproved. I have great doubts of propriety of congress to regulate Indian trade; you should not have assented to law for that purpose. *Draft.* 2¾ pp. [C.O.5, 1101, fos. 54–55d; entry, with Order in Council of 14 March 1770, in C.O.5, 1141, pp. 123–128]

265

14 April, Whitehall

Same to Lieut.-Governor Thomas Hutchinson (No. 35). You are to be appointed governor in room of Sir Francis Bernard; Mr Oliver to be lieut.-governor with the £200 allowance that was given to you; Nathaniel Rogers to be secretary. *Entry.* 1½ pp. [C.O.5, 765, pp. 91–92; draft in C.O.5, 759, fos. 55–56d]

266

14 April, Whitehall

Same to Governor William Tryon (No. 32), acknowledging Nos.
44–48. I agree that you should not consent to Tonnage Act whereby
inhabitants of North Carolina are put on better footing than H.M.'s
other subjects. Report requested on bills of credit outstanding. Gover-
norship of New York worth less than your present situation. Year's
leave granted. Plans for quitrents sent to Treasury. Memorial on naval
stores [No. 227] sent. *Draft.* 3¼ pp. [C.O.5, 313, fos. 43–45d; entry in
C.O.5, 332, pp. 46–48; entry of leave of absence, dated 10 May, in
C.O.324, 42, p. 184]

267

14 April, Whitehall

Same to Governor James Grant (No. 27), acknowledging No. 34, and
sending papers [Nos. 96, 97, 147]. Regiment which would have replaced
9th is now ordered to Pensacola; further proceeding on barracks at
St Augustine stopped. *Draft.* 1¼ pp. [C.O.5, 551, fos. 19–20d; entry
in C.O.5, 566, p. 30]

268

14 April, Whitehall

Same to Lieut.-Governor William Bull (No. 34), acknowledging Nos.
23–24. Little hope of finding Associate Judges for South Carolina
here. Additional instruction enclosed: Lords of Committee of Council
are considering prosecution of Treasurer. Agricultural and educational
endeavours approved. *Draft.* 2¼ pp. *Enclosed:*

* i. St James's, 14 April 1770. Additional instruction to Governor
   Lord Charles Montagu or in absence to Lieut.-Governor of South
   Carolina, to prevent Assembly from ordering issue of money from
   Treasury in illegal manner. *Copy.* 4 pp. [C.O.5, 393, fos. 28–33d;
   entry in C.O.5, 408, pp. 33–39]

269

14 April, Whitehall

Same to Governor James Wright (No. 30), acknowledging Nos. 39
and 40. H.M. approves appointment of Mr Hume to be Attorney-
General of Georgia in Mr Pryce's absence. *Draft.* ½ p. [C.O.5, 660,
fos. 86–87d; entry in C.O.5, 677, p. 42]

270

14 April, Whitehall

Same to Governor William Franklin (No. 24), acknowledging dispatches of 24 December and 12 February. *Draft.* ½ p. [C.O.5, 990, fos.
71–72d; entry in C.O.5, 1003, p. 27]

271

14 April, Whitehall

* Same to Sir William Johnson (No. 13), acknowledging No. 12. Security of frontiers to be principal object, but if possible without encouraging savages to attack each other. Congress reluctantly approved; General Gage to defray expenses. *Draft.* 2½ pp. [C.O.5, 71, Pt. 1, fos. 81–82d; entry in C.O.5, 241, pp. 272–275]

272

14 April, Whitehall

Same to John Stuart (No. 15, separate and private), recommending Lieutenant Thomas of Artillery to be deputy-superintendent of Indian affairs amongst Indians frequenting Mississippi. *Draft.* 1¼ pp. [C.O.5, 71, Pt. 1, fos. 77–78d; entry in C.O.5, 241, pp. 275–276]

273

14 April, Whitehall

Same to same (No. 16), acknowledging Nos. 18–19 and enclosing following. Report of Lords of Trade is not expected to favour extension of Virginia's boundary. Letter from Ross to Cameron shows iniquitous practice respecting lands at Fort Stanwix congress. Inducing Seminole Indians to reunite with Creeks and securing boundary lines of each province are desirable objects. Your desisting to solicit extension of East Florida line, approved. *Draft.* 2½ pp. *Enclosed :*

i. Whitehall, 16 March 1770. Commissioners for Trade and Plantations to Governor Lord Botetourt. *Entry,* of No. 208. 2¾ pp. [Covering letter in C.O.5, 71, Pt. 1, fos. 75–76d; entry, with enclosure, in C.O.5, 241, pp. 276–281]

274

14 April, Whitehall

Same to Captain Samuel Holland (No. 4), acknowledging No. 4 and approving reduction of surveys to smaller scale. New York–New Jersey boundary is before H.M. *Draft.* 1½ pp. [C.O.5, 71, Pt. 1, fos. 79–80d; entry in C.O.5, 241, pp. 281–283]

275

14 April, Whitehall

John Pownall to all governors of colonies in America, sending copy of Act of Parliament repealing duties granted in 7 George III on glass, red and white lead, painters colours, paper, etc. *Draft.* 1 p. [C.O.5, 71, Pt. 1, fos. 83–84d; entry in C.O.5, 241, p. 284]

276

14 April, Williamsburg

Governor Lord Botetourt to Earl of Hillsborough (No. 31). I do not understand your Nos. 22 and 26 if they do not authorize me to declare intentions of administration. I cannot help being astonished at reprehension in your No. 29. *Signed.* ¾ p. *Endorsed*, R, 4 June. [C.O.5, 1348, fos. 97–98d; signed duplicate in C.O.5, 1333, fos. 26–26A dorse; entry in C.O.5, 1372, p. 110]

277

15 April, Charleston

* Lieut.-Governor William Bull to Earl of Hillsborough (No. 26), acknowledging No. 33. Council objected to Tax Bill. Fourteen Bills presented to me 7th inst., whereupon Assembly determined to do no more business with Council and has addressed the King to appoint a branch of legislature independent of Council. Bills for schools and for encouragement of tobacco and flour not presented. Assembly prorogued to 5 June. *Signed.* PS. 16 April. *Gazettes* enclosed, 5 and 12 April. 2½ pp. *Endorsed*, R, 4 June. *Enclosed*:

> i. *South Carolina Gazette*, 5 April 1770. *Printed.* 4 large pp. [C.O.5, 393, fos. 39–42d; signed duplicate of covering letter in C.O.5, 379, fos. 115–116d; entry of covering letter in C.O.5, 409, pp. 103–107]

278

19 April, Whitehall

Earl of Hillsborough to Lords of Treasury, sending copy of letter from Governor Tryon and other papers relating to quitrents in North Carolina. *Draft.* ¾ p. [C.O.5, 313, fos. 48–49d; entry in C.O.5, 332, p. 49]

279

19 April, Whitehall

Same to Attorney- and Solicitor-General sending copy of presentment by grand jury at Boston, 21 November last, for consideration and report. *Draft.* 1 p. [C.O.5, 71, Pt. 1, fos. 89–90d; entry in C.O.5, 241, pp. 284–285]

280

19 April, Boston

Lieut.-Governor Thomas Hutchinson to Earl of Hillsborough (No. 7). House of Representatives has delayed granting lieut.-governor's salary. I have rejected their choice of John Hancock as Speaker, and will refuse consent to choice of Thomas Cushing as Commissary-General. I shall call next Assembly to Cambridge, but would have preferred Salem or Concord. Arrival of ships and goods from England with news that duties are likely to be taken off has brought on fresh ferment in Boston. Our deliverance depends entirely on measures taken in England. Trial of Captain Preston and soldiers put off. *Duplicate*. *Signed*. 2¼ small pp. *Endorsed*, R, 11 June, original not recd. [C.O.5, 759, fos. 152–153d; entry in C.O.5, 768, pp. 111–114; signed original in C.O.5, 894, pp. 45–48]

281

20 April, Pensacola

Lieut.-Governor Elias Durnford to Earl of Hillsborough (No. 10), explaining delay in letters. *Signed*. 1¼ pp. *Endorsed*, R, 23 July. [C.O.5, 587, pp. 277–280; entry in C.O.5, 620, pp. 250–251]

282

21 April, New Exchange Coffee-house, London

Montfort Browne to Earl of Hillsborough, asking for inquiry into his government of West Florida. *Signed*. 2 small pp. *Endorsed*, R, 21 April. [C.O.5, 587, pp. 231–234]

283

21 April, Boston

Lieut.-Governor Thomas Hutchinson to Earl of Hillsborough (No. 8). One Richardson, against the evidence and summing up of the court, has been found guilty of murder. Popular error and prejudice prevail against law and justice. Meeting of merchants, called for yesterday, was put off. *Signed*. 2 small pp. *Endorsed*, R, 11 June. [C.O.5, 759, fos. 154–155d; entry in C.O.5, 768, pp. 114–116]

284

23 April, Whitehall

Earl of Hillsborough to Postmaster-General, requesting packet-boat for Boston for dispatches of great importance. *Draft*. 1 p. [C.O.5, 71, Pt. 1, fos. 91–92d; entry in C.O.5, 241, pp. 285–286]

285

23 April, Admiralty

Lords of Admiralty to Earl of Hillsborough, enclosing the following. *Signed*, E. Hawke, Palmerston, F. Holburne. 1 p. *Enclosed*:

i. *Rose*, Boston, 14 March 1770. Captain Benjamin Caldwell to Philip Stephens, reporting shooting of 5 March and arrest of Captain Preston. I was present at Council when Lieut.-Governor Hutchinson agreed to comply with Council's advice and ask Lieut.-Colonel Dalrymple to withdraw the regiments. I have ordered *Beaver* and

Senegal here: they might help in relanding troops if General Gage orders them back to Boston. I understand the number of King's troops in this province fit for service does not much exceed 600. *Copy.* 3 pp. [C.O.5, 759, fos. 127–130d; entry in C.O.5, 768, pp. 99–102]

286

23 April, New York

Lieut.-General Thomas Gage to Earl of Hillsborough (No. 42), acknowledging Nos. 25 and 26. Reasons why St Augustine is inconvenient station for troops. Three regiments were appointed for southern district: proposes one in West Florida; of the second, eight companies at St Augustine, one company on detachment at Providence; third in reserve, to embark in emergency. Engineer's report from Providence under consideration. Lieutenant McDougall and inhabitants of Detroit will be informed of your opinion on possession of Hog Island. *Signed.* 3½ pp. *Endorsed*, R, 4 June. [C.O.5, 88, fos. 60–61d; entry in C.O.5, 234, pp. 62–66]

287

23 April, St Augustine

Governor James Grant to Earl of Hillsborough (No. 36), complaining of William De Brahm, Surveyor of East Florida, and recommending Frederick George Mulcaster to succeed him. *Signed.* 3 pp. *Endorsed*, R, 12 June. *Enclosed:*

i. Case of William Gerard De Brahm [June 1767]. *Copy.* 5¼ pp.

ii. St Augustine, 4 January 1768. Minutes of Council of East Florida, recording regulations for William De Brahm, Surveyor-General. *Copy.* 2 pp.

iii. St Augustine, 16–17 April 1770. Same, recording proceeding on complaint of William Haven against William De Brahm. *Copy.* 6¼ pp. [C.O.5, 551, fos. 25–36d; signed duplicate of covering letter, and copies of enclosures, in C.O.5, 544, fos. 171–182d; entry of covering letter in C.O.5, 567, pp. 147–150]

288

24 April, New York

Lieut.-General Thomas Gage to Earl of Hillsborough (No. 43). Mr Stuart is alarmed at Virginia's proposal to extend boundaries: similar problem with Northern Indians. Sir W. Johnson reports fears of Indians on the Wabash attacking the Illinois. Lieut.-Governor Durnford has asked for one regiment and company of artillery for West Florida and proposes re-establishment of Fort Bute. Reasons against this. Lieut.-Governor Penn's request for military aid in dispute between Pennsylvania and Connecticut has been deferred. General O'Reilly is to be

succeeded by Colonel Louis de Unzaga; there will be 562 troops left
in that province. A French company is designed for Illinois country.
Regimental movements proposed: 29th to New Jersey, 26th from New
Jersey here to replace 16th, now gone to Pensacola, 14th to stay at
Castle William. *Signed.* 6 pp. *Endorsed,* R, 4 June. *Enclosed :*

   i. Philadelphia, 6 April 1770. Lieut.-Governor John Penn to Lieut.-
   General Gage, asking for military aid to evict persons from Connecticut illegally settled on River Susquehannah, who have set up
   unlawful government, and begun riots in which one of them was
   killed and another wounded. *Copy.* 2½ pp.

   ii. New York, 15 April 1770. Reply to preceding. It would be improper for military to interfere without H.M.'s orders. *Copy.* 2 pp.
   [C.O.5, 88, fos. 62–69d; entry of covering letter in C.O.5, 234,
   pp. 67–74]

289

25 April, New York

Separate. Same to same, acknowledging secret letter of 17 February.
Accoutrements for New York light horse are probably to achieve
uniformity. Reported order from Boston will be inquired into. *Signed.*
2 pp. *Endorsed,* R, 4 June. [C.O.5, 88, fos. 70–71d; entry in C.O.5,
234, pp. 74–76]

290

25 April, Quebec

* Governor Guy Carleton to Earl of Hillsborough (No. 32), reporting
objections to ordinance sent with No. 28, and a reason for Charles
Grant's opposition to it. I cannot discover any foundation for repealing
any part of it. Within these 4 or 5 years 300–400 families have been
turned out of their houses and obliged to sell lands because of debts.
Signed. 7½ pp. *Endorsed,* R, 2 July. *Enclosed :*

   i. Quebec, 10 April 1770. Memorial of merchants and others of
   Quebec to Governor Carleton, protesting at ordinance of 22 March
   last and indulgence to debtors. Presented by Charles Grant, John
   Renaud, Stephen Moore, John Aitkin, Robert Bryan, J. Werden.
   Copy, certified by George Allsopp. *Signatories,* Robert Bryan and
   forty-nine others. 10½ pp. [C.O.42, 30, fos. 43–52d; entry of covering
   letter in C.O.43, 12, pp. 255–262; signed duplicate of covering letter,
   endorsed Read 22 August 1771, and copy of enclosure, in C.O.42, 8,
   fos. 3–10d; copy of covering letter and enclosure in C.O.42, 7,
   fos. 139–144d]

291

25 April, New York

* Lieut.-Governor Cadwallader Colden to Earl of Hillsborough (No.
10), acknowledging No. 37 and justifying assent to bill for emitting

bills of credit by reference to state of province at that time. Views of faction here and at Boston were same. Grand jury has found indictment against Alexander McDougall. Governments of Quebec and Pennsylvania have agreed to send commissioners here for regulating Indian trade. *Signed.* 4½ pp. *Endorsed,* R, 4 June. [C.O.5, 1101, fos. 56–58d; entry in C.O.5, 1138, pp. 142–146; signed duplicate in C.O.5, 1075, fos. 58–60d]

292

25 April, New York

Same to Commissioners for Trade and Plantations, sending Acts passed in New York last session, except that for emitting bills of credit formerly sent and since disallowed. Minutes of Council, journal of Assembly, and copy of letter to Lord Hillsborough, sent. *Signed.* 1 p. *Endorsed,* Recd. 5 June, Read 6 June 1770. *Enclosed :*

   i. New York, 21 February 1770. Lieut.-Governor Colden to Earl of Hillsborough (No. 9). *Duplicate,* of No. 140. *Signed.* 6¼ pp. *Endorsed,* as covering letter.

   ii. Agreement between Lieut.-Governor Colden and Lieut.-General Gage. *Copy,* of No. 140ii. 2 pp. *Endorsed,* Read 6 June 1770.

   iii. List of titles of fifty-nine Acts passed in New York in session 1769–1770. 9 pp. [C.O.5, 1074, fos. 217–230d]

293

25 April, Pensacola

Lieut.-Governor Elias Durnford to Earl of Hillsborough (No. 11). I have drawn two bills on Mr Ellis, provincial agent, for provincial contingent fund and for Indian department. *Signed.* 1 p. *Endorsed,* R, 23 July. [C.O.5, 587, pp. 281–284; signed duplicate, endorsed R, 12 September, in C.O.5, 577, pp. 441–444; entry in C.O.5, 620, p. 251]

294

26 April, Whitehall

Earl of Hillsborough to Lords of Admiralty. In consequence of affray at Boston on 5 March, H.M. commands that instructions be sent to commander-in-chief of H.M. ships, North American station, to give all aid to government there. *Entry.* 1 p. [C.O.5, 765, pp. 92–93; draft in C.O.5, 759, fos. 131–132d]

295

26 April, Whitehall

Same to Maj.-General Thomas Gage (No. 29). Following what passed at Boston on 5 and 6 March, you are to give all necessary aid to Lieut.-Governor Hutchinson. Enclosed are copy of letter of this date to him, and letter for Commodore Hood. *Draft.* 1¼ pp. [C.O.5, 88, fos. 53–54d; entry in C.O.5, 241, pp. 286–287]

296

26 April, Whitehall

*Same to Lieut.-Governor Thomas Hutchinson (No. 36). Measures to be taken consequential on transactions at Boston on 5 March are now being considered. If Captain Preston and soldiers should be convicted and condemned, respite execution till H.M.'s pleasure be known. Maj.-General Gage and Commodore Hood have been ordered to assist you to keep peace. Direct Attorney-General to enter *noli prosequi* to indictments of Maj.-General Gage and Sir F. Bernard. *Entry.* 3 pp. [C.O.5, 765, pp. 93–96; draft in C.O.5, 759, fos. 133–134d]

297

26 April, Halifax

Governor Lord William Campbell to Earl of Hillsborough (No. 58), acknowledging Nos. 34–36. Copies of laws are kept until safe conveyance is available. Captain Goold has written to resign commission in Marines; I recommend him. Assembly was dissolved 9th inst.; new one meets 6 June. *Signed.* 3 pp. *Endorsed*, R, 3 July. [C.O.217, 47, fos. 36–37d; signed duplicate, numbered 50, in C.O.217, 26, fos. 3–4d; entry in C.O.218, 17, pp. 235–237]

298

27 April, St James's

Order of King in Council, approving draft of commission for Thomas Hutchinson, appointed Governor of Massachusetts. *Copy.* 1 p. *Endorsed*, Recd. 12 December, Read 21 December 1772. [C.O.5, 894, pp. 447–450; sealed original in C.O.5, 26, fos. 103–104d]

299

27 April, St James's

Same, approving report of Committee for Plantation Affairs of 7th inst. recommending procedure to be followed by commissioners to settle New York–New Jersey boundary. *Copy.* 2½ pp. *Endorsed*, Recd., Read 29 April 1772. [C.O.5, 1075, fos. 195–196d]

300

27 April, Whitehall

Earl of Hillsborough to Lieut.-Colonel William Dalrymple, acknowledging narrative of transactions at Boston, and Captain Preston's case. I desire any further information you can give. *Draft.* ½ p. [C.O.5, 759, fos. 135–136d; entry in C.O.5, 241, p. 288]

301

27 April

John Pownall to Anthony Todd. Dispatch to General Gage is to go by express to Falmouth; packet-boat to sail with it for New York without delay. *Entry.* ¼ p. [C.O.5, 241, p. 286]

302

27 April, Boston

Lieut.-Governor Thomas Hutchinson to Earl of Hillsborough (No. 9), acknowledging Nos. 31 and 32. I have only the shadow of power without Council, and I have never been able to obtain their advice or consent to any proposal. I have used my negative power to refuse appointments, but I can remove none who are in office. They are attempting to compel importers of 'contraband goods' to send them back. Neglect by other colonies to proceed against associations makes me obnoxious to the people. H.M.'s commands acknowledged on petition of fishing towns and Law Officers' report on taxing Customs Commissioners. Assembly granted me £450 only and prepared a remonstrance, copy enclosed [*Marginal note:* not received with this letter which appears to be a duplicate, the original not received]. Boston principles obtain more and more in remote parts of the province and Representatives of seven-eighths of the towns appeared to be favourers of non-importation. Only vigorous measures in England can help. *Duplicate. Signed.* 4½ pp. *Endorsed,* R, 13 June, original not recd. *Enclosed:*

i. Proceedings of Assembly of Massachusetts. Lieut.-Governor Hutchinson's message to both Houses, 7 April 1770; answer of House of Representatives; and lieut.-governor's message of 26 April. *Printed.* 1 large p. [C.O.5, 759, fos. 158–161d; entry of covering letter in C.O.5, 768, pp. 116–124; signed original of covering letter in C.O.5, 894, pp. 71–76]

303

28 April, Burlington

Governor William Franklin to Earl of Hillsborough, acknowledging Nos. 21–23 and mandamus for Mr Skinner. Particulars of riots in Monmouth and Essex Counties are in enclosed papers. Rioters were entirely quelled; ringleaders have been or will be punished. Act for more effectual remedy against excessive costs in recovery of debts under £50 will stop clamour against lawyers and sheriffs, though I doubt if it will prove as satisfactory as expected. Assembly pressed me to give up appointment of coroners and let them be elected, as in England. *Signed.* 3 pp. *Endorsed,* R, 18 June. *Enclosed:*

i. Minutes of Council of New Jersey, 7–8 February 1770, relative to riots in Monmouth and Essex Counties. *Copy.* 17 pp.

ii. Journal of same at session of General Assembly, 14–27 March 1770. *Copy*. 31 pp.

iii. *Votes and Proceedings of General Assembly of New Jersey*, 14–27 March 1770. *Printed*, at Woodbridge, N.J., by James Parker. 23 pp. with table of Acts.

iv. 22 March 1770. Message of Assembly of New Jersey concerning appointment of coroners. *Copy. Signatory*, Richard Smith, clerk. ½ p.

v. 26 March 1770. Message of Governor Franklin in reply to preceding. *Copy*. 2 pp.

vi. 27 March 1770. Message of Assembly of New Jersey concerning same. *Copy. Signatory*, as No. iv. ¾ p. [Covering letter and enclosures iv–vi in C.O.5, 990, fos. 75–80d; enclosures i–iii, misplaced, in C.O.5, 990, fos. 12–61d; entry of covering letter in C.O.5, 1001, pp. 115–118]

304

29 April, Whitehall

William Pollock to Anthony Todd. Dispatch to General Gage to go by express to Falmouth for packet-boat to New York. *Entry*. ½ p. [C.O.5, 241, p. 289]

305

29 April, Charleston

Lieut.-Governor William Bull to Earl of Hillsborough (No. 27). Letters forwarded to Governors Shirley and Bruere, Mr Stuart and Mr De Brahm. Mr Stuart admitted to Council. I shall set out in few days on tour of back-settlements. On H.M.'s birthday I shall review three regiments of militia. *Unsigned*. 1½ pp. *Endorsed*, R, 12 June. [C.O.5, 393, fos. 47–48d; entry in C.O.5, 409, pp. 107–108]

306

29 April, St Augustine

William De Brahm to Earl of Hillsborough, reporting on his surveys and map-making. *Signed*. 2 pp. *Endorsed*, R, 30 July. [C.O.5, 71, Pt. 2, fos. 7–8d; entry in C.O.5, 227, pp. 246–248]

307

30 April, Whitehall

Earl of Hillsborough to Lords of Treasury, Lords of Admiralty and Viscount Barrington, enclosing following. *Entry*. ¼ p. *Enclosed*:

i. Address of House of Commons, 26 April, for papers regarding disputes or disturbances between H.M.'s troops in North America and inhabitants since 24 June last. *Entry*. 1 p. [C.O.5, 241, pp. 289–290; draft of covering letter in C.O.5, 71, Pt. 1, fos. 93–94d]

308

30 April, Whitehall

Same to same, enclosing following. *Entry.* ½ p. *Enclosed :*

i. Address of House of Lords, 30 April, for same papers. *Entry.* 1 p. [C.O.5, 241, pp. 291–292; draft of covering letter, dated 1 May, in C.O.5, 71, Pt. 1, fos. 95–96d]

309

30 April, Admiralty

Lords of Admiralty to Earl of Hillsborough, enclosing the following. *Signed,* E. Hawke, F. Holburne, C. J. Fox. 1 p. *Endorsed,* R, 1 May. *Enclosed :*

i. *Senegal* sloop, Newport, Rhode Island, 11 March 1770. Sir Thomas Rich to Philip Stephens, reporting news there of riots in Boston. *Copy.* 3¼ pp.

ii. *Rose,* Boston, 8 March 1770. Captain Benjamin Caldwell to Sir T. Rich, calling *Senegal* to Boston. *Copy.* ¾ p. [C.O.5, 759, fos. 137–142d; entry in C.O.5, 768, pp. 102–107]

310

30 April, Whitehall

John Pownall to Richard Jackson. Commissioners for Trade and Plantations are to consult you on all matters of law not of importance to require opinion of Attorney- and Solicitor-General. Acts sent, many of old date; your opinion desired, especially on those with suspending clauses and particularly those for naturalizing foreign Protestants. Extracts of commissions and instructions to governors, sent. Pennsylvania laws were presented to H.M. on 26 February; if not disallowed, they become irrevocable by Crown in six months. *Entry.* 2½ pp. [C.O.324, 18, pp. 368–370]

311

30 April, Charleston

John Stuart to Earl of Hillsborough (No. 20), acknowledging No. 12. *Signed.* 1 p. *Endorsed,* R, 12 June. [C.O.5, 71, Pt. 1, fos. 101–102d; entry in C.O.5, 227, p. 235]

312

[April]

The following papers were received 23 July 1770 from Lieut.-Governor Elias Durnford without any letter enclosing them.

i. Pensacola, 1 March 1770. Speech of Lieut.-Governor Durnford to Council and Assenbly of West Florida. *Copy.* 1¼ pp.

ii. 2 March 1770. Address of Upper House of Assembly to Lieut.-Governor Durnford. *Copy*. 2¼ pp.

iii. 2 March 1770. Message of Lieut.-Governor Durnford to Council. *Copy*. ½ p.

iv. 2 March 1770. Address of Assembly to Lieut.-Governor Durnford. *Copy*. 2 pp.

v. 2 March 1770. Message of Lieut.-Governor Durnford to Assembly. *Copy*. ½ p.

vi. Address of inhabitants of Pensacola to Lieut.-Governor Durnford. After the various scenes of misery and misfortunes in this unhappy province, we rejoice at your arrival. *Signed*, William Clifton and twenty-seven others. 2 pp.

vii. 26 December 1770 [*sic*, should be 1769]. Thanks for above address. *Copy*. ¼ p.

viii. Address of inhabitants of Mobile to Lieut.-Governor Durnford, to same effect as No. vi. *Signed*, William Gordon and twenty others. 1 p. [C.O.5, 587, pp. 285–302]

313

April

Cutting from (?) *Massachusetts Gazette*, reporting proceedings of House of Representatives of Massachusetts, 11, 12 April 1770; and message of Lieut.-Governor Hutchinson, 17 April 1770, signifying disapproval of choice of John Hancock to be Speaker in absence of Thomas Cushing. *Printed*. [C.O.5, 894, pp. 53–54]

314

1 May, Whitehall

Commissioners for Trade and Plantations to the King, proposing Chief Justice Martin Howard and Samuel Cornell to be of the Council in North Carolina in room of James Murray and Edward Brice Dobbs, who have vacated seats by long absence. *Entry*. *Signatories*, Soame Jenyns, John Roberts, Greville, W. Northey. 1 p. [C.O.5, 325, p. 427; draft in C.O.5, 305, fos. 41–42d]

315

1 May, St James's

Order of King in Council, appointing Martin Howard and Samuel Cornell to be of the Council in North Carolina in room of James Murray and Edward Brice Dobbs, who have vacated seats by long absence. *Copy*. 1 p. *Endorsed*, Recd. 12 December, Read 21 December 1772. [C.O.5, 302, fos. 212–213d, wrongly dated 1 May 1771; warrants for admission of Howard, dated 9 May, and Cornell, dated 10 May 1770, in C.O.324, 42, pp. 181–182]

316

1 May, Whitehall

John Pownall to Richard Jackson, sending copy of proclamation by governor of New Hampshire of 2 March 1769 for ascertaining rate of foreign coins, for his opinion in point of law. *Entry.* 1¾ pp. [C.O.5, 943, pp. 6–7; draft in C.O.5, 896, fos. 142–143d]

317

1 May, Whitehall

Same to same, sending bill passed in New York in 1769 for confirming estates claimed by or under aliens, for his opinion in point of law. Other papers sent. *Entry.* 1½ pp. [C.O.5, 1131, pp. 50–51; draft in C.O.5, 1080, pp. 355–358]

318

1 May, Charleston

John Stuart to Earl of Hillsborough (No. 21), acknowledging No. 13. *Signed.* 1 p. *Endorsed,* R, 12 June. [C.O.5, 71, Pt. 1, fos. 103–104d; entry in C.O.5, 227, pp. 235–236]

319

2 May, Admiralty

Lords of Admiralty to Earl of Hillsborough, inquiring if there is to be alteration in instructions for protection of Newfoundland fishery this year. *Signed,* Edward Hawke, Palmerston, F. Holburne. 1 p. *Endorsed,* R, 3d. [C.O.194, 29, fos. 1–2d; entry in C.O.195, 12, p. 86]

320

2 May, Charleston

* John Stuart to Earl of Hillsborough (No. 22), acknowledging No. 14 and reporting conference with Cherokees at the Congarees on 10 April. If their apprehensions on account of their lands were removed and traders to their nation regulated, there would be no danger of rupture with them. Delaware and Shawnese emissaries have been amongst Cherokees and Creeks. Report from West Florida suggests Indian irregularities caused by Spanish machinations. Reason for not paying Mr Westrop stated in enclosed. *Signed.* 4 pp. *Endorsed,* R, 12 June. *Enclosed :*

i. 10 April 1770. Report of conference with Cherokees at Congarees by John Stuart. *Copy.* 13¼ pp.

ii. Pearl River, 17 September 1769. M. De La Gautrais, late commissary in eastern part of Choctaw nation, to Charles Stuart, reporting attacks by Talapouche Indians, and by Biloxi, Pascagoula and Choctaw. Spanish intervention with Indians must be countered by English. *French,* with marginal notes in English. *Signed.* 8 pp.

iii. Pearl River, 14 September 1769. Declaration by Vaincant Rieux, English settler at Bayou Bonfouca. Party of sixty-eight Biloxi and other Indians, encouraged by Spaniards, attacked home of Mme. Duvernay. *French*. 6 pp.

iv. Undated letter from Charles Stuart to John Stuart, confirming No. iii. We will be much easier without French settlers. *Copy*. 1 p.

v. Pensacola, 30 September 1768. Lieut.-Governor Montfort Browne to John Stuart, reporting death of Mr Henderson. I have sent Lionel Becker Westrop to Mobile in his place. *Copy*. 1 p.

vi. Charleston, 7 February 1769. John Stuart to Lieut.Governor Browne. There are no funds to pay Mr Westrop. Extract sent of treaty concluded by me on 12 November last at Augusta with Lower Creeks, confirming cession of land by them in your province. Lines with Upper Creeks and Choctaws to be marked. *Copy*. 2¼ pp. [C.O.5, 71, Pt. 1, fos. 105–126d; entry of covering letter in C.O.5, 277, pp. 236–240]

321

3 May, Treasury

Grey Cooper to John Pownall. Papers requested in letters of 30 April and 1 May are not in this office. *Signed*. 1 p. [C.O.5, 71, Pt. 1, fos. 97–98d]

322

3 May, Boston

Lieut.-Governor Thomas Hutchinson to Earl of Hillsborough (No. 10), reporting opposition of overseers of Harvard College to holding Assembly in their public rooms; and asking for liberty to meet Assembly elsewhere. *Duplicate. Signed*. 1½ pp. *Endorsed*, R, 13 June, original not recd. [C.O.5, 759, fos. 162–163d; entry in C.O.5, 768, pp. 124–127; signed original in C.O.5, 894, pp. 71–76]

323

4 May, Whitehall

* Commissioners for Trade and Plantations to the King, replying to French complaints about Newfoundland fisheries. *Signed*, Greville, Soame Jenyns, William Fitzherbert, W. Northey. 10 pp. *Endorsed*, R, 8 May. *Enclosed*:

i. Answers by John Byron and Hugh Pallisser to French complaints. *Signed*. 11¼ pp.

ii. St John's, Newfoundland, 18 August 1768. Order by Hugh Pallisser that J. Hamont, master of French ship, is to forbear irregularities. *Copy*. 1¼ pp. [C.O.194, 29, fos. 13–26d; entry of covering letter in C.O.195, 12, pp. 88–94; another entry in C.O.195, 10, pp. 108–117]

324

4 May, Whitehall

Same to Committee of Privy Council for Plantation Affairs, recommending grant of 2000 acres of land in East Florida to Walter Humphreys, merchant. *Entry. Signatories,* Soame Jenyns, William Fitzherbert, Greville, Robert Spencer, William Northey. 2 pp. [C.O.5, 563, pp. 278–279]

325

4 May, Whitehall

Same to same, reporting on petition of Sir Francis Bernard for confirmation by H.M. of grant of island called Mount Desart made to him by General Court of Massachusetts on 27 February 1762. This Board recommended confirmation on 16 July 1764, but doubts arose about jurisdiction of General Court in territory of Sagadhoc. We propose that grant be confirmed, without prejudice to Crown's claims in Sagadhoc, which proviso corresponds to proposal by this Board on 6 June 1732. *Entry. Signatories,* as preceding. 4¾ pp. [C.O.5, 920, pp. 304–308; draft in C.O.5, 897, fos. 273–276d; petition in C.O.5, 114, fos. 113–114d]

326

4 May

List of twelve papers laid before House of Lords by Earl of Hillsborough respecting disturbances at Boston. *Entry.* 1½ pp. [C.O.5, 241, pp. 293–294]

327

4 May, Halifax

Governor Lord William Campbell to Earl of Hillsborough (No. 59), sending copies of laws passed in Nova Scotia last session and minutes of Council to 31 December last. *Signed.* 1 p. *Endorsed,* R, 3 July. [C.O.217, 47, fos. 38–39d; entry in C.O.218, 17, p. 237]

328

7 May

List of five papers laid before House of Commons by Vice-Chamberlain respecting Government's declaration of 13 May 1769 regarding Revenue Taxes in America. N.B. Above paper laid before House of Lords 15 May by Earl of Hillsborough. *Entry.* 1 p. [C.O.5, 241, p. 296]

329

7 May

List of nine papers laid before House of Commons by Vice-Chamberlain respecting disturbances at Boston. *Entry.* 1½ pp. [C.O.5, 241, pp. 294–295]

330

7 May, Brunswick

Governor William Tryon to Earl of Hillsborough (No. 53), enclosing following. *Signed.* ½ p. *Endorsed,* R, 2 August. *Enclosed:*

i. Lists of patents of land in North Carolina granted at Court of Claims in April 1770 by Governor Tryon. *Copy,* certified by John London, deputy secretary. 10 pp. [C.O.5, 313, fos. 77–78d, 81–86d; signed duplicate of covering letter in C.O.5, 301, fos. 144–145d; entry of covering letter in C.O.5, 328, p. 196; copy of enclosure in C.O.5, 320, fos. 106–111d]

331

8 May, Ordnance Office

Board of Ordnance to Earl of Hillsborough, enclosing following. *Signed,* H. S. Conway, Charles Frederick, W. H. Earle, A. Wilkinson, Charles Cocks. 1 p. *Endorsed,* R, 17 May. *Enclosed:*

i. Annapolis Royal, 12 January 1770. Extract of letter from Thomas Williams, storekeeper, to Board of Ordnance, asking for orders regarding garrison buildings that cannot be transported. *Copy.* ¾ p. [C.O.217, 47, fos. 27–30d; entry of covering letter and No. i in C.O.218, 17, pp. 233–234]

ii. Plan for fortifications and environs, Annapolis Royal. 1 large p. [M.P.G. 183]

332

8 May

Memorial of George Mercer to Commissioners for Trade and Plantations. Now that he has joined with Thomas Walpole, Thomas Pownall, Benjamin Franklin and Samuel Wharton for purchasing new province on Ohio, memorialist withdraws memorial presented 18 December last on behalf of Ohio Company. 1 p. *Endorsed,* Read 10 May. [C.O.5, 1332, fos. 184–185d]

333

9 May, London

Memorial of Robert Farmar, late major, 34th regiment, to Commissioners for Trade and Plantations, for confirmation of title to lands in Mobile, West Florida, which he holds by purchase from French and by Indian gift. *Signed.* 1½ pp. *Endorsed,* Recd., Read 21 May 1770. [C.O.5, 577, pp. 197–200]

334

10 May, Whitehall

Commissioners for Trade and Plantations to the King, recommending grant of 20,000 acres of land in New York to Josiah Martin, late lieut.-colonel, 68th regiment. *Entry. Signatories,* Soame Jenyns, William Fitzherbert, Robert Spencer. 1½ pp. [C.O.5, 1131, pp. 52–53; draft in C.O.5, 1080, pp. 359–362]

335

10 May

Leave of absence for Egerton Leigh, Attorney-General of South Carolina, in case ill-health shall absolutely require it. *Entry.* 1 p. [C.O.324, 42, p. 183]

336

10 May, Savannah

* Governor James Wright to Earl of Hillsborough (No. 43), acknowledging No. 29. No further notice was taken of letter from Speaker of House of Burgesses of Virginia, enclosing resolves of that House, beyond what I wrote in No. 37. The resolutions for non-importation were printed in the *Gazette,* but every attempt to get them signed proved abortive. *Duplicate. Signed.* 1¾ pp. *Endorsed,* R, 20 July, original not recd. [C.O.5, 660, fos. 96–97d; signed original, endorsed duplicate, in C.O.5, 651, fos. 24–25d; entry in C.O.5, 678, pp. 176–178]

337

10 May, Savannah

Same to John Pownall, acknowledging letter of 7 March with estimate for civil establishment of Georgia for 1769–1770. *Signed.* ½ small p. *Endorsed,* R, 23 July. [C.O.5, 660, fos. 94–95d]

338

10 May, Halifax

Arthur Goold to Earl of Hillsborough, acknowledging support in application for office of Register of Nova Scotia. *Signed.* 1 p. *Endorsed,* R, 3 July. [C.O.217, 43, fos. 34–35d]

339

10 May

Ordinance of Georgia reappointing Benjamin Franklin agent of the province for one year from 1 June next. *Entry.* 3½ pp. [C.O.324, 60, pp. 335–338]

340

11 May, Whitehall

Earl of Hillsborough to Governor John Byron. French are not to be obstructed in resorting to harbours in Newfoundland between Bonavista and Point Riche; they are not to be included within restrictions founded on 10 and 11 William III. You are to prevent private property being taken in lands etc. between Bonavista and Point Riche and take care that ships of both nations occupy beach only appropriate to number of their boats. Inquire into circumstances of whale, about which French complain. *Draft.* 3 pp. [C.O.194, 29, fos. 27–28d; entry, with opinion of law-officers, dated 21 March 1764, that 10 and 11 William III c.24 does not extend to parts of Newfoundland then in French possession, in C.O.195, 15, pp. 25–31]

341

11 May, Whitehall

Same to Lords of Admiralty, sending copy of No. 340, and requesting that instructions to Captain Byron shall correspond with it. *Draft.* 1 p. [C.O.194, 29, fos. 29–30d; entry in C.O.195, 15, pp. 32–33]

342

11 May, Whitehall

Same to Viscount Weymouth, sending copies of Nos. 323, 340 and 341. *Draft.* 1 p. [C.O.194, 29, fos. 31–32d; entry in C.O.195, 15, p. 33]

343

11 May, Savannah

* Governor James Wright to Earl of Hillsborough (No. 44), reporting on late session of Assembly. Out of twenty-five, there were fourteen new members, three of whom proved men of turbulent spirit, great liberty boys and men of bad hearts. Bill for regulating Indian affairs was laid aside. Negro bill passed but, though the Assembly agreed to suspending clause, they resolved on 14 March that such clauses were of pernicious consequence. Present ideas of liberty in America are high. Papers enclosed. On 23 March Assembly resolved that Council's address was unprovoked insult to them, and that the four southern parishes should be exempted from tax, being not represented in the House. No resolution made as to silk culture. I assented to eighteen bills and rejected two. We parted on good terms. No further notice

taken of Virginia resolution, and no resolutions for non-importation
have yet been signed. No illuminations on day of Wilkes's discharge.
There will always be some bad men. *Duplicate. Signed.* PS. In mine
of 26 December 1768 I wrote you on the very point taken up by Assembly relative to southern parishes, but had no answer. 5½ pp.
Endorsed, R, 20 July, original not recd. *Enclosed:*

i. Proceedings of Assembly of Georgia. Address to Governor, 16
November 1769, on need for representation in Assembly of parishes
of St David, St Patrick, St Thomas and St Mary, with Governor's
reply of same date. *Copy,* certified by John Simpson. 3 pp.

ii. Minutes of Council of Georgia, 27 November 1769. Recommendation that case of the four unrepresented parishes be stated to
government. *Copy,* certified by Charles Watson. 1 p.

iii. Proceedings of Assembly of Georgia. Address to Governor, 20
February 1770, on same subject, with Governor's reply of 21 February. *Copy,* certified by John Simpson, 3½ pp.

iv. Address of Council of Georgia to Governor, 12 March 1770,
justifying their recommendation in No. ii, with Governor's reply
of same date. *Copy,* certified by Charles Watson. 3 pp. [C.O.5, 660,
fos. 98–109d; signed original of covering letter, endorsed duplicate
and not containing postscript, and copies of enclosures, in C.O.5,
651, fos. 26–37d; entry of covering letter, containing postscript,
in C.O.5, 678, pp. 178–186]

344

12 May

Richard Jackson to Commissioners for Trade and Plantations, reporting
two private Acts passed in Virginia in 1769 concerning lands of Thomas
Fisher jnr. and of executors of Charles Carter, proper in point of law.
Signed. 1 p. *Endorsed,* Recd. 13 May, Read 21 May 1770. [C.O.5,
1332, fos. 186–187d]

345

12 May, Williamsburg

Governor Lord Botetourt to Earl of Hillsborough (No. 32), acknow-
ledging appointment of Commissary Horrocks to be of the Council.
Accounts enclosed. I rejoice in Lord North's destination. *Signed.* ¾ p.
Endorsed, R, 2 July. *Enclosed:*

i. Account of H.M.'s Revenue of 2s. per hogshead arising in Virginia, 25 October 1769–25 April 1770. *Copy. Signatory,* Richard
Corbin, deputy Receiver-General. Examined by John Blair, deputy
Auditor, and Lord Botetourt. 1½ pp. [C.O.5, 1348, fos. 101–104d;
signed duplicate of covering letter in C.O.5, 1333, fos. 27–27A
dorse, and entry in C.O.5, 1372, p. 111; copy of enclosure in C.O.5,
1333, fos. 38–39d]

346

13 May, Boston

Lieut.-Governor Thomas Hutchinson to Earl of Hillsborough (No. 11). Assembly meets 30th of this month at Cambridge. If they hear nothing from H.M. and Parliament disapproving principles avowed by Assembly last summer and by Council last winter, they will persevere. *Signed.* ¾ p. *Endorsed,* R, 13 June. [C.O.5, 759, fos. 192–193d; entry in C.O.5, 768, pp. 127–128; signed duplicate in C.O.5, 894, pp. 81–84]

347

14 May, New York

★ Lieut.-General Thomas Gage to Earl of Hillsborough (No. 44), reporting altercation between M. Rocheblave, commanding Spanish fort of St Genevieve opposite the Illinois, and Lieut.-Colonel Wilkins, and also troubles between Indians on Wabash River and traders. Disposition of regiments in southern district. Forts in West Florida weak. Mr Stuart's congress with Cherokees is over: they appear determined to continue the war with Western nations. Cherokees complain against traders and about boundary-line. *Signed.* 5½ pp. *Endorsed,* R, 18 June. *Enclosed:*

i. New Orleans, 27 January 1770. Orders by General Alexander O'Reilly for conduct of commanders towards the English. *Copy.* 2 pp. [C.O.5, 88, fos. 76–81d; entry of covering letter in C.O.5, 234, pp. 76–83]

348

16 May, New York

★ Lieut.-Governor Cadwallader Colden to Earl of Hillsborough (No. 11). By repeal of Act for emitting bills of credit there is deficiency of £1000 for supplying troops. Majority of merchants here and at Philadelphia are for importing from Great Britain, and will come to determination in few days. There was a procession last week to expose Boston importer who came to this place. *Signed.* 1½ pp. *Endorsed:* R, 18 June. [C.O.5, 1101, fos. 61–62d; entry in C.O.5, 1138, pp. 147–148; signed duplicate in C.O.5, 1075, fos. 61–62d]

349

18 May, Boston

★ Lieut.-Governor Thomas Hutchinson to Earl of Hillsborough (No. 12), enclosing papers. Instructions (enclosed) appear to be ravings of men in political frenzy. Hitherto, we have gone no further than to disown authority of Parliament; now even the King is allowed little or no share in government of the province. The lower class of people, called in as servants to intimidate those who refused to join combinations against imports, are now become the masters. Importers are intimidated. Support from England keeps up spirit here in the people, and encourages Council in their refusal to co-operate with me. *Signed.* 2¼ pp. *Endorsed,* R, 13 June. *Enclosed :*

i. Objections by Corporation of Harvard College, 3 May 1770, to meetings of Assembly there, with Lieut.-Governor Hutchinson's reply of 14 May. *Copy.* 2 pp.

ii. *Massachusetts Gazette and Boston Weekly Newsletter,* 17 May 1770, containing instructions to James Bowdoin, Thomas Cushing, Samuel Adams and John Hancock, by meeting of freeholders and others of Boston, 15 May 1770. *Printed.* 4 large pp. [C.O.5, 759, fos. 194–199d; entry of covering letter in C.O.5, 768, pp. 128–132; signed duplicate of covering letter, and copy of No. i, in C.O.5, 894, pp. 85–92]

350

19 May, Philadelphia

* Deputy Governor John Penn to Earl of Hillsborough (No. 21), acknowledging No. 21. I should have mentioned in my No. 17 the concurrence of merchants here in association against importation. They delayed to know outcome of Assembly's petitions to King and Parliament. They are now, on news that duties on paper, glass etc. are to be repealed but that on tea continued, waiting to know sentiments of neighbouring colonies. I am of opinion that they will prolong non-importation. *Duplicate. Signed.* 2 pp. *Endorsed,* R, 2 July, original not recd. [C.O.5, 1283, fos. 3–4d; signed original in C.O.5, 1278, fos. 13–14d; entry in C.O.5, 1300, pp. 349–352]

351

19 May, Philadelphia

Same to same (No. 22), acknowledging No. 22. *Duplicate. Signed.* ½ p. *Endorsed,* R, 2 July, original not recd. [C.O.5, 1283, fos. 5–6d; signed original in C.O.5, 1278, fos. 15–16d; entry in C.O.5, 1300, p. 352]

352

21 May, Whitehall

Commissioners for Trade and Plantations to the King, sending following. No material alteration from instructions given to Sir Henry Moore. *Entry. Signatories,* Soame Jenyns, John Roberts, William Fitzherbert, Robert Spencer, W. Northey. 6 pp. *Enclosed :*

i. General instructions for Earl of Dunmore, Governor of New York. *Entry.* 105 pp.

ii. Instructions to same, in pursuance of laws of Trade and Navigation. *Entry.* 61 pp. [C.O.5, 1131, pp. 54–255; draft of covering letter in C.O.5, 1080, pp. 363–370]

353

21 May, Whitehall

Same to same, recommending for approval two private Acts passed in Virginia in 1769. *Entry. Signatories,* Hillsborough, Soame Jenyns, William Fitzherbert, W. Northey, Robert Spencer. 1½ pp. [C.O.5, 1369, pp. 26–27; draft in C.O.5, 1336, fos. 164–165d]

354

21 May, Whitehall

Same to Committee of Council for Plantation Affairs. We see no reason to recommend compliance with petition of Edward Bell for lands in Virginia on Ohio River and elsewhere. *Entry. Signatories,* Hillsborough, Soame Jenyns, John Roberts, William Fitzherbert, William Northey, Robert Spencer. 1½ pp. [C.O.5, 1369, pp. 28–29; draft in C.O.5, 1336, fos. 166–167d]

355

21 May, Boston

Lieut.-Governor Thomas Hutchinson to Earl of Hillsborough (No. 13). On 18th inst. a tidesman in Customs who seized a coasting vessel for breach of Acts of Trade was tarred and feathered. No inquiry was made into this until I ordered one. This attack is not approved of by many who call themselves friends to liberty. Government here and at New York can be restored only by effectual measures to suppress illegal confederacies. *Signed.* 1½ pp. *Endorsed,* R, 1 July. *Enclosed :*

i. Bloomendale, 14 May 1770. Nathaniel Rogers to Lieut.-Governor Hutchinson, reporting activities of Sons of Liberty in New York and ferment on news that sixty of sixty-one Philadelphia merchants voted to import all goods but tea. *Copy* (?). 3 small pp. [C.O.5, 759, fos. 200–203d; entry of covering letter in C.O.5, 768, pp. 132–134]

356

22 May, Whitehall

John Pownall to all governors on continent and in islands, enclosing Acts of Parliament passed last session relating to America. *Entry.* ½ p. *Enclosed :*

i. Act to continue Act for importation of beef, etc. from Ireland and British dominions in America; Mutiny Act; Act to continue Act for encouraging indigo. [*Titles only*] *Entry.* 1 p. [C.O.5, 241, pp. 297–298]

357

23 May

Governor Walter Patterson to Earl of Hillsborough, seeking instructions how to act in case of proprietors in Island of St John who have not taken out patents from Nova Scotia. *Signed.* 1 small p. *Endorsed,* R, 28th [C.O.226, 4, fos. 18–19d; entry in C.O.227, 2, p. 2]

358

24 May, St James's

Order of King in Council, approving Act passed in Virginia in 1769 to dock entail of lands of Thomas Fisher, jnr. Like Order in respect of Act to empower executors of will of Charles Carter to sell lands. *Copy.* 1¼ pp. *Endorsed,* Recd. 12 December, Read 21 December 1772. [C.O.5, 1334, fos. 7–8d]

359

24 May, Boston

Lieut.-Governor Thomas Hutchinson to Earl of Hillsborough (No. 14), sending laws passed last session. I refused consent to several grants of townships but singled out that for Machias, between Penobscot and St Croix, the grantees being actual settlers. Colonel Goldthwaite, who commands at Fort Pownal, assures me that there are between 500 and 1000 families settled at Penobscot and eastwards. This part of province is asylum for debtors and criminals. Justices have been appointed. Proposal that Massachusetts quit claim to lands east of Penobscot and take lands between Kennebec and Penobscot as consideration. A fondness for land-jobbing in many of the Court might induce compliance. *Signed.* 3¼ small pp. *Endorsed,* R, 1 July. [C.O.5, 759, fos. 204–205d; entry in C.O.5, 768, pp. 134–138]

360

24 May, Boston

Same to John Pownall, sending exemplifications of laws passed in Massachusetts last session, with remarks thereon. I have not been able yet to procure minutes or journal of House of Representatives. *Signed.* 1 small p. *Enclosed:*

    i. Remarks on laws passed by Assembly of Massachusetts, March 1770. Temporary laws: Chs. 1–8. Perpetual laws, so called, or standing laws: Chs. 1–10. 3 pp. [C.O.5, 894, pp. 93–100; copy of No. i in Hutchinson's hand in C.O.5, 894, pp. 149–154]

361

25 May, Whitehall

Order of Committee of Council for Plantation Affairs, referring following to Commissioners for Trade and Plantations. *Seal. Signed,* Stephen Cottrell. ¾ p. *Endorsed,* Read 11 June 1770. *Enclosed :*

i. Petition of Thomas and Richard Penn, proprietors of Pennsylvania, alleging forcible entry of several inhabitants of Connecticut into Pennsylvania, and praying for directions for their removal and that H.M. may hear and determine right between Connecticut and Pennsylvania. *Copy.* 15 pp. [C.O.5, 1277, pp. 571–590]

362

25 May, Whitehall

Same, referring following to same. *Seal. Signed,* Stephen Cottrell. 1½ pp. *Endorsed,* Read 7 June 1770. *Enclosed :*

i. Memorial of Thomas Walpole, Benjamin Franklin, John Sargent, and Samuel Wharton, on behalf of selves and others, to King in Council. Treasury have accepted proposed purchase price and quit-rents for land-grants; memorialists renew their application, reserving all legal rights to lands within tract prayed for. *Copy.* 1½ pp.

ii. Definition of bounds of tract prayed for. *Copy.* ¾ p. [C.O.5, 1332, fos. 188–191d]

363

25 May, Whitehall

Same, referring following to same. *Seal. Signed,* Stephen Cottrell. ¾ p. *Endorsed,* Recd., Read 30 May 1770. *Enclosed :*

i. Petition of Lieut.-General Sir Jeffrey Amherst to the King for grant of estates of Jesuits in Canada. *Copy.* ¾ p. [C.O.42, 7, fos. 123–126d]

364

25 May, Ordnance-office

Board of Ordnance to Earl of Hillsborough, sending Captain Debbieg's plans for fortifying St John's, Newfoundland. Estimated cost: £71,736 13s. 3d. *Signed,* H. S. Conway, Charles Frederick, W. R. Earle, A. Wilkinson, Charles Cocks. PS. Captain Debbieg's report enclosed. 3½ pp. *Enclosed :*

i. Ordnance Office, 11 August 1769. John Boddington to Captain Debbieg, asking if plan will secure St John's harbour against sudden attack. *Copy.* ½ p.

ii. London, 18 October 1769. Hugh Debbieg to Board of Ordnance, replying to No. i. *Signed.* 8¼ pp. [C.O.194, 29, fos. 33–46d]

365

27 May, Boston

* Lieut.-Governor Thomas Hutchinson to Earl of Hillsborough (No. 15). On advice from Philadelphia that merchants there were disposed to import goods other than tea, near fifty merchants here declared willingness to join the Philadelphians; but a meeting of the popular party voted to adhere strictly to non-importation. I have desired Governor Penn and will desire Mr Colden to correspond with me. *Signed.* 2 small pp. *Endorsed,* R, 16 July. [C.O.5, 759, fos. 211–212d; entry in C.O.5, 768, pp. 138–139]

366

28 May, Whitehall

Earl of Hillsborough to Governor Walter Patterson. Persons holding Orders in Council for grants of land in Island of St John should have titles confirmed by patents under seal of said Island. *Draft.* ½ p. [C.O.226, 4, fos. 20–21d]

367

28 May

Richard Jackson to Commissioners for Trade and Plantations. Proclamation of 2 March 1769 by governor of New Hampshire for rating foreign coins is void. An Act of Assembly could prevent prejudice to private persons. *Signed.* 1¼ pp. *Endorsed,* Recd. 28 May 1770. [C.O.5, 930, fos. 78–79d]

368

28 May, Poole, Dorset

Memorial of persons interested in fishery of Newfoundland to Commissioners for Trade and Plantations, praying for recall of order for stopping brooks where salmon fishery is carried on, and enclosing following. *Signed,* Joseph White and fifteen others. 1 large p. *Endorsed,* Read 11 June 1770. *Enclosed:*

    i. Memorial of traders to Newfoundland, complaining of exorbitant Customs fees levied in Newfoundland and of stopping brooks where salmon fishery is carried on. With Governor Byron's reply; and list of Naval Officer's fees in Newfoundland, 24 July 1769. *Copy.* 3½ pp. [C.O.194, 18, fos. 71–75d]

369

28 May, Savannah

Governor James Wright to Earl of Hillsborough (No. 45), by Lauchlan McGillivray, who has resided the greater part of his time upwards of twenty years in the Creek nation, and will satisfy any inquiries you make. The Indians are ripe for mischief and some misconduct by our back-settlers made me lately apprehensive blood would be spilt, but it seems pretty well over. Anthony Stokes, Chief Justice, and Mr McGillivray, recommended to be of the Council; if Gray Elliott, on leave of absence, does not return, I recommend Mr Pryce, Attorney-General; if Mr Pryce does not return, whoever is appointed to succeed him. *Signed.* 2 pp. *Endorsed,* R, 27 July. *Enclosed:*

i. Supplement to *South Carolina Gazette,* 17 May 1770, reporting proceedings concerning non-importation. *Printed.* 4 pp. [C.O.5, 660, fos. 110–113d; entry of covering letter in C.O.5, 678, pp. 186–188]

370

[28 May]

Memorial of Adolphus Benzell, lieutenant, Royal Regiment, late director of works and fortifications at Crown Point, to Earl of Hillsborough, praying for grant of 13,000 acres of land in New York, including 100 acres forming peninsular opposite the fortress. *Copy.* 1 p. *Endorsed,* Recd. 28 May, Read 13 July 1770. [C.O.5, 1074, fos. 242–243d]

371

29 May, Detroit

Lieut. George McDougall to Earl of Hillsborough, declining to put his title to Hog Island to arbitration. *Signed.* 1 p. *Endorsed,* R, 17 August. *Enclosed:*

i. Memorial of same to same, setting out claim to Hog Island in Detroit River. 2½ pp.

ii. 29 August 1768. Extract of letter from General Gage to Captain Turnbull, requiring that Indians renounce claims to Mr McDougall. *Copy,* certified by T. Bruce, commanding Detroit. 1 p.

iii. Deed of sale of Hog Island by Indians to Lieutenant McDougall. *Copy,* certified as No. ii. 2 pp.

iv. Report by Captain George Turnbull, 68th regiment, and Lieutenant Daniel McAlpin, 60th regiment, on claim to Hog Island. It has these three years been looked on as the King's. *Copy,* certified as No. ii. 2¾ pp.

v. Detroit, 31 May 1770. Sworn declaration before Major Thomas Bruce by Pierre Emizier that Baptist Meloche said that he was forced by captains of militia at Detroit to sign memorial against Lieutenant McDougall, respecting Hog Island. *Signed,* T. Bruce, P. Emizier. 1 small p. [C.O.42, 30, fos. 55–63d; entry of covering letter in C.O.5, 227, pp. 249–250]

372

31 May, Ordnance Office

Board of Ordnance to Earl of Hillsborough. We have no authority to incur expense for fortifications in West Florida. Commander-in-chief in America is only judge of their necessity. Stores and tools demanded are valued at £6306 9s. 6d. As to paying artificers on the spot, standing rule in this office is that civil officers may stop pay or suspend artificers. Living expenses of engineers are not to be brought upon this office. *Signed,* H.S. Conway, Charles Frederick, W. R. Earle, A. Wilkinson, Charles Cocks. 2 pp. *Endorsed,* R, 4 June. [C.O.5, 587, pp. 235–238; entry in C.O.5, 620, pp. 244–246]

373

31 May, Williamsburg

Governor Lord Botetourt to Earl of Hillsborough (No. 33), enclosing following. *Signed.* ¾ p. *Endorsed,* R, 14 July. *Enclosed :*

    i. Address of House of Burgesses of Virginia to Governor Lord Botetourt, on extension of boundary, import of salt, and copper currency; with governor's reply. 1 large p. [C.O.5, 1348, fos. 107–109d; signed duplicate of covering letter, and copy of enclosure, in C.O.5, 1333, fos. 28–29d; entry of covering letter in C.O.5, 1372, pp. 111–112]

374

2 June, New York

Lieut.-General Thomas Gage to Earl of Hillsborough (No. 45). Regimental movements: 26th to New York, 29th from Castle William to New Jersey, 16th at Pensacola, three companies of 31st from West Florida to St Augustine. Spaniards intend to erect posts opposite every English post on Mississippi, but lose many troops by desertion. Inhabitants of New Orleans discontented, though trade there appears freer than was apprehended. Sir W. Johnson reports complaint of Shawnese and other Indians of Ohio against white traders. He has protracted the meeting between Six Nations and Cherokees as much as he can. Report from Fort Pitt of Indians hovering about fort. *Signed.* 4 pp. *Endorsed,* R, 2 July. *Enclosed :*

    i. New Orleans, 27 April 1770. Luis de Unzaga to General Gage, reporting his assumption of government of Louisiana and seeking friendly relations. *Copy.* 1½ pp. [C.O.5, 88, fos. 92–96d; entry of covering letter in C.O.5, 234, pp. 83–88]

375

2 June, Lancaster

Petition of merchants of Lancaster trading to Africa to Commissioners for Trade and Plantations, praying that Act passed in Virginia laying additional duty of five per cent. on negroes imported be prevented from becoming law. *Signed,* Thomas Hinde and fourteen others. 1 large p. *Endorsed,* Recd. 25 June, Read 2 July 1770. [C.O.5, 1332, fo. 192, 192d]

376

5 June, Whitehall

Earl of Hillsborough to Earl of Sandwich and Lord Le Despenser, Postmaster-General, requesting inquiry into delay of correspondence for New York. *Draft.* ½ p. [C.O.5, 71, Pt. 1, fos. 99–100d; entry in C.O.5, 241, p. 299]

377

5 June

Richard Jackson to Commissioners for Trade and Plantations, reporting that Act passed in South Carolina in 1769 to incorporate Fellowship Society is proper in point of law. *Signed.* 1 p. *Endorsed,* Recd. 5 June, Read 7 June 1770. [C.O.5, 379, fos. 93–94d]

378

5 June

Same to same, reporting that Act passed in New York in 1769 to confirm estate claimed by or under aliens is not in its present shape fit for assent of governor. *Signed.* 1¼ pp. *Endorsed,* Recd. 6 June, Read 7 June 1770. [C.O.5, 1074, fos. 231–232d]

379

5 June

Same to same, representing objections in law to three Acts passed in New York in 1767–1769, vizt. Acts to declare extension of Acts of Parliament; to prevent frauds by bills of sale; and to empower J.P.s etc. to try causes of £10 and under. No objection to three other Acts passed in 1769, vizt. Acts for preventing suits in Superior Court for sums less than £50; to explain Act for regulating elections to General Assembly; and for regulating sale of goods at auction. *Signed.* 2 pp. *Endorsed,* Recd. 6 June, Read 7 June 1770. [C.O.5, 1074, fos. 233–234d]

380

5 June, Charleston

Lieut.-Governor William Bull to Earl of Hillsborough (No. 28), soliciting pardon for William Fuste and Christopher Davis, sentenced to death for killing a mulatto, and remission of fine imposed on Robert Bussard, a German, convicted for his part in flagellation of persons of ill fame. *Signed.* 2 pp. *Endorsed,* R, 23 July. *Enclosed :*

i. Charleston, 28 April 1770. Warrant for reprieve of Christopher Davis. *Copy*. 1 large p.

ii. Same, for reprieve of William Fuste. *Copy*. 1 large p.

iii. Charleston, 3 May 1770. Warrant for suspension of fine on Robert Bussard. *Copy*. 1 large p. [C.O.5, 393, fos. 59–63d; entry of covering letter in C.O.5, 409, pp. 109–111]

381

6 June, St James's

Order of King in Council, disallowing Act passed in New Jersey in 1769 for striking £100,000 in bills of credit. Like Order disallowing Act passed in 1769 supplementary to Act for settling claims to common of Bergen. *Copy*. 1½ pp. *Endorsed,* Recd. 12 December, Read 21 December 1772. [C.O.5, 979, fos. 51–52d]

382

6 June, St James's

Same, disallowing Act passed in New York in 1770 declaring certain persons incapable of being members of Assembly. *Copy*. 1¼ pp. *Endorsed*, Recd. 12 December, Read 21 December 1772. [C.O.5, 1076, fos. 196–197d]

383

6 June, St James's

Same, approving draft of instructions to John, Earl of Dunmore, Governor of New York. *Copy*. 1 p. *Endorsed*, Recd. 12 December, Read 21 December 1772. [C.O.5, 1076, fos. 194–195d; sealed original in C.O.5, 26, fos. 111–112d; copy of instructions and instructions relating to trade and navigation, both dated 11 June, in C.O.5, 203, fos. 95–138d]

384

6 June, Charleston

Lieut.-Governor William Bull to Commissioners for Trade and Plantations, sending laws passed in South Carolina last session with list of titles; journals of Council to end of session; half-yearly account of grants passed. Journal of Assembly not ready. *Signed*. ¾ p. *Endorsed,* Recd. 23 July, Read 7 November 1770. *Enclosed :*

i. Lists of titles of fourteen Acts passed in South Carolina, 7 April 1770. Examined by Thomas Skottowe, secretary. 2 pp. [C.O.5, 379, fos. 148–151d]

385

6 June, Quebec

Samuel Holland to Earl of Hillsborough (No. 5), reporting surveying and map-making in Quebec and plans for eastern part of New England. Ensign George Sproule recommended. *Signed.* 2¼ pp. *Endorsed,* R, 17 August. [C.O.5, 71, Pt. 2, fos. 19–20d; entry in C.O.5, 227, pp. 250–252; signed duplicate in C.O.323, 27, pp. 47–50]

386

7 June, Whitehall

Commissioners for Trade and Plantations to Committee of Council for Plantation Affairs, recommending immediate stop to proclamation by governor of New Hampshire of 2 March 1769 for ascertaining rate of foreign coins, and preparation of Act of Assembly to prevent prejudice to private persons. *Entry. Signatories,* Soame Jenyns, John Roberts, William Fitzherbert, Robert Spencer, Greville, W. Northey. 2½ pp. [C.O.5, 943, pp. 8–10; draft in C.O.5, 896, fos. 144–145d]

387

7 June, Whitehall

Same to the King, recommending confirmation of Act passed in South Carolina in 1769 to incorporate the Fellowship Society. *Draft. Signatories,* as preceding. 2 pp. [C.O.5, 381, fos. 354–355d; entry in C.O.5, 404, pp. 432–433]

388

7 June, Whitehall

Same to Committee of Council for Plantation Affairs, reporting on Sir J. Amherst's petition to be granted Jesuit estates in Canada. Refer to reports of 30 May 1765 and 10 July 1769. It would be presumptuous to offer any arguments or objections. *Entry. Signatories,* as preceding. 3 pp. [C.O.43, 2, pp. 159–161]

389

7 June, Charleston

* Lieut.-Governor William Bull to Earl of Hillsborough (No. 29), reporting discussions with Governor Tryon on boundary between North and South Carolina. Report on three-hundred-and-fifty-mile tour of province by chariot: Santee River, Beaver Creek, conflux of Broad and Congaree Rivers, Cambden, Monks Corner. Militia at low ebb. Report on agriculture. Canal from Cooper River to Santee River contemplated. Three thousand waggons a year come to Charleston. A view of great growing prosperity to this province. *Signed.* PS. Assembly prorogued to 23 July. 6¼ pp. *Endorsed,* R, 23 July. [C.O.5, 393, fos. 64–67d; signed duplicate, endorsed R, 12 September, in C.O.5, 379, fos. 117–120d; entry in C.O.5, 409, pp. 112–120]

390

7 June, New Bern

Governor William Tryon to Earl of Hillsborough (No. 54), reporting visit to Charleston and failure to agree with Lieut.-Governor Bull on boundary between the two provinces, except on need to close the line in order to stop disorder on western frontier of both. I have removed into the palace. *Duplicate. Signed.* 2 pp. *Endorsed*, R, 24 August, original not recd. [C.O.5, 313, fos. 87–88d; signed original, endorsed duplicate, Read 7 November 1770, in C.O.5, 301, fos. 146–147d; entry in C.O.5, 328, pp. 196–198]

391

8 June, New Bern

Same to same, (No. 55), acknowledging No. 31. There is reason and justice in Council's application for allowance; I hope Treasury will approve. *Duplicate. Signed.* 1¼ pp. *Endorsed*, R, 24 August, original not recd. [C.O.5, 313, fos. 89–90d; signed original, endorsed duplicate, Read 7 November 1770, in C.O.5, 301, fos. 148–149d; entry in C.O.5, 328, pp. 198–199]

392

8 June, Boston

Lieut.-Governor Thomas Hutchinson to Earl of Hillsborough (No. 16), reporting elections for new Assembly, choice of Councillors, and election of Speaker. The House refuses to do business unless I remove them to Boston. I have obtained continuance of trial of Captain Preston and soldiers to last Tuesday in August. No. 36 acknowledged, with Order in Council, which has been recorded in Secretary's Office though not publicly communicated to House of Representatives. Appointment as governor acknowledged. Irregularities in Boston continue. Great part of the merchants wish them at end, but lowest class are now become their masters. *Signed.* 3 pp. *Endorsed*, R, 21 July. *Enclosed :*

    i. *Massachusetts Gazette and Boston Post-boy and Advertizer,* 4 June 1770, reporting elections to House of Representatives. *Printed.* 2 large pp.

    ii. Proceedings of Assembly of Massachusetts, Harvard, 30, 31 May, 5 June 1770. *Printed.* 1 p.

    iii. Same, 7 June 1770. *Printed.* 1 p. [C.O.5, 759, fos. 217–221d; entry of covering letter in C.O.5, 768, pp. 140–144; copies of Nos. ii and iii in C.O.5, 894, pp. 115–120]

393

8 June, Charleston

John Stuart to Earl of Hillsborough (No. 23). Choctaws and other Indians near Mississippi are reported well-disposed. Good prospect of peace between Creeks and Choctaws. Trouble reported between Lower Creeks and frontier inhabitants of Georgia, see enclosed message. Some Lower Creeks continue intercourse with Havana through Spanish fishing vessels on Florida peninsular. *Signed.* 2¼ pp. *Endorsed,* R, 23 July. *Enclosed:*

* i. Creek nation, 26 April 1770. Talk by Escotchaby or the Young Lieutenant to John Stuart; Stephen Forrester, interpreter. *Copy.* 2½ pp. [C.O.5, 71, Pt. 2, fos. 3–6d; entry of covering letter in C.O.5, 227, pp. 243–245]

394

8 June, Pensacola

Lieut.-Governor Elias Durnford to Earl of Hillsborough (No. 12), reporting visit of Piamatahaw, chief of Chickasaws. They want a commissary and a congress. Choctaws and Creeks are on point of making peace. Choctaws asked us to forget affair at the Natchez, and also asked pardon for an Indian who about three years ago accidentally killed a white man; which I promised. Creeks look on a congress as their due. *Signed.* 2½ pp. *Endorsed,* R, 12 September. [C.O.5, 587, pp. 315–318; entry in C.O.5, 620, pp. 251–253]

395

9 June, Pensacola

Same to same (No. 13), enclosing following. This place is far from being so unhealthy as it is industriously represented to be. *Signed.* 1 p. *Endorsed,* R, 12 September. *Enclosed:*

i. Register of burials at Pensacola, 26 June 1768–10 June 1770. Sixty-three burials. *Copy,* of register for town and garrison, examined by Nathaniel Cotton, rector of Pensacola and chaplain of garrison. 2 pp.

ii. Same of births and christenings, same date. Eighty-two christenings. *Copy,* examined as No. i. 3 pp. [C.O.5, 587, pp. 319–330; entry of covering letter in C.O.5, 620, pp. 253–254]

396

9 June, Pensacola

Rev. Nathaniel Cotton to Earl of Hillsborough. We need communion-cloths, prayer-books, and church built. Next schoolmaster should be in orders. I have no house: rent should be allowed me. I am unsettled. *Signed.* 2 small pp. *Endorsed,* R, 13 September. [C.O.5, 587, pp. 365–368; entry in C.O.5, 620, pp. 261–262]

397

11 June, Whitehall

Order of Committee of Council for Plantation Affairs on proclamation of 2 March 1769 by governor of New Hampshire. Draft instruction to Governor Wentworth to be prepared to stop operation thereof and to recommend to Assembly bill to prevent prejudice to private persons. *Seal. Signed,* Stephen Cottrell. 1¼ pp. *Endorsed,* Recd., Read 15 June 1770. [C.O.5, 930, fos. 80–81d]

398

11 June, Pensacola

Lieut.-Governor Elias Durnford to Earl of Hillsborough (No. 14). If part of the stream of Mississippi could be turned towards the lakes, it would be of advantage. Enclosed sketch is taken from Engineer Robertson's plan: he is well-informed of that part. Mr Gauld's plans are now complete to the westward of Mississippi and as far east as bounds of this province: they may be had at the Admiralty Office and are really worth seeing. Communication with Mississippi by the Iberville would be interrupted by Spaniards in case of rupture, but with proper force I should not doubt taking island of Orleans. *Signed.* 1¾ pp. *Endorsed,* R, 12 September. *Enclosed:*

  i. Map of communication between Iberville and the Mississippi. 1 large p. [M.P.G.359] [C.O.5, 587, pp. 331–335; entry of covering letter in C.O.5, 620, pp. 254–255]

399

12 June, Whitehall

Earl of Hillsborough to Lieut.-General Thomas Gage (No. 30), acknowledging Nos. 41–43 and separate letter of 25 April. Responsibility of the magistrates for Boston riots. Agrees to removal of 29th regiment from Castle William, but castle is to be strengthened as asylum in last extremity. Disposition of troops in southern station: one regiment in West Florida, two at St Augustine with detachment in Bahamas. West Florida to be supplied with stores and ordnance by you. Report on forts in Bahamas awaited. Indian affairs reported by Sir W. Johnson are disappointing. Appointment of French troops to Upper Mississippi is suspicious. Dispute between Pennsylvania and Connecticut needs to be examined here. *Draft.* 6¾ pp. [C.O.5, 88, fos. 72–75d; entry in C.O.5, 241, pp. 300–306]

400

12 June, Whitehall

Same to Governor Lord Botetourt (No. 32), acknowledging Nos. 30–31. Little doubt that commission for fixing boundary will be issued when

Pennsylvania and Virginia apply. Observation in my No. 29 about your speech was intended only to induce caution in use of King's name. Petition and papers sent, which will point out what Board of Trade contemplated in letter of 16 March desiring information of settlement in country between Mountains and Great Kanaway River. No final resolution will be taken on petition without attention to Virginia's interests. *Draft.* 2½ pp. [C.O.5, 1348, fos. 99–100d; entry in C.O.5, 1375, pp. 99–101]

401

12 June, Whitehall

Same to Governor Guy Carleton (No. 32). Ordinance sent with No. 28 approved. *Draft.* ½ p. [C.O.42, 30, fos. 29–30d; entry in C.O.43, 8, p. 81]

402

12 June, Whitehall

Same to Governor Peter Chester (No. 27), sending report of Board of Ordnance on demand for stores for West Florida [No. 372]. You are to apply to Lieut.-General Gage. *Draft.* 1 p. [C.O.5, 587, pp. 239–242; entry in C.O.5, 619, p. 60]

403

12 June, Whitehall

Same to Governor Lord William Campbell (No. 39), acknowledging No. 57. Salary paid to Mr Moreau to be continued to widow, until another missionary is found. *Draft.* 1 p. [C.O.217, 47, fos. 32–33d; entry in C.O.218, 25, pp. 76–77]

404

12 June, Whitehall

Same to Governor William Franklin (No. 25), sending two Orders in Council disallowing Acts passed in New Jersey. *Draft.* ½ p. [C.O.5, 990, fos. 73–74d; entry, with Orders of 6 June 1770, in C.O.5, 1003, pp. 28–32]

405

12 June, Whitehall

Same to Governor James Grant (No. 28), acknowledging No. 35. Spaniards fishing on coast of East Florida is not warranted by treaty; intelligence has been sent to Lord Weymouth to complain to Court of Spain. Two regiments, less small detachment for Providence, are to be stationed at St Augustine. *Draft.* 1½ pp. [C.O.5, 551, fos. 23–24d; entry in C.O.5, 566, pp. 31–32]

406

12 June, Whitehall

Same to same (No. 29), acknowledging No. 36 and complaint against Mr De Brahm. *Draft.* ½ p. [C.O.5, 551, fos. 37–38d; entry in C.O.5, 566, p. 32]

407

12 June, Whitehall

Same to Governor William Tryon (No. 33), acknowledging Nos. 49–53. I hope Assembly will fall on some method of quieting discontent and suppressing disorder in Rowan and Orange Counties, and that you will succeed in regulating Treasurer's office. *Draft.* 1 p. [C.O.5, 313, fos. 79–80d; entry in C.O.5, 332, pp. 49–50]

408

12 June, Whitehall

Same to Lieut.-Governor William Bull (No. 35), acknowledging Nos. 25–26 and letter of 6 April. Attorney- and Solicitor-General to be consulted in case of Mathew Turner. Assembly's support of resolution of 8 December regretted; I trust that H.M.'s indulgence in allowing matter to be settled on precedents they themselves established will end disagreement. Order in Council sent is additional proof of determination not to recede from just principles of constitution. *Draft.* 2 pp. [C.O.5, 393, fos. 43–44d; entry in C.O.5, 408, pp. 40–42]

409

12 June, Whitehall

Same to same (No. 36), acknowledging duplicate of No. 26 and unsigned No. 27. *Draft.* ½ p. [C.O.5, 393, fos. 45–46d; entry in C.O.5, 408, p. 42]

410

12 June, Whitehall

Same to Deputy Governor Robert Eden (No. 18), acknowledging No. 5. Proceedings in respect of *Good Intent* were atrocious. I lament want of authority and vigour in your government. Lord Proprietor is responsible for exertion of powers vested in him. *Draft.* 1 p. [C.O.5, 1283, fos. 28–29d; entry in C.O.5, 1301, pp. 10–11]

411

12 June, Whitehall

* Same to Lieut.-Governor Cadwallader Colden (No. 39), acknowledging No. 10. A governor who departs from instructions must fully explain such deviation. Order in Council disallowing Act declaring certain persons incapable of being members of Assembly, sent; also Act of Parliament to enable Assembly of New York to pass Act for emitting bills of credit. *Draft.* 2¾ pp. [C.O.5, 1101, fos. 59–60d; entry, with Order in Council of 6 June 1770, disallowing said Act, in C.O.5, 1141, pp. 128–133]

412

12 June, Whitehall

* Same to Lieut.-Governor Thomas Hutchinson (No. 37), acknowledging Nos. 6 and 7, and letter of 21 April. Measures to support civil government of Massachusetts will be ineffectual till that government itself has vigour and activity essential for civil constitutions. Meanwhile, General Gage has been ordered to put Castle William into state of security. Hopes that combinations against imports would be discontinued have proved delusive. *Entry.* 1¾ pp. [C.O.5, 765, pp. 114–115; draft in C.O.5, 759, fos. 156–157d]

413

12 June, Whitehall

Same to Governor James Wright (No. 31), acknowledging No. 42. *Draft.* ½ p. [C.O.5, 660, fos. 92–93d; entry in C.O.5, 677, pp. 42–43]

414

12 June, Whitehall

Same to John Stuart (No. 17), acknowledging Nos. 21–23. Disregard by Creeks and Cherokees of Shawnese and Delaware emissaries is fortunate. Final settlement of boundary between Cherokee and Virginia will be hastened. *Draft.* 1 p. [C.O.5, 71, Pt. 1, fos. 127–128d; entry in C.O.5, 241, pp. 299–300]

415

12 June, Pensacola

Lieut.-Governor Elias Durnford to Earl of Hillsborough (No. 15), enclosing papers concerning settlers who cleared from port in Maryland, mistook entrance to Mississippi, went a great way to westward, and were taken and kept prisoner for several months by Spaniards. H.M.S. *Druid,* Captain Jackson, and sloop *Florida* went to Vera Cruz to seek redress but were not allowed ashore for fear of contraband trade. *Signed.* 2½ pp. *Endorsed,* R, 12 September. *Enclosed:*

i. *Druid,* Pensacola, 20 April 1770. Captain John Jackson to [Lieut.-Governor Durnford], reporting failure at Vera Cruz. They have an English schooner stopped there. I will lay papers before Commodore Forrest in Jamaica. *Copy.* 3 pp.

ii. Vera Cruz, 22 March 1770. Juan Fernando de Palacio to Captain Jackson, enclosing following and ordering him to leave this coast. *Copy.* 1 p.

iii. Vera Cruz, 21 March 1770. Same to same, refusing entry to harbour and permission to land. Espionage suspected. *Copy.* 3¼ pp. [C.O.5, 587, pp. 337–352; entry of covering letter in C.O.5, 620, pp. 256–258]

416

13 June, Pensacola

Same to same (No. 16), sending minutes of Council of West Florida, 3 April–5 June 1770; eight Acts of last Assembly; with minutes of proceedings of Upper House of Assembly. *Signed.* ½ p. *Endorsed,* R, 12 September. [C.O.5, 587, pp. 353–356; entry in C.O.5, 620, pp. 258–259]

417

13 June, Pensacola

* Same to same, enclosing information of defences and troops at Vera Cruz, obtained by Mr Hodge. *Signed.* 1¼ pp. *Endorsed,* R, 12 September. Private. *Enclosed :*

  i. Vera Cruz, 18 March 1770. 2 ships said to be of 64 guns; 2 frigates, one having sailed to Havana; 6 large merchant galleons said to have 18 million dollars on board and much else; 11 gunners and 130 soldiers in fort; 4 companies of soldiers and some militia in town. In all New Spain, 5 regiments, a number of them stationed between mines of Mexico and their settlements near Mississippi. Irish regiment is now there. 1 small p. [C.O.5, 587, pp. 357–364; entry, with abstract of enclosure, in C.O.5, 620, pp. 259–260]

418

13 June, Halifax

Governor Lord William Campbell to Earl of Hillsborough (No. 60), acknowledging Nos. 33, 37–38. Assembly is now sitting: I do not discover licentious principle in them with which neighbouring colonies are infected. *Signed.* 1 p. *Endorsed,* R, 1 August. [C.O.217, 47, fos. 44–45d; entry in C.O.218, 17, p. 237]

419

13 June, Charleston

Lieut.-Governor William Bull to Earl of Hillsborough (No. 30), proposing Robert Pringle, Rawlins Lowndes, George Gabriel Powell and John Murray to be Associate Judges. *Signed.* ¾ p. *Endorsed,* R, 2 August. [C.O.5, 393, fos. 70–71d; signed duplicate, endorsed R, 12 September, in C.O.5, 379, fos. 117–120d; entry in C.O.5, 409, pp. 120–121]

420

14 June, Whitehall

Earl of Hillsborough to Viscount Weymouth, sending extract of letter from Governor Grant of East Florida, for complaint to Court of Spain if thought necessary. *Draft.* ½ p. [C.O.5, 551, fos. 39–40d; entry in C.O.5, 566, p. 33]

421

14 June, Whitehall

Same to Advocate-, Attorney- and Solicitor-General, sending papers in case of Mathew Turner. *Draft.* 1¼ pp. [C.O.5, 393, fos. 49–50d; entry in C.O.5, 408, p. 43]

422

14 June, Whitehall

John Pownall to Thomas Bradshaw, sending extract of Mr Stuart's letter on payment to Mr Westropp, appointed deputy-superintendent of Indian affairs by lieut.-governor of West Florida. *Draft.* ¾ p. [C.O.5, 587, pp. 243–246; entry in C.O.5, 619, p. 61]

423

15 June, St James's

Order of King in Council, confirming Act passed in South Carolina in 1769 for incorporation of Fellowship Society. *Copy.* ¾ p. *Endorsed,* Recd. 12 December, Read 21 December 1772. [C.O.5, 380, fos. 80–81d]

424

16 June, Whitehall

Commissioners for Trade and Plantations to the King, recommending disallowance of four Acts passed in New York, vizt. to declare extension of several Acts of Parliament; to empower J.P.s to try causes to value of £10; to prevent suits in Supreme Court for less than £50; and to explain Act for regulating elections of representatives to General Assembly. No comment on Act to prevent frauds by bills of sale and Act for regulating sale of goods at auction. *Entry. Signatories,* Hillsborough, Soame Jenyns, John Roberts, William Fitzherbert, Robert Spencer, Greville. 6 pp. [C.O.5, 1131, pp. 226–231; draft in C.O.5, 1080, pp. 371–378]

425

16 June

Commission to Phillips Callbeck to be Attorney-General of Island of St John. *Entry.* ¾ p. [C.O.324, 42, p. 186]

426

16 June, Treasury

Grey Cooper to John Pownall, regarding renewal of contract for transporting provisions and military stores at Niagara. *Signed.* 1 p. *Endorsed*, R, 19th. *Enclosed:*

> i. New York, 20 February 1770. Extract of letter from General Gage to Thomas Bradshaw, recommending against renewal of contract for term of years proposed. *Copy.* ½ p. [C.O.5, 88, fos. 82–85d; entry of covering letter in C.O.5, 227, pp. 240–241; copy of covering letter in C.O.5, 71, Pt. 1, fo. 129]

427

16 June, Treasury

Same to same, enclosing following. If Lord Hillsborough advises complying, expense should be included in estimate. *Signed.* ¾ p. *Endorsed*, R, 20th. *Enclosed:*

> i. Petition of proprietors of lands in Island of St John to Lords of Treasury, praying for provision for church, court-house and gaol in Charlotte Town. *Signed,* Walter Patterson and twenty-one others. 1 p. *Endorsed,* Read 6 June 1770. [C.O.226, 4, fos. 22–25d; entry of covering letter in C.O.227, 2, pp. 2–3]

428

16 June, Boston

* Lieut.-Governor Thomas Hutchinson to Earl of Hillsborough (No. 17), enclosing papers. It is influence of Boston which causes unconstitutional refusal of House of Representatives to do business at Cambridge. Leaders of the House seem to have no fear of consequences: the House in general is misled and imagine they are supporting their rights without seeing that they are subverting constitution. Disorders have increased in Boston. Mr Colden writes that New York merchants will import privately. *Duplicate. Signed.* 1¾ pp. *Endorsed,* R, 4 August, original nòt recd. *Enclosed:*

> i. *Massachusetts Gazette and Boston Weekly Newsletter,* 21 June 1770, reporting proceedings of House of Representatives in refusing to do business at Cambridge. *Printed.* 4 large pp.

> ii. *Boston Evening Post,* 18 June 1770, reporting address of Council to Lieut.-Governor Hutchinson, 12 June, and proceedings of House of Representatives and Council to 15 June. *Printed.* 4 pp., with fragment of supplement. [Covering letter and No. i in C.O.5, 759, fos. 224–227d; signed original of covering letter, with No. ii, in C.O.5, 894, pp. 101–110; entry of covering letter in C.O.5, 768, pp. 145–148]

429

20 June, Boston

Nathaniel Rogers to Earl of Hillsborough, acknowledging appointment as secretary of Massachusetts. *Signed.* 1½ small pp. *Endorsed,* R, 14 September. [C.O.5, 759, fos. 254–255d; entry in C.O.5, 768, pp. 155–156]

430

20 June, Charleston

Lieut.-Governor William Bull to Commissioners for Trade and Plantations, sending journal of Assembly of South Carolina for last session. *Signed.* ½ p. *Endorsed,* Recd. 28 July, Read 7 November 1770. [C.O.5, 379, fos. 152–153d]

431

21 June, Whitehall

Earl of Hillsborough to Lords of Treasury, notifying appointment of Earl of Dunmore as Governor of New York at £2000 a year payable out of duty on tea imported into America. *Draft.* 1 p. [C.O.5, 1101, fos. 63–64d; entry in C.O.5, 1141, pp. 134–135]

432

21 June, Whitehall

John Pownall to Clerk of Council in Waiting, transmitting enclosed for Privy Council. *Entry.* ½ p. *Enclosed:*

* i. State of the Disorders, Confusion and Misgovernment which have lately prevailed and do still continue in Massachusetts. Narrative of events since 1766 with appendix of sources from which it has been compiled. *Entry.* 51 pp. [C.O.5, 765, pp. 116–167; draft in C.O.5, 759, fos. 164–191d; another draft in C.O.5, 754, fos. 41–69d]

433

22 June

Richard Jackson to Commissioners for Trade and Plantations. Act passed in New York for naturalizing Garret Schotler and thirty other named persons is proper in point of law. *Signed.* 1 p. *Endorsed,* Recd. 24 June, Read 2 July 1770. [C.O.5, 1074, fos. 235–236d]

434

23 June, War Office

Viscount Barrington to Earl of Hillsborough enclosing following. *Signed.* ½ p. *Endorsed,* R, 26th. *Enclosed:*

i. Fort Chartres, 5 December 1769. Extract of letter from Lieut.-Colonel Wilkins, commanding 10th regiment in Illinois country, to Secretary at War, on bad siting of Fort Chartres. French still carry away trade of the Illinois. Good possibilities of Mississippi, Missouri and Wabash for furs, and of Illinois for settlement. 3,300 packs of furs might be obtained, valued at $231,000 or £53,900. Soil fertile, cotton flourishes, silk manufacture could be carried on, salt produced. Nature seems to have taken pride in formation of this country. Spanish troops expected here: if nothing is done we may expect annihilation of our trade, if not entire loss of the country. *Copy.* 6½ pp. [C.O.5, 88, fos. 86–91d]

435

23 June, Williamsburg

Governor Lord Botetourt to Earl of Hillsborough (No. 34), enclosing following. Ralph Wormely lives too far away to be of the Council; undated warrant requested for Dudley Digges for when vacancy occurs. I will send Captain Ferguson to England. *Duplicate. Signed.* 1 p. *Endorsed,* R, 13 August, original not recd. *Enclosed :*

i. Williamsburg, 21 June 1770. Governor Lord Botetourt to John Stuart. *Signed Copy,* of No. 505v. 1 p.

ii. Resolution of House of Burgesses of Virginia to address governor to take steps for treaty with Cherokees for lands. *Copy. Signatory,* G. Wythe, clerk. ½ p.

iii. Same, to address same to entreat Maryland to join with Virginia in erecting lighthouse on Cape Henry. *Copy. Signatory,* as No. ii. ½ p. [C.O.5, 1348, fos. 114–121d; signed original of covering letter in C.O.5, 1333, fos. 69–69A dorse, with copies of enclosures at fos. 35–37A dorse; entry of covering letter in C.O.5, 1372, pp. 112–113]

436

24 June, Williamsburg

Same to Commissioners for Trade and Plantations. Best information of patents will be sent as soon as procured. Acquaint me by first opportunity with lands which may immediately be granted in consequence of Treaty of Fort Stanwix. *Signed.* 1 p. *Endorsed,* Recd. 17 August, Read 4 November 1770. [C.O.5, 1333, fos. 46–46A dorse]

437

26 June, Treasury

Grey Cooper to John Pownall, sending memorial of inhabitants of Nova Scotia for payment of £3394 10s. 1d. for provisions supplied to Indians between 1761 and 1767 by order of civil and military officers. *Signed.* ¾ p. *Endorsed,* Recd. 29 June, Read 2 July. [C.O.217, 25, fos. 205–206d]

438

26 June, Boston

Lieut.-Governor Thomas Hutchinson to Earl of Hillsborough (No. 18), acknowledging Nos. 35 and 36. Measures in consequence of removal of troops are awaited with impatience. I have never asked Council's advice on expediency of applying for more troops and ships, and I have not applied for more. General Gage and Commodore Hood are advised of every transaction of moment. H.M.'s commands in case of verdict and sentence against Captain Preston and soldiers acknowledged. I will direct Attorney-General to enter a *noli prosequi* in suits against officers of the Crown for letters written to H.M.'s ministers. I have prorogued General Court to 25 July at Cambridge. Spirit of opposition will never expire until colonists are brought to know that their ancestors remained subjects of England when they removed to America. *Signed.* 1¾ pp. *Endorsed*, R, 4 August. *Enclosed:*

    i. *Massachusetts Gazette and Boston Weekly Newsletter,* 28 June 1770, reporting proceedings and prorogation of Assembly. *Printed.* 6 large pp.

    ii. Proceedings of Council of Massachusetts, 12 and 18 June 1770. *Printed.* 3 pp. [C.O.5, 759, fos. 228–233d; entry of covering letter in C.O.5, 768, pp. 148–151; signed duplicate of covering letter in C.O.5, 894, pp. 111–114]

439

27 June, Halifax

Governor Lord William Campbell to Earl of Hillsborough (No. 61), sending laws passed last session, journals of both Houses, and minutes of Council of Nova Scotia to 16 December last. *Signed. Endorsed*, R, 1 August. [C.O.217, 47, fos. 46–47d; entry in C.O.218, 17, p. 238]

440

[27 June]

* Petition of House of Burgesses of Virginia to the King, praying for total repeal of Acts of Parliament for raising revenue in America and exposing subjects to decisions of distant Admiralty Courts. *Signed,* Peyton Randolph, Speaker. 1 large p. [C.O.5, 1348, fo. 139; entry in C.O.5, 1372, pp. 116–120]

441

28 June, St James's

Letters patent constituting Walter Patterson Receiver-General and Collector of Revenues in Island of St John, Customs excepted. *Entry. Signatories,* North, C. Jenkinson, C. Townshend. Entered in office of Hon. and Rev. Robert Cholmondely, Auditor-General of Plantations, 30 June 1770: George Gillio. Enrolled in Remembrances of Exchequer,

Trinity Term, 10 George III, 39th roll: Martin. 2 pp. [C.O.5, 204, pp. 1–2]

442

28 June, Whitehall

John Pownall to Gamaliel Smithurst of Lancaster. In cases of denial of justice in courts in Plantations, the proper channel for redress is to H.M. in Privy Council. *Entry.* ½ p. [C.O.5, 241, p. 307]

443

29 June, Boston

Lieut.-Colonel William Dalrymple to Earl of Hillsborough. I am preparing narrative of ill-treatment of troops by magistrates and people of Boston, which may serve to put transaction of 5 March in proper light. I have accommodated at the castle several persons compelled to fly from Boston. *Signed.* 1½ pp. *Endorsed,* R, 8 August. [C.O.5, 759, fos. 243–244d]

444

30 June, Williamsburg

Governor Lord Botetourt to Earl of Hillsborough (No. 35). Assembly prorogued to 25 October: I passed forty-six bills and rejected one, on account of monies to be issued without my warrant. House of Burgesses directed their agent to lay before H.M. petition for total repeal of Revenue Act; many have signed Association. We are chiefly indebted for both to the patriots in England. *Duplicate. Signed.* 1 p. *Endorsed,* R, 13 August. *Enclosed :*

i. Governor's speech of prorogation to Assembly of Virginia. *Copy.* ¾ p.

ii. Williamsburg, 22 June 1770. Association for non-importation by gentlemen of House of Burgesses and body of merchants. *Printed. Signatories,* Peyton Randolph, Andrew Sprowle, and 163 others. 1 large p. [C.O.5, 1348, fos. 122–126d; copy of No. i in C.O.5, 1333, fos. 70–70A dorse; signed original of covering letter in C.O.5, 1333, fos. 30–30A dorse; entry of same in C.O.5, 1372, pp. 114–115]

445

30 June, Halifax

Governor Lord William Campbell to Earl of Hillsborough (No. 62). An inhabitant of Louisbourg last winter dug 500 chaldrons of coal. Soldiers were sent as guard, and I have made an offer for it for fuel for troops. *Signed.* 1½ pp. *Endorsed,* R, 1 August. [C.O.217, 47, fos. 48–49d; signed duplicate, endorsed Read 22 August 1771, in C.O.217, 26, fos. 64–65d; entry in C.O.218, 17, p. 238]

446

30 June, St Augustine

William De Brahm to Earl of Hillsborough (No. 11), complaining of difficulties and of Governor Grant's attempts to replace him. Six months leave and payment of salary requested. *Signed.* 4 pp. *Endorsed*, R, 17 September. Read by the King. [C.O.5, 71, Pt. 2, fos. 43–44d; entry in C.O.5, 227, pp. 264–272]

447

[June ?]

* Deputy Governor Robert Eden to Earl of Hillsborough (No. 6), enclosing following. Taking off duties on glass, paper and colours will not end Association. General voice is that duty on tea will stand as precedent. Taxing tea in England and not here would answer wishes of Americans. Assembly will meet in September. *Signed.* 3 pp. *Endorsed*, R, 17 August 1770. *Enclosed:*

i. *Proceedings of Committee appointed to examine importation of goods by Good Intent, in February 1770. Printed*, at Annapolis, by Anne Catherine Greene, 1770. xii + 27 pp.

ii. *Maryland Gazette*, 19 April 1770, reporting proceedings of said committee. *Printed.* 4 pp.

iii. *Maryland Gazette*, 26 April 1770, with letter on said subject. *Printed.* 4 pp. [C.O.5, 1283, fos. 30–57d; entry of covering letter in C.O.5, 1300, pp. 239–242]

448

2 July, Boston

Lieut.-Governor Thomas Hutchinson to John Pownall, enclosing following. There was another affair of same sort on 29 June, but the man insulted was determined to bring an action. *Signed.* ¾ small p. *Endorsed*, R, 4 August. *Enclosed:*

i. Proceedings of Council of Massachusetts, 21 May 1770. Owen Richards, tidesman, was tarred and feathered on 18 May. Justices to investigate. *Copy*, certified by John Cotton, deputy secretary. 1½ small pp.

ii. Proceedings of same, 21 June 1770. On 19 June one McMaster was seized in Boston and carted out of town ignominiously in broad daylight. *Copy*, certified as No. i. 1¼ pp.

iii. Proclamation by Lieut.-Governor Hutchinson, 28 June 1770, offering £50 reward for information against those who have threatened Henry Barnes for importing goods. *Printed.* 1 p. [C.O.5, 759, fos. 234–240d]

449

2 July, New Bern

Governor William Tryon to Earl of Hillsborough (No. 56), acknowledging No. 32 and enclosing following, by which it appears that there is £58,535 14s. 8d. outstanding. £20,000 of promissory notes issued in 1768 continue in circulation. Losing government of New York lamented; leave of absence acknowledged. Memorial respecting naval stores will be put before next Assembly. *Signed*. 2¼ pp. *Endorsed*, R, 24 August. *Enclosed:*

i. Estimate of monies emitting in North Carolina since 1748, showing purposes to which sums were applied and by what taxes sunk. 1 large p.

ii. Account of money paid into Treasury on sinking funds and burnt since 1749. Total: £37,162 7s. 4d. proclamation bills, £26,857 18s. interest notes. 1 p. [C.O.5, 313, fos. 93–97d; signed duplicate of covering letter and copies of enclosures, endorsed Read 7 November 1770, in C.O.5, 301, fos. 150–154d; entry of covering letter in C.O.5, 328, pp. 200–202]

450

2 July, New Bern

Same to John Pownall, acknowledging letter of 4 April and enclosures. *Signed*. ½ p. *Endorsed*, R, 24 August. [C.O.5, 313, fos. 91–92d; entry in C.O.5, 328, p. 200]

451

2 July, New York

List of twenty-three persons naturalized in New York, 18 April 1769 to end of April 1770, showing religious and temporal profession, place of abode and time of naturalization. *Certified*, by G. Banyar, deputy secretary. 1 large p. [C.O.5, 1075, fo. 63, 63d]

452

3 July, Whitehall

John Pownall to Anthony Todd. New York and Carolina packet-boats to be detained to Saturday. *Entry*. ½ p. [C.O.5, 241, p. 307]

453

4 July, Quebec

Governor Guy Carleton to Earl of Hillsborough (No. 33), enclosing following. *Duplicate. Signed.* ½ p. *Endorsed*, R, 13 September, original not recd. *Enclosed:*

i. Minutes of Council of Quebec, 18 April–29 June 1770. *Copy,* certified by George Allsopp, deputy clerk. *Countersigned,* Guy Carleton. 21 pp. [C.O.42, 30, fos. 64–75d; entry of covering letter in C.O.43, 12, p. 262; signed original of covering letter in C.O.42, 7, fos. 162–163d]

454

4 July, New York

Andrew Elliot to Earl of Hillsborough reporting adjournment to May next of commissioners for settling New York–New Jersey boundary. No other commissioner attended. *Signed.* 1 small p. *Endorsed,* R, 17 August. [C.O.5, 1101, fos. 76–77d; entry in C.O.5, 1138, pp. 148–149]

455

5 July, Whitehall

Order of Committee of Council for Plantation Affairs, referring following to Commissioners for Trade and Plantations. *Seal. Signed,* W. Blair. 1 p. *Endorsed,* Recd., Read 13 July 1770. *Enclosed :*

i. Petition of officers and soldiers to the King, praying that Governor Earl of Dunmore be permitted to grant lands in New York to those at whose expense they have already been located and surveyed, and to confirm to others grants already made. *Copy. Signatories,* John Murray, Francis Grant, Eglintowne, Joseph Wrightson, William Barr. 3 pp.

ii. List of officers referred to in above petition, with location of lands, taken from Surveyor-General's office at New York. *Copy.* 2 pp. [C.O.5, 1074, fos. 237–241d]

456

5 July, Whitehall

Commissioners for Trade and Plantations to Committee of Council for Plantation Affairs, enclosing following. *Entry. Signatories,* William Fitzherbert, Robert Spencer, Greville, Hillsborough, Edward Eliot, John Roberts. 1 p. *Enclosed :*

i. Additional instruction to Governor John Wentworth, to stop proclamation of 2 March 1769 for ascertaining rate of foreign coins. Assembly may prepare law to prevent prejudice. *Entry.* 1½ pp. [C.O.5, 943, pp. 11–13; draft in C.O.5, 896, fos. 146–149d]

457

5 July, Quebec

Governor Guy Carleton to Earl of Hillsborough (No. 34), enclosing papers on disagreement with Mr Ainslie, Collector of this port, arising from increase of fees. *Signed.* 1¼ pp. *Endorsed,* R, 13 September. *Enclosed :*

i. Quebec, 5 July 1770. Governor Carleton to Grey Cooper, sending papers on disagreement with Mr Ainslie. *Copy.* 1¼ pp.

ii. 1 August 1767. List of Custom-house fees at Quebec, conformable to those at New York. *Copy,* certified by George Allsopp, deputy clerk of Council. 1 p.

iii. 17 August 1769. List of same, as being the Halifax fees. *Copy,* certified as No. ii. 1 p.

iv. Quebec, 14 October 1769. George Allsopp to Customs-officers in province of Quebec, requiring list of fees: desist from demanding increased fees. *Copy,* certified as No. ii. 1 p.

v. Quebec, 16 October 1769. Deputy Collector Tom Mellish and Comptroller Thomas Scott to George Allsopp, enclosing list of fees, approved by Inspector-General. We shall observe governor's commands. *Copy,* certified as No. ii. 1 p.

vi. Quebec, 25 October 1769. Governor Carleton to Commissioners of Customs in Boston, reporting increased fees charged by Customs-officers at Quebec, apparently approved by Mr Hooton, the inspector. *Copy.* 1¾ pp.

vii. Quebec, 22 November 1769. Same to same, sending proceedings in Admiralty Court here, and requesting order to Mr Ainslie to return to duty or appoint deputy more conscientious than Mr Mellish. *Copy.* 1½ pp.

viii. Boston, 14 May 1770. Richard Reeve to Governor Carleton. Board has been under adjournment for some time. Meanwhile Collector of Quebec is returning to post. Table of fees at Halifax to be in force, copy enclosed. *Copy.* 1¼ pp.

ix. 23 December 1769. List of Customs fees at Halifax, N. Scotia, attested by Richard Reeve. *Copy,* certified as No. ii. 1 p.

x. Quebec, 14 June 1770. George Allsopp to Thomas Ainslie, sending copy of No. iv. H.E. is determined to suspend all who disobey orders in this letter. *Copy,* certified as No. ii. ¾ p.

xi. Quebec, 14 June 1770. Statement by Alexander MacCulloch that Thomas Ainslie refused to receive No. x because not addressed to him and Comptroller of Customs. 1 small p.

xii. Quebec, 14 June 1770. President H. T. Cramahé to [Customs-officers], returning No. x, directed as desired. *Copy.* 1 p.

xiii. Quebec, 15 June 1770. Tom Mellish and Thomas Scott to [President Cramahé]. Mr Ainslie is ill; he has communicated governor's order to Commissioners of Customs. *Copy.* 1 p.

xiv. Quebec, 23 June 1770. Thomas Ainslie to [Governor Carleton]. Nos. x, xii and xiii have been sent to Commissioners at Boston. I relinquish every fee until I hear from the Board. *Copy.* ½ p.

xv. Quebec, 23 June 1770. Thomas Scott to Governor Carleton. I acquiesce with your order and shall receive fees conformable to New York list. *Copy.* ¾ p.

* xvi. Quebec, 4 July 1770. Governor Carleton to Commissioners of Customs at Boston. New York is nearer Quebec by some hundred miles than Halifax. New York fees will be used here till H.M.'s pleasure is known. Mr Ainslie has been violent but at length obeyed. *Copy.* 6½ pp.

xvii. Quebec, 13 June 1770. Thomas Ainslie to Surveyor and Customer at Montreal. Governor has no power to dispense with law by which Customs fees are regulated; you are to receive fees agreeable to list delivered you by Collector. *Copy.* 1 p. [C.O.42, 30, fos. 76–110d; entry of covering letter in C.O.43, 12, pp. 263–265; signed duplicate of covering letter, and copies of enclosures, in C.O.42, 7, fos. 164–200d]

458

5 July, Halifax

Governor Lord William Campbell to Earl of Hillsborough (No. 63), enclosing following. Success of scheme for roads is doubtful. *Signed.* 1¼ pp. *Endorsed,* R, 15 October. *Enclosed:*

i. List of titles of sixteen Acts passed in Nova Scotia in session June–July 1770. 2¾ pp.

ii. Act for raising £1000 by lottery for building bridges and roads in Nova Scotia. *Copy.* 9¼ pp.

iii. Note comparing Nova Scotia law for lottery with Act of Parliament. 1 p. [C.O.217, 47, fos. 50–61d; signed duplicate of covering letter, and copies of enclosures, in C.O.217, 26, fos. 30–39d; entry of covering letter in C.O.218, 17, p. 239]

459

5 July, Charleston

John Stuart to Earl of Hillsborough (No. 24), acknowledging No. 16. Virginia will be blind to its interest not to acquiesce in line pointed out by H.M.'s instructions to me, while such territory may be obtained from Cherokees. *Signed.* 2 pp. *Endorsed,* R, 27 August. [C.O.5, 71, Pt. 2, fos. 21–22d; entry in C.O.5, 227, pp. 252–254; signed duplicate, endorsed R, 12 September, in C.O.323, 27, pp. 51–54]

460

6 July, St James's

* Order of King in Council, reciting and approving report of Committee for Plantation Affairs of 4th inst. on disorders in Massachusetts. Ordered that Boston be rendezvous of H.M. ships in North America

and fortress commanding that harbour be put in state of defence and garrisoned by regular troops. *Copy.* 4 pp. *Endorsed,* Recd. 12 December, Read 21 December 1772. [C.O.5, 894, pp. 459–466; another copy, without recital of report, same endorsement, at pp. 455–458]

461

6 July, Whitehall

Earl of Hillsborough to Lieut.-General Thomas Gage (No. 31), acknowledging Nos. 44 and 45. Altercations such as that between Lieut.-Colonel Wilkins and commander of Fort Genevieve should be avoided. Indian disorders will continue as long as colonies permit so loose a trade: all Crown can do is to see that the savages do not wrest interior country from us. Pensacola harbour should be defended by batteries. Deserters or emigrants from New Orleans should not be encouraged. Order in Council enclosed on 'State of the Disorders in Massachusetts'; possession of Castle William is to be delivered to officer appointed by you, and the fort put into state of defence. It will be for you to determine if the regiment now there will be sufficient for services intended. *Draft.* 4¼ pp. [C.O.5, 88, fos. 97–99d; entry in C.O.5, 241, pp. 308–311]

462

6 July, Whitehall

* Same to Lieut.-Governor Thomas Hutchinson (No. 38), acknowledging Nos. 9–14. Order in Council enclosed. Provincial company in Castle William to be withdrawn and fort delivered to Lieut.-General Gage's direction. Waste of timber and illegal grants in country east of River Sagadahoc is responsibility of the province. Your suggestion that the province should quit claim to lands east of Penobscot and take as compensation lands between that river and Kennebec deserves consideration. Removal of Colonel Goldthwaite from office of truckmaster by Assembly disapproved; he must remain in command of Fort Pownall. King approves summoning of General Court to Cambridge or wherever you think advisable, except Boston. *Entry.* 4 pp. *Enclosed:*

> * i. St James's, 6 July 1770. Order of King in Council on 'State of Disorders etc. in Massachusetts'. Boston to be rendezvous of H.M. ships in North America. Fortress commanding harbour there to be put in state of defence and garrisoned by regular troops. *Entry.* 5 pp. [C.O.5, 765, pp. 167–176; draft of covering letter in C.O.5, 759, fos. 206–208d]

463

6 July, Whitehall

Same to Governor Lord William Campbell (No. 40), acknowledging Nos. 58–59. I hope that new Assembly will adopt proper measures for supplying deficiencies of public funds in Nova Scotia and consider adequate permanent establishment for support of civil government. *Draft.* 1¼ pp. [C.O.217, 47, fos. 40–41d; entry in C.O.218, 25, pp. 77–78]

464

6 July, Whitehall

Same to Governor Guy Carleton (No. 33), acknowledging Nos. 30–32. Memorial in No. 32 will be sent to Board of Trade, which is considering ordinance for regulating courts of jurisdiction. *Draft.* 1 p. [C.O.42, 30, fos. 53–54d; entry in C.O.43, 8, p. 82]

465

6 July, Whitehall

Same to Governor Lord Botetourt (No. 33), acknowledging No. 32. I hope in next account of duty of 2s. per hogshead balance will be on other side. *Draft.* ¾ p. [C.O.5, 1348, fos. 105–106d; entry in C.O.5, 1375, p. 102]

466

6 July, Whitehall

Same to Governor John Wentworth (No. 31), acknowledging No. 30. I hope that when affair at Boston is truly represented, prejudices will be removed. Petition relative to late Revenue Act will be received if not disrespectful to legislature. Nothing can do more to restore peace than suppression of seditious publications. *Draft.* 2 pp. [C.O.5, 937, fos. 15–16d; entry in C.O.5, 947, pp. 47–48]

467

6 July, Whitehall

Same to Governor William Franklin (No. 26), acknowledging letter of 28 April. Zeal of magistrates and Council in suppressing riots in Essex and Monmouth Counties is commendable. You were right to refuse alteration in method of appointing coroners without H.M.'s consent. *Draft.* 1¼ pp. [C.O.5, 990, fos. 81–82d; entry in C.O.5, 1003, pp. 32–33]

468

6 July, Whitehall

Same to Deputy Governor John Penn (No. 23), expressing concern at disposition amongst Philadelphia merchants to concur in non-importation, which is now an evil of such magnitude as to require consideration of legislature. *Draft.* ¾ p. [C.O.5, 1283, fos. 7–8d; entry in C.O.5, 1301, p. 125]

469

6 July, Whitehall

Same to Lieut.-Governor Cadwallader Colden (No. 40), acknowledging
No. 11. I hope provision for troops will be made in paper currency bill
consequential on late Act of Parliament. *Draft.* ½ p. [C.O.5, 1101, fos.
65–66d; entry in C.O.5, 1141, p. 135]

470

6 July, Whitehall

Same to William De Brahm (No. 7), acknowledging letter of 1 November 1769 and map. Governor Grant has complained of your conduct
as Surveyor-General of East Florida. Confine your attention to General
Surveys and appoint person governor approves of to be deputy as
provincial Surveyor; otherwise you will be suspended. *Draft.* 1½ pp.
[C.O.5, 71, Pt. 1, fos. 132–133d; entry in C.O.5, 241, p. 312]

471

6 July, Whitehall

Same to Governor James Grant (No. 30), sending copy of No. 470 to
Mr De Brahm. Should he make difficulty in complying with these
directions, suspend him from office of provincial Surveyor. *Draft.* ¾ p.
[C.O.5, 551, fos. 41–42d; entry in C.O.5, 566, p. 33]

472

6 July, New York

Lieut.-General Thomas Gage to Earl of Hillsborough (No. 46),
acknowledging Nos. 27–29 and enclosures. Till H.M.'s pleasure is
received on proposals for disposition of brigade in southern district,
I am willing to postpone further work on barracks first proposed for
St Augustine. H.M.'s protection in matter of indictment at Boston
gratefully acknowledged. H.M.'s orders concerning cost of Sir W.
Johnson's congress with Northern Indians and assistance to be given
to Lieut.-Governor Hutchinson, will be obeyed. *Signed.* 2 pp. *Endorsed,*
R, 17 August. [C.O.5, 88, fos. 107–108d; entry in C.O.5, 234, pp. 89–90]

473

6 July, Quebec

Adam Mabane to Earl of Hillsborough, complaining of dismissal from
Council of Quebec by Lieut.-Governor Carleton in 1766. *Signed.*
2 small pp. *Endorsed,* R, September. [C.O.42, 30, fos. 145–146d]

474

7 July, Whitehall

Earl of Hillsborough to Lords of Admiralty. Directions to be given for Boston to be rendezvous for H.M. ships on North American station instead of Halifax. Object is to check violence, stop illicit trade and support revenue-officers and magistrates. *Entry*. 1 p. [C.O.5, 765, p. 177; draft in C.O.5, 759, fos. 209–210]

475

7 July

Richard Jackson to Commissioners for Trade and Plantations, reporting on eighteen Acts passed in Pennsylvania in 1769 [MS: 1759], proper in point of law. *Signed*. 3¼ pp. *Endorsed*, Recd. 7 July, Read 10 July 1770. [C.O.5, 1277, pp. 591–594]

476

7 July, New York

* Lieut.-General Thomas Gage to Earl of Hillsborough (No. 47). Annulling Act of New York for emitting bills of credit has caused deficiency in funds appropriated for supply of King's troops: see enclosed. Peace now being negotiated between Creeks and Choctaws through Mr Stuart's mediation. Creeks have visited Havana. Lieut.-Governor Durnford recommends that material from ruinous fort at Mobile be used for building barracks there and at Pensacola. Sir W. Johnson's congress not yet held. All quiet on Lakes as far as Detroit. Letters from Lieut.-Governor Hutchinson and Lieut.-Col. Dalrymple enclosed. Plan for removing prisoners at Boston to Castle William. Most people think they will be condemned. *Signed*. 5¼ pp. *Endorsed*, R, 17 August, *Enclosed*:

i. New York, 7 June 1770. Lieut.-Governor Cadwallader Colden to General Gage. Nothing remains in Treasury for providing for troops quartered in this province. I can have no hope of Assembly supplying deficiency. *Copy*. ¾ p.

ii. Boston, 22, 23 June 1770. Extracts of two letters from Lieut.-Governor Hutchinson to General Gage, expressing apprehensions that people of Boston will themselves execute sentence on Captain Preston and the soldiers, either when or before they are found guilty. *Copy*. 3 pp.

iii. Boston, 24 June 1770. Extract of letter from Lieut.-Colonel Dalrymple to General Gage, reporting attack on Mr Hulton's house. *Copy*. 1¼ pp. [C.O.5, 88, fos. 109–117d; entry in C.O.5, 234, pp. 91–101]

477

7 July, New York

Separate. Same to same. All I have discovered about order from Boston for military accoutrements is that officers of the militia desired a company of grenadiers in each regiment. *Signed.* 1 p. *Endorsed*, R, 17 August. [C.O.5, 88, fos. 118–119d; entry, dated 9 July, in C.O.5, 234, p. 101]

478

7 July, New York

* Lieut.-Governor Cadwallader Colden to Earl of Hillsborough (No. 12), acknowledging No. 38, and defending assent to Act disqualifying judges from sitting in Assembly and the meeting of commissioners to regulate Indian trade. I now suspect commissioners will not meet. Philadelphia merchants have been encouraged by a gentleman in England to persevere in non-importation. I believe merchants here are resolved to import. Men of property are sensible of dangers from riots. Opposite parties have taken their denomination from some distinguished person or family, but it is not in power of any one family to distress government while administration is conducted with prudence, which often requires compliance with popular humours. *Signed.* PS. Minutes of Council sent. 3½ pp. *Endorsed*, R, 17 August. [C.O.5, 1101, fos. 78–79d; entry in C.O.5, 1138, pp. 149–156]

479

[7 July]

Petition of merchants of Liverpool trading to Africa to Commissioners for Trade and Plantations, praying that Act passed in Virginia laying additional duty of five per cent. on negroes imported be not countenanced. *Signed,* Ralph Earle and fifty-five others. 1 large p. *Endorsed,* Recd. 7 July, Read 10 July 1770. [C.O.5, 1332, fo. 193, 193d]

480

8 July, St John's

Governor John Byron to Earl of Hillsborough. Merchants and principal adventurers in fishery complained last year and this of Customs fees at St John's, which were fixed at discretion of Customs officers. I have regulated them. Naval Officer needed at outports. *Signed.* 6½ pp. *Endorsed*, R, 30 July. *Enclosed :*

i. Fees payable at Custom-house, St John's, Newfoundland. 1 p.

ii. Fees taken at same, 1766–1767. 1 p.

iii. Fees taken by Naval Officer, St John's. 1 p.

iv. St John's, 1 July 1770. Petition of merchants, traders and adventurers to Governor Byron, complaining of Customs fees. *Copy.* *Signatories,* John Rogers and thirty-nine others. 1 large p.

v. 2 July 1770. Table of Customs fees payable at St John's, determined by Governor Byron. *Copy*. 1¼ large pp. [C.O.194, 29, fos. 47–62d; entry of covering letter in C.O.195, 12, pp. 94–99]

481

8 July, Pensacola

Lieut.-Governor Elias Durnford to Earl of Hillsborough (No. 17). Peace between Choctaws and Creeks was apparently concluded, but not accepted by Lower Creek towns. If they are not at variance, we shall find them troublesome. Northern Indians have been making overtures to our neighbours. I believe Spaniards from Havana have been tampering with Lower Creeks. *Signed*. 2¼ pp. *Endorsed*, R, 17 September. [C.O.5, 587, pp. 369–372; entry in C.O.5, 620, pp. 262–264]

482

9 July, Pensacola

Same to same (No. 18), enclosing following. Memorial prepared by some members of Assembly is to be delivered to Mr Hannay, their agent. I wish they may have weight to be of service to the province. *Signed*. 1½ pp. *Endorsed*, R, 17 September. *Enclosed :*

* i. Address of Council of West Florida to Earl of Hillsborough, asking for re-establishment of Fort Bute to help and secure settlement on Mississippi, and to secure fur-trade; for congress with Indians; for appointment of commissaries; for drawing of boundary-line between this and neighbouring colonies; and for church at Pensacola. *Signed*. William Clifton, James Bruce, David Hodge, James Jones, William Godley, Phillips Comyn. 3½ pp. [C.O.5, 587, pp. 373–380; entry in covering letter in C.O.5, 620, pp. 264–265]

483

9 July, Quebec

Petition to Governor Guy Carleton that fishing ports for sea-wolves should be reunited to Quebec, and that they should be free to take part in that fishery on coasts of Mingan and Labrador and in Gulf of St Lawrence, as formerly. *French. Signed*, Boucherville and ten others. 4 pp. *Endorsed*, Read 12 June 1772. [C.O.194, 18, fos. 130–132d]

484

10 July, New York

* Lieut.-General Thomas Gage to Earl of Hillsborough (No. 48), reporting resolution of merchants of this city to begin importing from Great Britain everything but tea and glass etc. until duty thereon expires. *Signed*. 1 p. *Endorsed*, R, 17 August. [C.O.5, 88, fos. 120–121d; entry in C.O.5, 234, p. 102]

485

10 July, St Augustine

Governor James Grant to Earl of Hillsborough (No. 37), acknowledging Nos. 25–26, and enclosing papers. Indians want meeting at Picolata. I want satisfaction for murders at St Mary's River three years ago, and return of runaway negroes. William Owen, acting Attorney-General, recommended to succeed if Mr Box dies. He practised law in Dublin, but was obliged to leave: his misfortunes are owing to a good disposition. *Signed.* 2½ pp. *Endorsed,* R, 15 October. *Enclosed:*

> i. Account of contingent expenses of East Florida, 25 June 1769–24 June 1770. *Signatory,* Alexander Skinner, clerk of public accounts. *Copy,* certified 13 July 1770 by David Yeats, deputy clerk to Council. 3 pp.

> ii. Plans and elevation of court-house, St Augustine. 2 pp. [M.P.G. 979]

> iii. Estimate of cost of repairs to court-house and gaol, St Augustine: £343. ½ p.

> iv. Naval Officer's list of vessels entering port of St Augustine, 24 June 1769–24 June 1770. 12 large pp.

> v. Same, of vessels leaving same, same dates. 12 large pp. [C.O.5, 551, fos. 45–66d; signed duplicate of covering letter, endorsed Account of contingent expenses sent to Auditor's office, 9 February 1773, in C.O.5, 544, fos. 183–184d; entry of covering letter in C.O.5, 567, pp. 151–154]

486

10 July, New York

* Lieut.-Governor Cadwallader Colden to Earl of Hillsborough (No. 13). After house-to-house inquiry, great majority declared for importing. *Signed.* PS. Printed advertisement enclosed. 1¼ small pp. *Endorsed,* R, 17 August. *Enclosed:*

> i. New York, 9 July 1770. It appears by return to committee of inspection that great majority is in favour of importation. It is expected that tea or other article subject to duty will not be shipped. *Printed. Signatory,* Isaac Low, chairman. 1 p. [C.O.5, 1101, fos. 80–82d; entry of covering letter in C.O.5, 1138, pp. 156–157]

487

10 July, Pensacola

Lieut.-Governor Elias Durnford to Earl of Hillsborough (No. 19), enclosing following. *Signed.* 1¼ pp. *Endorsed,* R, 17 September. *Enclosed:*

> i. Plan of encampment of detachment of 31st regiment at Red Cliffs, east side of Mobile Bay. 1 large p. [M.P.G. 359]

ii. Plan of site of new town, Mobile Bay. 1 large p. [M.P.G.359] [C.O.5, 587, pp. 381–386; entry of covering letter in C.O.5, 620, p. 266]

488

11 July, Whitehall

John Pownall to Grey Cooper, replying to letter of 16 June concerning contract for transport at Niagara. *Draft.* 1¾ pp. [C.O.5, 71, Pt. 2, fos. 1–2d; entry in C.O.5, 241, pp. 313–314]

489

11 July, Whitehall

Same to same, acknowledging letter of 26 June and memorial of persons in Nova Scotia seeking payment for provisions supplied to Indians. Expenditure was not authorized after 1764. The accounts have been regularly examined and audited, and it is for Treasury to decide whether persons performing public services by order of governor should be precluded from payment by want of authority in governor to give such orders. *Entry.* 4½ pp. [C.O.218, 7, pp. 282–286]

490

11 July, London

Petition of merchants of London trading to Quebec to Commissioners for Trade and Plantations, praying for suspension of ordinance of 22 March last. *Signed,* John Strettell and six others. 1¼ pp. *Endorsed,* Recd. 12 July, Read 13 July 1770. *Enclosed:*

i. Quebec, 11 and 15 April 1770. Extracts from two letters complaining of this ordinance. *Copy.* 2¼ pp. [C.O.42, 7, fos. 127–130d]

491

11 July, Pensacola

Lieut.-Governor Elias Durnford to Earl of Hillsborough (No. 20). I have drawn bills on Mr Ellis for provincial contingencies and Indian department. Provincial contingencies are now overdrawn, but Indian contingencies have favourable balance. Accounts enclosed. *Signed.* 1¼ pp. *Endorsed,* R, 17 September. *Enclosed:*

i. Accounts of West Florida: Provincial Contingencies and Indian Contingencies, 24 December 1769–24 March 1770. *Signed,* Elias Durnford, 11 July 1770. 2 pp. [C.O.5, 587, pp. 387–394; entry of covering letter in C.O.5, 620, p. 267]

492

12 July, Pensacola

Same to same (No. 21). Lieut.-governor of New Orleans has asked me to send back deserters from Spanish garrison, promising them free pardon; and offering to return our deserters. Several have sought asylum here. Our constitution will not permit their return by force. We have very few deserters from British troops. *Signed.* 2 pp. *Endorsed,* R, 17 September. [C.O.5, 587, pp. 395–398; entry in C.O.5, 620, pp. 268–269]

493

12 July, Johnson Hall

Sir William Johnson to Earl of Hillsborough, acknowledging Nos. 12–13. I set out for Indian congress tomorrow with cargo of Indian goods, got with difficulty from non-importers at New York. Provisions scarce. Fort Stanwix treaty will be ratified and explained at congress. I foresee much trouble and difficulty. *Signed.* 2½ pp. *Endorsed,* R, 17 September. [C.O.5, 71, Pt. 2, fos. 41–42d; entry in C.O.5, 227, pp. 259–264]

494

13 July, Whitehall

Commissioners for Trade and Plantations to Committee of Council for Plantation Affairs, reporting on petition of Thomas and Richard Penn, alleging forcible possession of lands in Pennsylvania by inhabitants of Connecticut. Agents of Connecticut have no instructions to avow the settlers' proceedings. Matter is entirely within Pennsylvania's jurisdiction. *Entry. Signatories,* Edward Eliot, John Roberts, William Fitzherbert, Robert Spencer. 4 pp. [C.O.5, 1296, pp. 350–353]

495

[13 July]

Petition of Thomas Martin to Commissioners for Trade and Plantations, for grant of 10,000 acres of land in East Florida. *Signed.* 1 p. *Endorsed,* Recd. 13 July 1770, Read 6 February 1771. [C.O.5, 545, fos. 1–2d]

496

14 July

Warrant to Governor Sir F. Bernard or to Lieut.-Governor of Massachusetts to insert additional clauses in letters patent to Francis Bernard and John Bernard to be Naval Officer of Massachusetts. *Entry.* 2 pp. [C.O.324, 42, pp. 191–192]

497

14 July

Warrant to Governor William Tryon to admit Samuel Strudwick to be Clerk of Pleas in North Carolina. *Entry.* 1 p. [C.O.324, 42, p. 193]

498

14 July, Pensacola

Lieut.-Governor Elias Durnford to Earl of Hillsborough (No. 22), reporting depredations by Choctaws near Mobile, and by Creeks at Mobile Bay near Dauphin Island. Further particulars later. *Signed.* 1¾ pp. *Endorsed,* R, 17 September. [C.O.5, 587, pp. 399–402; entry in C.O.5, 620, pp. 269–271]

499

14 July, Pensacola

Same to same, enclosing following, and sending minutes of Lower House of Assembly of West Florida 1767–1770. *Signed.* ½ p. *Endorsed,* R, 17 September. *Enclosed:*

    i. West Florida, Council minutes, 16 June 1770, recording objections to proceedings of some members of Lower House of Assembly regarding two memorials sent to provincial agent, to be laid before H.M.'s ministers. *Copy,* certified by Francis Poussett, 2 July 1770. 10¼ pp. [C.O.5, 587, pp. 403–418; entry of covering letter in C.O.5, 620, p. 271]

500

15 July, Boston

Lieut.-Governor Thomas Hutchinson to Earl of Hillsborough (No. 19). Party in favour of importation increases, but both sides wait to know the whole that will be done by Parliament. I meet Assembly at Cambridge on 25th inst., I am not sure they will proceed to business. *Signed.* ¾ p. *Endorsed,* R, 14 September. [C.O.5, 759, fos. 249–250d; entry in C.O.5, 768, p. 160]

501

16 July, Whitehall

Earl of Hillsborough to Earl of Dunmore, sending instructions as Governor of New York. Salary will be £2000 a year from date of commission payable out of duty on tea imported into America. No other salary or gift from Assembly to be accepted. Moiety of perquisites and emoluments to be paid to you from date of commission to date of your arrival. *Draft.* 1½ pp. [C.O.5, 1101, fos. 67–68d; entry in C.O.5, 1141, pp. 136–137]

502

16 July, Admiralty

Lords of Admiralty to Earl of Hillsborough, enclosing following.
Signed, E. Hawke, J. Buller, C. J. Fox. *Endorsed*, R, 17th. *Enclosed :*

    i. *Romney*, Halifax, 1 May 1770. Extract of letter from Captain
Hood to Philip Stephens. Everything was quiet at Boston five days
ago. *Copy*. ¾ p. [C.O.5, 759, fos. 213–216d; entry in C.O.5, 768,
pp. 139–140]

503

16 July, London

*Thomas Walpole to Earl of Hillsborough, reporting delay in con-
sideration by Board of Trade of his application. Unless stop be put to
grants of land by Virginia, country will be garbled for benefit of few.
Settlement of Middle Colonies will benefit extremities. Further delay
will increase difficulties. *Signed*. 4 pp. *Endorsed*, Read 18 July 1770.
Enclosed :

    i. London, 9 July 1770. Anonymous letter to [Thomas Walpole],
concerning lands granted by Virginia. *Copy*. 9½ pp. [C.O.5, 1332,
fos. 194–202d]

504

16 July, Charleston

Lieut.-Governor William Bull to Earl of Hillsborough (No. 31),
acknowledging No. 34 and additional instruction. I shall prorogue
Assembly to 6 August. Mr Motte, Treasurer, died 17 June; Henry
Perroneau appointed till next meeting of Assembly. I signified my
sentiments privately to Council on Commons' resolution of 8 December.
Act of Parliament repealing three articles in Revenue Act has not yet
altered non-importation plan. We are too apt to cast our eyes to the
north star of Boston. *Signed*. 2 pp. *Endorsed*, R, 12 September. [C.O.5,
393, fos. 74–75d; signed duplicate in C.O.5, 379, fos. 123–124d; entry
in C.O.5, 409, pp. 121–123]

505

16 July, Charleston

John Stuart to Earl of Hillsborough (No. 25), enclosing papers.
Emistisiguo, head-warrior of Upper Creeks, arrived Pensacola 13
June to conclude peace with Choctaws. Trade in every nation calls
for regulation. Cherokees convened for 5 October for cession to Virginia
of lands pointed out in H.M.'s instructions to me. *Signed*. 2½ pp.
Endorsed, R, 12 September. *Enclosed :*

    * i. Pensacola, 12 June 1770. Charles Stuart to John Stuart, reporting
peace-negotiations between Creeks and Choctaws. Report of clash
between Choctaws and traders at Natchez, none killed. Shawnese

should be watched. Instructions needed on conferment of honours and medals on Indians. Spaniards cannot do us much harm with Indians. Chickasaws complain of Northern Indians. General Haldimand and I propose visiting the lakes. Report that Creeks get arms from Havana will be inquired into. *Copy.* 8½ pp.

ii. Ninety Six, 27 June 1770. Abstract of letter from Alexander Cameron to John Stuart. Richard Paris and one Hight from Virginia are in Cherokee Lower towns trying to buy titles to land. *Copy.* 1½ pp.

iii. Keowee, 17 May 1770. John Watts, interpreter with Cherokees, to John Stuart, reporting activities of Richard Paris. *Copy.* 1½ pp.

iv. East side of Mobile Bay, 23 April 1770. Talk from Pai Mattaha to lieut.-governor of West Florida and deputy-superintendent for Indian affairs, requesting reappointment of beloved man to see justice done between white and red men; also gunpowder. *Copy.* 1½ pp.

v. Williamsburg, 21 June 1770. Governor Lord Botetourt to John Stuart, requesting treaty with Cherokees for cession of land. Costs to be within £2500 voted for the purpose. *Copy.* 1½ pp.

vi. 30 December 1769. Abstract of letter from Daniel McMurphy, trader with Creek nation. Governor of Havana has promised powder, bullets, rum and tobacco to Lower Creeks. *Copy.* ¾ p. [C.O.5, 71, Pt. 2, fos. 23–40d; entry of covering letter in C.O.5, 227, pp. 254–257]

506

[16 July]

Richard Jackson to Commissioners for Trade and Plantations, reporting on eight ordinances issued in Quebec in 1768–1769. No objection to seven of them; ordinance concerning baking in Quebec and Montreal is contrary to system of laws of this Kingdom and inconsistent with universal principles of trade. *Signed.* 2 pp. *Endorsed,* Recd. 16 July, Read 19 July 1770. [C.O.42, 7, fos. 145–146d]

507

18 July, Whitehall

John Pownall to Attorney- and Solicitor-General, enclosing following for consideration. *Entry.* 1 p. *Enclosed:*

i. Whether legislature of New York is warranted to make Acts of Naturalization such as they have for some time past, and whether such Acts are agreeable to laws of this Kingdom. *Entry.* 8 pp. [C.O.5, 1131, pp. 232–240; draft of covering letter and of case in C.O.5, 1080, pp. 379–392]

508

18 July

Richard Jackson to Commissioners for Trade and Plantations, recommending Act passed in New Jersey for regulating practice of law as unfit for H.M.'s approbation; and submitting to H.M.'s wisdom Act for choosing representatives of Morris, Cumberland and Sussex Counties and Act for septennial system of representatives. *Signed.* 2 pp. [C.O.5, 979, fos. 17–18d]

509

18 July

Same to same, recommending disallowance of Act of New Hampshire to restrain usury. Act for dividing province into counties alters system of judicature but seems highly proper. *Signed.* 2 pp. [C.O.5, 930, fos. 86–87d]

510

18 July

Same to same, recommending two Acts passed in Nova Scotia in 1768 and 1769 for H.M.'s approbation. *Signed.* 1½ large pp. [C.O.217, 25, fos. 207–208d]

511

18 July

Same to same, reporting on Act passed in West Florida in June 1769, to encourage settlements in lands west of Charlotte County. Not advisable that Act should be approved which in effect erects a subordinate province and allows free exercise of religion proscribed by Acts of Parliament. *Signed.* 1 p. [C.O.5, 577, pp. 201–204]

512

18 July

Same to same, reporting three Acts passed in Virginia in 1769 proper in point of law. Act, also passed in 1769, for laying additional duty on slaves imported is not objectionable in point of law; but it rests with you to determine how far it may be expedient in point of commercial policy. All such duties must raise price, but perhaps increase of negroes by importation where stock increases by procreation should be checked. *Signed.* 2 pp. [C.O.5, 1332, fos. 203–204d]

513

18 July, Lebanon

Governor Jonathan Trumbull to Earl of Hillsborough (No. 17), acknowledging No. 17. *Signed.* ½ small p. *Endorsed,* R, 17 September. [C.O.5, 1283, fos. 80–81d; entry in C.O.5, 1300, p. 127]

514

18 July, Lebanon

Same to same (No. 18), acknowledging No. 18. Copies of laws enclosed; journals of Assembly are not printed. Determinations of Assembly in cases between parties are entered in the public records. *Signed.* 2 small pp. *Endorsed,* R, 17 September. *Enclosed :*

  i. Hertford, 2 February 1769. William Pitkin to Earl of Hillsborough (No. 13). *Copy.* 1¼ small pp.

  ii. Acts passed in Connecticut 1768–1770. *Printed.* 15 pp. [C.O.5, 1283, fos. 82–93d; entry of covering letter in C.O.5, 1300, pp. 127–129]

515

18 July

Henry E. McCulloch to Earl of Hillsborough, resigning from Council in North Carolina. *Signed.* 1 small p. *Endorsed,* Recd., Read 18 July 1770. [C.O.5, 301, fos. 90–91d]

516

19 July, London

Lieutenant Adolphus Benzel to [John Pownall] enclosing and explaining following. *Signed.* 1 small p. *Endorsed,* R, 19 July. *Enclosed :*

  i. Petition of Adolphus Benzel to Earl of Hillsborough for confirmation by H.M. of grant by Governor Sir H. Moore in 1766 of 3000 acres of land near Crown Point, part of which is claimed by government of New Hampshire. 1 p. [C.O.5, 1101, fos. 69–73d]

  ii. Plan of Crown Point and environs showing lands granted to Lieutenant Benzel and to others. 1 large p. [M.P.G. 368]

517

20 July, New York

Earl of Hillsborough to Governor Earl of Dunmore (private), sending copy of Lieutenant Benzel's petition, which is to be confirmed subject to surrender to H.M. if needed for military purposes. *Draft.* 1 p. [C.O.5, 1101, fos. 74–75d; entry in C.O.5, 1141, pp. 137–138]

518

20 July, Whitehall

Commissioners for Trade and Plantations to the King, recommending approval of Act passed in Virginia for relief of insolvent debtors and Act to regulate suing out writs of replevin. *Entry. Signatories,* Hillsborough, Edward Eliot, William Fitzherbert, Greville, Robert Spencer. 2 pp. [C.O.5, 1369, pp. 30–31; draft in C.O.5, 1336, fos. 170–171d]

519

20 July, Whitehall

Same to same, recommending for disallowance Act passed in New Jersey in 1765 for regulating practice of law. *Entry. Signatories,* as preceding. 2 pp. [C.O.5, 999, pp. 230–231]

520

20 July, Whitehall

Same to same, recommending approbation of Acts passed in Nova Scotia in 1768 and 1769 to empower Supreme Court at Halifax to try felonies done in other counties, and to amend Act for partition of lands in coparcenary etc. and for more effectual collecting of H.M.'s quit-rents. *Entry. Signatories,* Hillsborough, Edward Eliot, William Fitzherbert, Greville, Robert Spencer. 2½ pp. [C.O.218, 7, pp. 287–289]

521

20 July, Whitehall

Same to same, recommending for disallowance Act passed in West Florida in 1769 to encourage settlement west of Charlotte County. *Entry. Signatories,* as preceding. 2 pp. [C.O.5, 660, pp. 212–213]

522

20 July, Whitehall

Same to same, recommending approbation of Act passed in New Hampshire in 1769 for dividing province into counties and more easy administration of justice. *Entry. Signatories,* as preceding. 1¾ pp. [C.O.5, 943, pp. 14–15; draft in C.O.5, 896, fos. 150–151d]

523

20 July, Whitehall

Same to same, recommending approbation of Act passed in New Hampshire in 1769 to restrain excessive usury, notwithstanding Mr Jackson's objections thereto. *Entry. Signatories,* as preceding. 3½ pp. [C.O.5, 943, pp. 16–19; draft in C.O.5, 896, fos. 152–153d]

524

20 July, Whitehall

Same to same, recommending approval of Act passed in Virginia in 1769 for exempting free negroes, mulattos and Indian women from payment of levies. *Entry. Signatories,* as preceding. 1¾ pp. [C.O.5, 1369, pp. 32–33; draft in C.O.5, 1336, fos. 172–173d]

525

20 July, Whitehall

* Same to Governor Lord Botetourt, sending papers concerning application by persons of wealth for grant of lands ceded to H.M. in Treaty of Fort Stanwix in 1768. Virginia has an interest in these lands. Information required on state of country in question. *Entry. Signatories,* as preceding. 2¾ pp. [C.O.5, 1369, pp. 34–36; draft in C.O.5, 1336, fos. 168–169d]

526

20 July, Whitehall

Same to Committee of Council for Plantation Affairs, submitting eighteen Acts passed in Pennsylvania in 1769. There may be some objection to Act to enable managers of contributions for relief of poor in Philadelphia to raise £14,000, and to Act for raising £16,000 for support of government; but Mr Jackson's opinion is that they are not contrary to Act of Parliament of 4 Geo. III. *Entry. Signatories,* as preceding. 10 pp. [C.O.5, 1296, pp. 354–363]

527

20 July, Whitehall

Same to the King, recommending for confirmation Act passed in New Jersey in 1768 for choosing representatives in Morris, Cumberland and Sussex Counties, notwithstanding objections to it. *Entry. Signatories,* Hillsborough, Soame Jenyns, Greville, William Northey. 4¼ pp. [C.O.5, 999, pp. 225–229]

528

20 July

Leave of absence for twelve months to Henry Yonge, Surveyor-General of Georgia. *Entry.* 1 p. [C.O.324, 42, p. 195]

529

20 July, Whitehall

John Pownall to Bamber Gascoyne, acknowledging memorial of merchants of Liverpool against Act passed in Virginia laying additional duty on slaves imported. Consideration postponed. *Entry.* 1½ pp. [C.O.5, 1369, pp. 37–38]

530

20 July, Whitehall

Same to Francis Reynolds, acknowledging memorial of merchants of Lancaster against Act passed in Virginia laying additional duty on slaves imported. Consideration postponed. *Entry.* 1½ pp. [C.O.5, 1369, pp. 39–40]

531

20 July, Savannah

* Governor James Wright to Earl of Hillsborough (No. 46). I have put an end to all present disputes between Indians and back-settlers. I have intelligence that Creek chiefs have gone to Mobile to ratify peace with Choctaws, which makes ir probable they will pick quarrel with us. A visit to England by one headman from Upper and one from Lower Creeks would be beneficial. South Carolina newspaper enclosed: such confederacy to destroy liberty was never known till 1766, and now, both times in Charleston. Can it be said law and government operate in South Carolina? I shall be obliged to delay going to England till next spring. Mr Stokes should be of the Council. Enclosed presentments were by a weak and infatuated grand jury. *Signed.* PS (1). Letters from Charleston confirm resolutions relative to West India islands. How far may not these people go, or where stop? PS (2). Paper now sent shows they have compelled Rhode Island vessel to return. 4¼ pp. *Endorsed*, R, 15 October. *Enclosed:*

i. 1 March 1766. Resolutions by fire-company of Charleston, relative to infernal Stamp Act and shipping of provisions to Georgia. *Copy.* 2¼ pp.

ii. July 1770. Statement by 'Georgians', denouncing declaration in South Carolina newspapers dated 19 June 1770. *Printed.* 1 p.

iii. *Georgia Gazette,* 27 June 1770, reporting presentments by grand jury at Savannah, 1769–1770; with supplement. *Printed.* 6 pp.

iv. *South Carolina Gazette,* 28 June 1770, reporting proceedings concerning non-importation. *Printed.* 4 pp.

v. *Georgia Gazette,* 4 July 1770. *Printed.* 4 pp.

vi. *South Carolina Gazette,* 5 July 1770, reporting proposal to extend non-importation to West India trade. *Printed.* 4 pp.

vii. *Georgia Gazette,* 11 July 1770, with supplement. *Printed.* 8 pp.

viii. *South Carolina and American General Gazette,* 11–18 July 1770, reporting sloop from Rhode Island not permitted to trade at Charleston. *Printed.* 4 pp. [Covering letter, with first postscript, and enclosures i-vii in C.O.5, 660, fos. 116–135d; signed duplicate of covering letter, with second postscript, and enclosure viii in C.O.5, 651, fos. 40–44d; entry of covering letter in C.O.5, 678, pp. 189–195]

532

23 July, Savannah

Same to same (No. 47), acknowledging No. 30. *Signed.* 1 small p. *Endorsed*, R, 15 October. [C.O.5, 660, fos. 136–137d; entry in C.O.5, 678, pp. 195–196]

533

23 July, Savannah

Same to Commissioners for Trade and Plantations, sending bills passed last session. Titles stated. Appointing to petty offices by ordinance adds to power of Assembly. H.M.'s disallowance of law regulating rates of wharfage and ordinance appointing harbour-master would prevent it for the future. Bill enclosed concerning representation in Assembly, which I was obliged to reject by my 17th instruction; but I am clear all the alterations proposed are beneficial and are what I proposed to Lord Hillsborough in 1768, except the limiting of Assembly to three years. Journals of Council as Upper House and Journals of Lower House, transmitted. *Signed.* PS. Proceedings of Council July–December 1769 transmitted. 7¼ pp. *Endorsed,* Recd. 1 November, Read 7 November 1770. *Enclosed:*

    i. Address of both Houses of Assembly of Georgia to Governor Wright, requesting him to seek instruction from H.M. to pass bill for amending Act to ascertain manner and form of elections to Commons House; with Governor Wright's reply. *Copy,* examined by Charles Watson. 1¼ pp.

    ii. Act to amend Act to ascertain manner and form of elections to Commons House of Assembly of Georgia. *Copy,* certified by John Simpson. 6 pp. [C.O.5, 651, fos. 38–39d, 45–53d]

534

24 July, Quebec

Memorial to Governor Guy Carleton for re-establishment of College of Quebec. *French. Signed,* Guillimine and twenty-one others. 5 pp. [C.O.42, 30, fos. 208–211d]

535

25 July, Whitehall

Earl of Hillsborough to Lords of Treasury, sending papers relative to fine imposed on Robert Bussard in South Carolina, and recommending remission. *Entry.* ½ p. [C.O.5, 408, p. 44]

536

25 July, Whitehall

John Pownall to Grey Cooper, sending letter from governor of North Carolina and enclosures respecting quitrents. *Entry.* ½ p. [C.O.5, 332, p. 50]

537

26 July, Boston

* Lieut.-Governor Thomas Hutchinson to Earl of Hillsborough (No 20). The New Yorkers having agreed to import (except tea) has distressed our combiners. Boston not being a corporation, the lowest class still have the rule. If Philadelphia follows New York, I think Boston will hold out no longer. Assembly met yesterday at Cambridge if they will not do business I must prorogue them. *Duplicate. Signed.* 1¼ pp. *Endorsed,* R, 14 September. Original not recd. *Enclosed :*

    i. Proceedings of Assembly of Massachusetts: Lieut.-Governor Hutchinson's speech of 25 July 1770. *Printed.* 1 p. [C.O.5, 759, fos. 251–253d; entry of covering letter in C.O.5, 768, pp. 154–155 signed original of covering letter, with enclosure, in C.O.5, 894 pp. 121–126]

538

27 July, Whitehall

Earl of Hillsborough to Board of Ordnance, acknowledging letter o 8 May. Materials and buildings at Annapolis Royal which cannot b used elsewhere are to be sold. *Draft.* ¾ p. [C.O.217, 47, fos. 42–43d entry in C.O.218, 25, p. 79]

539

27 July, Boston

Lieut.-Governor Thomas Hutchinson to Earl of Hillsborough. Hous of Representatives has voted to do no business, proof of design t wrest from the Crown every power the people think not convenient Parliament rising without any notice of us is discouraging to King' servants, but we are never to despair. *Entry.* ¾ p. [C.O.5, 768, pp 156–157]

540

28 July, Whitehall

Earl of Hillsborough to Lords of Treasury, sending copy of warran for fortifications to be erected at St John's, Newfoundland. *Entry* ½ p. [C.O.195, 15, p. 34]

541

29 July, Montreal

Pierre du Calvet to Earl of Hillsborough, criticizing ordinance con cerning administration of justice, which, as J.P., insults him, and which as citizen, he cannot accept because of articles against liberty an commerce. *French. Signed.* 3 pp. *Endorsed,* R, 13 September. [C.O.42 30, fos. 111–112d]

542

31 July, Whitehall

* Earl of Hillsborough to Lieut.-General Thomas Gage (No. 32), concerning state of British possessions on Mississippi. Unless intrusions from New Orleans are stopped, neither commerce nor dominion will be secure. Establishments at mouths of Ohio and Illinois rivers would be expensive; on the other hand, there are objections to colonizing Illinois country, which would not be as beneficial as colonizing unsettled parts of sea-coast. Fur trade of Mississippi via New Orleans cannot be guaranteed to Great Britain. The Iberville as alternative route for furs is insufficiently navigable: I should be glad to have your thoughts on cost of making it so. This is the dilemma. *Draft.* 8½ pp. [C.O.5, 88, fos. 100–104d; entry in C.O.5, 241, pp. 315–322]

543

31 July, Whitehall

Same to same (No. 33), sending warrant for fortifying harbour of St John's, Newfoundland, and copy of letter to Board of Ordnance with directions for disposal of materials at Annapolis Royal. *Draft.* ½ p. [C.O.5, 88, fos. 105–106d; entry in C.O.5, 241, p. 322]

544

31 July, Whitehall

Same to Governor Lord Botetourt (No. 34). Address of House of Burgesses of Virginia in your No. 33 has been laid before Council. Would copper coinage in same manner as Ireland's be agreeable to colony? *Draft.* 1 p. [C.O.5, 1348, fos. 110–111d; entry in C.O.5, 1375, pp. 102–103]

545

31 July, Whitehall

* Same to same (No. 35). Papers from Board of Trade will inform you of application for lands and separate government between Ohio and Alleghany Mountains. Desist from land-grants beyond limits in proclamation of 7 October 1763 till H.M.'s pleasure is signified. *Draft.* 1 p. [C.O.5, 1348, fos. 112–113d; entry in C.O.5, 1375, pp. 103–104]

546

31 July, Whitehall

Same to Governor James Grant (No. 31). H.M. has granted you leave of absence for fifteen months subject to state of colony. None of Council of East Florida is regularly appointed except Mr Woolridge, Dr Turnbull and Mr Jolly. *Draft.* 1½ pp. [C.O.5, 551, fos. 43–44d; entry in C.O.5, 566, pp. 34–35; entry of leave, dated 28 July, in C.O.324, 42, p. 201]

547

31 July, Whitehall

Same to Governor James Wright (No. 32), acknowledging Nos. 43–45.
I cannot but lament proceedings in last session of Assembly. Their
resolution respecting suspending clause is founded on mistaken construction of purpose of this regulation. You have done well to make the
letter of your instructions the rule of conduct. The appointing what
places shall send representatives to Assembly depends on H.M.'s
discretion. I shall converse with Mr McGillivray on Indian affairs.
Bishop of Norwich has requested seat for his brother in Council of
Georgia. *Draft.* 2¾ pp. [C.O.5, 660, fos. 114–115d; entry in C.O.5,
677, pp. 43–46]

548

31 July, Whitehall

* Same to Lieut.-Governor Thomas Hutchinson (No. 39), acknowledging Nos. 15 and 16. Combinations against British commerce would
have been ended without encouragement here. Refusal of Assembly
to do business except at Boston appears to be against constitution.
Gaining of further time in case of Captain Preston and others is
important. *Entry.* 3¼ pp. [C.O.5, 765, pp. 178–181; draft in C.O.5,
759, fos. 222–223d]

549

31 July, Whitehall

Same to Lieut.-Governor William Bull (No. 37), acknowledging Nos.
28–29. William Foust and Christopher Davis pardoned; fine on Robert
Bussard remitted. Useful and entertaining observations on South
Carolina in No. 29 acknowledged. Boundary between North and South
Carolina referred to Board of Trade. *Draft.* 1½ pp. [C.O.5, 393, fos.
68–69d; entry in C.O.5, 408, pp. 44–45; entry of pardons, dated 21
July, in C.O.324, 42, p. 202]

550

31 July, Whitehall

Same to John Stuart (No. 18), acknowledging No. 22. Disputes between
Indians and frontier inhabitants are to be expected. Papers enclosed
relating to complaint of M. Montault de Monberaut. *Draft.* 1½ pp.
Enclosed:

i. Memorial of M. Montault de Monberaut, with complaints against
Governor Johnston and Mr Stuart. *French. Copy.* 4 pp.

ii. Notes on same subject. *French.* 3 small pp.

iii. Mobile, 8 July 1765. M. de Monberaut to Chief Justice Clifton
and Attorney-General Wegg of West Florida, with complaints.
French. Copy. 3 pp.

iv. Inventory of possessions of M. de Monberaut in territory ceded
to English in 1763. *French.* 1 p. [C.O.5, 71, Pt. 2, fos. 11–18d;
entry of covering letter in C.O.5, 241, pp. 323–324; different version
of No. i, endorsed. Referred to Mr Stuart, in C.O.5, 587, pp. 303–
314]

551

31 July, Whitehall

Same to M. Francis. Case of Comte de Ricquebourg will be recommended to governor of Grenada; claims of Comte de Montault de
Monberaut will be inquired into. *Draft.* 1 p. [C.O.5, 71, Pt. 2, fos.
9–10d; entry in C.O.5, 241, pp. 324–325]

552

31 July, Whitehall

John Pownall to Anthony Todd. Packet-boats to be detained for Earl
of Hillsborough's dispatches. *Entry.* ½ p. [C.O.5, 241, p. 315]

553

31 July, Williamsburg

Governor Lord Botetourt to Earl of Hillsborough (No. 36), sending
forty-eight Acts of Virginia, journals of both Houses, minutes of
Council and other papers. Commissioners were appointed to meet
those from Northern colonies at New York on 10 July to form plan for
regulating Indian trade, but returned without entering upon business.
Signed. 1 p. *Endorsed,* R, 21 September. [C.O.5, 1348, fos. 131–132d;
entry in C.O.5, 1372, p. 115]

554

31 July, Williamsburg

Same to Commissioners for Trade and Plantations, enclosing following.
Signed. ½ p. *Endorsed,* Recd. 21 September, Read 14 November 1770.
Enclosed :

i. Account of Orders of Council of Virginia for granting lands, and of
petitions for lands, between Alleghany Mountains and line from
western boundary of Carolina line to confluence of Ohio and
Mississippi. Grants, 1745–1754: 34. Petitions postponed, 1747–1768:
9. Petitions lodged but not presented, 1754–1769: 34. *Certified,* by
N. Walthoe, clerk of Council. 15½ pp. [C.O.5, 1333, fos. 47–56d]

555

31 July

Same to Mr Conway, sending two witnesses against David Ferguson,
accused of murder on high seas, who is to be sent to England. They are

to be presented to Mr Pownall and Mr Stephens. *Signed.* 1 small p. *Addressed.* [C.O.5, 1348, fos. 129–130d]

556

31 July, Quebec

Petition of Indians of St Francois and other villages in Quebec, to the King, praying that their interpreter at Quebec should be paid. *French. Signatories,* Thomas and four other chiefs. *Certified,* by notary public, at Quebec, 31 July 1770. 1 large p. [C.O.42, 30, fo. 204, 204d]

557

4 August, Admiralty

Lords of Admiralty to Earl of Hillsborough, enclosing following. *Signed,* E. Hawke, J. Buller, F. Holburne. 1 p. *Endorsed,* R, 9th. *Enclosed:*

  i. *Romney,* Halifax, 29 June 1770. Commodore Hood to Philip Stephens. The lieut.-governor and the Commissioners have had as much naval force in Boston harbour as they have thought necessary. *Mermaid* and *Hussar* are there, *Martin* and *Bonetta* proceed thither to-morrow. I am told that the outrage of the people increases, and I have told the lieut.-governor that I am ready to go to Boston. *Copy.* 1½ pp. [C.O.5, 759, fos. 245–248d; entry in C.O.5, 768, pp. 152–154]

558

4 August, Whitehall

Earl of Hillsborough to Lieut.-Governor Thomas Hutchinson (No. 40), acknowledging Nos. 17 and 18. Your insistence on H.M.'s right to appoint place of meeting of Assembly approved. Doctrines of Assembly tend to destroy Crown's power and must not be suffered to have effect. *Entry.* 1½ pp. [C.O.5, 765, pp. 181–182; draft in C.O.5, 759, fos. 241–242d]

559

5 August, Boston

Lieut.-Governor Thomas Hutchinson to Earl of Hillsborough (No. 21), enclosing message from House of Representatives. The majority of House would have disapproved of it if they could have acted with freedom, uninfluenced by Boston. Assembly prorogued. *Signed.* 1 p. *Endorsed,* R, 17 September. *Enclosed:*

  i. Proceedings of Assembly of Massachusetts: Lieut.-Governor Hutchinson's speech to Council, 25 July 1770. *Printed.* 1 p.

ii. *Massachusetts Gazette and Boston Weekly Newsletter,* 9 August 1770, reporting message of House of Representatives to Lieut.-Governor Hutchinson, 31 July 1770, with his reply, 3 August 1770. *Printed.* 3 large pp. [C.O.5, 759, fos. 256–260d; entry of covering letter in C.O.5, 768, pp. 157–158; signed duplicate of covering letter, with copy of No. ii, in C.O.5, 894, pp. 127–134]

560

7 August, Annapolis

Deputy Governor Rovert Eden to Earl of Hillsborough (No. 7), acknowledging No. 17 and soliciting brevet of lieut.-colonel. I served H.M. fourteen years. Proceedings of Assembly of Maryland since my arrival and copies of laws enacted last year, sent; journals and laws since 1763 will be sent by next vessel. *Signed.* 1 p. *Endorsed,* R, 15 October. [C.O.5, 1283, fos. 60–61d; signed duplicate in C.O.5, 1278, fos. 29–30d; entry in C.O.5, 1300, pp. 242–243]

561

10 August

Richard Jackson to Commissioners for Trade and Plantations, advising that Act passed in Pennsylvania in 1769 to dissolve marriage of Curtis and Ann Grubb be referred to Attorney- and Solicitor-General. *Signed.* 1¾ pp. *Endorsed,* Recd. 18 August, Read 7 November 1770. [C.O.5, 1278, fos. 1–2d (damaged)]

562

10 August, Williamsburg

Governor Lord Botetourt to Earl of Hillsborough (No. 37), enclosing following. I have drawn on H.M.'s quitrents for additional sum for purchase of land from Indians. If you are of different opinion, I will pay out of my private fortune. *Signed.* ¾ p. *Endorsed,* R, 21 September. *Enclosed:*

* i. Charleston, 12 July 1770. John Stuart to Governor Lord Botetourt. I have called Cherokee chiefs to Lochaber on 5 October to obtain cession to Virginia of lands pointed out in H.M.'s instructions to me. Expenses will exceed estimate. *Copy.* 1¾ pp.

ii. Williamsburg, 9 August 1770. Governor Lord Botetourt to John Stuart, authorizing expenditure of £400 additional to £2500. Colonel Donelson will attend at Lochaber. *Signed Copy.* 1½ pp. [C.O.5, 1348, fos. 133–138d; entry of covering letter in C.O.5, 1372, p. 116]

563

14 August, Boston

Lieut.-Governor Thomas Hutchinson to Earl of Hillsborough (No. 22), notifying death of Nathaniel Rogers, probably brought on by troubles he met with from infatuated party. *Signed.* ¾ p. *Endorsed,* R, 17 September. [C.O.5, 759, fos. 261–262d; entry in C.O.5, 768, p. 159; signed duplicate in C.O.5, 894, pp. 135–138]

564

14 August, Quebec

President Hector Theophilus Cramahé to Earl of Hillsborough (No. 1), notifying entry into administration of government. *Duplicate. Signed.* 1½ pp. *Endorsed,* R, 25 September, original not received. *Enclosed:*

i. Quebec, 9 August 1770. Proclamation by President H. T. Cramahé, continuing officers. *Copy,* certified by George Allsopp, deputy secretary. 1¼ pp. [C.O.42, 30, fos. 113–116d; entry of covering letter in C.O.43, 12, pp. 265–266; signed original of covering letter, and copy of enclosure, in C.O.42, 7, fos. 201–204d]

565

14 August, Johnson Hall

* Sir William Johnson to Earl of Hillsborough (No. 14), reporting congress with Northern Indians. They demanded our assistance in war to test our friendship. Treaty of Fort Stanwix ratified. They complain of frontier inhabitants and traders, want of goods through non-importation, sale of rum, and lack of religious teachers. *Signed.* 7 pp. *Endorsed,* R, 17 October. *Enclosed:*

i. Report of proceedings at a treaty with the Six Nations, the Indians of Canada, the several dependant tribes, and deputies from the Cherokee nation, held at upper settlements near German Flatts in July 1770 by Sir William Johnson. *Copy,* examined by Richard Shuckburgh, secretary for Indian affairs. 39 pp. [C.O.5, 71, Pt. 2, fos. 93–118d; entry of covering letter in C.O.5, 227, pp. 275–287]

566

15 August, Treasury

Grey Cooper to John Pownall. Lords of Treasury have no objection to remission of fine on Robert Bussard. *Signed.* 1 p. *Addressed. Endorsed,* R, 18th. [C.O.5, 393, fos. 72–73d]

567

16 August, Charleston

Lieut.-Governor William Bull to Earl of Hillsborough (No. 32), soliciting remission of fine imposed on Daniel Price for murder of negro slave. Opinion of Attorney- and Solicitor-General that murder on high seas cannot be tried in Admiralty courts means sending offenders to Great Britain. Order in Council for prosecution of Treasurer received; Mr Motte died 19 June. *Signed.* 2½ pp. *Endorsed,* R, 15 October. *Enclosed:*

i. Charleston, 16 June 1770. Warrant for suspension of fine on Daniel Price. *Copy.* 1 large p. [C.O.5, 393, fos. 78–80d; signed duplicate of covering letter and copy of enclosure, in C.O.5, 379, fos. 125–127d; entry of covering letter in C.O.5, 409, pp. 123–126]

568

17 August, Charleston

Same to same (No. 33). Three Spanish ships arrived here to buy provisions to relieve famine in Yucatan. I gave them permission to buy all but rice; and with Council's advice, I gave license for 180 barrels of rice, paying Customs. *Signed.* 2¼ pp. *Endorsed,* R, 15 October. [C.O.5, 393, fos. 81–82d; signed duplicate in C.O.5, 379, fos. 128–129d; entry in C.O.5, 409, pp. 126–128]

569

17 August, St Augustine

William De Brahm to Earl of Hillsborough (No. 12), reporting progress of survey of East Florida. *Signed.* 1 p. *Endorsed,* R, 31 October. [C.O.5, 71, Pt. 2, fos. 119–120d; entry in C.O.5, 227, p. 287]

570

18 August, New York

★ Lieut.-General Thomas Gage to Earl of Hillsborough (No. 48, numbered by mistake), acknowledging No. 30. Lieut.-Governor Hutchinson judges it imprudent to put any but provincial troops into Castle William: 14th regiment is in barracks outside the fort. Materials for barracks will be sent to St Augustine as originally planned, and detachment sent to Bahamas as soon as possible. Engineer's report on Providence enclosed: part of stores for forts there will go in a few days. Enclosed letter shows that Brigadier Haldimand agrees with Lieut.-Governor Durnford regarding ruinous state of forts at Pensacola and Mobile. Necessary ordnance stores will be sent to Lieut.-Governor Durnford as far as the magazine allows. Company of 18th regiment arrived safely at Fort Chartres. Fifty men have arrived from New Orleans and been posted at Misere and St Louis. Spanish subjects are not encouraged to settle; if there are to be settlers in Illinois country, better British subjects than Spanish. Intelligence is that Shawnese and Delaware Indians seek to unite Northern, Southern and Western Indians in one general confederacy. Congress to take place soon at Scioto Plains. Sir W. Johnson has held congress with Six Nations and Northern Indians: proposed war is deferred. Affray between Indians and traders reported at Michilimackinac. Hog Island dispute to be put to Council. More desertions of Spanish troops and French merchants from New Orleans reported. *Signed.* 6¼ pp. *Endorsed,* R, 17 September. *Enclosed:*

i. Draft of Harbour of New Providence, by John Montressor, engineer. 1 large p. [M.P.G. 14]

ii. Plan of New Providence, by same. 2pp. [M.P.G. 15]

iii. Plan of Forts Nassau and Montagu, Island of New Providence, by same. 2 large pp. [M.P.G. 16]

iv. Report on repairs and additions to Forts Nassau and Montague and two water-batteries at New Providence, Bahamas, by same. 11½ pp.

v. Pensacola, 27 June 1770. Extract of letter from Brigadier Haldimand to General Gage, reporting on fortifications at Pensacola and Mobile. *French. Copy.* 2¾ pp. [C.O.5, 88, fos. 122–136d; entry of covering letter in C.O.5, 234, pp. 103–113]

571

18 August, New York

* Lieut.-Governor Cadwallader Colden to Earl of Hillsborough (No. 14), acknowledging No. 39. Equestrian gilt statue of the King erected Thursday last near fort. I am assured opponents of importation have themselves sent orders for goods. I am confident New York's example will be followed. Lord Dunmore daily expected. *Signed.* 2½ pp. *Endorsed,* R, 17 September. [C.O.5, 1101, fos. 89–90d; entry in C.O.5, 1138, pp. 158–160]

572

18 August, New York

Same to same (No. 15), reporting execution of Order in Council of 14 April 1769, and sending release and surrender by William Coxe and others, and letter of attorney. *Signed. Marginal note,* transmitted to Council Office, 26 September 1770. 1 p. *Endorsed,* R, 17 September. [C.O.5, 1101, fos. 91–92d; entry in C.O.5, 1138, p. 161]

573

19 August, Annapolis

* Deputy Governor Robert Eden to Earl of Hillsborough (No. 8), acknowledging No. 18. Committee called by advertisement in *Maryland Gazette* was to examine whether goods by *Good Intent* were shipped contrary to association. No disorder was committed. I wish to know how I could have hindered importers from re-shipping. It is mortifying that you think this was owing to want of vigour in my government. Partial repeal of Revenue Act has not ended difference between Britain and colonies. *Duplicate. Signed.* 2½ pp. *Endorsed,* R, 17 October, original not recd. [C.O.5, 1283, fos. 62–63d; signed original in C.O.5, 1278, fos. 31–32d; entry in C.O.5, 1300, pp. 243–247]

574

22 August, Savannah

Governor James Wright to Earl of Hillsborough (No. 48), acknowledging No. 31 and reporting affray between Indians and back-settlers
of Georgia about alleged horse-stealing: one Indian killed; two whites
missing, feared killed. Everything else is well, and as the principal
promoter of opposition is dead I think the other two will not attempt
it again. *Signed.* 1½ small pp. *Endorsed*, R, 31 October. *Enclosed:*

  i. Charleston, 28 July 1770. Satirical sheet concerning trial of John
  Stevenson, captain of watch-company. *Printed.* 1 p. [C.O.5, 660,
  fos. 138–140d; entry of covering letter in C.O.5, 678, p. 196]

575

22 August, Savannah

Same to John Pownall, acknowledging letter of 22 May and enclosures.
Signed. ½ small p. *Endorsed*, R, 31 October. [C.O.5, 660, fos. 141–142d;
entry in C.O.5, 678, p. 197]

576

23 August, Charleston

* Lieut.-Governor William Bull to Earl of Hillsborough (No. 34).
Assembly resumed consideration of resolutions 4 April last. All business
will go on except Tax Bill. Resolution of December last was hastily
passed, but they will adhere to it. If I mistake royal will, I request
favourable representation of my intentions. *Signed.* 3½ pp. *Endorsed*,
R, 15 October. *Enclosed:*

  i. 22 August 1770. Address of Commons House of Assembly of
  South Carolina to Lieut.-Governor Bull for copies of representations
  to H.M. or ministers on subject of H.M.'s additional instruction.
  Copy. Signatory, P. Manigault, Speaker. 1 small p.

  ii. 23 August 1770. Reply to preceding. No representation was made;
  and no letter would be laid before you on that subject without H.M.'s
  consent. *Copy.* 1¼ small pp. [C.O.5, 393, fos. 83–88d; signed duplicate of covering letter and copies of enclosures in C.O.5, 379, fos.
  130–133d; entry of covering letter in C.O.5, 409, pp. 128–132]

577

24 August, St Augustine

Governor James Grant to Earl of Hillsborough (No. 38), acknowledging No. 27 and enclosure. Large vessels come into this harbour
with ease: losses are infrequent since pilots were appointed. *Signed.*
1½ pp. *Endorsed*, R, 30 November. [C.O.5, 551, fos. 71–72d; entry in
C.O.5, 567, pp. 155–156]

578

25 August, Kittery, Piscataqua River

Samuel Holland to Earl of Hillsborough (No. 6), reporting surveys in progress at Casco Bay, in this river, and from Chaleur Bay to Baye Verte. *Canseaux* armed ship proceeds for England for repairs. *Signed.* 2½ pp. *Endorsed,* R, 15 October. [C.O.5, 71, Pt. 2, fos. 91–92d; entry in C.O.5, 227, pp. 272–274; signed duplicate, endorsed, Read 7 November 1770, in C.O.323, 27, pp. 55–58]

579

27 August, Williamsburg

Governor Lord Botetourt to Earl of Hillsborough (No. 38), acknowledging No. 32. Ferguson sent to England; witnesses sent many days ago. *Signed.* PS. I will compare grant desired by Mr Walpole with rights of this province. 1 p. *Endorsed,* R, 1 November. *Enclosed:*

i. Norfolk County Court, 19 January 1770. Remand of David Ferguson for trial for killing negro boy in this country and three men on high seas. *Copy.* 1½ pp.

ii. 22 January 1770. Walter Lyon to John Randolph, summarizing evidence against Ferguson. *Copy.* 2¾ pp. [C.O.5, 1348, fos. 143–148d; entry of covering letter in C.O.5, 1372, pp. 121–122]

580

28 August, Boston

Lieut.-Governor Thomas Hutchinson to Earl of Hillsborough (No. 23), acknowledging No. 37 and reporting letter received from General Gage and reply thereto, about putting King's troops into Castle William. I am glad the General did not take measures immediately as there is no apparent necessity more than for many months past. Trial of officer and soldiers comes on in a few days. Assembly prorogued to 25 September. I think I now have majority in Council. *Signed.* 3 small pp. *Endorsed,* R, 10 October. [C.O.5, 759, fos. 267–268d; entry in C.O.5, 768, pp. 161–163; signed duplicate in C.O.5, 894, pp. 139–142]

581

29 August, Boston

Same to John Pownall, enclosing following. New York's defection must weaken union of colonies. I still hope for effectual measures to prevent combinations formed in each colony and between several colonies, for they have eradicated all notions of subordination from minds of the people in most colonies. *Signed.* 1¾ small pp. *Endorsed,* R, 10 October. *Enclosed:*

i. 5 June 1770. Petition of James, Patrick and John McMasters of Boston, merchants, to Lieut.-Governor Hutchinson, praying for protection against intimidation by Dr Thomas Young and his associates. 1 p.

ii. Castle William, 27 June 1770. Petition of Patrick McMasters to Lieut.-Governor Hutchinson. After abuse and ill-treatment, petitioner has taken refuge in castle and prays for redress. Truth of facts stated sworn to, before Lieut.-Governor Hutchinson. 1¾ pp. [C.O.5, 759, fos. 269–274d]

582

30 August, Halifax

Governor Lord William Campbell to Earl of Hillsborough (No. 64), sending laws passed last session, journals of both Houses, and minutes of Council to 12 June last. *Signed.* ¾ p. *Endorsed,* R, 15 October. [C.O.217, 47, fos. 62–63d; entry in C.O.218, 17, p. 240]

583

30 August, Halifax

Same to same (No. 65), acknowledging No. 39 and copies of Acts relating to America. *Signed.* 1 p. *Endorsed,* R, 15 October. [C.O.217, 47, fos. 64–65d; signed duplicate in C.O.217, 26, fos. 26–27d; entry in C.O.218, 17, p. 240]

584

1 September, St Augustine

★ Governor James Grant to Earl of Hillsborough (No. 39). Greek settlement at Smyrnea in bad state. Last year's bounty saved them from starving. *Signed.* 2½ pp. *Endorsed,* R, 30 November. *Enclosed:*

i. Indent of clothing, tools etc. wanted for Greek settlement at Smyrnea under Andrew Turnbull. Total: £1050 10s. 8d. ½ p. [C.O.5, 551, fos. 73–76d; signed duplicate of covering letter, endorsed Read 22 August 1771, and copy of enclosure, in C.O.5, 545, fos. 17–20d; entry of covering letter in C.O.5, 567, pp. 156–158]

585

3 September, G.P.O.

Anthony Todd to John Pownall, enclosing following. *Signed.* 1 small p. *Endorsed,* R, 3 September. *Enclosed:*

★ i. G.P.O., New York, 11 July 1770. Alexander Colden to Anthony Todd, reporting resolution of merchants to import goods except tea, despite threats of faction including Isaac Sears, Captain McDougald 'the American Wilkes', and others. Packet detained to enable merchants to order. Death reported of James Parker, secretary and comptroller to G.P.O. in this district. *Copy.* 5½ pp. [C.O.5, 1101, fos. 83–88d]

586

5 September, Whitehall

John Pownall to Lieut.-General Thomas Gage, acknowledging Nos. 46–48 and separate letter of 9 July. *Entry.* ¼ p. [C.O.5, 241, p. 325]

587

5 September, Whitehall

Same to Governor Lord Botetourt, acknowledging in absence of Lord Hillsborough dispatches Nos. 34–35. *Entry.* ½ p. [C.O.5, 1375, p. 104]

588

5 September, Whitehall

Same to Lieut.-Governor Thomas Hutchinson. In absence of Earl of Hillsborough in Ireland, I send copies of his Nos. 39 and 40 and of his private letter of 4 August. *Entry.* ½ p. [C.O.5, 765, p. 183]

589

5 September, Whitehall

Same to Lieut.Governor Cadwallader Colden, acknowledging Nos. 12–13. *Entry.* ¼ p. [C.O.5, 1141, p. 138]

590

5 September, Whitehall

Same to Deputy Governor Robert Eden, acknowledging No. 6 without date. *Entry.* ¼ p. [C.O.5, 1301, p. 11]

591

5 September, Whitehall

Same to Lieut.-Colonel William Dalrymple, in absence of Earl of Hillsborough in Ireland, acknowledging dispatch of 29 June. *Entry.* ¼ p. [C.O.5, 765, p. 183]

592

5 September, Whitehall

Same to Samuel Holland, acknowledging No. 5. *Entry.* ¼ p. [C.O.5, 241, p. 325]

593

5 September, Philadelphia

★ Deputy Governor John Penn to Earl of Hillsborough (No. 23), acknowledging No. 23. Merchants here agreed on 5 June to continue non-importation. On news from New York of breach of agreement, they entered into enclosed resolve. There have always been some dry-goods merchants who would have imported all articles except those on which duty was laid. *Signed.* 1½ pp. *Endorsed, R,* 17 October. *Enclosed:*

> ★ i. Philadelphia, 19 July 1770. Report of meeting of inhabitants which resolved to continue non-importation and break off commercial intercourse with New York, with certain exceptions. 2¼ pp. [C.O.5, 1283, fos. 9–12d; signed duplicate of covering letter and copy of enclosure in C.O.5, 1278, fos. 17–20d; entry of both in C.O.5, 1300, pp. 352–356]

594

5 September

Lords of Admiralty to Earl of Hillsborough, sending papers regarding detention of negroes, property of British subjects, at Porto Rico. *Entry. Signatories,* E. Hawke, Lisburne, C. J. Fox. *Annotated,* eight enclosures, R, 5 September. 1 p. [C.O.5, 227, pp. 257–258]

595

6 September

Same to same, sending further paper regarding detention of negroes at Porto Rico. *Entry. Signatories,* E. Hawke, Lisburne, C. J. Fox. *Annotated,* 1 enclosure, R, 6 September. ½ p. [C.O.5, 227, pp. 258–259]

596

8 September, New York

★ Lieut.-General Thomas Gage to Earl of Hillsborough (No. 49), acknowledging No. 31 with enclosures. Orders sent to Lieut.-Governor Hutchinson to put garrison of King's troops into Castle William, and to Captain Montressor to make necessary repairs there. The fort is too small for more than one regiment; but it is weak towards the land, and if batteries were to be erected to defend Dorchester Point, two regiments would be needed. Lieut.-Colonel Dalrymple is empowered to call on reinforcements from Nova Scotia, and artillery detachment there has been ordered to join him. Rum has caused quarrels on frontiers of Pennsylvania and Virginia between Indians and whites. The colonies have not implemented the plan for taking into their own hands regulation of Indian trade, except West Florida. Mr Stuart has applied for officer to reside with Chickasaws, which Brigadier Haldimand thinks is necessary: salary would be about £150 a year. Stuart proposes to run the line between Virginia and Cherokees in October. Quebec works are bad: Brigadier Carleton and I think it best to postpone repairs and building of barracks there. Lieut.-Colonel Prevost will command in absence of Brigadier Carleton. *Signed.* 6 pp. *Endorsed, R,* 17 October. *Enclosed:*

i. Boston, 20 August 1770. Extract of letter from Lieut.-Colonel Dalrymple to General Gage, giving reasons why Castle William should be occupied by H.M.'s troops. *Copy.* 2½ pp. [C.O.5, 88, fos. 146–151d; entry in C.O.5, 234, pp. 114–121]

597

8 September, New York

Lieut.-Governor Cadwallader Colden to Earl of Hillsborough (No. 16), acknowledging No. 40. Agreement of merchants here to import has occasioned altercation. Earl of Dunmore expected; Assembly prorogued. *Signed.* 1 p. *Endorsed*, R, 17 October. [C.O.5, 1101, fos. 95–96d; entry in C.O.5, 1138, p. 162]

598

8 September, Charleston

★ Lieut.-Governor William Bull to Earl of Hillsborough (No. 35), enclosing papers. Assembly will adhere to right to issue money and application thereof to such purposes as they think proper. Assembly prorogued to 16 January. Summary history of alteration in manner of granting money and gradual increase of power of Assembly of South Carolina since 1736. *Signed.* 8¼ pp. *Endorsed*, R, 31 October. *Enclosed :*

i. 30 August 1770. Address of Commons House of Assembly of South Carolina to Lieut.-Governor Bull, to be shown any letter or representation made on subject of proceedings of this House. *Copy. Signatory*, P. Manigault, Speaker. 1½ small pp.

ii. 31 August 1770. Reply to preceding, refusing. *Copy.* ¾ p.

iii. 5 September 1770. Address of Commons House of Assembly, enclosing following. *Copy. Signatory*, as No. i. ½ small p.

iv. Report of Committee of Commons House, containing resolutions of rights in granting money. Agent to represent matter to H.M. in true light. *Copy.* 4 pp.

v. List of precedents from journals of Assembly of South Carolina, 1752–1769, of monies issued by resolutions of House, sent to Governor for assent and to Council for concurrence; of orders in Assembly for Treasurer to advance money on Governor's requis-. ition; and of orders where there was no requisition. 2½ pp. [C.O.5, 393, fos. 95–110d; signed duplicate of covering letter and copies of enclosures in C.O.5, 379, fos. 134–147d; entry of covering letter in C.O.5, 409, pp. 133–143]

599

8 September, Charleston

Same to Commissioners for Trade and Plantations, sending half-yearly return of grants, 8 November–2 May last. *Signed.* ¾ p. *Endorsed*, Recd. 1 November, Read 7 November 1770. [C.O.5, 379, fos. 154–155d]

600

12 September, Boston

* Lieut.-Governor Thomas Hutchinson to Earl of Hillsborough (No. 24), acknowledging receipt on 8 September, by express from General Gage, of letter of 6 July and Order in Council of same date. Council was notified of the Order next day and Castle William was committed to care of Lieut.-Colonel Dalrymple. Garrison in province's pay was ordered out. I told Council that the province's claim to contents of the castle remained entire. I never thought of superseding Colonel Goldthwaite: truckmastership is an office sunk almost to nothing. *Duplicate. Signed.* 4 small pp. *Endorsed,* R, 5 November. Original not recd. *Enclosed:*

> i. Boston, 9 September 1770. Same to General Gage. There can be no doubt of the King's authority to command his regular forces but it may be doubted whether a commission to command militia of this province can be granted, consistent with charter, by any person other than governor; and the governor's power by charter seems same with respect to forts as to militia. Captain Preston's trial appointed for 23 October. *Copy.* 2½ small pp.

> ii. Boston, 12 September 1770. Same to same. It would avoid any suspicion of violation of charter if garrison of Castle William were considered as under command of governor. Some provincial officers and soldiers withdrawn from garrison are objects of compassion. *Copy.* 3¼ pp.

> iii. Petition of Edmund Mooers and Thomas Fletcher to Lieut.-Governor Hutchinson. They have settled sixty people and made improvements on tract of land on east side of Penobscot River; and pray for grant thereof. 1 p. [C.O.5, 759, fos. 275–282d; entry of covering letter in C.O.5, 768, pp. 164–167]

601

13 September, Boston

Same to same (No. 25), enclosing following. *Duplicate. Signed.* ½ small p. *Endorsed,* R, 5 November. *Enclosed:*

> * i. Secret. Boston, 11 September 1770. Same to General Gage. I proposed, if jury found Captain Preston guilty, that counsel move arrest of judgement which would occasion less danger of violence than respiting sentence. But the court has put off business to latter part of October. Depositions having been sent to England by your order, and one or more persons present at the action having been examined by committee of [Privy] Council, royal pardon might be issued for use in case of necessity. *Copy.* 2 small pp. [C.O.5, 759, fos. 282–286d; entry of covering letter in C.O.5, 768, p. 168]

602

13 September, Ordnance-office

Board of Ordnance to Earl of Hillsborough. Warrant received for fortifying St John's, Newfoundland. Estimate of £71,736 13s. 3d. is on supposition that artificers and labourers will be furnished by troops in America; otherwise £6169 10s. to be added. Cost of ordnance etc. will be additional. *Signed,* H. S. Conway, Charles Frederick, Charles Cocks. 2 pp. *Endorsed,* R, do. [C.O.194, 29, fos. 63–64d; entry in C.O.195, 12, pp. 99–101; entry of warrant, dated 27 July 1770, in C.O.324, 42, pp. 198–200]

603

13 September, Charleston

Lieut.-Governor William Bull to Earl of Hillsborough, enclosing *Gazette* containing proceedings of Council relating to dispute between Council and Assembly of South Carolina. *Signed.* 1 small p. *Endorsed,* R, 26 December. *Enclosed:*

   i. *South Carolina and American General Gazette,* 3–10 September 1770. *Printed.* 4 large pp. [C.O.5, 393, fos. 125–128d; entry of covering letter in C.O.5, 409, p. 150]

604

20 September

John Pownall to Philip Stephens, concerning case of Ferguson, accused of murder on high seas. Two witnesses are to attend at Admiralty Office tomorrow. *Draft.* 2 pp. *Endorsed,* Read by the King. [C.O.5, 1348, fos. 127–128d; entry in C.O.5, 1375, pp. 105–107]

605

20 September, N.H.

Governor John Wentworth to Earl of Hillsborough (No. 31), acknowledging Nos. 28–29, *Gazette* of 17 March and proceedings of Parliament in consequence of remonstrance, address and petition to the King. H.M.'s subjects here detest such unwarrantable attempts. *Duplicate. Signed.* 2½ pp. *Endorsed,* R, 5 January 1771. [C.O.5, 937, fos. 19–20d; signed original in C.O.5, 930, fos. 101–102d; entry in C.O.5, 945, pp. 153–155]

606

20 September, N.H.

Same to same (No. 32), acknowledging No. 27, requesting powers to issue commissions for custody of idiots and to sell real estate of idiots in fee. *Duplicate. Signed.* 2 small pp. *Endorsed,* R, 5 January 1771. [C.O.5, 937, fos. 21–22d; signed original in C.O.5, 930, fos. 103–104d; entry in C.O.5, 945, pp. 155–156]

607

21 September, Halifax

Governor Lord William Campbell to Earl of Hillsborough (No. 66), acknowledging No. 40. Copies of Acts passed last session have been sent. *Duplicate. Signed.* ½ p. *Endorsed,* R, 20 November. [C.O.217, 47, fos. 68–69d; signed original in C.O.217, 26, fos. 28–29d; entry in C.O.218, 17; pp. 240–241]

608

[21 September]

Advocate-, Attorney- and Solicitor-General to Earl of Hillsborough. The only proper way to pardon Mathew Turner is under Great Seal, but practice has been introduced into colonies similar to circuit-pardons in England, and this may be sufficient. *Signed,* James Marriott, William de Grey, E. Thurlow. 1¼ pp. *Endorsed,* R, 21 September. *Enclosed :*

   i. Charleston, 5 May 1769. Reprieve of Mathew Turner. *Copy.* 2 pp.

   ii. Whitehall, 5 November 1761. John Pownall to Attorney- and Solicitor-General, with queries on murder trial in New York and answers dated 4 March 1762. *Copy.* 3 pp. [C.O.5, 393, fos. 51–58d]

609

22 September, Charleston

William De Brahm to Earl of Hillsborough (No. 13), reporting progress of surveys of East Florida, and complaining of Governor Grant. *Signed.* 7 pp. *Endorsed,* R, 30 November. [C.O.5, 71, Pt. 2, fos. 127–130d; entry in C.O.5, 227, pp. 288–302]

610

24 September, Whitehall

John Pownall to Philip Stephens, requesting names of H.M. ships destined for North America and West Indies, when they will be dispatched, and names of ships already on stations. *Draft.* 1 p. [C.O.5, 71, Pt. 2, fos. 45–46d; entry in C.O.5, 241, pp. 326–327]

611

24 September, Admiralty

Philip Stephens to John Pownall. *Kennington,* 20, and *Spy* sloop are destined for Leeward Islands; *Mercury,* 20, for Boston, then Carolina; *Guarland,* 24, and *Seaford,* 20, for Jamaica. *Seaford* will sail as soon as wind permits; others have been stopped by Lord Rochford's letter. *Signed.* 1 p. *Endorsed,* R, 25th. [C.O.5, 71, Pt. 2, fos. 47–48d]

612

24 September, Admiralty

John Pownall to Anthony Todd, asking how soon packet-boats at Falmouth may be ready for North America and West Indies. *Draft.* 1 p. [C.O.5, 71, Pt. 2, fos. 49–50d; entry in C.O.5, 241, p. 326]

613

24 September, G.P.O.

Anthony Todd to John Pownall. Packet-boats for New York, West Indies and Carolina will be ready at Falmouth on 3 October. *Signed.* 1½ small pp. *Endorsed,* R, 24 September. [C.O.5, 71, Pt. 2, fos. 51–52d]

614

24 September, Pensacola

Governor Peter Chester to Earl of Hillsborough (No. 1), reporting arrival on 10 August and acknowledging letters of 14 April and 22 May from Mr Pownall and No. 27 from Earl of Hillsborough. *Signed.* 1 p. *Endorsed,* R, 9 January 1771. [C.O.5, 588, pp. 1–4; signed duplicate, endorsed Read 22 August 1771, in C.O.5, 578, pp. 29–32; entry in C.O.5, 621, pp. 1–2]

615

25 September, Pensacola

Same to same (No. 2). Councillors appointed besides those in H.M.'s instructions, to make a quorum: Lieut.-Governor Durnford, Chief Justice William Clifton, James Bruce, Jacob Blackwell, David Hodge, James Jones, Phillips Comyn, George Raincock, Philip Livingston. May I, without transmitting reasons, supersede Councillors who do not take out mandamuses and pay office-fees? *Signed.* 1½ pp. *Endorsed,* R, 9 January 1771. [C.O.5, 588, pp. 5–8; signed duplicate in C.O.5, 578, pp. 55–58; copy, endorsed Recd., Read 27 March 1771, in C.O.5, 578, pp. 5–8; entry in C.O.5, 621, pp. 2–3]

616

25 September, Halifax

Governor Lord William Campbell to Earl of Hillsborough (No. 67), sending duplicates of laws passed in Nova Scotia last session, journals of both Houses, and minutes of Council to 12 June last. *Signed.* ½ p. *Endorsed,* R, 20 November. [C.O.217, 47, fos. 70–71d; entry in C.O.218, 17, p. 241]

617

26 September, Whitehall

John Pownall to Clerk of Council in Waiting, sending papers transmitted by Lieut.-Governor Cadwallader Colden in pursuance of Order
in Council of 14 April 1769. *Entry.* ¼ p. [C.O.5, 1141, p. 138]

618

26 September, Pensacola

* Governor Peter Chester to Earl of Hillsborough (No. 3). Council
of West Florida advised that settlers at Natchez be encouraged; Brig.-
General Haldimand not able to supply troops for their defence;
settlement there not displeasing to Indians; corn, powder, shot and
salt sent to settlers, out of contingent fund; talk sent to Indians. With
encouragement many would settle on Mississippi. Large vessels can
go up the river. Trade of Mississippi, Missouri and all the upper country
could be secured. Posts should be re-established at Fort Bute, Natchez
or elsewhere. When Commissioners for Trade and Plantations reported on 7 March 1768 in favour of abandoning those posts, Indian
trade, not settlement, was in view. Re-establishment would help
regulation of Indian trade and induce French to leave Spaniards and
come over to our side. If Iberville River were cleared of logs and canal
cut, communication with Mississippi by Lakes Maurepas and Pontchartrain would be practicable. I propose going to Fort Bute with
Lieut.-Governor Durnford. Another regiment for this province would
be required. Lands near the sea are not proper for cultivation: this,
and divisions in the colony, has prevented our being more than
garrison-town. East Florida has more countenance than West. *Signed.*
12½ pp. *Endorsed*, R, 19 January 1771. *Enclosed :*

i. Fort Natchez, 19 July 1770. John McIntire to [Governor of West
Florida]. Eighty souls arrived here from Fort Pitt; 100 families from
back parts of Virginia and Pennsylvania depend on our encouragement to set out for this place. Land good, but necessaries and defence
needed. *Copy.* 1¼ pp.

ii. 25 August 1770. Affidavit sworn before Governor Chester by
Daniel Huay of North Carolina. Deponent joined party of settlers for
Natchez at Muskingham River. Party was seventy-nine men,
women and children, and eighteen negroes, with tools and seed. Soil
at Natchez good. Others from North Carolina, Pennsylvania and
Virginia are interested in settling there. *Copy.* 2½ pp. [C.O.5, 588,
pp. 9–30; signed duplicate of covering letter and copies of enclosures
in C.O.5, 578, pp. 59–78; entry of covering letter in C.O.5, 621,
pp. 4–21]

619

27 September, Pensacola

Same to same (No. 4), enclosing following. My chariot and pictures of the King were lost on this ship. *Signed.* 1 p. *Endorsed*, R, 9 January 1771. *Enclosed :*

    i. Kingston, Jamaica, 28 August 1770. Thomas Gallimore to Governor Chester. Florida packet grounded off East Hispaniola, cargo stolen. *Copy.* 1¼ pp. [C.O.5, 588, pp. 31–38; signed duplicate of covering letter and copy of enclosure in C.O.5, 578, pp. 79–86; entry of covering letter in C.O.5, 621, pp. 22–23]

620

27 September, Pensacola

Attorney-General Edmund Rush Wegg to Earl of Hillsborough, complaining of improprieties in seizure by Customs of *Little Bob* in 1765, and making charges against Mr Blackwell. *Signed.* 3¼ pp. *Endorsed*, R, 9 January 1771. *Enclosed :*

    i. Extracts of three letters referring to above case. *Copy.* 3 pp. [C.O.5, 588, pp. 57–64; entry of covering letter in C.O.5, 621, pp. 23–28]

621

28 September, Whitehall

Most secret and confidential. Earl of Hillsborough to Governors of Quebec, Island of St John, Nova Scotia, New Hampshire, Massachusetts, New York, Virginia, North Carolina, South Carolina, Georgia, East Florida, West Florida, Bahamas, Bermuda, Barbados, Leeward Islands, Grenada, Jamaica, New Jersey, advising of possible breach with Spain over incident in Falkland Islands, and requiring attention to defence. *Draft.* 2 pp. [C.O.5, 71, Pt. 2, fos. 53–54d; entry, with postscript indicating that peace may still be preserved, in C.O.5, 241, pp. 327–328]

622

28 September, Whitehall

Separate and secret. Same to Lieut.-General Thomas Gage (No. 34). From Mr Rawle's information that he is unlikely to receive orders for arms and accoutrements, it seems that if there were designs of nature suspected they have been laid aside. *Draft.* ½ p. [C.O.5, 88, fos. 137–138d; entry in C.O.5, 241, pp. 331–332]

623

28 September, Whitehall

Same to same (No. 35), acknowledging Nos. 46–48. Your conduct approved. Hopes that Assembly of New York will now re-enact repealed law and that arrears on account of quartering will be discharged. Spaniards on Mississippi must be narrowly watched. Your suggestion to Lieut.-Governor Hutchinson for preserving Captain Preston appears very proper; presumably number of troops in Castle William is enough to ensure success. A union of Northern and Southern Indians might have fatal consequences, but I am more apprehensive of danger to West Florida from peace between Creeks and Choctaws. Intercourse between Spanish fishermen and Indians of Florida ought as much as possible to be prevented. *Draft.* 4½ pp. [C.O.5, 88, fos. 139–141d; entry in C.O.5, 241, pp. 332–338]

624

28 September, Whitehall

Most secret and confidential. Same to same (No. 36), informing him of possible breach with Spain over proceedings at Port Egmont, Falkland Islands. Considerable naval armament is to be prepared. PS. Further advice confirms hope that peace may be preserved. *Draft.* 1½ pp. [C.O.5, 88, fos. 142–143d; entry in C.O.5, 241, pp. 338–339]

625

28 September, Whitehall

Separate. Same to same. Board of Ordnance supposes that 650 artificers and labourers were to be furnished for erecting fort at St John's, Newfoundland, from military and naval forces in North America. Report your opinion how this may be done. *Draft.* 1½ pp. [C.O.5, 88, fos. 144–145d; entry in C.O.5, 241, pp. 340–341]

626

28 September, Whitehall

Secret and confidential. Same to Lords of Admiralty. Commanders-in-chief to be notified of possible breach with Spain over incident in Falkland Islands. A number of H.M.'s ships to be fitted out for sea. *Draft.* 2 pp. [C.O.5, 71, Pt. 2, fos. 57–58d; entry in C.O.5, 241, pp. 329–330]

627

28 September, Whitehall

Same to same, H.M.'s pleasure is that ships for North America and West Indies, stayed by Lord Rochford's letter, should depart as soon as may be. *Draft.* ½ p. [C.O.5, 71, Pt. 2, fos. 55–56d; entry in C.O.5, 241, p. 331]

628

28 September, Whitehall

Same to same. Report if fleet at St John's can furnish 300 men for work on fort there. *Draft.* 1½ pp. [C.O.194, 29, fos. 65–66d; entry in C.O.195, 15, pp. 34–35]

629

28 September, Whitehall

Same to Philip Stephens, sending packets for governor of Massachusetts; for lieut.-general of Leeward Islands; and for governor of Jamaica. To be entrusted to H.M. ships. *Entry.* ½ p. [C.O.5, 241, p. 341]

630

28 September, Boston

Lieut.-Governor Thomas Hutchinson to Earl of Hillsborough (No. 26). Assembly met 26th at Cambridge: my speech enclosed. Boston representatives have received from England copies of letters written by Lieut.-Governor Colden, Lieut.-Colonel Dalrymple and myself, presumably obtained from those laid before the House of Commons. I beg a way be found to prevent this: government is greatly hurt by it. *Signed.* 1 p. *Endorsed*, R, 5 November. *Enclosed :*

　i. Proceedings of Assembly of Massachusetts, Cambridge, 27 September 1770: speech of Lieut.-Governor Hutchinson. *Printed.* 1 p. [C.O.5, 759, fos. 287–289d; entry of covering letter in C.O.5, 768, pp. 168–169; unsigned duplicate with copy of No. i in C.O.5, 894, pp. 143–147]

631

29 September, Pensacola

Governor Peter Chester to Earl of Hillsborough (No. 5). Survey of Government-house enclosed: so ruinous as not to be habitable, now used for public worship and public affairs. Plan and estimate of new one enclosed. Terms of lease of Brigadier Haldimand's house, in which I now live, make it come dear; plan and terms of offer for sale sent. *Signed.* 3½ pp. *Endorsed*, R, 9 January 1771. *Enclosed :*

　i. 28 September 1770. Report of surveyors of Government-house, Pensacola. *Signed*, William Marshall and three others. ¾ p.

　ii. Pensacola, 25 September 1770. James Jones to Governor Chester, offering Brigadier Haldimand's house for sale. *Signed.* 3 small pp.

　iii. Pensacola, 27 September 1770. Elias Durnford to Governor Chester, sending report on Government-house (No. i). Price of new house: £2500 sterling. *Signed.* 1 small p.

　iv. Plans of Government-house, West Florida, and of proposed new house. [M.P.G. 611 (1–5)] [Covering letter and enclosures i–iii in C.O.5, 588, pp. 39–56; signed duplicate of covering letter, and copies of enclosures i–ii, in C.O.5, 578, pp. 87–98; copy of covering letter, endorsed Recd., Read 7 January 1771, and copies of enclosures i–iii in C.O.5, 577, pp. 449–466; entry of covering letter in C.O.5, 621, pp. 29–33, with note: Plans transmitted with above letter sent to Plantation Office]

632

29 September, Perth Amboy

★ Governor William Franklin to Earl of Hillsborough (No. 23), acknowledging Nos. 25 and 26. Assembly was greatly displeased at disallowance of Paper Money Act. Party may take advantage of this ill humour and prevail on Assembly not to grant money for King's troops. *Signed.* 2 pp. *Endorsed,* R, 9 November. *Enclosed :*

i. 28 September 1770. Governor Franklin's speech to Assembly of New Jersey. *Copy.* 1 p. [C.O.5, 990, fos. 83–86d; entry of covering letter in C.O.5, 1001, pp. 118–120]

633

1 October, Chatham Barracks

Lieut.-Colonel P. A. Irving to Earl of Hillsborough, enclosing following which is duplicate of what was sent to Commissioners for Trade and Plantations after dismissal from Council of Quebec. *Signed.* 2 small pp. *Endorsed,* R, 4 October. *Enclosed :*

i. Memorial of Lieut.-Colonel Irving and A. Mabane, surgeon to Quebec garrison, members of Council of Quebec, to Commissioners for Trade and Plantations, complaining of arbitrary conduct of Lieut.-Governor Carleton. *Signed.* 7½ pp.

ii. Quebec, 15 October 1766. P. A. Irving and four other members of Council of Quebec, to Lieut.-Governor Carleton, protesting at calling only part of Council. *Copy.* 2 small pp.

iii. Quebec, 28 November 1766. Reply to preceding. *Copy.* 2 small pp.

iv. 3 December 1766. P. A. Irving to Walter Murray and others, sending and commenting on No. iii. *Copy.* 2 small pp.

v. Comments on No. iii. 1½ small pp.

vi. Quebec, 29 November 1766. Lieut.-Governor Carleton to P. A. Irving, explaining why he would not interpose to have bail accepted for Captain Fraser and others. *Copy.* 3 pp.

vii. Statement giving motives for Lieut.-Colonel Irving and Mr Mabane signing the application for bail. 1¼ small pp.

viii. Quebec, 6 December 1766. P. A. Irving to Lieut.-Governor Carleton, commenting on No. iii. *Copy.* 1 small p.

ix. Quebec, 5 December 1766. Adam Mabane to Lieut.-Governor Carleton, replying to No. iii. *Copy.* 1½ pp.

x. Affidavit, sworn before James Potts, J.P., by Captain George Etherington to effect that Adam Mabane did not persuade M. de L'Obbiniere to sign petition on behalf of prisoners. *Copy.* 1 p.

xi. [P. A. Irving, Lieut.-Colonel Jones and Captain Morris] to Lieut.-Governor Carleton, justifying petition for release of prisoners. *Copy.* 3½ pp. [C.O.42, 30, fos. 121–144d; entry of covering letter in C.O.43, 12, pp. 266–268]

634

1 October, St Augustine

Governor James Grant to Earl of Hillsborough (No. 40). We shall ship double last year's quantity of indigo. Bounty favours production of inferior indigo. Without troops a new colony could not exist, certainly not get on. Materials for barracks arrived yesterday. *Duplicate. Signed.* 1½ pp. *Endorsed,* R, 26 December. [C.O.5, 551, fos. 83–84d; signed original in C.O.5, 545, fos. 21–22d; entry in C.O.5, 567, pp. 158–161]

635

2 October, St Augustine

Same to same (No. 41), acknowledging No. 30 and explaining circumstances of Mr De Brahm's suspension. I have appointed Frederick G. Mulcaster Surveyor till H.M.'s pleasure be known: he is married to Mr De Brahm's only daughter, but Mr De Brahm is at variance with him as he is with all mankind. *Duplicate. Signed.* 2½ pp. *Endorsed,* R, 26 December. *Enclosed :*

i. Charleston, 24 September 1770. William De Brahm to Governor Grant. I have told Lord Hillsborough it is not my inclination to disobey orders. *Copy.* ½ p.

ii. St Augustine, 4 October 1770. Governor Grant to William De Brahm, suspending him from office of Land Surveyor of East Florida. *Copy.* 1 p. [C.O.5, 551, fos. 85–90d; signed original, and copies of enclosures, in C.O.5, 545, fos. 23–28d; entry of covering letter in C.O.5, 567, pp. 161–165]

636

2 October, London

Paul Wentworth to John Pownall, soliciting seat in Council of New Hampshire as recommended by Governor John Wentworth. *Signed.* 2 small pp. *Addressed. Endorsed,* Recd. October, Read 7 November 1770. [C.O.5, 930, fos. 95–96d]

637

3 October, Whitehall

Earl of Hillsborough to John Stuart (No. 19), acknowledging Nos. 24–25. Contrary to impression given in your letter of 5 July, Indian affairs in West Florida appear to be in much confusion, requiring your immediate presence there. Peace between Choctaws and Creeks is dangerous to West Florida. *Draft.* 2½ pp. [C.O.5, 71, Pt. 2, fos. 59–60d; entry in C.O.5, 241, pp. 343–344]

638

3 October, Whitehall

Same to Governor Peter Chester (No. 29). From Lieut.-Governor Durnford's letters, Indian affairs in West Florida appear to be in much confusion: I have directed Mr Stuart to go to Pensacola. Members of Assembly have their own interests too much in view and much time has been wasted in altercations with Council on matters of privilege. Council has deliberated on matters not referred to them, and by address to the King's servants has assumed correspondence that should be confined to governor. You are to correct these irregularities. I shall pay no regard to representations made by agent grounded on instructions from members of Assembly without concurrence of Council, or made after dissolution. Further information required from you and General Gage regarding re-establishment of Fort Bute and settlement on Mississippi. *Draft.* 3¾ pp. [C.O.5, 587, pp. 419–424; entry in C.O.5, 619, pp. 62–66]

639

3 October, Whitehall

* Same to Governor Lord Botetourt (No. 37), acknowledging Nos. 34–37. There is little doubt but that association for non-importation and petition on revenue laws were encouraged by persons in England. It is pleasing that House of Burgesses receded from claim of Cherokee land in address of December last and closed with my proposal of 13 May 1769. King acquiesces in your drawing on quitrents but this is not to be precedent. Appointment to Council of Mr Digges is to await vacancy. *Draft.* 3¼ pp. [C.O.5, 1348, fos. 140–142d; entry in C.O.5, 1375, pp. 107–110]

640

3 October, Whitehall

Same to Governor William Tryon (No. 35), acknowledging Nos. 54–56. Sum of paper currency outstanding appears large, and will I hope be sufficient until prejudices of the people admit, and circumstances of colony induce, currency of better credit. *Draft.* ¾ p. [C.O.5, 313, fos. 98–99d; entry in C.O.5, 332, p. 51]

641

3 October, Whitehall

Same to Governor Jonathan Trumbull (No. 19), acknowledging No. 18 [MS: 17] and copy of No. 13. First law sent might have been questioned for restraining freedom of trade had it not been repealed. *Draft.* 1 p. [C.O.5, 1283, fos. 94–95d; entry in C.O.5, 1301, pp. 270–271]

642

3 October, Whitehall

* Same to Lieut.-Governor Thomas Hutchinson (No. 42), acknowledging Nos. 19–22. Your speech of 25 July to Assembly commended; from the answer it is apparent that they really mean to distress the mother-country. No time should be lost in deliberating on measures to prevent independence. Avoid as much as possible entering into arguments with them. Mr Rogers's death lamented. *Entry*. 3 pp. [C.O.5, 765, pp. 184–186; draft in C.O.5, 759, fos. 263–264d]

643

3 October, Whitehall

Same to Lieut.-Governor William Bull (No. 39), acknowledging Nos. 30–31, and inquiring if persons proposed as Associate Judges are attached to H.M.'s government. I hope Assembly will have seen error of conduct. Appointment of Treasurer approved. Attested copy of pardon for Mathew Turner sent. *Draft*. 2½ pp. [C.O.5, 393, fos. 76–77d; entry in C.O.5, 408, pp. 46–48; entry of pardon in C.O.324, 42, p. 205]

644

3 October, Whitehall

* Same to Deputy Governor Robert Eden (No. 19), acknowledging No. 6. I hope that resolution of New York merchants will extend to Maryland. Meanwhile, persevere in removing prejudice. *Draft*. 1½ pp. [C.O.5, 1283, fos. 58–59d; entry in C.O.5, 1301, pp. 12–13]

645

3 October, Whitehall

Same to President H. T. Cramahé (No. 35), acknowledging No. 1. *Draft*. ¾ p. [C.O.42, 30, fos. 119–120d; entry in C.O.43, 8, p. 83]

646

3 October, Whitehall

Same to Sir William Johnson (No. 14), acknowledging letter of 12 July last. Prejudice in mind of savages by idle and wicked report that the King has ordered no more goods to be sent should be removed. Any design for union between Northern and Southern Indians must be defeated. *Draft*. 1½ pp. [C.O.5, 71, Pt. 2, fos. 63–64d; entry in C.O.5, 241, pp. 346–348]

647

3 October, Whitehall

Same to Lieut.-Colonel William Dalrymple. Your protection of persons compelled to seek refuge in Castle William approved. Your narrative of events of 5 March expected. *Entry.* 1½ pp. [C.O.5, 765, pp. 187–188; draft in C.O.5, 759, fos. 265–266d]

648

3 October, Whitehall

Same to William De Brahm (No. 8), acknowledging No. 11. Request for leave refused. H.M.'s service must not be obstructed by differences with Governor Grant. *Draft.* 1 p. [C.O.5, 71, Pt. 2, fos. 61–62d; entry in C.O.5, 241, pp. 345–346]

649

3 October, Whitehall

Same to Andrew Elliot, acknowledging letter of 4 July concerning New York-New Jersey boundary commission. Order in Council has been issued, I hope no further delay will happen. *Draft.* ½ p. [C.O.5, 1101, fos. 93–94d; entry in C.O.5, 1141, p. 139]

650

3 October, Whitehall

Same to Lieutenant George McDougal. Since you do not acquiesce in arbitration, dispute between you and inhabitants of Detroit concerning Hog Island must be determined by H.M. in Council. *Draft.* ½ p. [C.O.42, 30, fos. 117–118d; entry in C.O.43, 8, p. 83; another entry in C.O.5, 241, p. 341]

651

3 October, Whitehall

John Pownall to Anthony Todd. Packet-boats to be detained for dispatches ready tomorrow. *Entry.* ½ p. [C.O.5, 241, p. 342]

652

4 October, St Augustine

Frederick G. Mulcaster to Earl of Hillsborough. I was this day sworn as Surveyor-General of East Florida in room of Mr De Brahm, suspended. *Signed.* 1¼ small pp. *Endorsed*, R, 30 November. [C.O.5, 551, fos. 77–78d; entry in C.O.5, 227, pp. 302–303]

653

5 October, New York

* Lieut.-Governor Cadwallader Colden to Earl of Hillsborough (No. 17). Party opposing government was defeated last week in struggle to turn out elective magistrates favourable to government. Mr Ludlow, puisne judge of Supreme Court, and Mr Banyar, deputy secretary, have been supports of administration. I beg to be excused from naming opponents. Rioting is greatly discouraged. *Signed.* 2¾ pp. *Endorsed,* R, 9 November. [C.O.5, 1101, fos. 97–98d; entry in C.O.5, 1138, pp. 163–165]

654

6 October, New York

Lieut.-General Thomas Gage to Earl of Hillsborough (No. 50), acknowledging No. 33. All moveable stores and materials at Annapolis Royal have been moved to Halifax. Detachment of 14th regiment has relieved provincial company in Castle William which at first caused consternation in Boston, but no commotion. Repairs are going on and plans drawn for defence of the landing. One regiment appears sufficient. Return of ordnance stores for Bahamas enclosed. Notice received from West Florida of arrival of Governor Chester there, and of arrival and settlement of eighty people with eighteen negroes at Natchez. Mining company on Lake Superior have built stockaded fort at falls of St Mary, commanding pass from Lake Huron to Lake Superior, which has aroused jealousy of traders who apprehend that real design is to monopolize all the northern trade. *Signed.* 6½ pp. *Endorsed,* R, 9 November. *Enclosed :*

    i. Return of ordnance stores sent to Providence, 21 September 1770. *Copy.* 1½ pp. [C.O.5, 88, fos. 152–157d; entry of covering letter in C.O.5, 234, pp. 121–130]

655

6 October, New York

Separate. Same to same, acknowledging No. 32, which requires much reflection. *Signed.* 1 p. *Endorsed,* R, 9 November. [C.O.5, 88, fos. 158–159d; entry in C.O.5, 234, p. 131]

656

7 October, New Bern

Governor William Tryon to Earl of Hillsborough (No. 57), acknowledging No. 33 and enclosures. Samuel Cornell admitted to Council. Insurrection of Regulators at Hillsborough on 24–25th of last month during sitting of Superior Court: Mr Henderson, Associate Judge, escaped at night. *Signed.* 1½ pp. *Endorsed,* R, 9 January 1771. [C.O.5, 314, fos. 1–2d; signed duplicate, endorsed Read 22 August 1771, in C.O.5, 302, fos. 5–6d; entry in C.O.5, 328, pp. 203–205]

657

7 October, Montreal

Chartier de Lolbiniere to Earl of Hillsborough, complaining of difficulties in obtaining possession of two seigneuries on Lake Champlain.

'rench. *Signed.* 2 small pp. *Endorsed,* R, 19 November. [C.O.42, 30,
>s. 162–163d; entry in C.O.43, 12, pp. 269–270; copy in C.O.42, 8,
>s. 17–18d]

58

October, Savannah

;overnor James Wright to Earl of Hillsborough (No. 49), acknow-
:dging No. 32. I have had petition for representation in Assembly
·om twenty-six inhabitants of St David's parish: the three other
arishes will probably apply at next meeting. I am not apprehensive of
nything but this interrupting harmony and good humour; I wish I
·ere authorized to issue writs of election. Two whites were killed by
ndians, but it is yet doubtful if the Indian was killed. Talk enclosed;
thers sent to Lower and Upper Creeks. Some of party I sent to search
fter two missing men burned Indian huts on Oconee River: the
ndians do not look on this as one of their regular towns and will not
link anything of its being burned, though they may pretend to. Mr
'onge, Surveyor-General, recommended to be of Council. *Signed.*
½ pp. *Endorsed,* R, 10 December. *Enclosed:*

   i. Talk by Salliqea and Young Lieutenant at the Euchees, 5 September 1770, denying involvement in Little River affair and suggesting
that Upper Creeks did it. Hope trade will not be stopped. 1½ pp.
Endorsed [by Governor Wright], Talk from Coweta Lieutenant and
Selechee, 5 September 1770, recd. 23 September. [C.O.5, 660, fos.
149–151d; signed duplicate of covering letter, endorsed Read 22
August, in C.O.5, 651, fos. 64–65d; entry of covering letter in C.O.5,
678, pp. 202–205]

59

October, Halifax

;overnor Lord William Campbell to Earl of Hillsborough (No. 68),
nclosing following. Lands granted to Alexander McNutt and others
ave been resumed after verdict by jury of non-performance of con-
itions. I beg instruction to grant them and all such tracts to persons
ble to settle them; and orders to meet expenses of process from quit-
:nts. *Signed.* 2½ pp. *Endorsed,* R, 27 November. *Enclosed:*

   i. Estimate of civil establishment of Nova Scotia proposed for 1771.
Total, £4239 0s. 5d. 2 pp. [C.O.217, 47, fos. 72–75d; signed duplicate
of covering letter, and copy of enclosure, in C.O.217, 26, fos. 66–69d;
entry of covering letter in C.O.218, 17, pp. 241–242]

60

October, Boston

.ieut.-Governor Thomas Hutchinson to Earl of Hillsborough (No.
7). The House voted by fifty-nine to twenty-nine to proceed to busi-
:ss: Council in general were in favour of it. House is preparing

remonstrance which will probably pass. Heads of opposition are very wrath, but body of the people will be more quiet in their minds. *Signed.* ½ p. *Endorsed,* R, 7 November. [C.O.5, 759, fos. 290–291d; entry in C.O.5, 768, pp. 169–170]

661

9 October, Quebec

President H. T. Cramahé to Governor Guy Carleton, sending address[1] to H.M. However desirous the Canadians are to see their ancient laws and customs restored, they thought it sufficient to have it signed by a few principal hands. *Signed.* 1¼ small pp. *Endorsed,* R, 21 November. [C.O.42, 30, fos. 164–165d; entry in C.O.43, 12, p. 268]

662

10 October

Warrant for appointment of Henry Preston and Charles Pryce as Clerk of Crown and Peace in Georgia. *Entry.* 1 p. [C.O.324, 42, p. 209]

663

10 October

Same for same as Clerk of Pleas in Georgia. *Entry.* 1 p. [C.O.324, 42, p. 210]

664

10 October, N.H.

Governor John Wentworth to Earl of Hillsborough (No. 33), acknowledging No. 30. I hope Lords of Trade will confirm Act dividing New Hampshire into counties and will secure guarantees on west side of Connecticut River. *Duplicate. Signed.* 2 pp. *Endorsed,* R, 5 January 1771. [C.O.5, 937, fos. 23–24d; signed original in C.O.5, 930, fos. 105–106d; entry in C.O.5, 945, pp. 156–157]

665

10 October, Quebec

President H. T. Cramahé to Earl of Hillsborough (No. 2), enclosing following. *Signed.* ¾ p. *Endorsed,* R, 19 November. *Enclosed :*

　　i. Minutes of Council of Quebec, 16 July–28 September 1770 *Copy,* certified by G. Allsopp, deputy clerk. 11 pp. [C.O.42, 30, fos 153–161d; signed duplicate of covering letter in C.O.42, 8, fos. 19–20d; entry of covering letter in C.O.43, 12, p. 270]

1 Probably No. 889 below.

666

10 October, Quebec

Thomas Ainslie to John Pownall, complaining of irregularities by Richard Murray, Vendue-Master of Quebec and deputy Collector of Customs. *Signed.* 3 small pp. *Endorsed,* R, 26 March 1771. [C.O.42, 31, fos. 3–4d]

667

12 October, Whitehall

Lord Rochford to Earl of Hillsborough, enclosing following. *Signed.* 1 p. *Endorsed,* R, 15 October. *Enclosed:*

i. *Description of the Manner of Making Tar in Sweden* with *Description of Manner of Making Pitch. English* and *French. Printed.* 31 pp. with diagrams. [C.O.5, 71, Pt. 2, fos. 65–82B]

668

15 October, Williamsburg

President William Nelson to Earl of Hillsborough, reporting death of Lord Botetourt. John Blair declining on account of age, Council this day swore me in as commander-in-chief. *Signed.* 2½ pp. *Endorsed,* R, 7 December. *Enclosed:*

i. 15 October 1770. Proceedings of Council of Virginia on death this morning of Governor Lord Botetourt. *Copy,* certified by John Blair, jnr., clerk. 1¼ pp.

ii. Williamsburg, 15 October 1770. Proclamation by President Nelson, continuing officers. *Copy.* 1 p. [C.O.5, 1348, fos. 153–158d; signed duplicate of covering letter, two copies of No. i, and copy of No. ii, in C.O.5, 1333, fos. 71–76d; entry of covering letter in C.O.5, 1372, pp. 122–125]

669

15 October, Charleston

William De Brahm to Earl of Hillsborough (No. 14), notifying suspension from office by Governor Grant and requesting leave to defend himself in England. *Signed.* 1 p. *Endorsed,* R, 8 January 1771. *Enclosed:*

i. Charleston, 24 September 1770. William De Brahm to Governor Grant, notifying Lord Hillsborough's order to appoint deputy. George Rolfe appointed. *Copy.* 1 small p.

ii. St Augustine, 4 October 1770. Extract of minutes of Council of East Florida, recording suspension of William Gerard De Brahm from office of Land Surveyor-General, and appointment of Frederick George Mulcaster in his place. George Rolfe, deputy Surveyor-General, to deliver up papers appertaining to office. *Copy.* 1 p.

iii. St Augustine, [4] October 1770. Governor Grant to William D
Brahm, suspending him from office of Land Surveyor of Eas
Florida. *Copy. Counter-signatory*, David Yates, deputy clerk. 1 ɪ

iv. St Augustine, 4 October 1770. Frederick George Mulcaster t
William De Brahm, notifying his having been sworn into office c
Surveyor. *Copy*. 1 small p.

v. Charleston, 15 October 1770. William De Brahm to his son-in
law, Frederick G. Mulcaster. Earl of Hillsborough's letter has bee
misconstrued. *Copy*. 2¼ small pp. [C.O.5, 72, fos. 3–11d; entry ɑ
covering letter in C.O.5, 227, pp. 345–347]

670

16 October, Whitehall

Earl of Hillsborough to Lords of Admiralty. Thomas Hutchinson beiɴ
appointed Captain-General and Governor-in-Chief of Massachusett
he is to be granted such powers usually granted to captains-general ɑ
American colonies. *Entry*. ½ p. [C.O.5, 765, p. 188]

671

16 October, Whitehall

Same to Lord Chamberlain, requesting customary allowance of plaɪ
for Thomas Hutchinson, Governor-in-Chief of Massachusetts. *Entrʲ*
½ p. [C.O.5, 765, p. 189]

672

16 October, Whitehall

John Pownall to Clerk of Council in Waiting, sending papers froɪ
governor of Quebec (now in London) pursuant to Order of 28 Augu
1767. *Draft*. ½ p. *Enclosed:*

i. Inventory of papers accompanying letter dated Quebec, ɪ
September 1769, from Goverɴor Carleton to Earl of Hillsboroug
Papers concerned state of laws and judicature in Quebec; laws ɑ
property; criminal laws; police laws; extracts of edicts in force ɪ
colonies of Canada; copies of various commissions and edicts. 3½ p
[C.O.42, 30, fos. 147–150d; entry in C.O.43, 8, pp. 84–87]

673

16 October, Charleston

Lievt.-Governor William Bull to Commissioners for Trade aɴ
Plantations, sending journals of Commons House of Assembly of Souɪ
Carolina, 14 August–8 September. Henry Middleton has resigɴe
from Council: Gabriel Manigault, John Savage and David Deas aɪ
of large estates and undoubted loyalty. *Signed*. 1 p. *Endorsed*, Recɑ
30 November, Read 6 February 1771. [C.O.5, 380, fos. 1–2]

674

18 October, Virginia

* President William Nelson to Earl of Hillsborough (No. 2), acknowledging letter of 20 July to Lord Botetourt, and answering allegations
in anonymous letter of 9 July to Mr Walpole about concern of members
of Council of Virginia in large grants of land west of Alleghany Mountains. Papers enclosed. Proposals of Mr Walpole and associates critic-
ized. When back of Virginia is sufficiently populated, new colony may
be wise measure. *Signed.* 10 pp. *Endorsed,* R, 22 December. *Enclosed:*

i. 12 July 1749. Minutes of Council of Virginia, recording permission
to named persons to survey 200,000 acres of land on south side of
River Allegane, otherwise Ohio. *Copy,* certified by John Blair, clerk.
1 p.

ii. Williamsburg, 19 February 1754. Proclamation by Lieut.-Governor
Robert Dinwiddie. To encourage raising of troops, 200,000 acres of
land is to be set aside on Ohio for grants to volunteers. *Copy,* certified as No. i. 1 p.

iii. 6 December 1769. Account by Nathaniel Walthoe, clerk, of all
orders of Council for granting lands between Alleghany Mountains
and line from western boundary of Carolina line to confluence of
Ohio and Mississippi. 1745–1754: thirty-four grants with names of
grantees.
    Nine more grants, 1743–1760, which escaped Mr Walthoe's
observation. *Signed,* John Blair, jnr., clerk. 9½ pp.

iv. Memorandum by John Blair, clerk, that Council journals record
no grant since 27 August 1754 of more than 1000 acres west of mountains, and no grant of any quantity since 7 October 1763. *Signed.*
1¼ pp.

* v. Mount Vernon, 5 October 1770. George Washington to Governor
Lord Botetourt. Grant of lands solicited by Mr Walpole will give
fatal blow to interests of this country. I ask for favourable representation to H.M. of case of officers and soldiers claiming in accordance
with order of 18 February 1754 and proclamation of 19 February
1754. Order of Council and proclamation annexed. PS. Troops
raised in consequence of this proclamation conducted themselves
so as to receive their country's thanks. *Copy,* certified by John Blair,
jnr., clerk of Council. 3½ pp.

vi. 15 October 1770. Proceedings of Council of Virginia. *Copy,*
of No. 668i, certified as No. v. 1 p. [C.O.5, 1348, fos. 161–180d;
signed duplicate of covering letter and copies of Nos. i and v, in
C.O.5, 1333, fos. 77–85d; copy of covering letter in C.O.5, 1333,
fos. 135–142d; entry of same in C.O.5, 1372, pp. 125–137]

675

19 October, Whitehall

★ Earl of Hillsborough to Lieut.-Governor William Bull (No. 40), acknowledging Nos. 32–34. David [*sic,* should be Daniel] Pryce's fine remitted. Steps taken regarding Spanish vessels require serious consideration. You are forbidden by additional instruction of 14 April to assent to any Act for defraying expenses for services not arising in colony. If there are innocent sufferers, H.M. would authorize separate bill for indemnification. *Draft.* 2 pp. [C.O.5, 393, fos. 89–90d; entry in C.O.5, 408, pp. 48–49]

676

19 October, Whitehall

Same to Lieut.-Colonel P. A. Irving, acknowledging letter of 1 October. Case was decided when H.M. approved General Carleton's conduct in dismissing you from Council of Quebec. *Draft.* 1¼ pp. [C.O.42, 30, fos. 151–152d; entry in C.O.43, 8, pp. 87–89]

677

19 October

Warrant for appointment of Thomas Flucker as Secretary of Massachusetts. *Entry.* 1 p. [C.O.324, 42, pp. 212–213]

678

19 October, St Augustine

★ Governor James Grant to Earl of Hillsborough (No. 42), acknowledging No. 31. My absence at present would be inexpedient. There is precedent in Barbados for senior Councillor, though appointed by Governor, assuming government. John Moultry has been considered President of Council in East Florida for seven years: recommended to be lieut.-governor. Mr Wooldridge is despised by everybody, Mr Jolly has left the province, Dr Turnbull resides at Smyrnea. *Signed.* 4½ pp. *Endorsed,* R, 26 December. [C.O.5, 551, fos. 91–94d; signed duplicate in C.O.5, 545, fos. 29–32d; entry in C.O.5, 567, pp. 165–172]

679

20 October

Richard Jackson to Commissioners for Trade and Plantations, reporting thirty-four Acts passed in Virginia in 1769 proper in point of law. *Signed.* 3½ pp. *Endorsed,* Recd. 23 October, Read 7 November 1770. [C.O.5, 1333, fos. 40–42d]

680

20 October, New Bern

* Governor William Tryon to Earl of Hillsborough (No. 58), enclosing papers respecting outrages of Regulators. I have inquired of officers commanding militia regiments what number of volunteers will turn out, and what number can be ordered out. It must be by aid of legislature that I can expect to extinguish this dangerous flame. *Duplicate. Signed.* 1¼ pp. *Endorsed*, R, 9 January 1771, original not recd. *Enclosed :*

i. New Bern, 16 October 1770. Minutes of Council of North Carolina. *Copy,* certified by John London. 8½ pp.

* ii. Granville, 29 September 1770. Richard Henderson to Governor Tryon, describing riot at Hillsborough on Monday last. Number of insurgents when riot began about 150, but constantly increased. PS. Express from Hillsborough: insurgents left Wednesday, having done little mischief. Enclosed petition printed here. *Copy.* 5¼ pp.

iii. Hillsborough, 30 September 1770. Several inhabitants of Hillsborough to Governor Tryon, calling for action against Regulators. *Copy. Signatories,* James Watson and six others. 1¾ pp.

iv. Orange County, 30 September 1770. Affidavit sworn before Robert Lytle, J.P., by Josiah Lyons. In Hillsborough on 25th inst. Regulators drank Damnation to King George and success to the Pretender. *Copy.* ½ p.

v. New Bern, 9 October 1770. Affidavit sworn before Robert Palmer by Ralph McNair, concerning riot at Hillsborough on 24–25 September last by Herman Husband and others called Regulators. *Copy.* 1½ pp.

vi. New Bern, 30 September 1770. Charter granted to inhabitants of Hillsborough. *Copy. Signatory,* William Tryon. 2½ pp.

* vii. Petition of inhabitants of Orange County to Chief Justice Martin Howard and Associate Judges Maurice Moore and Richard Henderson, complaining of extortions and want of justice. 174 subscribers, names not given. *Copy.* 4½ pp. [C.O.5, 314, fos. 3–24d; signed original of covering letter, and copy of Nos. ii-vii, in C.O.5, 302, fos. 7–22d; entry of covering letter in C.O.5, 328, pp. 205–207]

681

20 October, Charleston

* Lieut.-Governor William Bull to Earl of Hillsborough (No. 36), acknowledging No. 37. *Gazette* enclosed, Journals of Assembly sent to Commissioners for Trade and Plantations. Public discontent continues. Subscribers to non-importation threaten vengeance against violaters of association. Associators forbid any subscriber to use wharves of non-subscribers. Mr Middleton has resigned from Council.

It is difficult to prevail on men of spirit and ability to accept a seat. Now only five Councillors, besides Mr Stuart. *Signed.* 3¼ pp. *Endorsed,* R, 30 November. *Enclosed :*

> i. *South Carolina and American General Gazette,* 24 September–31 October 1770, reporting proceedings of Assembly of South Carolina. *Printed.* 4 large pp. [C.O.5, 393, fos. 119–122d; entry of covering letter in C.O.5, 409, pp. 144–149]

682

22 October, Portsmouth, N.H.

* John Wentworth, Surveyor-General of Woods, to Earl of Hillsborough, reporting measures taken to protect H.M.'s timber in the late province of Maine, choice of a tract of timber in Nova Scotia fit for ship-building, and prosecution of James Potter for waste in Vice-Admiralty Court at Boston. Report on timber between Rivers Damarascoti and St Croix: settlement should be stopped, which would help the fishery. Report on trespasses committed at Windsor on New York side of Connecticut River, in which Samuel Wells, Judge of Common Pleas of New York and J.P. for Cumberland County, was principal agent. Trespassers were convicted. Various enclosures sent: Mr Wells should be dismissed the King's service. There are many tracts of timber in interior of New York to which I have asserted the King's right, despite claims of proprietors. Instructions required concerning tracts of land on both sides of Kennebec River. Schooner of 60–100 tons needed for the service. Vice-Admiralty Court's district should be enlarged. Acts of Parliament for preservation of timber should be strengthened. Instructions required about disposal of white pine timber unfit for masts, yards or bowsprits. *Entry.* 35½ pp. *Annotated,* twenty enclosures. R, 5 January 1771. NB. The original letter and enclosures sent to the Board of Trade. [C.O.5, 227, pp. 310–345]

683

24 October, New York

Governor Earl of Dunmore to Earl of Hillsborough (No. 1), reporting arrival 18th inst. and hopes of peaceful administration. *Signed.* 1 small p. *Endorsed,* R, 27 November. [C.O.5, 1101, fos. 99–100d; entry in C.O.5, 1138, p. 166; signed duplicate, dated 12 November 1770, endorsed Read 22 August 1771, in C.O.5, 1075, fos. 91–92d]

684

24 October, Charlotte Town, I. of St John

* Governor Walter Patterson to Earl of Hillsborough (No. 1), reporting arrival on 30 August, and reporting resources of Island of St John. French inhabitants are mostly kept by British employers. About 125 families arrived this summer; one ship wrecked but no lives lost. Chief Justice Duport has leave to go to Halifax. Ship daily expected from London, another from Ireland. No provisions are to be brought here. *Signed*. 6 pp. *Endorsed*, R, 1 January 1771. [C.O.226, 4, fos. 26–29d; entry in C.O.227, 2, pp. 3–8; signed duplicate, endorsed Read 22 August 1771, in C.O.226, 1, fos. 11–14d]

685

25 October, Charlotte Town, I. of St John

Same to same (No. 2). Phillips Callbeck, John Russel Spence, Thomas Wright and Patrick Fergus, appointed to Council of Island of St John; Wright recommended to be Surveyor-General. Act enclosed. *Signed*. 2¾ pp. *Endorsed*, R, 1 January 1771. *Enclosed*:

    i. Council at Charlotte Town, 25 September 1770. Act for better regulating sea-cow fishery. *Copy*, certified by Phillips Callbeck. 1 p. [C.O.226, 4, fos. 30–32d; entry of covering letter in C.O.227, 2, pp. 8–11; signed duplicate of covering letter in C.O.226, 1, fos. 15–16d]

686

25 October, Charlotte Town, I. of St John

Same to same (No. 3). Church, gaol and court-house needed here: labour is expensive, I imagine cost would be £3000. Communications in Island of St John are bad; to make the roads passable would cost £500. Soldiers needed, for public works as well as defence. *Signed*. 6½ pp. *Endorsed*, R, 1 January 1771. [C.O.226, 4, fos. 33–36d; entry in C.O.227, 2, pp. 11–17; signed duplicate in C.O.226, 1, fos. 17–20d; extract, endorsed Read 17 January 1771, in C.O.226, 1, fos. 7–9d]

687

25 October, Treasury

John Robinson to John Pownall. Lords of Treasury have no objection to remission of fine imposed on Daniel Price. *Signed*. 1 p. *Addressed*. *Enclosed*:

    i. Charleston, 10 August 1770. Lieut.-Governor William Bull to Lords of Treasury, recommending for pardon Daniel Price, found guilty of killing a negro in a passion and fined £350 currency. *Copy*. 1¼ pp. [C.O.5, 393, fos. 91–94d]

688

25 October

Vote of Council of Massachusetts appointing William Bollan agent, to act agreeable to instructions of Council or committee authorized for that purpose. *Entry*. 1 p. [C.O.324, 60, p. 192]

689

28 October, N.H.

* Governor John Wentworth to Earl of Hillsborough (No. 34), acknowledging No. 31. I have succeeded in removing prejudice in people's minds after affair in Boston. Principal men resolved never to submit to anarchy. Few attended meeting of Sons of Liberty in Portsmouth. Boston voted to exclude this province from all intercourse, to starve it into their combinations. I had to prevent a Boston Son of Liberty being tarred and feathered. Theodore Atkinson appointed secretary of New Hampshire. *Duplicate. Signed.* 9 small pp. *Endorsed*, R, 5 January 1771. [C.O.5, 937, fos. 25–30d; signed original in C.O.5, 930, fos. 107–112d; entry in C.O.5, 945, pp. 158–165]

690

28 October, Montreal

Pierre du Calvet to Earl of Hillsborough, soliciting favours and enclosing papers. *French. Signed.* 2 pp. *Endorsed*, R, 14 December. *Enclosed:*

i. Petition of same to the King, soliciting royal bounty in recognition of attachment to Protestant cause. *French. Signed.* 1½ pp.

ii. Observations on ordinance of February last. *French.* 3½ pp.

iii. Memorial on judicial system in Quebec, with special reference to Pierre du Calvet; with copies of letters, in French and English, to and from him. 48 pp. [C.O.42, 30, fos. 168–199d; signed duplicate of covering letter, and copies of Nos. i–ii, in C.O.42, 8, fos. 11–16d; signed copy of No. i in C.O.5, 114, fos. 213–214d]

691

30 October, Boston

* Governor Thomas Hutchinson to Earl of Hillsborough (No. 28). Captain Preston was acquitted this morning. Behaviour of the people was remarkably decent. Trial of the soldiers will not come on this fortnight: there is room to expect that at most they can be found guilty of manslaughter. Proceedings of Council against Mr Oliver enclosed. Assembly is sitting at Cambridge, doing the common business of the province. *Signed.* 1¼ pp. *Endorsed*, R, 8 December. *Enclosed:*

i. *Massachusetts Gazette and Boston Postboy*, 29 October 1770, reporting proceedings of House of Representatives, 23 October 1770; and proceedings of Assembly of South Carolina for August 1770. *Printed.* 4 pp.

ii. 30 October 1770. Certificate by Lieut.-Governor Hutchinson that Joseph Lee and William Kneeland are J.P.s of Middlesex County, Massachusetts, and John Cotton deputy-secretary of the province. *Seal. Signed. Countersigned*, Andrew Oliver, secretary. 1 p.

iii. Proceedings of Council of Massachusetts, 4–24 October 1770, on information that affidavit by Andrew Oliver, secretary, was printed in a pamphlet, published in London, in which members of Council were represented as having made a declaration respecting plan formed by the people to remove the troops.

The documents in the case comprise: petition of Andrew Oliver (5 October); affidavit of John Cotton (9 October); affidavit of Francis Skinner (9 October); affidavit of Benjamin Caldwell (12 October); affidavit of William Dalrymple (12 October); sworn statements of Samuel Danforth (12 October), John Erving, James Pitts and Samuel Dexter (12 October), Thomas Hubbard and James Russell (12 October), Harrison Gray (9 October), Royall Tyler (12 October); petition of Andrew Oliver (16 October); report of Council's committee of inquiry; resolution of Council (24 October) that Andrew Oliver by taking secret minutes at Council is guilty of breach of trust, and that he has injured and abused members of Council. *Copies*, certified by persons named in No. ii. 46 pp. [C.O.5, 759, fos. 300–330d; entry of covering letter in C.O.5, 768, pp. 170–171]

692

31 October, Ordnance-office

Board of Ordnance to Earl of Hillsborough, requesting to know H.M.'s pleasure on fort to be built at St John's, Newfoundland. *Signed*, H. S. Conway, Charles Frederick, W. R. Earle, Charles Cocks. PS. Treasury have called for our estimates. 1½ pp. *Endorsed*, R, 1 November. [C.O.194, 29, fos. 67–68d; entry in C.O.195, 12, pp. 101–102]

693

31 October, Virginia

President William Nelson to Earl of Hillsborough (No. 3), acknowledging No. 34. Legislature wishes copper currency to be of best sort, that is, of intrinsic value. *Signed*. 1 p. *Endorsed*, R, 5 January 1771. [C.O.5, 1349, fos. 7–8d; signed duplicate in C.O.5, 1333, fos. 89–89A dorse; entry in C.O.5, 1372, pp. 143–145]

694

31 October, Virginia

Same to same (No. 4), acknowledging No. 35. Contravention of H.M.'s proclamation of 1763 in grants of land between Alleghanies and Ohio, denied. *Signed*. 1 p. *Endorsed*, R, 5 January 1771. *Enclosed:*

i. 12 February 1755. Notice by Governor and Council of Virginia of H.M.'s instruction authorizing grants west of Alleghanies. 10 April 1766; proclamation by Lieut.-Governor Fauquier requiring observance of H.M.'s proclamation of 7 October 1763. Memorandum by John Blair, jnr., to same effect as No. 674iv. *Copy*. 2 pp. [C.O.5,

1349, fos. 9–12d; signed duplicate of covering letter in C.O.5, 1333, fos. 90–90A dorse, copy of enclosure at fos. 88–88A dorse; entry of covering letter in C.O.5, 1372, pp. 145–146]

695

1 November, Whitehall

John Pownall to Philip Stephens, sending Ferguson, late master of *Betsey*, accused of murder on high seas; with papers. *Draft.* 1½ pp. [C.O.5, 1348, fos. 149–150d; entry in C.O.5, 1375, pp. 110–111]

696

2 November, Quebec

President H. T. Cramahé to Earl of Hillsborough (No. 3), acknowledging Nos. 32–33 and enclosing following. Everything is quiet here and in upper country. *Signed.* 1 p. *Endorsed,* R, 14 December. *Enclosed:*

  i. Report of state of manufactures in Quebec, 2 November 1770. *Signed,* H. T. Cramahé. 2½ pp. [C.O.42, 30, fos. 200–203d; entry of covering letter in C.O.43, 13, pp. 1–2; signed duplicate of covering letter, and copy of No. i, in C.O.42, 8, fos. 21–24d]

697

4 November, N.H.

* Governor John Wentworth to Earl of Hillsborough (No. 35), sending journals and Acts of Assembly of New Hampshire by hand of Lieut.-Governor Temple. Comments on Acts and journals, and on petition of Dr Eleazer Wheelock for incorporation of Dartmouth College. More than £10,000 has been raised in Great Britain, for education of Indians, missionaries and furtherance of learning. *Signed.* 18½ small pp. *Endorsed,* R, 5 January 1771. [C.O.5, 937, fos. 31–40d; signed duplicate in C.O.5, 930, fos. 113–120d; entry in C.O.5, 945, pp. 166–177]

698

5 November, Burlington

* Governor William Franklin to Earl of Hillsborough (supposed to be No. 24). Assembly resolved not to provide for H.M.'s troops in New Jersey but were persuaded to grant £500 for supply during winter; they have left appointment of barrack-master to Governor and made the money liable to be drawn by warrant from Governor and Council. *Signed.* 2 pp. *Endorsed,* R, 15 December. *Enclosed:*

  i. 25 October 1770, Governor Franklin's message to Assembly of New Jersey; with Assembly's answer of 26 October. *Copy.* 1½ pp. [C.O.5, 990, fos. 91–94d; entry of covering letter in C.O.5, 1001, pp. 121–122]

699

6 November

Richard Jackson to Commissioners for Trade and Plantations, reporting on forty-eight Acts passed in North Carolina in 1768. Act for dividing province into six districts and establishing superior court in each is not objectionable but could be improved. Act to encourage importation of British halfpence and Act for declaring certain lots in New Bern taken up by trustees for public school saved and improved, are unfit for H.M.'s approbation. Act for providing for payment of forces raised to suppress insurrection on western frontier is not improper in point of law; whether the emergency was sufficient reason for passing it is not for me to determine. No objection in point of law to other forty-four Acts. *Signed.* 6 pp. *Endorsed,* Recd. 8 November, Read 21 November 1770. [C.O.5, 301, fos. 155–158d]

700

6 November

Same to same, reporting on thirteen Acts passed in South Carolina in 1767–1769. Act for issuing £106,500 in bills of credit is repugnant in law and unfit for approbation. No objection to others, except that Act for establishing ferry on Savannah River does not appear to make provision for purchase of land. *Signed.* 2½ pp. [C.O.5, 379, fos. 156–157d]

701

7 November

Same to same, reporting seven Acts passed in Virginia in 1770 proper in point of law. *Signed.* 1½ pp. *Endorsed,* Recd. 8 November, Read 14 November 1770. [C.O.5, 1333, fos. 43–44d]

702

8 November, G.P.O.

Anthony Todd to John Pownall. Packet-boats from Falmouth to America are detained for Earl of Hillsborough's dispatches. *Signed.* 1½ small pp. *Endorsed,* R, 8 November. [C.O.5, 71, Pt. 2, fos. 121–122d]

703

9 November

Richard Jackson to Commissioners for Trade and Plantations, reporting Act passed in Virginia in 1770 proper in point of law. *Signed.* 1 p. *Endorsed,* Recd. 8 [*sic*] November, Read 14 November 1770. [C.O.5, 1333, fos. 45–45A dorse]

704

9 November

Leave of absence for twelve months to James Wooldridge, Provost Marshal of East Florida. *Entry.* ¾ p. [C.O.324, 42, p. 216]

705

9 November, Virginia

President William Nelson to Earl of Hillsborough (No. 5), enclosing following. £400 sterling p.a. would make the old gentleman happy for rest of his days. Printed Acts passed last session and journals sent. *Duplicate. Signed.* 1¼ pp. *Endorsed,* R, 31 December 1770. *Enclosed:*

  i. Memorial of Council of Virginia to the King, soliciting pension for John Blair. *Signed,* William Nelson and nine others. 2 small pp.

  ii. Accounts of revenue of 2s. per hogshead arising in Virginia, 25 April–25 October 1770. *Signed,* Richard Corbin, deputy Receiver-General. Examined by John Blair, deputy Auditor, and William Nelson. 1½ pp. [Covering letter and No. i in C.O.5, 1348, fos. 181–184d; signed original of covering letter and copy of No. i in C.O.5, 1333, fos. 91–93A dorse; No. ii in C.O.5, 1333, fos. 94–95d; entry of covering letter in C.O.5, 1372, pp. 137–139]

706

10 November, New York

* Lieut.-General Thomas Gage to Earl of Hillsborough (No. 51), giving views on British possessions on Mississippi. The French first adopted plan of forts and settlements. Advantages we are supposed to reap by forts. They are not, except Michilimackinac, marts of trade. They may keep Indians in awe, but are disliked. They do not draw the savages away from settlements in time of war. They do keep French in subjection. Advantages of colonization at such a distance are questionable: millions of acres on sea-coast are uncultivated. Settlement might mean war with Indians. To procure all the commerce the country will afford, and at as little expense as we can, is only object we should have in view. Indians need our goods; all we should do is prevent frauds of traders and follow methods taken in the southern district. On Mississippi, forts at junction of Ohio and Illinois Rivers might stop intrusions from Louisiana but would be expensive. Canadian traders on the Wabash sell cheaper than those from Louisiana. Best peltry comes from Upper Mississippi about Fort Chartres, but British traders do not go after it. Suggestion of drawing trade from Mississippi by a canal joining it with the Iberville needs to be carefully examined. Advantages we might gain from civil and military establishments at mouths of Ohio and Illinois Rivers would be greatly disproportionate to expense. One reason for French settlement was to supply New Orleans with provisions, which they otherwise had to get from British colonies or from Europe. *Signed.* 16½ pp. *Endorsed,* R, 14 December. [C.O.5, 88, fos. 164–173d; entry in C.O.5, 234, pp. 132–156]

707

10 November, New York

Lieut.-Governor Cadwallader Colden to Earl of Hillsborough, protesting against Earl of Dunmore's claim to moiety of perquisites and emoluments of the government from date of his commission to his arrival, a claim not made since 1732 and then dropped. Attorney-General has been commanded to file bill in Chancery for recovery of these emoluments. *Signed.* 5 pp. *Endorsed,* R, 14 December. [C.O.5, 1101, fos. 103–105d; entry in C.O.5, 1138, pp. 172–179]

708

12 November, St James's

Patent of appointment of Thomas Flucker to be Secretary of Massachusetts. *Entry.* 2¼ pp. [C.O.324, 51, pp. 387–389]

709

12 November, New York

* Lieut.-General Thomas Gage to Earl of Hillsborough (No. 52), reporting Siota congress of Indians of western confederacy. Western tribes agreed to make peace with Cherokees. War likely between northern and southern leagues: western tribes are exasperated against Six Nations for the lands they have ceded. Captain Preston is acquitted, but there are suits for damages against him: he is recommended for H.M.'s consideration. Evidence of provocation of the troops before 5 March enclosed. Engineers hope to complete works and plans of Castle William by end of this month. *Signed.* 4 pp. *Endorsed,* R, 14 December. *Enclosed :*

i. 3 October 1770. Certificates by Lieut.-Governor Thomas Hutchinson that James Murray is J.P. for Suffolk County, Massachusetts. *Seal. Signed,* A. Oliver, Secretary. ½ p.

ii. Affidavit sworn at Castle William, 25 August 1770, before James Murray, J.P., by Alexander Ross, lieutenant, 14th regiment. In July 1769 he was charged with riot and rescue of John Riley from custody, insulted and threatened by Justice Dana at his trial, acquitted, presented for same offence by grand jury, found guilty, and in March 1770 fined £20. *Signed.* James Murray. 4 pp.

iii. Same, same date, by Captain Charles Fordyce, 14th regiment, to same effect as parts of No. ii. *Signed,* James Murray. 2½ pp.

iv. Same, same date, by John Phillips, sergeant, 14th regiment. John Riley was arrested on misdirected warrant in July 1769, fined 13s. 4d. which he could not pay, and escaped from the court. Lieutenant Ross tried to stop this escape but was charged with assisting it, and abused by Justice Dana at the trial. *Signed,* James Murray. 4 pp.

v. Same, same date, by Samuel Heale, corporal, 14th regiment. On 13 July 1769 John Riley struck Winship, a butcher, only after much abuse. *Signed*, James Murray. 2 pp.

vi. Same, same date, by Jonathan Stevenson, soldier, 14th regiment. On 14 July 1769 at Riley's trial, Lieutenant Ross ordered Riley to remain in court. During examination, gross invective was used against the troops. *Signed*, James Murray. 1½ pp.

vii. Same, same date, by John Ness, ensign, 14th regiment. Following riot on 24 October 1769, he was brought before Justice Dana and insulted. No person appeared to support accusation against him, and his case was dismissed. On 26 October he was again arrested, again abused by the justices, bailed, and acquitted at superior court. *Signed*, James Murray. 7 pp.

viii. Same, same date, by James Hichman, sergeant, 14th regiment, to same effect as parts of No. vii. For using his halberd to stop a rioter, he was brought before Justice Dana, abused, bailed, and has not yet been brought to trial. *Signed*, James Murray. 2½ pp.

ix. Same, same date, by Michael Groves, Robert Adamson, John Stevens, William Coleman and John Thorpe, soldiers, 14th regiment. At riot on 24 October 1769 when the mob threw stones, they were ordered by their officers not to offer any violence to inhabitants. *Signed*, James Murray. 1 p.

x. Same, same date, by William Fowler, soldier, 14th regiment. In riot of 24 October he was struck by brick bat thrown by Obadiah Whiston, blacksmith, but was unable to have his complaint upheld before the justices on ground that soldiers' evidence was insufficient. *Signed*, James Murray. 2¾ pp.

xi. Same, same date, by John Kirk, soldier, 14th regiment. On 7 March last he was knocked down and abused by a man at head of mob in Boston. *Signed*, James Murray. ½ p.

xii. Same, same date, by Daniel Mattear, lieutenant, and Cornelius Smelt, ensign, 14th regiment, to effect that Ensign Ness was abused and insulted at Justice Dana's court on 24 October 1769. *Signed*, James Murray. 1 p.

xiii. Same, same date, by Thomas McFarland, corporal, Samuel Bish and Stephen Cheslett, 14th regiment. On 27 October 1769 Robert Pierpoint offered to give them 200 dollars and procure their discharge from army if they would testify against Ensign Ness. *Signed*, James Murray. ¾ p.

xiv. Same, same date, by Thomas Light, sergeant, 14th regiment. On 29 October 1769 a mob abused sentries of the fortifications guard in Boston. *Signed*, James Murray. ¾ p.

xv. Same, same date, by James Unwin and Jesse Lindley, soldiers, 14th regiment, the sentries referred to in No. xiv. One of the mob said 'Give me the club, I will soon drive the dogs from thence for we know they dare not fire'. *Signed*, James Murray. ¾ p.

xvi. Same, same date, by John Park, Thomas Shearwood, Robert Holbrook and William Marburn, soldiers, 14th regiment. In riot led by Robert Pierpoint on 24 October 1769 when William Fowler was injured, they were ordered by their officers not to offer violence to any inhabitant. *Signed,* James Murray. 2 pp.

xvii. Same, same date, by Richard Ratcliff, soldier, 14th regiment. Mob assembled on 17 October 1769 before main guard, Boston. One Pitt damned him for a lobster scoundrel, bloody back dog. *Signed,* James Murray. 1 p.

xviii. Same, same date, by John Woodhouse, soldier, 14th regiment. Stones were thrown at him by mob on 29 October 1769 before main guard, Boston. *Signed,* James Murray. 1 p.

xix. Same, same date, by William Lake, corporal, 14th regiment. He was knocked down by mob the later end of November. *Signed,* James Murray. ¾ p.

xx. Same, same date, by Thomas Hoult, sergeant, John Gregory, drummer, Thomas Smith, soldier, 14th regiment. In December 1768 they were set on by mob in Boston with cries of 'Lobsters, show them no mercy', and blows. *Signed,* James Murray. ¾ p.

xxi. Same, same date, by Hardress Grey, sergeant, 14th regiment. They were assaulted by mob in January 1769. *Signed,* James Murray. 1¾ pp.

xxii. Same, same date, by John Norfolk, sergeant, 14th regiment, concerning affray between soldiers and townspeople of Boston on or about 22 February 1769 in which Ruddock, who said he was a J.P., took a leading part. *Signed,* James Murray. 1½ pp.

xxiii. Same, same date, by William McCracken, soldier, 14th regiment. He was assaulted and knocked down by townsmen in Boston on 6 January last. *Signed,* James Murray. ½ p.

xxiv. Same, same date, by William Brown, soldier, 14th regiment. He was assaulted and knocked down by townspeople in Boston on or about 14 February last. *Signed,* James Murray. ½ p.

xxv. Same, same date, by Joseph Whitehouse, soldier, 14th regiment. He was assaulted by townsmen in Boston in late February 1769, called 'Lobster, bloody back'd dog'. He saw assault on Captain Goldfinch on 5 March last. *Signed,* James Murray. ¾ p.

xxvi. Same, same date, by Robert Balfour, corporal, 14th regiment. On 14 July 1769 he was assaulted by townspeople of Boston who said 'God damn him for a bloody back'd scoundrel'. *Signed,* James Murray. ½ p.

xxvii. Same, same date, by David Young, soldier, 14th regiment. He was knocked down on 22 September 1769 while on duty at main guard, Boston. *Signed,* James Murray. ½ p.

xxviii. Same, same date, by William Banks, soldier, 14th regiment. He was knocked down and insulted in Boston in April last. *Signed,* James Murray. ½ p.

xxix. Same, same date, by William Holam, soldier, 14th regiment. He was attacked by townspeople in Boston on 4 November 1769, 24 May last and 4 June last. *Signed,* James Murray. 1 p.

xxx. Same, same date, by Thomas Podger and Richard Henley, soldiers, 14th regiment. While sentries at the neck-guard, Boston, in November 1769, they were insulted. *Signed,* James Murray. ½ p.

xxxi. Same, same date, by John Arnold, corporal, James Shelley, Dennis Towers, Jacob Brown, soldiers, 14th regiment. They were insulted by one Hines and other fishermen in Boston in November 1769. *Signed,* James Murray. ¾ p.

xxxii. Same, same date, by Thomas Thornley, sergeant, 14th regiment. He and the neck-guard were insulted by large mob on 5 November 1769. They were obliged to fix bayonets. *Signed,* James Murray. ¾ p.

xxxiii. Same, same date, by John Shelton, corporal, James Botham, William Mabbot, soldiers, 14th regiment. They were attacked by mob on 25 December 1769 who, swore 'they would murder these bloody back'd rascals'. *Signed,* James Murray. ½ p.

xxxiv. Same, same date, by William Wilson, soldier, 14th regiment. In February 1769 he was knocked down in streets of Boston. Next night he saw three men at barrack door who said 'Damn the King, Damn the Governor, Officers and Soldiers' and ran off. *Signed,* James Murray. ½ p.

xxxv. Same, same date, by William Barker, soldier, 14th regiment. While on duty at main guard, Boston, in December 1769, he was knocked down by mob and much hurt. *Signed,* James Murray. ½ p.

xxxvi. Same, same date, by Gavin Thomson, soldier, 14th regiment. On 29 May last he was assaulted and kicked off Boston Common. *Signed,* James Murray. ½ p.

xxxvii. Same, same date, by John Ridings, sergeant, 14th regiment. He was struck and insulted by mob on 6 March last. *Signed,* James Murray. 1 p.

xxxviii. Same, same date, by John Eyley, sergeant, 14th regiment. On 17 October 1769 he saw sentries at main guard, Boston, insulted by mob. *Signed,* James Murray. ¾ p.

xxxix. Same, same date, by George Smith, soldier, 14th regiment. In February last, in Boston, he met a number of well-dressed persons, one of whom said 'The King of England had no more business with them than any other man, and if they imagined any person present thought so they would tar and feather him immediately and afterwards cut off his head and stick it up on the highest post in the town'. *Signed,* James Murray. 1 p.

xl. Same, same date, by John Care, soldier, 14th regiment. In Boston in March last, he was called 'Lobster and bloody back', and threatened. *Signed,* James Murray. ½ p.

xli. Same, same date, by William Henderson, sergeant, William Leeming and Eustace Merryweather, soldiers, 14th regiment. They were insulted and forced off Boston Common by mob on 29 May last. *Signed,* James Murray. ¾ p.

xlii. Same, same date, by Edward Osbaldeston, soldier, 14th regiment. On 29 May last on Boston Common townspeople gathered about him and said 'Damn the King of Great Britain, Damn the Ministry and all the scoundrels who ordered the lobsters to Boston and drinking a health to King Hancock, hoping King George would not be long on the throne'. *Signed,* James Murray. ½ p.

xliii. Same, same date, by Jacob Moor, soldier, 14th regiment. He was insulted and threatened by a rope-maker in Green's Lane, Boston, in March last. *Signed,* James Murray. ½ p.

xliv. Same, same date, by George Barnett, soldier, 14th regiment. He was insulted and assaulted by mob in Boston in March last. *Signed,* James Murray. ½ p.

xlv. Affidavit sworn at Perth Amboy, New Jersey, 12 August 1770, before Frederick Smyth, Chief Justice, by Alexander Mall, ensign, 29th regiment. On 5 March last he saw inhabitants of Boston attack two soldiers with loaded bludgeons. Mob threatened to break into barracks. Bells were rung as signal to assemble. Vast numbers came in from country. This was all, or mostly, prior to shooting in King's Street. Mob was incited by Mr Dana, magistrate. Insults by inhabitants of Boston were so common as generally to pass unnoticed. *Signed,* Frederick Smyth, 2¼ pp.

xlvi. Affidavit sworn in Somerset County, 24 July 1770, before James Hude, J.P., by William Godson, soldier, 29th regiment. He was attacked by mob while on barrack-guard. *Signed,* James Hude. ¾ p.

xlvii. Same, same date, by Henry Malone, soldier, 29th regiment. In Boston on 5 March 1770 he was prevented from carrying message by a man with a sword, who threatened him. *Signed,* James Hude. ¾ p.

xlviii. Same, same date, by William Normanton, soldier, 29th regiment. On 5 March last in Boston he was attacked by Peter Winslow and wounded with hatchet. *Signed,* James Hude. ¾ p.

xlix. Same, same date, by Cornelius Murphy, soldier, 29th regiment. He was insulted and stoned by mob assembled outside Lieut.-Colonel Carr's house where he was sentry. His piece was not loaded: he used butt-end to push crowd back. *Signed,* James Hude. 1 p.

l. Same, same date, by Thomas Smilie, sergeant, 29th regiment. He was assaulted on 8 June 1769 by John Ruddock, son of a magistrate at Boston. In previous April, Mr Jervais at head of mob drove the sentry from barrack gate, and said to the sergeant of guard

'Damn you, bloody back rascals, our town is free, we will have no soldiers in it but ourselves, which we think better soldiers than you'. *Signed,* James Hude. 1 p.

li. Affidavit sworn as No. xlv, 28 July 1770, by Alexander McCartney, corporal, 29th regiment. He was knocked down and beaten by two townsmen in Boston on 2 March last. *Signed,* Frederick Smyth. ½ p.

lii. Same, same date, by Patrick Donally, soldier, 29th regiment. He was attacked by townspeople in Boston on 2 March last. *Signed,* Frederick Smyth. ½ p.

liii. Same, same date, by John Rodgers, soldier, 29th regiment. He was knocked down by Joseph Shed and others opposite the Ropewalks, Boston, on 3 March last. His skull was fractured and arm broken. *Signed,* Frederick Smyth. ½ p.

liv. Same, 24 July 1770, by Hugh Broughton, sergeant, 29th regiment. On 5 March last Captain Preston sent a party from main guard to save sentry at Custom-house from the mob, and went there with them. It was a considerable time before deponent heard shots. He heard voices cry 'Fire you boogars if you dare'. *Signed,* Frederick Smyth. 1¼ pp.

lv. Same, same date, by John Dumphrey, soldier, 29th regiment. While on sentry at Green's barracks, Boston, last winter he was attacked and clubbed. *Signed,* Frederick Smyth. ¾ p.

lvi. Same, same date, by James McKaan, soldier, 29th regiment. While on guard at the Neck, Boston, on 25 December 1769 he was struck by a football and brickbat. He made to strike a young lad who went after the ball but did not reach him. To avoid arrest and imprisonment he had to abscond. *Signed,* Frederick Smyth. 1 p.

lvii. Same, same date, by John Croker, soldier, 29th regiment. Shortly after regiment landed in Boston, an inhabitant tried in a public house to persuade him to desert. *Signed,* Frederick Smyth. ½ p.

lviii. Same, 28 July, by John Fitzpatrick, corporal, 29th regiment. He was assaulted and insulted by mob in Boston some time before 5 March last. *Signed,* Frederick Smyth. ½ p.

lix. Same, same date, by Hugh McCann, corporal, 29th regiment. Before 5 March last he was insulted and assaulted by mob while on duty in Boston. On 5 March he was assaulted by Mr Pierpoint with mob, who said that 'the soldiers were murdering the townspeople at the town-house'. Later on same night, deponent and party had to fix bayonets to keep off crowd. *Signed,* Frederick Smyth. 1¼ pp.

lx. Same, 24 July, by James Corkrin, soldier, 29th regiment. Winter after the troops came to Boston, he was offered £50 a year by a countryman to go to the country and teach their men exercise and discipline of regular troops. *Signed,* Frederick Smyth. ½ p.

lxi. Same, same date, by Thomas Burgess, corporal, 29th regiment. Before 5 March last, he was interfered with in performance of his duties as sentry at Custom-house by mob which had tarred and feathered a man they had in a cart whom they called an informer. He hoped that loading his firelock would frighten the mob, but it had no effect. *Signed*, Frederick Smyth. 1¼ pp.

lxii. Same, 28 July 1770, by Joshua Williams, soldier, 29th regiment. In June 1769, a few days after he joined regiment at Boston, he was knocked down by mob. His skull was fractured and a pike or other weapon driven into his temple. *Signed*, Frederick Smyth. 1 p.

lxiii. Same, same date, by William Jones and Richard Pearsall, sergeants, 29th regiment. They, and Mrs Jones, were attacked and struck at the ferry, on returning to Boston, in summer 1769. It was then General Mackay's order that no N.C.O. or soldier should strike an inhabitant on any pretence, but should complain to him; which they did, and produced witnesses. General Mackay gave them half a guinea for good behaviour and advised them to drop all proceedings as no redress could be got for a soldier in Boston. *Signed*, Frederick Smyth. 1½ pp.

lxiv. Same, same date, by John Timmins, soldier, 29th regiment. On 14 June 1769 he was attacked and beaten in streets of Boston. He was told that three of his attackers were John Reed, Josiah Davis and John Paymount, all wigmakers of Boston. He could get no redress. *Signed*, Frederick Smyth. 2 pp.

lxv. Same, same date, by Henry Cullin, corporal, 29th regiment. While sentry at barrack gate in Boston in summer 1769, he defended himself against two men who tried forcibly to enter. He was brought before Justice Dana who abused him and threatened the soldiers. *Signed*, Frederick Smyth. 1¼ pp.

lxvi. Same, same date, by Patrick Walker, soldier, 29th regiment. He was assaulted in late February last at the Ropewalks, Boston, by about twelve inhabitants, supposed to be ropemakers. *Signed*, Frederick Smyth. ½ p.

lxvii. Same, same date, by William Murray, corporal, 29th regiment. He was stoned by townspeople when on guard at Custom-house, Boston. They said 'Damn the King and Commissioners and them that sent the troops there'. *Signed*, Frederick Smyth. ¾ p.

lxviii. Same, same date, by Richard Johnson, Robert Ward and John Addicott, soldiers, 29th regiment. They were knocked down and beaten by mob on 3 March last. *Signed*, Frederick Smyth. ½ p.

lxix. Same, same date, by George Irwin, soldier, 29th regiment. He was knocked down and beaten by townspeople in Green's Lane, Boston, on 2 March last. *Signed*, Frederick Smyth. ½ p.

lxx. Affidavit sworn at New Brunswick, New Jersey, 25 July 1770, before William Oake, mayor, by Henry Dougan, surgeon's mate, 29th regiment. On 7 March in Boston he met a number of inhabitants who said 'that they had but one life to lose and that they were willing to lose it for their country, and they also said that Mr Handcock said that he had but one life to lose and that he would lose it for his country, and why should not they, and that they would oppose the troops and prevent them from taking the damned bougers out of jail'. *Signed*, William Oake. ½ p.

lxxi. Same, same date, by Gilbert Carter, ensign, 29th regiment. He was insulted, threatened and stoned on several occasions from first night regiment landed in Boston. On 5 March 1770, when he had the neck-guard, the mob said they would have 10,000 or 12,000 men from the country that night to tear the soldiers in pieces. *Signed*, William Oake. 1 p.

lxxii. Same, same date, by Captain Jeremiah French, 29th regiment. He saw riot on 5 March from roof of British Coffee House in King Street, Boston, and judged there were 300 or 400 people there when first shot was fired. There was a long interval between first shot and those fired afterwards. Deponent did not see Captain Preston and party till after the firing. Lieut.-Colonel Maurice Carr and Captain William Monsell, 29th regiment, were also in the coffee-house and could not leave until escort was sent to protect them. Captain Dashwood, an inhabitant, called out several times 'Damn the rascals, are we to be shot down like pigeons? I will fight them all from the colonel down. Let us take to our arms, let us set fire to the beacon.' *Signed*, William Oake. ¾ p.

lxxiii. Affidavit sworn as No. xlvi, same date, by John Eustace, corporal, 29th regiment. On 5 March last, in Boston, he was set on and beaten by Mr Pierpoint, with many threatening words. *Signed*, James Hude. ¾ p.

lxxiv. Same, same date, by Thomas Walker, drummer, 29th regiment. On 2 March, Patrick Walker was attacked and wounded by ropemakers in Boston. Deponent and two others with him were also attacked and cut about the head. *Signed*, James Hude. 1 p. [C.O.5, 88, fos. 174–262d; entry of covering letter in C.O.5, 234, pp. 156–161]

710

12 November, New York

* Governor Earl of Dunmore to Earl of Hillsborough (No. 2), enclosing following papers. Riots in Cumberland and Gloucester counties were instigated by people of New Hampshire. Restriction on governor of New York granting lands there gives sort of sanction to disorder, and should be taken off. Project for colony on the Ohio condemned here, on grounds of distance, expense of defence, and probable jealousy of Ohio Indians. *Signed*. PS. Plague reported on Hispaniola. 4 pp. *Endorsed*, R, 14 December. *Enclosed*:

i. New York, 25 October 1770. Address of congratulation to Earl of Dunmore by grand jurors of New York City and County, with answer. *Copy. Signatory*, Isaac Low, foreman. 1¼ pp.

ii. 26 October 1770. Same, by Chamber of Commerce of City of New York, with answer. *Copy. Signatory,* Hugh Wallace, president. 1½ pp.

iii. New York, 29 October 1770. Same, by minister, elders and deacons of Reformed Protestant German Church of City of New York, with answer. *Copy. Signatory,* Michael Kern. 2 pp.

iv. New York, 27 October 1770. Same, by Justices of Supreme Court, counsellors and officers of law in New York province, with answer. *Copy.* 2¼ pp.

v. 29 October 1770. Same, by Mayor, Aldermen and Commonalty of City of New York, with answer. The Corporation presented H.E. with freedom of the City. *Copy. Signatory,* Augustus Cortland, clerk. 2 pp.

vi. Same, by ministers, elders and deacons of United Presbyterian Churches of City of New York, with answer. *Copy.* 2½ pp.

vii. New York, 25 October 1770. Same, by minister, trustees, and wardens of German Evangelical Lutheran Church in Montgomery's Ward, City of New York, with answer. *Copy. Signatory,* John Siegfried Gerock, minister. 2¼ pp.

viii. New York, 25 October 1770. Same, by rector and inhabitants of City of New York in communion of Church of England, with answer. *Copy. Signatory,* Samuel Auchmuty, rector. 2¾ pp.

ix. Same, by minister, elders and deacons of Reformed Protestant French Church in City of New York, with answer. *Copy. Signatories,* Adam de Martel [MS. Martlet] and five others. 2¼ pp.

x. Same, by Marine Society of City of New York, with answer. *Copy.* 2 pp.

xi. New York, 25 October 1770. Same, by Old Church of Jesus Christ baptized on personal profession of faith, with answer. *Copy. Signatory,* John Carman, clerk. 1½ pp.

xii. New York, 24 October 1770. Same, by minister, churchwardens and vestrymen of Ancient Lutheran Church of City of New York, with answer. *Copy. Signatory,* Bernard Michael Houseal. 2¼ pp.

xiii. New York 25 October 1770. Same, by minister, elders and deacons of Reformed Protestant Dutch Church of City of New York, with answer. *Copy. Signatory,* Archibald Laidlie. 2 pp.

xiv. New York, 1 November 1770. Proclamation by Governor Earl of Dunmore for apprehension of rioters who on 26 September 1770 interrupted work of commissioners of New York appointed to partition land called Wallumschaack on east side of Hudson River in Albany County. *Printed.* 1 large p.

xv. New York, 11 November 1770. Affidavit sworn before Whitehead Hicks, mayor, by William Bedlow of New York, mariner. It was reported at Kingston that between twenty and twenty-five people a day were dying of plague in Port au Prince, Leogane, and elsewhere in St Domingue. *Signed.* 1½ pp. [C.O.5, 1101, fos. 106–137d; entry of covering letter in C.O.5, 1138, pp. 166–172; signed duplicate of covering letter, dated 5 December 1770, and copies of Nos. i–ii, iv–vi, viii, xiii–xiv, in C.O.5, 1075, fos. 93–110d]

711

14 November, Whitehall

Commissioners for Trade and Plantations to the King, recommending Paul Wentworth to be of the Council in New Hampshire. *Signatories,* Hillsborough, Soame Jenyns, William Fitzherbert, Robert Spencer, W. Northey. 1 p. [C.O.5, 943, p. 20; draft in C.O.5, 896, fos. 154–155d]

712

14 November, Whitehall

Same to Governor Lord Botetourt, requiring explanation of omission from Act to divide Hamilton parish of provision for disposal of money from sale of glebe. *Entry. Signatories,* Hillsborough, William Fitzherbert, Robert Spencer, William Northey. 1 p. [C.O.5, 1369, p. 41; draft in C.O.5, 1336, fos. 174–175d]

713

14 November

John Pownall to Attorney- and Solicitor-General, requesting opinion on Act passed in Pennsylvania to dissolve marriage of Curtis and Ann Grubb. *Entry.* 1½ pp. [C.O.5, 1296, pp. 364–365]

714

15 November, Whitehall

Earl of Hillsborough to Lieut.-General Thomas Gage (No. 37), acknowledging Nos. 49 and 50. Your conduct in executing Order in Council of 6 July approved. Sir W. Johnson has in some measure averted dangerous Indian confederacy that appeared to be forming. Brigadier Carleton has not yet applied for building citadel at Quebec. Grant to Mining Adventurers has not yet been completed. *Draft.* 2½ pp. [C.O.5, 88, fos. 160–161d; entry in C.O.5, 241, pp. 352–354]

715

15 November, Whitehall

Same to Governor James Grant (No. 33). Your appointments of members of Council of East Florida will be confirmed by H.M. with seniority now held; but until then they cannot be considered senior to those who have the King's warrant and government in your absence cannot devolve on them. *Draft.* 2 pp. [C.O.5, 551, fos. 67–68d; entry in C.O.5, 566, pp. 35–37]

716

15 November, Whitehall

Same to same (No. 34), acknowledging No. 37. Bills drawn for repair of court-house will be accepted by Crown agent. In any future treaty with Indians, return of runaway slaves will be proper stipulation. *Draft.* 1¼ pp. [C.O.5, 551, fos. 69–70d; entry in C.O.5, 566, p. 38]

717

15 November, Whitehall

Same to Governor Lord Charles Montagu. In present delicate situation, you are to repair immediately to your government. *Draft.* ½ p. [C.O.5, 393, fos. 113–114d; entry in C.O.5, 408, p. 51]

718

15 November, Whitehall

* Same to Governor Thomas Hutchinson (No. 43), acknowledging Nos. 23–27. Your measures relative to Castle William approved. Resolution of Assembly to sit at Cambridge induces hope that disorders are drawing to a period. No intention of making public letters to this office which can inconvenience you. *Entry.* 1½ pp. [C.O.5, 765, pp. 189–190; draft in C.O.5, 759, fos. 292–293d]

719

15 November, Whitehall

Same to Governor Lord William Campbell (No. 42), acknowledging Nos. 63–65 and papers. *Draft.* ½ p. [C.O.217, 47, fos. 66–67d; entry in C.O.218, 25, p. 80]

720

15 November, Whitehall

Same to Governor Lord Botetourt (No. 38). Person mentioned in your No. 38 has been delivered to me. *Draft.* ½ p. [C.O.5, 1348, fos. 151–152d; entry in C.O.5, 1375, p. 112]

721

15 November, Whitehall

Same to Governor James Wright (No. 34), acknowledging Nos. 46–48. Your attention to preventing introduction to Georgia of Boston doctrines, approved. Disputes between Indians and back-settlers are to be expected as long as colonial legislatures fail to enact necessary laws. I cannot advise sending Creek headmen to England. *Draft.* 1½ pp. [C.O.5, 660, fos. 143–144d; entry in C.O.5, 677, pp. 47–48]

722

15 November, Whitehall

Same to Governor William Franklin (No. 27), acknowledging No. 23. *Draft.* ½ p. [C.O.5, 990, fos. 87–88d; entry in C.O.5, 1003, p. 34]

723

15 November, Whitehall

Same to Lieut.-Governor William Bull (No. 41), acknowledging No. 35. Resolutions of Lower House of Assembly of South Carolina on Committee's report are as ill-founded as they are unbecoming. However, their agent will be given every facility. Adhere to directions in exercise of negative in passing money-bills. *Draft.* 1 p. [C.O.5, 393, fos. 111–112d; entry in C.O.5, 408, p. 50]

724

15 November, Whitehall

Same to Deputy Governor John Penn (No. 24), acknowledging No. 23. Resolutions of 19 July are expressed in unbecoming terms but I am happy to find by late advices that example has in some degree removed prejudice. *Draft.* ½ p. [C.O.5, 1283, fos. 13–14d; entry in C.O.5, 1301, p. 126]

725

15 November, Whitehall

Same to Deputy Governor Robert Eden (No. 20), acknowledging Nos. 7–8. I am sorry that expressions in my No. 19 were considered as conveying censure of your conduct. Military rank must be solicited elsewhere. Some of the laws you sent require very mature consideration. *Draft.* 1¼ pp. [C.O.5, 1283, fos. 64–65d; entry in C.O.5, 1301, pp. 14–15]

726

15 November, Whitehall

Same to Sir William Johnson (No. 15), acknowledging No. 14. Advantage of preventing Six Nations from engaging in war with Western Indians and confederating with Southern Indians depends on answer given by Six Nations to proposals of Western Indians. *Draft.* 1¾ pp. [C.O.5, 71, Pt. 2, fos. 87–88d; entry in C.O.5, 241, pp. 354–355]

727

15 November, Whitehall

Same to Samuel Holland (No. 5), acknowledging Nos. 5–6, with plans. Your leaving Mr Wright to survey coast from Chaleur Bay to Bay Verte was proper. *Draft.* 1 p. [C.O.5, 71, Pt. 2, fos. 89–90d; entry in C.O.5, 241, p. 356]

728

15 November, Whitehall

* Circular. Same to Governors of Quebec, New York, New Jersey, Virginia, North Carolina and Pennsylvania, notifying complaints of Six Nations against traders and frontier inhabitants. Colonies must find some means of regulating Indian affairs. *Draft.* 2 pp. [C.O.5, 71, Pt. 2, fos. 83–84d; entry in C.O.5, 241, pp. 350–351]

729

15 November, Whitehall

Circular. Same to General Gage and governors of colonies, sending copy of King's speech to Parliament on 13th inst. Spanish matter is still in doubt. *Draft.* 1 p. [C.O.5, 71, Pt. 2, fos. 85–86d; entry in C.O.5, 241, p. 349]

730

15 November, Virginia

President William Nelson to Earl of Hillsborough (No. 6). Since 1749 there has been no competent jurisdiction in colony for trial of pirates: sending accused to England is expensive, and in Ferguson's case principal witnesses absconded. We have no regular means of removing scandalous clergy. *Signed.* 3 pp. *Endorsed*, R, 31 December. *Enclosed:*

   i. Query: whether General Court of Virginia can suspend or deprive clergy. 1 small p. [C.O.5, 1348, fos. 185–188d; entry of covering letter in C.O.5, 1372, pp. 139–143]

731

16 November, St James's

Order of King in Council, appointing Paul Wentworth to be of the Council in New Hampshire. *Copy.* ¾ p. *Endorsed,* Recd. 12 December, Read 21 December 1772. [C.O.5, 930, fos. 156–157d; entry of warrant, dated 20 November, in C.O.324, 42, p. 222; sealed original of Order in C.O.5, 26, fos. 131–132d]

732

17 November, Portsmouth

Governor John Byron to Earl of Hillsborough. Complaints received that French in Newfoundland deny bait to English. I shall send King's ship earlier next year. Measures have been taken to stop interruption of French fishery on Sundays. *Signed.* 2½ pp. *Endorsed*, R, 19 November. *Enclosed:*

   i. 8 May 1769. Order by Governor Byron regulating the taking of bait. *Printed.* 1 p. [C.O.194, 29, fos. 71–73d; entry of covering letter in C.O.195, 12, pp. 103–104]

733

17 November, Bath

Governor Lord Charles Montagu to Earl of Hillsborough. I am ready
to obey H.M.'s commands. My health is better but far from established.
Signed. 1 small p. *Endorsed,* R, 19 November. [C.O.5, 393, fos. 115–
116d; entry in C.O.5, 409, p. 144]

734

19 November, New York

Governor Earl of Dunmore to Earl of Hillsborough (No. 3), enclosing
following. *Signed.* 1 p. *Endorsed,* R, 7 January 1771. *Enclosed:*

i. 17 November 1770. Minutes of Council of New York recording
consideration of petition of Frederick Philips, proprietor of manor of
Philipsburg, Westchester County, seeking lease of royal mines in that
manor. Council considered a former petition in 1763. *Copy,* certified
by G. Banyar, deputy clerk. 1¼ pp.

ii. 15 June 1763. Same, recording consideration of petition of Charles
Scott and Henry Holding, both of London, and memorial of Frederick Philipse. *Copy,* certified as No. i. 5¾ pp. [C.O.5, 1102, fos. 3–10d;
entry of covering letter in C.O.5, 1138, pp. 180–181; copy of covering
letter, endorsed Recd., Read 13 February 1771, and copies of
enclosures, in C.O.5, 1075, fos. 68–74d; signed duplicate of covering
letter, dated 5 December 1770, endorsed Original not recd., and
copies of enclosures, in C.O.5, 1075, fos. 111–118d]

735

20 November, Boston

* Governor Thomas Hutchinson to Earl of Hillsborough (No. 29),
reporting prorogation of General Court to 2 January, and proceedings
thereof. Council have chosen Mr Bollan as agent, and House of Representatives Dr Franklin or, in case of refusal, Dr Lee. Distinct agents
for the two branches of legislature is unnecessary and unconstitutional.
Inventory of stores at Castle William and minutes of evidence of Captain Preston's trial, enclosed. Trial of the soldiers has been delayed
some days. *Signed.* 1½ pp. *Endorsed,* R, 24 December. *Enclosed:*

i. Inventory of stores at Castle William at entry of regular troops,
taken by John Phillips and Joseph Goldthwait. *Copy.* 29 pp.

ii. 24–27 October 1770. Summary of evidence in the King *v.* Preston
on indictment for murder.
  Witnesses for the King: Edward Garrish, Colonel Marshall,
Thomas Hubbard, Ebenezer Hinkley, Peter Cunningham, Cruik-
shanks, Wyat, John Cole, Theodore Bliss, Henry Knox, Benjamin
Burdise, Fullerton, Daniel Calef, Robert Godard, Obadiah Whiston,
Diman Morton, Nathaniel Fosdick, Austin, Langsford, Archbald,
Isaac Pierce, Joseph Belknap, Jonathan Mason.

Witnesses for the prisoner: William Johnson, Edward Hill, Benjamin Davis, Joseph Edwards, John Frost, Bemjamin Lee, Richard Palmes, Theodore Bliss (recalled), Matthew Murray, Andrew, a negro servant, John Coffin, Theodore Bliss (recalled), Jack, a negro servant, Daniel Cornwall, William Sawyer of Bolton, Jane Whitehouse, Newton Prince, negro, James Woodall, Joseph Helyer, Captain James Gifford, Thomas Handaside Peck, John Gillespie, Lieut.-Governor Hutchinson. 25¼ pp.

iii. Proceedings of Council and House of Representatives of Massachusetts, 10–20 November 1770, concerning land east of Sagadahoc. *Copy*, certified by John Cotton, deputy-secretary. 3 pp.

iv. *Massachusetts Gazette and Boston Weekly Newsletter*, 22 November 1770, reporting proceedings of Assembly. *Printed*. 4 pp.

v. Accounts of Harrison Gray, Treasurer and Receiver-General of Massachusetts, May 1770–May 1771. *Copy*, certified by Thomas Flucker, secretary. 19 large pp. [Covering letter and enclosures i–iv in C.O.5, 759, fos. 335–372d; enclosure v, signed duplicate of covering letter, and copies of enclosures iii and iv, in C.O.5, 894, pp. 219–250; entry of covering letter in C.O.5, 768, pp. 172–174]

736

21 November, Whitehall

Earl of Hillsborough to Governor Lord Charles Montagu. In present situation in South Carolina, it is important that the governor be on the spot. How soon will you be ready to embark? *Draft*. ¾ p. [C.O.5, 393, fos. 117–118d; entry in C.O.5, 408, pp. 51–52]

737

21 November, Whitehall

Commissioners for Trade and Plantations to the King, recommending disallowance of Act passed in South Carolina in 1767 for establishing parish of St Luke in Granville County, parish of All Saints in Craven County, and chapel of ease in parish of St Frederick, which augments number of Assembly by allowing each parish to send two representatives. *Draft. Signatories*, Hillsborough, Soame Jenyns, W. Fitzherbert, Robert Spencer, Greville, W. Northey. 1½ pp. [C.O.5, 381, fos. 358–359d; entry in C.O.5, 404, pp. 436–437]

738

21 November, Whitehall

Same to same, recommending approval of private Act passed in Virginia in 1765 and of eight others passed in 1770. *Entry. Signatories*, as preceding. 3½ pp. [C.O.5, 1369, pp. 42–45; draft in C.O.5, 1336, fos. 178–179d]

739

21 November, Whitehall

Same to same, recommending approval of Act passed in Virginia in 1764 to dock entail of lands of Richard Todd. *Entry. Signatories,* as preceding. 1½ pp. [C.O.5, 1369, pp. 46–47; draft in C.O.5, 1336, fos. 176–177d]

740

21 November, Whitehall

Same to same, recommending disallowance of Act passed in South Carolina in 1769 for issuing £106,500 in bills of credit. *Draft. Signatories,* as preceding. 1¼ pp. [C.O.5, 381, fos. 356–357d; entry in C.O.5, 404, pp. 434–435]

741

[21 November]

Memorial of Edward Bell to Commissioners for Trade and Plantations, praying for grant of 80,000 acres of waste land in back-lands of Virginia. ½ large p. *Endorsed,* Read 21 November 1770. [C.O.5, 1333, fos. 57–57A dorse]

742

23 November, Whitehall

Commissioners for Trade and Plantations to the King, recommending disallowance of Act passed in Virginia in 1769 for paying Burgesses for last convention and present session of Assembly. Convention was illegal and unconstitutional. *Entry.* 2 pp. *Signatories,* Hillsborough, Soame Jenyns, William Fitzherbert, Robert Spencer, Greville, W. Northey. 2 pp. [C.O.5, 1369, pp. 48–49; draft in C.O.5, 1336, fos. 180–181d]

743

23 November, Whitehall

* Same to same, recommending disallowance of Act passed in Virginia in 1769 for laying additional duty on slaves imported. Act for better support of contingent charges of government to be permitted to expire by its own limitations. Governor to be instructed not to assent to any law increasing duty on slaves imported. *Entry. Signatories,* as preceding. 5 pp. [C.O.5, 1369, pp. 50–54; draft in C.O.5, 1336, fos. 182–185d, copy at fos. 186–188d]

744

23 November, Whitehall

Same to same, reporting on bill to amend manner of electing members in Commons House of Georgia, passed in 1770 by Assembly, assented to by Council but rejected by Governor Wright as contrary to his instructions. We have no objection to bill except to clause limiting duration of Assembly to three years. *Entry. Signatories,* Soame Jenyns, William Fitzherbert, Greville, Robert Spencer, W. Northey. 5 pp. [C.O.5, 674, pp. 347–351]

745

23 November, Whitehall

Same to same, reporting on bill passed by Council and Assembly of Georgia in 1770 which alters elections by allowing vote to proprietors of town-lots, taxable equal to fifty acres of land; by directing voting to be by ballot; by qualifying persons possessed of £300 value in houses, town-lots etc. or lands to serve as representatives; and by limiting duration of Assembly to three years. The governor rejected it, but thinks all alterations beneficial except the last. Propose that the governor be empowered to consent to such a bill, save only for clause limiting duration. *Seal. Signed,* as preceding. 5 pp. [C.O.5, 660, fos. 145–148d; entry in C.O.5, 678, pp. 197–201]

746

[23 November]

Petition of Helen Maria Timberlake, widow of Lieutenant Henry Timberlake, to Commissioners for Trade and Plantations, for 6000 acres of land in West Florida. *Signed.* 1 p. *Endorsed,* Recd., Read 23 November 1770. [C.O.5, 577, pp. 445–448]

747

26 November, St James's

Order of King in Council, approving Act passed in Virginia in 1770 to vest lands in David Meade in fee simple. Like Orders confirming nine private Acts passed in Virginia 1764–1770. *Copy.* 2¼ pp. *Endorsed,* Recd. 12 December, Read 21 December 1772. [C.O.5, 1334, fos. 9–10d]

748

26 November, Whitehall

Earl of Hillsborough to Board of Ordnance. I am waiting to hear from Admiralty and Lieut.-General Gage whether men can be made available for works on fort at St John's. Meanwhile, begin on fortified battery and barracks, and insert in estimates sums necessary for them. *Draft.* 2 pp. [C.O.194, 29, fos. 69–70d; entry in C.O.195, 15, pp. 36–37]

749

26 November, Whitehall

Same to Postmaster-General. American packet-boats at Falmouth to be prepared for sea. Dispatches will be ready in three or four days. *Draft.* ½ p. [C.O.5, 71, Pt. 2, fos. 123–124d; entry in C.O.5, 241, p. 357]

750

26 November, Charleston

Lieut.-Governor William Bull to Earl of Hillsborough (No. 37), soliciting remission of fine imposed on Gilbert Campbell for killing a negro boy. *Signed.* 2 pp. *Endorsed,* R, 9 January 1771. [C.O.5, 394, fos. 3–4d; entry in C.O.5, 409, pp. 162–164]

751

27 November, Whitehall

Order of Committee of Council for Plantation Affairs referring following to Commissioners for Trade and Plantations. *Seal. Signed,* W. Blair. ¾ p. *Endorsed,* Recd. 27 November, Read 28 November 1770. *Enclosed:*

> i. Memorial of Earl of Dartmouth, on behalf of himself, Hon. George Legge, Charles Legge, William Legge and Hennage Legge, to the King, praying for grant of 100,000 acres of land in East Florida, to make settlements. *Copy.* 1 p. [C.O.5, 544, fos. 185–188d]

752

28 November, Whitehall

Commissioners for Trade and Plantations to the King, recommending that petition of Helen Maria Timberlake, widow of Lieutenant Henry Timberlake, for 6000 acres of land in West Florida, be granted. *Entry. Signatories,* Hillsborough, Soame Jenyns, William Fitzherbert, W. Northey. 2 pp. [C.O.5, 600, pp. 214–215]

753

28 November, Whitehall

John Pownall to Clerk of Council in Waiting, sending extract of letter from General Gage concerning mining company on Lake Superior, and address of House of Burgesses of Virginia relating to copper coin. *Draft.* ¾ p. [C.O.5, 71, Pt. 2, fos. 125–126d; entry in C.O.5, 241, pp. 357–358]

754

28 November, Treasury

John Robinson to John Pownall, sending papers relating to Engineer

John Campbell's application for payment for surveys of Mississippi, Iberville etc., and asking if payment should be made. *Entry.* 1¼ pp. [C.O.5, 620, pp. 271–272]

755

28 November, Charleston

* John Stuart to Earl of Hillsborough, reporting congress with Cherokees at Lochaber on 18 October and sharp practice by Virginians to get land. I did not obtain all within my instructions. Indians offered land on Ohio, which I refused. *Signed.* 3½ pp. *Endorsed,* R, 9 January 1771. *Enclosed :*

> * i. Lochaber, 18 October 1770. Report of meeting of principal chiefs and warriors of Cherokee nation with John Stuart. *Copy.* 12½ pp.

> ii. Treaty, same date, made at this congress for cession of land to Virginia. *Copy. Signatories,* John Stuart, Occonnastotah, Kittagusta, Attahkullakulla, Kaheatoy, Wolf of Keowee, Uka Youla, Chukanuctas, Teutchkee, Kinnatitah, Tiftoy, Tarrapin, Ecuij, Skahloske, Chinista, Chinista Watoga, Otacite of Higwassie, William Ogilvy, secretary. 4½ pp.

> iii. Further report of proceedings of this congress. *Copy.* 4¼ pp.

> iv. 17 August 1770. Extract of minutes of Council of Virginia, concerning cession of land, letter of Occonnastotah, and governor's reply. *Copy.* 7½ pp.

> v. 18 August 1770. Governor Lord Botetourt to Occonistotoh, head warrior of Cherokees, concerning cession of land. *Copy.* 1 p.

> vi. Williamsburg, 18 August 1770. Same to Colonel Andrew Lewis, notifying forthcoming meeting with John Stuart and Cherokees. *Copy.* ½ p.

> * vii. New York, 16 October 1770. General Thomas Gage to John Stuart, reporting congress at Siota by Shawnese and Western Indians. Scheme of Shawnese to form confederacy of all Western and Southern Indians is a notable piece of policy. At congress of Six Nations and Northern Indians war against Western Indians was strongly proposed. PS. I am informed Cherokee deputies engaged for their nation with Six Nations and Northern Indians. *Copy.* 2¾ pp. [C.O.5, 72, fos. 20–42d; entry of covering letter in C.O.5, 228, pp. 1–5]

756

29 November, Charleston

Same to same, acknowledging No. 18. M. de Monberaut was appointed deputy for Indian affairs in West Florida in 1764. His memorial is indecent, illiberal and scurrilous. Account of his conduct in office. *Signed.* 10½ pp. *Endorsed,* R, 9 January 1771. *Enclosed :*

i. New York, 31 March 1764. Abstract of letter from General Gage to John Stuart recommending M. de Monberaut. *Copy*. 1 p.

ii. Mobile, 3 January 1765. Abstract of letter from John Stuart to General Gage, notifying M. de Monberaut's appointment as deputy. *Copy*. 1 p.

iii. Mobile, 24 January 1765. Abstract of letter from John Stuart to John Pownall, reporting above appointment. *Copy*. 1½ pp.

iv. Undated instruction by John Stuart to M. de Monberaut, relative to Indian affairs. *Copy*. 2½ pp.

v. Receipts by M. de Monberaut for sums paid for salary and stores. *Copy*. 3 pp.

vi. Charleston, 30 August 1765. Abstract of letter from John Stuart to General Gage, notifying M. de Monberaut's suspension from office. *Copy*. 3½ pp.

vii. Pensacola, 15 July 1765. Governor George Johnston to John Stuart, notifying M. de Monberaut's suspension. *Copy*. 1½ pp.

viii. Mobile, 19 June 1765. Chevalier de Montaut de Monberaut to Governor Johnston and John Stuart, complaining. *French. Copy.* 7 pp.

ix. Pensacola, 26 June 1765. Governor Johnston to M. de Monberaut, replying to No. viii article by article. *Copy*. 15¼ pp.

x. Pensacola, 27 June 1765. Letter from Governor Johnston. The question is how to get rid of M. de Monberaut with best grace. *Copy*. 2½ pp.

xi. New Orleans, 29 July 1765. Letter from M. de Monberaut, defending his character and attacking John Stuart's. *French. Copy.* 3 pp.

xii. New York, 26 February 1767. Abstract of letter from General Gage to John Stuart, notifying claims for money by M. de Monberaut, who intends to complain to H.M. *Copy*. 1½ pp.

xiii. 24 March 1767. Abstract of letter from John Stuart to General Gage, recounting circumstances of M. de Monberaut's dismissal. *Copy*. 5 pp.

xiv. New York, 8 May 1767. Abstract of letter from General Gage to John Stuart. It appears that M. de Monberaut has been very well paid for his services. *Copy*. ½ p. [C.O.5, 72, fos. 43–80d; entry of covering letter in C.O.5, 228, pp. 6–20]

757

29 November, Falmouth

George Beale to Anthony Todd. *Duke of Cumberland, Eagle* and *Anna Teresa* packet-boats are preparing for sea. *Entry*. ¾ p. [C.O.5, 247, pp. 2–3]

758

30 November, Ordnance-office

★ Board of Ordnance to Earl of Hillsborough. Captain Debbieg informed us it will require three years to finish battery at St John's, two years to finish barracks, four years for whole works if done with masonry; or three years, including barracks, if fort is done with earth. In which mode should works be carried on? It may be proper to make matter subject to subsequent and separate estimates, the annual estimate being required on Monday. *Signed,* H. S. Conway, Charles Frederick, W. R. Earle, Charles Cocks, A. Wilkinson. 4½ pp. *Endorsed,* R, 1 December. [C.O.194, 29, fos. 74–77d; entry in C.O.195, 12, pp. 105–108]

759

30 November, Boston

Governor Thomas Hutchinson to Earl of Hillsborough (No. 30), enclosing following. I have written to sheriff of Lincoln County to appoint deputy at Machias. If not checked, these settlers may be as dangerous as Regulators in North Carolina. I cannot find spoil has yet been made on trees fit for masts or bowsprits. No disposition yet in Council or House of Representatives to eject intruders. *Signed.* 1¼ pp. *Endorsed,* R, 30 December. *Enclosed:*

i. Machias, 8 November 1770. Petition of Jonathan Longfellow, J.P. for Lincoln County, to Lieut.-Governor Hutchinson, setting forth difficulties of his office. He has been attacked and beaten, and unless supported must resign. *Signed.* 2¼ pp.

ii. Machias, 9 November 1770. Petition of inhabitants to Lieut.-Governor Hutchinson, representing disorders of the place especially attack on Jonathan Longfellow and absolute necessity of another J.P. in this place. *Signed.* 3 pp. [C.O.5, 759, fos. 373–378d; entry of covering letter in C.O.5, 768, pp. 175–177; signed duplicate of covering letter in C.O.5, 894, pp. 251–254]

760

30 November, Charleston

★ Lieut.-Governor William Bull to Earl of Hillsborough (No. 38), reporting on present state of South Carolina. Counties and judicial divisions described. Church of England: how clergy are appointed. Dissenters strong in back country. Council slightly regarded by Assembly. Courts of justice described: six circuit-courts to be established for remote parts. No Court of Exchequer. Laws regarding slaves; no insurrection since 1739. Militia about 10,000 men in 10 regiments. Defences of Charleston described. 1292 houses, 5030 whites, 5831 blacks, in Charleston. Defences of Port Royal described. Literature in infancy: no good grammar-school. Charleston Library near 2000 volumes. Agriculture very prosperous. Rice crop: 120–140,000 barrels.

Indigo: 500,000 lbs a year. Hemp, flax, tobacco, madder, silk, olives, vines, apples produced. When land of province is all taken up, it may be proper to buy land from Cherokee boundary westward to Keowee. Negroes: 72,178. Land: 2,678,454 acres, and several hundred thousand more granted, perhaps chiefly to non-residents. Commerce keeps pace with agriculture: near 500 sail employed and 3–4000 negroes imported annually. Interest, eight per cent. Exchange with England: £700 currency to £100 sterling. Cherokees more important politically than commercially, as barrier to Indians on Ohio and Illinois, and counterbalance to Creeks. No Indians, except a few Cattawbas within 300 miles of coast. Public spirit in office-holding. *Signed.* 30 pp. *Endorsed,* R, 9 January 1771. [C.O.5, 394, fos. 5–20d; entry in C.O.5, 409, pp. 165–208]

761

[*30 November*]

Memorial of Lieutenant Benjamin Roberts, late commissary of Indian affairs under Sir W. Johnson, to Earl of Hillsborough, setting forth his services since 1759 and soliciting employment in that department or elsewhere. *Signed.* 7¼ pp. *Enclosed,* R, 30 November. [C.O.5, 114, fos. 90–93d; receipt noted in C.O.5, 620, p. 273]

762

1 December, Charleston

John Thomas, deputy superintendent of Indian affairs for Mississippi, to Earl of Hillsborough, acknowledging appointment. Hopes to bring Arkansas to act in conjunction with Chickasaws and form barrier to protect East and West Florida. Mr Stuart has four deputy superintendents for his district; Spaniards have superintendent and three deputies for Mississippi alone, all French officers. *Signed.* 1 p. *Endorsed,* R, 9 January 1771. [C.O.5, 72, fos. 16–17d; entry in C.O.5, 227, pp. 354–356]

763

2 December, Charleston

* John Stuart to Earl of Hillsborough (No. 28), acknowledging No. 19. By enclosed letters, it appears that there was no ground for apprehending danger from Indians in West Florida. I shall continue inquiry into two whites found dead between Creek nation and Pensacola. Mediation between Choctaws and Creeks justified. Commissaries to restrain traders are needed, also deputy for small Indian nations of the Mississippi, also presents for Indians. Lieut.-Governor Durnford wants an extended boundary, Choctaws want a congress. *Signed.* PS. Report on murder of two whites last summer at Occonni in affray between hunting Indians and back-settlers of Georgia. Whites were the aggressors. 8 pp. *Endorsed,* R, 9 January 1771. *Enclosed:*

* i. Pensacola, 17 June 1770. Charles Stuart to John Stuart, reporting meeting with Emistisiguo. *Copy.* 6 pp.

* ii. Mobile, 26 August 1770. Abstract of letter from same to same. Euchees have attacked Choctaws. Bad consequences of liquor trade. Spaniards not troublesome as to Indian matters. Indians press for congress. Eighty Virginians and North Carolinians have settled at Natchez. *Copy.* 4½ pp.

iii. Pensacola, 27 September 1770. Abstract of letter from same to same. Uncertainty of peace between Creeks and Choctaws. Congress expected. No more news of Western Indians. I wish you could send to Latchaway Indians and Lower Creeks to stop them going to war against Choctaws. *Copy.* 2 pp.

iv. Mobile, 26 August 1770. Talk from Charles Stuart to headmen and warriors of Creek nation, sending talk from Choctaws and counselling peace. *Copy.* 1½ pp.

v. New York, 19 September 1770. Abstract of letter from General Gage to John Stuart. Proposal for additional £150 a year for officer in Chickasaw nation has been mentioned to Lord Hillsborough. *Copy.* ½ p.

vi. September 1770. Abstract of talk from Creek Indians to Charles Stuart, in reply to No. iv. *Copy. Signatory,* Emistisiguo. 2¼ pp.

vii. Great Tallassie, 1 October 1770. Talk from headmen and warriors of Creek nation. Neither we nor the Choctaws can live without English assistance. It is not the people but renegades that create disturbances. *Copy.* 1¾ p.

viii. Estimate by John Stuart of annual cost of deputy for Indian affairs on the Mississippi Lakes Pontchartrain and Maurepas: £602 12s. 10d. ½ p.

* ix. Charleston, 25 November 1770. Talk from John Stuart to head warriors of Upper Creeks. Line between Virginia and Cherokees has been settled. Murders, as at Occoni, must be punished. Pains I have been at to reconcile Creeks and Choctaws must convince you that your white brethren have never acted as instruments of dissension with red. Talks with Shawnese and other Western Indians should have been communicated to me. *Copy.* 2¾ pp.

x. Downs, 11 September 1769. Abstract of letter from Lieut.-Governor Durnford to John Stuart, on need for congresses in West Florida with Choctaws and Creeks. *Copy.* ½ p.

xi. Augusta, 5 October 1770. Abstract of letter from Samuel Thomas, trader in Creek nation, reporting investigation of murder of two whites by Upper Creeks and burning of Indians' houses at Occoni. Expenses sought. *Copy.* ½ p.

* xii. Undated talk from Emistisiguo to Charles Stuart, sending token of friendship to be presented to Choctaws. *Copy.* 1¼ pp.

xiii. Undated talk [from Creeks to Choctaws] explaining token of friendship, and hoping for peace. *Copy.* 3½ pp. [C.O.5, 72, fos. 81–114d; entry of covering letter in C.O.5, 228, pp. 21–32]

764

3 December, Whitehall

Earl of Hillsborough to Attorney- and Solicitor-General, requesting opinion whether H.M. may in time of peace lay embargo on ships in colonial ports laded with provisions and warlike stores, and if so how. *Draft.* 1 p. [C.O.5, 71, Pt. 2, fos. 131–132d; entry in C.O.5, 241, p. 358]

765

3 December, Whitehall

Same to Board of Ordnance. Begin with construction of battery at St John's, Newfoundland, and destruction of cove at Quiddi-Viddi. Construction is to be in such manner as that the service may be completed as soon as possible. *Draft.* 1 p. [C.O.194, 29, fos. 78–79d; entry in C.O.195, 15, p. 38]

766

3 December, Whitehall

John Pownall to Messrs. Makens of Ypres. Your letter will be laid before Privy Council. *Draft.* ½ p. [C.O.5, 71, Pt. 2, fos. 137–138d; entry in C.O.5, 241, p. 359]

767

3 December, Whitehall

Same to Clerk of Council in Waiting, enclosing following to be laid before H.M. in Council. *Draft.* ½ p. *Enclosed :*

i. Ypres, 16 November 1770. Messieurs Makens & Co. to Commissioners for Trade and Plantations, requesting permission to ship rags to London. *Copy.* 2 pp. [C.O.5, 71, Pt. 2, fos. 133–136d; entry of covering letter in C.O.5, 241, p. 359]

768

4 December, Whitehall

Order of Committee of Council for Plantation Affairs, directing Commissioners for Trade and Plantations to prepare draft of additional instruction for governor of Virginia not to assent to any law whereby duty on slaves imported shall be increased. *Seal. Signed,* Stephen Cottrell. 1 p. *Endorsed,* Recd., Read 5 December 1770. [C.O.5, 1333, fos. 58–58A dorse]

769

4 December

Attorney- and Solicitor-General to Earl of Hillsborough. H.M. may lay embargo before war is declared, either by proclamation or by Order in Council. *Signed,* William de Grey, E. Thurlow. 1½ pp. *Endorsed,* R, 7 December. [C.O.5, 71, Pt. 2, fos. 139–140d; entry in C.O.5, 227, pp. 303–305]

770

4 December, Whitehall

John Pownall to Anthony Todd. American packets at Falmouth to be detained to Saturday. *Entry.* ½ p. [C.O.5, 241, p. 360]

771

5 December, Whitehall

Commissioners for Trade and Plantations to Committee of Privy Council for Plantation Affairs, recommending grant of 20,000 acres of land in East Florida to each of the following: Earl of Dartmouth, Hon. George Legge commonly Lord Lewisham, Charles Legge, William Legge, and Hennage Legge. *Entry. Signatories,* Hillsborough, Soame Jenyns, W. Northey, William Fitzherbert. 3 pp. [C.O.5, 563, pp. 280–282]

772

5 December, Whitehall

Same to same, enclosing following. *Entry. Signatories,* as preceding. 1 p. *Enclosed :*

i. Draft of additional instruction to Governor Lord Botetourt, not to assent to any law whereby duty on slaves imported is increased or importation obstructed. *Entry.* 2½ pp. [C.O.5, 1369, pp. 55–58; draft in C.O.5, 1336, fos. 189–192d]

773

5 December, New York

Separate. Lieut.-General Thomas Gage to Earl of Hillsborough, acknowledging duplicate of separate letter of 28 September respecting labour for building in Newfoundland. Garrison at Halifax might in peacetime supply men required for labour, but not artificers. Contract with people in New Hampshire might be cheaper. Because of climate, season for mason's work in Newfoundland is May to August, and ground is too hard for the spade by end of September. *Signed.* 1¾ pp. *Endorsed,* R, 7 January 1771. [C.O.5, 89, fos. 7–8d; entry in C.O.5, 234, pp. 161–163]

774

5 December, Boston

Governor Thomas Hutchinson to Earl of Hillsborough (No. 31). Six soldiers are acquitted, two found guilty of manslaughter. By evidence as I have received it there was no room for the distinction. The judges conducted with great firmness and explained the law in most public manner. Mr Murray and Captain Preston go for England. Minutes of evidence, though inaccurately taken, are enclosed; correct account of trial is preparing for the press. Face of affairs more favourable than for eighteen months past. *Signed.* 2½ small pp. *Endorsed,* R, 30 December. *Enclosed:*

i. 27–29 November 1770. Summary of evidence in King *v.* Mathew Kilroy *et al.*, soldiers in 29th regiment, on five indictments for murder.

Witnesses: Jonathan William Austin, Ebenezer Bridgeham, James Dodge, Samuel Clarke, Edward Langsford, town watchman, Francis Archbald jnr., James Brewer, Samuel Commons, James Baily, Richard Palmes, John Danbrook, Jedediah Bass, Thomas Wilkinson, Josiah Simpson [*Marginal note:* this witness delivered his evidence as a schoolboy does his lesson and no credit was given to it], Nathaniel Fosdick, Samuel Hemmingway, Joseph Helyer, Nicholas Ferreter, Benjamin Burdick, Robert Williams, Bartholomew Kneeland, Nathaniel Thayer, Nathaniel Appleton, John Appleton, Colonel Marshall, Joseph Croswell, James Carter, Jonathan Cary, James Crawford, Archibald Gould, William Hunter, David Michelson, John Short, Benjamin Davis, Shubael Hughes, James Selkrig, Archibald Bowman, William Dickson, John Gillespie, Thomas Knight, James Cookson, William Strong, Dr Richard Hirons, Captain Goldfinch, Benjamin Davis jnr., James Thompson, Alexander Crookshanks, Lieutenant William Carter, Patrick Keaton, William Davis, sergeant-major, 14th regiment, Nathaniel Russell, John Cox, Henry Knox, John Buckley, Benjamin Leigh, John Frost, William Boatswain, James Whaddell, Daniel Cornwall, John Ruddock, Newton Prince, Gregory Townsend, Andrew, Oliver Wendell's negro, Oliver Wendell (as to Andrew's character), William Whittington, Joseph Hinkley, Harrison Gray, Charles Willis, Mathew Murray, Thomas Simmons, William Parker, John Gridley, John Williams, Catherine Field, John Mansfield, Dr John Jeffries, Captain Edmund Mason, Thomas Hall, Captain O'Hara, Theodore Bliss, Henry Bass, Edward Paine. 38½ pp. [C.O.5, 759, fos. 379–402d; entry of covering letter in C.O.5, 768, pp. 177–179; signed duplicate of covering letter in C.O.5, 894, pp. 255–258]

775

5 December, Boston

Same to Earl of Hillsborough (No. 32), repeating part of letter relating to trial of the soldiers. Six were acquitted, two found guilty of man-

slaughter; clergy will be allowed. Sentence not yet passed. *Signed.*
1 small p. *Endorsed,* R, 7 January 1771. [C.O.5, 760, fos. 3–4d; entry
in C.O.5, 768, p. 179]

776

5 December, New York

Governor Earl of Dunmore to Earl of Hillsborough (private), reporting
Mr Colden's refusal to give up half the emoluments of government
between date of governor's commission and arrival in New York.
Attorney-General advises suit in King's name. Mr Colden should be
made to comply with order to account for emoluments, even though
he may be allowed to keep a part. *Duplicate. Signed.* PS. Proxy for
House of Lords with Earl of Hillsborough's name, requested. 1¾ pp.
Endorsed, R, 7 January 1771. [C.O.5, 1102, fos. 15–16d; entry in C.O.5,
1138, pp. 181–183]

777

5 December, New York

Same to same (private). In orders sent on Mr Colden's refusal to
comply with order respecting emoluments of government, no intimation should be made of my particular interest; otherwise there
would be no way of prosecuting the cause in court of Chancery. State
of case enclosed, drawn by Mr Smith. *Duplicate. Signed.* 1 p. *Endorsed,*
R, 7 January 1771. *Enclosed:*

    i. State of the case. 2 small pp. [C.O.5, 1102, fos. 17–20d; entry of
    covering letter in C.O.5, 1138, pp. 183–184]

778

5 December, Charleston

John Stuart to Earl of Hillsborough (No. 29, private), reporting arrival
of Lieutenant Thomas. *Signed.* 1 p. *Endorsed,* R, 9 January 1771.
[C.O.5, 72, fos. 115–116d; entry in C.O.5, 228, pp. 20–21]

779

5 December, Charleston

* Lieut.-Governor William Bull to Earl of Hillsborough (No. 38,
private), acknowledging Nos. 38–39. Names of Mr Pringle, Mr Lowndes and Mr Powell withdrawn from nominees as Associate Judges;
Wellins Calcott, George Milligen and William Henry Drayton proposed instead, all well-affected. Mr Middleton has resigned from
Council. John Bremar proposed as Master in Chancery in place of
William Burrows who has factious connexions. Robert Raper, deputy
naval officer, active in formenting discontent, and William Hales,
his clerk, deserve admonition. Of merchants, Miles Brewton is active

supporter of the resolutions; John Edwards Hawkins, James Laurens and John Marsh are chief of those in this interest for private advantage. John Neufville, chairman, is rather a man of straw. First movers are Thomas Lynch, Christopher Gadsden and John Mackenzie. General meeting summoned by these people for 13th inst. *Signed.* 8 pp. *Endorsed,* R, 13 January 1771. [C.O.5, 394, fos. 21–25d; entry in C.O.5, 409, pp. 150–162]

780

[*5 December*]

Memorial of Edward Bell to Commissioners for Trade and Plantations, setting out claim to receive grant of land in Virginia, with evidence of character. 2½ pp. *Endorsed,* Recd. 5 December, Read 12 December 1770. [C.O.5, 1333, fos. 59–60d]

781

6 December

Richard Jackson to Commissioners for Trade and Plantations, reporting no substantial objection to Act passed in Virginia in 1770 to dock entail of lands whereof Sarah Rootes is seised. *Signed.* 1½ pp. *Endorsed,* Recd. 11 December 1770, Read 7 January 1771. [C.O.5, 1333, fos. 61–62d]

782

6 December, New York

Separate. Lieut.-General Thomas Gage to Earl of Hillsborough, acknowledging No. 34, separate and secret. I shall continue to inquire into supply of arms to people of Boston. *Signed.* ¾ p. *Endorsed,* R, 7 January 1771. [C.O.5, 89, fos. 9–10d; entry in C.O.5, 234, p. 163]

783

6 December, New York

* Governor Earl of Dunmore to Earl of Hillsborough (No. 4), acknowledging duplicate of private and confidential letter, No. 41 not yet to hand. Defences of this city in bad condition, militia unexercised, season too late for works. Further disorders in lands disputed between New York and New Hampshire, paper enclosed. *Signed.* PS. Report of plague in Hispaniola now contradicted. 2¼ pp. *Endorsed,* R, 7 January 1771. *Enclosed:*

i. Albany, 22 November 1770. Affidavit sworn before John R. Bleecker and Abraham Ten Broeck, justices of peace, by Jeremiah Gardner. On 19th inst. deponent was assisting John Wallworth to build house at Walomsack when they were interrupted by armed men [seventeen named], who forced him to fly and destroyed house.

Signed. 2½ pp. [C.O.5, 1102, fos. 11–14d; entry in C.O.5, 1138, pp. 185–188; signed duplicate of covering letter, dated 29 December 1770, with copy of enclosure, in C.O.5, 1075, fos. 119–122d]

784

6 December, New York

Lieut.-Governor Cadwallader Colden to Earl of Hillsborough, asserting his right to emoluments of government claimed by Earl of Dunmore, who has begun action in King's name in Chancery, where he is sole judge. *Signed.* 3½ pp. *Endorsed*, R, 7 January 1771. [C.O.5, 1102, fos. 21–22d; entry in C.O.5, 1138, pp. 188–194]

785

7 December, Whitehall

Earl of Hillsborough to Lords of Treasury, notifying Andrew Oliver's appointment as Lieut.-Governor of Massachusetts at £300 a year out of duty on tea imported into America. *Entry.* ½ p. [C.O.5, 765, p. 193; draft in C.O.5, 759, fos. 294–295d]

786

7 December, Whitehall

Same to same, notifying Thomas Hutchinson's appointment as Governor of Massachusetts at £1500 a year out of duty on tea imported into America, and half-pay when on leave. *Entry.* 1 p. [C.O.5, 765, p. 192; draft in C.O.5, 759, fos. 296–297d]

787

7 December, Whitehall

Same to Governor Thomas Hutchinson, transmitting commission as Governor of Massachusetts. General instructions will be prepared; meanwhile those to Sir F. Bernard should rule your conduct. *Entry.* 1 p. [C.O.5, 765, p. 191; draft in C.O.5, 759, fos. 298–299d]

788

7 December, Whitehall

John Pownall to Anthony Todd. The King has commanded that packet-boats be detained to Tuesday on application of Secretary at War. *Entry.* ½ p. [C.O.5, 241, p. 360]

789

7 December

Richard Jackson to Commissioners for Trade and Plantations, reporting on six Acts passed in New Jersey in 1768 and twenty-three passed in 1769, proper in point of law, though there are objections to Act for relief of insolvent debtors and to Act for laying duty on purchasers of slaves imported. Act to erect courts for trial of causes of £10 and under should, at this time at least, be disallowed. *Signed*. 6¼ large pp. *Endorsed*, Read 12 December 1770. [C.O.5, 979, fos. 19–22d]

790

7 December, New York

* Lieut.-General Thomas Gage to Earl of Hillsborough (No. 53), acknowledging duplicate of No. 35. It is doubtful whether Assembly of New York will re-enact repealed law concerning emission of paper-money; they will be the only sufferers. In case of war, I apprehend requisitions of troops may be made on the province, who can support them only by such emission. I hope batteries in West Florida are far advanced. My information from West Florida contains no bad reports concerning Indians. I have already informed you of troops needed for Castle William and of state of Indian confederacies. While Sir W. Johnson was in Seneca country, a party of Six Nations returned with four Choctaw scalps given them by Cherokees. Whether Cherokees mean war is uncertain. Report from Lieut.-Colonel Wilkins on rigidity of Spaniards at the Illinois; on Illinois trade; and on clearance of *Florida Packet* with peltry for London, with suggestion of illicit trading. Fort Chartres, by wearing away of banks of Mississippi, will in a few years stand on a peninsular. Illinois garrison sickly. *Signed*. 5 pp. *Endorsed*, R, 7 January 1771. *Enclosed*:

i. Detroit, 9 October 1770. Petition of Lieutenant John Nordberg, 60th Regiment, to Earl of Hillsborough, for promotion, as ordered by H.M. in 1764. *Signed* (?). 1 p.

ii. [1764] Petition of same to Earl of Halifax, for recognition of services. *Signed* (?). 3 pp.

iii. Cavendish Square, 9 February 1758. Lord Barrington to Maj.-General Abercrombie, recommending Captain Nordberg. *Copy*. 1 p. [C.O.5, 89, fos. 11–19d; entry of covering letter in C.O.5, 234, pp. 163–171]

791

7 December, New York

* Same to same (No. 54), acknowledging duplicate of No. 36, most secret and confidential. I shall immediately consider security of colonies and arrangements for operations, in case of rupture with Spain. O.C. Illinois at Fort Chartres and Brig.-General Haldimand at Pensacola have been put on guard: I shall direct O.C. Quebec, O.C. Nova Scotia and commanders on the Lakes to be watchful. *Signed*. 1½ pp. *Endorsed*, R, 7 January 1771. [C.O.5, 89, fos. 20–21d; entry in C.O.5, 234, pp. 171–172]

792

7 December, New York

* Private. Same to same, acknowledging private and secret letter of 3 October. If the letter I have written reaches Boston before Captain Preston sails, I shall settle all matters with him as you desire. When originals of your letters by the *Mercury* arrive, your No. 35 shall be destroyed and the rest renumbered to correspond with duplicates. I believe it will depend on war or peace [with Spain] whether this Assembly passes bill for emitting paper currency. People of Boston still retain a sour disposition, but I have not heard of noise or tumult. King's troops taking possession of Castle William mortified them. *Signed.* 2 small pp. *Endorsed,* R, 7 January 1771. [C.O.5, 89, fos. 22–23d]

793

8 December, Savannah

Governor James Wright to Earl of Hillsborough (No. 50). I believe that no satisfaction will be given by Creeks for murder of two whites at the Oconees. The delinquents made off to the Cherokees. It's high time those wretches should know that they shall not be suffered to murder H.M.'s subjects. I have written to Captain Stuart to tell him that making peace between Creeks and Choctaws is making war between Indians and us. We can do nothing in this province without assistance. So many provinces are concerned in the Indian trade that they will never agree to stop the trade with the Creeks or on any other proper regulation, without peremptory orders from home. *Signed.* PS. What I formerly mentioned of inviting some chiefs to go home may not now be practicable or advisable. 2¾ pp. *Endorsed,* R, 29 January 1771. *Enclosed:*

i. Savannah, 2 October 1770. Governor Wright to Lieutenant of the Cowetas, Selichee, and all other headmen and warriors in the Lower Creek country, demanding satisfaction according to Treaty of Augusta for the two murders in the settlement between Augusta and Little River. *Copy,* certified by J. Wright. 3 pp. Copy sent to Upper Creeks.

ii. Talk by headmen and warriors of Lower Creeks to Governor Wright. The murders were done by people from the Upper Towns. We hope the trade will not be stopped. *Copy,* certified by J. Wright. *Signatories,* Young Lieutenant, Salechee, Cusseta King, Second Man, Kill the Yard, Talpekee, Cussita Head Warrior. 2 pp. [C.O.5, 661, fos. 1–6d; signed duplicate of covering letter, and copies of enclosures, in C.O.5, 651, fos. 66–71d; entry of covering letter in C.O.5, 678, pp. 205–208]

794

8 December, Bath

Lord Charles Montagu to Earl of Hillsborough. I shall be ready to sail when a ship is ready. *Signed.* 1 small p. *Endorsed,* R, 15 January 1771. [C.O.5, 394, fos. 30–31d; entry in C.O.5, 409, p. 210]

795

9 December, St James's

Order of King in Council, approving Act passed in New Jersey in 1768 for choosing representatives in Morris, Cumberland and Sussex Counties. Earl of Hillsborough to send to governor of New Jersey circular instruction of 1768 requiring governors of colonies not to assent to laws enlarging Assemblies. *Copy.* 4½ pp. *Endorsed,* Recd. 12 December, Read 21 December 1772. [C.O.5, 979, fos. 57–60d]

796

9 December, St James's

Same, disallowing four Acts passed in New York in 1767–1769 vizt. for trial of causes of less than £10; to prevent suits in Supreme Court for less than £50; to extend Acts of Parliament not therein declared to extend to the Plantations; to explain Act for regulating elections of Representatives. *Copy.* 1¾ pp. *Endorsed,* Recd. 12 December, Read 21 December 1772. [C.O.5, 1076, fos. 198–199d]

797

9 December, St James's

Same, confirming two Acts passed in Nova Scotia in 1768 and 1769. *Copy.* 1½ pp. *Endorsed,* Recd. 12 December, Read 21 December 1772. [C.O.217, 26, fos. 132–133d]

798

9 December, St James's

Same, disallowing Act passed in New Jersey in 1765 for regulating practice of law. *Copy.* 1¼ pp. *Endorsed,* Recd. 12 December, Read 21 December 1772. [C.O.5, 979, fos. 55–56d]

799

9 December, St James's

Same, approving Act passed in New Jersey in 1768 for choosing representatives in Morris, Cumberland and Sussex Counties. *Copy.* 1¼ pp. *Endorsed,* Recd. 12 December, Read 21 December 1772. [C.O.5, 979, fos. 53–54d; sealed original in C.O.5, 26, fos. 133–136d]

800

9 December, St James's

Same, approving draft of additional instruction to Governor John Wentworth of New Hampshire to stop proclamation of 2 March 1769 for rating foreign coins and to provide if necessary for law for preventing prejudice to private persons. *Copy.* 1 p. *Endorsed*, Recd. 12 December, Read 21 December 1772. [C.O.5, 930, fos. 158–159d; sealed original of order, with draft of instruction, in C.O.5, 26, fos. 137–140d]

801

9 December, St James's

Same, approving Act passed in New Hampshire in 1769 for dividing province into counties. Like Order confirming Act passed in 1769 to restrain excessive usury. *Copy.* 1½ pp. *Endorsed*, Recd. 12 December, Read 21 December 1772. [C.O.5, 930, fos. 160–161d]

802

9 December, St James's

Same, disallowing Act passed in West Florida in 1769 to encourage settlement west of Charlotte County. *Copy.* 1½ pp. *Endorsed*, Recd. 12 December, Read 21 December 1772. [C.O.5, 579, pp. 159–162]

803

9 December, St James's

Same, disallowing Act passed in South Carolina in 1769 for emitting £106,500 in bills of credit. *Copy.* 1½ pp. Like Order of same date, disallowing Act passed in South Carolina in 1767 for establishing parishes of St Luke and All Saints and creating chapel of ease in parish of St Frederick. ¼ p. *Endorsed*, Recd. 12 December, Read 21 December 1772. [C.O.5, 380, fos. 82–83d]

804

9 December, St James's

Same, referring following to Commissioners for Trade and Plantations. *Seal. Signed*, W. Blair. 1 p. *Endorsed*, Recd., Read 20 February 1771. *Enclosed*:

★ i. Piccadilly, 29 November 1770. Petition of Charles Garth, agent of South Carolina, to the King, praying for withdrawal of additional instruction to governor of South Carolina of 14 April 1770; and for communication in future of all representations from governors relating to proceedings of Commons House of Assembly. *Copy.* 5½ pp. [C.O.5, 380, fos. 3–8d]

805

9 December, St James's

Same, approving draft of additional instruction to governor of Virginia not to assent to any law whereby duty on slaves imported shall be increased, or importation prohibited or obstructed. *Copy.* 1¼ pp.

Endorsed, Recd. 12 December, Read 21 December 1772. [C.O.5, 1334, fos. 11–12d; sealed original of order, with draft of instruction, in C.O.5, 26, fos. 141–144d]

806

9 December, St James's

Same, disallowing Act passed in Virginia in 1769 laying additional duty on slaves imported. *Copy.* 1½ pp. *Endorsed,* Recd. 12 December, Read 21 December 1772. [C.O.5, 1334, fos. 13–14d]

807

9 December, St James's

Same, confirming Act passed in Virginia in 1769 exempting free negroes, mulattos and Indian women from payment of levies. Like Orders in respect of Act to amend law for relief of debtors and Act to regulate suing out writs of replevin. *Copy.* 1½ pp. *Endorsed,* Recd. 12 December, Read 21 December 1772. [C.O.5, 1334, fos. 15–16d]

808

9 December, St James's

Same, disallowing Act passed in Virginia in 1769 for paying Burgesses. *Copy.* 1¼ pp. *Endorsed,* Recd. 12 December, Read 21 December 1772. [C.O.5, 1334, fos. 17–18d]

809

9 December, War Office

Viscount Barrington to Earl of Hillsborough. House of Commons having voted augmentation to forces, recruiting in North America might go on better if recommended to governors of colonies. *Signed.* 1 p. *Endorsed,* R, 11 December. [C.O.5, 71, Pt. 2, fos. 141–142d; entry in C.O.5, 234, pp. 131–132]

810

10 December, Whitehall

John Pownall to Clerk of Council in Waiting, sending copy of report from Attorney- and Solicitor-General on power of Crown to lay embargo in time of peace on ships clearing from Plantations with provisions and warlike stores for any foreign port. *Entry.* ½ p. [C.O.5, 241, p. 361]

811

11 December, Whitehall

Earl of Hillsborough to Lieut.-General Thomas Gage (No. 38). Spain's reply upon Falkland Islands proceedings is unsatisfactory:

preparation should not be relaxed. Defensive and offensive plans should be considered. Copy of circular to governors on recruiting in colonies, sent. *Draft.* 1¾ pp. [C.O.5, 88, fos. 162–163d; entry in C.O.5, 243, pp. 1–2]

812

11 December, Whitehall

Same to Governor William Franklin (No. 28), sending two Orders of 9th inst. disallowing one Act passed in New Jersey and confirming another. Copy of instruction to governors in 1767 not to consent to enlargement of Assemblies sent. *Draft.* 2¼ pp. [C.O.5, 990, fos. 89–90d; entry, with Orders, in C.O.5, 1003, pp. 34–40]

813

11 December, Whitehall

Same to Governor Lord William Campbell (No. 43), acknowledging Nos. 66–68. Lands formerly granted to McNutt and others are not to be re-granted until you have sent proposals for settlement. Order in Council of 9th inst. sent. *Draft.* 1½ pp. [C.O.217, 47, fos. 76–77d; entry, with Order, in C.O.218, 25, pp. 81–84]

814

11 December, Whitehall

Same to Governor John Wentworth (No. 33), sending Order confirming Act dividing New Hampshire into counties and Act for restraining usury. Case of townships west of Connecticut River delayed; governor of New York has been instructed to forbear passing grants till H.M.'s pleasure be known; lose no time in sending state mentioned in your No. 29. Additional instruction in consequence of proclamation rating foreign coins, sent. Paul Wentworth appointed of the Council in New Hampshire. *Draft.* 2¼ pp. [C.O.5, 937, fos. 17–18d; entry of letter, of Order of 9 December 1770, and of additional instruction of 10 December 1770, in C.O.5, 947, pp. 49–55]

815

11 December, Whitehall

Same to Governor Earl of Dunmore (No. 1), acknowledging No. 1 and notifying death of Lord Botetourt and Dunmore's appointment to succeed him. Commission and instructions are preparing. Order in Council sent disallowing four Acts passed in New York in 1767–1769; Board of Trade's representation thereon sent for private information. *Draft.* 1½ pp. [C.O.5, 1101, fos. 101–102d; entry, with Order of 9 December 1770, in C.O.5, 1141, pp. 140–143]

816

11 December, Whitehall

Same to Governor Peter Chester (No. 1), sending Order in Council disallowing Act passed in West Florida in June 1769 to encourage settlement west of Charlotte County. *Draft.* ½ p. [C.O.5, 587, pp. 425–428; entry, with Order of 9 December 1770, in C.O.5, 619, pp. 67–69]

817

11 December, Whitehall

Same to Governor James Grant (No. 35), acknowledging Nos. 38–39. I cannot authorize further expense on behalf of Greeks at New Smyrna but will send your letter to Treasury. No explanation received from you of suspension of Mr De Brahm. *Draft.* 2½ pp. [C.O.5, 551, fos. 79–80d; entry in C.O.5, 566, pp. 39–40]

818

11 December, Whitehall

Same to Governor Thomas Hutchinson (No. 1), acknowledging letter of 30 October and news of acquittal of Captain Preston. Censuring of Mr Oliver by Council for giving information to the King is disrespect to H.M. His Majesty's approval of Mr Oliver's conduct is to be declared to Council, but you may use your discretion whether to have it entered in journals. *Entry.* 1¾ pp. [C.O.5, 765, pp. 194–195; draft in C.O.5, 759, fos. 331–332d]

819

11 December, Whitehall

Same to same (No. 2). Mr Oliver appointed Lieut.-Governor of Massachusetts. H.M.'s approval of his conduct as secretary is to be publicly declared at full meeting of Council and entered in journals. *Entry.* 1 p. [C.O.5, 765, pp. 195–196; draft in C.O.5, 759, fos. 333–334d; entry of commission, dated 19 October, in C.O.324, 42, pp. 211–212]

820

11 December, Whitehall

Same to Governor James Wright (No. 35), acknowledging No. 49. H.M. approves your issuing writs to the four new parishes for election of representatives in Assembly of Georgia, if you think fit. Copy of representation by Commissioners of Trade and Plantations on election bill, sent: you may assent to alteration in law as regards qualification of electors and elected, and ballot, but not for limiting duration of Assembly. *Draft.* 1¼ pp. [C.O.5, 660, fos. 152–153d; entry in C.O.5, 677, p. 49]

821

11 December, Whitehall

Same to Lieut.-Governor William Bull (No. 42), acknowledging No. 36. I believe artifices of Associators will soon cease to have effect. Agent has presented petition for revocation of additional instruction of 14 April. Council's conduct approved. Lord Charles Montagu commanded to return to South Carolina. Order in Council of 9th inst. sent, disallowing two Acts passed in South Carolina in 1767 and 1769: objection to former is that it increases number of Assembly. *Draft.* 2¼ pp. [C.O.5, 393, fos. 123–124d; entry, with Order, in C.O.5, 408, pp. 52–59]

822

11 December, Whitehall

Same to President William Nelson (No. 39), acknowledging letter of 15 October. Earl of Dunmore appointed Governor of Virginia. Five Orders in Council of 26 November and 9 December on laws passed in 1769, sent. If any bill be presented to you increasing duty on slaves or prohibiting importation, pay strict attention to additional instruction now sent. *Draft.* 2½ pp. [C.O.5, 1348, fos. 159–160d; entry, with Orders, in C.O.5, 1375, pp. 112–127]

823

11 December, Whitehall

Same to President H. T. Cramahé (No. 36), acknowledging No. 2. Affairs of Quebec are now under consideration; there is prospect of removal of difficulties and obstructions. *Draft.* ¾ p. [C.O.42, 30, fos. 166–167d; entry in C.O.43, 8, p. 89]

824

11 December, Whitehall

Circular. Earl of Hillsborough to all governors of colonies except Bermuda, St John, and Newfoundland, recommending recruitment for army in America. *Draft.* 1½ pp. [C.O.5, 71, Pt. 2, fos. 143–144d; entry in C.O.5, 241, p. 362]

825

11 December, Virginia

President William Nelson to Earl of Hillsborough (No. 7), sending another copy of Acts passed last session with journal of House of Burgesses and quarterly accounts of Naval Officer to October last. *Signed.* 1 small p. *Endorsed,* R, 4 April 1771. [C.O.5, 1349, fos. 70–71d; entry in C.O.5, 1372, p. 164]

826

[*11 December*]
Petition of James Reed of Bristol, merchant, to Commissioners for Trade and Plantations, praying for grant of Madelaine Islands to further interest in sea-cow fishery. *Signed.* 2¼ pp. *Endorsed,* Recd. 11 December, Read 12 December 1770. [C.O.194, 18, fos. 76–77d]

827

12 December, Whitehall

Commissioners for Trade and Plantations to the King, recommending disallowance of two Acts passed in North Carolina in 1768, vizt. to encourage importation of copper halfpence and for declaring certain lots in Newbern, taken up by trustees for public school, saved and improved. *Entry. Signatories,* Hillsborough, Soame Jenyns, William Fitzherbert, Greville, 4½ pp. [C.O.5, 325, pp. 437–441; draft in C.O.5, 305, fos. 50–53d]

828

12 December, Whitehall

* Same to Governor William Tryon of North Carolina, requesting that amendments be made in Superior Court Act and Act for appointment of sheriffs. Act for introducing copper halfpence and Act for declaring certain lots in Newbern, taken up by trustees for public school, saved and improved according to law, have been proposed to H.M. for disallowance. Act for payment of forces to suppress insurrections is liable to objections, but reasons you state for assenting to it are cogent and we must rely on them as excuse for permitting operation of the law. *Entry. Signatories,* Hillsborough, Soame Jenyns, William Fitzherbert, W. Northey, Greville. 8½ pp. [C.O.5, 325, pp. 428–436; draft in C.O.5, 305, fos. 43–49d]

829

12 December, St Augustine

* Governor James Grant to Earl of Hillsborough (No. 43), acknowledging circular (No. 32). Spanish fishing on this coast could be interrupted by sloop. In war Spaniards will do everything to draw Indians into war with H.M.'s subjects. New barrack rises fast. Forty vessels in this port in past two months, and not a single accident. *Signed.* 3½ pp. *Endorsed,* R, 1 March 1771. *Enclosed:*

  i. St Augustine, 26 April 1766. Extract of letter from Governor Grant to H. S. Conway. Spaniards look on Florida Keys as Spanish property. *Copy.* ½ p. [C.O.5, 552, fos. 5–8d; signed duplicate of covering letter, and copy of enclosure, in C.O.5, 545, fos. 33–36d; entry of covering letter in C.O.5, 567, pp. 173–177]

830

12 December, Boston

Governor Thomas Hutchinson to Earl of Hillsborough (No. 33), acknowledging letter of 3 October and duplicate of letter of 28 September, original not received. General Gage notified of repairs necessary at Castle William. Mr Manwaring, Customs officer, and three others acquitted to-day on charge of firing on the people from Custom-house. Crown gave up case. Suspicion of subornation of witness. *Signed.* 1 p. *Endorsed*, R, 1 February 1771. [C.O.5, 760, fos. 5–6d; entry in C.O.5, 768, pp. 180–181; signed duplicate in C.O.5, 894, pp. 259–262]

831

13 December, Whitehall

John Pownall to Grey Cooper, sending copy of letter from Governor Grant urging further royal bounty to Greek settlement in East Florida. *Draft.* ¾ p. [C.O.5, 551, fos. 81–82d; entry in C.O.5, 566, p. 41]

832

13 December, Savannah

* Governor James Wright to Earl of Hillsborough (No. 51). This province is weak and defenceless. The militia, 2500–3000, is scattered, not under discipline, and not one-half to be depended on. Although present crop of rice is expected to be 25,000 barrels, we can do nothing warlike. Fort George on Cockspur Island is decaying, a new fort would cost £2500 or more. A regiment stationed here, under the direction of the governor, is necessary to deal with the Creeks and with our back-settlers. Troops at St Augustine are of no use to Georgia. A ship and sloop of war stationed here would be a material part of our security. Those stationed from Carolina to Florida do not come here. If there is war, convoys ordered for Carolina should take charge of our merchant ships, too. *Signed.* 5 pp. *Endorsed*, R, 28 January 1771. [C.O.5, 661, fos. 7–10d; signed duplicate in C.O.5, 651, fos. 72–75d; entry in C.O.5, 678, pp. 209–216]

833

13 December, N.H.

Governor John Wentworth to Earl of Hillsborough (No. 36), acknowledging duplicate of No. 33. Confirmation of County Act would facilitate provision for repair of Castle William and Mary at mouth of Piscataqua River and enlargement of garrison. *Signed.* 4 small pp. *Endorsed*, R, 4 February 1771. [C.O.5, 937, fos. 41–42d; signed duplicate in C.O.5, 930, fos. 121–122d; entry in C.O.5, 945, pp. 177–180]

834

13 December, Charleston

* Lieut.-Governor William Bull to Earl of Hillsborough (No. 39), reporting meeting this day of planters, merchants and mechanics. Only article now talked of as not proper to be imported is tea. I apprehend Association will now be wholly at an end: talk of new Association on principles of sumptuary laws is to preserve appearance. *Signed.* 1½ pp. *Endorsed,* R, 1 March 1771. [C.O.5, 394, fos. 34–35d; signed duplicate, endorsed Read 22 August 1771, in C.O.5, 380, fos. 18–19d; entry in C.O.5, 409, pp. 210–211]

835

14 December, Whitehall

Commissioners for Trade and Plantations to the King, enclosing following. *Entry. Signatories,* Hillsborough, Soame Jenyns, William Fitzherbert, Greville. 1 p. *Enclosed:*

i. Draft of commission to John, Earl of Dunmore, to be Governor of Virginia. *Entry.* 28 pp. [C.O.5, 1369, pp. 61–89; draft of covering letter in C.O.5, 1336, fos. 193–194d]

836

14 December, Whitehall

Same to same, enclosing following, conformable to commission to late governor. *Entry. Signatories,* as preceding. 1 p. *Enclosed:*

i. Draft commission to William Tryon to be Governor of New York. *Entry.* 34 pp. [C.O.5, 1131, pp. 241–275; draft of covering letter in C.O.5, 1080, pp. 393–396]

837

14 December, Whitehall

Same to same, enclosing following, which is conformable to that given to late governor. *Entry. Signatories,* as preceding. 1 p. *Enclosed:*

i. Draft commission to Josiah Martin to be Governor of North Carolina. *Entry.* 33 pp. [C.O.5, 325, pp. 442–475; draft of covering letter in C.O.5, 381, fos. 360–361d]

838

14 December, Ordnance Office

Board of Ordnance to Earl of Hillsborough, requesting to know under whose orders the two engineers in East Florida and the two in West Florida are to act. *Signed,* H. S. Conway, Charles Frederick, A. Wilkinson, Charles Cocks. 1¾ pp. *Endorsed,* R, 15 December. [C.O.5, 71, Pt. 2, fos. 145–146d; entry in C.O.5, 227, pp. 305–306]

839

14 December, St Augustine

Governor James Grant to Earl of Hillsborough (No. 44). Indigo samples sent to Charleston well thought of; sugar also. Road needed from here to the Mosquettoes. I shall fit up Spanish bishop's palace for Council and Assembly and officers of government: I hope to pay for it from balances saved since first establishment of province. *Signed.* 3 pp. *Endorsed,* R, 1 March 1771. *Enclosed:*

    i. Charleston, 30 November 1770. Extract of letter from merchant in Charleston to Governor Grant, praising indigo samples. *Copy.* ½ p. [C.O.5, 552, fos. 9–12d; signed duplicate of covering letter, and copy of enclosure, in C.O.5, 545, fos. 37–40d; entry of covering letter in C.O.5, 567, pp. 178–181]

840

15 December, Whitehall

Earl of Hillsborough to Lord Chamberlain, requesting customary allowance of plate etc. for Josiah Martin, appointed Governor of North Carolina. *Entry.* ½ p. [C.O.5, 332, p. 52]

841

15 December, Whitehall

Same to same, requesting same for John, Earl of Dunmore, appointed Governor of Virginia. *Entry.* ½ p. [C.O.5, 1375, p. 128]

842

15 December, Whitehall

Same to same, requesting same for William Tryon, appointed Governor of New York. *Entry.* ½ p. [C.O.5, 1141, p. 144]

843

15 December, Whitehall

Same to Lords of Admiralty, requesting grant of usual powers to Josiah Martin, appointed Governor of North Carolina. *Entry.* ½ p. [C.O.5, 332, p. 52]

844

15 December, Whitehall

Same to same, requesting same to John, Earl of Dunmore, appointed Governor of Virginia. *Entry.* ½ p. [C.O.5, 1375, p. 127]

845

15 December, Whitehall

Same to same, requesting same to William Tryon, appointed Governor of New York. *Entry.* ½ p. [C.O.5, 1141, p. 143]

846

15 December, Whitehall

John Pownall to Clerk of Council in Waiting, sending extract of letter from Governor Earl of Dunmore, dated 12 November, notifying report of plague in St Domingue. *Draft.* 1 p. [C.O.5, 1101, fos. 138–139d; entry in C.O.5, 1141, p. 144]

847

15 December, Charleston

Lieut.-Governor William Bull to Earl of Hillsborough (No. 40). James Johnston appointed Clerk of Court of Common Pleas in place of Douglas Campbell, presumed dead. *Duplicate. Signed.* 2 pp. *Endorsed,* R, 1 March 1771, original not received. [C.O.5, 394, fos. 36–37d; signed original in C.O.5, 380, fos. 20–21d; entry in C.O.5, 409, pp. 212–213]

848

15 December, Virginia

President William Nelson to Earl of Hillsborough (No. 8), enclosing following. Indians have cut us short on Holston River; it is a pity their offer of equivalent was refused. Colonel Donelson is to attend to running the line in May. We are using every precaution against plague. *Signed.* 2 small pp. *Endorsed,* R, 7 February 1771. *Enclosed:*

i. Lochaber, 18 October 1770. Treaty with Cherokees for cession to Virginia. *Copy* of No. 755ii, certified by John Blair, jnr. 1 large p.

* ii. Lochaber, 25 October 1770. John Stuart to Governor Lord Botetourt, reporting congress with Cherokees. Indians say Young Warrior's talk was forgery. Charge of misrepresentation in Colonel Lewis's letter should be supported or I shall expect redress. *Copy,* certified as No. i. 2 pp.

iii. 12 December 1770. Minutes of Council of Virginia, recording proceedings on plague precautions and Cherokee cession. *Copy,* certified as No. i. 1½ pp. [C.O.5, 1349, fos. 17–23d; entry of covering letter in C.O.5, 1372, pp. 154–156]

849

15 December, Virginia

Same to same (No. 9), enclosing following. *Signed.* 1 small p. *Endorsed,* R, 7 February 1771. *Enclosed:*

i. Account of H.M.'s quitrents in Virginia in 1769. *Copy. Signatory,* Richard Corbin, deputy Receiver-General. Examined by John Blair, deputy Auditor, and William Nelson. 3½ pp.

ii. Minutes of Council of Virginia, 6 August–8 November 1770. *Copy,* certified by John Blair, jnr., clerk. 13½ pp. [C.O.5, 1349, fos. 24–37d; entry of covering letter in C.O.5, 1372, pp. 156–157]

850

17 December, Treasury

John Robinson to John Pownall, inquiring if surveys of Mississippi, Iberville etc., made by Engineer John Campbell, and for which he has sought payment, were made on Lord Hillsborough's orders or orders of lieut.-governor of West Florida, and if service has been performed so as to deserve reward. *Signed.* 1 p. *Endorsed,* R, 17 December. [C.O.5, 587, pp. 429–432; entry in C.O.5, 620, pp. 273–274]

851

17 December, Whitehall

John Pownall to John Robinson. Surveys by Engineer Campbell were at orders of lieut.-governor of West Florida, not of Lord Hillsborough. Survey may be useful to the public and Mr Campbell ought to be rewarded. *Draft.* 1¼ pp. [C.O.5, 587, pp. 433–436; entry in C.O.5, 619, pp. 69–70]

852

17 December, Whitehall

Same to John Ellis, agent for West Florida, requesting presence at Board of Trade and Plantations on 19th inst., and statement of balance in hand for service of West Florida. *Entry.* ¾ p. [C.O.5, 600, p. 223]

853

17 December, Whitehall

Same to Anthony Wheelock, agent for East Florida, requesting attendance at Board of Trade to state balance of grants for service of province. *Entry.* 1 p. [C.O.5, 563, p. 283]

854

17 December, Whitehall

Same to John Campbell, agent for Georgia, desiring his attendance at Board of Trade and state of balances for Georgia. *Entry.* ½ p. [C.O.5, 674, p. 363]

855

17 December

Same to Richard Cumberland, agent for Nova Scotia, desiring his presence at Board of Trade on 19th inst. to state balances of Parliamentary grant. *Entry.* ¾ p. [C.O.218, 7, p. 300]

856

17 December

Warrant for appointment of Arthur Goold as Register of Grants, Patents etc. in Nova Scotia. *Entry.* 1½ pp. [C.O.324, 42, pp. 227–228]

857

18 December, Queen Square, London

John Campbell, agent for Georgia to John Pownall. Accounts of the province to midsummer 1769 are before the auditor, and the balance cannot be stated till their final liquidation. *Signed.* 1 small p. *Endorsed,* Read, 17 January 1771. [C.O.5, 651, fos. 54–55d]

858

19 December, Queen's House

Order of King in Council, approving draft of commission to John, Earl of Dunmore, to be Governor of Virginia. *Copy.* 1 p. *Endorsed,* Recd. 12 December, Read 21 December 1772. [C.O.5, 1334, fos. 19–19A dorse; sealed original in C.O.5, 26, fos. 147–148d; entry of commission, dated 21 December, in C.O.5, 1375, pp. 129–147]

859

19 December, Queen's House

Same, approving draft of commission to Josiah Martin to be Governor of North Carolina. *Copy.* 1 p. *Endorsed,* Recd. 12 December, Read 21 December 1772. [C.O.5, 302, fos. 206–207d; sealed original of Order in C.O.5, 26, fos. 151–152d; entry of commission, dated 21 December, in C.O.5, 332, pp. 53–82]

860

19 December, Queen's House

Same, approving draft of commission to William Tryon to be Governor of New York. *Copy.* 1 p. *Endorsed,* Recd. 12 December, Read 21 December 1772. [C.O.5, 1076, fos. 200–201d; sealed original in C.O.5, 26, fos. 149–150d; entry of commission, dated 21 December, in C.O.5, 1141, pp. 145–169]

861

19 December, Whitehall

* Commissioners for Trade and Plantations to the King, reporting on Act passed in New Jersey in 1769 to erect courts for trial of causes of £10 and under. Mr Jackson reports that it should, at this time at least, be disallowed; and this opinion and the Act are laid before H.M. *Entry. Signatories,* Hillsborough, Soame, Jenyns, William Fitzherbert, Greville. 6 pp. [C.O.5, 999, pp. 232–237]

862

19 December, London

Balances in hand of John Ellis, Agent for West Florida. Bounties for encouraging commerce, £21 5s. Indian presents, £514 15s. 7d. Provincial contingencies £563 0s. 10d. ½ p. *Endorsed,* Read 7 January 1771. [C.O.5, 577, pp. 467–470]

863

19 December, Virginia

President William Nelson to Earl of Hillsborough (No. 10), acknowledging No. 37. Spirit of Association seems to be cooling every day. Mr Wormely and Mr Digges are both well-qualified to succeed Mr Blair in Council. *Signed.* 2 pp. *Endorsed,* R, 7 February 1771. [C.O.5, 1349, fos. 38–39d; entry in C.O.5, 1372, pp. 157–159]

864

19 December, Virginia

Same to same, acknowledging No. 36. Should it be necessary, every effort will be exerted in defence. *Signed.* 1 small p. *Endorsed,* R, 7 February 1771. [C.O.5, 1349, fos. 40–41d; entry in C.O.5, 1372, pp. 159–160]

865

19 December, Kittery, Piscataqua River

Samuel Holland to Earl of Hillsborough, acknowledging No. 4. Country between St John's River, Nova Scotia and York County, Massachusetts, is fit to be a separate province. *Signed.* 3½ pp. *Endorsed,* R, 4 March 1771. [C.O.5, 72, fos. 139–140d; entry in C.O.5, 228, pp. 37–43] *Enclosed:*

   i. Sketch of country between New Hampshire and Nova Scotia. 1 large p. [M.P.G. 346]

866

20 December, Halifax

Arthur Gould to Earl of Hillsborough. I have had no answer to request to Admiralty to be suspended, in order to take office of Register of Nova Scotia. *Signed.* 2 small pp. *Endorsed*, R, 15 May 1771. [C.O.217, 48, fos. 19–20d; entry in C.O.218, 17, pp. 246–247]

867

21 December, Boston

Governor Thomas Hutchinson to John Pownall, sending Acts passed in last session of General Court of Massachusetts. Packet goes by Lady Bernard. *Signed.* ¾ p. *Endorsed*, Recd. 11 February, Read 20 February 1771. *Enclosed:*

i. Remarks by Governor Hutchinson on laws passed last session. 3 pp. *Endorsed*, Read 20 February 1771. [C.O.5, 894, pp. 159–166]

868

22 December, Treasury

John Robinson to John Pownall, enclosing following. *Signed.* ½ p. *Endorsed*, Recd. 22 December 1770, Read 17 January 1771. *Enclosed:*

i. 7 December 1770. Report by Robert Cholmondely, Auditor-General of Plantations, to Lords of Treasury on Quitrent Act passed in New York last session and its inadequacies. *Copy.* 2¾ pp. [C.O.5, 1075, fos. 64–67d]

869

22 December, Halifax

Governor Lord William Campbell to Earl of Hillsborough (No. 69), enclosing following. Settlement proposed is from Orkneys. It would be beneficial. *Signed.* 1½ pp. *Endorsed*, R, 1 April 1771. *Enclosed:*

i. London, 12 June 1770. Dr Hugh Bailley, Hugh Bailley and Allan Auld to George Walker, empowering him to apply to government of Nova Scotia for grant of 30,000 acres of land in Bay of Chaleur and 30,000 more on River Rustiga with fishing rights; 10,000 more at Nepesiquet in Bay of Chaleur, with fishery; and 1000 more at Belldown with beach and pond. *Copy.* 2 pp. [C.O.217, 48, fos. 7–10d; signed duplicate of covering letter in C.O.217, 26, fos. 70–71d; copy of enclosure in C.O.217, 26, fos. 76–77d; entry of covering letter in C.O.218, 17, pp. 243–244]

870

22 December, Halifax

* Same to same (No. 70), notifying plan of Mr Bailly, missionary, to form settlement of Indians near this town. Mr Bailly recommended.

Signed. 2½ pp. *Endorsed,* R, 1 April 1771. [C.O.217, 48, fos. 11–12d; signed duplicate in C.O.217, 26, fos. 74–75d; entry in C.O.218, 17, pp. 244–245]

871

22 December, Boston

Governor Thomas Hutchinson to Earl of Hillsborough (No. 34). Commissioners of Customs have left Castle and hold boards in town. Salem, Marblehead and Falmouth (Maine) need defences. Our defence must be H.M. ships. *Signed.* 1½ small pp. *Endorsed,* R, 19 February 1771. [C.O.5, 760, fos. 11–12d; entry in C.O.5, 768, pp. 181–182]

872

22 December, Boston

Andrew Oliver to John Pownall, sending journal of General Court to 3 August last, and Treasurer's accounts. *Signed.* 1 small p. *Endorsed,* Recd. 11 February, Read 20 February 1771. *Enclosed:*

i. Accounts of Harrison Gray, Treasurer and Receiver-General of H.M.'s Revenue in Massachusetts Bay, 31 May 1769–31 May 1770. *Copy,* examined by A. Oliver, secretary. 33 large pp. [C.O.5, 894, pp. 167–206]

873

23 December, Pensacola

Governor Peter Chester to Earl of Hillsborough (No. 6). Ill-health has made me defer tour of Mississippi until February. *Signed.* 1½ pp. *Endorsed,* R, 6 March 1771. [C.O.5, 588, pp. 69–72; signed duplicate in C.O.5, 578, pp. 99–102; entry in C.O.5, 621, pp. 33–34]

874

24 December, Admiralty

Lords of Admiralty to Earl of Hillsborough, enclosing following. *Signed,* E. Hawke, Palmerston, F. Holburne. 1 p. *Endorsed,* R, 26 December. *Enclosed:*

i. London, 18 December 1770. Petition of merchants trading to South Carolina and Georgia to Lords of Admiralty, for convoy to sail from Charleston by 21 March next in event of war with Spain. *Copy. Signatories,* John Nutt, Samuel Carne, James Strachan, Alexander Watson, William Roberts & Co., James Poyas, George Curling, Greenwood & Higginson, Ogilvie & Michie, Thomas & Richard Shubrick, John Nicholson, Newfuille & Rolleston, Graham Clark & Co., Basil Cowper, William Thomson. 2 pp. [C.O.5, 393, fos. 129–131d; entry in C.O.5, 227, pp. 306–309]

875

24 December

Richard Jackson to Commissioners for Trade and Plantations, reporting on eight Acts passed in New Hampshire in 1767–1769: all proper in point of law, except that crime to be punished by Act to prevent disorders on 5 November ought to be more distinctly described. *Signed.* 2 pp. *Endorsed,* Recd. 26 December 1770, Read 30 January 1771. [C.O.5, 930, fos. 97–98d]

876

24 December, Pensacola

* Governor Peter Chester to Earl of Hillsborough (No. 7). There being seven companies at Pensacola and two companies at Mobile, instead of two regiments for defence of West Florida, will discourage settlement. East Florida now has two regiments: as disorders in colonies seem now subsided, one of these could be put here. *Signed.* 3 pp. *Endorsed,* R, 6 March. [C.O.5, 588, pp. 73–78; signed duplicate in C.O.5, 578, pp. 103–106; entry in C.O.5, 621, pp. 35–38]

877

25 December, Pensacola

Same to same (No. 8), sending copies of laws passed last session, minutes of Council, and journals of Houses of Assembly. Comments on Act for preventing fraudulent mortgages and conveyances (concerning *femmes couverts*) and Act for regulating Indian trade. Proposes disallowance of Act for granting licences to retailers of liquor (January 1767); Act to erect Mobile into a county and establish Court of Common Pleas (January 1767); Act for order and government of slaves (June 1767); Act to confirm and regulate Court of Requests (January 1768). *Signed.* 4½ pp. *Endorsed,* R, 6 March. [C.O.5, 588, pp. 77–82; signed duplicate in C.O.5, 578, pp. 111–114; copy, endorsed Recd., Read 27 March 1771, in C.O.5, 578, pp. 9–12; entry in C.O.5, 621, pp. 38–43]

878

26 December, Whitehall

Earl of Hillsborough to Board of Ordnance. Engineers in Florida are to be instructed according to Secretary at War's letter to Earl of Halifax of 9 February 1765. *Draft.* 1 p. [C.O.5, 71, Pt. 2, fos. 147–148d; entry in C.O.5, 243, p. 2]

879

26 December, Pensacola

Governor Peter Chester to Earl of Hillsborough (No. 9). Non-resident public officers should reside or be suspended. I recommend Mr Livingston, my private secretary, to succeed to office of Secretary and

Register of the province if post becomes vacant: he is at present deputy to Mr MacPherson, the patentee. *Signed.* 2 pp. *Endorsed,* R, 6 March. [C.O.5, 588, pp. 83–86; signed duplicate, endorsed Read 22 August 1771, in C.O.5, 578, pp. 115–118; entry in C.O.5, 621, pp. 43–45]

880

26 December, Pensacola

Philip Livingston, jnr., to Earl of Hillsborough, soliciting post of Secretary and Register of West Florida, should Mr Macpherson be removed for non-residence. Fees as deputy were formerly more considerable than now: very large tracts were granted as jobs. *Duplicate. Signed.* 2¼ pp. [C.O.5, 578, pp. 107–110]

881

28 December, Whitehall

Earl of Hillsborough to Lords of Admiralty, requesting names of H.M. ships for Newfoundland next year; they are to be fitted for sea with all possible dispatch. *Draft.* ¾ p. [C.O.194, 29, fo. 80; entry in C.O.195, 15, p. 39]

882

29 December, Bristol

James Reed to Commodore John Byron, asking that following be conveyed to Mr Pownall. *Signed.* 1½ small pp. *Addressed. Enclosed:*

    i. Magdalen Islands, 19 October 1770. Samuel Gridley to James Reed, reporting interruption of sea-cow fishery by whalers and other fishermen. *Signed.* 2¼ pp. *Annotated,* Received 24 December. *Addressed.* [C.O.194, 18, fos. 78–81d]

883

31 December, Admiralty

Lords of Admiralty to Earl of Hillsborough, replying to letter of 28 September. Men should not be compelled to work on fortifications at St John's; if employed, they should be paid. *Signed,* E. Hawke, Palmerston, F. Holburne. 1¼ pp. *Endorsed,* R, 2 January 1771. *Enclosed:*

    i. Welbeck Street, 6 December 1770. Governor John Byron to [Philip Stephens]. If H.M.S. *Antelope* lays up at St John's in fishing season, she could spare men for works there. Other ships cannot spare men. *Copy.* 2 pp. [C.O.194, 30, fos. 1–4d; entry in C.O.195, 12, pp. 108–110]

884

31 December, Welbeck-st., London

Governor John Byron to Earl of Hillsborough, enclosing following. *Signed.* ½ p. *Endorsed,* R, 2 January 1771. *Enclosed:*

i. General Scheme of Fishery and Inhabitants of Newfoundland in 1770. Fish made by British fishing ships, 252,910 quintals; by byboatmen, 118,768 quintals; by inhabitants, 277,820 quintals. Carried to foreign markets: 610,910 quintals. *Signed*, J. Byron. 1 large p.

ii. General Account of French Fishery at Newfoundland, St Pierre and Miquelon, Gulf of St Lawrence, and on the Banks, for 1770; with observations. Fish made: 435,340 quintals (no certain information about St Pierre and Miquelon, and Gulf). *Signed*, J. Byron. 1 large p. [C.O.194, 30, fos. 5–8d; entry of covering letter in C.O.195, 12, p. 111]

885

31 December, New York

Governor Earl of Dunmore to Earl of Hillsborough (No. 5). [This letter, in Secretary of State's records, is dated 18 January 1771 and has been entered in the *Calendar* accordingly. See below, No. 932]

886

Proceedings of Council and House of Representatives of Massachusetts relative to holding the General Assembly at Cambridge, 30 May–25 June 1770. Printed by Edes and Gill, printers to House of Representatives, Boston, 1770. *Printed.* 83 pp. On fly-leaf: Rt. Hon. Earl of Hillsborough. [C.O.5, 760, fos. 200–240d]

887

A Continuation of the Proceedings of the House of Representatives of Massachusetts relative to holding the General Assembly at Cambridge. Printed by Edes and Gill, printers to House of Representatives, Boston, 1770. 66 pp. [C.O.5, 760, fos. 241–274d]

888

Undated petition of British freeholders, merchants and traders in Quebec to the King, praying for the calling of General Assembly at Quebec in same manner as is used in provinces in America. *Signed*, Henry Taylor and thirty others. 1 large p. [C.O.42, 30, fo. 205, 205d]

889

Undated petition of Canadians of Quebec to the King, praying to be judged and governed according to the laws, customs and ordinances under which they were born. *French. Signed*, Berthelot and fifty-four others. 1 large p. [C.O.42, 30, fo. 206, 206d]

890

Undated petition of inhabitants of Quebec to Governor Guy Carleton, praying for re-establishment of College of Quebec. *French. Signed*, Guillemine and sixty-eight others. 1 large p. [C.O.42, 30, fo. 207, 207d]

891

2 January, Whitehall

Separate. Earl of Hillsborough to Lieut.-General Thomas Gage (No. 39), acknowledging Nos. 51 and 52. I concur with you as regards influence which posts in the interior and on Mississippi are supposed to have on commerce and politics, but posts on the Lakes appear to me of very great importance, especially now. We should avoid as much as possible meddling in disputes between one Indian confederacy and another. Captain Preston's acquittal gives universal satisfaction. Make allowances to the two officers appointed to Castle William by Governor Hutchinson. *Draft.* 2½ pp. [C.O.5, 89, fos. 5–6d; entry in C.O.5, 243, pp. 3–4]

892

2 January, Whitehall

Most secret. Same to same. Much reason to apprehend war with Spain. Defensive and offensive plans must be considered, beginning with attack on New Orleans. Practicability and force needed must depend on your judgement. King's present intention is that you should command the expedition in person. Commander-in-chief of Jamaica Squadron to co-operate. It may be advisable to collect together a large body of troops, but those in Quebec, Newfoundland and West Florida are not to be diminished, nor posts on the lakes left insecure. Correspondence concerning fortification of St John's, Newfoundland, sent. Copy of Sir J. Amherst's circular of 1763 to provincial governors, sent: it may contain hints for recruiting regiments in America. *Draft.* 5¼ pp. [C.O.5, 89, fos. 1–4d; entry in C.O.5, 243, pp. 20–22]

893

2 January, Whitehall

Same to Governor Thomas Hutchinson (No. 3), acknowledging Nos. 29–31. Proceedings of Assembly before prorogation seem to be merely to save the credit of party. Your refusal to concur in votes for payments to Mr Bollan and Mr De Berdt, and your appointment of officers in Castle William, approved. Repeat recommendations to Assembly on disturbances in Eastern country, which tend to dissolution of society. Results of prosecution of the soldiers give ground to hope that the colony is returning to order and tranquillity. *Entry.* 2½ pp. [C.O.5, 765, pp. 197–199; draft in C.O.5, 760, fos. 1–2d]

894

2 January, Whitehall

Same to Governor James Grant (No. 36), acknowledging Nos. 40–42. Mode of distributing parliamentary bounty on indigo needs alteration, but merchants are of contrary opinion. Suspension of Mr De Brahm justified. Recommendation of Mr Moultrie to be Lieut.-Governor will be put before H.M. *Draft.* 1½ pp. [C.O.5, 552, fos. 1–2d; entry in C.O.5, 566, pp. 42–43]

895

2 January, Whitehall

* Same to Governor William Franklin (No. 29), acknowledging No. 24. King could not have given concurrence to Paper Currency Act of New Jersey without violating law and constitution. *Draft.* ½ p. [C.O.5, 991, fos. 1–2d; entry in C.O.5, 1003, p. 41]

896

2 January, Whitehall

Same to Governor Walter Patterson (No. 2), acknowledging Nos. 1–3. No objection to regulation of sea-cow fishery, if licences are not a burden. Application from Mr Wright to be Surveyor-General will be considered. I will try to obtain provision for buildings and roads, but no hope at present of troops. *Draft.* 2¼ pp. [C.O.226, 4, fos. 37–38d]

897

2 January, Whitehall

Same to Governor Earl of Dunmore (No. 2), acknowledging No. 2. Board of Trade are considering matter of lands on Connecticut River. Reports from Jamaica give different account of sickness at Port au Prince. *Draft.* 1½ pp. [C.O.5, 1102, fos. 1–2d; entry in C.O.5, 1141 pp. 170–171]

898

2 January, Whitehall

Same to Lieut.-Governor William Bull (No. 43), acknowledging letter of 13 September and *South Carolina Gazette* of 10 September. *Draft* ¾ p. [C.O.5, 394, fos. 1–2d; entry in C.O.5, 408, p. 60]

899

2 January, Whitehall

Same to President Hector Theophilus Cramahé (No. 37), acknowledging No. 3. When Parliament reassembles bill will be proposed granting legislative powers to Governor and Council of Quebec for limited time and under restrictions. *Draft.* 1 p. [C.O.42, 31, fos. 1–2d entry in C.O.43, 8, p. 90]

900

2 January, Whitehall

Same to President William Nelson (No. 40), acknowledging No. 2 and duplicates of Nos. 5–6. Attention will be given to equitable claims o

ettlers whose possession derives from grants in 1754 to Ohio Company
nd Lieut.-Governor Dinwiddie's proclamation. Pirates can be tried
n colonies, but not murder on high seas. Bishop of London has
xercised episcopal authority in colonies by ancient usage: only Dr
Gibson took out commission for this purpose. *Draft.* 2½ pp. [C.O.5,
349, fos. 1–2d; entry in C.O.5, 1375, pp. 147–150]

01

January, Whitehall

Same to Lords of Admiralty. In case of necessity for convoys, trade to
nd from South Carolina and Georgia will be protected. *Draft.* ¾ p.
C.O.5, 72, fos. 1–2d; entry in C.O.5, 241, p. 363]

02

January, Whitehall

ame to Bishop of London, sending extract of letter from President
Nelson and reply thereto, relating to jurisdiction over clergy in Virginia.
Draft. 1 p. [C.O.5, 1349, fos. 5–6d; entry in C.O.5, 1375, p. 151]

03

January, Whitehall

ohn Pownall to Mr Montagu, agent for Virginia, sending extract of
tter from President Nelson and Lord Hillsborough's reply respecting
ommissions for trial of pirates. *Draft.* ½ p. [C.O.5, 1349, fos. 3–4d;
ntry in C.O.5, 1375, pp. 150–151]

04

January, Quebec

resident H. T. Cramahé to Earl of Hillsborough (No. 4), enclosing
ollowing. Road between New York and Quebec begun by Mr Sleeper
s far as River a la Moelle. We want means of completing it. *Signed.*
½ pp. *Endorsed,* R, 22 April. *Enclosed:*

i. Minutes of Council of Quebec, 10 November 1770, concerning
road. *Copy,* certified by George Allsopp, deputy clerk. 1½ pp.

ii. Petition of Samuel Sleeper to President Cramahé, seeking financial
support for road. *Copy.* 2 pp.

iii. Plan of Lake Champlain. 1 p.

iv. Plan of Onion River. 1 p. [C.O.42, 31, fos. 9–16d; entry of
covering letter in C.O.43, 13, pp. 3–4; signed duplicate of covering
letter, and copies of Nos. ii-iv, in C.O.42, 8, fos. 25–30d]

905

4 January

Richard Jackson to Commissioners for Trade and Plantations, reporting nine Acts passed in Nova Scotia in 1768 proper in point of law. *Signed* 1½ pp. *Endorsed*, Read 23 January 1771. [C.O.217, 26, fos. 48–49d]

906

[4] January

Same to same, reporting Act passed in Nova Scotia in 1770 to raise £1000 by lottery sufficiently proper in point of law. *Signed*. 1 p *Endorsed*, Read 23 January 1771. [C.O.217, 26, fos. 46–47d]

907

5 January

Same to same, reporting no objection in point of law to Act passed in Virginia in 1770 to dock entail of lands whereof John Wormeley i seised. *Signed*. 1 p. *Endorsed*, Read 17 January 1771. [C.O.5, 1333 fos. 63–64d]

908

6 January, Charleston

William De Brahm to Earl of Hillsborough (No. 15), acknowledging No. 8, reporting surveys of Florida, sending map of northernmost par of East Florida, and complaining of difficulties between himself and Governor Grant. *Signed*. 3 pp. *Endorsed*, R, 19 September. [C.O.5 72, fos. 308–309d; entry in C.O.5, 228, pp. 76–80]

909

6 January, Barr Hall

Edward Savage to Earl of Hillsborough, sending recommendation o himself by Chief Baron Foster. *Entry*. ½ p. [C.O.5, 246, p. 1]

910

7 January, Admiralty

Philip Stephens to John Pownall, enclosing following. Several ar originals, which please return. *Signed*. 1 p. *Endorsed*, R, 9th. *Enclosed*

    i. Admiralty, 7 January 1771. Lords of Admiralty to Earl of Hills borough, sending report on collection of Greenwich Hospital dutie in Massachusetts. *Signed*, E. Hawke, Palmerston, Francis Holburne 2½ pp. *Endorsed*, R, 9th. [C.O.5, 72, fos. 12–15d; entry in C.O.5 227, pp. 348–354, with note of twenty-seven enclosures]

911

8 January

Richard Jackson to Commissioners for Trade and Plantations, giving
opinion on six Acts passed in Georgia in 1768, which are proper in
point of law. Titles stated. I have also considered an Act passed in 1768
for granting duty on raw neat hides, and submit that it may be material
to consider how far it may be proper to give way to colonies laying
duties on export of raw materials, which in many cases gives preference
to colonial manufacture against that of Great Britain. *Signed.* 1½ pp.
Endorsed, Read 8 March 1771. [C.O.5, 651, fos. 60–61d]

912

9 January

Same to same, recommending for repeal three Acts passed in West
Florida in 1767 and 1769, vizt. Acts concerning attachments; for
making estates of absentee debtors liable to attachment; empowering
magistrates and freeholders of Charlotte County to prohibit sale of rum
to Indians. Reasons stated. Following Acts passed in 1767–1769 are
proper in point of law, vizt. Acts for clearing streets of Pensacola; to
regulate markets; for order and government of slaves; to amend Act
concerning coasters; to prevent sale of flour otherwise than by weight;
to regulate Court of Requests; for relief of debtors; for appointing
vestries and parish officers; to prevent fires in Pensacola; to prevent
stealing of horses and cattle. *Signed.* 2½ pp. *Endorsed,* Read, 13 February
1771. [C.O.5, 578, pp. 1–4]

913

9 January, Lord Chamberlain's Office

Earl of Hertford to Earl of Hillsborough, requesting H.M.'s determination of allowance of pictures of their Majesties to colonial governors. *Signed.* 1 p. *Endorsed,* R, 9 January. [C.O.5, 72, fos. 18–19d;
entry in C.O.5, 227, p. 357]

914

9 January, Admiralty

Philip Stephens to John Pownall, enclosing following, made at order of
Captain Hood who has acquainted Lords of Admiralty that fullest
credit may be given to it. *Signed.* 1 p. *Endorsed,* Read 17 January 1771.
Enclosed:

i. Halifax, 20 July 1770. William Johns, master shipwright, to
Commodore Hood, reporting a voyage, 31 May to 17 July 1770,
in *Hawke* schooner, along Nova Scotia coast and timber resources
thereof. *Copy.* 3 pp. *Endorsed,* Read 17 January 1771.

ii. Halifax Careening Yard, 20 July 1770. Same to same, reporting
timber prices in Nova Scotia. *Copy.* 1 p. *Endorsed,* as No. i. [C.O.217,
26, fos. 40–45d]

915

10 January, N.J.

Chief Justice Frederick Smyth to Earl of Hillsborough, tendering resignation from Council of New Jersey; which meets fifty miles from where I have fixed myself. *Signed*. 1 p. *Endorsed*, R, 6 March. [C.O.5, 991, fo. 3, 3d]

916

11 January, London House

* Bishop of London to Earl of Hillsborough. From want of proper ecclesiastical jurisdiction in colonies doubts will arise in whom power of disciplining clergy is lodged. After Gibson, Bishop Sherlock confined himself to ordaining and licencing ministers. Until there is resident bishop in America, instructions to governor should provide for proper procedure. I am ready to part with the shadow of a power I cannot discharge with any effect. *Signed*, Ric. London. 6¼ pp. *Endorsed*, R, 15th. [C.O.5, 1349, fos. 13–16d; entry in C.O.5, 1372, pp. 146–154]

917

12 January, Lebanon

Governor Jonathan Trumbull to Earl of Hillsborough (No. 19), acknowledging No. 19. *Signed*. 1 small p. *Endorsed*, R, 24 April. [C.O.5, 1284, fos. 106–107d; entry in C.O.5, 1300, pp. 129–130]

918

14 January

Richard Jackson to Commissioners for Trade and Plantations, reporting eleven Acts passed in Massachusetts proper in point of law; with comments on Assessment Act, Plymouth Harbour Lighthouse Act and Tonnage Act. *Signed*. 2½ pp. *Endorsed*, Read 30 January 1771. [C.O.5, 894, pp. 155–158]

919

14 January, Burlington

* Governor William Franklin to Earl of Hillsborough (No. 25), acknowledging circulars of 28 September and 15 November. I shall endeavour in case of war to prevail on Assembly to put the province in better state of defence. I shall represent Indian trade to Council and Assembly: colonies principally concerned will never agree on effectual measures of regulation. Minutes of Council, proceedings of Assembly and Acts passed last session, sent. John Ladd died 20 December, leaving vacancy in Council; Daniel Cox of Trenton and John Lawrence of Burlington recommended. Balance in Council between East and West Jersey should be considered. *Signed*. 4 pp. *Endorsed*, R, 22 April. [C.O.5, 991, fos. 4–6d; entry in C.O.5, 1001, pp. 123–127]

920

15 January, New York

Governor Earl of Dunmore to Earl of Hillsborough (No. 6), acknowledging circulars of 15 November and secret letter of 28 September 1770. I will represent to Council and Assembly the Indian complaints but doubt if separate regulation by provinces will answer end proposed. Further applications from distressed officers and soldiers concerning New Hampshire lands. H.M.'s pleasure requested on enclosed Act. *Signed.* 1¾ pp. *Endorsed,* R, 4 March. *Enclosed:*

i. Act passed in New York, 27 January 1770, to enable H.M.'s subjects by birth or naturalization to inherit and hold real estate notwithstanding defect of purchase before naturalization. *Copy,* certified, 17 January 1771, by G. Banyar, deputy secretary. 2½ pp.

ii. Speech of Governor Earl of Dunmore to Council and Assembly of New York, 11 December 1770, recommending security of province in event of war with Spain. *Printed.* 1 p.

iii. Address of Council of New York to Governor Earl of Dunmore, 13 December 1770, with governor's answer. *Copy. Signatory,* Daniel Horsmanden. 2¼ pp.

iv. Address of Assembly of New York to same, 18 December 1770, with governor's answer. *Copy. Signatory,* John Cruger, Speaker. 2½ pp. [C.O.5, 1102, fos. 31–40d; entry of covering letter in C.O.5, 1138, pp. 196–199; signed duplicate, dated 9 March 1771, and copies of enclosures i-ii, in C.O.5, 1075, fos. 129–134d]

921

15 January, Treasury

John Robinson to John Pownall, reporting departure for America of *Jenny* and *Ceres,* both suspected of illicit trade. *Signed.* 1 p. *Endorsed,* R, 15 January. [C.O.5, 72, fos. 117–118d; entry in C.O.5, 228, p. 35]

922

16 January, Treasury

Same to same. Lords of Treasury think it reasonable Engineer John Campbell should receive £450 for surveys in West Florida. Board of Trade to provide for it in next application to Parliament. *Signed.* ¾ p. *Endorsed,* Read 17 January 1771. [C.O.5, 577, pp. 471–474]

923

16 January, New York

* Lieut.-General Thomas Gage to Earl of Hillsborough (No. 55), acknowledging No. 37, and reporting Indian conference at Fort Pitt, attended by deputies of Northern and Western leagues, both peaceably disposed. Shawnese report forty large boats of Spanish troops and

French officers on Mississippi: they may have been traders. Land-jobbers have impeded Mr Stuart's treaty with Cherokees, fixing boundary of Virginia. Clashes reported between people of Georgia and Creeks. Western Indians continue incursions in Cherokee country. No great likelihood of peace between Creeks and Choctaws lasting long. Congress with Indians in West Florida is unavoidable. New York is so desirous of striking money that Assembly will be obliged to pass bill for emitting paper currency. Plan of Castle William and other papers enclosed. *Signed.* 3½ pp. *Endorsed,* R, 4 March. *Enclosed :*

i. Plans of Castle William, Boston, by John Montressor, engineer; New York, 16 January 1771. [M.R. 19]

ii. New York, 16 January 1771. Report to Lieut.-General Gage of work carried out at Castle William. *Signed,* John Montressor. 5 pp. *Signed,* John Montressor. 4 pp.

iii. 15 October 1770. Return of ordnance in garrison of Castle William.

iv. 26 September 1770. Return of ordnance and stores on island of Castle William. *Signed,* John Montressor. 29 pp. [C.O.5, 89, fos. 33–65d; entry of covering letter in C.O.5, 234, pp. 173–177]

924

17 January, New York

Same to same (No. 56), acknowledging circular of 15 November. I shall wait with some impatience to know decision of matter of war with Spain. *Signed.* 1 p. *Endorsed,* R, 4 March. [C.O.5, 89, fos. 66–67d; entry in C.O.5, 234, pp. 177–178]

925

17 January, Boston

* Governor Thomas Hutchinson to Earl of Hillsborough (No. 34), acknowledging letter of 15 November and original of letter of 28 September. I knew that enemies to government here and opposition in England would take advantage of any unguarded step in affair of the Castle. Two officers placed in Castle are unprovided for. Printed trial of soldiers enclosed. General Court prorogued. Copies of letters sent from England were those laid before House of Commons last session. *Signed.* 2¼ pp. *Endorsed,* R, 13 March. *Enclosed :*

i. *Trial of William Wemms, James Hartegan, William M'Cauley, Hugh White, Matthew Killroy, William Warren, John Carrol, and Hugh Montgomery, soldiers in 29th regiment, for the Murder of Crispus Attucks, Samuel Gray, Samuel Maverick, James Caldwell and Patrick Carr,* taken in shorthand by John Hodgson. With Appendix on trial of Edward Manwaring, John Munro, Hammond Green, and Thomas Greenwood, for aiding and abetting in murder of Crispus Attucks. Printed at Boston, by J. Fleeming, and sold at his printing office in Newbury Street. *Printed.* 217 pp. [C.O.5, 760, fos. 13–120d; entry of covering letter in C.O.5, 768, pp. 183–185]

926

17 January, Charleston

Lieut.-Governor William Bull to Earl of Hillsborough (No. 41), acknowledging Nos. 40–41, and circular. Kindness to Spaniards in August was long before we knew of insult in Falkland Islands. Expected movements of H.M.S. *Fowey* and H.M. sloop *Bonetta*. *Signed*. PS. 22 January. *Bonetta* arrived here yesterday, *Fowey* sails today for Virginia. 2¼ pp. *Endorsed*, R, 6 March. [C.O.5, 394, fos. 38–39d; entry in C.O.5, 409, pp. 214–215]

927

[17 January]

Unsigned note [*Query:* in handwriting of William Knox]. There is surplus of £2500 in East Florida account arising chiefly from savings on Indian presents. Submitted that sum appropriated to contingencies be augmented to £1000 and all Indian expenses charged thereon. 1½ pp. *Endorsed*, Read 17 January 1771. [C.O.5, 544, fos. 189–190d]

928

18 January, Whitehall

Earl of Hillsborough to Lords of Treasury. Good part of peltry exported through the Mississippi is carried to foreign markets. Case, notified by General Gage, sent for investigation. *Draft*. 1¼ pp. [C.O.5, 72, fos. 119–120d; entry in C.O.5, 241, pp. 364–365]

929

18 January, Whitehall

Same to Secretary at War, sending papers on Lieutenant Nordberg for H.M.'s directions. *Draft*. ½ p. [C.O.5, 89, fos. 24–25d; entry in C.O.5, 243, p. 4]

930

18 January, Whitehall

Same to Viscount Barrington, enclosing following, it being H.M.'s intention that Captain Preston should be reimbursed. *Draft*. ¼ p. *Enclosed:*

 i. Expenses incurred in defence of Captain Thomas Preston, Corporal Wemys, and seven privates of 29th regiment, on account of prosecution by people of Boston for riot on 5 March 1770. Total, £264 7s. Items include: To certain people employed to inquire about town privately and collect evidences, £25 10s.; To small presents to particular people in Boston, £21. *Copy. Signatory*, Thomas Preston. 1 p. [C.O.5, 89, fos. 26–29d; entry in C.O.5, 243, p. 5]

931

18 January, Whitehall

Same to Lord Chamberlain. Regulation regarding allowance of their Majesties' pictures covers governors of Plantations and ambassadors. *Draft.* 1 p. [C.O.5, 72, fos. 121–122d; entry in C.O.5, 241, p. 365]

932

18 January, New York

Governor Earl of Dunmore to Earl of Hillsborough (No. 5), enclosing following. *Duplicate. Signed.* PS. Another petition of like nature is forming. H.M. frigate *Mercury* arrived here with dispatches to Commodore Gambier at Boston. Anxiety about Falkland Islands. 1¼ pp. *Endorsed*, R, 4 March. *Enclosed :*

> i. Petition of Giles Alexander of Boston, for self and others, to Governor Earl of Dunmore for grants of land by New York in townships of New Stanford, Draper and New Fane, where they have made settlements, and elsewhere in the Green Mountains, which they were deluded into thinking were in New Hampshire's jurisdiction. *Copy.* 4 pp.

> ii. Schedule of forty-six townships in which petitioners are interested. 1 p.

> iii. Schedule of names of sixty-nine petitioners. 1 p. [C.O.5, 1102, fos. 25–30d; entry of covering letter in C.O.5, 1138, pp. 195–196; signed original of covering letter, dated 31 December 1770, and copies of enclosures, in C.O.5, 1075, fos. 123–128d]

933

18 January, Savannah

Governor James Wright to Earl of Hillsborough (No. 52), acknowledging No. 34, and giving substance of letter from Captain Stuart on subject of peace between Choctaws and Creeks, and reply thereto. I have appointed Alexander Wylly to be Clerk of the Council in place of Mr Watson, dead; see enclosed recommendation. *Duplicate. Signed.* 2¼ pp. *Endorsed*, R, 19 April, original not received. *Enclosed :*

> i. Savannah, 26 December 1770. James Habersham and eight others to Governor Wright, recommending Alexander Wylly. *Copy.* 2 small pp. [C.O.5, 661, fos. 17–20d; entry of covering letter in C.O.5, 678, pp. 216–219]

934

18 January, Savannah

Same to same (No. 53), acknowledging circular of 15 November. *Signed.* ¾ small p. *Endorsed*, R, 19 April. [C.O.5, 661, fos. 21–22d; entry in C.O.5, 678, p. 220]

935

22 January, Whitehall

Circular. Earl of Hillsborough to Lieut.-General Thomas Gage and all governors of colonies in America. The King has accepted the Spanish King's disavowal of expedition against Port Egmont. To General Gage only: desist from further steps in consequence of letter of 2nd inst. PS. Great Seal given to Mr Justice Bathurst; Mr De Grey, Chief Justice of Common Pleas; Mr Thurloe, Attorney-General; Mr Wedderburn, Solicitor-General; Privy Seal delivered to Lord Suffolk; seals of Secretary of State to Lord Halifax. *Draft.* 1½ pp. [C.O.5, 72, fos. 127–128d; entry in C.O.5, 241, pp. 367–368]

936

22 January, Whitehall

Earl of Hillsborough to Lords of Admiralty. Commanders of H.M. ships on American stations to be advised that the King has accepted the Spanish King's disavowal of expedition against Port Egmont. *Draft.* 1 p. [C.O.5, 72, fos. 123–124d; entry in C.O.5, 241, p. 366]

937

22 January, Whitehall

Same to same. Two warships to be prepared to convey to commander-in-chief and governors in America news contained in preceding document. *Draft.* 1 p. [C.O.5, 72, fos. 125–126d; entry in C.O.5, 241, pp. 366–367]

938

22 January, Boston

* Governor Thomas Hutchinson to Earl of Hillsborough (private). Disorders in colonies have been caused, not by forms of government, but by false notion of government, admitting individuals to judge bounds of authority. Since last private letter there have been changes. Britain's resentment is expected; if omitted, we shall go back to disorders. Changing garrison at Castle began cure. King's magazine on Fort Hill proposed. Acts of Parliament every session to control America would familiarize us with its authority. Threat of making Maine separate province could be used as security for good behaviour, or to show resentment. When Massachusetts charter is considered, H.M. might be enabled to end election of Councillors. Act permitting issue of bills of credit at New York maintains Parliament's authority. Two officers at Castle kept in pay; Captain Phillips, late commander there, was greatest sufferer, his paper sent herewith. It must be a bad constitution which is not preferred to savage state of some years past. *Entry.* 5½ pp. *Annotated*, R, 30 March. [C.O.5, 246, pp. 2–7]

939

22 January, Charleston

Lieut.-Governor William Bull to Earl of Hillsborough (No. 42). Assembly opened on 16th inst. Council gave assurances that they will not permit any bill to come to me for assent not comformable to instruction of 14 April. But something extraordinary may be expected. Two regiments reported at Porto Rico from Cadiz. Many privateers at St Eustatius waiting for war to be declared. *Signed.* 1½ pp. *Endorsed,* R, 6 March. *Enclosed:*

> i. 16 January 1771. Speech of Lieut.-Governor Bull to Council and Assembly of South Carolina. *Signed.* 2¼ pp. [C.O.5, 394, fos. 40–43d; entry of covering letter in C.O.5, 409, pp. 216–217]

940

22 January, London

Memorial of merchants of London to Commissioners for Trade and Plantations, seeking aid in procuring additional bounty on timber and deals, and bounty on white oak staves and heading imported from North America. *Signed,* Watson & Rashleigh; John Fraser & Co.; Champion & Dickason; Lane, Long & Fraser; Hunter & Baily; Davis, Strachan & Co.; Anthony Vialers. 1 p. *Endorsed,* Read 23 January 1771. [C.O.323, 27, pp. 59–62]

941

23 January, Admiralty

Lords of Admiralty to Earl of Hillsborough, enclosing following. Orders will be given to fit them out with all possible dispatch. *Signed,* Sandwich, J. Buller, Palmerston, J. Spencer. 1 p. *Endorsed,* R, 25 January. *Enclosed:*

> i. 23 January 1771. List of ships intended for Newfoundland this year. ½ p. [C.O.194, 30, fos. 13–16d; entry of covering letter in C.O. 195, 12, p. 111]

942

24 January, Lord Chamberlain's Office

Earl of Hertford to Earl of Hillsborough, acknowledging letter of 18 January, and returning papers. *Signed.* ½ p. [C.O.5, 72, fos. 129–130d]

943

24 January, Treasury

John Robinson to John Pownall. Lords of Treasury think fine on Gilbert Campbell in South Carolina should be remitted. *Signed.* ¾ p. *Endorsed,* R, 25 January. *Enclosed:*

i. Charleston, 25 November 1770. Lieut.-Governor Bull to Lords of Treasury, giving facts of above case. *Signed.* 1¼ pp. *Endorsed,* Recd. 14 January, Read 15 January 1771. [C.O.5, 394, fos. 26–29d; entry of covering letter in C.O.5, 409, p. 209]

944

24 January, Tom's Coffee House, London

Robert Allen to Richard Sutton. Convey to Lord Rochford concern of committee of Canada Reconnoissances that notice be taken of their demands in negotiation with Court of France. *Signed.* 1 small p. [C.O.5, 43, fos. 243–244d]

945

25 January, Whitehall

Commissioners for Trade and Plantations to the King, recommending approval of Act passed in Virginia in 1770 to dock entail of lands of John Wormeley. *Entry. Signatories,* Hillsborough, Soame Jenyns, John Roberts, William Fitzherbert, Greville. 1½ pp. [C.O.5, 1369, pp. 59–60; draft in C.O.5, 1336, fos. 195–196d]

946

25 January, Whitehall

John Pownall to Grey Cooper, sending following. *Entry.* 1 p. *Enclosed:*

i. Estimate of expense of General Surveys in North America for 1771: £1885 14s. *Entry.* 1 p.

ii. Observations on estimates for Nova Scotia, Georgia, East Florida, West Florida, General Surveys. *Entry.* 2 pp. [C.O.324, 18, pp. 371–374]

947

25 January

Warrant for appointment of Theodore Atkinson as Secretary of New Hampshire. *Entry.* 1 p. [C.O.324, 42, p. 240]

948

28 January, New Bern

Governor William Tryon to Earl of Hillsborough (No. 59), recommending Colonel Hugh Waddell, Marmaduke Jones and Sir Nathaniel Dukinfield to be of the Council in North Carolina. *Signed.* 1½ pp. *Endorsed,* R, 19 April. [C.O.5, 314, fos. 27–28d; signed duplicate in C.O.5, 302, fos. 23–24d; entry in C.O.5, 328, pp. 207–208]

949

30 January, Whitehall

Commissioners for Trade and Plantations to the King, enclosing following. No material alteration from instructions to Governor Tryon. *Entry. Signatories,* Hillsborough, Soame Jenyns, John Roberts, William Fitzherbert, Greville. 2½ pp. *Enclosed:*

  i. Draft general instructions to Josiah Martin, Governor of North Carolina. *Entry.* 119 pp.

  ii. Draft instructions to same in pursuance of laws of Trade and Navigation. *Entry.* 55 pp. [C.O.5, 326, pp. 1–177; draft of covering letter in C.O.5, 305, fos. 54–55d]

950

30 January, Whitehall

Same to same, enclosing following. No material alteration from instructions to late governor; detailed changes stated. *Entry. Signatories,* as preceding. 1½ pp. *Enclosed:*

  i. Draft general instructions for John, Earl of Dunmore, Governor of Virginia. *Entry.* 89 pp.

  ii. Draft instructions for same in pursuance of laws of Trade and Navigation. *Entry.* 51 pp. [C.O.5, 1369, pp. 93–234; draft of covering letter in C.O.5, 1336, fos. 198–199d]

951

30 January, Whitehall

Same to same, enclosing following. No material alteration from instructions to late governor. *Entry. Signatories,* as preceding. 1½ pp. *Enclosed:*

  i. General instructions to William Tryon, Governor of New York. *Entry.* 95 pp.

  ii. Instructions to same in pursuance of laws of Trade and Navigation. *Entry.* 46 pp. [C.O.5, 1131, pp. 276–418; draft of covering letter in C.O.5, 1080, pp. 397–400]

952

30 January, Whitehall

Same to same, recommending Ralph Wormeley to be of the Council in Virginia in room of John Blair, resigned. *Entry.* 1 p. *Signatories,* as preceding. [C.O.5, 1369, p. 92; draft in C.O.5, 1336, fos. 197–197A dorse]

953

30 January, Whitehall

Same to same, recommending for approval Act passed in Virginia in 1770 to dock entail of lands of Sarah Rootes. *Entry. Signatories,* as preceding. 1½ pp. [C.O.5, 1369, pp. 90–91; draft in C.O.5, 1336, fos. 200–201d]

954

30 January, Whitehall

John Pownall to Grey Cooper, sending memorial of London merchants on bounties on timber, staves and heading from North America, and resolution of Commissioners for Trade and Plantations that proposed bounties will be of national benefit. *Entry.* 1½ pp. [C.O.324, 18, pp. 375–376]

955

30 January, Halifax

Governor Lord William Campbell to Earl of Hillsborough (No. 71), acknowledging No. 41, secret and confidential, and No. 42. *Signed.* 1 p. *Endorsed,* R, 15 May. [C.O.217, 48, fos. 17–18d; signed duplicate in C.O.217, 26, fos. 78–79d; entry in C.O.218, 17, p. 246]

956

31 January, New Bern

★ Governor William Tryon to Earl of Hillsborough (No. 60). Principal matters recommended to Assembly have been duly considered, and all done that could be for reformation of abuses and restoration of tranquillity. I rejected six bills and passed forty-four. Hermon Husbands, late representative of Orange County, expelled the House 20 December, and arrested. Response from militia favourable. Bill to prevent riots enclosed; principal rioters to be indicted under this law next week. Situation unsettled. *Signed.* 2¾ pp. *Endorsed,* R, 19 April. *Enclosed:*

i. Proceedings of Assembly of North Carolina, 20 December 1770, against Hermon Husbands. *Copy,* signed by J. Green, jnr., clerk. 2 pp.

ii. Governor Tryon's speech to Council and Assembly of North Carolina [5 December 1770]. *Copy.* 5 pp.

iii. Act of North Carolina for preventing tumults and riotous assemblies, passed 15 January 1771. *Copy,* certified by Robert Palmer, secretary. *Signatories,* William Tryon, James Hasell, President, Richard Caswell, Speaker. 5 large pp.

iv. Address of Council of North Carolina to Governor Tryon [December 1770]. *Copy,* signed by James Hasell. 4 pp.

v. Address of Assembly of North Carolina to Governor Tryon
[December 1770]. *Copy*, signed by R. Caswell, Speaker. 3 pp.
[C.O.5, 314, fos. 29–44d; signed duplicate of covering letter in C.O.5,
302, fos. 24–25d; entry of covering letter in C.O.5, 328, pp. 209–212]

957

31 January, Quebec

President H. T. Cramahé to Earl of Hillsborough (No. 5, secret),
acknowledging Nos. 34–35. No reason to apprehend stir among
Canadians while Spain only is concerned. *Signed*. 2 pp. *Endorsed*,
R, 22 April. [C.O.42, 31, fos. 17–18d; entry in C.O.43, 13, pp. 5–6]

958

1 February, New Bern

Governor William Tryon to Earl of Hillsborough (No. 61), requesting
repeal of Act of Parliament restricting emission of paper currency for
North Carolina. Ports of this province have been open ever since repeal
of Stamp Act for every kind of British manufacture. *Signed*. 1½ pp.
Endorsed, R, 19 April. *Enclosed :*

i. 26 January 1771. Address of Assembly of North Carolina to Governor Tryon on need for repeal of Act of Parliament restricting
emission of paper currency. *Copy*. *Signatory*, Richard Caswell,
Speaker. By order, J. Green, jnr., clerk. 1¼ pp.

ii. 24 January 1771. Address of same to same on same subject. *Copy*.
Signatory, Richard Caswell, Speaker. Sent by Mr Jacob Blount and
Mr Thomson. 1 p.

iii. New Bern, 26 January 1771. Governor Tryon's reply to No. ii.
Copy. 1 p. [C.O.5, 314, fos. 45–52d; signed duplicate of covering
letter and copies of enclosures in C.O.5, 302, fos. 26–34d; entry of
covering letter in C.O.5, 328, pp. 213–214]

959

4 February, Boston

Governor Thomas Hutchinson to Earl of Hillsborough (No. 35). From
enclosed, you may judge most townships east of the Penobscot. Elsewhere we are peaceable. I meet Assembly at Cambridge middle of next
month. *Signed*. 1 small p. *Endorsed*, R, 26 March. *Enclosed :*

* i. Petition of inhabitants of 5th Township, commonly called
Pleasant River, to Governor Hutchinson, asking for appointment as
J.P. of Captain Wilmot or other person, to stop lawlessness. *Copy*.
Signatories, Moses Plumer and thirty-one others. 2 pp. [C.O.5, 760,
fos. 121–124d; entry of covering letter in C.O.5, 768, p. 186; signed
duplicate of covering letter, and copy of enclosure, in C.O.5, 894,
pp. 263–270]

960

4 February

[Same to same] (private). Repairs at Castle William should not be delayed. Exclusion of governor from direction of these repairs is derogatory in eyes of people. *Entry.* 1½ pp. *Annotated*, R, 30 March. [C.O.5, 246, pp. 7–9]

961

5 February, Whitehall

John Pownall to Clerk of Council in Waiting, sending copy of letter from Governor Wentworth respecting custody of idiots. *Draft.* ½ p. [C.O.5, 937, fos. 43–44d; entry in C.O.5, 947, pp. 57–58]

962

5 February, New Bern

Governor William Tryon to Earl of Hillsborough (No. 62), reporting manufactures set up since 1 December 1769: two still-houses; two furnaces for iron-works making pig iron only, third will soon be at work. Ore very good. Works on Trent River not resumed. *Signed.* 1 p. *Endorsed*, R, 26 April. [C.O.5, 314, fos. 55–56d; signed duplicate, endorsed R, 15 May, in C.O.5, 302, fos. 35–36d; entry in C.O.5, 328, p. 216]

963

5 February, Virginia

* President William Nelson to Earl of Hillsborough (No. 11), acknowledging circular of 15 November. Commissioners went to New York to meet those from other provinces for consideration of Indian trade, but no others came. I almost despair of success in stopping traders from carrying rum to Indians. Papers enclosed. Boundary between H.M. and Mr Penn is worthy of consideration. *Signed.* 2 pp. *Endorsed*, R, 2 April. *Enclosed:*

i. Letters on plan for meeting of commissioners to regulate Indian trade: 5 March 1770, John Penn to Lord Botetourt; 24 March 1770, Lord Botetourt to John Penn; 21 April 1770, John Penn to Lord Botetourt; 13 March 1770, Governor Carleton to Cadwallader Colden; 16 April 1770, Cadwallader Colden to John Penn. *Copy*, certified by John Blair, jnr. 3¼ pp.

ii. 3 October 1769–20 February 1770. Extracts of minutes of Council of Virginia, recording proceedings on murders of Indians by Black Boys, particularly Henry Judey, John Ryan, and Ingman. *Copy*, certified as No. i. 2½ pp.

iii. 21 May–30 May 1770. Extract of journal of House of Burgesses of Virginia, recording proceedings on bill for appointing commissioners to form plan to regulate Indian trade. *Copy*, certified as No. i, with copy of bill. 2¼ pp. [C.O.5, 1349, fos. 56–65d; entry of covering letter in C.O.5, 1372, pp. 160–163]

964

5 February, Virginia

Same to same (supposed to be No. 12), acknowledging No. 38. *Signed*. 1 small p. *Endorsed*, R, 2 April. [C.O.5, 1349, fos. 66–67d; entry in C.O.5, 1372, p. 163]

965

5 February, Virginia

Same to same (No. 13), acknowledging circular of 15 November. I observe that event of peace or war with Spain remains doubtful. *Signed*. 1 small p. *Endorsed*, R, 2 April. [C.O.5, 1349, fos. 68–69d; entry in C.O.5, 1372, p. 163]

966

6 February, St James's

Order of King in Council, appointing Ralph Wormeley to be of the Council in Virginia in room of John Blair, resigned. *Copy*. 1 p. *Endorsed*, Recd. 12 December, Read 21 December 1772. [C.O.5, 1334, fos. 22–23d; warrant, dated 7 January 1771, in C.O.324, 42, pp. 242–243; sealed original of Order in C.O.5, 27, fos. 14–15d]

967

6 February, St James's

Same, approving draft of instructions to John, Earl of Dunmore, Governor of Virginia. *Copy*. 1½ pp. *Endorsed*, Recd. 12 December, Read 21 December 1772. [C.O.5, 1334, fos. 24–25d; copy of instructions in C.O.5, 203, fos. 170–198d, 234–235d; sealed original of Order in C.O.5, 27, fos. 8–9d]

968

6 February, St James's

Same, approving Act passed in Virginia in 1770 to dock entail of lands of John Wormeley. Like Order in respect of Act to dock entail of lands of Sarah Rootes. *Copy*. 1¼ pp. *Endorsed*, Recd. 12 December, Read 21 December 1772. [C.O.5, 1334, fos. 20–21d]

969

6 February, St James's

Same, approving draft instructions to William Tryon, Governor of New York. *Copy*. 1¼ pp. *Endorsed*, Recd. 12 December, Read 21 December 1772. [C.O.5, 1076, fos. 202–203d; sealed original in C.O.5, 27, fos. 10–11d]

970

6 February, St James's

Same, approving draft instructions to Josiah Martin, Governor of North Carolina. Articles 14 and 19 restrain the governor on certain conditions from assenting to Acts increasing number of Assembly inconsistent with H.M.'s right, or whereby lotteries are instituted. Minor alterations noted. *Copy*. 2 pp. *Endorsed*, Recd. 12 December, Read 21 December 1772. [C.O.5, 302, fos. 208–209d; copy of instructions in C.O.5, 203, fos. 199–235d; sealed original of Order in C.O.5, 27, fos. 12–13d]

971

6 February, Whitehall

Commissioners for Trade and Plantations to the King, recommending that governor of Nova Scotia be empowered to pass Act for raising £1000 by lottery for bridges and roads. *Seal. Signed*, Soame Jenyns, William Fitzherbert, Greville, Thomas Whately. 1¾ pp. [C.O.217, 48, fos. 1–2d; entry in C.O.218, 7, pp. 296–297]

972

6 February, Whitehall

Same to same, recommending disallowance of Act passed in Nova Scotia in 1768 for taking special bails on actions in Supreme Court. *Entry. Signatories*, Hillsborough, Soame Jenyns, William Fitzherbert, Greville, Thomas Whately. 2½ pp. [C.O.218, 7, pp. 293–295]

973

6 February, New Bern

Governor William Tryon to Earl of Hillsborough (No. 63), enclosing following. *Unsigned*. ½ p. *Endorsed*, R, 15 May. *Enclosed :*

i.List of patents of land in North Carolina granted at Court of Claims, New Bern, 30 November 1770. *Copy*, certified by Robert Palmer, secretary. 14½ pp. [C.O.5, 314, fos. 59–68d; signed duplicate of covering letter in C.O.5, 302, fos. 37–38d; entry of covering letter in C.O.5, 328, pp. 216–217; copy of enclosure in C.O.324, 54, fos. 189–197d]

974

8 February, Whitehall

Commissioners for Trade and Plantations to the King, recommending grant of 10,000 acres of land in East Florida to Thomas Martin. *Entry. Signatories,* Hillsborough, Soame Jenyns, William Fitzherbert, Greville. 2 pp. [C.O.5, 563, pp. 285–286]

975

10 February, New Bern

Governor William Tryon to Earl of Hillsborough (No. 64), sending minutes of Council of North Carolina, 19 November 1770 to 7 February 1771. *Signed.* ¾ p. *Endorsed,* R, 15 May. [C.O.5, 314, fos. 69–70d; signed duplicate in C.O.5, 302, fos. 39–40d; entry in C.O.5, 328, p. 217]

976

11 February, St James's

Order of King in Council, referring following to Commissioners for Trade and Plantations, for report. *Seal. Signed,* Stephen Cottrell. ¾ p. *Endorsed,* Recd. 14 February, Read 21 February 1771. *Enclosed:*

　i. List of twenty Acts passed in Pennsylvania in 1769–1770. 2½ pp. [C.O.5, 1278, fos. 33–36d]

977

11 February, Whitehall

Earl of Hillsborough to Lieut.-General Thomas Gage (No. 40), acknowledging Nos. 53 and 54 and separate letters of 5 and 6 December. Papers sent regarding cargo of peltry from Illinois country, and Lieutenant Norberg. Your letter relative to fortifications at St John's, Newfoundland, will be communicated to Board of Ordnance. If necessary to hold a congress with Indians in West Florida, and if you are of opinion cost should not be defrayed out of Mr Stuart's allowance, it should be paid for by you and placed to account of Army Contingencies in America; also cost of deputy-superintendent on Mississippi and commissary with Chickasaws, if you agree they are necessary. Indian meeting at Scioto to be closely attended to. Your report on Fort Chartres makes it necessary to decide whether or not we ought to maintain establishment in Illinois country; and, if affirmative, where to take post. *Draft.* 3¼ pp. [C.O.5, 89, fos. 30–32d; entry in C.O.5, 243, pp. 6–7]

978

11 February, Whitehall

Same to Governor Earl of Dunmore (No. 3), acknowledging Nos. 3 and 4. Papers relative to Mr Philipse's application for lease of royal mines sent to Board of Trade. *Draft.* ½ p. [C.O.5, 1102, fos. 23–24d; entry in C.O.5, 1141, p. 171]

979

11 February, Whitehall

Same to same (No. 1), sending commission and instructions as Governor of Virginia. Lose no time in repairing thither. Commission and instructions for Governor Tryon, New York, and same for Governor Martin, North Carolina, also sent. *Draft.* 1 p. [C.O.5, 1349, fos. 42–43d; entry in C.O.5, 1375, pp. 154–155]

980

11 February, Whitehall

Same to Governor Lord William Campbell (No. 44), sending copy of No. 971 and H.M.'s permission to consent to the bill. *Draft.* ¾ p. [C.O.217, 48, fos. 3–4d; entry in C.O.218, 25, p. 85]

981

11 February, Whitehall

Same to Governor James Grant (No. 37). Mr Moultrie appointed Lieut.-Governor of East Florida. *Draft.* ½ p. [C.O.5, 552, fos. 3–4d; entry in C.O.5, 566, p. 45; entry of commission, dated 25 January 1771, in C.O.324, 42, p. 237]

982

11 February, Whitehall

Same to Governor William Tryon (No. 36), acknowledging Nos. 57–58. Hopes that same zeal which has stopped like riots on former occasion will be exerted against lawless and savage disturbers of public tranquillity. Your commission to be Governor of New York, with instructions, sent to Earl of Dunmore; lose no time in repairing thither. *Draft.* 1½ pp. [C.O.5, 314, fos. 25–26d; entry in C.O.5, 332, pp. 82–83]

983

11 February, Whitehall

Same to Governor Peter Chester (No. 2), acknowledging Nos. 1–5. You cannot remove members of Council without reason being assigned. No objection to settlement at Natchez or use of contingent fund to help settlers. Report on that country awaited. Lords of Trade have proposed that £2550 be allowed for building new Government-house. *Draft.* 3 pp. [C.O.5, 588, pp. 65–68; entry in C.O.5, 619, pp. 70–73]

984

11 February, Whitehall

Same to Governor James Wright (No. 36), acknowledging Nos. 50 and 51. I hope justice will be obtained for the murders by the Creeks. Best security we can have is the good will of the savages, which ought to be cultivated by strict adherence to principles of justice and humanity. *Draft.* 1 p. [C.O.5, 661, fos. 11–12d; entry in C.O.5, 677, pp. 50–51]

985

11 February, Whitehall

* Same to Governor Thomas Hutchinson (No. 4), acknowledging Nos. 32 and 33. Perjury of those who appeared against Manwaring and three others, now acquitted, should be detected and punished. Your instructions are being prepared by Board of Trade, who are impressed with necessity of declaring against Council's claim to act separately from governor. Possession of King's Castle at Boston by King's troops is to be considered as a trust committed to them by the governor on the King's order. *Entry.* 2 pp. [C.O.5, 765, pp. 199–201; draft in C.O.5, 760, fos. 7–8d]

986

12 February, Whitehall

Same to same (No. 5), transmitting copy of royal pardon for Ebenezer Richardson, convicted of murder by a court at Boston in March last. *Entry.* 1 p. [C.O.5, 765, pp. 201–202; draft in C.O.5, 760, fos. 9–10d; entry of pardon, directed to Recorder of City of London, with certification by William Pollock, 1st Clerk in Secretary of State's office for Department of the Colonies, in C.O.324, 42, pp. 244–245]

987

11 February, Whitehall

Same to Lieut.-Governor William Bull (No. 44), acknowledging Nos. 37–38 and separate letter of 30 November. Fine on Gilbert Campbell remitted. Robert Knox Gordon appointed Chief Justice of South Carolina, Edward Savage an Associate Judge. Mr Gordon and William H. Drayton to be of Council in South Carolina. *Draft.* 2 pp. [C.O.5, 394, fos. 32–33d; entry in C.O.5, 408, pp. 61–62; entry of warrant for Gordon's appointment as Chief Justice, dated 25 January, in C.O.324, 42, p. 239; same for Edward Savage, dated 25 March 1771, in C.O.324, 42, pp. 256–257]

988

11 February, Whitehall

Same to President William Nelson (No. 41), acknowledging Nos. 3–4, 8–10 and letter of 19 December. No. 7 not received. Papers on copper coinage enclosed, which subject still needs consideration. In the consideration of propositions to settle beyond line prescribed in 1763, attention will be given to rights of H.M.'s subjects in Virginia. Question of discipline of clergy needs examination: avoid discussion thereon. I hope that settlement of Cherokee line will be followed by regulation to prevent contravention of treaty. Ralph Wormely appointed to be of the Council. *Draft.* 2¾ pp. *Enclosed :*

i. 13 May 1760. Warrant to William Chetwynd, Master of Mint, to provide copper coinage for Ireland. *Copy.* 7 pp.

ii. 18 August 1768. Warrant to Viscount Townshend to circulate copper coinage in Ireland. *Copy.* 5 pp.

iii. London, 23 December 1769. Invoice of copper halfpence sent to Dublin. *Copy.* 1 p. [C.O.5, 1349, fos. 44–55d; entry of covering letter in C.O.5, 1375, pp. 152–154]

989

11 February, Whitehall

Same to John Stuart (No. 20), acknowledging Nos. 28–29 and separate letters of 28 and 29 November. Your conduct in settling line between Virginia and Cherokees approved. It was necessary to remove any suspicion of our acting as incendiaries in war between Creeks and Choctaws. Confederacies may endanger West Florida. Extract of letter to General Gage sent, regarding allowance for deputy among small tribes of Mississippi and commissary in Chickasaw nation. *Draft.* 3 pp. [C.O.5, 72, fos. 131–132d; entry in C.O.5, 241, pp. 369–371]

990

11 February, Whitehall

Same to John Wentworth, Surveyor of Woods, acknowledging letter of 22 October. Your conduct approved; your report to be considered by Board of Trade. *Draft.* 1 p. [C.O.5, 72, fos. 133–134d; entry in C.O.5, 241, pp. 371–372]

991

12 February, Whitehall

John Pownall to Governor James Wright, enclosing estimate on which House of Commons vote for civil establishment of Georgia for 1770–1771 is based. *Entry.* ½ p. *Enclosed :*

i. Estimate, as above. Total, £3086. Principal items: salaries of Governor (£1000), Chief Justice (£500), agent (£200), Surveyor of

Lands (£150), Attorney-General (£150); contingent expenses
(£500). *Entry.* 1 p. [C.O.5, 677, pp. 51–52; another entry of estimate,
dated 23 January, in C.O.5, 674, p. 352; draft of covering letter in
C.O.5, 72, fos. 135–136d]

992

12 February, Whitehall

Same to Governor James Grant, enclosing following. *Entry.* ½ p.
Enclosed:

i. Estimate of civil establishment of East Florida, 24 June 1770–24
June 1771. Total, £4350. Principal items: salary of Governor, £1200;
Indians and other contingencies, £1000; salary of Chief Justice and
encouragement of vines, silk etc., £500 each; salary of agent, £200.
Entry. 1 p. [C.O.5, 566, pp. 43–44; another entry of estimate in
C.O.5, 563, p. 284; draft of covering letter in C.O.5, 72, fos. 135–
136d]

993

12 February, Whitehall

Same to Governor Lord William Campbell, enclosing following.
Entry. ¼ p. *Enclosed:*

i. Estimate of civil establishment for Nova Scotia for 1771. Total,
£5796 10s. 5d. Principal items: as for 1770 but including £1500,
part of £3000, allowed for building church, court-house and gaol
at Charlotte Town, Island of St John. *Entry.* 1¾ pp. [C.O.218, 25,
pp. 85–87; another entry of enclosure in C.O.218, 7, pp. 290–292;
draft of covering letter in C.O.5, 72, fos. 135–136d]

994

12 February, Whitehall

Same to Governor Peter Chester, sending copy of estimates on which
vote of £6100 for civil establishment of West Florida for 24 June
1770–24 June 1771 is based. Principal items: Governor's salary £1200;
contingencies and Indian presents £1000 each; house for governor £850
on account; Chief Justice's salary £500; Engineer Campbell, reward for
survey, £450; agent's salary £200; Attorney-General's and Secretary's
salaries £150 each. *Entry.* 1½ pp. [C.O.5, 619, pp. 74–75; another entry
in C.O.5, 600, p. 224; draft in C.O.5, 72, fos. 135–136d]

995

12 February, Whitehall

Same to Samuel Holland and William Gerard De Brahm, notifying
vote of House of Commons for 1771 for surveys: £1885 5s. *Draft.* 1 p.
[C.O.5, 72, fos. 135–136d; entry, with estimates, in C.O.5, 241, pp.
372–373]

996

12 February, Treasury

John Robinson to John Pownall, notifying Treasury's readiness to pay gratuity to Dr Marriott, Advocate-General, above the fee for his reports. *Signed.* 1½ pp. *Endorsed,* R, 13th. [C.O.5, 72, fos. 135–136d; entry in C.O.5, 228, pp. 35–37]

997

13 February, Whitehall

Commissioners for Trade and Plantations to the King, proposing Robert Knox Gordon and William H. Drayton to be of the Council in South Carolina. *Draft. Signatories,* Soame Jenyns, W. Fitzherbert, Greville, Thomas Whately. 1 p. [C.O.5, 381, fos. 362–363d; entry in C.O.5, 404, p. 438]

998

15 February, St Augustine

Governor James Grant to Earl of Hillsborough (No. 45), acknowledging Nos. 33–34 and circular of 15 November. State of Council in East Florida enclosed. Samples of sugar, rum, cotton, sent. Wine not as good as could be wished. Indigo samples will be sent; quantity made is not considerable but quality very fine. Bills drawn on account of Greek settlers. *Signed.* 2 pp. *Endorsed,* R, 4th May. *Enclosed :*

i. Account of H.M.'s bounty to Greek settlement, 1769. *Signed,* James Grant. 1 p.

ii. Sundries shipped by John Gordon of Charleston, for Greek settlement. Acknowledged by A. Turnbull. 3 pp.

iii. Governor Grant's account with John Gordon for sundries for Greek settlement. 1 p.

iv. State of Council of East Florida, with dates of appointment. 1 p.

v. Invoice of sundries shipped by James Wallace from Charleston, 1 August 1769, for Greek settlement. Acknowledged by A. Turnbull. 1 p.

vi. Invoice of Indian corn shipped by Adam Bishop, 1 August 1769, for Greek settlement. Acknowledged by A. Turnbull. 1 p. [C.O.5, 552, fos. 19–30d; copy of No. iv in C.O.5, 545, fos. 13–14d; entry of covering letter in C.O.5, 567, pp. 183–185]

999

16 February, Treasury

John Robinson to John Pownall, enclosing following. *Signed.* ¾ p. *Endorsed,* Recd. 16 February, Read 20 February 1771. *Enclosed :*

i. Custom-house, London, 2 May 1770. Commissioners of Customs to Lords of Treasury, reporting that it would be difficult to ascertain dimensions and qualities of staves and headings from North America to determine bounty thereon. We cannot recommend bounty. *Copy.* *Signatories,* J. Jeffreys, Edward Hooper, J. Frederick, Thomas Boone. 2½ pp. [C.O.323, 27, pp. 63–70]

1000

18 February

Warrant for appointment of William Haven, Naval Officer of Georgia. *Entry.* 1½ pp. [C.O.324, 42, pp. 245–246]

1001

18 February, Tom's Coffee House, London

Robert Allen and William Tooke to [Lord Rochford], requesting immediate settlement of claims of proprietors of Canada Reconnoissances. *Signed.* 1½ pp. [C.O.5, 43, fos. 245–246d]

1002

18 February, Johnson Hall

* Sir William Johnson to Earl of Hillsborough (No. 15), acknowledging Nos. 14–15, and reporting on council at Sioto, prospects of confederacy between Northern and Southern Indians, and prospects of Indian war with whites. *Signed.* 3½ pp. *Endorsed,* R, 22 April. [C.O.5, 72, fos. 183–185d; entry in C.O.5, 228, pp. 43–49]

1003

[18] February, London

Petition of Frederick Dutens of London, merchant, to Commissioners for Trade and Plantations, for grant, according to terms of French grants, of 14,000 acres in Bay of Chaleur for carrying on fishery. *Signed.* 1½ pp. *Endorsed,* Recd. 18 February, Read 8 March 1771. [C.O.42, 7, fos. 205–206d]

1004

[18 February]

Memorial of Lieutenant John Campbell to Commissioners for Trade and Plantations, praying for 10,000 acres of land in West Florida. *Signed.* ¾ p. *Endorsed,* Recd. 18 February, Read 10 May 1771. [C.O.5, 578, pp. 21–24]

1005

20 February, Whitehall

Commissioners for Trade and Plantations to the King, recommending that David Hodge, appointed by Governor Chester to be of Council in West Florida, be confirmed. *Entry. Signatories,* Hillsborough, Soame Jenyns, William Fitzherbert, Greville, Thomas Whately. 1 p. [C.O.5, 600, p. 220]

1006

20 February, Whitehall

Same to same, recommending for disallowance three Acts passed in West Florida in 1767 and 1769, vizt. Acts concerning attachments; for making estates of absent debtors liable to attachment; empowering magistrates and freeholders of Charlotte County to prohibit sale of rum to Indians. *Entry. Signatories,* as preceding. $3\frac{1}{2}$ pp. [C.O.5, 600, pp. 216–219]

1007

20 February

Richard Jackson to Commissioners for Trade and Plantations, reporting seventeen acts passed in Massachusetts in April 1770 proper in point of law. Act for preventing currency of bills of credit of Connecticut, New Hampshire and Rhode Island is not repugnant to law of this kingdom but imposes oath on members of Council and officers of Massachusetts. *Signed.* $2\frac{1}{2}$ large pp. *Endorsed,* Recd. 22 February, Read 8 March 1771. [C.O.5, 894, pp. 207–210]

1008

20 February

John Pownall to Richard Jackson, sending twenty Acts passed in Pennsylvania in 1769–1770 for opinion in point of law. *Entry.* 1 p. [C.O.5, 1296, p. 366]

1009

21 February

Richard Jackson to Commissioners for Trade and Plantations. Act passed in Georgia in 1770 for ordering and governing slaves is proper in point of law. *Signed.* 1 p. *Endorsed,* Recd. 22 February, Read 6 March 1771. [C.O.5, 651, fos. 58–59d]

1010

22 February, Whitehall

Commissioners for Trade and Plantations to Committee of Council for Plantation Affairs, recommending lease of royal mines in Manor of Philipseburgh to Frederick Philipse, on conditions. *Entry. Signatories,* Soame Jenyns, William Fitzherbert, Greville. 6 pp. [C.O.5, 1131, pp. 419–424; draft in C.O.5, 1080, pp. 401–408]

1011

23 February, Treasury

John Robinson to John Pownall, enclosing following, from contractors for supplying masts etc. from North America to Royal Navy. *Signed.* ¾ p. *Endorsed,* Recd. 23 February, Read 27 March 1771. *Enclosed:*

    i. Lime-street, 21 February 1771. John Durand, for self and Anthony Bacon, to Lords of Treasury, asking leave to import masts from New England for East India Company's ships, as permitted to the late contractors. *Copy.* 1½ pp. [C.O.323, 27, pp. 77–84]

1012

24 February, St James's

Order of King in Council, appointing David Hodge to be of the Council in West Florida. *Copy.* 1 p. *Endorsed,* Recd. 12 December, Read 21 December 1772. [C.O.5, 579, pp. 163–166; warrant, dated 27 February, in C.O.324, 42, p. 252; sealed original of Order in C.O.5, 27, fos. 24–25d]

1013

24 February, St James's

Same, appointing Robert [MS: Thomas] Knox Gordon and William Henry Drayton to be of the Council in South Carolina. *Copy.* ¾ p. *Endorsed,* Recd. 12 December, Read 21 December 1772. [C.O.5, 380, fos. 84–85d; warrants for admission of Gordon, dated 26 February, and Drayton, dated 27 February, in C.O.324, 42, p. 251; sealed original of Order in C.O.5, 27, fos. 22–23d]

1014

27 February, Whitehall

Commissioners for Trade and Plantations to the King, recommending Henry Yonge and Anthony Stokes to be of the Council in Georgia. *Entry. Signatories,* Hillsborough, Thomas Whately, Soame Jenyns, Greville. 1 p. [C.O.5, 674, p. 353]

1015

27 February, Virginia

President William Nelson to Earl of Hillsborough (No. 14), enclosing following. H.M.'s subjects in Virginia have been easy during my short administration. *Signed.* 1 p. *Endorsed,* R, 29 April. *Enclosed:*

    i. Spring Hill, 11 July 1770. Lieut.-Governor Cadwallader Colden to Richard Bland and Patrick Henry. We are disappointed in general meeting of commissioners. *Copy.* 1 p.

ii. New York, 12 July 1770. Record of meeting of commissioners of Virginia and New York for forming plan for Indian trade. No commissioners attended from other colonies. *Copy. Signatories,* Richard Bland, Patrick Henry, Isaac Low, William McAdam, John Thurman. 1 p.

iii. Williamsburg, 24 March 1770. Governor Lord Botetourt to Governor Penn. I will lay before Assembly your letter and Act of Pennsylvania for appointing commissioners to form plan for Indian trade. *Copy.* ½ p.

iv. Annapolis, 9 May 1770. Robert Eden to John Penn. Our Assembly is prorogued to 7 August; inform me of regulations proposed by commissioners who meet. *Copy.* 1 p.

v. Quebec, 30 May 1770. Guy Carleton to Cadwallader Colden. Commissioners can be sent only in winter. We will consider general plan. *Copy.* 1 p.

vi. Williamsburg, 17 June 1770. Governor Lord Botetourt to Governor Penn, sending Act of Virginia for appointment of commissioners. *Copy.* ½ p.

vii. Philadelphia, 28 June 1770. John Penn to Cadwallader Colden. Commissioners of this province have deferred determining whether to attend. *Copy.* 1 p. [C.O.5, 1349, fos. 72–79d; entry of covering letter in C.O.5, 1372, pp. 164–166]

1016

28 February, London

Memorial of merchants of London to Commissioners for Trade and Plantations, answering objections by Commissioners of Customs to proposed bounty on staves and heading from North America. *Signed,* as No. 940, with John Woodbridge & Co.; John Edwin. 1½ large pp. *Endorsed,* Read 1 March 1771. [C.O.323, 27, pp. 71–72]

1017

28 February, Savannah

Governor James Wright to Earl of Hillsborough (No. 54), acknowledging circular of 11 December. If any recruiting parties come into this province, I shall assist them. From the great scarcity of men, I apprehend very few recruits will be met with here. *Signed.* ¾ small p. *Endorsed,* R, 26 April. [C.O.5, 661, fos. 23–24d; signed duplicate in C.O.5, 651, fos. 76–77d; entry in C.O.5, 678, pp. 220–221]

1018

28 February, Savannah

* Same to same (No. 55), acknowledging No. 35 and permission to issue writs to form new parishes for election of members in the Assem-

bly. The difficulty is on account of these parishes not being particularly represented. Assembly resolved not to order in a tax bill for the present year on that account, and ordered the Speaker to issue a warrant to commit the deputy-secretary to gaol for refusing an oath. They suppose their privileges and powers equal to those of the House of Commons. I dissolved them. Assembly's existence and authority arise from H.M.'s commission and instructions to me, not from charter. Northern Indians have been among the Cherokees. In the event of rupture with Indians, this province will need troops or it will be severely distressed. *Signed.* PS. 2 March. This matter of the parliamentary power of Assembly should be brought to a point. I have heard to-day that there were seventy Indians in the Cherokee country, partly Northern, partly Western, pressing Cherokees to join against the whites. They declined, but Creeks seem wanton. It is reported that Spaniards at New Orleans have invited headmen of Creeks there. 5 pp. *Endorsed, R, 26 April. Enclosed:*

> i. Proceedings of Assembly of Georgia, 24, 26 October 1770, 25 January, 2 February 1771, on representation in Assembly of parishes of St David, St Patrick, St Thomas, St Mary. *Copy,* attested by John Simpson, Clerk of Assembly. 2½ pp.
>
> ii. Same, 30 January, 18, 20 February 1771, on inquiry into state of public offices. Order to commit Thomas Moodie to gaol for refusing to take oath. *Copy,* attested as No. i. 2½ pp.
>
> iii. Proceedings of Council of Georgia, 23, 25 February 1771. Speech of Governor Wright, address of Council, Governor's answer. *Copy,* certified by Alexander Wylly. 8½ pp. [C.O.5, 661, fos. 25–38d; signed duplicate of covering letter, and copies of enclosures, in C.O.5, 651, fos. 78–89d; entry of covering letter in C.O.5, 678, pp. 221–230]

1019

28 February, Philadelphia

Deputy Governor John Penn to Earl of Hillsborough (No. 24), acknowledging No. 24 and circular of 15 November. Since 1769 I have recommended to Assembly of Pennsylvania need for regulating Indian trade. They appointed commissioners to meet those of other colonies, but no meeting took place. Another attempt should be made. *Signed.* 3½ pp. *Endorsed, R, 22 April. Enclosed:*

> i. 16 January 1769. Deputy Governor Penn's message to Assembly recommending regulation of Indian trade. *Copy.* 1½ pp.
>
> ii. 10 February 1769. Reply by Assembly to No. i. *Copy. Signatory,* Joseph Galloway, Speaker. ½ p.
>
> iii. 28 January 1771. Deputy Governor Penn's message to Assembly on same subject. *Copy.* 1½ pp.

iv. 1 February 1771. Reply by Assembly to No. iii. *Copy. Signatory,* as No. ii. 3½ pp. [C.O.5, 1284, fos. 1–10d; entry of covering letter in C.O.5, 1300, pp. 357–361]

1020

[*28 February*]

Petition of Charles William Mackinnan of Georgia to Commissioners for Trade and Plantations, for 5000 acres of land in Georgia, where he moved from Antigua three years ago. 1 small p. *Endorsed,* Recd. 28 February, Read 6 do. [*sic,* March?] [C.O.5, 651, fos. 56–57d]

1021

[*February*]

State of Canada Reconnoissances. It would be better for H.M.'s ministers to take some steps before matter is brought before Parliament. *Draft.* 5¼ pp. [C.O.5, 43, fos. 326–328d; copy at fos. 330–333d]

1022

1 March, St James's

Order of King in Council, appointing Henry Yonge and Anthony Stokes to be of the Council in Georgia. *Copy.* 1 p. *Endorsed,* Recd. 12 December, Read 21 December 1772. [C.O.5, 651, fos. 201–202d; warrants for admission of Yonge, dated 4 March, and of Stokes, dated 5 March, in C.O.324, 42, p. 254; sealed original of Order in C.O.5, 27, fos. 28–29d]

1023

1 March, Whitehall

John Pownall to John Robinson, sending memorial in which London merchants answer objections of Commissioners of Customs to proposed bounty on staves from America. Commissioners for Trade and Plantations are of opinion that the answers are full and satisfactory. *Entry.* 1½ pp. [C.O.324, 18, pp. 376–377]

1024

1 March, New York

Josiah Martin to Earl of Hillsborough, acknowledging letter of 13 December and appointment as Governor of North Carolina. *Signed.* 2 small pp. *Endorsed,* R, 22 April. [C.O.5, 314, fos. 53–54d; entry in C.O.5, 328, p. 215]

1025

4 March, G.P.O.

Anthony Todd to John Pownall. *Lord Hyde* packet, Captain Goddard, is ready to sail. No boat on this side for Carolina or West Indies. *Entry.* ½ p. [C.O.5, 247, p. 3]

1026

4 March, Charleston

* Lieut.-Governor William Bull to Earl of Hillsborough (No. 43), acknowledging circulars of 15 November and 11 December, No. 42 and Order in Council for repeal of two Acts. I consented to Act for exchanging £106,500 because I considered it continuation of Act of 1748. History of paper-bills in South Carolina since 1723. Papers enclosed on Assembly's opposition to late additional instruction. Council attached to H.M. Lord Charles Montagu expected in spring. *Signed.* 4 pp. *Endorsed, R, 19 April. Enclosed :*

i. 25 January 1771. Address of Commons House of Assembly of South Carolina to Lieut.-Governor Bull on additional instruction, and other matters. *Copy. Signatory,* P. Manigault, Speaker. 3 pp.

ii. 25 January 1771. Answer to preceding. *Copy.* 1½ pp.

iii. 25 January 1771. Message in reply to preceding. *Copy. Signatory,* as No. i. ½ p.

iv. 31 January 1771. Same, conveying resolution for payment of money. *Copy. Signatory,* as No. i. ½ p.

v. 7 February 1771. Message of Lieut.-Governor Bull to Commons House on same subject. *Copy.* 1½ pp.

vi. 13 February 1771. Message of Commons House to Lieut.-Governor Bull on same subject. *Copy. Signatory,* as No. i. 2 pp.

vii. 15 February 1771. Reply to preceding. *Copy.* 2½ pp.

viii. 27 February 1771. Message of Commons House to Lieut.-Governor Bull on same subject. *Copy. Signatory,* as No. i. 3½ pp.

ix. 21 January 1771. Message of Lieut.-Governor Bull to Commons House on lack of money in Treasury. *Copy.* 1 p.

x. 24 January 1771. Reply to preceding. *Copy.* 1 p. [C.O.5, 394, fos. 46–68d; signed duplicate of covering letter in C.O.5, 380, fos. 22–24d; entry of covering letter in C.O.5, 409, pp. 217–224]

1027

4 March, Charleston

Same to Commissioners for Trade and Plantations, sending half-yearly list of grants and copy of ordinance appointing Henry Peronneau and Benjamin Dart joint-Treasurers of South Carolina. *Signed.* ½ p. *Endorsed,* Recd., Read 19 April 1771. [C.O.5, 380, fos. 14–15d]

1028

5 March

Richard Jackson to Commissioners for Trade and Plantations, reporting sixteen Acts passed in New York in December 1769 proper in point of law. Act of 1770 for providing £2000 for troops is in part rendered impracticable by repeal of bill for emitting £120,000 on loan; no other objection to it. Act of 1770 to enable persons to recover debts on promissory notes recommended for repeal. Act of 1770 to enable H.M.'s subjects by birth or naturalization to inherit real estate notwithstanding defect of purchase before naturalization, is not improper for approval. Act of 1770 for relief of insolvent debtors has on the whole had its effect; repeal will do little good; submitted whether to repeal for sake of example. Act of 1770 for relief of James De Peyster and others recommended for repeal. Thirty-four other Acts passed in New York in 1770 are proper in point of law. *Signed.* 6¼ pp. *Endorsed,* Recd. 5 March, Read 6 March 1771. [C.O.5, 1075, fos. 75–78d]

1029

5 March, London

Observations and answers by Thomas Walpole on President William Nelson's letter to Earl of Hillsborough of 18 October 1770. The reply, paragraph by paragraph, to Nelson's letter contains strictures on Colonel George Washington's letter of 5 October 1770, enclosed with Nelson's. 22 pp. *Endorsed,* Read 25 March 1772. *Enclosed:*

i. London, 9 July 1770. Letter to Thomas Walpole, with allegations about land grants in Virginia. With remarks on the letter. *Copy.* 9 small pp.

ii. Extracts of journals of House of Burgesses of Virginia, 24 November and 13 December 1766, on subject of land grants. *Copy.* 3¼ pp.

iii. 28 May 1770. [Thomas Walpole] to John Pownall, commenting on No. iv, and why it cannot affect his application. *Copy.* 2¼ pp.

iv. Representation by House of Burgesses to the King, on need to encourage settlement of frontiers. *Copy. Signatory,* Peyton Randolph. 2 pp.

v. New York, 10 November 1770. Extract of letter from Lieut.-General Thomas Gage to Earl of Hillsborough, concerning settlement of interior country of America. *Copy.* 5 pp. *Endorsed,* Read 25 March 1772.

vi. New York, 12 November 1770. Extract of letter from Earl of Dunmore to Earl of Hillsborough concerning proposed colony on Ohio. *Copy.* 2¼ pp. *Endorsed,* as No. v. [C.O.5, 1333, fos. 143–173d; probably Nos. v–vi were not enclosures but were filed here as relevant papers]

1030

5 March, Charleston

Lieut.-Governor William Bull to Earl of Hillsborough (No. 44). Henry Peronneau and Benjamin Dart appointed by ordinance joint-Treasurers of South Carolina. Form of bond altered to conform to additional instruction. *Signed.* PS. No gaols or court-houses for circuit courts yet finished. 1½ pp. *Endorsed*, R, 19 April. *Enclosed :*

 i. Bond by Benjamin Dart for performance of duties. *Copy, Signatories*, Peter Manigault and nine others. 1 p. [C.O.5, 394, fos. 69–71d; signed duplicate of covering letter and copy of enclosure in C.O.5, 380, fos. 25–27d; entry of covering letter in C.O.5, 409, pp. 224–226]

1031

5 March, Philadelphia

Deputy Governor John Penn to Earl of Hillsborough, acknowledging circular of 11 December. All possible assistance will be given to recruiting parties. *Signed.* ½ p. *Endorsed*, R, 22 April. [C.O.5, 1284, fos. 11–12d; signed duplicate, endorsed Read 22 August 1771, in C.O.5, 1278, fos. 51–52d; entry in C.O.5, 1300, pp. 361–362]

1032

5 March, Charleston

John Stuart to Earl of Hillsborough (No. 30), reporting Indian affairs in West Florida. Endeavours at reconciliation between Creeks and Choctaws have been defeated. Strange Indians amongst Cherokees caused traders to panic, papers enclosed. Creeks are more attached to us than to Spaniards. *Signed.* 3¼ pp. *Endorsed*, R, 19 April. *Enclosed :*

 i. Mobile, 12 December 1770. Talk from Charles Stuart to Creek Indians. I will do what I can to reconcile you and Choctaws. Bad white men must be taken to governor for punishment. Murders lately committed near Augusta show there are still madmen among you. *Copy.* 1¾ pp.

 * ii. Charleston, 23 February 1771. John Stuart to Alexander Cameron. I wish you may succeed in turning arms of Cherokees from Chickasaws. Northern Indians do not want to strike at whites; Western confederacy, headed by Shawnese, do. Our interest is to unite Cherokees and Northern confederacy. *Copy.* 2¼ pp.

 * iii. Fort Prince George, 8 February 1771. Alexander Cameron to John Stuart. Frontier inhabitants are in panic, unnecessarily because Northern Indians and Cherokees have gone against Chickasaws. Some Creek headmen have gone to New Orleans. *Copy.* 2 pp.

 iv. Long Canes, 1 February 1771. Abstract of letter from Richard King, clerk, to John Caldwell, trader to Cherokee nation, reporting apprehensions of attack on whites, especially by Creeks. Some Creeks have been at New Orleans. *Copy.* $2\frac{1}{4}$ pp.

v. Silver Bluff, Savannah River, 19 February 1771. George Galphin to John Stuart. Young Lieutenant of Cowetas says he was invited to Havana but would not go. He says the young people are mad but he will hold them as long as he can. *Copy.* $\frac{3}{4}$ p.

vi. Long Canes, 23 January 1771. Abstract of letter from Alexander Cameron to [John Stuart], reporting Spanish activity amongst Creeks, and arrival of Nottowegas and some Shawnese. *Copy.* 1 p.

* vii. Pensacola, 26 December 1770. Charles Stuart to John Stuart, reporting his contriving postponement of peace between Creeks and Choctaws. Abuses by white hunters in Chickasaw nation and want of justice reported. *Copy.* 8 pp. [C.O.5, 72, fos. 165–182d; entry of covering letter in C.O.5, 228, pp. 50–53]

1033

6 March, Whitehall

Earl of Hillsborough to Lieut.-General Thomas Gage (No. 41), acknowledging Nos. 55 and 56. Your attention to Indian affairs in interior country approved. *Draft.* $\frac{1}{2}$ p. [C.O.5, 89, fos. 68–69d; entry in C.O.5, 243, p. 8]

1034

6 March, Whitehall

Same to Governor Earl of Dunmore (No. 4), acknowledging Nos. 5 and 6. Delay in determining on law regarding naturalized persons was owing to vacancy of office of counsel to Board of Trade. Mr Jackson now appointed, Act is before H.M. for approbation. *Draft.* $1\frac{1}{4}$ pp. [C.O.5, 1102, fos. 41–42d; entry in C.O.5, 1141, p. 172]

1035

6 March, Whitehall

Same to Governor Walter Patterson (No. 3), sending copy of estimate for Nova Scotia for next year, in which Parliament has included sum for buildings in Island of St John. Wait until I send plans. *Draft.* 1 p. [C.O.226, 4, fos. 39–40d]

1036

6 March, Whitehall

Same to Governor Lord William Campbell (No. 45). Estimate for civil establishment for Nova Scotia sent you by Mr Pownall shows why bill for £100 drawn by you in 1769 for making roads cannot be paid. I can suggest no method of relieving you unless Assembly think fit the sum

should be reimbursed by Act for providing fund for roads by lottery
Draft. 1½ pp. [C.O.217, 48, fos. 5–6d; entry in C.O.218, 25, pp. 88–89

1037

6 March, Whitehall

Commissioners for Trade and Plantations to the King, enclosing
following. The following articles in instructions to late governor have
been omitted: article 25, relating to Surveyor-General of Customs
article 38, recommending law for punishing mutiny and desertion
article 43, directing governor to watch the French and Indians in their
interest; article 49, concerning payment of governor's salary by legislature there. Additional articles included: article 5, to stop Council from
meeting without summons from, and presence of, governor; article 16
to forbid governor to consent to any vote for payment of money to
agents except such as shall be appointed by Act of whole legislature
article 27, to direct governor not to assent to law taxing salaries, no
being paid out of moneys granted by legislature there, of persons in
H.M.'s service whose offices have no peculiar relation to Massachusetts
article 43, relative to Castle William, to remove any doubts that it was
H.M.'s intention to take from governor command of that fort. No
alteration in instructions relating to Acts of Trade. *Entry. Signatories*
Soame Jenyns, William Fitzherbert, Edward Eliot, Greville. 6 pp
Enclosed:

> i. Draft instructions for Thomas Hutchinson, Governor of Massa-
> chusetts. *Entry* of draft. 48¼ pp.

> ii. Draft instructions for same, relating to Acts of Trade, *Entry, o*
> draft. 42 pp. [C.O.5, 920, pp. 309–405; draft of covering letter in
> C.O.5, 897, fos. 277–282d]

1038

8 March, Whitehall

Same to same, recommending confirmation of Act passed in New
York in 1770 to enable H.M.'s subjects, by birth or naturalization, to
hold real estates notwithstanding defect of purchase before natural
ization. *Entry. Signatories,* Soame Jenyns, William Fitzherbert
Greville, Thomas Whately. 1 p. [C.O.5, 1131, p. 425; draft in C.O.5
1080, pp. 409–412]

1039

8 March, Whitehall

Same to same, recommending royal allowance of Act passed in Georgia
in 1770 for ordering and governing slaves, whereby slaves are declared
to be chattels as in South Carolina. *Entry. Signatories,* Soame Jenyns
William Fitzherbert, Greville, Thomas Whately. 2 pp. [C.O.5, 674
pp. 354–355]

1040

8 March, Whitehall

Same to same, recommending grant of 5000 acres of land in Georgia to Charles William Mackinnen. *Entry. Signatories*, Soame Jenyns, William Fitzherbert, Greville, Thomas Whately. 2 pp. [C.O.5, 674, pp. 356–357]

1041

8 March, Treasury

John Robinson to John Pownall. No further money to be authorized for Greek colonists in East Florida. *Signed.* 1 p. *Endorsed*, R, 13th. [C.O.5, 552, fos. 13–14d; entry in C.O.5, 567, pp. 182–183]

1042

8 March, Pensacola

* Governor Peter Chester to Earl of Hillsborough (No. 10), acknowledging No. 28. The 16th regiment at present consists of 401 men for defence against Spaniards and Indians. At New Orleans Spaniards have 380 regular troops, 1500 militia, and upwards of 4000 negroes used to muskets and the woods; more militia and negroes elsewhere. Spanish posts re-established opposite Fort Bute and at Point Coupee on Mississippi; they expect regiment from Havana. Report on fortifications here enclosed. Mobile fort ruinous; bricks could be used for other works. *Signed.* 3¼ pp. *Endorsed*, R, 21 June. *Enclosed :*

i. 10 March 1771. Return of troops in West Florida, by Francis Hutcheson, acting major of brigade. Four captains, 14 subalterns, 8 staff officers, 27 sergeants, 20 drummers, 401 rank and file. 1 p.

ii. Pensacola, 13 March 1771. T. Sowers, engineer, to Governor Chester, reporting on condition of fortifications in West Florida. *Copy.* 2½ small pp. [C.O.5, 588, pp. 91–102; signed duplicate of covering letter, and copies of enclosures, in C.O.5, 578, pp. 119–128; entry of covering letter in C.O.5, 621, pp. 45–49]

1043

[8 March]

Petition of John Evans of Tallysarn, Cardiganshire, Wales, to the King, requesting order to mine gold and silver in vicinity of Mississippi and Ohio Rivers, and elsewhere in North America, paying one-tenth to H.M. *Signed.* 1 p. *Endorsed*, Read 8 March 1771. [C.O.323, 27, pp. 73–76; entry in C.O.5, 228, pp. 33–34]

1044

9 March, New York

Lieut.-General Thomas Gage to Earl of Hillsborough (No. 57), acknowledging No. 38 and circular to governors recommending recruitment. I have ordered recruiting-parties from every regiment, except Royal American, to embark for Great Britain. Recruiting parties will receive money-allowance. Timber will be supplied for repairing gun-platforms and carriages at Quebec. Batteries, gun-carriages etc. at Halifax in ruinous state. Powder sent to St Augustine but more needed than I can spare. No news from West Florida, but I cannot doubt that every measure will be taken for its defence; fleet at Jamaica is its surest defence. Report from Fort Chartres: they had rumour of difference between Great Britain, France and Spain, but no attention paid to it; no knowledge of Spanish boats on Mississippi reported by Indians. Enclosed received: there are two engineers at St Augustine but not under my command. *Signed.* 3¾ pp. *Endorsed,* R, 22 April. *Enclosed:*

> i. Bermuda, 9 January 1771. Extract of letter from Governor Bruere to General Gage, applying for company of soldiers and for engineers to inspect fortifications, which need repair. *Copy.* 1 p. [C.O.5, 89, fos. 72–76d; entry of covering letter in C.O.5, 234, pp. 178–183]

1045

9 March, New Bern

Governor William Tryon to Earl of Hillsborough (No. 65), enclosing six bills rejected last session, with comments. I offered, if Assembly would pass effectual quitrent law, to give up arrears. Bill to this effect, copy enclosed, was unsatisfactory. Should H.M. approve, it might be carried in future without objectionable clause. Greatest opposition was from representatives in Lord Granville's district. *Signed.* 3½ pp. *Endorsed,* R, 15 May. *Enclosed:*

> i. Act for securing titles of freeholders in North Carolina. *Copy.* 2½ pp.

> ii. Act to empower churchwardens and vestrymen of parish of St Gabriel's to sell the glebe. *Copy.* 1 p.

> iii. Act for restraint of vagrants. *Copy.* 4 pp.

> iv. Act to amend Act for establishing town of Campbelton. *Copy.* 1 p.

> v. Bill for more easy collection of quitrents in North Carolina. *Copy.* 8 pp.

> vi. Act additional to Act for regulation of elections to General Assembly of North Carolina. *Copy.* 7 pp.

> vii. Act to amend Act for regulation of town of Wilmington. *Copy.* 5 pp. [C.O.5, 314, fos. 71–90d; signed duplicate of covering letter in C.O.5, 302, fos. 41–43d; entry of covering letter in C.O.5, 328, pp. 217–223]

1046

9 March, Pensacola

* Governor Peter Chester to Earl of Hillsborough (No. 11). Mr Stuart awaited here. Indian discontent arises from freedom of trade and too lavish presents when the French were here. Creeks and Choctaws not yet at peace. Act regulating Indian trade not effective. Southern colonies should pass bill to limit goods and rum carried to Indians, for settling a reasonable tariff, to allow Indian evidence etc. Commissaries residing with each nation needed to enforce regulation and supply information of Indian intentions. Congress with Lower Creeks will restore friendship, and we might obtain cession of interior country. *Signed.* 6¼ pp. *Endorsed*, R, 21 June. *Enclosed:*

> i. Undated affidavit sworn before Governor Chester by William Smith and William Gregory, servants to Robert Mackay, Indian trader, reporting designs against whites among Upper Creeks, and their refusal to give satisfaction to Governor Wright for two whites killed by Ofusky people. *Copy.* 2 pp. [C.O.5, 588, pp. 103–114; signed duplicate of covering letter in C.O.5, 578, pp. 129–136; copy of enclosure, endorsed (wrongly) in Governor Chester's No. 19 of 15 April 1771, in C.O.5, 578, pp. 165–168; entry of covering letter in C.O.5, 621, pp. 49–57]

1047

9 March, New York

* Governor Earl of Dunmore to Earl of Hillsborough (No. 7), acknowledging letter of 11 December. Whole province except lawyers dissatisfied at H.M.'s disallowance of four Acts of Assembly. Assembly have not discharged arrears on account of troops and are inflexible in refusing to admit Judge Livingston to seat. Address from Assembly on Indian affairs, speeches from Oneida Indians, and proposals of Germans to form company of militia, enclosed. Country between Hudson River, Lakes George and Champlain on west, Connecticut River on east, northern line of Massachusetts and 45th degree of latitude, is a fine country, clearly within limits of New York. Disorders there are originated by persons in power in New Hampshire, papers enclosed. There can be no tranquillity until order prohibiting grants by New York of lands before patented under New Hampshire is rescinded. Inhabitants amount to 6 or 700 families, of which 450 odd have petitioned to be continued in this government and 200 to be under New Hampshire. *Signed.* PS. Joseph Reade, of Council, dead. Affidavits enclosed concerning disorders promoted by people of greatest power in New Hampshire. 9¼ pp. *Endorsed*, R, 22 April. *Enclosed:*

> i. 15 February 1771. Address of Assembly of New York to Governor Earl of Dunmore. Commissioners to meet those from other provinces to regulate Indian trade were appointed in 1770, but only those from New York and Virginia met in July last. Bill will be prepared when

Assembly is informed of regulations heretofore practised in Indian country. *Signed*, John Cruger, Speaker. 2¾ pp.

ii. Oneide, 31 December 1770. Speech from chiefs of Oneida Indians to Governor Earl of Dunmore, asking for blacksmith to teach trade, and tools. *Copy. Signatories*, Tagawarou, Ojekheda, Tekeengo, Suhnagearat, Giwi, Shinhari, Siskete, Tegawe. Interpreted by Samuel Kirkland, missionary. 2½ pp.

iii. New York, 25 January 1771. Memorial of Frederick William Hecht and 5 others on behalf of German Protestants of City of New York, to Governor Earl of Dunmore, proposing German company of militia of 120 men including officers, at their own expense. *Copy.* 2 pp.

iv. New York, 7 March 1771. Attorney-General J. T. Kemp to Earl of Hillsborough, exposing errors in petition by inhabitants of lands now by H.M.'s order in New York but formerly esteemed in New Hampshire, and vindicating actions of government of New York. With references to documents Nos. 1–42 described below, Nos vii–1. *Signed.* 21 pp.

v. Fort George, 8 March 1771. Certificate by Governor Earl of Dunmore that persons attesting following affidavits are public officers of New York. *Signed.* 1¼ pp.

vi. New York, 8 March 1771. Certificate by Goldsbrow Banyar, deputy secretary and deputy clerk of Council of New York, of authenticity of following copies and extracts. *Signed.* 1 p.

vii. Extract of letters patent to James, Duke of York, 4 November 1674. (No. 1). *Copy.* ½ p.

viii. 3 July 1742. Commission to Benning Wentworth to be Governor of New Hampshire, with definition of bounds. *Copy,* attested, 17 November 1749, at Portsmouth, New Hampshire, by Theodore Atkinson, Secretary. (No. 2). *Copy.* ¾ p.

ix. New York, 10 April 1765. Minutes of Council (No. 3) recording:

x. St James's, 20 July 1764. Order of King in Council declaring western banks of Connecticut River to be boundary between New York and New Hampshire. (No. 4). *Copy.* ¾ p.

xi. 10 April 1765. Proclamation by Lieut.-Governor Colden notifying above order. (No. 5). *Copy.* 1 p.

xii. 28 December 1763. Proclamation by same, requiring judges and other officers of New York to exercise jurisdiction as far as banks of Connecticut River, undoubted eastern limit of New York. (No. 6). *Copy.* 2 pp.

xiii. Portsmouth, 17 November 1749. Governor Benning Wentworth to Governor George Clinton, claiming western line of New Hampshire to be from three miles north of Pautucket Falls, striking Hudson

River about eighty poles [*sic*] between where Mohawk River comes into Hudson River. (No. 7). *Copy.* 1 p.

xiv. New York, 3 April 1750. Minutes of Council of New York. On reading No. xiii and extract of No. viii, Council advised Connecticut River to be eastern boundary of New York. (No. 8). *Copy.* ¾ p.

xv. Portsmouth, 25 April 1750. Governor Wentworth to Governor Clinton on same subject. (No. 9). *Copy.* 1 p.

xvi. New York, 5 June 1750. Minutes of Council of New York. No. xv read. (No. 10). *Copy.* ½ p.

xvii. New York, 6 June 1750. Governor Clinton to Governor Wentworth on same subject. (No. 11). *Copy.* ¾ p.

xviii. Portsmouth, 22 June 1750. Governor Wentworth to Governor Clinton, proposing that both provinces make representation to H.M. (No. 12). *Copy.* ¾ p.

xix. New York, 24 July 1750. Minutes of Council of New York. No. xviii read, representation to H.M. advised. (No. 13). *Copy.* 1 p.

xx. New York, 25 July 1750. Governor Clinton to Governor Wentworth, agreeing with proposal. (No. 14). *Copy.* ¼ p.

xxi. Portsmouth, 2 September 1750. Governor Wentworth to Governor Clinton, proposing exchange of copies of representations to H.M. *Copy.* ¼ p.

xxii. New York, 19 September 1750. Minutes of Council of New York. No. xxi read. (No. 15). *Copy.* ¼ p.

xxiii. Whitehall, 22 December 1752. Thomas Hill to Robert Charles, agent of New York, sending Governor Wentworth's proposal for running boundary between New York and New Hampshire. (No. 16). *Copy.* ¼ p.

xxiv. 23 March 1751. Governor Wentworth to Board of Trade, proposing that commissioners settle northern as well as eastern boundary of New York. (No. 17). *Copy.* 1 p.

xxv. New York, 22 May 1765. Minutes of Council of New York. Resolved not to dispossess persons settled under grant from New Hampshire on lands which by Order in Council of 20 July 1764 are in New York. (No. 18). *Copy.* ½ p.

xxvi. New York, 28 February 1770. Minutes of Council of New York. Read, petition of 120 persons on lands west of Connecticut River, for constitution of new county to north of Cumberland County for protection against lawless banditti of felons and criminals. (No. 19). 1 p.

xxvii. 4 March 1771. Declaration by Alexander Colden, Surveyor-General of New York, that the order of 22 May 1765 [*see* No. xxv] has been strictly observed. No return of survey has been made of any land under grant from New Hampshire east of Green Mountain except for persons holding grants of New Hampshire; except 8 tracts of 500 acres each allotted by Governor Benning Wentworth for himself, 4 of which were surveyed for Lieutenant Thomas Etherington and 4 for Lieut. William Lesley. (No. 20). *Copy.* 1¼ pp.

xxviii. New York, 20 January 1764. [Lieut.-Governor Cadwallader Colden to Commissioners for Trade and Plantations], giving history of New York's claim to lands west of Connecticut River. (No. 21). *Copy.* 6 pp.

xxix. Map of environs of Lakes Champlain and George, showing Cumberland and Gloucester Counties and boundary between New York and New Hampshire, made by Simon Metcalfe. Sworn, 6 March 1771, before Daniel Horsmanden. *Signed.* 1 large p. [M.P.G. 365]

xxx. New York, 12 December 1769. Proclamation by Lieut.-Governor Colden for apprehension of rioters who on 19 October 1769 interrupted survey of lands called Wallumschaack, on east side of Hudson River. (No. 22). *Printed.* 1 p.

xxxi. New York, 1 November 1770. Proclamation by Governor Earl of Dunmore for apprehension of rioters who on 26 September 1770 interrupted work of commissioners of New York appointed to partition Wallumschaack. (No. 23). *Printed.* 1 p.

xxxii. New York, 10 June 1767. Minutes of Council of New York. Read, letter from Earl of Shelburne, 11 April 1767, and petitions from Society for Propagating Gospel and Samuel Robinson of Bennington for self and more than 1000 grantees of land on west side of Connecticut River, alleging that their lands have been granted away by government of New York. Allegations denied. (No. 24). *Copy.* 3½ pp.

xxxiii. Petition of inhabitants of land now by H.M.'s order in New York, formerly esteemed to be in New Hampshire, to the King, praying for relief. (No. 25). *Copy.* 2¼ pp.

xxxiv. New York province, 21 January 1771. Affidavit sworn before Simon Stephens, J.P., by Willard Stevens of Charles Town, New Hampshire, that No. xxxiii is true copy. (No. 26). *Copy.* ¼ p.

xxxv. Cumberland County, 2 February 1771. Affidavit sworn before Samuel Wells, J.P., by Malachi Church of Brattleborough, concerning methods used in collection of signatures for New Hampshire petition, No. xxxiii. (No. 27). *Copy.* 6 pp.

xxxvi. New York, 6 March 1771. Affidavit sworn before Daniel Horsmanden by John Kelly of New York, concerning collection of signatures for New Hampshire petition. With list of patents issued by Governor Benning Wentworth, 1749–1764, from map in deponent's possession. (No. 28). *Copy.* 2½ pp.

* xxxvii. New York, 27 February 1771. Affidavit sworn as preceding by Ebenezer Cole, who settled at Shaftsbury six years ago last

spring, when there were only two persons settled north of him on grants from New Hampshire. Description of events in the district 1764 to present. (No. 29). *Copy.* 4½ pp.

* xxxviii. New York, 27 February 1771. Affidavit sworn as preceding by John Munro of Fowlis, Albany County, J.P., concerning riot of 19 October 1769 and other matters. (No. 30). *Copy.* 4½ pp.

xxxix. New York, 2 March 1771. Affidavit sworn as preceding by Simon Stevens of Charles Town, New Hampshire, member of Assembly of New Hampshire, concerning designs of Governor John Wentworth to recover for New Hampshire lands west of Connecticut River. (No. 31). *Copy.* 3 pp.

xl. New York, 2 March 1771. Affidavit sworn as preceding by Samuel Wells, J.P. of Brattleborough, concerning collection of signatures of New Hampshire petition and other matters. (No. 32). *Copy.* 2 pp.

xli. New York, 1 March 1771. Affidavit sworn as preceding by Joseph Blanchard, member of House of Representatives of New Hampshire, concerning designs of Governor John Wentworth in lands west of Connecticut River. (No. 33). *Copy.* 4½ pp.

xlii. New York, 2 March 1771. Affidavit sworn as preceding by Oliver Willard, Assistant Judge of Inferior Court of Common Pleas for Cumberland County, inhabitant of Hertford in that county, concerning Governor Wentworth's intention to grant five islands in Connecticut River, the New Hampshire petition, and other matters. (No. 34). *Copy.* 2¾ pp.

xliii. New York, 4 March 1771. Affidavit sworn as preceding by James Van Cortlandt of the Yonkers, Westchester County, concerning riot in 1764 in patents of Rensslaerswyck and Hoseck. (No. 35). *Copy.* ¾ p.

xliv. Albany, 7 November 1769. Affidavit sworn before Abraham C. Cuyler, Alderman, by John Bleeker of Albany, concerning riot at Wallumsach on 19 October 1769. (No. 36). *Copy.* 2¾ pp.

xlv. Albany, 17 November 1769. Affidavit sworn before J. Roorbach, alderman, by Nanning Vischer of Albany, concerning same. (No. 37). *Copy.* 1¼ pp.

xlvi. Albany, 17 November 1769. Affidavit sworn before John H. Ten Eyck, Recorder, by Thomas Hun of Albany, concerning same. (No. 38). *Copy.* 2½ pp.

xlvii. Albany, 17 November 1769. Affidavit sworn before J. Roorback, alderman, by Peter Lansingh of Albany, concerning same. (No. 39). *Copy.* 1½ pp.

xlviii. Albany, 8 October 1770. Affidavit sworn before Volchert P. Douw, Mayor, by John Bleeker, Peter Lansingh, Thomas Hun and Nanning Vischer, concerning interruption of work of commissioners for deciding Wallomsack patent by Simon Hathaway and others on 12 September 1770. (No. 40). *Copy*. 1½ pp.

* xlix. New York, 9 August 1770. Affidavit sworn before Daniel Horsmanden, by John Grout of Chester, Cumberland County, attorney, concerning affray in May last between posse of Daniel Whipple, Sheriff of Cumberland County, and riotous body of forty armed persons. Deponent was captured and held prisoner. (No. 41). *Copy*. 2½ pp.

* l. New York, 9 August 1770. Affidavit sworn as preceding by Samuel Wells concerning same. (No. 42). *Copy*. 4 pp.

li. New York, 1 November 1770. Petition of subscribers, for selves and others, inhabitants of Cumberland and Gloucester Counties, New York, on west side of Connecticut River, to the King, complaining of riots and opposing petition to transfer to jurisdiction of New Hampshire. *Signed*, Abner Reeve, William Syme, Silas Hamilton, Samuel Wells, and 432 others [*some names illegible*]. One large page, with some signatures on dorse. Also on dorse: Cumberland County, 1 February, 1771. Affidavit sworn before Samuel Wells, J.P., by Israel Curtis, Malachi Church and John Kelly, vouching for authenticity of signatures to this petition and that subscribers, with exceptions, are residents in said counties. *Signed*. ½ large p.

lii. New York, 3 December 1770. Petition of inhabitants of lands on west side of Connecticut River, New York, to Governor Earl of Dunmore. Hope to remain within government of New York. *Signed*, Thomas Chandler and 411 others [*some names illegible*]. 2 large pp.

liii. Gloucester County, 10 January 1771. Affidavit sworn before Abner Fowler, J.P., by John Taplin. Deponent was told by Jonathan Grout that Samuel Chase of Cornish, New Hampshire, told him that the rioters at Windsor, Cumberland County, were advised by Governor Wentworth not to obey laws of New York. *Signed*. 1 p.

liv. Same, 12 January 1771. Affidavit sworn before Thomas Sumner, J.P., by Nathaniel Martin, David Davies, James Aiken, Samuel McDufrey, Hezekiah Sillaway and William Bell, residents of Mooretown, Gloucester County. The town was granted by letters patent of New York last spring, previous to which, farms and possessions of deponents and other inhabitants were reserved to them by order of Council of New York. *Signed*. ½ p.

lv. Same, 9 January 1771. Affidavit sworn before John Taplin, J.P., by John Peters of Mooretown, Gloucester County. Colonel Jacob Bayley influenced and prevented inhabitants of Newbury from signing petition for continuing jurisdiction of New York on west side of Connecticut River. *Signed*. 1 p.

lvi. Same, 12 January 1771. Affidavit sworn before John Peters by Thomas Sumner to same effect. *Signed*. ½ p.

lvii. Cumberland County, 2 February 1771. Affidavit sworn before Samuel Wells by Malachi Church, to same effect. *Signed.* ¾ p.

lviii. Same, 23 January 1771. Affidavit sworn before Samuel Wells, J.P., by John Peters and Malachi Church. They were told by Nathan Stone, of Windsor, of Governor Wentworth's designs to recover for New Hampshire lands west of Connecticut River. *Signed.* 2¾ pp. [C.O.5, 1102, fos. 49–123d; entry of covering letter in C.O.5, 1138, pp. 199–210]

1048

9 March, New York

William Bayard to Earl of Hillsborough. Acts passed in New York and New Jersey concerning boundary between the provinces will, if confirmed, reduce quitrents to Crown by £1163 sterling a year. Solicits place of Joseph Read, deceased. *Copy.* 2 pp. *Endorsed,* R, 22 April. [C.O.5, 1102, fos. 124–125d; entry in C.O.5, 1138, pp. 211–213; copy in C.O.5, 1075, fo. 135, 135d]

1049

10 March, New Bern

Governor William Tryon to Earl of Hillsborough (No. 66), sending journals of Council of North Carolina as Upper House. *Signed.* ½ p. *Endorsed,* R, 15 May. [C.O.5, 314, fos. 91–92d; signed duplicate in C.O.5, 302, fos. 44–45d; entry in C.O.5, 328, p. 223]

1050

11 March, New Bern

Same to same (No. 67), reporting on last session of Assembly and resolves passed in this House respecting Associate Judge Henderson. He is friend to government and had his house and effects burnt last winter. Great difficulty in raising money for operations against insurgents. *Signed.* 1½ pp. *Endorsed,* R, 15 May. *Enclosed:*

i. Account of fees received by Governor Tryon on each instrument issued by him. *Copy,* of account laid before Assembly of North Carolina, certified by J. Edwards. 1½ pp.

ii. North Carolina. Bill for more easy and certain collection of quitrents. *Copy.* 5½ pp. *Endorsed,* Read 22 August 1771. [Covering letter in C.O.5, 314, fos. 93–94d; signed duplicate, with enclosures, in C.O.5, 302, fos. 46–53d; entry of covering letter in C.O.5, 328, pp. 224–226]

1051

10 March, Pensacola

Governor Peter Chester to Earl of Hillsborough (No. 12). Assembly's assuming nomination of Treasurer was indecent attack on Crown's prerogative. I shall be industrious to prevent Council's deliberating on measures not referred to them. I hope members of next Assembly will know better. Mr Hannay's appointment as agent was by Council and Assembly and should have been by Act. *Signed.* 2½ pp. *Endorsed,* R, 21 June. [C.O.5, 588, pp. 115–118, signed duplicate in C.O.5, 578, pp. 137–140; entry in C.O.5, 621, pp. 57–59]

1052

11 March, Pensacola

Same to same (No. 13). General Gage has desired Brigadier Haldimand to have proposed cut between Mississippi and Iberville surveyed; Mr Durnford will go. I do not think it prudent to leave this place. *Signed.* 2 pp. *Endorsed,* R, 21 June. [C.O.5, 588, pp. 119–122; signed duplicate in C.O.5, 578, pp. 141–144; entry in C.O.5, 621, pp. 60–61]

1053

12 March, G.P.O.

Anthony Todd to John Pownall, enclosing the following. It appears extraordinary that the governor of a province should be so indifferent to the correspondence of his people as to desire no more mails might be sent even to the capital until a postmaster should be appointed. *Signed.* I small p. *Endorsed,* R, 13th. *Enclosed:*

i. Savannah, 1 December 1770. Governor James Wright to Peter De Lancey, deputy P.M.G. of Carolina, reporting impossibility of finding anyone to deal with the mail without a salary. No more mail to be sent until an appointment is made. *Copy.* 1¼ small pp. [C.O.5, 661, fos. 13–16d; entry in C.O.5, 247, pp. 1–2]

1054

12 March, Pensacola

Governor Peter Chester to Earl of Hillsborough (No. 14), acknowledging letter of 15 November and enclosures. *Signed.* 1 p. *Endorsed,* R, 21 June. [C.O.5, 588, pp. 123–126; signed duplicate in C.O.5, 578, pp. 145–148; entry in C.O.5, 621, pp. 61–62]

1055

12 March, New Bern

Governor William Tryon to Earl of Hillsborough (No. 68), sending Acts passed in North Carolina last session with comments. *Signed.* 3¼ pp. *Endorsed,* R, 15 May. [C.O.5, 314, fos. 95–96d; signed duplicate, endorsed Read 12 December 1771, in C.O.5, 302, fos. 54–55d; entry in C.O.5, 328, pp. 226–231]

1056

13 March, New Bern

Same to same (No. 69), acknowledging Nos. 34–35 and letters of 15 and 15 November and 11 December. Tonnage Act not obtained but grant made by resolve for purchase of gunpowder and lead. Every possible encouragement will be given to recruiting parties. *Duplicate. Signed.* 1½ pp. *Endorsed,* R, 24 June, original not recd. [C.O.5, 314, fos. 103–104d; signed original, endorsed R, 16 August, Read 12 December 1771, in C.O.5, 302, fos. 56–57d; entry in C.O.5, 328, pp. 232–233]

1057

13 March, Pensacola

Governor Peter Chester to Earl of Hillsborough (No. 15). Alexander Macullagh has been appointed to execute office of deputy Provost Marshal for Samuel Hannay, patentee, in place of David Doig who was charged with rape of a child and absconded. *Signed.* 1 p. *Endorsed,* R, 21 June. [C.O.5, 588, pp. 127–130; signed duplicate in C.O.5, 578, pp. 149–152; entry in C.O.5, 621, pp. 62–63]

1058

14 March, Pensacola

Same to same (No. 16), sending minutes of Council from his arrival to 11 February, and enclosing register of births and burials in this place. *Signed.* ½ p. *Endorsed,* R, 21 June. *Enclosed :*

i. Copy of register of births and burials, 24 June–24 December 1770. Thirty-eight burials, forty-two christenings. *Signed,* Nathaniel Cotton, rector. 6 pp. [C.O.5, 588, pp. 131–142; signed duplicate of covering letter in C.O.5, 578, pp. 153–156; entry of covering letter in C.O.5, 621, p. 63]

1059

14 March, Pensacola

Same to same, enclosing following. *Signed.* ¾ p. *Endorsed,* R, 21 June. *Enclosed :*

i. Treasury Chambers, 7 November 1770. John Robinson to [Governor Chester], asking for list of fees taken by Customs officers. *Copy.* 1¼ pp.

ii. Pensacola, 14 March 1771. Governor Chester to Lords of Treasury, enclosing following. *Duplicate. Signed.* ¾ p.

iii. List of Naval Officer's fees. *Signed*(?), James Ferguson, Naval Officer. 1 p.

iv. Fees received by Comptroller of Customs, Pensacola. *Signed*(?), J. Martin. ½ p.

v. Pensacola, 3 April 1771. Fees of Collector of Customs. *Signed*(?), James Bruce, Collector. 1 p.

vi. Fees of Collector of Customs at Mobile. *Signed*(?), Jacob Blackwell, Collector. 1 p. [C.O.5, 588, pp. 143–164; signed duplicate of covering letter and copy of No. i in C.O.5, 578, pp. 157–164; entry of covering letter in C.O.5, 621, pp. 63–64]

1060

15 March, Whitehall

Commissioners for Trade and Plantations to the King, recommending disallowance of three Acts passed in New York in 1770, vizt. Acts for relief of insolvent debtors; to enable persons to recover debts on promissory notes; for relief of James De Peyster, insolvent debtor. Reasons stated. *Entry. Signatories*, Soame Jenyns, John Roberts, William Fitzherbert, Thomas Whately, Greville. 4 pp. [C.O.5, 1131, pp. 426–429; draft in C.O.5, 1080, pp. 413–418]

1061

15 March, Whitehall

Same to same, recommending disallowance of Act passed in Georgia in 1768 for granting duty on raw neat hides exported. *Entry. Signatories*, Soame Jenyns, John Roberts, William Fitzherbert, Thomas Whately, Greville. 1½ pp. [C.O.5, 674, pp. 358–359]

1062

15 March, Ordnance-office

Board of Ordnance to Earl of Hillsborough, requesting orders to Commodore, Newfoundland, and O.C. land forces at St John's, to furnish men for work on battery to be erected there. *Signed*, H. S. Conway, A. Wilkinson, Charles Cocks. 1 p. *Endorsed*, R, 16 May. [C.O.194, 30, fos. 17–18d; entry in C.O.195, 12, p. 112]

1063

15 March, Burlington

Governor William Franklin to Earl of Hillsborough (No. 26), acknowledging No. 28, Orders and additional instruction, which will be obeyed. *Signed*. 1 p. *Endorsed*, R, 17 June. [C.O.5, 991, fos. 13–14d; entry in C.O.5, 1001, pp. 127–128]

1064

15 March, Charleston

William De Brahm to Earl of Hillsborough (No. 16), reporting progress in survey and mapping of East Florida. *Signed*. 2 pp. *Endorsed*, R, 15 May. *Enclosed:*

i. Sketch of southermost part of promontory formerely called Tegeste, now East Florida. Drawn by William Gerard De Brahm, Surveyor-General for South District of North America. 1 large p. [M.P.G. 347] [covering letter in C.O.5, 72, fos. 192–193d; entry in C.O.5, 228, pp. 54–56]

1065

18 March, St Germain

Marquise de Vaudreuil to [? Earl of Hillsborough], soliciting help in obtaining revenue reserved on two estates in Canada, sold by her husband to M. de Lobiniere in 1763. *French. Entry.* 1½ pp. [C.O.5, 246, pp. 10–11]

1066

20 March, St Augustine

Governor James Grant to Earl of Hillsborough (No. 46), acknowledging Nos. 35–36 and circular of 11 December. Army in America may be completed on this continent, though southern provinces contribute little; recruiting parties from 21st and 31st regiments to go to England. Support for Greek settlement requested. *Duplicate. Signed.* 1¼ pp. *Endorsed*, R, 19 June, original not recd. [C.O.5, 552, fos. 33–34d; signed original in C.O.5, 545, fos. 41–42d; entry in C.O.5, 567, pp. 185–186]

1067

20 March, St Augustine

Same to same (No. 47). Owing to ill health, I shall go home. Dr Turnbull is at Smyrnea and will not interfere with Mr Moultrie, who will probably receive H.M.'s mandamus in few weeks. *Duplicate. Signed.* 1 p. *Endorsed*, R, 19 June, original not recd. [C.O.5, 552, fos. 35–36d; signed original in C.O.5, 545, fos. 43–44d; entry in C.O.5, 567, p. 187]

1068

21 March, London

Memorial of Thomas Ainslie, Collector of Customs at Quebec, to Earl of Hillsborough, complaining of irregularities by Richard Murray, Vendue-Master of Quebec, concerning sale of *Charming Peggy* and cargo. 1 p. [C.O.42, 31, fos. 5–6d]

1069

22 March

Richard Jackson to Commissioners for Trade and Plantations, reporting twenty-one Acts passed in Nova Scotia in 1769 and 1770 proper in point of law. Act granting H.M. excise on tea, coffee and playing-cards is not contrary to law but is commercially objectionable. Act for benefit of fishery on coasts of Nova Scotia is void inasmuch as Assembly is not competent to make laws punishing offences three leagues from shore. *Signed.* 3 large pp. *Endorsed,* Recd. 8 April, Read 10 May 1771. [C.O.217, 26, fos. 60–61d]

1070

[22 March]

Memorial of William Markham, late major, 47th regiment, to Commissioners for Trade and Plantations, requesting grant of 5000 acres of land in New York. *Copy.* 2 pp. *Endorsed,* Recd. 22 March, Read 27 March 1771. [C.O.5, 1075, fos. 79–80d]

1071

26 March, Treasury

John Robinson to John Pownall, sending petition of Lieutenant Roberts, late commissary of Indian affairs under Sir W. Johnson, for opinion of Commissioners for Trade and Plantations thereon. *Signed.* ¾ p. *Endorsed,* Recd. 2 May, Read 10 May 1771. [C.O.323, 27, pp. 85–88]

1072

27 March, Whitehall

Commissioners for Trade and Plantations to Committee of Council for Plantation Affairs. We have considered petition of Charles Garth, agent of South Carolina, for withdrawal of additional instruction to governor of South Carolina of 14 April 1770 and for H.M. to enjoin communication to Commons House of all representations to H.M. relating to proceedings of that House. We do not recommend the petition in either point. *Entry. Signatories,* Soame Jenyns, Edward Eliot, William Fitzherbert, Thomas Whately. 4 pp. [C.O.5, 404, pp. 439–442]

1073

27 March, Whitehall

Same to Governor Thomas Hutchinson. Material objection to bill passed in Massachusetts for preventing the currency in that province of bills of credit of Connecticut, New Hampshire and Rhode Island, is that a new test for admission to offices is established. We have not proposed disallowance, as law is limited to three years, trusting that at expiration some other means will be found. *Entry. Signatories,* as preceding. 2 pp. [C.O.5, 920, pp. 406–407; draft in C.O.5, 897, fos. 283–284d]

1074

27 March, Whitehall

Same to Governor James Wright, explaining objections to Act for laying duty on raw hides exported, recommended for disallowance, and to Act to prevent spreading of smallpox, which should be amended if further continued. *Entry. Signatories,* Soame Jenyns, Edward Eliot, William Fitzherbert, Thomas Whately. 3 pp. [C.O.5, 674, pp. 360–362]

1075

27 March, London

Petition of Frederick Dutens of London, merchant, to Commissioners for Trade and Plantations, for grant of 50,000 acres of land in Bay of Chaleur. *Signed.* 1½ pp. *Endorsed,* Recd. 8 April, Read 10 April 1771. [C.O.42, 7, fos. 207–208d]

1076

27 March, Burlington

Governor William Franklin to Earl of Hillsborough (No. 27), acknowledging circular of 11 December and enclosing following. Assembly will meet 17 April to provide for troops. *Signed.* PS. No. 29 acknowledged. John Smith died yesterday, making two vacancies in Council, which I hope will be supplied by Daniel Cox and John Lawrence. 1½ pp. *Endorsed,* R, 14 June. *Enclosed:*

 i. Burlington, 26 March 1771. Proclamation by Governor Franklin requiring assistance for recruiting to H.M.'s forces. *Printed.* 1 p. [C.O.5, 991, fos. 15–17d; entry of covering letter in C.O.5, 1001, pp. 129–130]

1077

27 March, Virginia

President William Nelson to Earl of Hillsborough (No. 15), acknowledging letter of 11 December. I shall assist recruiting parties. *Signed.* 1 p. *Endorsed,* R, 6 June. [C.O.5, 1349, fos. 80–81d; entry in C.O.5, 1372, p. 166]

1078

27 March, Virginia

Same to same (No. 16), acknowledging No. 39. I hope Earl of Dunmore will arrive by 10 April when General Court begins. I shall obey H.M.'s additional instruction respecting import duty on slaves. Observations enclosed on Mr Jackson's reasoning on disallowed Acts. *Signed.* 1¾ pp. *Endorsed,* R, 6 June. *Enclosed:*

 i. Observations on two Acts of Assembly of Virginia. 3½ pp.

 ii. Remarks on Mr Jackson's observations on Act of Virginia exempting negroes from paying levies. 1 small p. [C.O.5, 1349, fos. 82–86d; entry of covering letter in C.O.5, 1372, pp. 167–169]

1079

27 March, Virginia

Same to Commissioners for Trade and Plantations, acknowledging letter of 14 November. Glebe of Hamilton parish was to be sold so that proceeds could be divided between two vestries; if they were guilty of misappropriation, Assembly would supply remedy. *Signed.* 1½ pp. *Endorsed,* Recd. 5 June, Read 12 June 1771. [C.O.5, 1333, fos. 67–68d]

1080

28 March, St James's

Order of King in Council, reciting and approving report of Committee for Plantation Affairs of 26th inst. on draft instructions for Governor Thomas Hutchinson, Massachusetts. Differences from former instructions noted. *Copy.* 4¾ pp. *Endorsed,* Recd. 12 December, Read 21 December 1772. [C.O.5, 894, pp. 467–474; copy of instructions in C.O.5, 203, fos. 236–252d; sealed original of Order in C.O.5, 27, fos. 30–33d]

1081

28 March, St James's

Same, confirming grant by General Court of Massachusetts in 1762 to Sir F. Bernard, Bt., of island called Mount Desart on north east of Penobscot Bay within bounds of Sagadhock, without prejudice to Crown's rights there. *Copy.* 3¼ pp. *Endorsed,* Recd. 12 December, Read 21 December 1772. [C.O.5, 894, pp. 475–482]

1082

30 March, Soho, London

William Bollan to Earl of Hillsborough. Governor Hutchinson has refused consent to grant to me for service from July 1769; it is suggested that this refusal was conformable to your sentiments. No governor or other person can justly obstruct payment for this service. *Signed.* 4 small pp. [C.O.5, 760, fos. 125–128d]

1083

30 March, Tom's Coffee House, London

Robert Allen and William Tooke to [Lord Rochford]. They expect no success from Lord Harcourt's manner of treating affairs of proprietors of Canada Reconnoissances, and hope to be enabled to apply to Parliament. *Signed.* 3 small pp. *Endorsed,* R, do. *Enclosed:*

    i. Paris, 18 March 1771. MM. Tourton and Baur to Robert Allen. French Ambassador in London is empowered to negotiate. *French.* *Signed.* 2 small pp. *Addressed.* [C.O.5, 43, fos. 248–251d]

1084

1 April, Whitehall

Earl of Hillsborough to Lieut.-General Thomas Gage (No. 42), sending copy of article 43 of instructions to Governor Hutchinson regarding custody of Castle William. Continue to act in concord with him. You are to direct commander at St John's, Newfoundland, to furnish men for building battery or tower at entrance to harbour there, on request from the engineer appointed. *Draft.* 1½ pp. [C.O.5, 89, fos. 70–71d; entry in C.O.5, 243, pp. 8–9]

1085

1 April, Whitehall

* Same to Governor Thomas Hutchinson (No. 6), acknowledging dispatches of 22 December and 17 January, both numbered 34. Your instructions will be very full regarding establishment and command of Castle William. Works at castle should be restricted, both on ground of expense and to avoid causing suspicion. Appearance of a general disposition to promote order and submission to government is pleasing to H.M. Disorders in Eastern country call for interposition of government: Treasury has appointed surveyors to report whether any parts of it should be reserved for supply of naval stores. Meanwhile further settlement should be avoided and magistrates appointed to restrain disorder. *Entry.* 3½ pp. [C.O.5, 765, pp. 202–205; draft in C.O.5, 760, fos. 129–131d]

1086

1 April, Whitehall

Same to Governor James Grant (No. 38), acknowledging Nos. 43–44. Attention to indigo culture approved. Surplus in agent's hands on parliamentary grant will be available for approved purposes. Copy of Treasury's refusal of further support of Greek colonists sent. *Draft.* 1½ pp. [C.O.5, 552, fos. 15–16d; entry in C.O.5, 566, pp. 45–46]

1087

1 April, Whitehall

Same to Governor Peter Chester (No. 3), acknowledging Nos. 6–9. No hope of augmenting defence of West Florida beyond one regiment. Laws referred to counsel. No probability of vacancy in office of Secretary. *Draft.* 1½ pp. [C.O.5, 588, pp. 87–90; entry in C.O.5, 619, pp. 75–76]

1088

1 April, Whitehall

Same to Lieut.-Governor William Bull (No. 45), acknowledging Nos.

39–42. Lord Charles Montagu will embark shortly. Your correspondence and conduct approved. Charles M. Coslett and John Murray appointed Assistant Judges. Commissioners for Trade and Plantations have represented that Agent Garth's petition be not complied with. *Draft.* 2½ pp. [C.O.5, 394, fos. 44–45d; entry in C.O.5, 408, pp. 63–65; entry of warrants for appointment of Coslett, dated 30 March, and Murray, dated 1 April, in C.O.324, 42, p. 258]

1089

1 April, Whitehall

Same to Samuel Holland (No. 6), acknowledging letter of 19 December 1770. Remarks on Eastern New England noted. *Draft.* ¾ p. [C.O.5, 72, fos. 142–143d; entry in C.O.5, 241, p. 374]

1090

1 April, New York

William Bayard to Earl of Hillsborough, alleging irregularities in proceeding of New York Assembly regarding boundary between New York and New Jersey, and injustice to himself in payment of expenses. *Copy.* 4 pp. *Endorsed,* R, 15 May. [C.O.5, 1102, fos. 155–157d; entry in C.O.5, 1138, pp. 217–222]

1091

2 April, New York

Lieut.-General Thomas Gage to Earl of Hillsborough (No. 58), acknowledging No. 39. Posts on the Lakes are in general in very defensible state. Ordnance stores and artillerymen are going to Fort Chartres, and Fort Pitt is to be reinforced from Philadelphia. Much disturbance by Indians in Fort Pitt quarter. Enclosed letter suggests plan to attack us, but, unless the Nations have deceived us, affairs cannot be as dangerous as represented; Sir W. Johnson informed. No disturbances reported from Fort Pitt or Niagara, but bad news from Cherokee country. Mr Stuart writes that this is the effect of Shawnese machinations. Creek-Choctaw war goes on. Ordnance and stores sent to Brig.-General Haldimand at Pensacola. Report on works completed in West Florida; I hope batteries are finished. There are about 450 Spanish troops in Louisiana, 350 at New Orleans and the rest in posts on Mississippi; 500 more expected from Havana. Regiments in Nova Scotia and Boston are to recruit east of Connecticut River; the corps in Canada, the Lakes, New York and Jersey, west of that river and down to Potomac; regiments in the Floridas, in Virginia, Carolina and Georgia. Circular sent to governors soliciting help in recruiting. *Signed.* 6 pp. *Endorsed,* R, 15 May. *Enclosed:*

i. Fort Pitt, 7 March 1771. Information [sent by Captain Edmonstone to Lieut.-General Gage], reporting intelligence from Indians of general plan to attack western posts and frontiers of Virginia and Carolina, negotiated principally by Shawnese and Delawares. *Copy.* 3¼ pp.

ii. Same, without date, with more details of same. *Copy.* 2¼ pp.

iii. List of ordnance sent to Pensacola. *Copy.* *Signatory,* Thomas James, Lieut.-Colonel, R.R.A. 3½ pp.

iv. New York, 22 March 1771. List of engineer's stores sent to Pensacola. *Copy.* *Signatory,* John Montressor. 1 p. [C.O.5, 89, fos. 80–91d; entry of covering letter and enclosures i–ii in C.O.5, 234, pp. 183–196]

1092

2 April, New York

* Same to same (No. 59), acknowledging most secret letter of 2 January, with enclosures. Attack on Louisiana is very practicable, approach by Mississippi being judged most advantageous. Your letter did not arrive till 21 March. I shall assemble troops at New York. 64th and 65th regiments will embark from Halifax to Boston and march thence. I propose to post 21st regiment from St Augustine to Philadelphia. When these arrive, I shall be able to assemble 14th, 21st, 26th, 29th, 64th and 65th regiments, with small train of artillery: about 2000 rank and file, less detachment to garrison Castle William. In event of war, provincial troops will be required for Halifax and Quebec. It is absolutely necessary that H.M. ships convoy troops from New York and proper that frigates go up Mississippi. The six companies of 59th regiment at Halifax will not be able to spare labour for batteries to be raised at St John's, Newfoundland, unless reinforced by provincial troops. *Signed.* 4¼ pp. *Endorsed,* R, 15 May. [C.O.5, 89, fos. 92–94d; entry in C.O.5, 234, pp. 197–201]

1093

2 April, New York

* Governor Earl of Dunmore to Earl of Hillsborough (No. 8), acknowledging No. 2. I hope royal declaration of 1764 concerning New York-New Hampshire borders will be confirmed. Paper enclosed on capture by Spaniards. Lieut.-Colonel Bradstreet claims to have evidence that the patent of 1706 to Johannes Hardenberg and others is invalid; Council has granted him 20,000 acres out of this land as compensation for his expenses. Petitions received from officers and others for land in this location. Land in question is about 1,500,000 acres, not 10 families settled on it. *Signed.* 3¼ pp. *Endorsed,* R, 15 May. *Enclosed:*

i. 27 March. Extract of letter recounting taking by Spanish *guarda-costa* off St Domingo of *Sally,* Ephraim Peate, master, and three sloops, all of Dartmouth, on whaling voyage. *Copy.* 1¼ small pp.

ii. New York, 25 March 1771. Petition of Andrew Anderson and thirty-one others to Governor Earl of Dunmore, for grants of land on south side of Pagtagkan branch of Delaware River, and enclosing state of case of grant of 1706. *Copy. Signatories,* Andrew Anderson and thirty others. 3 pp.

iii. List of petitioners in No. ii and number of acres they claim by H.M.'s proclamation in favour of reduced officers: twenty-nine names. 1 p.

iv. State of case to show that patent to Johannes Hardenbergh and others, commonly called the Great Patent, was issued on false suggestions and that Council of New York in some proceedings thereon did not have required quorum. With references to enclosed evidences Nos. 1–13, v-xvii below. $6\frac{1}{4}$ pp.

v. Petition of Johannes Hardenbergh and company to Governor Viscount Cornbury, 1706. (No. 1). *Copy,* certified by G. Banyar. 1 p.

vi. Minutes of Council of New York, 18 July 1706. Present, governor and four councillors. Hardenberg's petition read, licence to be prepared. (No. 2). *Copy,* certified by G. Banyar. $\frac{1}{2}$ p.

vii. New York, 17 March 1706/7. Petition of Johannes Hardenberg and others to Governor Viscount Cornbury. (No. 3). *Copy,* certified by G. Banyar. $1\frac{3}{4}$ pp.

viii. New York, 19 June 1707. Petition of same to same. (No. 4). *Copy,* certified by G. Banyar. 1 p.

ix. New York, 19 June 1707. Minutes of Council of New York. Present, governor and five councillors. Petitions of inhabitants of Hurley, Ulster County, and of J. Hardenbergh and company, ordered to lie on table. (No. 5). *Copy,* certified by G. Banyar. 1 p.

x. New York, 4 February 1707/8. Petition of J. Hardenbergh and others to Governor Viscount Cornbury. (No. 6). *Copy,* certified by G. Banyar. $1\frac{1}{2}$ pp.

xi. New York, 5 February 1707[/8]. Minutes of Council of New York. Present, governor and six councillors. Hardenbergh and the inhabitants of Hurley to be heard on their respective petitions. (No. 7). *Copy,* certified by G. Banyar. 1 p.

xii. New York, 18 March 1707/8. Same. Present, governor and four councillors including T. Wenham. Petition of inhabitants of Hurley referred to gentlemen of Council. Attorney-General to prepare letters patent for lands petitioned for by J. Hardenbergh and company. (No. 8). *Copy,* certified by G. Banyar. 1 p.

xiii. New York, 15 April 1708. Same. Present, governor and four councillors including T. Wenham. Warrant for patent to J. Hardenbergh and company signed. Quitrent, £3. (No. 9). *Copy,* certified by G. Banyar. $\frac{1}{2}$ p.

xiv. 12 January 1708. Extract of release by Robert Lurting of New York, merchant, to Thomas Wenham of New York, merchant, of one-seventh part of lands in Ulster and Albany Counties granted to Johannes Hardenbergh and six others, of whom Lurting was one. (No. 10). *Copy*, certified by G. Banyar. 1¼ pp.

xv. Instruction to Governor Lord Lovelace of New York not to act without quorum of five councillors unless on extraordinary emergencies. (No. 11). *Copy*, certified by G. Banyar. ¼ p.

xvi. 3 May 1702. Minutes of Council of New York recording actions of Governor Viscount Cornbury when only four members of Council were present. (No. 12). *Copy*, certified by G. Banyar. 1 p.

xvii. 20 April 1708. Extract of letters patent to J. Hardenbergh and others, granting land in Ulster and Albany Counties. (No. 13). *Copy*, certified by G. Banyar. ¾ p.

xviii. Schedule of 26 lots totalling 1,120,617 acres granted to J. Hardenbergh and company in 1708, commonly called the Great Patent. Plus 25,000 acres in dispute with Rochester and 350,000 acres claimed by patentees 41 years later. Claimants also claim parts of other patents. 1½ pp.

xix. Map of lands between Hudson River and Fishkill or main branch of Delaware River, claimed under patent of 20 April 1708 to J. Hardenbergh and six others. Drawn 30 March 1771 by Simon Metcalfe, deputy Surveyor. 1 large p. [M.P.G. 365]. [C.O.5, 1102, fos. 128–154d; entry of covering letter in C.O.5, 1138, pp. 213–217; signed duplicate of covering letter, dated 7 May 1771, in C.O.5, 1075, fos. 136–137d]

1094

2 April, Boston

Governor Thomas Hutchinson to Earl of Hillsborough (No. 1), acknowledging separate letter of 7 December and commission, which was published here in usual form. I have avoided asking or receiving grants from government since last April and shall continue to do so. I have received civility and respect from all but a few. Nos. 1–3 and circular of 11 December received. I see no inconvenience in entering No. 2 on Council's journals. I shall refuse grants to agents. I hope for better success relating to Eastern Country. Proclamation issued requiring civil officers to aid recruiting parties. Allowance to two officers at Castle acknowledged. Party against government will not be able again to carry vote against doing business in Assembly; if they should, I shall end session. *Signed.* 2¼ pp. *Endorsed,* R, 25 May. [C.O.5, 760, fos. 134–135d; entry in C.O.5, 768, pp. 186–189; signed duplicate in C.O.5, 894, pp. 271–274]

1095

2 April, Charleston

Lieut.-Governor William Bull to Earl of Hillsborough (No. 45). I assented to two Acts and one Ordinance. Assembly adjourned to 7 May. James Simpson appointed Attorney-General in absence of Mr Leigh. *Signed.* 1¼ pp. *Endorsed,* R, 15 May. [C.O.5, 394, fos. 74–75d; signed duplicate in C.O.5, 380, fos. 28–29d; entry in C.O.5, 409, pp. 227–228]

1096

3 April, Whitehall

Circular. John Pownall to Governors of Quebec, Nova Scotia, New Hampshire, Massachusetts, New Jersey, New York, Pennsylvania and Virginia, enclosing to each ten copies of following. *Draft.* ¾ p. *Enclosed,*

i. *Description of the Manner of Making Tar in Sweden;* with *Description of the Manner of Making Pitch. Printed.* 31 pp., with 4 pp. of diagrams. [C.O.5, 72, fos. 144–164d; entry of covering letter in C.O.5, 241, p. 375]

1097

3 April, Paris

Extract of letter from Lord Harcourt to Lord Rochford. No present expectation of success in Canada Reconnoissances business. *Copy.* ¾ p. [C.O.5, 43, fos. 252–253d]

1098

4 April, Annapolis

Deputy Governor Robert Eden to Earl of Hillsborough (No. 9), acknowledging circular of 11 December. Recruiting parties will be assisted. Proceedings of Assembly enclosed: I cannot boast of great harmony amongst us. Reduction of officers' fees and clergymen's salaries in new Inspection law was stumbling block. Maryland has little to do with Indian trade. No. 20 acknowledged. *Signed.* 3¼ pp. *Endorsed,* R, 1 June. *Enclosed:*

i. *Votes and Proceedings of Lower House of Assembly of Maryland,* 25 September–2 November 1770. *Printed.* 55 pp.

ii Same, 5–21 November 1770. *Printed.* 34 pp.

iii. *Laws of Maryland,* passed September–November 1770. *Printed.* 33 pp. [C.O.5, 1284, fos. 33–95d; entry of covering letter in C.O.5, 1300, pp. 247–251]

1099

5 April, Old Jewry, London

Memorial of Samuel Smith, agent of Island of St John, to Commissioners for Trade and Plantations, asking when second moiety of quitrents payable by proprietors of the colony is to commence. 1 p. *Endorsed*, Recd. 8 April, Read 10 April 1771. [C.O.226, 1, fos. 10–10A dorse]

1100

5 April, Pensacola

Governor Peter Chester to Earl of Hillsborough (No. 17), acknowledging circular of 11 December 1770. I shall attend to security of this province. *Signed.* ½ p. *Endorsed*, R, 21 June. [C.O.5, 588, pp. 165–168; signed duplicate, endorsed Read 12 December 1771, in C.O.5, 578, pp. 169–172; entry in C.O.5, 621, p. 65]

1101

6 April, Pensacola

Same to same (No. 18), acknowledging No. 1 and disallowance of Act to encourage settlement west of Charlotte County, which was contradictory to spirit of the constitution. I wonder how it could ever have been framed. *Signed.* 1¼ pp. *Endorsed*, R, 21 June. [C.O.5, 588, pp. 169–172; signed duplicate, endorsed Read 12 December 1771, in C.O.5, 578, pp. 173–176; entry in C.O.5, 621, pp. 65–66]

1102

6 April

Richard Jackson to Commissioners for Trade and Plantations, reporting nineteen Acts passed in Massachusetts in November 1770 proper in point of law, though there is a seeming indecorum in Impost Act. *Signed.* 2½ large pp. *Endorsed*, Recd. 8 April, Read 10 May 1771. [C.O.5, 894, pp. 211–214]

1103

6 April

Same to same, reporting on six Acts passed in New Hampshire in 1770, proper in point of law. *Signed.* 1½ pp. *Endorsed*, Recd. 8 April, Read 15 May 1771. [C.O.5, 930, fos. 99–100d]

1104

8 April

Same to same. Ordinance issued in Quebec in February 1770 for more effectual administration of justice is fit to pass into law unless you think it falls under description of law of new and extraordinary nature. *Signed.* 1 p. *Endorsed,* Recd. 8 April, Read 26 April 1771. [C.O.42, 7, fos. 209–210d]

1105

8 April, Whitehall

John Pownall to Richard Jackson, sending extract of letter from Governor Chester with observations on Acts of West Florida. Reconsider Acts on which you have already reported in light of these observations. *Entry.* 1 p. [C.O.5, 600, p. 221]

1106

8 April, Halifax

Governor Lord William Campbell to Earl of Hillsborough (No. 72), enclosing following. *Signed.* 1¼ pp. *Endorsed,* R, 17 June. *Enclosed:*

    i. Halifax, 6 April 1771. Report by Chief Engineer W. Spry to Lieut.-Colonel Thomas Bruce, O.C. troops, Nova Scotia, on defences of Halifax. *Copy,* certified by W. Spry. 5 pp.

    ii. Halifax, 6 April 1771. Resolution by Governor Lord William Campbell, Lieut.-Colonel Bruce, Major Fleming, commanding 64th regiment, Captain Spry, and Richard Bulkeley, Secretary of province, to repair batteries defending Halifax. *Copy.* 1 p. [C.O.217, 48, fos. 27–34d; entry of covering letter in C.O.218, 17, pp. 247–248]

1107

8 April, Buckingham-street, London

Michael Francklin to Joshua Sharpe. It is true that I am to go out with Admiral Montagu or in one of his squadron, but I shall not return to America without knowledge and approbation of Captain Hughes. *Signed.* 1 small p. *Addressed.* [C.O.217, 34, fos. 225–226d]

1108

[8 April]

Memorial of Nicholas Darby of London, merchant, to Commissioners for Trade and Plantations. Memorialist has engaged in fishery on coast of Labrador since 1764 but suffered damages by Eskimos, and at hands of Samuel Davis, Lieutenant of Marines, commander at York Fort. Prays for relief. *Copy.* 4½ pp. *Endorsed,* Recd. 8 April, Read 10 April 1771. [C.O.194, 18, fos. 82–85d]

1109

9 April

Richard Jackson to Commissioners for Trade and Plantations, reporting on seven Acts passed in New Jersey in March 1770, proper in point of law. Act to explain Act for relief of insolvent debtors is recommended for disallowance. *Signed.* 2¼ large pp. *Endorsed,* Read 10 May 1771. [C.O.5, 979, fos. 23–24d]

1110

10 April, Whitehall

Earl of Hillsborough to Lords of Admiralty, requesting orders to Commodore, Newfoundland, to furnish men for work on battery at entrance to St John's harbour. *Draft.* 1 p. [C.O.194, 30, fos. 19–20d; entry in C.O.195, 15, pp. 39–40]

1111

10 April, Whitehall

Commissioners for Trade and Plantations to the King, recommending grant of 5000 acres of land in New York to William Markham, late major, 47th regiment. *Entry. Signatories,* Soame Jenyns, John Roberts, William Fitzherbert, Thomas Whately. 1½ pp. [C.O.5, 1131, pp. 430–431; draft in C.O.5, 1080, pp. 419–422]

1112

10 April, Whitehall

Same to same, recommending that James Jones, appointed by Governor Chester to be of Council in West Florida, be confirmed. *Entry. Signatories,* Hillsborough, Soame Jenyns, John Roberts, William Fitzherbert, Thomas Whately. 1 p. [C.O.5, 600, p. 222]

1113

[10 April]

Petition of Lieut.-Colonel Thomas Howard to Commissioners for Trade and Plantations, requesting grant of 10,000 acres of land in New

York on usual terms. *Copy.* ¾ p. *Endorsed,* Recd., Read 10 April 1771. [C.O.5, 1075, fos. 81–82d]

1114

11 April, Ordnance-office

John Boddington to John Pownall. Unless the soldiers of garrison in Newfoundland are obliged to assist in works, little progress can be made in erecting battery at St John's harbour. Board desires Commodore will inquire into inhabitants' claims on account of destroying entrance to Quiddy Viddy. *Signed.* 1¼ pp. *Endorsed,* R, 12th. *Enclosed:*

  i. Kensington, 12 February 1699. Order that soldiers be obliged to work in fortifications at St John's, Newfoundland. *Copy.* 1 p. [C.O.194, 30, fos. 21–24d; entry of covering letter in C.O.195, 12, pp. 112–113]

1115

11 April, Halifax

Governor Lord William Campbell to Earl of Hillsborough (No. 73), acknowledging No. 43 and circular on recruiting. Expenses of proceedings on vacation of McNutt's grant not yet met: order for payment out of quitrents requested. Minutes of Council of Nova Scotia, July–December last, sent. *Duplicate. Signed.* 1½ pp. *Endorsed,* R, 15 June, original not recd. *Enclosed:*

  i. Minutes of Council of Nova Scotia, 19 September 1770, recording fees to be taken in Court of Escheats. *Copy.* 1¼ pp. [C.O.217, 48, fos. 23–26d; signed original of covering letter in C.O.217, 26, fos. 80–81d, and entry in C.O.218, 17, pp. 257–258; copy of enclosure in C.O.217, 26, fos. 72–73d]

1116

12 April, Whitehall

Commissioners for Trade and Plantations to the King, recommending grant of 10,000 acres of land in New York to Lieut.-Colonel Thomas Howard. *Entry. Signatories,* Hillsborough, Soame Jenyns, William Fitzherbert, Thomas Whately. 1½ pp. [C.O.5, 1131, pp. 432–433; draft in C.O.5, 1080, pp. 423–426]

1117

12 April, Whitehall

John Pownall to Clerk of Council in Waiting, sending addresses and petitions of inhabitants of Quebec. *Draft.* ¾ p. [C.O.42, 31, fos. 7–8d; entry in C.O.43, 8, p. 91]

1118

12 April, Whitehall

Same to John Boddington, sending papers showing directions given in respect of troops to be employed as workmen on fortifications at St John's, Newfoundland. *Draft.* ¾ p. [C.O.194, 30, fos. 25–26d; entry in C.O.195, 15, pp. 40–41]

1119

12 April, New Bern

* Governor William Tryon to Earl of Hillsborough (No. 70), reporting proceedings against Hermon Husbands. I am raising militia to march against insurgents. General Waddell commands militia from western counties. I have asked General Gage for two field-pieces. Papers enclosed. Governor Bull and President Nelson informed. *Signed.* 4¼ pp. *Endorsed*, R, 21 June. *Enclosed:*

* i. Mecklenberg County, 8 March 1771. Affidavit sworn before William Harris, J.P., by Waighstill Avery, taken prisoner by Regulators on 6 March. *Copy.* 2¼ pp.

ii. 15 March 1771. Presentment by grand jury of New Bern of Regulators as enemies to H.M.'s person and government and to liberty of his subjects. *Copy.* 1½ pp.

iii. Terms of association to support civil government in North Carolina. *Copy.* ¾ p.

* iv. Salisbury, 18 March 1771. John Frohock and Alexander Martin to Governor Tryon, reporting meeting with Regulators on 6–7 March. We agreed to appointment of arbitrators. *Copy.* 3½ pp.

v. New Bern, 19 March 1771. Governor Tryon to commanding officers of militia regiments, calling for men to be embodied. *Copy.* 2½ pp.

* vi. New Bern, 5 April 1771. Governor Tryon to John Frohock and Alexander Martin. Mode of your agreement with insurgents is unconstitutional, dishonourable and dangerous to society. *Copy.* 1 p. [C.O.5, 314, fos. 105–120d; signed duplicate of covering letter and copies of Nos. i–ii and iv–vi, in C.O.5, 302, fos. 58–71d; entry of covering letter in C.O.5, 328, pp. 234–239]

1120

13 April, New Bern

Same to same (No. 71), enclosing following. *Signed.* ½ p. *Endorsed*, R, 21 June. *Enclosed:*

i. Minutes of Council of North Carolina, 13 February–19 March 1771. *Copy*, certified by Robert Palmer. 13½ pp. [C.O.5, 314, fos.

121–136d; signed duplicate of covering letter in C.O.5, 302, fos. 72–73d; entry of covering letter in C.O.5, 328, p. 239]

1121

13 April, Pensacola

Governor Peter Chester to Earl of Hillsborough (No. 19), enclosing following. John Stuart daily expected. I believe there is no intention in these savages to commence hostilities against us; ill behaviour was from riotous young men returning from war. Because boundary between Indians and us has not been settled, I cannot say if disturbances took place in the province. Henry Le Fleur appears to have grounds for enclosed demands, but your directions needed. *Signed.* 3½ pp. *Endorsed*, R, 21 June. *Enclosed :*

i. Undated letter from Charles Stuart to Governor Chester, recounting grievances of Chickasaws, Choctaws and Creeks. Superintendent has appointed person to manage tribes inhabiting lakes and banks of Mississippi. *Copy.* 5 pp.

ii. West Florida, 12 April 1771. Affidavit sworn before Philip Livingston jnr., J.P., by Andrew Hamton, reporting Indian disturbances on east side of Alabama River. *Copy.* 3 pp.

iii. West Florida, 12 April 1771. Same, by Thomas Fleming, reporting same events. *Copy.* 3 pp.

iv. Pensacola, 10 April 1771. Memorial of Henry Le Fleur to Governor Chester, seeking payment for services as interpreter at Natchez. *Copy.* 1½ pp.

v. Pensacola, 26 November 1768. Lieut.-Governor Montfort Browne to Henry Le Fleur, appointing him to above post. *Copy.* 1 p. [C.O.5, 588, pp. 173–200; signed duplicate of covering letter, endorsed Read 12 December, and copies of enclosures in C.O.5, 578, pp. 177–204; entry of covering letter in C.O.5, 621, pp. 66–70]

1122

13 April, Halifax

Governor Lord William Campbell to Earl of Hillsborough, applying for leave to return to England or go elsewhere in America for recovery of health, eyesight particularly. *Duplicate. Signed.* 2 small pp. *Endorsed,* R, 24 June, original not recd. *Enclosed :*

i. Note of Lord William Campbell's services in India and North America. 1 small p. [C.O.217, 48, fos. 41–44d; entry in C.O.218, 18, pp. 2–3]

1123

13 April, Quebec

President H. T. Cramahé to Earl of Hillsborough (No. 6), enclosing following. *Signed.* ½ p. *Endorsed,* R, 12 July. *Enclosed :*

i. Minutes of Council of Quebec, 5 January–14 February 1771. *Copy*, certified by George Allsopp, deputy clerk. 9 pp. [C.O.42, 31, fos. 29–35d; entry of covering letter in C.O.43, 13, p. 8; signed duplicate of covering letter in C.O.42, 8, fos. 31–32d]

124

4 April, Williamsburg

Richard Starke to [Earl of Hillsborough], concerning Vice-Admiralty Court in Virginia. *Signed.* 1½ small pp. *Endorsed*, R, 4 June. [C.O.5, 54, fo. 9, 9d]

125

5 April, St James's

Order of King in Council, appointing James Jones to be of the Council in West Florida. *Copy.* 1 p. *Endorsed*, Recd. 12 December, Read 21 December 1772. [C.O.5, 579, pp. 167–170; warrant, dated 17 April, in C.O.324, 42, p. 260; sealed original of Order in C.O.5, 27, fos. 36–37d]

126

5 April, Whitehall

Earl of Hillsborough to Earl of Rochford, sending following. Walton & Co. were formerly contractors for provisions to Spanish garrison of St Augustine. *Draft.* 1 p. *Enclosed :*

i. Fort George, 1 August 1769. Governor Sir H. Moore to Earl of Hillsborough, enclosing following. Application to governor of Havana was without success. *Signed.* 1 p. *Endorsed*, Received from Mr Blackburn, agent for parties named, in March 1771.

ii. Memorial of John Blackburn of London, merchant, agent for William and Jacob Walton of New York, praying for relief. 1¼ pp. [C.O.5, 1102, fos. 43–48d; entry of covering letter in C.O.5, 1141, p. 173]

127

6 April

Opinion of Richard Jackson that the King may confer dignity of Baronet on one of his new subjects in Canada. *Signed.* 3 pp. [C.O.5, 43, fos. 264–265d]

128

[6 April]

Petition of Alexander Duncan to Commissioners for Trade and Plantations, for grant of 5000 acres of land in East Florida. *Signed.* 1 p. *Endorsed*, Recd. 16 April, Read 10 May 1771. [C.O.5, 545, fos. 3–4d]

1129

[*16 April*]

Petition of Adam Duncan to Commissioners for Trade and Plantations, for grant of 5000 acres of land in East Florida. *Signed.* 1 p. *Endorsed,* Recd. 16 April, Read 10 May 1771. [C.O.5, 545, fos. 5–6d]

1130

[*16 April*]

Petition of George Ramsay to Commissioners for Trade and Plantations, for grant of 5000 acres of land in East Florida. *Signed.* 1 p. *Endorsed,* Recd. 16 April, Read 10 May 1771. [C.O.5, 545, fos. 7–8d]

1131

17 April, Admiralty

Lords of Admiralty to Earl of Hillsborough, inquiring if there is to be alteration in instructions for protection of Newfoundland fishery this year. *Signed,* Sandwich, Palmerston, A. Hervey. 1 p. *Endorsed,* R, 19 April. [C.O.194, 30, fos. 27–28d; entry in C.O.195, 12, p. 14]

1132

17 April

Warrant for appointment of James Macpherson as Secretary and Clerk of Council of West Florida. *Entry.* ¾ p. [C.O.324, 42, pp. 258–259]

1133

17 April, Virginia

President William Nelson to Earl of Hillsborough (No. 17), acknowledging No. 40. No commission for trial of pirates was received here. Since Bishop Gibson's death, commissaries have been appointed by letters from Bishops of London, which they have not thought sufficient authority. Cause has been lately instituted against minister for immorality. *Signed.* 2½ pp. *Endorsed,* R, 6 June. [C.O.5, 1349, fos. 87–88d; entry in C.O.5, 1372, pp. 169–171]

1134

[*17 April*]

Memorial of Lieut.-Colonel Douglas, on half-pay, to Earl of Hillsborough. Land allotted to him in Island of St John is unfavourable; prays for grant of 20,000 acres of land in East Florida where he proposes to settle families from the Levant. 1 small p. *Endorsed,* Recd. 17 April, Read 10 May 1771. [C.O.5, 545, fos. 9–10d]

1135

[*17 April*]

Memorial of Francis Edward Douglas, merchant in Calcutta and Bengal, to Earl of Hillsborough, for grant of 20,000 acres of land in East Florida where he proposes to settle families from Greek Islands. 1 p. *Endorsed*, Recd. 17 April, Read 10 May 1771. [C.O.5, 545, fos. 11–12d]

1136

18 April, Halifax

Governor Lord William Campbell to Earl of Hillsborough (No. 74). Orders came today for removal of 64th and 65th regiments to Boston; I have not received least intimation of it myself. *Signed*. 1 p. *Endorsed*, R, 17 June. [C.O.217, 48, fos. 35–36d; entry in C.O.218, 17, pp. 248–249]

1137

19 April, Boston

* Governor Thomas Hutchinson to Earl of Hillsborough (No. 2), enclosing oration which, with other publications, confirms people in disrespect to supreme authority. Persons of best character and estates are outvoted by men of lowest order at town meeting. I shall end General Court in few days. Council's conduct unexceptionable. I hope attempts of majority of House to perplex affairs of government will produce change of members. *Signed*. 1¼ pp. *Endorsed*, R, 31 May. *Enclosed :*

i. *Oration Delivered 2 April 1771 to Commemorate the Bloody Tragedy of 5 March 1770*, by James Lovell, A.M. Printed at Boston by Edes and Gill, by order of town of Boston. *Printed*. 19 pp.

ii. *Massachusetts Gazette and Boston Weekly Newsletter*, 19 April 1771, reporting addresses of Council, Justices of Common Pleas and Justices of General Sessions to Governor Hutchinson. *Printed*. 4 pp. [C.O.5, 760, fos. 136–149d; entry of covering letter in C.O.5, 768, pp. 190–191; signed duplicate of covering letter, endorsed Read 12 December 1771, in C.O.5, 894, pp. 293–296]

138

19 April]

etition of John Noble of Bristol and Andrew Pinson of Dartmouth, erchants and partners, to Commissioners for Trade and Plantations. hey have fished on Newfoundland and Labrador coasts for seven years, nd pray for use of Temple Bay, near Pitts Harbour, for erection of ages etc. and liberty to extend nets from Whale Island to shores of ay. *Copy*. 1½ pp. *Endorsed*, Read 19 April 1771. [C.O.194, 18, fos. 6–87d]

1139

[*19 April*]

Petition of Allan Auld, attorney for George Walker, formerly comman
der-in-chief of royal family's private ships of war, to Commissioners fo
Trade and Plantations, praying for grant to Walker of 15,000 acres o
land in Nova Scotia. *Signed.* ½ p. *Endorsed,* Recd. 19 April, Rea
10 May 1771. [C.O.217, 26, fos. 50–51d]

1140

[*19 April*]

Petition of Hugh Baillie, late of Bengal, to same for same. *Signed.* ½ p
Endorsed, as preceding. [C.O.217, 56, fos. 52–53d]

1141

[*19 April*]

Petition of William Semple, late of Bengal, to same for same. *Signed.* ½ p
Endorsed, as preceding. [C.O.217, 56, fos. 54–55d]

1142

[*19 April*]

Petition of Hugh Baillie, Doctor of Laws, to same for same. *Signed.* ½ p
Endorsed, as preceding. [C.O.217, 56, fos. 56–57d]

1143

[*19 April*]

Petition of Allan Auld, merchant in London, to same for same. *Signe*
½ p. *Endorsed,* as preceding. [C.O.217, 56, fos. 58–59d]

1144

20 April, Whitehall

Earl of Hillsborough to Lords of Admiralty. No change is necessar
in Mr Byron's instructions this year. *Draft.* ½ p. [C.O.194, 30, fo
29–30d; entry in C.O.195, 15, p. 41]

1145

20 April, Whitehall

Same to Governor Lord Charles Montagu (private), recommendin
Mr Bell, native of Lisburn, Ireland, for grant of land in South Carolin
Entry. ½ p. [C.O.5, 246, p. 1]

1146

20 April

Richard Jackson to Commissioners for Trade and Plantations, reporting on two Acts passed in Pennsylvania in 1769, proper in point of law. Act for relief of John Relfe and Abraham Howel, prisoners, and Act for relief of John Galbreath, prisoner, lack clauses which insolvency Acts should have. *Signed.* 2 pp. *Endorsed,* Read 24 April 1771. [C.O.5, 1287, fos. 39–40d]

1147

20 April

Warrant for appointment of John Fewtrell as Assistant Judge in South Carolina. *Entry.* ¼ p. [C.O.324, 42, p. 263]

1148

22 April

Richard Jackson to Commissioners for Trade and Plantations, reporting on fourteen Acts passed in Pennsylvania in 1770, proper in point of law. Act for sale of goods distrained needs to be amended. Act for relief of prisoners should be repealed unless you deem it sufficient for this year to rely on control given to the court. *Signed.* 3 pp. *Endorsed,* Read 24 April 1771. [C.O.5, 1278, fos. 37–38d]

1149

23 April, Halifax

John Duport to Earl of Hillsborough, describing Island of St John and arrival of governor, and soliciting payment of and addition to salary as Chief Justice. *Signed.* 4 pp. *Endorsed,* R, 17 June. [C.O.226, 4, fos. 41–43d]

1150

24 April, Whitehall

Commissioners for Trade and Plantations to the King, recommending that present instructions relating to granting lands in Quebec be revoked and governor authorized to grant lands, with advice of Council, in fief and seigneurie, as hertofore, but omitting *haute, moyenne* and *basse justice,* exercise whereof has been long disused. *Entry. Signatories,* Hillsborough, Soame Jenyns, John Roberts, William Fitzherbert, Greville, Thomas Whately. 3 pp. [C.O.43, 2, pp. 162–164]

1151

24 April, Whitehall

Same to Committee of Council for Plantation Affairs. We have considered papers on boundary between North and South Carolina and petition of Charles Garth on this subject, and propose that the governors be instructed to appoint commissioners to continue the boundary from Salisbury Road, where it now ends, along said road to Catawba lands, along south, east and north boundaries of said lands, to Catawba River, thence along said river to confluence of north and south branches thereof, thence due west to Cherokee boundary. *Draft. Signatories*, Soame Jenyns, John Roberts, W. Fitzherbert, Greville, Thomas Whately. 4 pp. [C.O.5, 381, fos. 364–366d; entry in C.O.5, 404, pp. 443–446]

1152

26 April, Whitehall

Same to the King, proposing Barnard Elliot and David Deas to be of the Council in South Carolina. *Draft. Signatories*, Hillsborough, Soame Jenyns, Edward Eliot, W. Fitzherbert, Greville. 1 p. [C.O.5, 381, fos. 367–368d; entry in C.O.5, 404, p. 447]

1153

26 April, Whitehall

Same to same, proposing William Axtell to be of the Council of New York in room of Joseph Reade, deceased. *Entry. Signatories*, Soame Jenyns, Edward Eliot, William Fitzherbert, Greville. ½ p. [C.O.5, 1131, p. 434; draft in C.O.5, 1080, pp. 427–430]

1154

26 April, Whitehall

Same to same, proposing Sir Nathaniel Duckenfield and Marmaduke Jones to be of the Council in North Carolina. *Entry. Signatories*, Soame Jenyns, Edward Eliot, Greville, Thomas Whately. 1 p. [C.O.5, 326, p. 178; draft in C.O.5, 305, fos. 56–57d]

1155

26 April, Whitehall

Same to same, recommending Daniel Coxe to be of the Council in New Jersey in room of John Ladd, deceased. *Entry. Signatories*, Soame Jenyns, Edward Eliot, William Fitzherbert, Greville, Thomas Whately. 1 p. [C.O.5, 999, p. 238]

1156

26 April, Tom's Coffee House, London

Robert Allen and William Tooke to [Lord Rochford], enclosing case and petition which they propose to present to Parliament. *Signed*. 1 p. *Endorsed*, R, do. *Enclosed*:

    i. Memorial of holders of Reconnoissances given in exchange for Canada paper, to House of Commons for relief. 2½ pp. [Covering letter in C.O.5, 43, fos. 266–267d; enclosure at fos. 296–297d; another copy at fos. 314–315d; similar memorial to Lord Weymouth, at fos. 312–313d; similar memorial to House of Lords, at fos. 316–317d]

1157

27 April, Charleston

* John Stuart to Earl of Hillsborough (No. 31). Dissatisfaction of Western Indians at extensive cessions of land at Fort Stanwix congress induced them to promote confederacies. Want of regulation of traders gives rise to many disorders. Cherokees lately proposed to give land to pay debts. I embark for Pensacola tomorrow. Mr Cameron has gone to mark Virginia boundary. *Signed.* 4 pp. *Endorsed,* R, 21 June. *Enclosed :*

i. Charleston, 11 December 1770. Abstract of letter from John Stuart to Alexander Cameron. Present of land to your son was improper. *Copy.* ½ p.

ii. Lochaber, 23 January 1771. Extract of letter from Alexander Cameron to John Stuart, justifying gift of land to his son by Cherokees. *Copy.* 1½ pp.

iii. Toqueh, 4 March 1771. Alexander Cameron to John Stuart, reporting on Cherokees. I am at a loss to judge the Great Warrior's real sentiments. No parties have gone against Chickasaws. Cherokees wish to dispose of land for debts. *Copy.* 3¼ pp.

* iv. Toqueh, 19 March 1771. Same to same, reporting suspected negotiation between Cherokees and Creeks for alliance against whites. Cherokees resent extension of Virginia's frontier. Parties of Northern and Western Indians continually coming and going. *Copy.* 3 pp.

v. Keowee, 12 February 1771. Talk from headmen of Lower Towns (Cherokee) to warriors and beloved men over the hills, expressing hopes for peace. *Copy.* 1 p.

* vi. Toqueh, 12 February 1771. Talk from Ouconnastotah to John Stuart, inquiring if Northern Indians have, as they say, Sir William Johnson's liberty to go against Choctaws. *Copy.* 1 p.

vii. Toqueh, 28 February 1771. Talk from Alexander Cameron to Overhill Cherokee chiefs, warning them against ceding lands to traders, and against Western Indians. *Copy.* 1¼ pp.

viii. Toqueh, 3 March 1771. Report of speeches by Great Warrior, Judd's Friend, The Prince and The Corn Tassel at convention of Overhill Cherokee chiefs. *Copy. Signatory,* Alexander Cameron. 2¼ pp.

ix. Chote, Cherokee Nation, Upper Hills, 22 February 1771. Cession of land by Cherokee sachems and warriors to their traders. Land begins at mouth of Kayugas and is five measures long and five measures broad—sixty square miles. *Copy. Signatories,* Oconastato, his mark; and marks of Willanawaw, Judd's Friend or Ostonego, Villanota, Kenatita, Hyentty-tisky, Scattielesky, Ugy-Youlgy. *Witnessed,* by John Godfrey Riegger, John Walker, Richard Field. 1 large p. [C.O.5, 72, fos. 210–229d; entry of covering letter in C.O.5, 228, pp. 62–67]

1158

27 April, Charleston

John Stuart to Earl of Hillsborough (No. 32, private), asking for leave in England on account of illness. *Signed.* 1 p. *Endorsed,* R, 21 June. [C.O.5, 72, fos. 230–231d; entry in C.O.5, 228, p. 68]

1159

29 April, Whitehall

Order of Committee of Council for Plantation Affairs, approving report of Commissioners for Trade and Plantations of 22 February on petition of Frederick Philipse for lease of mines in Manor of Philipseburgh, New York. Draft instruction to governor to be prepared. *Seal. Signed,* Stephen Cottrell. 1¼ pp. *Endorsed,* Recd. 2 May, Read 10 May 1771. [C.O.5, 1075, fos. 83–84d]

1160

29 April

Warrant to Master-General and Board of Ordnance for appointment of engineers for building fortifications at St John's, Newfoundland. *Entry.* 1 p. *Attached:*

    i. Establishment of engineers for Newfoundland. *Entry.* ¼ p. [C.O. 324, 42, pp. 264–265]

1161

29 April, Quebec

President H. T. Cramahé to Earl of Hillsborough (No. 7), acknowledging circulars of 15 November and 11 December. No violence committed on Indians on this frontier. Notice of last July's projected meeting of commissioners for Indian regulation arrived too late; meeting to be concerted for December or January next. Regiments can expect few recruits here. *Signed.* 2 pp. *Endorsed,* R, 12 July. [C.O.42, 31, fos. 36–37d; entry in C.O.43, 13, pp. 9–10; signed duplicate, endorsed Read 12 December 1771, in C.O.42, 8, fos. 33–34d]

1162

29 April, Charleston

John Thomas to Earl of Hillsborough, notifying his departure shortly for Pensacola and offer to General Gage to take New Orleans in event of war. *Signed.* 1 p. *Endorsed*, R, 21 June. *Enclosed:*

i. Charleston, 28 April 1771. John Stuart to John Thomas, ordering him to Pensacola. *Copy.* ½ p. [C.O.5, 72, fos. 206–209d; entry of covering letter in C.O.5, 228, pp. 61–62]

1163

30 April, Whitehall

Circular. John Pownall to Governors of North Carolina, South Carolina, Georgia, East Florida, West Florida, sending to each twelve copies of printed account of how pitch and tar are made in Sweden. *Draft.* ½ p. [C.O.5, 72, fos. 186–187d; entry in C.O.5, 241, p. 375]

1164

30 April, Whitehall

John Pownall to Anthony Todd, requesting detention of American packet-boats for Earl of Hillsborough's dispatches. *Entry.* ¼ p. [C.O.5, 247, p. 2]

1165

30 April, Savannah

* Governor James Wright to Earl of Hillsborough (No. 56). I met new Assembly on 24 April. On 25th they absolutely denied H.M.'s right to negative their choice of Speaker, see enclosures. On all occasions they declare they are entitled to all rights and powers of House of Commons. If not restrained, they will become petty tyrants and set up a kind of court of inquisition. Parliamentary inquiries in our little sphere are totally unnecessary. I expect to see you in August. *Signed.* 3 pp. *Endorsed*, R, 21 June. *Enclosed:*

i. Journal of Commons House of Assembly of Georgia, 23–26 April 1771, particularly concerning choice of Speaker; election returns; appointment of committee of grievances; resolution of House that Governor's rejection of Noble B. Jones as Speaker is not to be a precedent; and dissolution. *Copy,* certified by John Simpson. 19½ pp.

ii. Journal of Upper House of Assembly of Georgia, 23–26 April 1771. *Copy,* certified by Alexander Wylly. 6¼ pp.

iii. Minutes of Council of Georgia, 23–26 April 1771. *Copy,* certified as No. ii. 3 pp. [C.O.5, 661, fos. 41–60d; signed duplicate of covering letter, endorsed Read 12 December 1771, in C.O.5, 651, fos. 131–132d; entry of covering letter in C.O.5, 678, pp. 230–233]

1166

30 April, Burlington

Governor William Franklin to Earl of Hillsborough (No. 28). Assembly refused money for supply of troops, alleging inability of colony to pay.

I believe that they will grant the money next session. *Duplicate. Signed.* 1½ pp. *Endorsed,* R, 10 June, original not recd. *Enclosed :*

i. 18 April 1771. Governor Franklin's speech to Assembly of New Jersey. *Printed.* 1 large p.

ii. 20 April 1771. Address of Council of New Jersey to Governor Franklin. *Printed.* 1 p.

iii. 20 April 1771. Address of Representatives of New Jersey to Governor Franklin, stating inability of province to pay for King's troops. *Copy. Signatory,* Stephen Crane, Speaker. 1½ pp.

iv. 23 April 1771. Governor Franklin's message in reply to preceding. *Printed.* 4 pp.

v. 25 April 1771. Reply of Representatives of New Jersey to preceding. *Printed.* 2¾ pp.

vi. 29 April 1771. Governor Franklin's message in reply to preceding. *Printed.* 4 pp. [Covering letter in C.O.5, 991, fos. 9–10d, with entry in C.O.5, 1001, pp. 130–131; enclosures i, iii-vi in C.O.5, 991, fos. 18–25d; signed original of covering letter, endorsed Read 22 August 1771, and enclosures i-vi, in C.O.5, 979, fos. 23–38d]

1167

30 April, Quebec

* President H. T. Cramahé to Earl of Hillsborough (No. 8), acknowledging Nos. 36–37. Contrary to newspaper reports, there is no symptom of insolence among Canadians at prospect of war with Spain. Three soldiers have been hanged for robbery; perfect harmony between civil and military. *Signed.* 2½ pp. *Endorsed,* R, 12 July. [C.O.42, 31, fos. 38–39d; entry in C.O.43, 13, pp. 10–12; signed duplicate, endorsed Read 12 December 1771, in C.O.42, 8, fos. 35–36d]

1168

[April]

Papers in case in Court of Chancery of New York against Lieut.-Governor Cadwallader Colden on his refusal to account for moiety of emoluments to the governor. *Vide* Lord Hillsborough's letter to Governor Earl of Dunmore dated 16 July 1770. *Enclosed :*

i. Bill of complaint of Attorney-General John Tabor Kemp. 10½ pp.

ii. Answer of Lieut.-Governor Colden. 33 pp.

iii. Replication of Attorney-General. 69 pp.

iv. Rejoinder of Lieut.-Governor Colden. 103 pp.

v. Second replication of Attorney-General. 32 pp.

vi. Second rejoinder of Lieut.-Governor Colden. 29 pp.

vii. New York, 3 April 1771. Opinion of Justice Robert R. Livingston, given at request of Earl of Dunmore. *Signed.* 11½ pp.

viii. New York, 3 April 1771. Like opinion of George D. Ludlow. *Signed.* 7½ pp.

ix. New York, 17 April 1771. Like opinion of Daniel Horsmanden. *Signed.* 2 pp.

x. New York, 17 April 1771. Like opinion of David Jones. *Signed.* 1 p. [C.O.5, 1102, fos. 330–489d]

1169

1 May, St James's

Order of King in Council, appointing Daniel Coxe to be of the Council in New Jersey in room of John Ladd, deceased. *Copy.* 1 p. *Endorsed,* Recd. 12 December, Read 21 December 1772. [C.O.5, 979, fos. 61–62d; sealed original in C.O.5, 27, fos. 44–45d; entry of warrant, dated 4 May, in C.O.324, 42, pp. 274–275]

1170

1 May, St James's

Same, referring the following to Commissioners for Trade and Plantations. *Seal. Signed,* Stephen Cottrell. 1½ pp. *Endorsed,* Recd. 21 November, Read 18 December 1771. *Enclosed:*

i. Petition of several inhabitants of Georgia to the King. They hold land by allotment from Trustees for Georgia and by grants made to soldiers in General Oglethorpe's regiment when it was disbanded. Sir William Baker claimed the same land by grant from Lord Proprietors of South Carolina: his heirs now propose that they should be bought out. Petitioners are too poor to defend their titles at law, and pray that attorney-general of Georgia may defend them at H.M.'s expense, or that grant of land elsewhere may be made to Sir W. Baker's heirs. 2½ pp. [C.O.5, 651, fos. 139–142d]

1171

1 May, St James's

Same, appointing William Axtell to be of the Council in New York in room of Joseph Read, deceased. *Copy.* 1 p. *Endorsed,* Recd. 12 December, Read 21 December 1772. [C.O.5, 1076, fos. 204–205d; sealed original in C.O.5, 27, fos. 40–41d; entry of warrant, dated 4 May, in C.O.323, 42, p. 71]

1172

1 May, St. James's

Same, appointing Sir Nathaniel Duckenfield and Marmaduke Jones to be of the Council in North Carolina. *Copy.* 1 p. *Endorsed,* Recd. 12

December, Read 21 December 1772. [C.O.5, 302, fos. 210–211d; warrants for admission of Duckenfield, dated 3 May, and Jones, dated 4 May, in C.O.324, 42, p. 273; sealed original of Order in C.O.5, 27, fos. 42–43d]

1173

1 May, St James's

Same, appointing Barnard Elliot and David Deas to be of the Council in South Carolina. *Copy.* 1 p. *Endorsed,* Recd. 12 December, Read 21 December 1772. [C.O.5, 380, fos. 86–87d; warrants for admission of Barnard Elliot, dated 3 May, and David Deas, dated 4 May, in C.O.324, 42, p. 272; sealed original of Order in C.O.5, 27, fos. 46–47d]

1174

1 May, Treasury

John Robinson to John Pownall, sending memorial of Lieutenant Benjamin Roberts, seeking support in lawsuits, and requesting information and opinion of Commissioners for Trade and Plantations. *Signed.* 1 p. *Endorsed,* Recd. 2 May, Read 10 May 1771. [C.O.323, 27, pp. 89–92]

1175

1 May, Boston

* Governor Thomas Hutchinson to Earl of Hillsborough (No. 3). I dissolved Assembly and issued writs for new election, though I find no clause in charter making new House of Representatives necessary every year. Party in opposition have failed in many points. Council showed good disposition until I communicated your letter respecting lieut.-governor's conduct when secretary. I refused assent to five bills, enclosed for H.M.'s pleasure. I negatived election of Speaker, of Mr Hancock and Mr Adams to manage Indian trade, and of two persons as truckmaster. They renewed grants to Mr De Berdt and Mr Bollan, agents, which I again declined. They declined repair of governor's house. Favourable account of Eastern part of province, but intruders multiply every day. *Signed.* 4 pp. *Endorsed,* R, 15 June. *Enclosed :*

i. Bill to incorporate Marine Society. *Copy.* 3 pp.

ii. Bill to grant £1300 to Governor. *Copy.* ½ p.

iii. Bill to grant £506 to Governor for services while Lieut.-Governor. *Copy.* ½ p.

* iv. Bill to prevent importation of negro slaves. Such importation is not only of no real advantage to H.M.'s subjects but gives occasion to most cruel and barbarous practices in Africa. *Copy.* 1¾ pp.

v. Bill for regulating militia. *Copy.* 2 pp.

vi. 23, 26 April 1771. Extracts from minutes recording proceedings of Council on reading of Earl of Hillsborough's letter of 11 December 1770 expressing H.M.'s approval of Mr Oliver's conduct as secretary. *Copy*, certified by Thomas Flucker, secretary. 3 pp.

vii. *Massachusetts Gazette and Boston Weekly Newsletter*, 2 May 1771, reporting proceedings of House of Representatives, 24–26 April 1771. *Printed*. 4 pp. [C.O.5, 760, fos. 152–167d; entry of covering letter in C.O.5, 768, pp. 192–197; signed duplicate of covering letter in C.O.5, 894, pp. 275–280]

1176

2 May, Tom's Coffee House, London

Robert Allen and William Tooke to [Lord Rochford], pressing claims for proprietors of Canada Reconnoissances. *Signed*. 1½ pp. *Endorsed*, R, 3 May. [C.O.5, 43, fos. 268–269d]

1177

3 May

Robert Allen to Mr Porten, hoping that yesterday's letter will answer purpose of meeting called by Lord Rochford. ½ p. *Endorsed*, R, do. [C.O.5, 43, fo. 270, 270d]

1178

4 May, Whitehall

Earl of Hillsborough to Lieut.-General Thomas Gage (No. 43) acknowledging No. 57. Allowance for recruiting parties appears reasonable. Part of your letter relating to state of batteries at Halifax and gunpowder needed at St Augustine, sent to Board of Ordnance. I agree with you that what has been done for security of West Florida is enough. Governor Bruere's request for company at Bermuda refused. Allowance of £150 a year to Pierre Sinnot, appointed lieut.-governor of Niagara, to be inserted in estimates of military contingencies in North America. Copy of dispatch from Governor Shirley, Bahamas, sent: signify to Captain Hodgson that the governor, and not he, commands forts and garrisons except as regards regimental detail of troops. Admonish Captain Hodgson. *Draft*. 3¼ pp. [C.O.5, 89, fos. 77–78d; entry in C.O.5, 243, pp. 9–11]

1179

4 May, Whitehall

Same to Governor of New York, acknowledging Earl of Dunmore's No. 7, and approving Assembly's attention to regulating Indian trade and proposal to form German company of militia. Reports on disorders in eastern part of province communicated to Board of Trade. William Axtell recommended by Board of Trade to be of Council of New York in place of Mr Read. *Draft*. 2½ pp. [C.O.5, 1102, fos. 126–127d; entry in C.O.5, 1141, pp. 174–177]

1180

4 May, Whitehall

Same to Governor Josiah Martin (No. 1), acknowledging Nos. 59–62 from Governor Tryon. Proceedings against representative of Orange County approved. Ground to hope that dangerous views of insurgents in North Carolina will be defeated. Lords of Trade have recommended Sir N. Dukenfield and Marmaduke Jones to be of the Council. *Draft.* 1½ pp. [C.O.5, 314, fos. 57–58d; entry in C.O.5, 332, pp. 84–85]

1181

4 May, Whitehall

⋆ Same to Governor of Newfoundland. Take account and make valuation of houses, stages etc. in Quiddy Viddy for compensation for destruction in connection with fortifications at St John's. Urge to them that proposed works are in their interests. Stop fishing at Magdalene Islands without licence from you and payment of rent. *Draft.* 3 pp. [C.O.194, 30, fos. 31–32d; entry in C.O.195, 15, pp. 42–44]

1182

4 May, Whitehall

Same to Governor Lord William Campbell (No. 46), acknowledging Nos. 69–70. Proposals for settlement by George Walker are under Board of Trade's consideration. Encourage settlement of Indians near Halifax, but not at public expense. *Draft.* ¾ p. [C.O.217, 48, fos. 13–14d; entry in C.O.218, 25, pp. 90–91]

1183

4 May, Whitehall

Same to Governor James Wright (No. 37), acknowledging Nos. 52–55. Mr Wylly's conduct and principles must have been considerably altered from what they were, to induce Council's recommendation of him; which I do not think fit to make the ground of recommendation to H.M. Assembly's conduct was unwarrantable in a subordinate colony. Your dissolution approved, H.M.'s disapprobation of late Assembly's measures to be signified to new Assembly. Council's behaviour on that occasion approved. No leave of absence to be allowed to governors except when their services are required elsewhere or for sickness. *Draft.* 2¾ pp. [C.O.5, 661, fos. 39–40d; entry in C.O.5, 677, pp. 53–55]

1184

4 May, Whitehall

Same to Governor James Grant (No. 39). No governor in future is to have leave of absence except for ill-health or where his service is required elsewhere. *Draft.* 1 p. [C.O.5, 552, fos. 17–18d; entry in C.O.5, 566, p. 47]

1185

4 May, Whitehall

Same to same (No. 40), acknowledging No. 45. Names of Councillors of East Florida will be laid before Lords of Trade. *Draft.* ½ p. [C.O.5, 552, fos. 31–32d; entry in C.O.5, 566, p. 48]

1186

4 May, Whitehall

Same to Governor William Franklin (No. 30), acknowledging No. 25. Indian trade is not the only instance evincing absolute necessity of general superintending power over British dominions in America. Mr Coxe to be of the Council in New Jersey. *Draft.* 2¼ pp. [C.O.5, 991, fos. 7–8d; entry in C.O.5, 1003, pp. 42–43]

1187

4 May, Whitehall

Same to Governor Thomas Hutchinson (No. 7), transmitting general instructions and instructions relative to trade. *Entry.* ½ p. [C.O.5, 765, p. 206; draft in C.O.5, 760, fos. 132–133d]

1188

4 May, Whitehall

Same to Governor Jonathan Trumbull (No. 20), acknowledging No. 19. H.M. has full confidence in assurances of loyalty by Governor and Company of Connecticut. *Draft.* ½ p. [C.O.5, 1284, fos. 108–109d; entry in C.O.5, 1301, p. 272]

1189

4 May, Whitehall

Same to Lieut.-Governor William Bull (No. 46), acknowledging Nos. 43–44. Ship for Lord Charles Montagu not yet ready. *Draft.* ½ p. [C.O.5, 394, fos. 72–73d; entry in C.O.5, 408, p. 65]

1190

4 May, Whitehall

Same to Deputy Governor John Penn (No. 25), acknowledging letters of 28 February and 5 March. Your attention to orders and Assembly's zeal to remedy Indian complaints, approved. *Draft.* ½ p. [C.O.5, 1284, fos. 13–14d; entry in C.O.5, 1301, p. 127]

1191

4 May, Whitehall

Same to President H. T. Cramahé (No. 38), acknowledging Nos. 4–5.

Assist road building by private subscription; no public expenditure authorized. State of Quebec is still under consideration. *Draft.* 1¼ pp. [C.O.42, 31, fos. 19–20d; entry in C.O.43, 8, pp. 92–93]

1192

4 May, Whitehall

* Same to Sir William Johnson (No. 16), acknowledging No. 15. Natural enmities between one Indian nation and another, without our interference, are our security. *Draft.* 2¼ pp. [C.O.5, 72, fos. 188–189d; entry in C.O.5, 241, pp. 376–378]

1193

4 May, Whitehall

* Same to John Stuart (No. 21), urging as little interference in Indian affairs as possible. *Draft.* 2¾ pp. [C.O.5, 72, fos. 190–191d; entry in C.O.5, 241, pp. 378–380]

1194

4 May

Commission to Pierre Sinnot to be Lieut.-Governor of Niagara. *Entry.* 1 p. [C.O.324, 42, pp. 269–270]

1195

4 May

Warrant for appointment of Arthur Gordon as Attorney-General of East Florida. *Entry.* 1¼ pp. [C.O.324, 42, pp. 275–276]

1196

4 May, Welbeck-st., London

Governor John Byron to [Earl of Hillsborough], soliciting salary for Michael Gill who has resided at St John's, Newfoundland, for thirty or forty years and been indefatigable in offices of J.P. etc. *Signed.* 2 pp. *Endorsed,* R, 15th. *Enclosed*(?) :

i. Dartmouth, 3 March 1771. John Holdsworth to Governor Byron, soliciting help for Mr Gill. I have obtained petition on his behalf. *Signed.* 1½ small pp.

ii. Petition of merchants and adventurers of Dartmouth and Teignmouth in Newfoundland fishery on behalf of Mr Gill and his son. *Signed,* Robert Newman, jnr., and thirty-three others. 1 large p.

iii. St John's, Newfoundland, 19 November 1770. Memorial of Michael Gill to Governor Byron, praying for pittance or that his son be appointed Naval Officer. 1 small p. *Endorsed,* Much recommended by Mr Byron, 9 April 1771. [C.O.5, 154, fos. 1–6d; entry of covering letter and No. i in C.O.5, 246, pp. 9, 11–12; no proof that Nos. i–iii are enclosures to covering letter]

1197

4 May, Burlington

Governor William Franklin to Earl of Hillsborough (No. 29), acknowledging circular of 22 January. *Signed.* 1 p. *Endorsed, R,* 10 June. [C.O.5, 991, fos. 11–12d; entry in C.O.5, 1001, p. 132]

1198

6 May, Treasury

John Robinson to John Pownall. Commissioners for Trade and Plantations are to include salary of Receiver-General of quitrents in East Florida in estimate of civil expenditure for ensuing year. *Signed.* 1 p. *Endorsed,* Recd., Read 27 June 1771. [C.O.5, 545, fos. 15–16d]

1199

6 May, Charleston

William De Brahm to Earl of Hillsborough (No. 17), reporting surveys and complaining of suspension from his provincial office. *Signed.* 3½ pp. *Endorsed, R,* 21 June. [C.O.5, 72, fos. 203–205d; entry in C.O.5, 228, pp. 57–60]

1200

7 May, Whitehall

Lieut.-General Thomas Gage to Earl of Hillsborough (No. 60), acknowledging circular of 22 January and Nos. 40 and 41, with enclosures. All operations undertaken in consequence of your letter of 2 January were discontinued. I have ordered 64th and 65th regiments back to Nova Scotia; 25th or another regiment will return to St Augustine as soon as convenient. Lieutenant Nordberg will be informed of reception of his memorial. *Florida Packet* reported back in Mississippi, from French Islands. I believe there is British contraband trade on that river. Mr Stuart should now be at Pensacola, holding congress with Choctaws, conferring with Chickasaws, and trying to engage tribes on Mississippi in our interest. These services are beyond ordinary allowance of the department. Commissary in Chickasaw nation is necessary; one on Mississippi would be useful. There are hopes of preserving Fort Chartres by facing river banks; I cannot at present point out a more healthy spot in the Illinois, whole country being reported full of marshes. Preparations for temporary works at Quebec and Halifax have been relaxed. Three regiments sent out recruiting parties, not without success. Every objection to proposed canal to establish communication with Mississippi should be fully considered. Sir W. Johnson, while apprehending possible rupture with Indians, does not think Six Nations so inclined: he thinks it proper, however, to call their chiefs to account. Fears in South Carolina of hostilities with Cherokees soon subsided. I have sent two light field-pieces to Governor Tryon who intended to march against insurgents in North Carolina about

20 April. *Signed.* 7½ pp. *Endorsed,* R, 10 June. [C.O.5, 89, fos. 99–102d; entry in C.O.5, 234, pp. 202–209]

1201

7 May, New York

Governor Earl of Dunmore to Earl of Hillsborough (No. 9), acknowledging Nos. 3 and 4, No. 1 of 11 February and circular of 22 January. Commission and instructions received. Colonel Martin's illness will not permit him to repair to his government without risk. *Signed.* 1½ pp. *Endorsed,* R, 10 June. [C.O.5, 1102, fos. 162–163d; entry in C.O.5, 1138, pp. 222–223; signed duplicate, dated 4 June 1771, endorsed Read 12 December 1771, in C.O.5, 1075, fos. 138–139d]

1202

7 May, Charleston

Lieut.-Governor William Bull to Earl of Hillsborough (No. 46), acknowledging circular of 22 January. *Signed.* 1 p. *Endorsed,* R, 21 June. [C.O.5, 394, fos. 76–77d; signed duplicate, endorsed Read 12 December 1771, in C.O.5, 380, fos. 30–31d; entry in C.O.5, 409, pp. 228–229]

1203

7 May, Charleston

Same to same (No. 47), acknowledging No. 44. Appointment of Mr Gordon as Chief Justice welcomed. Lord Charles Montagu daily expected. Assembly prorogued to 3 June. Vines from Madeira are being sent to Hillsborough and Londonborough townships. *Signed.* 2 pp. *Endorsed,* R, 21 June. [C.O.5, 394, fos. 78–79d; signed duplicate, endorsed Read 12 December 1771, in C.O.5, 380, fos. 32–33d; entry in C.O.5, 409, pp. 229–231]

1204

7 May, New York

Josiah Martin to Earl of Hillsborough, acknowledging commission as Governor of North Carolina, with instructions. I am indisposed. *Signed.* 1 small p. *Endorsed,* R, 10 June. [C.O.5, 314, fos. 99–100d; entry in C.O.5, 328, p. 232]

1205

8 May, Savannah

Governor James Wright to Earl of Hillsborough (No. 57), acknowledging circular of 22 January. *Signed.* 1 small p. *Endorsed,* R, 21 June. [C.O.5, 661, fos. 61–62d; signed duplicate, endorsed Read 12 December 1771, in C.O.5, 651, fos. 133–134d; entry in C.O.5, 678, p. 234]

1206

8 May, Savannah

Same to same (No. 58), acknowledging No. 36. Creeks talk of making satisfaction, but we are not in a capacity to compel them to give it. I have always treated the Indians with humanity and kindness and done them ample justice: they often tell the traders that I have not two tongues. But the unlimited number of traders take advantage of them and cheat them, as do outsettlers in back parts of the province. *Signed.* 2 small pp. *Endorsed*, R, 21 June. [C.O.5, 661, fos. 63–64d; signed duplicate, endorsed Read 12 December 1771, in C.O.5, 651, fos. 135–136d; entry in C.O.5, 678, pp. 234–235]

1207

8 May, Savannah

Same to John Pownall, acknowledging letter of 12 February and vote for civil establishment of Georgia. *Signed.* ½ small p. *Endorsed*, R, 21 June. [C.O.5, 661, fos. 65–66d; entry in C.O.5, 678, p. 236]

1208

10 May, Whitehall

* Commissioners for Trade and Plantations to Committee of Council for Plantation Affairs, submitting twenty Acts passed in Pennsylvania in 1769–1770. There are objections to Act for relief of John Relfe and Abraham Howel, prisoners; to Act for relief of John Galbreath, prisoner; to Act for relief of prisoners; and to Act for sale of goods distrained. Proprietaries of Pennsylvania should not be styled in laws true and absolute proprietaries of Three Lower Counties. *Entry.* *Signatories*, Hillsborough, Soame Jenyns, Edward Eliot, John Roberts. 7¼ pp. [C.O.5, 1296, pp. 367–374]

1209

[10 May]

Memorial of Charles Murray to King in Council, praying for 3000 acres of land in West Florida. *Signed.* ¾ p. *Endorsed*, Read 10 May 1771. [C.O.5, 578, pp. 13–16]

1210

[10 May]

Same to same, for 2000 acres of land in West Florida. *Signed.* ¾ p. *Endorsed*, Read 10 May 1771. [C.O.5, 578, pp. 17–20]

1211

11 May, Whitehall

Commissioners for Trade and Plantations to the King, recommending disallowance of Act passed in New Jersey in 1770 to explain and amend Act for relief of insolvent debtors. *Entry. Signatories,* Hillsborough, Edward Eliot, John Roberts, Greville, Thomas Whately. 3½ pp. [C.O.5, 999, pp. 239–242]

1212

11 May, Whitehall

John Pownall to John Robinson, acknowledging letters of 26 March. By Sir W. Johnson's letter it appears that Lieutenant Roberts discharged his duty with diligence and fidelity. No information in this office about alleged lawsuit: he should be supported for what he did by direction of superiors. His claim for allowance for losses and expenses, relating principally to military service, should be referred to General Gage; something in advance suggested. *Entry.* 4 pp. [C.O.324, 18, pp. 379–382]

1213

12 May, St Augustine

Lieut.-Governor John Moultrie to Earl of Hillsborough (No. 1). Governor Grant sailed for England three days ago. No. 37 to Governor Grant acknowledged. Promise of plentiful crop. *Signed.* 2½ pp. *Endorsed,* R, 15 July. [C.O.5, 552, fos. 39–40d; signed duplicate, endorsed Read 12 December 1771, in C.O.5, 545, fos. 45–46d; entry in C.O.5, 567, pp. 188–189]

1214

13 May, Whitehall

John Pownall to John Boddington, sending extract of General Gage's letter of 9 March relative to ruinous state of batteries in Nova Scotia and want of gunpowder at St Augustine. *Draft.* ½ p. [C.O.217, 48, fos. 15–16d; entry in C.O.5, 243, p. 12]

1215

14 May, Welbeck St., London

Governor John Byron to Earl of Hillsborough, recommending Michael Gill for recognition of long service in Newfoundland. *Entry.* 1½ pp. *Annotated,* R, 15th. [C.O.5, 246, pp. 11–12]

1216

15 May, Whitehall

Commissioners for Trade and Plantations to Committee of Council for Plantation Affairs, enclosing following. *Entry. Signatories,* Soame Jenyns, Edward Eliot, John Roberts, William Fitzherbert, Greville,

Thomas Whately. 1 p. *Enclosed :*

i. Draft of additional instruction to Governor William Tryon of New York, directing grant of lease of royal mines in Manor of Philipseburgh to Frederick Philipse, on conditions. *Entry.* 4 pp. [C.O.5, 1131, pp. 435–439; draft in C.O.5, 1080, pp. 431–442]

1217

15 May, Boston

Governor Thomas Hutchinson to Earl of Hillsborough (No. 4), acknowledging Nos. 4–5 and circular of 22 January. Expresses and packets take much longer than merchant vessels. Had your circular arrived in usual time, expense of transporting two regiments from Halifax and back would have been saved. They arrived about ten days ago and are preparing to return in few days. Recruiting parties are returning to their corps. Some judges of Superior Court were struck by informality of royal pardon sent for Richardson, and have deferred determination to June. *Signed.* 1¾ pp. *Endorsed,* R, 20 June. [C.O.5, 760, fos. 168–169d; entry in C.O.5, 768, pp. 198–200]

1218

15 May, Newport

Commission by Governor Joseph Wanton to Henry Marchant to be joint agent of Rhode Island with Joseph Sherwood. *Entry.* 3¼ pp. [C.O.324, 60, pp. 410–413]

1219

16 May, Whitehall

Earl of Hillsborough to Board of Ordnance. Report what sum is reasonable to allow soldiers and seamen working on fortifications at St John's, Newfoundland. *Draft.* ¾ p. [C.O.194, 30, fos. 37–38d; entry in C.O.195, 15, p. 46]

1220

16 May, Whitehall

Same to Governor John Byron. Warrant for fortifications at St John's, sent. You are to direct troops that can be spared to work thereon. Mr Gill's services merit attention. *Draft.* 1¼ pp. [C.O.194, 30, fos. 35–36d; entry in C.O.195, 15, p. 45]

1221

16 May, Whitehall

John Pownall to Richard Jackson, sending extract of Mr Wentworth's letter concerning claim of Kennebec Proprietors and copies of reports by Law Officers in 1726 and by Richard West in 1718. Your opinion requested, whether by 2 Geo.II c.35 white pine trees of twenty-four inches diameter growing on land possessed under grant from Plymouth Council may or may not be felled without Crown licence. *Entry*. 3 pp. [C.O.324, 18, pp. 383–385]

1222

16 May

General H. S. Conway to Earl of Hillsborough, asking for directions on sum to be paid to troops employed on works at St John's, Newfoundland. 3½ small pp. [C.O.194, 30, fos. 33–34d; entry in C.O.5, 246, pp. 13–14]

1223

16 May, Boston

Governor Thomas Hutchinson to John Pownall, sending laws passed in Massachusetts last session. Many new towns were created out of new territory: House of Representatives will soon swell to enormous size. *Signed*. ¾ p. *Endorsed,* Recd. 12 July, Read 12 December 1771. [C.O.5, 894, pp. 281–284]

1224

[16 May]

Petition of Samuel Stennett D.D., on behalf of Baptists of Ashfield, New England, to Commissioners for Trade and Plantations, praying disallowance of Act passed in Massachusetts in 1768. They are forced to support Independent church in Ashfield. 3 small pp. *Endorsed,* Recd. 16 May, Read 22 May 1771. [C.O.5, 894, pp. 215–218]

1225

17 May, Whitehall

Earl of Hillsborough to Lord North (private), concerning salary of Governor of Grenada. *Draft*. 2½ pp. [C.O.5, 154, fos. 7–8d; entry in C.O.5, 246, pp. 15–16]

1226

18 May, Great Alamance Camp, N.C.

★ Governor William Tryon to Earl of Hillsborough [No. 72], reporting victory over Regulators on 16 May. We lost about sixty men, killed, missing and wounded, one officer killed, one dangerously wounded. Detail will be sent as soon as I have settled the country. My army was upwards of 1100; rebels 2000. Field-pieces from General Gage were of infinite service. *Signed*. PS. General Waddell with 250 men was surrounded by Regulators and obliged to retreat to Salisbury. 1½ pp. *Endorsed*, R, 29 July. *Enclosed:*

    i. 17 May 1771. Governor Tryon's orders after battle of Alamance. *Copy.* 1 p. [C.O.5, 314, fos. 141–144d; signed duplicate of covering letter, endorsed Read 12 December 1771, in C.O.5, 302, fos. 76–77d; another signed duplicate, without postscript, in C.O.5, 302, fos. 74–75d; entry of covering letter in C.O.5, 328, pp. 240–243]

1227

18 May, Virginia

President William Nelson to Earl of Hillsborough, enclosing following. *Signed.* ½ p. *Endorsed*, R, 12 July. *Enclosed:*

    i. Account of revenue of 2s. a hogshead, 25 October 1770–25 April 1771. *Copy. Signatory*, Richard Corbin, deputy Receiver-General. Examined by John Blair, deputy Auditor, and William Nelson. 1½ pp. [C.O.5, 1349, fos. 91–93d; entry of covering letter in C.O.5, 1372, p. 172]

1228

19 May, Burlington

Governor William Franklin to Earl of Hillsborough (No. 30), enclosing following, great part of which is taken up with inquiry into complaint of John Hatton, Collector of Customs of Salem, against J.P.s at Cape May. Council found no foundation for complaint. Commissioners at Boston should remove him. *Signed.* 1½ pp. *Endorsed*, R, 12 July. *Enclosed:*

    i. Minutes of Council of New Jersey, 8 January–26 March 1771. *Copy*, certified by Charles Pettit, deputy clerk. 27 pp.

    ii. Evidences in inquiry into John Hatton's complaint. (1) Notes and observations by deputy secretary of New Jersey. (2) Same on examination of John Hatton, 23 February. (3) Same on examination of John Hatton, jnr., 23 February. (4) 26 March, Commissioners of Customs at Boston to Governor Franklin. (5) 10 April, Governor Franklin's reply. (6) Philadelphia, 7 June 1769, Inspector-General John Williams to Commissioners of Customs. *Copy.* 21 pp. [C.O.5, 991, fos. 28–56d; entry of covering letter in C.O.5, 1001, pp. 132–133]

1229

20 May, Pennsylvania

President James Hamilton to Commissioners for Trade and Plantations. John Penn embarked for Britain fortnight since; I and Council have entered on administration. *Signed.* 1 p. *Endorsed*, R, 9 July. [C.O.5, 1284, fos. 17–18d; entry in C.O.5, 1300, pp. 362–363]

1230

21 May, Admiralty

Philip Stephens to John Pownall, requesting that orders be given to Captain Holland to let Lieutenant Henry Mowat copy plans of Holland's surveys. *Signed.* 1 p. *Endorsed,* Recd. 21 May, Read 23 May 1771. [C.O.323, 27, pp. 97–100]

1231

22 May, Whitehall

Commissioners for Trade and Plantations to Governor Lord William Campbell. We should have proposed disallowance of Act passed in Nova Scotia in June last granting excise on tea, coffee and playing-cards but for the almost bankrupt state of Treasury in Nova Scotia. Do not consent to like bill for future. *Entry. Signatories,* Edward Eliot, John Roberts, William Fitzherbert, Thomas Whately. 2 pp. [C.O.218, 7, pp. 298–299]

1232

22 May, Ordnance-office

Board of Ordnance to Earl of Hillsborough, recommending that troops to be employed on works at St John's be paid 6d. a day with promise, if necessary, of 9d. a day if General Gage does not object. *Signed,* H. S. Conway, Charles Frederick, A. Wilkinson, Charles Cocks. 1½ pp. *Endorsed,* R, 23 May. [C.O.194, 30, fos. 39–40d; entry in C.O. 195, 12, pp. 114–116]

1233

22 May, London

Petition of Dr John Breynton, Rector of St Paul's, Halifax, N. Scotia, to Commissioners for Trade and Plantations, praying for financial help for church. *Signed.* 2 pp. *Endorsed,* Recd., Read 29 May 1771. [C.O.217, 26, fos. 62–63d]

1234

23 May, Whitehall

Order of Committee of Council for Plantation Affairs, referring following to Commissioners for Trade and Plantations. *Seal. Signed,* Stephen Cottrell. 1 p. *Endorsed,* Recd., Read 29 May 1771. *Enclosed:*

    i. Petition of Lieutenant Donald Campbell, late 60th regiment for grant of 100,000 acres of land in New York. *Copy.* 2½ pp. [C.O.5, 1075, fos. 85–88d]

1235

23 May, Whitehall

Same, referring following to Commissioners for Trade and Plantations, who are to consider their report of 17 July 1769. *Seal. Signed,* Stephen Cottrell. ¾ p. *Endorsed,* Recd. 3 June, Read 6 June 1771. *Enclosed:*

   i. New York, 6 October 1770. Extract of letter from Lieut.-General Gage to Earl of Hillsborough relating to Mining Company on Lake Superior. *Copy.* 1½ pp. [C.O.323, 27, pp. 109–116]

1236

23 May, Whitehall

Earl of Hillsborough to Board of Ordnance, accepting proposals about payment of troops for works at St John's, Newfoundland, in letter of 22 May. *Draft.* 1 p. [C.O.194, 30, fos. 41–42d; entry in C.O.195, 15, p. 47]

1237

23 May, Whitehall

Same to Lieut.-General Thomas Gage (No. 44), sending papers concerning troops to be used as artificers and labourers in works at St John's, Newfoundland. *Draft.* 1 p. [C.O.5, 89, fos. 95–96d; entry in C.O.5, 243, pp. 12–13, where the papers are stated to be: note from General Conway; Lord Hillsborough to Board of Ordnance, 16 May 1771; Board of Ordnance to Lord Hillsborough, 22 May 1771; Lord Hillsborough to Board of Ordnance, 23 May 1771; Earl of Marlborough to Governor Byron, 23 May 1771]

1238

23 May, Whitehall

Same to Governor John Byron, sending papers about payment of troops for works at St John's, Newfoundland. *Draft.* ½ p. [C.O.194, 30, fos. 43–44d; entry in C.O.195, 15, p. 48]

1239

23 May

* Richard Jackson to Commissioners for Trade and Plantations, reporting on claim of Kennebec Proprietors, and whether by 2 Geo.II c.35 white pine trees of twenty-four inches diameter or upwards on land possessed under grant from Plymouth Council may be felled without Crown licence. I am of opinion that in case the soil was private property before 7 October 1690 they may cut without licence. If the title of Kennebec Company is well-derived, they are exempt from penalties of 2 Geo.II. But white pine trees not growing within limits of some township seem to come within 8 Geo.I c.12. *Signed.* 2 pp. *Endorsed,* Read 24 May 1771. [C.O.323, 27, pp. 101–104]

1240

23 May, Whitehall

John Pownall to Captain Samuel Holland. You are to permit Lieutenant Mowat to take copies for Admiralty's use of your plans and surveys. *Entry.* 1 p. [C.O.324, 18, p. 386]

1241

23 May, Charlotte Town, I. of St John

Governor Walter Patterson to Earl of Hillsborough (No. 1, should be 4), acknowledging letters. *Signed.* 1 p. *Endorsed,* R, 13 September. [C.O.226, 4, fos. 46–47d; entry in C.O.227, 2, pp. 17–19; signed duplicate, endorsed Read 12 December 1771, in C.O.226, 1, fos. 21–22d]

1242

23 May, Charlotte Town, I. of St John

Same to same (No. 2, should be 5), acknowledging No. 2. Winter was mild. I gave licence for sea-cow fishing to an inhabitant: fees shall not exceed 10s. Surveyor needed, Mr Wright willing. *Signed.* 2½ pp. *Endorsed,* R, 13 September. [C.O.226, 4, fos. 48–49d; entry in C.O.227, 2, pp. 19–22; signed duplicate, endorsed Read 12 December 1771, in C.O.226, 1, fos. 23–24d]

1243

23 May, St Augustine

Lieut.-Governor John Moultrie to Earl of Hillsborough (No. 2). Indigo in Georgia and South Carolina is an annual; here, at least biennial. Rice plants live through winter in southern part of province. Indian expenses have been small since Picolata congress in 1767, but may be greater. Seventy Indians recently visited Smyrnea and were well-behaved. *Duplicate. Signed.* 5 pp. *Endorsed,* R, 1 August, original not recd. [C.O.5, 552, fos. 43–45d; entry in C.O.5, 567, pp. 189–194]

1244

24 May, St James's

Order of King in Council, allowing nineteen Acts passed in Pennsylvania in 1769–1770 and disallowing Act passed in 1770 for sale of goods distrained. *Copy.* 9½ pp. *Endorsed,* Recd. 12 December, Read 21 December 1772. [C.O.5, 1278, fos. 106–111d]

1245

24 May, St James's

Same, approving draft of additional instruction to governor of New York authorizing grant of mines in Manor of Philipseburgh to Frederick

Philipse. *Copy.* 1¼ pp. *Endorsed,* Recd. 12 December, Read 21 December 1772. [C.O.5, 1076, fos. 206–207d; sealed original in C.O.5, 27, fos. 50–51d; entry of instruction, dated 30 May, in C.O.5, 1141, pp. 178–181]

1246

25 May, Whitehall

Order of Committee of Council for Plantation Affairs, approving report of Commissioners for Trade and Plantations of 24th ult. on boundary between North and South Carolina. Draft instructions to governors of both provinces to be prepared. *Seal. Signed,* Stephen Cottrell. 1 p. *Endorsed,* Recd. 28 May, Read 29 May 1771. [C.O.5, 301, fos. 159–160d]

1247

25 May, Downing St., London

Lord North to Earl of Hillsborough, about salary of Governor of Grenada. *Entry.* 1 p. [C.O.5, 246, p. 17]

1248

27 May, Virginia

President William Nelson to Earl of Hillsborough, acknowledging circular of 22 January. Nothing is so destructive of true interest of tobacco planter as war. *Signed.* ½ p. *Endorsed,* R, 2 August. [C.O.5, 1349, fos. 94–95d; entry in C.O.5, 1372, p. 173]

1249

27 May, Virginia

★ Same to same (No. 18), acknowledging No. 41. John Norton appointed agent for obtaining copper for this colony. Matter of ecclesiastical jurisdiction may arise from meeting of clergy of Virginia summoned by Commissary to consider expediency of applying for American episcopate. Good progress made in marking Cherokee line. Mr Wormely not yet sworn at Council. *Signed.* 2½ pp. *Endorsed,* R, 2 August. [C.O.5, 1349, fos. 98–99d; entry in C.O.5, 1372, pp. 174–177]

1250

29 May, Whitehall

Commissioners for Trade and Plantations to Committee of Council for Plantation Affairs, enclosing following. *Entry. Signatories,* Hillsborough, Soame Jenyns, William Fitzherbert, Greville, Thomas Whately. 1 p. *Enclosed:*

i. Draft of additional instruction to Governor Josiah Martin of North Carolina for determination of boundary with South Carolina. *Entry.* 3 pp. [C.O.5, 326, pp. 179–182; draft in C.O.5, 305, fos. 58–61d;

like letter of same date and draft of like instruction to Governor Lord Charles Montagu of South Carolina, in C.O.5, 404, pp. 448–451]

1251

29 May, Charleston

William De Brahm to Earl of Hillsborough (No. 18), reporting on surveys and suspension from provincial office, and claiming payment. *Signed.* 3¼ pp. *Endorsed*, R, 15 July. [C.O.5, 72, fos. 249–250d; entry in C.O.5, 228, pp. 70–73]

1252

29 May, Connecticut

* Church of England Clergy of Connecticut to Earl of Hillsborough, imploring influence towards obtaining American episcopate, for which pitiable state of Church pleads. Our clergy want somebody to superintend them, our youth want confirmation, our candidates want holy orders without travelling 3000 miles. *Signed,* Jeremiah Leaming, secretary to convention. 2¼ pp. *Endorsed*, R, 4 May 1772. [C.O.5, 1284, fos. 112–113d; entry in C.O.5, 1300, pp. 130–133]

1253

29 May, Bermuda

Richard Washington to Earl of Hillsborough, on subject of illicit trade at Bermuda and other matters concerning trade of that island. *Entry.* 2¼ pp. [C.O.5, 246, pp. 23–25]

1254

29 May

Petition of Major Robert Rogers to Commissioners for Trade and Plantations for grant of 20,000 acres of land in New York. 1 p. *Endorsed,* Recd., Read 29 May 1771. [C.O.5, 1075, fos. 89–90d]

1255

30 May, Whitehall

John Pownall to Philip Stephens, sending copy of No. 1240. *Entry.* ¾ p. [C.O.324, 18, p. 387]

1256

30 May, Whitehall

Same to Richard Jackson, asking if white pine trees, growing on land in Massachusetts not erected into township, can under 8 Geo.I c.12 be cut or destroyed without licence from Crown. *Entry.* 1 p. [C.O.5, 920, p. 408; draft in C.O.5, 897, fos. 285–286d]

1257

30 May

Richard Jackson to Commissioners for Trade and Plantations. I have reconsidered Act of West Florida for order and government of slaves and Act to regulate Court of Requests; and have considered Act for licensing retailers of liquor and Act to erect Mobile into county and establish Court of Common Pleas there; with Governor Chester's letter objecting to these Acts. There is weight in his objection to Act to erect Mobile into county, which should be disallowed, but his objections to others are insufficient for disallowance. *Signed.* $2\frac{1}{4}$ pp. *Endorsed*, Recd. 30 May, Read 6 June 1771. [C.O.5, 578, pp. 25–28]

1258

30 May, Boston

Governor Thomas Hutchinson to John Pownall, sending *Massachusetts Gazette* of 30 May 1771 with account of election. I wished to avoid negatives and offered privately, before the choice, if they would bring in the Secretary, to take Hancock with him, but they would not be prevailed upon; I thought it would be giving too much to take him without. House has to-day desired me to carry them to Boston, giving up claim of right and urging only inconvenience from sitting at Cambridge. I will send their message to Lord Hillsborough in hopes of obtaining H.M.'s leave to hold next session at Boston if this one goes as I hope. *Entry.* $\frac{3}{4}$ p. *Annotated*, R, 9 July. [C.O.5, 768, pp. 200–201]

1259

31 May, Whitehall

Commissioners for Trade and Plantations to the King, proposing confirmation of membership of Council in East Florida of Lieut.-Governor John Moultrie, John Stuart, Robert Catherwood, John Holmes, Rev. John Forbes, William Drayton, Witter Cuming, Andrew Turnbull, Sir Charles Burdett, Bart., Martin Jollie. *Entry. Signatories,* Hillsborough, Thomas Whately, Greville, Edward Eliot. $1\frac{1}{2}$ pp. [C.O.5, 563, pp. 287–288]

1260

31 May, Whitehall

Same to same, recommending disallowance of Act passed in Massachusetts in June 1768 additional to Act for erecting town of Ashfield, whereby all persons of whatever religion are taxed for support of Independent Church. Out of seventeen families at first settlement, twelve were Anti-pedobaptists. *Entry. Signatories,* Soame Jenyns, Edward Eliot, William Fitzherbert, Greville, Thomas Whately. 2 pp. [C.O.5, 920, pp. 409–410; draft in C.O.5, 897, fos. 287–289d]

1261

31 May, Whitehall

Same to Committee of Council for Plantation Affairs. We have considered petition of Lieutenant Donald Campbell, 60th regiment, for grant of 100,000 acres in lieu of 35,000 acres of land in New York granted by Order of 10 September 1766. No new objection. *Entry.* *Signatories*, Hillsborough, Thomas Whately, Greville, Edward Eliot. 2½ pp. [C.O.5, 1131, pp. 440–442; draft in C.O.5, 1080, pp. 443–446]

1262

1 June, Whitehall

★ Earl of Hillsborough to Governor Thomas Hutchinson (No. 8), acknowledging Nos. 1 and 2. Your conduct approved. Endeavours of incendiaries at Boston to keep up in the lower sort disrespect of government and an opinion of their own independence are lamentable, but there are hopes that more respectable inhabitants will counteract these intentions. *Entry.* 1½ pp. [C.O.5, 765, pp. 206–207; draft in C.O.5, 760, fos. 150–151d]

1263

1 June, Burlington

★ Governor William Franklin to Earl of Hillsborough (No. 31). Assembly again refused to provide for troops. I shall prorogue them from time to time until I know H.M.'s pleasure; only inconvenience thereby would be depriving officers of salaries. *Signed.* 3¼ pp. *Endorsed,* R, 12 July. *Enclosed:*

i. 29 May 1771. Governor Franklin's message to Assembly of New Jersey, requesting provision for troops. *Copy.* ½ p.

ii. 31 May 1771. Extract of journal of Assembly of New Jersey, recording refusal to provide for troops. *Copy.* 4½ pp.

iii. 1 June 1771. Extract of minutes of Council of New Jersey, recording advice to Governor Franklin to prorogue Assembly. *Copy. Signatory,* Charles Pettit, deputy clerk. 1¾ pp. [C.O.5, 991, fos. 57–65d; entry of covering letter in C.O.5, 1001, pp. 134–137]

1264

1 June, Charlotte Town, I. of St John

Governor Walter Patterson to Earl of Hillsborough (No. 3, should be 6), enclosing following. Liquor has been immoderately used and wages paid in it. Council minutes and copies of commissions enclosed. *Signed.* 1½ pp. *Endorsed,* R, 13 September. *Enclosed:*

i. Charlotte Town, 24 September 1770. Commission to John Duport to be Chief Justice of Island of St John. *Copy.* 1¼ pp.

ii. Charlotte Town, 8 November 1770. Commission of Peace to Thomas Debrisay, Phillips Callbeck, Thomas Wright and George Burn. *Copy.* 2½ pp.

iii. Charlotte Town, 4 January 1771. Commission to Phillips Callbeck to be Surrogate-General and Judge of Probates. *Copy.* 1 p.

iv. Form of appointment of David Higgins to keep office to prevent transport of persons from Island of St John without pass. *Copy.* 1½ pp.

v. Minutes of Council of Island of St John, 19 September 1770–1 June 1771. *Copy.* 12 pp.

vi. 15 November 1770. Ordinance prohibiting sale of liquor in Island of St John without licence. *Copy,* certified by Phillips Callbeck. 4½ pp.

vii. 20 February 1771. Ordinance prohibiting transport of persons out of Island of St John without licence. *Copy,* certified by Thomas Debrisay. 5½ pp. [C.O.226, 4, fos. 50–75d; entry of covering letter in C.O.227, 2, pp. 23–24; signed duplicate of covering letter, endorsed Read 12 December 1771, and copies of enclosures i–iv, in C.O.226, 1, fos. 25–33d; another copy of No. iii in C.O.226, 1, fos. 47–48d]

1265

2 June, Plymouth

Governor John Byron to Earl of Hillsborough. H.M.S. *Panther* was forced to put back here by losing mainmast. *Signed.* 1¼ pp. *Endorsed,* R, 5 June. [C.O.194, 30, fos. 45–46d; entry in C.O.195, 12, pp. 116–117]

1266

4 June, Whitehall

* Lieut.-General Thomas Gage to Earl of Hillsborough (No. 61), acknowledging No. 42 and enclosure regarding Castle William. My objection to King's officers receiving provincial commissions was soon settled: Mr Hutchinson and I have always acted in concert. O.C. St John's, Newfoundland, will be ordered to furnish every man he can spare for battery. 64th and 65th regiments, all but four companies, have gone back to Halifax. Recruiting parties have returned to their corps: most of those embarking for Great Britain were stopped. Engineer given bad report on state of buildings at Pensacola. Two batteries there are finished and three more marked out. Report and plans are in preparation. Indian problems in West Florida, the Lakes and Fort Pitt, reported. Vessels on Lakes Erie and Huron are reported too bad to be repaired; though one is being patched up at Detroit for summer navigation. I hope by next spring two others will be built. Two new vessels for Lakes Ontario and Champlain, I conclude finished by this time. Castle William likely to become expensive, papers enclosed. *Signed.* 6 pp. *Endorsed,* R, 12 July. *Enclosed:*

i. Boston, 15 May 1771. Governor Thomas Hutchinson to General Gage. Flags at Castle William need replacing, and storm has carried away part of glacis. Repairs needed. *Copy.* 1 p.

ii. New York, 3 June 1771. Estimate by John Montressor, engineer, of cost of repairs at Castle William. Total £5463 16s. 4¾d. 1 p.

iii. 1 June 1771. Estimate by same of cost of new platforms and carriages for Castle William. Total: £1320 7s. 11¾d. ¾ p. [C.O.5, 89, fos. 113–122d; entry of covering letter in C.O.5, 234, pp. 210–216]

1267

4 June, New York

Governor Earl of Dunmore to Earl of Hillsborough (No. 10), acknowledging Mr Pownall's letter and pamphlets which have been distributed. Copies of Acts passed last session sent. Comments on Act for emitting £120,000 in bills of credit; Act to explain duty of loan-officers; Act for establishing boundary with New Jersey (adding three members of Assembly to agents in this controversy); Act to confirm ancient conveyances (concerning *femmes couverts*); Act to prevent abuses by tenants before legal title is obtained; Act to prevent inconveniences from delays of causes; Act for apprehending persons in any county or place by warrants from J.P.s of any other county or place; Act for better regulation of election of officers in City of New York. Removal of instruction forbidding governor to consent to law establishing lotteries proposed; hospital and other conveniences needed which cannot be accomplished otherwise. *Signed.* P.S. If I have done wrong in assenting to any of above Acts, I beg you to consider it an error of judgement. 6 pp. *Endorsed,* R, 12 July. [C.O.5, 1102, fos. 168–171d; entry in C.O.5, 1138, pp. 223–229; signed duplicate dated 2 July, endorsed Read 12 December 1771, in C.O.5, 1075, fos. 140–143d; list of papers sent in C.O.5, 1075, fos. 144–145d]

1268

4 June, New York

⋆ Same to same (private). According to your advice, I shall try to compromise with Mr Colden. I continue in inclination to remain in this government. If Mr Tryon repairs here, I shall remain till I know issue of my application. *Duplicate. Signed.* 2 small pp. *Endorsed,* R, 12 July, original not recd. [C.O.5, 154, fo. 10, 10d; entry in C.O.5, 246, pp. 19–20]

1269

4 June, Boston

⋆ Governor Thomas Hutchinson to Earl of Hillsborough (No. 5), acknowledging No. 6. General Gage can do no more than represent to H.M. repairs necessary at Castle. Part of glacis against the sea being gone, there is danger of devastation by storm. New Assembly is sitting at Cambridge. I accepted two of the Councillors chosen and negatived two others. Assembly has given up claim to determine place of sitting. Inconveniences of holding it out of Boston; I submit I should be allowed to prorogue it to Boston. I doubt if the two Houses will take proper measures for removing intruders from Eastern Country. *Signed.* 2½ pp. *Endorsed*, R, 23 July. *Enclosed :*

i. Cambridge, 30 May 1771. Speech of Governor Hutchinson to Council and House of Representatives of Massachusetts. *Copy.* 2¼ pp.

ii. Cambridge, 29 May 1771. Address of House of Representatives to Governor Hutchinson, asking for Court to be adjourned or prorogued to Boston; with Governor's answer of 30 May. *Copy.* 2¼ pp. [C.O.5, 760, fos. 174–179d; entry of covering letter in C.O.5, 768, pp. 201–204; signed duplicate of covering letter, endorsed Read 12 December 1771, in C.O.5, 894, pp. 297–300]

1270

5 June, Whitehall

Earl of Hillsborough to Lieut.-General Thomas Gage (No. 45), acknowledging Nos. 58 and 59. I am surprised my letter of 22 January, acquainting you that H.M. had accepted Spain's disavowal of expedition against Port Egmont, had not reached you before 2 April. I cannot think that there is immediate danger of Indians uniting to attack the colonies. Prince born this morning. *Draft.* 2 pp. [C.O.5, 89, fos. 97–98d; entry in C.O.5, 243, pp. 13–14]

1271

5 June, Whitehall

* Same to Governor William Tryon (No. 2), acknowledging Earl of Dunmore's No. 8. Board of Trade have prepared report on lands west of Connecticut River; directions may be expected before the fall. Grant to Lieut.-Colonel Bradstreet of 20,000 acres of land patented to Hardenberg in 1706 was irregular: until further explanation, I cannot advise H.M. to consent to petitions for grants of those lands. Prince born this morning. *Draft.* 2¼ pp. [C.O.5, 1102, fos. 158–159d; entry in C.O.5, 1141, pp. 182–184]

1272

5 June, Whitehall

Same to Governor Josiah Martin (No. 2). Governor Tryon's conduct approved. Bill for better collection of quitrents deserves attention; I will try to obtain Treasury's consideration, and send you instructions thereon. Prince born this morning. *Draft.* 2 pp. [C.O.5, 314, fos. 97–98d; entry in C.O.5, 332, pp. 85–86]

1273

5 June, Whitehall

Same to Governor Lord William Campbell, recommending Mme Dechevry, returning to Cape Breton to recover her late husband's possessions. *Entry.* 1 p. [C.O.5, 246, p. 18]

1274

5 June, Whitehall

Same to same (No. 47), acknowledging No. 71. Prince born this morning. *Draft.* ½ p. [C.O.217, 48, fos. 21–22d; entry in C.O.218, 25, p. 91]

1275

5 June, Whitehall

Same to Governor John Byron, sending copy of letter of 23 May. Prince born this morning. *Draft.* 1 p. [C.O.194, 30, fos. 47–48d; entry in C.O.195, 15, p. 49]

1276

5 June, Whitehall

* Same to Deputy Governor Robert Eden (No. 21), acknowledging No. 9. Indian trade does not require congress of commissioners. Prince born this morning. *Draft.* 1¾ pp. [C.O.5, 1284, fos. 96–97d; entry in C.O.5, 1301, pp. 15–16]

1277

5 June, Whitehall

Same to William Bayard, acknowledging letter of 1 April concerning expenses of New York–New Jersey boundary, which will be considered by Lords of Trade. *Draft.* ½ p. [C.O.5, 1102, fos. 160–161d; entry in C.O.5, 1141, p. 184]

1278

5 June, Whitehall

Circular. Same to Governors in America, announcing birth of prince. *Draft.* ½ p. [C.O.5, 72, fos. 195–196d; entry in C.O.5, 241, p. 381]

1279

5 June, Whitehall

Circular. John Pownall to Governors in America, enclosing copies of four Acts (five for East and West Florida) passed last session in Parliament which relate to America. *Draft.* ½ p. *Enclosed :*

i. List of Acts, vizt. for continuing two Acts made in 6 and 9 George

III for punishing mutiny etc.; for continuing Act made in 8 George
III concerning import of salt-beef from Ireland and British dominions; for explaining Act made in 8 George III for encouraging
import of naval stores; for granting bounty on import of white oak
staves and heading from American colonies; for amending Act
made in last session for extending to East and West Florida same
liberty in exporting rice to Southern Europe as already granted to
Carolina and Geogia. *Draft.* 1¼ pp. [C.O.5, 72, fos. 197–198d;
entry of covering letter in C.O.5, 241, pp. 382–384]

1280

5 June

Richard Jackson to Commissioners for Trade and Plantations, reporting
28 Acts passed in Virginia in June 1770 [MS: 1771] proper in point
of law. Act for regulating election of Burgesses extends privileges to
members of Assembly to matters inconvenient to course of justice.
Act to explain jurisdiction of court of hustings of Williamsburg is
open to objections: it rests with you whether to advise disallowance.
Act to amend Act to divide Hamilton parish seems improper. Act for
dissolving vestries: there are laws for compelling vestries to do their
duty, which should have been tried first. *Signed.* 3½ pp. *Endorsed,*
Recd. 5 June, Read 12 June 1771. [C.O.5, 1333, fos. 64–66d]

1281

5 June

* Same to same. White pine trees on any lands in Massachusetts not
erected into a township cannot, under 8 Geo.I c.12, be felled without
Crown licence. Though the law as it now stands protects trees on
private property, it deprives them of another protection (the vigilance
and care of the owner) that might perhaps have been more efficacious.
Signed. 2½ pp. *Endorsed,* Recd. 5 June, Read 6 June 1771. [C.O.323,
27, pp. 105–108]

1282

5 June, Charleston

Lieut.-Governor William Bull to Earl of Hillsborough (No. 48),
acknowledging No. 45. Commissions to Chief Justice Gordon and
Assistant Judge Savage published 3rd inst. *Signed.* 1¼ pp. *Endorsed,*
R, 15 July. [C.O.5, 394, fos. 80–81d; signed duplicate, endorsed Read
12 December 1771, in C.O.5, 380, fos. 34–35d; entry in C.O.5, 409,
pp. 232–233]

1283

6 June, Whitehall

* Commissioners for Trade and Plantations to Committee of Council
for Plantation Affairs, reporting on petition of officers and soldiers

who seek grants and confirmation of grants of lands in northern New York and west of Connecticut River, disputed by claimants under New Hampshire. Proposals for upholding claims of petitioners but saving rights of *bona fide* settlers claiming under New Hampshire grants antecedent to warrants of survey to petitioners. We advise that no further grants be made in this district until it has been surveyed and white pines and other timber reserved to H.M. Claim of S.P.G. under New Hampshire grants to be compensated. *Entry. Signatories,* Hillsborough, Soame Jenyns, Edward Eliot, John Roberts, William Fitzherbert, Thomas Whately. 14 pp. [C.O.5, 1131, pp. 443–455; draft in C.O.5, 1080, pp. 447–474]

1284

6 June, Whitehall

Same to Governor Peter Chester. We referred laws of West Florida mentioned in your letter to Earl of Hillsborough of 25 December last to counsel, copy of report sent. Act for erecting Mobile into county is recommended to H.M. for disallowance, as is Act for better government of slaves. No action on other laws. *Entry. Signatories,* Soame Jenyns, John Roberts, William Fitzherbert. 2 pp. [C.O.5, 600, pp. 225–226]

1285

6 June, London

Memorial of Jeremiah Terry to Earl of Hillsborough, complaining of difficulties in collecting debts from Spaniards in West Florida. *Signed.* 2½ pp. *Endorsed,* R, 12 June. Copy referred to Earl of Rochford, 3 July 1771. *Enclosed:*

    i. Above New Orleans, 4 September 1769. Jeremiah Terry to General O'Reilly, asking leave to enter New Orleans to collect debts. *Copy.* ½ p.

    ii. Same, 5 September 1769. Same to same, with list of debts due from inhabitants of New Orleans. *Copy.* 1½ pp. [C.O.5, 72, fos. 199–202d]

1286

6 June, Virginia

President William Nelson to John Pownall, acknowledging letter of 3 April. Description of making tar in Sweden will be distributed. First method is nearly agreeable to present practice; second, by kilns, will be thought too expensive as most tar is made in Virginia by poor people. *Signed.* 1 p. *Endorsed,* R, 19 August. [C.O.5, 1349, fos. 100–101d; entry in C.O.5, 1372, p. 182]

1287

7 June, St James's

Order of King in Council that in commissions to future governors of colonies clause be inserted empowering them as Chancellors to issue commissions for custody of idiots. *Copy.* 1½ pp. *Endorsed*, Read 21 December 1772. [C.O.323, 27, pp. 301–304; sealed original in C.O.5, 27, fos. 74–75d]

1288

7 June, St James's

Same, approving draft instructions to governors of North and South Carolina concerning boundary between the two provinces. *Copy.* 1 p. *Endorsed*, Recd. 12 December, Read 21 December 1772. [C.O.5, 302, fos. 214–215d; sealed original, with drafts of instructions, in C.O.5, 27, fos. 76–81d; entry of instruction to governor of North Carolina, dated 10 June, in C.O.5, 332, pp. 87–88; entry of same to governor of South Carolina, dated 10 June, in C.O.5, 408, pp. 66–67]

1289

7 June, St James's

Same, approving Act passed in New York in 1770 to enable H.M.'s subjects by birth or naturalization to inherit and hold real estate notwithstanding defect of purchase before naturalization. *Copy.* 1½ pp. *Endorsed*, Recd. 12 December, Read 21 December 1772. [C.O.5, 1076, fos. 210–211d]

1290

7 June, St James's

Same, disallowing three Acts passed in New York in 1770, vizt. for relief of insolvent debtors; to enable recovery of debts on promissory notes; to relieve James de Peyster, debtor. *Copy.* 1½ pp. *Endorsed*, Recd. 12 December, Read 21 December 1772. [C.O.5, 1076, fos. 208–209d]

1291

7 June, St James's

Same, directing Commissioners for Trade and Plantations to prepare draft additional instruction to governor of Quebec authorizing him to grant lands in fief and seigneurie as practised heretofore, omitting *haute, moyenne, basse justice. Seal. Signed*, Stephen Cottrell. 2 pp. *Endorsed*, Recd. 11 June, Read 19 June 1771. [C.O.42, 8, fos. 1–2d]

1292

7 June, St James's

Same, dismissing petition of Charles Garth, agent of South Carolina, for withdrawal of additional instruction of 14 April 1770 and for direction to governor of South Carolina to communicate to Commons House all representations transmitted relative to proceedings of that House.

Entry. Signatory, Stephen Cottrell. 3 pp. [C.O.5, 408, pp. 68–70; copy, endorsed Recd. 12 December, Read 21 December 1772, in C.O.5, 380, fos. 88–89d; another copy in C.O.5, 27, fos. 72–74d]

1293

7 June, St James's

Same, disallowing two Acts passed in North Carolina in 1768, vizt. to encourage import of British copper halfpence; and for declaring lots in New Bern taken up by trustees for promoting public school saved and improved. *Copy.* 1½ pp. *Endorsed,* Recd. 12 December; Read 21 December 1772. [C.O.5, 302, fos. 216–217d]

1294

7 June, St James's

Same, approving report of Committee for Plantation Affairs that forcible intrusion by inhabitants of Connecticut alleged by proprietors of Pennsylvania is matter entirely within jurisdiction of Pennsylvania and that it is unnecessary and improper to interpose H.M.'s authority. *Copy.* 2½ pp. *Endorsed,* Recd. 12 December, Read 21 December 1772. [C.O.5, 1278, fos. 104–105d]

1295

7 June, St James's

Same, disallowing three Acts passed in West Florida in 1767 and 1769, vizt. Act concerning attachments, Act making estates of absent debtors liable to attachment, Act empowering magistrates and freeholders of Charlotte County to prohibit sale of rum to Indians. *Copy.* 1½ pp. *Endorsed,* Recd. 12 December, Read 21 December 1772. [C.O.5, 579, pp. 171–174]

1296

7 June, St James's

Same, disallowing Act passed in New Jersey in 1770 to amend Act for relief of insolvent debtors. *Copy.* 1½ pp. *Endorsed,* Recd. 12 December, Read 21 December 1772. [C.O.5, 979, fos. 63–64d]

1297

7 June, St James's

Same, disallowing Act passed in New Jersey in 1769 to erect courts for trial of causes of £10 and under. *Copy.* 1½ pp. *Endorsed,* Recd. 12 December, Read 21 December 1772. [C.O.5, 979, fos. 65–66d]

1298

7 June, St James's

Same, approving Act passed in Georgia in 1770 for ordering and governing slaves. *Copy.* 1½ pp. *Endorsed,* Recd. 12 December, Read 21 December 1772. [C.O.5, 651, fos. 203–204d]

1299

7 June, St James's

Same, disallowing Act passed in Georgia in 1768 for granting duties on raw neat hides exported. *Copy.* 1½ pp. *Endorsed,* Recd. 12 December, Read 21 December 1772. [C.O.5, 651, fos. 205–206d]

1300

7 June, St James's

Same, confirming appointment to Council in East Florida of John Moultrie, John Stuart, Robert Catherwood, John Holmes, John Forbes, clerk, William Drayton, Witter Cuming, Andrew Turnbull, Sir Charles Burdett, Bt., Martin Jollie. *Copy.* 1¼ pp. *Endorsed,* Recd. December, Read 21 December 1772. [C.O.5, 545, fos. 107–108d; warrant for admission of John Moultrie, dated 10 June 1771, in C.O.324, 42, p. 285; sealed original of Order in C.O.5, 27, fos. 68–69d]

1301

8 June, Whitehall

Earl of Hillsborough to Governor Earl of Dunmore (No. 2). I have received Nos. 15–17 from President Nelson about copper coin, ecclesiastical jurisdiction, and pension for Mr Blair. Difficulties about pension. *Draft.* 1 p. [C.O.5, 1349, fos. 89–90d; entry in C.O.5, 1375, pp. 155–156]

1302

8 June, Whitehall

Same to Judge Livingston. I have postponed taking any step on subject of your petition in hope that new governor of New York will fall on method of inducing Assembly to desist. *Entry.* ½ p. [C.O.5, 246, p. 19]

1303

9 June .

Richard Jackson to Commissioners for Trade and Plantations, reporting on seventeen Acts passed in Maryland in 1769, proper in point of law. Act for relief of certain prisoners is defective; and Act supplementary to Act to prevent concealing felons, though of real public utility, is improper for H.M.'s allowance. *Signed.* 3 pp. *Endorsed,* Recd. 11 June, Read 12 June 1771. [C.O.5, 1278, fos. 41–42d]

1304

9 June, Plymouth

Governor John Byron to Earl of Hillsborough, acknowledging letter of 5 June. *Panther* will be ready to sail for Newfoundland in two or three days. *Signed.* 1 p. *Endorsed*, R, 12 June. [C.O.194, 30, fos. 49–50d; entry in C.O.195, 12, p. 117]

1305

10 June, Charlotte Town, Island of St John

Thomas Wright to Earl of Hillsborough, soliciting appointment as Surveyor-General of this island, for which office there is absolute necessity. Survey of coast of Nova Scotia opposite this island finished; distances taken to complete general projection of Gulf of St Lawrence. I am about to join Captain Holland in survey of New England. *Signed.* 2 pp. *Endorsed*, R, 13 September. [C.O.5, 154, fos. 22–23d]

1306

11 June, Boston

Governor Thomas Hutchinson to Commissioners for Trade and Plantations, acknowledging letter of 27 March and explaining purpose and circumstances of law for preventing currency of bills of credit of Connecticut, New Hampshire and Rhode Island in this province. Newspaper sent. *Signed.* 2¼ pp. *Endorsed*, Recd. 27 July, Read 21 February. [C.O.5, 894, pp. 321–324]

1307

12 June, Whitehall

Commissioners for Trade and Plantations to the King, recommending disallowance of Act passed in Virginia in 1770 for appointing commissioners to meet commissioners of neighbouring colonies to form plans for regulation of Indian trade. *Entry. Signatories*, Hillsborough, Soame Jenyns, John Roberts, William Fitzherbert. 1½ pp. [C.O.5, 1369, pp. 235–236; draft in C.O.5, 1336, fos. 202–203d]

1308

12 June, Whitehall

John Pownall to John Robinson, sending copy of bill for better collection of quitrents in North Carolina for Treasury's opinion thereon. *Draft.* 1 p. [C.O.5, 314, fos. 101–102d; entry in C.O.5, 332, p. 89]

1309

13 June

Richard Jackson to Commissioners for Trade and Plantations, reporting on sixteen Acts passed in South Carolina in 1770–1771, proper in point of law. Act passed in 1770 for issuing £70,000 for building court-houses in similar to Act of New York disallowed two years ago. Act passed is 1771 for causeway and ferry in parish of Prince George is open to objection but insufficient to condemn it. *Signed.* 3 pp. *Endorsed,* Recd. 18 June, Read 19 June 1771. [C.O.5, 380, fos. 16–17d]

1310

13 June, Boston

Governor Thomas Hutchinson to Earl of Hillsborough (No. 6), enclosing following, part of which is copied from *Cape Fear Mercury.* *Signed.* ½ p. *Endorsed,* R, 24 July. *Enclosed:*

i. *Massachusetts Gazette and Boston Weekly Newsletter,* 13 June 1771, printing extract from *North Carolina Gazette* and other reports of battle at Almansee. *Printed.* 4 pp. [C.O.5, 760, fos. 180–183d; entry of covering letter in C.O.5, 768, p. 204; signed duplicate of covering letter, endorsed Read 12 December 1771, in C.O.5, 894, pp. 301–304]

1311

13 June, St Augustine

Lieut.-Governor John Moultrie to Earl of Hillsborough (No. 3). Dr Turnbull and settlers at Smyrnea were frightened by Indian visit, notwithstanding his earlier letter, copy enclosed. Indians demanded provisions at store on way to Musquito, but we never had less to fear from them. I asked O.C. troops in this province to reinforce detachment at Smyrnea; he declined. *Signed.* 4 pp. *Endorsed,* R, 1 August. *Enclosed:*

i. Smyrnea, 9 May 1771. Andrew Turnbull to Governor Grant or Lieut.-Governor. Upper Creek chiefs with seventy-two warriors and young men came here, on false report that there was a settlement by Spaniards and Yamassees on Cape Florida. No irregularities. Party of 31st regiment here should be reinforced. *Copy.* 2½ pp.

ii. St Augustine, 6 June 1771. Lieut.-Governor Moultrie to Major Alexander Mackenzie, asking for reinforcement at Smyrnea. *Copy.* 1½ pp.

iii. St Augustine, 6 June 1771. Major Mackenzie to Lieut.-Governor Moultrie, refusing. Refer to General Gage. *Copy.* 1 p. [C.O.5, 552, fos. 46–54d; entry of covering letter in C.O.5, 567, pp. 194–200]

1312

14 June, St James's

Order of King in Council, disallowing Act passed in Virginia in 1770 appointing commissioners to meet commissioners of neighbouring colonies to form plan for regulating Indian trade. *Copy.* 1½ pp. *Endorsed,* Recd. 12 December, Read 21 December 1772. [C.O.5, 1334, fos. 26–27d]

1313

14 June, St James's

Same, referring following to Commissioners for Trade and Plantations. *Seal. Signed,* Stephen Cottrell. 1 p. *Endorsed,* Recd. 18 June, Read 19 June 1771. *Enclosed:*

    i. Petition of James and Normand Macdonald of Isle of Skye, on behalf of themselves and others, to the King, praying for grant of 40,000 acres of land in North Carolina where they design to form a settlement. *Copy.* 1 p. [C.O.5, 302, fos. 1–4d]

1314

14 June, Whitehall

Commissioners for Trade and Plantations to the King, proposing disallowance of Act passed in West Florida in 1767 to erect Mobile into county; and submitting whether it may not be advisable to disallow also Act passed in West Florida in 1767 for order and government of slaves on ground that there should have been inserted a clause saving power to judges to stay execution of death sentences. *Entry. Signatories,* Hillsborough, Edward Eliot, John Roberts, William Fitzherbert. 5½ pp. [C.O.5, 600, pp. 227–232]

1315

14 June, Whitehall

Same to President William Nelson, acknowledging letter of 27 March. In future, care is to be taken to avoid objection to law for sale of glebe land, which your letter has not removed. *Entry. Signatories,* Edward Eliot, John Roberts, William Fitzherbert. 1¼ pp. [C.O.5, 1369, pp. 237–238; draft in C.O.5, 1336, fos. 207–208d]

1316

14 June, Virginia

* President William Nelson to Earl of Hillsborough (No. 19), reporting floods. I have called Assembly for 11 July. It is by far most dreadful catastrophe since first settlement. *Duplicate. Signed.* 1½ pp. *Endorsed,* R, 13 August, original not recd. *Enclosed:*

    i. Memorial of merchants and others on James River to President

Nelson, applying for assistance in distress caused by floods. *Copy,* certified by John Blair, jnr. *Signatories,* William Mitchell and 112 others. 1 large p.

ii. Minutes of Council of Virginia, 12–13 June 1771, recording proceedings on No. i. *Copy,* certified as No. i. 1½ pp. [C.O.5, 1349, fos. 102–106d; signed original of covering letter and copies of enclosures, in C.O.5, 1333, fos. 96–100d; entry of covering letter in C.O.5, 1372, pp. 180–182]

1317

15 June, Halifax

Governor Lord William Campbell to Earl of Hillsborough (No. 75), acknowledging circular and Nos. 43–44. *Signed.* 1 p. *Endorsed,* R, 24 July. [C.O.217, 48, fos. 57–58d; signed duplicate in C.O.217, 26, fos. 82–86d; entry in C.O.218, 18, p. 3]

1318

18 June

Richard Jackson to Commissioners for Trade and Plantations, reporting on seven Acts passed in New Jersey, proper in point of law. Act for support of government and Act for provision of £500 for support of H.M.'s troops are proper in point of law, but need amendment in future. Act supplementary to Act enabling creditors to recover debts should be disallowed. Act to enable H.M.'s subjects to inherit real estate notwithstanding purchase before naturalization is objectionable; it will be grace in H.M. either to leave it not disallowed or to signify intention to allow like Act with suspending clause. *Signed.* 3¼ large pp. *Endorsed,* Recd., Read 29 June 1771. [C.O.5, 979, fos. 25–26d]

1319

19 June, Whitehall

Commissioners for Trade and Plantations to the King, recommending disallowance of Act passed in Virginia in 1770 to explain jurisdiction of court of hustings of Williamsburg, which disallowance has been solicited by merchants of London. *Entry. Signatories,* Hillsborough, Edward Eliot, John Roberts, William Fitzherbert. 3 pp. [C.O.5, 1369, pp. 239–241; draft in C.O.5, 1336, fos. 204–206d]

1320

19 June, Whitehall

Same to same, enclosing following. *Entry. Signatories,* as preceding. ¾ p. *Enclosed :*

    i. Additional instruction to Governor of Quebec to grant lands, with advice of Council and subject to royal ratification, in fief and seigneurie as heretofore, but omitting the reservation of exercise of such judicial powers as have been long disused. *Entry.* 2½ pp. [C.O.43, 2, pp. 165–168]

1321

19 June, Pensacola

Governor Peter Chester to Earl of Hillsborough (No. 20), acknowledging circular of 22 January and Mr Pownall's of 12 February, with estimate. *Signed.* 1 p. *Endorsed,* R, 26 August. [C.O.5, 588, pp. 229–232; signed duplicate, endorsed Read 12 December 1771, in C.O.5, 578, pp. 205–208; entry in C.O.5, 621, pp. 72–73]

1322

20 June, Admiralty

Lords of Admiralty to Earl of Hillsborough. *Granby* sloop is said to have been lost for want of light in Halifax lighthouse. Complaints are frequent. *Signed,* Sandwich, J. Buller, C. J. Fox. 1¼ pp. *Endorsed,* R, 21st. *Enclosed :*

  i. *Salisbury,* Boston, 12 May 1771. Commodore James Gambier to Philip Stephens, reporting loss of *Granby* with all hands through, it is believed, want of light in lighthouse. *Copy.* 4 pp. [C.O.217, 48, fos. 37–40d; entry of covering letter in C.O.218, 18, p. 1]

1323

20 June, Treasury

John Robinson to John Pownall, enclosing following. *Signed.* ½ p. *Endorsed,* R, 21 June. *Enclosed :*

  i. Treasury, 11 June 1771. Minute on Governor Carleton's memorial. Military government of Quebec town is to be re-annexed to civil government of province, when former falls vacant. Meanwhile Governor Carleton is to receive £10,202 2s. 5½d. in respect of 1766–1770, and £2000 a year until re-annexation. After re-annexation, governor's salary is to be £1500 a year. *Copy.* 2 pp. [C.O.42, 31, fos. 21–24d; entry in C.O.43, 13, pp. 6–8]

1324

20 June

Richard Jackson to Commissioners for Trade and Plantations, giving opinion that fifteen Acts passed in Georgia in 1770 are proper in point of law. Titles stated. I have also considered Act of same year for granting £3355 9s. 0¼d. for support of government, which is objectionable because it imposes tax on imports for sale without excepting manufactures and produce of this kingdom. Other objections stated. It is, however, of little utility to declare it void as it must have had its full effect by now. I have also considered Act of same year assessing inhabitants of Savannah, which is open to objection. *Signed.* 3 pp. *Endorsed,* Recd. 21, Read 27 June 1771. [C.O.5, 651, fos. 62–63d]

1325

20 June, Pensacola

Governor Peter Chester to Earl of Hillsborough (No. 21), acknowledging No. 2. Mr Durnford has not yet returned. Settlement of lands on Mississippi highly necessary. *Signed.* 2¼ pp. *Endorsed,* R, 26 August. [C.O.5, 588, pp. 233–236; signed duplicate, endorsed Read 12 December 1771, in C.O.5, 578, pp. 209–212; entry in C.O.5, 621, pp. 73–75]

1326

20 June, New York

Governor Earl of Dunmore to Earl of Hillsborough, enclosing following, which may be first account of Colonel Tryon's victory over these lawless rascals. I hope to receive H.M.'s orders to remain where I am. Best respects to Lady Hillsborough and the young ladies. *Signed.* 1 small p. *Endorsed,* private. *Enclosed:*

* i. Extract of letter, dated New Bern, 6 June 1771, from Samuel Cornell to Elias Debrosses, merchant, in New York, giving account of campaign and battle against Regulators. *Copy.* 5 pp. [C.O.5, 154, fos. 15–18d; entry of covering letter in C.O.5, 246, p. 21]

1327

21 June, Whitehall

Commissioners for Trade and Plantations to the King, recommending disallowance of two Acts passed in New Jersey in 1770, vizt. Act supplementary to Act for enabling creditors to recover just debts and Act to enable H.M.'s subjects by birth or naturalization to inherit real estate notwithstanding purchase before naturalization; and proposing additional instruction to governors of all colonies not to assent to any law by which lands, goods etc. of persons who have never resided in the colony are made liable to attachment. *Entry. Signatories,* Hillsborough, Edward Eliot, John Roberts, William Fitzherbert. 4 pp. [C.O.5, 999, pp. 243–246]

1328

21 June, Whitehall

Same to same, recommending disallowance of two Acts passed in South Carolina in 1770, vizt. for issuing £70,000 for expense of courthouses and gaols; and to encourage making of flax, linen and thread. Second gives bounty on linen, which ought to be discouraged. *Draft. Signatories,* as preceding. 3½ pp. [C.O.5, 381, fos. 369–372d; entry in C.O.5, 404, pp. 452–454]

1329

21 June, Whitehall

Same to Committee of Council for Plantation Affairs, recommending discountenance of petition of James and Normand Macdonald of Isle of Skye for land in North Carolina. Emigration of inhabitants of Great Britain must lessen strength, and prejudice landed interest and manufactures, of these kingdoms. *Entry. Signatories,* as preceding. 3½ pp. [C.O.5, 326, pp. 183–186; draft in C.O.5, 305, fos. 62–64d]

1330

21 June, Whitehall

Same to Governor William Franklin, notifying recommendation to H.M. of disallowance of Act of New Jersey supplementary to Act for enabling creditors to recover just debts and Act for confirming titles derived from grants by aliens. Besides these, Act for support of government is open to objections; to avoid doubt, future Acts should state quantities of paper bills remaining in Treasury under different emissions and periods fixed for redemption. We have long hoped House of Representatives of New Jersey would recede from claim of sole right of appointing agent: we can never admit any person to appear as agent, not appointed by Act of whole legislature. *Entry. Signatories,* as preceding. 3½ pp. [C.O.5, 999, pp. 247–250]

1331

21 June

Warrant for appointment of James Trail to office of Prothonotary and Chief Clerk of General Court of Pleas in South Carolina. *Entry.* 1 p. [C.O.324, 42, p. 290]

1332

21 June, Tom's Coffee House, London

Committee of Canada Reconnoissances to Richard Sutton, enclosing following. ½ p. *Endorsed,* R, do. *Enclosed:*

i. 21 June 1771. Same to Lord Rochford, desiring meeting. ¼ p. *Endorsed,* R, do. [C.O.5, 43, fos. 271–274d]

1333

21 June, Pensacola

Governor Peter Chester to Earl of Hillsborough (No. 22), enclosing following. *Signed.* ½ p. *Endorsed,* R, 26 August. *Enclosed:*

i. Pensacola, 8 April 1771. Certificate by Governor Chester that Alexander Macullagh is deputy Clerk of Council of West Florida. *Signed.* Countersigned by Ph. Livingston jnr. 1 p.

ii. Minutes of Council of West Florida, 11 February–8 April 1771. *Copy*, certified by Alexander Macullagh. 35 pp. [C.O.5, 588, pp. 237–278; signed duplicate of covering letter, endorsed Read 12 December 1771, in C.O.5, 578, pp. 213–216; entry of covering letter in C.O.5, 621, p. 75]

1334

22 June, Boston

* Governor Thomas Hutchinson to Earl of Hillsborough (No. 7), enclosing following. One-third of the House, men of best characters, opposed; most of others seem to have come into it from ignorance. Real spring is from heads of party that makes clamour at Court's being held out of Boston. It is already considered by many as miserable effort of few despairing men. *Signed*. 1½ pp. *Endorsed*, R, 24 July. *Enclosed:*

i. *Massachusetts Gazette and Boston Weekly Newsletter*, 20 June 1771, reporting text of protest by House of Representatives, passed 63–35, reconsidered, redrafted, and passed 63–31. *Printed*. 4 pp. [C.O.5, 760, fos. 184–187d; entry of covering letter in C.O.5, 768, pp. 205–206]

1335

22 June, Pensacola

Governor Peter Chester to Earl of Hillsborough (No. 23). Number of grantees of lands near Pensacola wish to exchange for lands elsewhere. There was mistake in terms of letters patent to James Bruce in 1768; I told him in Council that this should be rectified, but have not complied with Council's advice that he be allowed to change location of his grant, which I thought bad precedent. *Signed*. 2½ pp. *Endorsed*, R, 26 August. *Enclosed:*

i. Pensacola, 8 June 1771. Petition of James Bruce to Governor Chester and Council of West Florida. Condition in his grant of land not agreeable to H.M.'s mandamus. Requests to be allowed to exchange for like tract elsewhere in province. *Copy*. 2½ pp.

ii. Pensacola, 28 July 1766. Minutes of Council of that date and 11 June 1771, recording proceedings on above petition. *Copy*, certified by Alexander Macullagh, deputy Clerk of Council. 2½ pp. [C.O.5, 588, pp. 279–290; signed duplicate of covering letter and copies of enclosures, endorsed Read 12 December 1771, in C.O.5, 578, pp. 217–228; entry of covering letter in C.O.5, 621, pp. 76–78]

1336

23 June, Pensacola

* Same to same (No. 24). Lieut.-Governor Durnford has returned from Mississippi. Laying out townships in country contiguous to Mississippi is prevented by former injudicious grants of great tracts, on which no improvements have been made and no quitrents paid. Terms of such grants enclosed: can they be vacated by proclamations requiring cultivation in six or twelve months? Troops needed to protect settlers in this country, Spanish complaints, copy sent, are against licentious traders for selling rum. *Signed.* 3½ pp. *Endorsed,* R, 26 August. *Enclosed:*

★ i. Pensacola, 23 June 1771. Lieut.-Governor Elias Durnford to Governor Chester. Survey in preparation. Lands from Perle River to west and from junction of Manchack or Iberville Creek are good; also those between Mississippi and Amit Rivers. Application to Parliament needed for allowance for surveys proposed. Townships needed. Very few residents on lands granted on Mississippi, which prevents those inclined to settle. Troops needed to assist magistrates. I hope the cut may be done but it will be expensive. Pascagoulas, Mobiliens and Tensas, small Indian tribes, have been induced to move to Spanish side. Spanish complaints sent. *Copy.* 3½ pp.

ii. Blank form of letters patent for grants of land in West Florida. *Printed.* 1 p. [C.O.5, 588, pp. 291–300; signed duplicate of covering letter and copy of enclosure i, both endorsed Read 12 December 1771, and copy of enclosure ii, in C.O.5, 578, pp. 229–238; entry of covering letter in C.O.5, 621, pp. 79–82]

1337

23 June, [*S. Carolina*]

W. Wragg to Earl of Hillsborough, acknowledging introduction to Mr Gordon and Mr Savage. *Signed.* 2 small pp. *Endorsed,* R, 1 August. [C.O.5, 154, fo. 19, 19d; entry in C.O.5, 246, pp. 21–22]

1338

27 June, St James's

Order of King in Council, approving draft of additional instruction to governor of Quebec concerning manner of granting land. *Copy.* 1½ pp. *Endorsed,* Recd. 12 December, Read 21 December 1772. [C.O.42, 8, fos. 97–98d; sealed original, with draft of instruction, in C.O.5, 27, fos. 84–87d; entry of instruction, dated 2 July (★), in C.O.43, 8, pp. 93–94]

1339

27 June, Whitehall

Commissioners for Trade and Plantations to the King, recommending John Lawrence to be of the Council in New Jersey in room of John Smith, deceased. *Entry. Signatories,* Hillsborough, Edward Eliot, John Roberts, William Fitzherbert, Thomas Whately. 1 p. [C.O.5, 999, p. 251]

1340

27 June, Whitehall

Same to same, recommending disallowance of Act and four ordinances passed in Georgia in 1770, in order to stop practice of passing ordinances for appointment to offices. Governor to be instructed not to assent to like laws. *Entry. Signatories,* Hillsborough, Edward Eliot, W. Fitzherbert, Thomas Whately. 3½ pp. [C.O.5, 674, pp. 364–367]

1341

27 June, Whitehall

Same to Committee of Council for Plantation Affairs. We have reconsidered our report of 17 July 1769 relative to application of Henry Bostwick and others for grant of mines on Lake Superior. Gentlemen interested deny design imputed by General Gage: fort commanding Pass of St Mary was a quarter-acre fenced in to secure agent from drunken Indians. We think clause should be inserted in grant, if H.M. makes it, restraining the Adventurers from interfering in peltry-trade; from mining or having any post within twenty miles of passage from Lake Huron to Lake Superior; and from erecting fortifications. *Entry. Signatories,* as preceding. 4 pp. [C.O.324, 18, pp. 388–391]

1342

29 June, St Augustine

Lieut.-Governor John Moultrie to Earl of Hillsborough (No. 4), enclosing following and sending journals of Council. Agricultural prospects are good. Indians are friendly: they have returned seven runaway negroes, reward given. Allowance to Provost Marshal discontinued now that he has salary. *Signed.* 4 pp. *Endorsed,* R, 11 October. *Enclosed:*

i. General account of contingent expenses of East Florida, 25 June 1770–24 June 1771. *Signatory,* Alexander Skinner, clerk of accounts. *Copy,* certified 29 June 1771 by David Yeats, deputy clerk of Council. 3 pp. [C.O.5, 552, fos. 55–59d; entry of covering letter in C.O.5, 567, pp. 200–203]

1343

29 June, New Bern

Governor William Tryon to Commissioners for Trade and Plantations, acknowledging dispatch of 12 December 1770. I shall leave it to Governor Martin to get amendments in laws you recommend. *Signed.* ½ p. *Endorsed,* Recd. 11 October 1771, Read 21 February 1772. [C.O.5, 302, fos. 92–93d; signed duplicate, endorsed R, 13 September, in C.O.5, 314, fos. 149–150d]

1344

29 June, New Bern

Same to Earl of Hillsborough (No. 73), acknowledging dispatches up to No. 36 inclusive and circulars of 15 and 15 November, 11 December and 22 January. I embark for New York tomorrow; dispatches will be sent from there. *Duplicate. Signed.* 1 p. *Endorsed,* R, 13 September. [C.O.5, 314, fos. 147–148d; signed original, endorsed Read 12 December 1771, in C.O.5, 302, fos. 78–79d; entry in C.O.5, 328, p. 243]

1345

30 June, New Bern

Same to same (No. 75), enclosing minutes of Council of North Carolina and rules of precedency, which relate to claims between Sir Nathaniel Duckinfield, Bart., and H.M.'s Council. *Signed.* 1 p. *Endorsed,* R, 13 September. *Enclosed :*

i. Minutes of Council of North Carolina, 5–19 April 1771. *Copy,* certified by Robert Palmer, secretary. 6 pp.

ii. Same, 29 June 1771. *Copy,* certified as No. i. 3½ pp.

iii. Rules of precedency adjusted from Acts and Statutes in England, by Joseph Edmondson, Mowbray Herald. 1 p. [C.O.5, 314, fos. 151–164d; signed duplicate of covering letter, endorsed Read 15 May 1772, and copies of Nos. ii-iii, in C.O.5, 302, fos. 101–109d; entry of covering letter in C.O.5, 328, p. 244]

1346

30 June, New Bern

Same to same (No. 76), enclosing following. *Signed.* 1 p. *Endorsed,* R, 13 September. *Enclosed :*

i. List of patents of land granted at Court of Claims, New Bern, 10 April 1771. *Copy.* 10 pp. [C.O.5, 314, fos. 165–174d; signed duplicate of covering letter, endorsed Read 15 May 1772, in C.O.5, 302, fos. 110–111d; entry of covering letter in C.O.5, 328, p. 245; another copy of enclosure in C.O.324, 54, fos. 92–99d]

1347

1 July, Virginia

President William Nelson to Earl of Hillsborough (No. 20), soliciting remission of fine on James Anderson. Earl of Dunmore writes that there is to be meeting at New York in December for settling Indian trade. *Signed.* 1½ pp. *Endorsed,* R, 12 August. [C.O.5, 1349, fos. 107–108d; signed duplicate in C.O.5, 1333, fos. 101–102d; entry in C.O.5, 1372, pp. 178–179]

1348

2 July, Treasury

John Robinson to John Pownall, sending petition of Alice, widow of Benjamin Heron, late deputy secretary of North Carolina, for recognition of trouble in forming abstract of land grants, for opinion thereon. *Signed.* ¾ p. *Endorsed,* R, 3d. [C.O.5, 314, fos. 137–138d; entry in C.O.5, 328, p. 240]

1349

2 July, New York

Lieut.-General Thomas Gage to Earl of Hillsborough (No. 62), acknowledging No. 43. I hope my answer to Captain Hodgson will prevent further dispute between him and Governor Shirley of Bahamas. I have ordered artillery detachment back from Bahamas to St Augustine. Orders establishing lieut.-governor of Niagara received. Reports enclosed on fort and buildings at Pensacola and on Fort Charlotte and buildings at Mobile, with estimates of further works and plans. I await H.M.'s approbation of what is now proposed for accommodation of troops at Pensacola. I have ordered an assistant engineer from the Illinois to Pensacola to assist the works, and given him instructions to make certain observations on his route that may be of use. Assembly of New Jersey has refused to supply troops stationed there, see enclosed. *Signed.* 3½ pp. *Endorsed,* R, 9 August. *Enclosed:*

i. Report of survey of buildings and fort at Pensacola, 5 April 1771, by Captain Thomas Sowers, engineer. *Signed* (?). 1½ pp.

ii. New York, 27 June 1771. Report by same of works necessary for protection of harbour and town of Pensacola. *Signed* (?). 2¼ pp.

iii. New York, 27 June 1771. Estimate by same of cost of five new batteries with blockhouses etc. at Pensacola. Total: $11,290 or £2634 6s. 8d. sterling. *Signed* (?). 1 p.

iv. New York, 27 June 1771. Estimate by same of cost of building barracks etc. at Pensacola. Total: $34,106 or £7958 1s. 4d. sterling. *Signed* (?). 2 pp.

v. New York, 27 June 1771. Estimate by same of cost of repairs for provision and powder magazines and building new stockaded fort at Pensacola. Total: $1900 or £443 6s. 8d. sterling. *Signed* (?). ½ p.

vi. Report of survey by same of Fort Charlotte and public buildings at Mobile, 13 January 1771. *Signed* (?). 3½ pp.

vii. New York, 27 June 1771. Report by same of repairs necessary at Fort Charlotte, Mobile. *Signed* (?). 1½ pp.

viii. New York, 27 June 1771. Estimate by same of cost of repairs of officers' square of barracks at Mobile, agreeable to contract with Peter Rochan of Mobile, and of stockading. Total: $2395¾ or £558 18s. 5d. sterling. *Signed* (?). 1 p.

ix. Burlington, 3 June 1771. Governor William Franklin to General Gage, reporting Assembly's refusal to grant money for supply of King's troops in New Jersey. *Copy.* 1 p.

x. Plan, by Thomas Sowers, drawn by William Brasier, of entrance to Pensacola harbour, showing situation of new batteries. 1 large p. [M.P.G. 9]

xi. Plans, elevations and sections, by same, drawn by same, of new barracks designed for troops at Pensacola. 2 large pp. and 3 pp. [M.P.G. 10]

xii. Plan and section, by same, drawn by same, of batteries at Pensacola. 1 large p. [M.P.G. 11]

xiii. Plan, by same, of Fort Charlotte, Mobile. 1 large p. [M.P.G. 12] [C.O.5, 89, fos. 127–152d; entry of covering letter in C.O.5, 234, pp. 217–222]

1350

2 July, New York

Governor Earl of Dunmore to Earl of Hillsborough (No. 11), acknowledging No. 1 to Governor Tryon. I hope to discharge arrears on account of supplying troops out of savings of the £2000 granted by Assembly, which I hope may be a sure fund. Commissioners from different provinces to regulate Indian affairs will meet on 1 December. Disorders on New Hampshire borders will continue till H.M. removes all doubt. *Signed.* PS. Enclosed just received. 2½ pp. *Endorsed,* R, 9 August. *Enclosed :*

i. 2 July 1771. Address of thanks by principal body of German Protestants in City of New York to Governor Earl of Dunmore, for permission to form militia-company. *Signed,* F. W. Hecht and five others. 1¾ pp. [C.O.5, 1102, fos. 174–177d; entry of covering letter in C.O.5, 1138, pp. 230–231]

1351

2 July, New York

* Same to same (private), acknowledging private letter of 4 May. I grant Virginia's advantage in point of emolument but climate will oblige me to live without my family. Here there is harmony between me and the people. I have referred your letter to Mr Tryon; if he agrees to change, I shall be pleased to remain in New York. *Signed.* 1½ pp. *Endorsed,* R, 9 August. [C.O.5, 154, fos. 20–21d; entry in C.O.5, 246, pp. 22–23]

1352

3 July, Whitehall

Earl of Hillsborough to Earl of Rochford, forwarding Jeremiah Terry's memorial. *Draft.* 1 p. [C.O.5, 72, fos. 238–239d; entry in C.O.5, 241, p. 384]

1353

3 July, Whitehall

Same to Lieut.-General Thomas Gage (No. 46), acknowledging No. 60. No news of *Florida Packet*, Treasury informed. From Governor Chester's correspondence, differences with savages in West Florida have become alarming. Removal from Fort Chartres to any other place seems useless as long as it can be secured from the river. I hope it will keep French in subjection, without new establishment at Kascasquies, until resolution is taken on expediency of continuing remote establishments. I await Mr Durnford's report on channel of the Iberville. Indian designs can never occasion much mischief without support of Six Nations. Supply of artillery to Governor Tryon in North Carolina, approved. *Draft.* 4¾ pp. [C.O.5, 89, fos. 103–106d; entry in C.O.5, 243, pp. 15–17]

1354

3 July, Whitehall

Same to same (No. 47), enclosing following. Give possession to memorialist, if house is unconnected with King's works. *Draft.* ½ p. *Enclosed:*

i. Monday morning. Letter from Lieut. P. Sinclair, 15th regiment, for Earl of Hillsborough, requesting occupation of house in Detroit as mode of repaying his expenses. *Signed* (?). 1½ small pp. *Endorsed,* R, 22 May 1771.

ii. Memorial of same to same. Memorialist built several houses near Detroit for troops employed on H.M.'s vessel on the lake; they are no longer serviceable. Prays possession of Crown's house there in lieu. 1½ small pp. [C.O.5, 89, fos. 107–112d; entry of covering letter in C.O.5, 243, p. 17]

1355

3 July, Whitehall

Same to Governor William Franklin (No. 31), acknowledging Nos. 26–29. Mr Lawrence recommended to be of the Council in New Jersey. Your perseverance in demanding provision for troops, approved. Two Orders disallowing Acts passed in New Jersey, sent. *Draft.* 1½ pp. [C.O.5, 991, fos. 26–27d; entry, with Orders of 7 June 1771, in C.O.5, 1003, pp. 44–49]

1356

3 July, Whitehall

★ Same to Governor Peter Chester (No. 4), acknowledging Nos. 10–19. Your conduct approved. Security of West Florida in event of war

would have depended on offensive operations. Enlargement of boundaries of West Florida would be dangerous at this time. Engagements
made for frequent meetings with Indians should be preserved. Board
of Trade's ideas for regulation of Indian trade correspond with your
own. Boundary line between West Florida and Indians should be
ascertained. Mr Le Fleur's claims to be inquired into. Order in Council
disallowing three Acts passed in West Florida in 1767 and 1769, with
Board of Trade's representation thereon, sent. *Draft.* 6 pp. [C.O.5,
588, pp. 201–208; entry, with Order, in C.O.5, 619, pp. 83–85]

1357

3 July, Whitehall

* Same to Governor Thomas Hutchinson (No. 9), acknowledging
Nos. 3 and 4. Your conduct in dissolving Assembly of Massachusetts,
issuing writs for new election, and withholding consent from three bills,
approved. Bill for establishing Marine Society may be assented to.
Your conduct in negativing persons elected to manage the Indian trade
and payments to Mr De Berdt and Mr Bollan, and in refusing to move
Assembly to Boston, approved. You do not explain surprise of Supreme
Court judges at pardon for Ebenezer Richardson: same mode of
pardon has been long in use. *Entry.* 3 pp. [C.O.5, 765, pp. 208–210;
draft in C.O.5, 760, fos. 170–171d]

1358

3 July, Whitehall

Same to same (No. 10), ordering him to assist Mr Scammell, appointed
Inspector of Lands and Surveyor of White Pines in eastern part of
Massachusetts and in Nova Scotia north of Bay of Fundy. *Entry.* ½ p.
[C.O.5, 765, p. 211; draft in C.O.5, 760, fos. 172–173d]

1359

3 July, Whitehall

Same to Governor Lord William Campbell (No. 48), acknowledging
Nos. 72–74. Expense on military works should not be incurred without
approval of commander-in-chief. Expenses of Court of Escheats
could be met by sale of fortified lands; Treasury to be notified. Extract
of Mr Wentworth's letter [See No. 682] sent; ensure that tract of
timber is reserved to H.M. No grant of any land to be made in Nova
Scotia until Surveyor of Woods or deputy has surveyed the district
for timber for Royal Navy. Inquire strictly into Halifax lighthouse.
Draft. 3 pp. [C.O.217, 48, fos. 45–46d; entry in C.O.218, 25, pp. 92–95]

1360

3 July, Whitehall

Same to same (No. 49). You have H.M.'s leave to go to any other colony in North America for recovery of health. *Draft.* ¾ p. [C.O.217, 48, fos. 47–48d; entry in C.O.218, 25, pp. 95–96]

1361

3 July, Whitehall

Same to same (No. 50, separate), enclosing following, and recommending it subject to military considerations. *Draft.* ¾ p. *Enclosed :*

i. Memorial of Detliffe Christopher Jessen of Lunenburg, Nova Scotia, to Earl of Hillsborough, praying for grant of small piece of land on which Boscawn Battery formerly stood. *Copy.* 2 pp. [C.O.217, 48, fos. 53–54d; entry in C.O.218, 25, p. 97]

1362

3 July, Whitehall

Same to same (No. 51), desiring countenance for Mr Scammell, Inspector of Lands and Surveyor of White Pines. *Draft.* ½ p. [C.O.217, 48, fos. 53–54d; entry in C.O.218, 25, p. 97]

1363

3 July, Whitehall

Same to Governor James Grant (No. 41), sending copy of No. 1374 to Mr De Brahm. *Draft.* ½ p. [C.O.5, 552, fos. 37–38d; entry in C.O.5, 566, p. 49]

1364

3 July, Whitehall

Same to Governor James Wright (No. 38), sending two Orders in Council of 7 June last, confirming Act passed in Georgia in May 1770 for ordering and governing slaves, and disallowing Act passed in March 1768 for laying duty on raw neat hides exported. *Draft.* ½ p. [C.O.5, 661, fos. 67–68d; entry, with Orders, in C.O.5, 677, pp. 56–60]

1365

3 July, Whitehall

Same to Governor of New York (No. 3), acknowledging Earl of Dunmore's No. 9. Delay in considering laws of the colony is principally to be attributed to neglect in transmitting transcripts, which should be remedied. Two Orders in Council of 7 June sent, one confirming Act passed in 1770, the other disallowing three Acts passed in same session. Representation of Board of Trade thereon, sent. *Draft.* 1½ pp. [C.O.5, 1102, fos. 164–165d; entry, with Orders, in C.O.5, 1141, pp. 185–190]

1366

3 July, Whitehall

Same to same (No. 4), desiring countenance for Mr Bentzell, appointed Inspector of Lands and Surveyer of White Pines in Quebec and in that part of New York on Lake Champlain; and also for Mr Ruggles, appointed to like office in New Hampshire and that part of New York between Connecticut River and Hudson River. *Draft.* ½ p. [C.O.5, 1102, fos. 166–167d; entry in C.O.5, 1141, pp. 190–191]

1367

3 July, Whitehall

Same to Governor Earl of Dunmore (No. 3), sending Order of 14 June disallowing Act passed in Virginia. *Draft.* ½ p. [C.O.5, 1349, fos. 96–97d; entry, with Order, in C.O.5, 1375, pp. 156–158]

1368

3 July, Whitehall

Same to Governor of North Carolina (No. 3), sending Order in Council of 7 June disallowing two Acts passed in North Carolina in 1768, with Board of Trade's representation thereon. *Draft.* ½ p. [C.O.5, 314, fos. 139–140d; entry, with Order, in C.O.5, 332, pp. 90–92]

1369

3 July, Whitehall

Same to Deputy Governor John Penn (No. 26), sending Order of 24 May, instrument voiding Act of Pennsylvania, and another instrument passed in 1766 voiding Act passed in 1764. *Draft.* 1 p. [C.O.5, 1284, fos. 15–16d; entry, with Order, in C.O.5, 1301, pp. 128–140]

1370

3 July, Whitehall

Same to President H. T. Cramahé (No. 39). King has appointed you Lieut.-Governor of Quebec. Privy Council has given orders for steps to be taken to settle affairs of Quebec. *Draft.* 1 p. [C.O.42, 31, fos. 25–26d; entry in C.O.43, 8, p. 95; entry of commission, dated 6 June, in C.O.324, 42, pp. 281–282]

1371

3 July, Whitehall

Same to same (No. 40). You are to give assistance to Mr Bentzell, appointed Inspector of Lands and Surveyor of White Pines in Quebec and part of New York on Lake Champlain. *Draft.* ½ p. [C.O.43, 31, fos. 27–28d; entry in C.O.43, 8, pp. 95–96]

1372

3 July, Whitehall

* Same to John Stuart (No. 22), acknowledging No. 31. General Indian war is improbable. Time not favourable for extension of West Florida's limits, but boundary lines already agreed must be ascertained. Law regulating Indian trade, framed by you and communicated to governors might remedy evil. Cessions of lands by Indians to traders to be discountenanced. *Draft*. 3½ pp. [C.O.5, 72, fos. 240–242d; entry in C.O.5, 241, pp. 385–387]

1373

3 July, Whitehall

Same to same (No. 23), refusing home leave but consenting to his going to a northern colony for recovery of health. *Draft*. 1 p. [C.O.5, 72, fos. 243–244d; entry in C.O.5, 241, p. 388]

1374

3 July, Whitehall

Same to William De Brahm (No. 9), summoning him to England to answer complaints. *Draft*. ¾ p. [C.O.5, 72, fos. 245–246d; entry in C.O.5, 241, pp. 388–389]

1375

3 July, Whitehall

Same to John Duport, Chief Justice of Island of St John. I hope agent will procure payment of quitrents so as to enable payment of salaries of officers; I cannot recommend payments beyond what quitrents will answer. *Draft*. 1¼ pp. [C.O.226, 4, fos. 44–45d]

1376

3 July, Whitehall

Same to John Wentworth, Surveyor-General of Woods. No final representation yet from Board of Trade on your report, but your conduct approved. Reports by Mr Jackson on questions stated by Board of Trade, sent. *Draft*. 1½ pp. [C.O.5, 72, fos. 247–248d; entry in C.O.5, 241, pp. 389–390]

1377

3 July, Treasury

John Robinson to John Pownall, notifying waste committed on unappropriated lands in Lake Champlain region. *Signed*. 1 p. *Endorsed*, R, 3 July. *Enclosed*:

i New York, 9 March 1771. Adolphus Benzell, Inspector of White

Pines in America, to Grey Cooper, reporting facts as above. Plan of region is being prepared. *Signed.* 1¼ pp. *Endorsed,* Recd. 22 April, Read 25 June 1771.

ii. No date. Same to Earl of Dunmore, asking for trespass and waste in Lake Champlain region to be forbidden. *Copy.* 1½ pp. [C.O.5, 72, fos. 232–237d; entry of covering letter in C.O.5, 228, pp. 69–70]

1378

3 July, R.I.

Governor Joseph Wanton to Earl of Hillsborough, acknowledging letter of 17 February 1770 and sending laws of Rhode Island from time last sent. Recruiting parties have been assisted. Letter of 22 January last acknowledged. *Signed.* 2¼ pp. *Endorsed,* R, 14 October. [C.O.5, 1284, fos. 148–149d; entry in C.O.5, 1300, pp. 27–28]

1379

4 July, New Bern

President James Hasell to Earl of Hillsborough (No. 1). Governor Tryon embarked for New York four days ago. Troops returned 2nd inst. Above 6000 rebels submitted. Governor Martin indisposed at New York. *Signed.* 2 pp. *Endorsed,* R, 11 October. [C.O.5, 314, fos. 269–270d; signed duplicate, endorsed Read 12 December 1771, in C.O.5, 302, fos. 80–81d; entry in C.O.5, 328, pp. 253–254]

1380

6 July, Boston

★ Governor Thomas Hutchinson to Earl of Hillsborough (No. 8), acknowledging No. 7. I informed House of Representatives that my instructions would not allow consent to Tax and Treasury bills, and received answer which is open denial of H.M.'s right to appoint Commissioners of Customs or raise money from colonies, a principle gaining strength in this and other colonies. I prorogued Court yesterday. *Signed.* 1½ pp. *Endorsed,* R, 19 August. *Enclosed :*

i Cambridge, 4 July 1771. Message of Governor Hutchinson to House of Representatives on Tax Bill, with House's answer. *Copy,* certified by Thomas Flucker. 2½ pp.

ii. Cambridge, 5 July 1771. Speech of Governor Hutchinson to both Houses of Assembly. *Copy,* certified as No. i. [C.O.5, 760, fos. 188–195d; entry of covering letter in C.O.5, 768, pp. 206–208]

1381

8 July, Quebec

President H. T. Cramahé to Earl of Hillsborough (No. 9), acknowledging circular of 22 January. This event has enabled province to make greater export of corn than ever since first settlement. *Signed.* 1 p. *Endorsed*, R, 4 September. [C.O.42, 31, fos. 42–43d; entry in C.O.43, 13, p. 12; signed duplicate, endorsed Read 12 December 1771, in C.O.42, 8, fos. 37–38d]

1382

9 July, Quebec

Same to same (No. 10), sending minutes of Council of Quebec to 30 June. Two attempts made to set fire to this town; no discovery yet made. *Signed.* 2 pp. *Endorsed*, R, 4 September. [C.O.42, 31, fos. 44–45d; entry in C.O.43, 13, pp. 12–13; signed duplicate, endorsed Read 12 December 1771, in C.O.42, 8, fos. 39–40d]

1383

9 July, New York

Governor Earl of Dunmore to Earl of Hillsborough (No. 12), reporting arrival of Governor Tryon. I shall prepare to go to Virginia. *Signed.* 1¼ pp. *Endorsed*, R, 17 August. [C.O.5, 1102, fos. 178–179d; entry in C.O.5, 1138, p. 232]

1384

9 July, Charleston

Lieut.-Governor William Bull to Earl of Hillsborough (No. 49), acknowledging No. 46. Pamphlets concerning tar-making in Sweden have been distributed. *Signed.* 1½ small pp. *Endorsed*, R, 26 August. [C.O.5, 394, fos. 82–83d; signed duplicate, endorsed Read 12 December 1771, in C.O.5, 380, fos. 36–37d; entry in C.O.5, 409, p. 233]

1385

9 July, Charleston

Same to same (No. 50), enclosing and recommending following. *Signed.* 1½ pp. *Endorsed*, R, 26 August. *Enclosed :*

  i. Charleston, 5 July 1771. Memorial of George Milligen, surgeon to garrison in South Carolina, to the King, for additional salary. *Signed.* 2 small pp. [C.O.5, 394, fos. 84–87d; signed duplicate of covering letter and copy of enclosure, endorsed Read 12 December 1771, in C.O.5, 380, fos. 38–41d; entry of covering letter in C.O.5, 409, pp. 234–235]

1386

9 July, New York

Governor William Tryon to Earl of Hillsborough (No. 1), reporting arrival on 7 inst. *Signed.* PS. Governor Martin is recovering and sails for North Carolina in a few days. 2 pp. *Endorsed*, R, 17 August. [C.O.5,

1102, fos. 180–181d; entry in C.O.5, 1138, pp. 233–234; signed duplicate, endorsed Read 12 December 1771, in C.O.5, 1075, fos. 146–147d]

1387

10 July, Charleston

Lieut.-Governor William Bull to John Pownall, acknowledging pamphlets on tar-making in Sweden. *Signed.* 1 small p. *Endorsed*, R, 26 August. [C.O.5, 394, fos. 88–89d; entry in C.O.5, 409, pp. 235–236]

1388

10 July, Quebec

President H. T. Cramahé to John Pownall, acknowledging accounts of tar-making in Sweden which shall be dispersed. *Signed.* ¾ p. *Endorsed*, R, 4 September. [C.O.42, 31, fos. 46–47d; entry in C.O.43, 13, p. 13]

1389

12 July, Mobile

Rev. William Gordon to Earl of Hillsborough, soliciting appointment to succeed Mr Cotton at Pensacola. *Signed.* 1 small p. *Endorsed*, R, 5 December. [C.O.5, 588, pp. 439–442; entry in C.O.5, 621, p. 98]

1390

13 July, Whitehall

Earl of Hillsborough to Viscount Barrington, sending extract of letter from General Gage concerning Lieutenant Nordberg. *Draft.* ½ p. [C.O.5, 89, fos. 123–124d; entry in C.O.5, 243, p. 18]

1391

13 July, Whitehall

Same to Lords of Treasury, sending extract of letter from Lieut.-General Gage concerning *Florida Packet* and export of peltry to foreign market. *Draft.* ½ p. [C.O.5, 72, fos. 251–252d; entry in C.O.5, 241, p. 391]

1392

13 July, Whitehall

Same to same, proposing that cost of Court of Escheats in Nova Scotia be met by sale at auction of forfeited lands. *Draft.* 1 p. [C.O.217, 48, fos. 55–56d; entry in C.O.218, 25, pp. 97–98]

1393

13 July, Treasury

John Robinson to John Pownall, enclosing papers concerning outrages on Customs officers in America and neglect of governors to give
protection. *Signed.* ¾ p. *Endorsed*, R, 15 July. *Enclosed :*

i. 9 December 1768. Extract of letter from Collector and Comptroller of Rhode Island, reporting smuggling of wine. *Copy.* 2¾ pp.

ii. Philadelphia, 9 April 1769. Extract of letter from Inspector-
General John Williams to Commissioners of Customs, Boston,
reporting smuggling and want of support from governor. *Copy.* 1¼ pp.

iii. 24 April 1769. Extract of letter from William Sheppard, Surveyor and Searcher at Philadelphia, to Commissioners of Customs,
reporting smuggling, riotous assembly and assault. *Copy.* 8 pp.

iv. 13 October 1769. Extract of letter from John Swift, Deputy
Collector at Philadelphia, to Commissioners of Customs, reporting
assault by mob on Customs informer. *Copy.* 3 pp.

★ v. 20 December 1770. Extract of letter from John Swift and Alexander Barclay, Comptroller at Philadelphia, to Commissioners of
Customs. Government is not strong enough to stop smuggling. *Copy.*
2½ pp.

vi. Perth Amboy, 25 December 1770. John Hatton, Collector at
Salem etc. to Commissioners of Customs, notifying smuggling, and
accusing Read, Collector at Burlington. I am obliged to keep con-
cealed by day and when I travel it is all by night. *Copy.* 2½ pp.

vii. 7 December 1770. Same to Governor Franklin, reporting impossibility of discharging his office and proceedings against him by
magistrates. *Copy.* 4¾ pp.

viii. 25 December 1770. Opinion of Cortland Skinner, Attorney-
General of East Jersey, to John Hatton. Magistrates at Cape May
have no authority in transaction occurring on high seas. Apply to
Admiralty. *Copy.* ½ p.

ix. Perth Amboy, 25 December 1770. Cortland Skinner to Charles
Petit. Magistrates at Cape May exceeded their jurisdiction. Governor
would be justified in dismissing them. *Copy.* 1½ pp.

x. 6 December 1770. Warrant by James Whillden, Thomas Learning
and John Leonard, justices, to Sheriff of Cape May County to bring
John Hatton before court to give security to appear at next Quarter
Sessions. *Copy.* 1½ pp.

xi. Same date. Same by same to same to bring Ned, a mulatto, before
court for same purpose. *Copy.* 1½ pp.

xii. Cooper's Ferry, opposite Philadelphia, 30 December 1770. John
Hatton to Commissioners of Customs. Governor Franklin has
granted a *non ultimo prosequi* for me but not for my negro. *Copy.* 1¾ pp.

* xiii. Newport, Rhode Island, 11 April 1771. Charles Dudley, Collector of Customs at Newport, to Commissioners of Customs, reporting assault and hindrances on 3rd inst. following his attempt to examine ship *Polly. Copy.* 11½ pp. [C.O.5, 72, fos. 253–289d; entry of covering letter in C.O.5, 228, pp. 74–76]

1394

13 July, Treasury

Same to same, enclosing following. *Signed.* ¾ p. *Endorsed*, R, 15 July. *Enclosed :*

i. Custom-house, Boston, 7 September 1769. Richard Reeve to Thomas Bradshaw, enclosing following. *Copy.* ½ p.

ii. Extract of letter, dated 1 September 1769, from Collector and Comptroller of Rhode Island, making charges against Naval Officer of Rhode Island. *Copy. Signatories,* Charles Dudley, Collector, John Nicoll, Comptroller. 3½ pp. [C.O.5, 1284, fos. 123–130d; entry of covering letter in C.O.5, 1300, p. 23]

1395

15 July, Virginia

President William Nelson to Earl of Hillsborough (No. 21). Assembly met to consider flood relief. If they emit paper money it will not exceed £25–£30,000 and shall be agreeable to royal instruction. *Duplicate. Signed.* 1½ pp. *Endorsed*, R, 3 September. *Enclosed :*

i. President Nelson's speech to Assembly of Virginia on flood disaster. *Copy.* 1¾ pp.

ii. Address of Council to President Nelson on same subject, with his answer. *Printed.* 1 p.

iii. Same of Burgesses to same, on Lord Botetourt's death and flood disaster. *Copy.* 1 large p. [C.O.5, 1349, fos. 109–114d; signed original of covering letter, and copies of Nos. ii–iii, in C.O.5, 1333, fos. 103–107d; entry of covering letter in C.O.5, 1372, pp. 183–184]

1396

16 July, Boston

Governor Thomas Hutchinson to Commissioners for Trade and Plantations, sending exemplifications of laws passed in Massachusetts last session with remarks, and duplicates of laws passed preceding session. *Signed.* 1 small p. *Endorsed*, Recd. 6 September, Read 12 December. *Enclosed :*

i. Remarks by Governor Hutchinson on laws passed in Massachusetts in 1771. 1¼ small pp. *Endorsed*, Read 12 December 1771. [C.O.5, 894, pp. 285–292]

1397

17 July, Southampton-Street, London

James Marriot to John Pownall, requesting for Lord Chancellor copy of ordinance of Canada of March 1770 concerning courts of justice. *Entry.* ¼ p. [C.O.5, 246, p. 20]

1398

17 July

Declaration by Thomas and John Penn that H.M.'s approval of Richard Penn to be deputy governor of Pennsylvania and Three Lower Counties shall not diminish Crown's claims to Three Lower Counties. *Seals. Signed. Witnesses,* Henry Wilmot, John Lancaster. ¾ p. *Endorsed,* Recd., Read 23 July 1771. [C.O.5, 1278, fos. 45–46d]

1399

18 July, Boston

* Governor Thomas Hutchinson to Earl of Hillsborough (No. 9). I communicated to Council H.M.'s 5th and 16th instructions. Council do not pretend to meet without governor, but I told them I should not object to referring matters to committees to report to me in Council. Other instruction relates to agents. Correspondence by both Houses with their agents has contributed to jealousies. I hope when agents find they are not to be paid, this will cease. *Signed.* 1½ pp. *Endorsed,* R, 24 August. *Enclosed :*

  i. *Massachusetts Gazette and Boston Weekly Newsletter,* 18 July 1771. *Printed.* 4 pp. [C.O.5, 760, fos. 196–199d; entry of covering letter in C.O.5, 768, pp. 208–210; signed duplicate of covering letter, endorsed Read 12 December 1771, in C.O.5, 894, pp. 305–308]

1400

19 July, St James's

Order of King in Council, appointing John Lawrence to be of the Council in New Jersey in room of John Smith, deceased. *Copy.* 1 p. *Endorsed,* Recd. 12 December, Read 21 December 1772. [C.O.5, 979, fos. 67–68d; sealed original in C.O.5, 27, fos. 88–89d; entry of warrant, dated 19 July, in C.O.324, 42, p. 303]

1401

19 July, St James's

Same, approving appointment of Richard Penn as deputy or lieut.-governor of Pennsylvania and Three Lower Counties. Commissioners for Trade and Plantations to take security for his observing Acts of Trade and obeying H.M.'s instructions. *Seal. Signed,* W. Blair. 1½ pp. *Endorsed,* Recd. 20 July, Read 23 July 1771. [C.O.5, 1278, fos, 43–44d;

copy, endorsed Recd. 12 December, Read 21 December 1772, at fos. 112–113d]

1402

19 July, Whitehall

Earl of Hillsborough to Lieut.-General Thomas Gage (No. 48), acknowledging No. 61. Works proposed at Castle William are to be executed. Assembly of New Jersey persists in refusal to provide for troops stationed there: extract of letter to Governor Franklin sent. Only two measures can be effectual: interposing the authority of Parliament, or withdrawing the troops. If it can be done without appearance of yielding, withdrawal would perhaps be most eligible. Report your sentiments on this. *Draft.* $2\frac{1}{4}$ pp. [C.O.5, 89, fos. 125–126d; entry in C.O.5, 243, pp. 18–19]

1403

19 July, Whitehall

Same to Governor William Franklin (No. 32), acknowledging Nos. 30–31. Examination of Mr Hatton's complaint approved. Assembly's refusal to provide for troops is reprehensible: asserting inability to pay adds mockery to insult. Renew endeavours to persuade them. *Draft.* $1\frac{1}{2}$ pp. [C.O.5, 991, fos. 66–67d; entry in C.O.5, 1003, pp. 49–50]

1404

19 July, Whitehall

Same to Governor of New York (No. 5), acknowledging Earl of Dunmore's No. 10 and Acts passed last session. *Draft.* $\frac{1}{2}$ p. [C.O.5, 1102, fos. 172–173d; entry in C.O.5, 1141, p. 191]

1405

19 July, Whitehall

Same to Governor Earl of Dunmore (private), acknowledging private letter of 11 June [*Query:* No. 1268] relative to affair of Mr Colden; which seems at present to be in such state that it is impossible to give opinion of it. *Draft.* $1\frac{1}{4}$ pp. [C.O.5, 154, fos. 11–12d]

1406

19 July, Whitehall

Same to Lieut.-Governor John Moultrie (No. 42), acknowledging No. 1. $\frac{1}{2}$ p. [C.O.5, 552, fos. 41–42d; entry in C.O.5, 566, p. 49]

1407

19 July, Whitehall

Same to Governor and Company of Rhode Island (No. 21). It appears that outrages have been committed on Customs officers, particularly at Newport in April last, and no support given by government. *Draft*. 2 pp. [C.O.5, 1284, fos. 133–134d; entry in C.O.5, 1301, pp. 444–446]

1408

19 July, Whitehall

★ Same to Proprietaries of Pennsylvania. Acts of violence have been committed with impunity, particularly in Philadelphia in April and October 1769 on occasion of lawful seizures by Customs officers. *Draft*. 2 pp. [C.O.5, 1284, fos. 19–20d; entry in C.O.5, 1301, pp. 141–142]

1409

19 July, Whitehall

Same to Lieut.-Governor H.T. Cramahé (No. 41), acknowledging Nos. 6–8. King does not approve of congresses for regulating Indian trade. *Draft*. 1½ pp. [C.O.42, 31, fos. 40–41d; entry in C.O.43, 8, pp. 96–97]

1410

19 July, Whitehall

★ Same to Attorney- and Solicitor-General, sending copy of representation of Collector and Comptroller of Rhode Island relative to office of Naval Officer, for report whether the claim of governor of Rhode Island to be Naval Officer is warranted or whether Crown may appoint. *Draft*. 3¼ pp. [C.O.5, 1284, fos. 135–137d; entry in C.O.5, 1301, pp. 446–449]

1411

19 July

Warrant for appointment of Henry Kneller as Attorney-General of Quebec. *Entry*. 1 p. [C.O.324, 42, p. 302]

1412

19 July, Whitehall

John Pownall to John Robinson, sending papers on cases of Naval Officer at Rhode Island and Customs officers at Philadelphia. Papers have been received from Governor of New Jersey putting John Hatton's case in different light; but if Lords of Treasury are not satisfied, Earl of Hillsborough will concur in further measures. *Draft*. 1½ pp. [C.O.5, 72, fos. 290–291d; entry in C.O.5, 241, pp. 391–392; another draft in C.O.5, 1284, fos. 131–132d]

1413

20 July, Whitehall

Same to James Marriot, sending for Law Officers copy of ordinance published in Quebec on 1 February 1770 for regulating law proceedings. *Entry.* ¼ p. [C.O.5, 246, p. 20]

1414

20 July, London

Francis Mackay to Earl of Hillsborough, begging not to be deprived of office of Surveyor of Woods in Quebec for which Mr De Lanaudiere has applied. *Signed.* 1 p. *Endorsed*, private. [C.O.5, 154, fos. 13–14d]

1415

20 July, Burlington

* Governor William Franklin to Earl of Hillsborough (No. 32), acknowledging No. 30 and sending Votes of Assembly of New Jersey. A member of Assembly resigned, being insolvent; the House ordered writ for new election, which I refused as a matter affecting prerogative. *Signed.* PS. Copies of process of making tar and pitch in Sweden acknowledged. 2½ pp. *Endorsed*, R, 13 September. [C.O.5, 991, fos. 68–69d; entry in C.O.5, 1001, pp. 137–140]

1416

20 July, Charleston

Lieut.-Governor William Bull to Earl of Hillsborough, introducing and recommending M. Mesnil de St Pierre who intends to recruit *vignerons* in France. *Entry. Annotated*, R, 26 October. 1¼ pp. [C.O.5, 246, pp. 30–31]

1417

22 July, Virginia

President William Nelson to Earl of Hillsborough (No. 22). Assembly was prorogued on 21 July. *Signed.* 1 p. *Endorsed*, R, 23 October. [C.O.5, 1349, fos. 115–116d; signed duplicate, endorsed Read 12 December 1771, in C.O.5, 1333, fos. 108–108A dorse; entry in C.O.5, 1372, p. 184]

1418

22 July, Newport R.I.

* John, Thomas and Samuel Freebody to Earl of Hillsborough. In 1769 we obtained two judgments of King and Council against Jahleel Brenton but could not obtain execution in Rhode Island. Judgements were upheld by Superior Court in March 1770 but set aside in Michaelmas 1770. Governor and Company of Rhode Island approve of this disobedience to King's order. *Signed.* PS. Application to governor

would be in vain. 4 large pp. *Endorsed*, R, 8 November. *Enclosed :*

i. Newport, 29 July 1771. Sworn declaration, attested by Charles Bardin, by John, Thomas and Samuel Freebody that at Superior Court in March 1770 Henry Marchant said that the judgements of King and Council were contrary to law. *Signed.* 1 p. [C.O.5, 1284, fos. 150–153d]

1419

[22 July]

Richard Penn to Commissioners for Trade and Plantations, proposing David and John Barclay, of London, merchants, as security for observance of Acts of Trade. *Signed.* ½ p. *Endorsed*, Recd. 22 July, Read 23 July 1771. [C.O.5, 1278, fos. 47–48d]

1420

23 July, Whitehall

John Pownall to Grey Cooper. David and John Barclay are to be securities for Richard Penn to be deputy Governor of Pennsylvania. Draft of bond sent. *Entry.* 2 pp. [C.O.5, 1296, pp. 386–387]

1421

23 July

Bond in £2000 by David and John Barclay of London, merchants, security that Richard Penn, Lieut.-Governor of Pennsylvania, observes Acts of Trade. *Entry.* 11 pp. [C.O.5, 1296, pp. 375–385]

1422

24 July, Tom's Coffee House, London

John Marlar, for Robert Allen, and William Tooke to Lord Rochford, sending case of proprietors of Canada Reconnoissances [See No. 1427i] *Signed.* 1½ small pp. *Endorsed*, R, do. [C.O.5, 43, fos. 275–276d]

1423

24 July, Charlotte Town, I. of St John

Governor Walter Patterson to Earl of Hillsborough (No. 4, should be 7), acknowledging No. 3. Grant of £1500 for buildings will encourage settlement. Roads needed: I have had one of thirty-three miles laid out at my own risk. Plan of Charlotte Town altered to give every house southern aspect and more land. *Signed.* 3 pp. *Endorsed*, R, 13 September. [C.O.226, 4, fos. 76–77d; entry in C.O.227, 2, pp. 25–30; signed duplicate, endorsed Read 12 December 1771, in C.O.226, 1, fos. 34–35d] *Enclosed :*

i. Plan of Charlotte Town, Island of St John, by Thomas Wright, surveyor. 1 large p. [M.P.G. 257]

1424

26 July, Virginia

President William Nelson to Earl of Hillsborough (No. 23), enclosing following. *Signed.* ¾ p. *Endorsed*, R, 23 October. *Enclosed :*

i. Remarks on four Acts passed in late session of Assembly. 2½ pp.

ii. Journals of Council of Virginia, 12 December 1770–1 May 1771. *Copy*, certified by John Blair, jnr. 39 pp.

iii. Same, 11–20 July 1771. *Copy*, certified as No. ii. 8½ pp.

iv. Journal of House of Burgesses, 11–20 July 1771. *Copy*, certified by G. Wythe, clerk. 40 pp. [C.O.5, 1349, fos. 117–170d; signed duplicate of covering letter, endorsed Read 12 December 1771, copy of No. i and copy of part of No. iv, in C.O.5, 1333, fos. 109–113d; copy of No. iii in C.O.5, 1333, fos. 129–134B dorse; entry of covering letter, wrongly dated 22 July, in C.O.5, 1372, p. 185]

1425

27 July

Attorney- and Solicitor-General to Earl of Hillsborough. We are of opinion that charter does not empower governor of Rhode Island to appoint Naval Officer, but Acts of 15 Charles II and 7 & 8 William III recognize his power to do so. We know of no checks in execution of office other than those in 7 & 8 William III and common law. *Signed*, E. Thurlow, A. Wedderburn. 3¼ pp. *Endorsed*, R, 29 July. [C.O.5, 1284, fos. 138–139d; entry in C.O.5, 1300, pp. 24–27]

1426

29 July, Treasury

John Robinson to John Pownall, enclosing following and expressing Treasury's astonishment that an Act directly contrary to Act of Parliament should be passed. *Signed.* ¾ p. *Endorsed*, R, 2 August. *Enclosed :*

i. Custom-house, Boston, 12 February 1771. Richard Reeve to Grey Cooper, enclosing following. *Signed.* ½ p. *Endorsed*, Recd. 1 May, Read 11 July 1771. Write to Mr Pownall. Minute. Done.

ii. Act of West Florida to prevent masters of vessels from carrying off persons in debt from this province and for improving coastal trade. Passed Assembly, 8 May 1770, E. R. Wegg, Speaker. By order of Upper House, William Clifton, President. Assented to, 14 May 1770, by Elias Durnford. *Copy*, certified by Francis Poussett. 6½ pp.

iii. Protest at above bill by James Bruce. *Copy*, certified 11 June 1770 by Francis Poussett. 1½ pp. [C.O.5, 588, pp. 209–228; copy of covering letter, endorsed Recd. 25 November, Read [blank], and copies of enclosures in C.O.5, 578, pp. 33–54; entry of covering letter in C.O.5, 621, pp. 71–72]

1427

30 July, Tom's Coffee House, London

Committee of Canada Reconnoissances to Lord Rochford, enclosing following. ½ p. *Enclosed :*

i. Case of Merchants trading to and interested in trade of Canada, holders of Canada Bills. *Copy.* 16 large pp. [C.O.5, 43, fos. 277–286d]

1428

30 July, Fogo

Address of congratulations by merchants and planters of Fogo, Twilingate, Tiltin and other fishing places in Newfoundland, to Governor John Byron. *Signed*, William Lane, thirteen other planters, and fifteen merchants. 3 small pp. *Endorsed*, R, 3 December 1771. [.C.O.194, 30, fos. 78–79d]

1429

31 July, St James's

Order of King in Council disallowing Act passed in Massachusetts in 1768 additional to Act for erecting Huntstown into town of Ashfield. *Copy.* 1 p. *Endorsed*, Recd. 12 December, Read 21 December 1772. [C.O.5, 894, pp. 483–486]

1430

31 July, Quebec

President H. T. Cramahé to Earl of Hillsborough (No. 11), acknowledging No. 38. Road proposed by Mr Sleeper could not have been perfected without support from government. Canadians eagerly wish for settlement of this province. Meeting of commissioners from colonies concerned in Indian trade is set for 1 December at New York. *Signed.* 2½ pp. *Endorsed*, R, 10 September. [C.O.42, 31, fos. 48–49d; entry in C.O.43, 13, pp. 14–16; signed duplicate, endorsed Read 12 December 1771, in C.O.42, 8, fos. 41–42d]

1431

July

* Colonel Goldthwait's talk with a Mataugwesannack Indian, now among the Penobscot Indians. *Copy.* 8¼ pp. [C.O.42, 87, fos. 207–212d]

1432

[July?]

* Anonymous letter to Earl of Hillsborough, complaining of attempt to usurp attributes of God. *Signed*, A Servant. 1 p. *Addressed. Endorsed*, R, 8 November, postmarked Newport, R.I. [C.O.5, 1284, fos. 154–155d]

1433

1 August, New York

* Governor William Tryon to Earl of Hillsborough (No. 77), relating principal events attending success of battle of Alamance on 16 May. Proclamation of pardon was made to rebels who submitted; by 19 June 3300 had come into camp. On 4 June army effected junction with General Waddell who on 8 June marched westward to suppress insurrection. Of prisoners tried, two were acquitted, twelve capitally convicted: six executed, six respited till H.M.'s pleasure be known. H.M.'s indulgence solicited for widow and children of Benjamin Merril, executed. Eastern counties raised no men owing to Northern Treasurer's refusal of my warrants on him. Cost of pay, provisions etc. estimated at £40,000 currency which province is incapable of discharging unless by new emission of currency or aid of Parliament. Papers enclosed. *Signed.* PS. Few, an outlaw, was hanged in camp; houses and plantations of outlaws were laid waste. 8½ pp. *Endorsed*, R, 13 September. *Enclosed:*

> * i. Petition of inhabitants of Orange County to Governor Tryon, asking that their petitions be heard and grievances redressed. Delivered to H. E. at Alamance Camp, 15 May 1771, six o'clock in evening. *Copy. Signatories,* John Williams, Samuel Law, James Wilson, Joseph Scott, Samuel Clark. 2¾ pp.

> * ii. Great Alamance Camp, 16 May 1771. Governor Tryon's reply to preceding, calling on rebels to surrender in one hour. *Copy.* 1 p. [C.O.5, 314, fos. 175–184d; entry of covering letter in C.O.5, 328, pp. 245–251]

1434

2 August, New York

Same to same (No. 78), enclosing following. Army pursued no further than small plantation in rear of rebels. *Signed.* 1 p. With note of casualties in H.M.'s forces on 16 May: nine killed, sixty-one wounded. *Endorsed*, R, 13 September. *Enclosed:*

> i. Plan of camp at Alamance, 14–19 May 1771. Drawn by C. J. Sauthier. 1 large p.

> ii. Plan of camp and battle of Alamance, 16 May 1771. Drawn as No. i. 1 large p.

> iii. Orders by Governor Tryon to provincials of North Carolina, 1 May–20 June 1771. *Copy.* 67 pp.

> iv. Governor Tryon's letters, October 1770–June 1771. Entries of letters or extracts of letters to the following persons. 17 October 1770, Richard Henderson; James Watson and others. 8 October 1770, Alexander McCullock; Thomas McGuire. 19 October 1770, colonels of Orange and Rowan regiments; colonels of every other regiment. 20 November 1770, Captain Robert Howe; Colonel John

Simpson; Colonel Richard Caswell and Colonel John Hinton. 4 December 1770, Colonel John Simpson. 17 December 1770, Colonel John Simpson. 22 December 1770, Colonel John Simpson. 24 December 1770, Colonel Joseph Leech. 26 January 1771, Colonel John Frohock. 28 January 1771, Captain Robert Howe (2). 2 February 1771, Colonel Edmund Fanning. 6 February 1771, Colonel Joseph Leech. 17 February 1771, colonels of Dobbs, Johnston, Wake regiments; Colonel Edmund Fanning; Colonel Richard Henderson; Colonel John Ashe; Colonel William Cray; Colonel John Simpson (2). 8 February 1771, Colonel Joseph Leech. 9 February 1771, Colonel Joseph Leech; Colonel William Thomson. 13 February 1771, Thomas McGuire. 13 January 1771, Richard Henderson. 19 February 1771, Colonel Richard Caswell (*). 21 February 1771, Colonel John Ashe; Colonel William Cray; Christopher Neale; Colonel Richard Caswell; Colonel William Cray. 27 February 1771, Francis Nash; Colonel Hinton and Colonel Byam; Maurice Moore; Thomas McGuire(*). 1 March 1771, Sheriffs of Counties. 16 March 1771, Thomas Hart. 19 March 1771, Orders for raising 2550 men; colonels raising 100 men and upwards(*); colonels raising 50 men; Colonel John Harvey; Colonel Moses Alexander. 25 March 1771, Colonel James Moore. 30 March 1771, Colonel Robert Schaw; Colonel John Ashe and Colonel James Rutherford; Colonel James Sampson; Colonel James Moore; colonels of Rowan, Mecklenburg, Tryon and Anson regiments. 1 April 1771, Colonel William Cray. 2 April 1771, Colonel William Hayward. 3 April 1771, colonels of counties; Colonels Robert Palmer, John Simpson and John Smith; John Burgwin. 4 April 1771, Colonel Richard Caswell (2), Colonel Needham Bryan; Colonel John Hinton. 5 April 1771, Colonel William Thomson; John Frohock and Alexander Martin. 6 April 1771, Colonel Edmund Fanning; Colonel Joseph Leech. 12 April 1771, Colonel Edward Vail; Colonel Edward Buncombe. 13 April 1771, Colonel John Ashe; Thomas McGuire; Colonel Benjamin Nynns and other colonels; Thomas Hart. 18 April 1771, Colonel Edward Buncombe; Colonel Edward Vail; Captain Farquhard Campbell; Colonel John Ashe (2). 21 April 1771, Richard Blackledge. 22 April 1771, Jacob Mitchell. 23 April 1771, Colonel Joseph Leech; Colonel Thomson; Captain Christopher Neale; Richard Blackledge. 25 April 1771, Colonel Leech. 26 April 1771, Colonel Fanning. 1 May 1771, General Waddell (*). 13 May 1771, Chief Justice and Associate Judges. 14 May 1771, Thomas McGuire; Marmaduke Jones. 18 May 1771, General Waddell. 21 May 1771, Chief Justice and Associate Judges. 23 May 1771, General Waddell; Colonel Martin Armstrong. 24 May 1771, Colonel Fanning. 10 May 1771, General Waddell (*). 23 May 1771, Captain Simon Bright. List of requisitions from settlements. 25 May 1771, General Waddell. 26 May 1771, General Waddell; Colonel Fanning; General Waddell. 27 May 1771, Robert Hogg, Archibald Maclaine and William Hooper. 7 June 1771, General Waddell. 20 June 1771, Colonel John Ashe. List of warrants drawn on Treasurers for various services. 81 pp. [C.O.5, 314, fos. 185–268d; entry of covering letter in C.O.5, 328, p. 252]

1435

2 August, Whitehall

Earl of Rochford to Governor William Tryon, acknowledging, in Lord Hillsborough's absence, letter of 18 May and news of battle of Alamance. Your conduct approved; H.M.'s thanks to troops. I trust that this event will lay foundations for such measures of lenity and moderation as may convince deluded people of error. *Draft.* 2½ pp. [C.O.5, 314, fos. 145–146d; entry in C.O.5, 332, pp. 93–95]

1436

3 August, Savannah

President James Habersham to Earl of Hillsborough (No. 1), acknowledging letter of 22 January, duplicate of No. 37 and letter of 5 June. Governor Wright received original of No. 37 before he left, communicated it to Council, and left it with me to obey H.M.'s commands when it may be proper to call new Assembly, for which at present there appears no urgent necessity. *Signed.* 2½ pp. *Endorsed*, R, 18 November. [C.O.5, 661, fos. 71–72d; signed duplicate, endorsed Read 12 December 1771, in C.O.5, 651, fos. 137–138d; entry in C.O.5, 678, pp. 237–240]

1437

3 August, Savannah

Same to John Pownall. Governor Wright departed on 10th of last month and the government of Georgia has devolved on me. I received your letter of 5 June. Governor Wright has acquitted himself with great uprightness and honour. *Signed.* ¾ small p. *Endorsed*, R, 20 November. [C.O.5, 661, fos. 69–70d; entry in C.O.5, 678, pp. 236–237]

1438

4 August, Annapolis

Deputy Govenor Robert Eden to Earl of Hillsborough (No. 10), acknowledging No. 21. Back-parts of Virginia and North Carolina need regulation. Bounty on white oak staves will give satisfaction. I congratulate you on return of confidence between the different sides of the Atlantic. *Signed.* 2½ pp. *Endorsed*, R, 19 October. [C.O.5, 1284, fos. 98–99d; signed duplicate, endorsed Read 12 December 1771, in C.O.5, 1278, fos. 53–54d; entry in C.O.5, 1300, pp. 251–254]

1439

5 August, G.P.O.

Anthony Todd to John Pownall. *Lord Hyde*, Captain Goddard, for New York, and *Le Despencer*, Captain Pond, for Carolina, are ready to sail. *Entry.* ¼ p. [C.O.5, 247, p. 5]

1440

5 August, New York

Governor William Tryon to Earl of Hillsborough (No. 2), acknowledging duplicate of No. 1 and original No. 2. Addresses enclosed. Earl of Dunmore left me H.M.'s additional instruction of 4 December 1769, No. 33 to Sir H. Moore, Nos. 38–40 to Lieut.-Governor Colden, and No. 1 to Governor of New York. *Signed*. PS. German Protestants are sensible of honour done them. 2¼ pp. *Endorsed*, R, 13 September. *Enclosed:*

i. New York, 12 July 1771. Address of congratulation to Governor Tryon by rector and inhabitants of city in communion of Church of England. *Signed*, Samuel Auchmuty, rector. 2 pp.

ii. Same, 13 July 1771. Same, by minister, elders and deacons of United Presbyterian Churches in the city. *Signed*, John Rodgers, Joseph Freakin, ministers. 1¾ pp.

iii. Same, 15 July 1771. Same, by minister, elders and deacons of Reformed Protestant Dutch Church in the city. *Signed*, Archibald Laidlie. 1 p.

iv. Same, 15 July 1771. Same, by minister, churchwardens and vestrymen of Ancient Lutheran Church in the city. *Signed*, Bernard Michael Houseal. 2½ pp.

v. Same, 15 July 1771. Same, by minister, elders and deacons of Reformed Protestant German Church in the city. *Signed*, John Michael Kern. 1 p.

vi. Same, 16 July 1771. Same, by minister, elders and deacons of Reformed Protestant French Church in the city. *Signed*, J. Adam de Martel. 2 pp.

vii. Same, 17 July 1771. Same, by minister, trustees and wardens of German Evangelical Lutheran Church in the city. *Signed*, John Siegfried Gerock. 2 pp.

viii. Same, 17 July 1771. Same, by Old Church of Jesus Christ Baptized on personal profession of faith. *Signed*, John Carman, clerk. 1 p.

ix. Same, 18 July 1771. Same, by Mayor, Aldermen and Commonalty of city. 1¾ pp.

x. Same, 22 July 1771. Same, by Chamber of Commerce of the city. *Signed*, Elias Derbrosser, president. 1 p.

xi. Same, 22 July 1771. Same, by Marine Society of the city. *Signed*, Leonard Lispinaro, president. 1¾ pp.

xii. Albany, 22 July 1771. Same, by rector and inhabitants of Albany in communion of Church of England. *Signed*, Henry Munro, rector, and six others. 1½ pp.

xiii. Schenectady, 22 July 1771. Same, by minister, churchwardens and inhabitants of Schenectady in communion of Church of England. *Signed*, William Andrews, minister, and five others. 1¾ pp.

xiv. New York, 23 July 1771. Same, by president, professors etc. of College of New York. 1¾ pp.

xv. Same, 6 August 1771. Address by German Protestants of the city to Governor Tryon, expressing thanks for H.M.'s consent to formation of militia company. *Signed*, F. W. Hecht and five others. 1¾ pp.

xvi. Same, 16 July 1771. Address of congratulation to Governor Tryon by United Brethren in city and province of New York (Moravians). *Signed*, George Neisser. 3 pp.

xvii. Address of congratulation to Governor Tryon by Judges, Attorney-General, practisers and officers of Supreme Court of New York. 1½ pp.

xviii. New York, 5 August 1771. Governor Tryon's thanks for the above addresses. *Signed*. 22½ pp. [C.O.5, 1102, fos. 182–228d; entry of covering letter in C.O.5, 1138, pp. 234–235; signed duplicate of covering letter, endorsed Read 12 December 1771, in C.O.5, 1075, fos. 148–149d]

1441

6 August, New York

Lieut.-General Thomas Gage to Earl of Hillsborough (No. 63), acknowledging Nos. 44 and 45. Copy of letter to Governor Byron enclosed: I have strong objections against deviating from regulations for payment of soldiers employed in public works. Increase in pay in Newfoundland would be demanded elsewhere. Batteries in West Florida have been forwarded diligently: Brig.-General Haldimand hopes Pensacola harbour will soon be the best fortified in America. Plans of passage from West Florida to New Orleans, preferable to that by bayou of St John, are hoped for. Haldimand needs artificers for boat-building. Arkansa nation have asked permission to settle on English side of Mississippi. Tribes have been quarrelling at Michilimackinac. Repairs wanted at all posts: timber of this country has no duration. Castle William barracks in bad condition, see enclosed. Prospect of war with Spain did not stop friendly intercourse between the two shores of Mississippi at Fort Chartres, but Spanish commander was remarkably attentive to the savages. Lieut.-Colonel Wilkins has changed his opinion respecting the Illinois, and sends me new plan for demolishing Fort Chartres and reducing the number of troops. My dispatches from the Illinois contain accusations against trading company, Baynton, Wharton & Morgan, of Philadelphia. I do not trouble you with these papers, full of dirt, invective, law and indecencies: they must be left to Lords of Council or perhaps Courts at Westminister.

I strongly disapprove of parts of the commanding officer's conduct. Powers are wanting to determine controversies in Illinois country. *Signed.* 8½ pp. *Endorsed,* R, 13 September. *Enclosed :*

i. Boston, 19 July 1771. Extract of letter from Governor Thomas Hutchinson to General Gage, notifying bad condition of barracks at Castle William. *Copy.* ½ p.

ii. New York, 30 July 1771. Lieut.-General Gage to Governor Byron, Newfoundland. Regulated allowance for soldiers employed in King's works is 9d. a day for artificers, 6d. a day for labourers. I can give no reason for increasing it. Any alteration would spread from regiment to regiment. *Copy.* 1½ pp. [C.O.5, 89, fos. 153–161d; entry of covering letter in C.O.5, 234, pp. 222–234]

1442

7 August, Whitehall

John Pownall to Governor Thomas Hutchinson, in absence of Lord Hillsborough in Ireland, acknowledging Nos. 5–7. *Entry.* ¼ p. [C.O.5, 765, p. 211]

1443

7 August, Whitehall

Same to Governor Lord William Campbell, acknowledging No. 75. *Entry.* ¼ p. [C.O.218, 25, p. 99]

1444

7 August, Whitehall

Same to Governor Earl of Dunmore, acknowledging in Lord Hillsborough's absence dispatch of 20 June. *Entry.* ¼ p. [C.O.5, 1375, p. 159; another entry in C.O.5, 1141, p. 191]

1445

7 August, Whitehall

Same to President William Nelson, acknowledging in Lord Hillsborough's absence dispatch of 27 May and one numbered 18. *Entry.* ¼ p. [C.O.5, 1375, p. 159]

1446

7 August, Whitehall

Same to [Governor Thomas Hutchinson], enclosing following. *Entry.* ½ p. *Enclosed :*

i. St James's, 31 July 1771. Order in Council [See No. 1429]. *Entry.* 1½ pp. [C.O.5, 765, pp. 212–213]

1447

7 August, Whitehall

Same to Lieut.-Governor John Moultrie, acknowledging Nos. 2–3.
Entry. ½ p. [C.O.5, 566, p. 50]

1448

7 August, G.P.O.

Postmaster-General to Earl of Hillsborough. *Diligence* and *Comet*
perform four voyages a year between Jamaica, Pensacola and Charleston, at £150 a voyage with no allowance for demurrage. We request you
order governors to pay £2 a day when they detain these boats. *Signed*,
Le Despencer, W. F. Thynne. *Endorsed*, R, 9 August. [C.O.5, 134, fos.
287–288d; entry in C.O.5, 247, p. 4]

1449

7 August, Charleston

Lieut.-Governor William Bull to Earl of Hillsborough (No. 51),
acknowledging circular of 5 June. *Signed.* ½ p. *Endorsed*, R, 11 October.
[C.O.5, 394, fos. 90–91d; entry in C.O.5, 409, p. 236]

1450

7 August, Charleston

Same to same (No. 52), Edward Savage appointed Judge of Vice-
Admiralty Court in room of James Simpson, resigned. *Signed.* 1 p.
Endorsed, R, 11 October. [C.O.5, 394, fos. 92–93d; entry in C.O.5, 409,
p. 237]

1451

8 August, St Augustine

Lieut.-Governor John Moultrie to Earl of Hillsborough (No. 5),
acknowledging Nos. 38–40 and copies of method of making tar in
Sweden, which will be distributed. Best materials for tar and pitch
are in this province; I am certain turpentine also can be made here. In
time we can supply naval stores. Roads needed. Indigo does well.
Signed. 3½ pp. *Endorsed*, R, 18 November. [C.O.5, 552, fos. 60–61d;
signed duplicate, endorsed Read 12 December 1771, in C.O.5, 545,
fos. 47–49d; entry in C.O.5, 567, pp. 203–206]

1452

8 August, New Bern

President James Hasell to John Pownall, acknowledging twelve copies
of process of making tar in Sweden, which shall be distributed. *Signed.*
¾ p. *Endorsed*, R, 14 October. [C.O.5, 314, fos. 271–272d; entry in
C.O.5, 329, p. 1]

1453

8 August

Massachusetts Gazette and Boston Newsletter, 8 August 1771, containing open letter from 'Benevolus' to Governor Thomas Hutchinson. *Printed.* 4 pp. [C.O.5, 894, pp. 309–312]

1454

9 August

Commission to James Morden to be barrack-master at Halifax. *Entry.* 1 p. [C.O.324, 42, p. 307]

1455

9 August, Boston

Governor Thomas Hutchinson to Earl of Hillsborough (No. 10), acknowledging duplicate of No. 8, original not yet received, and circular of 5 June. *Signed.* 1 p. *Endorsed*, R, 13 September. [C.O.5, 760, fos. 275–276d; entry in C.O.5, 768, pp. 210–211]

1456

9 August, New Bern

* President James Hasell to Earl of Hillsborough (No. 2), acknowledging No. 1 to Governor Martin, not yet arrived. This province is now returned to peace. Hermon Husbands, chief ringleader of rebels, with eight or ten associates, reported in Maryland; I sent a young man to identify him. Assistance in apprehending him has been requested from President Nelson and President Hamilton. *Duplicate. Signed.* 2 pp. *Endorsed*, R, 14 October. [C.O.5, 314, fos. 273–274d; entry in C.O.5, 329, pp. 1–3]

1457

9 August, Johnson Hall

* Sir William Johnson to Earl of Hillsborough (No. 16), acknowledging No. 16, and reporting congress at Johnson Hall on 14 July with chiefs of Six Nations and investigation of suspicion that Six Nations were exciting Shawnese and Delawares to make war on us. Some Senecas may be doubtful but in general Six Nations are faithful. Jealousies amongst Indian nations are in our interest. *Signed.* 3½ pp. *Endorsed*, R, 14 October. *Enclosed :*

    i. Report of part of above-mentioned congress. *Copy.* 3 pp. [C.O.5, 72, fos. 310–314; entry of covering letter in C.O.5, 228, pp. 80–84]

1458

12 August

Certificate by George Arbuthnot, King's Remembrancer, that Richard Penn gave security for execution of his office of deputy Governor of Pennsylvania. *Signed.* ¼ p. *Endorsed*, Recd., Read 22 August 1771. [C.O.5, 1278, fos. 49–50d]

1459

12 August, Charlotte Town, I. of St John

Address of thanks of Grand Jury of Island of St John to the King for creating separate government. *Signed*, David Higgins and fourteen others. 1¾ pp. *Endorsed*, Read by the King, 30 November. [C.O.226, 4, fos. 88–89d; entry in C.O.227, 2, pp. 36–37]

1460

[?13] August, Boston

* Governor Thomas Hutchinson to John Pownall, sending newspapers. Same spirit which denied Parliament's authority now denies King's. Mr Robinson, a Commissioner of Customs, has appealed against verdict for £2000 damages against him at suit of Mr Otis. Attested copy of Newgate pardon may be sufficient for discharge of Richardson. *Entry.* 3 pp. *Annotated*, R, 13 September [C.O.5, 246, pp. 25–28]

1461

15 August, New Bern

Governor Josiah Martin to Earl of Hillsborough (No. 1), reporting arrival on 11th inst. and acknowledging Nos. 1–2 and other papers. I meet Assembly on 10 October. Charge of raising forces computed at £40,000 currency, met by issue of promissory notes. Only remedy appears to be new emission of paper currency. Upwards of 6000 persons took oath in consequence of Governor Tryon's proclamation. Perfect tranquillity now. Council has thirteen members but only two live in or near New Bern. Oath of abjuration not in use here. Many outlaws have taken sanctuary in back parts of South Carolina. I shall try to revive quitrent bill. *Signed.* 8 pp. *Endorsed*, R, 14 October. [C.O.5, 314, fos. 275–279d; signed duplicate, endorsed Read 12 December 1771, in C.O.5, 302, fos. 82–85d, 88, 88d; entry in C.O.5, 329, pp. 3–10]

1462

15 August, Boston

Governor Thomas Hutchinson to John Pownall, commending Commodore Gambier. *Entry.* ¼ p. *Annotated*, R, 29 October. [C.O.5, 246, p. 33]

1463

19 August

John Pownall to Anthony Todd, requesting that mail for Ireland be detained for dispatch for Lord Hillsborough, which should be ready in one hour. *Entry.* ¼ p. [C.O.5, 247, p. 5]

1464

19 August, Charleston

Lieut.-Governor William Bull to Earl of Hillsborough (No. 53). William H. Drayton appointed Deputy P. M. G. for Southern District of North America in place of Peter De Lancey, shot dead in duel. *Duplicate. Signed.* 1 p. *Endorsed*, R, 17 October, original not received. [C.O.5, 394, fos. 94–95d; signed original, endorsed Read 12 December 1771, in C.O.5, 380, fos. 42–43d; entry in C.O.5, 409, p. 238]

1465

20 August, N.H.

⋆ Governor John Wentworth to Earl of Hillsborough (No. 37), enclosing and recommending following. *Signed.* 5½ pp. *Endorsed*, R, 26 December. *Enclosed :*

⋆ i. 16 August 1771. Report of Council of New Hampshire to Governor Wentworth on history of Connecticut River grants and present grievances of inhabitants. *Copy,* certified by Theodore Atkinson, secretary. *Signatories,* Daniel Peirce, George Jaffrey, Daniel Rogers. 18½ pp. [C.O.5, 937, fos. 47–59d; entry of covering letter in C.O.5, 945, pp. 180–183]

1466

22 August, Whitehall

Commissioners for Trade and Plantations to the King. Richard Penn, Lieut.-Governor of Pennsylvania, has given security for execution of office. Draft of instructions enclosed: no alteration from those given for direction of late lieut.-governor. *Entry. Signatories,* Thomas Whately, John Roberts, Edward Eliot, William Fitzherbert. 2 pp. *Enclosed :*

i. Draft instructions to Thomas and John Penn, proprietors, for direction of Richard Penn, Lieut.-Governor. *Entry.* 52 pp. [C.O.5, 1296, pp. 388–441]

1467

23 August, Halifax

Governor Lord William Campbell to Earl of Hillsborough (No. 76). Assembly sat 5 June–6 July; Acts and journals sent. *Signed.* 1 p.

Endorsed, R, 23 October. [C.O.217, 48, fos. 59–60d; signed duplicate, endorsed Read 15 May 1772, in C.O.217, 26, fos. 104–105d; entry in C.O.218, 18, pp. 3–4]

1468

23 August, Virginia

President William Nelson to Earl of Hillsborough (No. 24), acknowledging Nos. 1–2 to Earl of Dunmore, and papers sent by Mr Pownall. With respect to copper money, I flatter myself that my No. 18 and steps taken by Treasurer will be satisfactory. *Signed.* 1 p. *Endorsed*, R, 1 November. [C.O.5, 1349, fos. 171–172d; entry in C.O.5, 1372, pp. 185–186]

1469

23 August, Boston

Governor Thomas Hutchinson to John Pownall, sending journal of House of Representatives. Secretary has sent proceedings of General Court and minutes of Council. *Signed.* ½ small p. *Endorsed*, Recd. 31 October, Read 12 December 1771. [C.O.5, 894, pp. 313–316]

1470

24 August, Burlington

Governor William Franklin to Earl of Hillsborough (No. 33), enclosing following. *Signed.* ½ p. *Endorsed*, R, 14 October. *Enclosed:*

i. Journal of proceedings of Council of New Jersey at session of General Assembly, 18 April–1 June 1771. *Seal.* 18 pp.

ii. Minutes of Council of New Jersey, 23 April–21 August 1771. *Seal. Copy*, certified by Charles Pettit, deputy clerk. 20 pp. [C.O.5, 991, fos. 70–91d; entry of covering letter in C.O.5, 1001, p. 141]

1471

24 August, Pensacola

Governor Peter Chester to Earl of Hillsborough (No. 25), acknowledging No. 3 and Mr Pownall's of 30 April. Books on Swedish manufacture of pitch and tar will be distributed. *Signed.* ½ p. *Endorsed*, R, 5 December. [C.O.5, 588, pp. 301–304; signed duplicate, endorsed Read 18 December 1771, in C.O.5, 578, pp. 239–242; entry in C.O.5, 621, p. 83]

1472

25 August, Pensacola

Same to same (No. 26). Rev. Nathaniel Cotton died 3 July, we now have no clergyman. Salary is £100, perquisites inconsiderable. Were Mr Cotton's successor also chaplain to garrison, at further £100 a year, it would afford comfortable maintenance. Mr Gordon, minister at Mobile, has applied but is an unpopular preacher. *Signed*. 2 pp. *Endorsed*, R, 5 December. [C.O.5, 588, pp. 305–308; signed duplicate, endorsed Read 18 December 1771, in C.O.5, 578, pp. 243–246; entry in C.O.5, 621, pp. 83–85]

1473

25 August, Boston

* Governor Thomas Hutchinson to Earl of Hillsborough (private), recommending Henry Barnes, sufferer by refusal to comply with non-importation scheme. It is thought that five-sixths of tea consumed in America the last two years has been illegally imported. Price in England should be reduced and cruising vessels given larger rewards for seizures. *Entry*. 2¼ pp. *Annotated*, R, 29 October. [C.O.5, 246, pp. 31–33]

1474

26 August, Pensacola

Governor Peter Chester to Earl of Hillsborough (No. 27), enclosing following. *Signed*. ½ p. *Endorsed*, R, 5 December. *Enclosed:*

i. Copy of register of burials for Pensacola, 24 December 1770–24 June 1771: seventeen burials. *Signed*, Nathaniel Cotton. 1 p.

ii. Same of christenings for same period: twelve christenings. *Signed*, as No. i. 1 p. [C.O.5, 588, pp. 309–316; signed duplicate of covering letter and copies of enclosures, all endorsed Read 18 December 1771, in C.O.5, 578, pp. 247–254; entry of covering letter in C.O.5, 619, p. 85]

1475

27 August, Pensacola

Same to same (No. 28), reporting disagreement between himself and Brig.-General Haldimand as to who should give the word when the brigadier is absent from Pensacola. I shall continue to avoid disputes. *Signed*. 2 pp. *Endorsed*, R, 5 December. [C.O.5, 588, pp. 317–320; signed duplicate, endorsed Read 18 December 1771, in C.O.5, 578, pp. 255–258; entry in C.O.5, 621, pp. 85–87]

1476

27 August, New York

Memorial of Daniel Frisby, mariner, of New York, to Governor William Tryon. He was master of *Hawke* of New York, seized by Spanish *guardacosta* five leagues from Point Espada, N. E. Hispaniola. Released on payment of fine, but robbed. *Copy*. 3½ pp. *Endorsed*, R, 16 December, from Governor Tryon. NB. The proceedings of Governor and Council of New York on this memorial was enclosed in Governor Tryon's No. 7 [No. 1549]. [C.O.5, 1102, fos. 314–316d]

1477

28 August, St James's

Order of King in Council, approving draft instructions for Richard Penn, Lieut.-Governor of Pennsylvania and Three Lower Counties. *Entry.* 2½ pp. [C.O.5, 1301, pp. 143–145; sealed original in C.O.5, 27, fos. 92–93d]

1478

28 August, Pensacola

Governor Peter Chester to Earl of Hillsborough (No. 29), sending journals of Council and Assembly last session and copies of Acts. Comments on Acts for continuing Tax Bill; Act for establishing method of appointing constables; Act for regulation of taverns (repealing an Act proposed for disallowance in my No. 8); Act for punishment of vagabonds; Act for granting certain duties and appointing same to providing for clerks and messengers of Council and Assembly, and for ferries, bridges, an express to Mobile and pilot-boat at Pensacola. No provision made for expenses of courts of oyer and terminer. *Signed.* 4¾ pp. *Endorsed*, R, 5 December. [C.O.5, 588, pp. 321–326; signed duplicate, endorsed Read 18 December 1771, in C.O.5, 578, pp. 259–264; entry in C.O.5, 621, pp. 87–91]

1479

29 August, Pensacola

Same to same (No. 30). Brig.-General Haldimand refuses to allow building of Government-house within the garrison, letters enclosed. H.M.'s commission gives me power over forts. H.M.'s pleasure requested in this dispute. *Signed.* 4 pp. *Endorsed*, R, 5 December. *Enclosed :*

i. Pensacola, 23 August 1771. Governor Chester to Brig.-General Frederick Haldimand asking where in the garrison the barracks are to be built so that Government-house and barracks may not interfere with one another. *Duplicate. Signed.* 3½ small pp.

ii. Red Cliffs Battery, near Pensacola, 29 August 1771. Brig.-General Haldimand to Governor Chester. The fort is entrusted to my care and I cannot authorize building in it. I have asked for General Gage's directions. *Copy.* 1½ small pp. [C.O.5, 588, pp. 455–468; signed duplicate of covering letter, endorsed Read 18 December 1771, and copies of enclosures, in C.O.5, 578, pp. 265–278; entry of covering letter in C.O.5, 621, pp. 92–96]

1480

29 August, Halifax

Governor Lord William Campbell to Earl of Hillsborough (No. 77), acknowledging Nos. 46–47 and papers. On Mr Bailly's return I shall take steps to effect Indian settlements: no major expense therein

foreseen. *Signed*. PS. Mr Goold recommended to be of the Council.
1½ pp. *Endorsed*, R, 23 October. [C.O.217, 48, fos. 61–62d; signed
duplicate, endorsed Read 12 December 1771, in C.O.217, 26, fos.
84–85d; entry in C.O.218, 18, pp. 4–5]

1481

30 August, New York

Governor William Tryon to Earl of Hillsborough (No. 3), enclosing
following, presented on my visiting King's College in this city. *Signed*.
1 p. *Endorsed*, R, 14 October. *Enclosed :*

> * i. Address of students of King's College to Governor Tryon, by
> Roebuck. Poems in praise of Governor Tryon by Edward Stevens,
> Barclay, John Jauncey, and Frederick Philipse. 10 pp. [C.O.5, 1102,
> fos. 229–236d; entry of covering letter in C.O.5, 1138, p. 236; signed
> duplicate of covering letter, endorsed Read 12 December 1771, and
> copy of enclosure, in C.O.5, 1075, fos. 150–159d]

1482

30 August, Pensacola

Governor Peter Chester to Earl of Hillsborough (No. 31). Mr Stuart
has arrived and directed his deputies to bring down Indians. Creeks
expected in ten days, Chickasaws and Choctaws in November or
December. *Signed*. ¾ p. *Endorsed*, R, 5 December. [C.O.5, 588, pp.
469–472; signed duplicate, endorsed Read 18 December 1771, in
C.O.5, 578, pp. 279–282; entry in C.O.5, 621, p. 96]

1483

30 August, Pensacola

Lieut.-Governor Elias Durnford to Earl of Hillsborough. At John
Stuart's arrival with letters from you, I was requested to furnish extracts
of my correspondence relating to Indian affairs for his guidance, and
wish to know how far I am justified for my attention to these matters.
Signed. 2½ pp. *Endorsed*, R, 5 December. [C.O.5, 588, pp. 451–454;
entry in C.O.5, 621, pp. 99–100]

1484

30 August, Pensacola

Same to same, asking for twelve months leave in England. *Signed*.
1 small p. *Endorsed*, R, 5 December. [C.O.5, 588, pp. 447–450; entry
in C.O.5, 621, pp. 100–101]

1485

31 August, Pensacola

Same to same. I have given plans and reports of western part of province
to the governor. No surveys of interior part have been made. By an

allowance of £1200 for one year, certain knowledge would be gained. *Signed.* 2 small pp. *Endorsed,* R, 5 December. [C.O.5, 588, pp. 443–446; entry in C.O.5, 621, pp. 101–102]

1486

31 August, Treasury

John Robinson to John Pownall, enclosing following. *Signed.* ½ p. *Endorsed,* R, 9th September. Read by the King. *Enclosed:*

i. Custom-house, London, 31 May 1771. Edward Stanley to John Robinson, enclosing representation relating to *Florida Packet,* Robert Roberts master, reported arrived with peltry from Illinois country. *Copy.* 1 p.

ii. Custom-house, London, 31 May 1771. Report by Inspectors of the River, of arrival of *Florida Packet* and result of examination of her papers. *Copy. Signatories,* R. Weskett, Alexander Abery. 1½ pp.

iii. Custom-house, London, 14 March 1771. Edward Stanley to John Robinson. *Florida Packet* not so far reported in London or outports. *Copy.* ½ p.

iv. Treasury Chambers, 19 January–14 August 1771. Extract of minutes in case of *Florida Packet. Copy.* 4½ pp.

v. Custom-house, Edinburgh. Commissioners of Customs of Scotland to John Robinson. No report of arrival of *Florida Packet. Copy. Signatories,* M. Cardonnel, George Clerk Maxwell, Basil Cochrane. ½ p.

vi. Custom-house, London, 12 August 1771. Edward Stanley to John Robinson. *Florida Packet* is now fitting out for another voyage. If proof can be got of delivery of lading from Illinois country to foreign plantation, the vessel may be seized. *Copy.* 1 p. [C.O.5, 72, fos. 292–307d; entry of covering letter in C.O.5, 621, p. 82]

1487

31 August, Pensacola

Governor Peter Chester to Earl of Hillsborough (No. 32). Considerable sums due for quitrents in West Florida: Philip Livingston jnr. appointed Receiver-General. Allowance needed for him. *Signed.* 1¼ pp. *Endorsed,* R, 5 December. [C.O.5, 588, pp. 473–476; signed duplicate, endorsed Read 18 December 1771, in C.O.5, 578, pp. 283–286; entry in C.O.5, 621, pp. 96–97]

1488

31 August, New York

* Governor William Tryon to Earl of Hillsborough (private). I refused Earl of Dunmore's offer of exchange of government of Virginia for this, for public and private reasons. *Signed.* 4 pp. *Endorsed,* R, 9 November. [C.O.5, 154, fos. 25–27d]

1489

1 September, Pensacola

Governor Peter Chester to Earl of Hillsborough (No. 33), enclosing following. *Signed.* ½ p. *Endorsed*, R, 5 December. *Enclosed:*

i. Pensacola, 20 August 1771. Return of troops in West Florida. 16th regiment: 13 officers, 41 N.C.O.s, 351 drummers, fifers and privates. 31st regiment: 2 officers, 4 N.C.O.s, 23 drummers, fifers and privates. Royal Artillery: 1 officer, 1 sergeant, 2 bombardiers, 2 gunners, 16 mattrosses. Staff: 2 adjutants, 1 surgeon, 2 mates. *Signed*, Francis Hutchinson, acting major of brigade. 1 p.

ii. Pensacola, 31 August 1771. Remain of ordnance and ordnance stores at fort. *Signed*, Benjamin Gower. 2½ pp.

iii. Pensacola, 31 August 1771. Return of ordnance and ordnance-stores received from New York by General Gage's order. *Signed*, J(?). Watkins. 3½ pp. [C.O.5, 588, pp. 477–490; signed duplicate of covering letter, endorsed Read 18 December 1771, with copies of enclosures in C.O.5, 578, pp. 287–300; entry of covering letter in C.O.5, 621, pp. 97–98]

1490

2 September, New York

Governor William Tryon to Earl of Hillsborough (No. 4), enclosing following. *Signed.* 1 p. *Endorsed*, R, 14 October. *Enclosed:*

i. New York, 14 August 1771. Minutes of Council of New York, recording proceedings on petition of Colonel John Bradstreet and associates for grant of lands. *Copy*, certified 6 [*sic*] August 1771 by G. Banyar, deputy clerk. 8½ pp. [C.O.5, 1102, fos. 237–244d; entry of covering letter in C.O.5, 1138, p. 237; signed duplicate of covering letter, endorsed Read 12 December 1771, in C.O.5, 1075, fos. 160–161d]

1491

2 September, New York

* Same to same (No. 5), enclosing papers relating to office of Surrogate and Register of Prerogative Court of New York, which I have given to Mr Fanning in testimony of his service and losses in North Carolina. *Signed.* 2 pp. *Endorsed*, R, 14 October. *Enclosed:*

i. New York, 17 August 1771. Memorial of Goldsbrow Banyar, on behalf of George Clarke, Secretary of New York, to Governor Tryon, claiming the office. *Signed.* 7 pp.

ii. Kensington, 8 May 1758. Order in Council granting nomination to office of clerk of Council of Jamaica to Secretary of that colony, as heretofore. *Copy.* 2½ pp.

iii. New York, 19 August 1771. Governor Tryon to Goldsbrow Banyar, rejecting Secretary's claim to office of Surrogate and Register, and requiring surrender of the seal. *Copy.* 1 p. [C.O.5, 1102, fos. 245–255d; entry of covering letter in C.O.5, 1138, pp. 238–239; signed duplicate of covering letter, endorsed Read 12 December 1771, and copies of Nos. i and iii, in C.O.5, 1075, fos. 162–169d]

1492

3 September, New York

Same to same (No. 6), acknowledging Nos. 3–4 and enclosures. *Signed.* 1 p. *Endorsed,* R, 14 October. [C.O.5, 1102, fos. 256–257d; entry in C.O.5, 1138, pp. 239–240; signed duplicate, endorsed Read 12 December 1771, in C.O.5, 1075, fos. 170–171d]

1493

3 September, New York

Lieut.-General Thomas Gage to Earl of Hillsborough (No. 64), acknowledging Nos. 46 and 47. 26th and 29th regiments will draw for St Augustine station, and one will go thither next month: barracks are finished. I fear that strengthening river-bank at Fort Chartres will be an annual labour and expense. I will inquire at Detroit about house for Lieutenant Sinclair. I have annulled all grants of lands made at Detroit and the Illinois by commanding officers who have no power to make them. Party of Kickapous who dwell on Wabash have killed three or four people at the Illinois: Sir W. Johnson thinks their chastisement can be effected by encouraging tribes who dislike them. Report from Michilimackinac on mining company in Lake Superior: I don't find other traders are obstructed by them. O. C. Michilimackinac complains of traders in general not reporting to fort. Commissaries deputed by the provinces to agree on general regulations for Indian trade are soon to meet: means of stopping these abuses will no doubt be considered. Some repairs carried out in Quebec province: others deferred until Governor Carleton's return. I reviewed and was satisfied with 26th and 29th regiments and will shortly review Scots Fusiliers who arrived in Pennsylvania from St Augustine in the spring. *Signed.* 5¾ pp. *Endorsed,* R, 14 October. [C.O.5, 89, fos. 166–169d; entry in C.O.5, 234, pp. 235–240]

1494

3 September, Charlotte Town, I. of St John

Governor Walter Patterson to Earl of Hillsborough (No. 5, should be 8), enclosing following. Proprietors are backward to pay quitrents. *Signed.* 1¼ pp. *Endorsed,* R, 23 October. *Enclosed:*

i. Ordinance for recovering of H.M.'s quitrents in Island of St John. *Copy*, certified by Phillips Callbeck, acting secretary. 5 pp. [C.O.226, 4, fos. 79–84d; entry of covering letter in C.O.227, 2, pp. 30–31; signed duplicate of covering letter, endorsed Read 29 July 1772, in C.O.226, 1, fos. 45–46d]

1495

3 September, Burlington

Governor William Franklin to Earl of Hillsborough (No. 34), acknowledging letters of 5 and 21 June and 3 July, and Mr Pownall's with copies of Acts of Parliament. *Signed.* ¾ p. *Endorsed*, R, 14 October. [C.O.5, 991, fos. 92–93d; entry in C.O.5, 1001, p. 141]

1496

3 September, Boston

Lieut.-Governor Andrew Oliver to Earl of Hillsborough, acknowledging letter of 31 May and favour. *Entry.* ½ p. *Annotated*, R, 29 October. [C.O.5, 246, p. 34]

1497

3 September, Fort Amherst, Island of St John

Chief Justice John Duport to Earl of Hillsborough. Few settlers arrived this summer. Ordinance for collecting quitrents will not answer purpose. Officers should be paid out of certain funds. My situation distressed. Drooping state of fishery at Cape Breton is chiefly owing to duty on liquor in Nova Scotia; it might be advantageous to annex Cape Breton to this government. *Signed.* 5 small pp. *Endorsed*, R, 23 October. [C.O.226, 4, fos. 85–87d; entry in C.O.227, 2, pp. 31–35; signed duplicate, endorsed Read 12 December 1771 in C.O.226, 1, fos. 36–38d]

1498

4 September, G.P.O.

Anthony Todd to John Pownall. *Hillsborough* packet-boat, Captain Blackwell, for West Indies, and *Eagle*, Captain Nicholls, for Charleston, are ready to sail; *Harriot*, Captain Oake, for New York, not ready. *Entry.* ½ p. [C.O.5, 247, p. 5]

1499

4 September, Whitehall

John Pownall to Lieut.-General Thomas Gage, acknowledging No. 62, in absence of Lord Hillsborough in Ireland. *Entry.* ¼ p. [C.O.5, 243, p. 19]

1500

4 September, Whitehall

Same to Governor Earl of Dunmore, acknowledging Nos. 11–12. *Entry.* ¼ p. [C.O.5, 1141, p. 193]

1501

4 September, Whitehall

Same to Governor William Tryon, acknowledging dispatches of 18 May from North Carolina and 9 July from New York. *Entry.* ½ p. [C.O.5, 1141, p. 192]

1502

4 September, Whitehall

Same to Governor Thomas Hutchinson, acknowledging Nos. 8 and 9. *Entry.* ¼ p. [C.O.5, 765, p. 214]

1503

4 September, Whitehall

Same to Governor Peter Chester, acknowledging Nos. 20–24. *Entry.* ¼ p. [C.O.5, 619, p. 85]

1504

4 September, Whitehall

Same to Lieut.-Governor William Bull, acknowledging Nos. 49–50. *Entry.* ½ p. [C.O.5, 408, p. 71]

1505

4 September, Whitehall

Same to President William Nelson, acknowledging dispatches Nos. 8–9. *Entry.* ¼ p. [C.O.5, 1375, p. 159]

1506

4 September, New Bern

Governor Josiah Martin to Earl of Hillsborough (No. 2). Assembly prorogued to 15 November. Climate malign: one of my children has died and my house is a perfect hospital. *Signed.* 2 pp. *Endorsed*, R, 5 December. [C.O.5, 314, fos. 284–285d; signed duplicate, endorsed Read 18 December 1771, in C.O.5, 302, fos. 86–87d; entry in C.O.5, 329, pp. 10–11]

1507

6 September, Philadelphia

President James Hamilton to Earl of Hillsborough (No. 25), acknowledging No. 25, circular of 5 June, and two letters from Mr Pownall. *Signed.* 1 p. *Endorsed,* R, 8 November. [C.O.5, 1284, fos. 21–22d; signed duplicate, endorsed Read 12 December 1771, in C.O.5, 1278, fos. 55–56d; entry in C.O.5, 1300, p. 364]

1508

9 September, Boston

Governor Thomas Hutchinson to Earl of Hillsborough (No. 11), acknowledging Nos. 9–10. Difficulty of the judges is that they cannot be possessed of original pardon. Would there be inconveniences in warrant under sign manual to governor, as in other capital cases? Mr Scammell gone to Eastern part of province. From general view of those who made the inquiry (report enclosed), coast from Kennebec to St Croix is all taken possession of, and all east of Penobscot, by those with no colour of title except grant of General Court of Massachusetts. *Signed.* 2½ pp. *Endorsed,* R, 29 October. *Enclosed:*

    * i. Boston, 12 September 1771. Report on Eastern Country by Committee of Council of Massachusetts, to Governor Hutchinson. (1) Land at Machias very good. (2) Pine trees are saplings not capable of making masts. (3) Authority should be strengthened and gaol established at Fort Pownall. (4) They need a preacher. (5) There are about 150 males of 16 upwards and about 60 families. (6) At Goldsboro land is not very extraordinary, but very good at Frenchman's Bay. No pines there fit for R.N. Lands in other townships good, but same as Machias and Goldsboro with respect to pine trees. At least 500 families in the 13 granted townships, with fine trees fit to mast R.N. in rear. Land good at Mount Desart, many trees fit for masts. (7) Settlers intend to stay. Not true that they went there only for sake of timber. (8) Not much spoil made by cutting trees fit for masts. (9) River St Croix, east of Peshamaquoda River, is true River St Croix and eastern boundary of this province, notwithstanding grants of land west of it by governor of Nova Scotia. *Copy,* certified by T. Flucker. *Signatories,* William Brattle, James Bowdoin, Thomas Hubbard. 5½ pp. [C.O.5, 760, fos. 277–282d; entry of covering letter in C.O.5, 768, pp. 213–216]

1509

10 September, Boston

* Same to same (private), acknowledging private letter of 30 May. Massachusetts is estimated to consume 2400 chests of tea (of about 340 lbs) a year, whole continent 19,200 chests. Much Dutch tea consumed. Collector at Falmouth acknowledges that Acts of Trade are broken there; he suggests cruising schooners, officers of which should share in forfeitures. *Entry.* 2 pp. *Annotated,* R, 29 October. [C.O.5, 246, pp. 34–36]

1510

12 September, Philadelphia

President James Hamilton to Earl of Hillsborough (No. 26), acknowledging No. 26. I have issued proclamation disallowing laws referred to. *Signed.* 1 p. *Endorsed*, R, 8 November. [C.O.5, 1284, fos. 23–24d; signed duplicate, endorsed Read 12 December 1771, in C.O.5, 1278, fos. 57–58d; entry in C.O.5, 1300, p. 365]

1511

13 September, G.P.O.

Anthony Todd to John Pownall. *Hillsborough* and *Eagle* have sailed; *Duke of Cumberland* arrived from New York and will be ready next Tuesday. *Entry.* ½ p. [C.O.5, 247, p. 6; with entry of reply]

1512

16 September, G.P.O.

Same to same. *Duke of Cumberland*, Captain Goodridge, for New York, will be ready on arrival of tomorrow's letters. *Entry.* ¼ p. [C.O.5, 247, p. 6]

1513

16 September, Halifax

Governor Lord William Campbell to Earl of Hillsborough (No. 78), acknowledging Nos. 48–51. Repair of batteries was recommended by General Gage. Sale of forfeited lands would bring in little. Tract proposed by Mr Wentworth, when forfeited, will be reserved to H.M. Reservation of 10,000 acres of best woodland to H.M. in every 100,000-acre tract, proposed as best method of securing timber. Not granting lands until surveyed by Surveyor of Woods would be discouragement. Halifax lighthouse to be inquired into. *Signed.* PS. Estimate for next year enclosed. Charles Procter appointed to succeed Mr Foye, dead, as Provost Marshal. 4½ pp. *Endorsed*, R, 23 October. *Enclosed :*

> i. Estimate of charge of civil establishment of Nova Scotia proposed for 1772. Total, £4296 10s. 2 pp. [C.O.217, 48, fos. 63–67d; signed duplicate of covering letter, and copy of enclosure, in C.O.217, 26, fos. 86–90d; entry of covering letter in C.O.218, 18, pp. 5–6]

1514

16 September, Halifax

Same to Commissioners for Trade and Plantations, acknowledging letter respecting Excise Act. It was never understood that instruction against duties on importation of British goods extended to prevent excises. *Signed.* 1½ pp. *Endorsed*, Recd. 23 October 1771, Read 5 February 1772. [C.O.217, 26, fos. 99–100d]

1515

16 September, Portsmouth N.H.

Samuel Holland to John Pownall, acknowledging letter of 23 May. I beg you will procure order to Mr Desbarres, employed by Admiralty in surveying coast of Nova Scotia, to let me copy his surveys. Coast from west of Cape Anne to east of Kennebec River is surveyed. Connecticut River and Winnipissiokee Lake surveyed last winter. Copies of these surveys and Mr Wright's will be sent. *Duplicate. Signed.* 2 small pp. *Endorsed,* Read 12 December 1771. [C.O.323, 27, pp. 117–120]

1516

17 September, War Office

Viscount Barrington to Earl of Hillsborough, enclosing following. *Signed.* 1 small p. *Endorsed,* R, 17 September. *Enclosed:*

 i. Long Island, New York, 6 August 1771. Lieut. John Thompson, half-pay officer, to Lord Barrington, complaining of not getting land he has right to by H.M.'s proclamation. *Signed.* 1 p. *Addressed. Endorsed,* R, 13 September. [C.O.5, 89, fos. 162–165d]

1517

17 September, Whitehall

John Pownall to Lieut.-General Thomas Gage, acknowledging No. 63, in absence of Lord Hillsborough in Ireland. *Entry.* ¼ p. [C.O.5, 243, p. 20]

1518

17 September, Whitehall

Same to Governor William Tryon, acknowledging Nos. 73–78 from North Carolina and No. 2 from New York. *Entry.* ½ p. [C.O.5, 1141, p. 192]

1519

17 September, Whitehall

Same to Governor Thomas Hutchinson, acknowledging No. 10. *Entry.* ¼ p. [C.O.5, 765, p. 214]

1520

17 September, Whitehall

Same to Lieut.-Governor H. T. Cramahé, acknowledging dispatches Nos. 9–11. *Entry.* ¼ p. [C.O.43, 8, p. 97]

1521

18 September, G.P.O.

Anthony Todd to John Pownall, requesting that all papers be sent hither in the office bag to stop abuse of giving or selling covers to booksellers. *Signed.* 2 small pp. *Enclosed:*

    i. Franked cover, addressed to General Montague, Windsor, from Maynard, stationer, Lower Brook Street. [C.O.5, 134, fos. 289–291d]

1522

20 September, Whitehall

John Pownall to Lieut.-Governor John Moultrie, recommending M. Tavel, from Berne, who proposes to settle in East Florida. *Entry.* ½ p. [C.O.5, 246, p. 28]

1523

23 September, N.H.

* Governor John Wentworth to Earl of Hillsborough (No. 38), sending Acts and enclosing journals of Assembly of New Hampshire and Naval Officer's transcripts. Decay of governor's power in matters of trade and decline of Naval Officer's authority require regulation. Confirmation of County Act gratefully acknowledged. Proclamation rating foreign coins declared void, but Assembly has granted Supply Bill referring currency to proclamation and Act of Queen Anne. Captain Holland has begun survey of the province, and I hope will complete a map: Assembly refused to contribute to this service. No new manufacture; every mechanic branch has diminished except linen, potash and pearlash. Many roads made; collection of quitrents improved. Settlement of New Hampshire wilderness discourages New England manufactures. Encouragement of agriculture is impediment to manufacture. Militia is 12,000 foot and 1000 horse, insufficiently armed. *Duplicate. Signed.* 24 pp. *Endorsed*, R, 21 February 1772. *Enclosed:*

    i. Certificate by Governor Wentworth that Theodore Atkinson is Secretary of New Hampshire, 10 September 1771. *Seal. Signed.* ¾ p.

    ii. Minutes of General Assembly of New Hampshire, 13 November 1770–19 January 1771. *Copy*, certified by Theodore Atkinson. 23 pp.

    iii. 10 September 1771. Certificate, as No. i. *Seal. Signed.* ¾ p.

    iv. Minutes of General Assembly of New Hampshire, 19 March 1771–13 April 1771. *Copy*, certified as No. ii. 16 pp.

    v. Naval Officer's list of shipping entering port of Piscataqua, New Hampshire, 10 October 1770–5 January 1771, by Eleazer Russell, deputy Naval Officer. *Signed*, John Wentworth. 1 large p.

    vi. Same, of shipping clearing from same; same dates. *Signed*, as No. v. 2 large pp.

vii. Same, of shipping entering same, 5 January 1771–5 April 1771. *Signed*, as No. v. 2 large pp.

viii. Same, of shipping clearing from same; same dates. *Signed*, as No. v. 2 large pp.

ix. Same, of shipping entering same, 5 April 1771–5 July 1771. *Signed*, as No. v. 2 large pp.

x. Same, of shipping clearing from same; same dates. *Signed*, as No. v. 2 large pp. [C.O.5, 937, fos. 62–103d; signed original of covering letter, endorsed Read 15 May 1772, in C.O.5, 930, fos. 123–135d; entry of covering letter in C.O.5, 945, pp. 184–208]

1524

23 September, Pensacola

John Stuart to Earl of Hillsborough (No. 33). Cession of land by Cherokees to traders was without application to me as superintendent. Bad consequences must be expected. Only West Florida has law confirming boundaries agreed by treaties and making it penal to purchase or accept land beyond such boundaries. *Signed*. 2½ pp. *Endorsed*, R, 23 December. *Enclosed*:

i. Fort Charlotte, 4 June 1771. Extract of letter from Edward Keating to Andrew McLean, merchant at Augusta, concerning cession of land by Cherokees. *Copy*. 4 pp.

ii. 8 June 1771. Report of meeting of party of Cherokee and most of the Cherokee traders, near Fort Charlotte. *Copy*. 2½ pp.

iii. 21 June 1771. Abstract of letter from Andrew McLean concerning cession of land by Cherokees. *Copy*. 1¾ pp. [C.O.5, 72, fos. 326–333d; entry of covering letter in C.O.5, 228, pp. 84–88]

1525

24 September, Pensacola

Same to same (No. 34), acknowledging Nos. 20–21. Hopes to survey and mark Indian boundaries before leaving West Florida. Surveys of lines behind Virginia, the Carolinas and Georgia are being made. Our interference in Choctaw-Creek quarrel has had no bad consequence: there never was less appearance of peace between them. Encroachment beyond line stipulated by Treaty of Pensacola, up Alabama River, has given disgust to Creeks. Congresses with Choctaws and Chickasaws have been called to Mobile. Indian trade should be regulated, but there is no prospect of the provinces doing it. Spaniards from Cuba fish on western side of Florida peninsular. Mr Thomas on the Mississippi. *Signed*. 4¾ pp. *Endorsed*, R, 23 December. *Enclosed*:

i. Sketch of Cherokee boundaries with Virginia and North Carolina, 1771. 1 large p. [M.P.G.348]

ii. Pensacola, 1 August 1771. John Stuart to Governor Peter Chester, requesting extracts of letters to Lord Hillsborough on Indian affairs. *Copy.* ¾ p.

iii. Pensacola, 3 August 1771. Extract of minutes of Council of West Florida, with extracts of letters from Lieut.-Governor Elias Durnford to Earl of Hillsborough relating to Indian affairs, of 18 February, 8 June, 8, 9 and 14 July 1770; with observations thereon by John Stuart. *Signed*, by John Stuart. 8½ pp.

iv. Oakchoy, 1 May 1771. Talk from headmen and warriors of Upper Creek nation to John Stuart, with speeches by Emistisiguo and Old Gun Merchant recalling former undertakings by whites and encroachments on boundaries. Satisfaction sought for murder of Indian on Savannah River. *Copy.* 3½ pp.

* v. Tallassies, 15 July 1771. Talk from same to same, with speech by Emistisiguo about boundary lines. *Copy.* 1½ pp.

* vi. Pensacola, 30 August 1771. John Stuart to Governor Peter Chester, putting questions on Indian affairs. Cession from Six Nations contained hunting grounds of Western tribes and Cherokees. Cherokees have ceded to traders land claimed by Creeks. *Copy.* 2½ pp.

* vii. Pensacola, 10 September 1771. Govenor Chester to John Stuart, replying to questions on boundary with Creeks and relations with Choctaws. *Copy.* 8 pp.

viii. Pensacola, 31 August 1771. John Stuart to Governor Chester, sending copies of letters from Lord Hillsborough, by which it appears he wishes that congress with Choctaws etc. could be avoided. Is congress necessary? Should Choctaws be treated with for lands on Mississippi or titles obtained from the small tribes there? *Copy.* 1 p.

ix. Mobile, 8 September 1771. René Roi, interpreter, to John Stuart. Spaniards at New Orleans have sent for fourteen Choctaw chiefs. *Copy.* translated from French. 1½ pp.

x. Pensacola, 4 September 1771. Instructions by John Stuart to John McIntosh to arrange meetings with Choctaws and Chickasaws at Mobile about 10 November. Enter in your journal Indian names of geographical features. *Copy.* 1¾ pp.

* xi. Pensacola, 17 August 1771. Instructions by John Stuart to John Thomas to go to New Orleans, up Mississippi to Natchez, to report on small tribes and to reside on Mississippi, cultivating good understanding with Indians there. *Copy.* 3¼ pp.

xii. Pensacola, 10 August 1771. John Stuart to Emistisiguo and other chiefs of Upper Creek Nation, replying to Nos. iv–v, and arranging meeting. *Copy.* 1½ pp. [C.O.5, 72, fos. 334–365d; entry of covering letter in C.O.5, 228, pp. 89–98]

1526

25 September, St Augustine

Lieut.-Governor John Moultrie to Earl of Hillsborough (No. 6), acknowledging No. 41. Twenty miles of road towards Musquito is now finishing; for £250–£300 it could be completed to Musquito River, and for another £500 the thirty miles to Smyrnea. *Signed.* 3 pp. *Endorsed*, R, 5 December. [C.O.5, 552, fos. 64–65d; signed duplicate, endorsed Read 18 December 1771, in C.O.5, 545, fos. 50–52d; entry in C.O.5, 567, pp. 207–209]

1527

26 September, Savannah

President James Habersham to Earl of Hillsborough (No. 2), acknowledging No. 38. I have not issued writs for new Assembly, which would pursue same measures as their predecessors. Talk from headman of Lower Creeks enclosed. Cherokees some time ago proposed to Governor Wright ceding lands in compensation for debts due to traders, and observed that if Creeks laid claim to those lands they would try to get them to give it up. Insinuation in the talk that the whites asked for these lands is incorrect. Lands are of best quality and would be a grand addition of territory and security from Indian incursions. *Signed.* 4 pp. *Endorsed*, R, 5 December. *Enclosed:*

i. Cussiters, Lower Creeks, 20 August 1771. Talk by Emisteseco to Governor Wright, Captain Stuart and George Galphin. *Copy*, certified by A. Wylly. *Signatories*, Emisteseco, Seleche, Parachickala King, Hitcheter King, Cussiter King, Young Lieutenant. *Witnesses*, J. Barrington, John Millar. 2 pp. [C.O.5, 661, fos. 75–79d; signed duplicate of covering letter, endorsed Read 18 December 1771, and copy of enclosure, in C.O.5, 651, fos. 143–147d; entry of covering letter in C.O.5, 678, pp. 240–244]

1528

26 September, Charleston

Governor Lord Charles Montagu to Earl of Hillsborough, notifying arrival on 16th inst. Assembly met 18th. Regarding £1500 sent to England in 1769 by order of House of Assembly, scarcely above two members but what in private condemn it, yet from pride find it difficult to recede. Charleston much increased in buildings since I left. H.M.S. *Mercury*, *Tartar* and *Bonetta* in harbour. P. De Lancey killed in duel, William H. Drayton appointed postmaster. *Signed.* 2 pp. *Endorsed*, R, 18 November. *Enclosed:*

i. 19 September 1771. Address of Council of South Carolina to Governor Lord Charles Montagu. *Copy.* 1¼ pp.

ii. 19 September 1771. Address of Commons House of Assembly to same. *Copy. Signatory*, P. Manigault. 2 pp. [C.O.5, 394, fos. 96–101d; entry of covering letter in C.O.5, 409, pp. 239–241]

1529

26 September, Pensacola

Governor Peter Chester to Earl of Hillsborough (No. 34), acknowledging circular of 5 June. *Signed.* 1 p. *Endorsed,* R, 23 December. [C.O.5, 588, pp. 491–494; signed duplicate, endorsed Read 15 May 1772, in C.O.5, 578, pp. 305–308; entry in C.O.5, 621, p. 103]

1530

27 September, Pensacola

Same to same (No. 35), acknowledging Acts of Parliament sent by Mr Pownall. *Signed.* ½ p. *Endorsed,* R, 23 December. [C.O.5, 588, pp. 495–498; signed duplicate, endorsed Read 15 May 1772, in C.O.5, 578, pp. 321–324; entry in C.O.5, 621, p. 103]

1531

27 September

John Pownall to President James Habersham. It is request of several persons of great consideration that Attorney-General Pryce be given leave of absence when he has settled his affairs in Georgia; Mr Hume to officiate during absence. *Entry.* ¾ p. [C.O.5, 246, p. 29]

1532

28 September, Treasury

John Robinson to John Pownall, sending extract of letter from Governor Bruere of Bermuda in which he requests payment of money due for interest from sale of land. *Signed.* ¾ p. *Endorsed,* R, 4 October. [C.O.5, 145, fos. 4–5d]

1533

28 September, Halifax

Governor Lord William Campbell to Earl of Hillsborough (No. 79). Halifax lighthouse is supported by duty of 6d. a ton on vessels entering harbour; manager receives the duty and is responsible for maintaining the light. *Signed.* 3 pp. *Endorsed,* R, 23 October. *Enclosed :*

i. Minutes of Council of Nova Scotia, 27 September 1771. Complaint about Halifax lighthouse was well-founded, arising partly from carelessness, partly from fog. Present fund insufficient; Commodore Gambier is to represent to government need for assistance. *Copy.* 2¼ pp. [C.O.217, 48, fos. 68–71d; signed duplicate of covering letter, endorsed Read 12 December 1771, and copy of enclosure, in C.O.217, 26, fos. 91–94d; entry of covering letter in C.O.218, 18, pp. 7–8]

1534

28 September, Halifax

Same to Earl of Hillsborough (No. 80), acknowledging leave of absence. *Signed*. 1 p. *Endorsed*, R, 23 October. [C.O.217, 48, fos. 72–73d; signed duplicate, endorsed Read 12 December 1771, in C.O.217, 26, fos. 95–96d; entry in C.O.218, 18, p. 8]

1535

28 September, Pensacola

* Governor Peter Chester to Earl of Hillsborough (No. 36), enclosing five maps [*Marginal note :* These maps will be found in the Collection of Maps] of lands near Fort Bute, Rivers Mississippi, Iberville, Amit and Comit, with remarks. In one map, plan of town is laid out to be called Harwich. Mr Durnford reports that the Iberville is blocked by logs and that nothing is wanting but to destroy by fire when the river is dry. Proposed cut marked on map; Mr Durnford thinks it practicable but expensive. Report on River Amit: good land. Indians say there is a communication from Amit to Lake Maurepas and with very little land-carriage to Bay of St Louis and Lake Pontchartrain. Such inland navigation would be beneficial to a township on Amit, fifteen miles to Baton Rouge. Troops needed for defence: estimate of cost of establishing ourselves on Mississippi enclosed. I think that, instead of incurring expense of the cut, government should grant annual sum for transporting settlers from Europe or southern colonies. Objection is that, without a communication between this place and the lakes, these settlements would in war be a sacrifice to Spain; but if Indians are in our interest, inhabitants would be secure, West Florida would flourish, and in war New Orleans could be secured. Report on small Indian tribes on Mississippi: 237 warriors in all. Lieutenant Thomas is to invite back those who retired to Spanish side of the river. Three maps enclosed of parts of this province, one showing grants of greatest part of Mississippi front from Manchac to Natchez to persons who have made no improvements; this land is fit to be regranted in small tracts. *Signed*. 13¼ pp. *Endorsed*, R, 23 December. *Enclosed :*

i. Estimate by Elias Durnford, engineer for West Florida, of expense of proposed cut from River Mississippi to River Iberville: £9150. *Copy*. 1¾ pp. [C.O.5, 588, pp. 499–518; signed duplicate of covering letter, and copy of enclosure, endorsed Read 15 May 1772, in C.O.5, 578, pp. 309–320, 325–330; entry of covering letter in C.O.5, 621, pp. 103–113]

1536

29 September, Pensacola

Same to same (No. 37), enclosing following. Mr Stuart seemed in doubt what measures you wished should be pursued with the Indians, and requested extracts of letters, which were furnished him. Council's opinion on two letters I received from him is entered in minutes; my reply enclosed. One reason for holding congress with Choctaws was grounded on apprehension that Spaniards at New Orleans had been negotiating with them, reported by Mr McIntosh, Indian merchant at Mobile, but unconfirmed. *Signed.* 2½ pp. *Endorsed*, R, 23 December. *Enclosed:*

i. Pensacola, 10 September 1771, Governor Chester to John Stuart. *See* No. 1525vii. *Duplicate. Signed.* 9 pp.

ii. Mobile, 12 September. Extract of letter from Alexander McIntosh to [Governor Chester]. Choctaws have gone to Orleans. *Copy.* ½ small p. [C.O.5, 588, pp. 519–536; signed duplicate of covering letter and copies of enclosures in C.O.5, 578, pp. 331–346; entry of covering letter in C.O.5, 621, pp. 114–116]

1537

29 September, Charlotte Town, I. of St John

Governor Walter Patterson to John Pownall, acknowledging letter of 5 June. *Signed.* ½ small p. *Endorsed*, R, 17 December. [C.O.226, 4, fos. 97–98d]

1538

30 September, G.P.O.

Anthony Todd to John Pownall. *Harriot* packet for New York and *Grenville* for West Indies will be ready on arrival of next Wednesday's mails. *Entry.* ½ p. [C.O.5, 247, p. 7]

1539

30 September, New Bern

Governor Josiah Martin to Earl of Hillsborough (No. 3), acknowledging No. 3 and reporting arrival of *Sta Catherina*, Spanish vessel in distress, with troops board. Provisions sold to them. Ship sailed, leaving some troops here. Some violence on individuals reported from back-country but in general people seem well-disposed. *Signed.* 6 pp. *Endorsed*, R, 13 December. [C.O.5, 314, fos. 286–287d; signed duplicate, endorsed Read 15 May 1772, in C.O.5, 302, fos. 112–114d; entry in C.O.5, 329, pp. 11–17]

1540

30 September, St John's, Newfoundland

Governor John Byron to Earl of Hillsborough, enclosing following. I have sent orders to Captain Gower of *Pearl* at Magdalen Islands to stop disorders by New England vessels. *Signed.* 3 pp. *Endorsed*, R, 13 November. *Enclosed:*

i. St John's, 31 August 1771. Report by Captain Hugh Debbieg on compensation fixed by arbitration to be paid to owners of property at Quiddi Viddi. Total claim: £2170. *Signatories*, John Livingston and eleven others. *Counter-signatories*, John Byron and seven others. *Copy*. 6½ pp. [C.O.194, 30, fos. 51–56d; signed duplicate of covering letter, endorsed Read 12 December 1771, and copy of enclosure, in C.O.194, 18, fos. 92–98d; entry of covering letter in C.O.195, 12, pp. 118–119]

1541

30 September, St John's, Newfoundland

Same to Earl of Hillsborough, enclosing following from governor of St Pierre, and other letters. Number of seamen and mariners furnished from *Panther* for work on fortifications prevented me visiting outposts. Letters enclosed on allowances to troops; on receipt of General Gage's, wages were reduced from 9d. to 6d. *Signed*. 3 pp. *Endorsed*, R, 13 November. *Enclosed*:

i. St Pierre, Terre-Neuve, 14 August 1771. M. D'Angeac to Governor Byron, protesting at seizure yesterday of ten French chaloupes. *French. Copy*. 2 pp.

ii. *Aeolus*, 16 August 1771. Captain William Bennett to Governor Byron, reporting seizure of French fishing boats for trespass. *Copy*. 2¾ pp.

iii. *Panther*, St John's, 4 September 1771. Governor Byron to Governor of St Pierre. Seizure was for fishing without limits prescribed by treaty. Boats will be returned to owners. Any other found without limits will be confiscated. *Copy*. 4 pp.

iv. [9 August 1771]. Captain Hugh Debbieg to Governor Byron. Small wages are not most economical way to carry on King's works. Soldier cannot support himself on 6d. Pending arrival of General Gage's answer, shall I use discretionary power to pay 9d? PS. Troops employed at Chatham in 1756 were paid 8d. a day. *Copy*. 3 pp.

v. *Panther*, St John's, 9 August 1771. Governor Byron to Captain Debbieg. I never heard that a common labourer was hired here at less than 2s. a day. 9d. is least soldier could be expected to work for with spirit. *Copy*. 3¼ pp.

vi. New York, 30 July 1771. Lieut.-General Thomas Gage to Governor Byron. Regulated allowances are 6d. a day for labourers, 9d. for artificers; I can give no reason for increasing them in Newfoundland. *Copy*. 3 pp.

vii. St John's, 7 September 1771. Captain Debbieg to Governor Byron, asking that contents of General Gage's letter be communicated to soldiers, seamen and marines. It will be hard on them. *Copy*. 2½ pp.

viii. St John's, 7 September 1771. Governor Byron to Lieut.-General Gage. Pay of troops on works here has been reduced to regulated sum. *Copy*. 1½ pp. [C.O.194, 30, fos. 57–75d; signed duplicate of covering letter, endorsed Read 12 December 1771, and copies of enclosures, in C.O.194, 18, fos. 99–120d; entry of covering letter in C.O.195, 12, pp. 119–121]

1542

30 September, Pensacola

Governor Peter Chester to Earl of Hillsborough (No. 38). Creeks have put off visit on account of expedition against Choctaws; now expected next month. *Signed.* 1½ pp. *Endorsed*, R, 23 December. [C.O.5, 588, pp. 537–540; signed duplicate, endorsed Read 15 May 1772, in C.O.5, 578, pp. 347–350; entry in C.O.5, 621, pp. 116–117]

1543

30 September, Pensacola

Lieut.-Governor Elias Durnford to Earl of Hillsborough, with schemes in the event of war with Spain for capturing New Orleans with two regiments from the Ohio, and for attacking Vera Cruz and Havana with troops from West Florida. *Signed.* 4¼ pp. *Endorsed*, R, 23 December. [C.O.5, 588, pp. 541–546; entry in C.O.5, 621, pp. 117–121]

1544

30 September, Savannah

President James Habersham to Earl of Hillsborough (No. 3). John Wortsch of Ebenezer has shipped 438 lbs of raw silk to London, last year 291 lbs. He assures me the people of Ebenezer are determined to prosecute culture of silk. I have given him the use of a few basons and reels out of repair in the filature here. *Signed.* 2½ pp. *Endorsed*, R, 5 December. [C.O.5, 661, fos. 80–81d; signed duplicate, endorsed Read 18 December 1771, in C.O.5, 651, fos. 148–149d; entry in C.O.5, 678, pp. 244–246]

1545

1 October, New York

* Lieut.-General Thomas Gage to Earl of Hillsborough (No. 65). I hope you have received from Mr Durnford his plan for junction of Mississippi and Iberville rivers. Mr Stuart at Pensacola hoped to avoid ceremonies and name of a congress. Batteries at Pensacola need facing: Ensign Hutchins, whom I hoped to send by way of Mississippi in hopes of obtaining intelligence, lately arrived here and will go to Pensacola to assist. He thinks it will cost £250 this year and £100 a year thereafter to save Fort Chartres. Copy of his remarks on Illinois enclosed: it appears to agree in general with others I have thought mostly to be depended on. If his estimation of exports of peltry is accurate, expense of new settlement at Cap au Grais and fort would exceed profits. Kikapous have done more mischief, killing a white man and slave and taking another white man prisoner, six miles from Fort Chartres.

They seem bent on war with whites. Pouteatamies of St Joseph also killed some of our people. French traders and French deserters from Spaniards are thick upon the Ouabache at Post St Vincent. The foundation of intelligence in my No. 58 was that a troublesome tribe of Senecas, without knowledge of Six Nations as a whole, had invited Western tribes to unite against the English; they have now been confounded. I fear we shall have to reduce the Pouteatamies and Ouabache Indians by force: I hope Spanish governor of Louisiana is not encouraging them. I have ordered troops at the Illinois to train for service of the woods, and propose if requisite to concert with Mr Stuart about obtaining aid of Cherokees and Chickasaws. Indians continue to complain of rum and encroachments by whites beyond the boundary; settled in 1768. Major Hamilton will replace Lieut.-Colonel Wilkins, going on leave, in command of the Illinois. *Signed.* 8 pp. *Endorsed*, R, 8 November. *Enclosed:*

> ★ i. Extracts of remarks on Illinois country by Ensign Hutchins, 60th regiment, assistant engineer. Description of Kaskaskias, La Prairie Du Rocher, Peorias, St Philips, Cahokia, St Louis, St Genevieve, Saline, Cape Aux Gris. Exports from British and Spanish territory 1769–1770. Report on navigation of Mississippi. *Copy.* 5½ pp. [C.O.5, 89, fos. 170–177d; entry of covering letter in C.O.5, 234, pp. 240–248]

1546

1 October, Boston

★ Governor Thomas Hutchinson to Earl of Hillsborough (No. 12). Report on Eastern Country, enclosed with last, is evidently calculated to justify the two Houses' neglect. I have no doubt that greater part of inhabitants are employed in lumbering. There are fine beech trees, which I have heard is as serviceable as oak. I expect nothing from General Court. *Signed.* PS. Mr Story, who felt resentment of the populace in 1765, is bearer of my dispatches. 2 small pp. [C.O.5, 760, fos. 283–284d; entry in C.O.5, 768, pp. 216–217]

1547

2 October, Admiralty

Lords of Admiralty to Earl of Hillsborough, enclosing following. *Signed*, Sandwich, J. Buller, Lisburne. 1 p. *Endorsed*, R, 4th. *Enclosed:*

> i. Receiver's office for Greenwich Hospital, Tower Hill, 18 September 1771. Commissioners for Collecting Sixpenny Duties to Philip Stephens. Mr Hulton, our deputy receiver at Boston, has again asked for directions on collection of duty from vessels in fishery from Salem and Marblehead. *Copy. Signatories*, Thomas Hicks, George Marsh. 1 p. [C.O.5, 119, Pt. 1, fos. 1–4d; entry in C.O.5, 768, pp. 211–212]

1548

2 October

John Pownall to Grey Cooper, requesting issue of £100 for copying maps and plans and preparing them for publication. *Draft.* ½ small p. [C.O.5, 154, fo. 24]

1549

2 October, New York

★ Governor William Tryon to Earl of Hillsborough (No. 7), enclosing following. Claimants of land on Lake Champlain under French grants are expected here this month. Further disorders reported on New Hampshire frontier. Satisfaction required of Governor of St Domingo for injuries to Daniel Frisby. Patent granted to Frederick Philipse for royal mines in manor of Philipsburgh. *Signed.* 3 pp. *Endorsed*, R, 8 November. *Enclosed :*

i. Minutes of Council of New York, 9 July 1771–23 September 1771. *Copy*, certified by G. Banyar, deputy clerk. 41½ pp.

ii. Minutes of Council of New York in Department of Lands, 7 August 1771–18 September 1771. *Copy*, certified as No. i. 21½ pp.

iii. New York, 17 August 1771. Proclamation by Governor Tryon calling for evidence of titles of claimants to lands under French grant on Lake Champlain in New York province to be sent to Secretary's office within three months. *Printed.* 1 p.

★ iv. Brattleborough, 18 September 1771. Samuel Wells to John Tabor Kemp, notifying survey initiated by Governor of New Hampshire to show that Connecticut River comes from so much to the east as not to joint 45th degree of northern latitude. Contributions were taken for this purpose from persons near the river bank. *Copy*, certified by G. Banyar. 2 pp.

v. Cumberland County, 18 September 1771. Affidavit sworn before Samuel Wells by Nehemiah Howe of Putney in Cumberland County, concerning survey of Connecticut River. *Copy*, certified as preceding. 1¾ pp.

★ vi. New York, 2 October 1771. Governor Tryon to Governor Wentworth, concerning survey last winter by Whiting and Grant of easterly branch of Connecticut River. Grantees under New Hampshire have lately dispossessed persons settled under titles from New York, encouraged by assurances ascribed to you that jurisdiction will be altered. I hope you will undeceive them. *Copy.* 3 pp.

vii. New York, 30 September 1771. Governor Tryon to Governor of St Domingo, demanding redress for Daniel Frisby, master of *Hawke* of New York, seized by armed Spanish sloop on 27 June in passage from Curaçao to New York with cargo of salt and hides; and punishment of officer responsible. *Copy.* 3 pp. [C.O.5, 1102, fos. 258–310d;

entry of covering letter in C.O.5, 1138, pp. 240–242; signed duplicate of covering letter, endorsed Read 18 December 1771, with PS. explaining that second copies of minutes of Council are not sent, with copies of Nos. iii–vii, in C.O.5, 1075, fos. 174–185d]

1550

3 October, Williamsburg

Governor Earl of Dunmore to Earl of Hillsborough (No. 1), reporting arrival on 25 ult. [MS: inst.] I shall try to follow in Lord Botetourt's steps. Accounts of discontent among Indians make me wish for plan, at home, to remove it. *Signed.* 2 pp. *Endorsed*, R, 30 November. [C.O.5, 1349, fos. 173–174d; signed duplicate, dated 12 October, endorsed Read 12 December 1771, in C.O.5, 1333, fos. 114–115d; entry in C.O.5, 1372, pp. 186–188]

1551

4 October, Whitehall

Order of Committee of Council for Plantation Affairs, referring twenty-five Acts passed in Massachusetts in April–July 1771 to Commissioners for Trade and Plantations. *Seal. Signed*, Stephen Cottrell. *Endorsed*, Recd. 4 October, Read 18 December 1771. [C.O.5, 894, pp. 317–320]

1552

4 October, Admiralty

Lords of Admiralty to Earl of Hillsborough, enclosing following. *Signed*, Sandwich, J. Buller, Lisburne. 1 p. *Endorsed*, R, 7th. *Enclosed :*

   i. State of island of Tobago, 25 June 1771, showing white and negro population, number of runaways, arms, ammunition, produce etc. *Copy*. 1 p. [C.O.5, 119, Pt. 1, fos. 5–8d; entry of covering letter in C.O.5, 247, p. 7]

1553

8 October, Halifax

Governor Lord William Campbell to Earl of Hillsborough. John Cunningham has acted in Major Gorham's place during his absence on Indian affairs, and is recommended for favour. *Signed.* 1½ pp. *Endorsed*, R, 13 December. [C.O.217, 48, fos. 86–87d; entry in C.O.218, 18, p. 10]

1554

8 October, Quebec

Lieut.-Governor H. T. Cramahé to Earl of Hillsborough (No. 12), acknowledging No. 39 and commission as lieut.-governor. Canadians rely on H.M.'s paternal regard. Proclamation enclosed. *Signed.* 2½ pp. *Endorsed*, R, 23 November. *Enclosed :*

i. Quebec, 26 September 1771. Proclamation by Lieut.-Governor Cramahé, notifying his appointment and continuing officers. *Copy*, certified by George Allsopp, deputy clerk. 1 p. [C.O.42, 31, fos. 50–53d; entry of covering letter in C.O.43, 13, pp. 16–17; signed duplicate of covering letter, endorsed Read 12 December 1771, and copy of enclosure, in C.O.42, 8, fos. 43–46d]

1555

8 October, Quebec

Same to same (No. 13), acknowledging No. 40. Mr Bentzell has been here; and shall be supported. *Signed.* 1 p. *Endorsed*, R, 23 November. [C.O.42, 31, fos. 54–55d; entry in C.O.43, 13, p. 18; signed duplicate, endorsed Read 12 December 1771, in C.O.42, 8, fos. 47–48d]

1556

8 October, London

William De Brahm to John Pownall, complaining. *Signed.* 2 small pp. [C.O.5, 154, fo. 28, 28d]

1557

9 October, St James's

Order of King in Council, referring following to Commissioners for Trade and Plantations. *Seal. Signed*, Stephen Cottrell. ¾ p. *Endorsed*, Recd. 10 October, Read 18 December 1771. *Enclosed :*

i. List of titles of twenty-one Acts passed in Pennsylvania in 1771. 2¼ pp. [C.O.5, 1278, fos. 59–62d]

1558

9 October, Halifax

Governor Lord William Campbell to Earl of Hillsborough, enclosing and recommending following. I have frequent complaints of Indians since Fort Frederick at entrance of St John's River was dismantled. Strong blockhouse would check them. *Signed.* 2 pp. *Endorsed*, R, 12 March 1772. *Enclosed :*

i. Halifax, 27 August 1771. Memorial of Charles Newland Godfrey Iadis, late Capt./Lieut., 52nd regiment, to Governor Lord William Campbell, setting forth destruction of his store on St John's River by fire, attributed to Indians, and praying for assistance. *Signed.* 2½ pp.

ii. Account of effects lost in fire. 2 pp. *Endorsed*, Read in Council, 2 September 1771; ordered that inquiry be made; signed by Richard Bulkeley. [C.O.217, 48, fos. 90–95d; entry of covering letter in C.O.218, 18, pp. 11–13]

1559

9 October, Quebec

Lieut.-Governor H. T. Cramahé to Earl of Hillsborough (No. 14), enclosing following. *Signed.* ½ p. *Endorsed,* R, 23 November. *Enclosed:*

i. Minutes of Council of Quebec, 12 July–30 September 1771. *Copy,* certified by George Allsopp, deputy clerk. 12 pp. [C.O.42, 31, fos. 56–64d; entry of covering letter in C.O.43, 13, p. 18; signed duplicate of covering letter, endorsed Read 12 December 1771, in C.O.42, 8, fos. 49–50d]

1560

9 October, Quebec

Same to John Pownall, acknowledging letter of 5 June. *Signed.* ½ small p. *Endorsed,* R, 23 November. [C.O.42, 31, fos. 65–66d; entry in C.O.43, 13, p. 18; signed duplicate, endorsed Read 12 December 1771, in C.O.42, 8, fos. 51–52d]

1561

12 October

Richard Jackson to Commissioners for Trade and Plantations, reporting four Acts passed in Virginia in 1767, 1769, 1770, proper in point of law. *Signed.* 1½ pp. *Endorsed,* Recd. 13 November, Read 18 December 1771. [C.O.5, 1333, fos. 116–117d]

1562

12 October, New York

Address of governors of College of New York to Earl of Hillsborough, seeking assistance in becoming a university and financial aid. *Seal.* 1 p. *Endorsed,* R, 3 February 1772. [C.O.5, 1103, fos. 14–15d; entry in C.O.5, 1138, pp. 249–250]

1563

12 October, New York

* Memorial of Church of England clergy of New York and New Jersey to Earl of Hillsborough, on need for bishops in America. *Signed,* Samuel Auchmuty, D.D., Thomas B. Chandler, D.D., John Ogilvie, D.D., Charles Inglis, A.M. 3½ pp. *Endorsed,* R, 3 February 1772, by Dr Cooper. [C.O.5, 73, fos. 4–6d; entry in C.O.5, 228, pp. 99–103]

1564

15 October, Williamsburg

Governor Earl of Dunmore to Earl of Hillsborough (No. 2), adding his solicitations to those already made for pension for Mr Blair. *Signed.* 2½ pp. *Endorsed,* R, 11 December. [C.O.5, 1349, fos. 182–183d; entry in C.O.5, 1372, pp. 188–190]

1565

15 October, Fort Amherst, Island of St John

Chief Justice John Duport to Earl of Hillsborough, acknowledging letter of 3 July. Since my last, nine families have arrived at Charlotte Town and about seventy persons at Magree. *Signed.* 1 small p. *Endorsed,* R, 9 December. [C.O.226, 4, fos. 93–94d; entry in C.O.227, 2, pp. 39–40]

1566

16 October, Halifax

Governor Lord William Campbell to Earl of Hillsborough (No. 81). Construction of lanthorn at Halifax lighthouse has been changed to permit free emission of smoke. *Signed.* 1 p. *Endorsed,* R, 22 November. [C.O.217, 48, fos. 74–75d; signed duplicate, endorsed Read 15 May 1772, in C.O.217, 26, fos. 106–107d; entry in C.O.218, 18, p. 9]

1567

16 October, St Augustine

Lieut.-Governor John Moultrie to Earl of Hillsborough (No. 7), acknowledging No. 42. Indigo should be double, probably treble, last year's. *Signed.* 2 pp. *Endorsed,* R, 23 December. [C.O.5, 552, fos. 66–67d; signed duplicate, endorsed Read 15 May 1772, in C.O.5, 545, fos. 61–62d; entry in C.O.5, 567, pp. 209–210]

1568

18 October, Whitehall

John Pownall to Anthony Todd, sending copy of letter from Lieut.-Governor William Bull, notifying death of Peter De Lancey and appointment of W. H. Drayton to execute office of deputy P.M.G., Southern District. *Entry.* ½ p. [C.O.5, 250, p. 1]

1569

18 October, Boston

Governor Thomas Hutchinson to Earl of Hillsborough (No. 13), acknowledging Order in Council disallowing Act passed in 1768 for erecting town of Ashfield. *Signed.* 1 small p. *Endorsed,* R, 21 November 1771. [C.O.5, 760, fos. 285–286d; entry in C.O.5, 768, p. 218]

1570

18 October, New Bern

* Governor Josiah Martin to Earl of Hillsborough (No. 4), enclosing list of six rebels recommended for mercy. Amongst six executed, Robert Matear was egregious offender but his parents were good people and H.M.'s bounty is solicited to grant them his lands and

goods. Sheriff of Guilford County reports some continuing spirit of resistance. Petitions on behalf of Hunter and two other outlaws received from Orange and Guilford Counties. Husbands reported in Pennsylvania. Proclamations enclosed. Act of grace by H.M. will be attended with good effect. *Duplicate. Signed.* 3 pp. *Endorsed*, R, 21 February, original not recd. *Enclosed :*

i. Names of respited criminals: Forrester Mercer, James Stewart, James Emmerson, Hermon Cox, William Brown, James Copeland. 1 small p.

ii. 17 May 1771. Proclamation by Governor William Tryon, offering pardon to those in arms who submit before 21st inst. except outlaws and those now prisoners. *Copy.* 1 p.

iii. 21 May 1771. Same, extending time to 24th inst. *Copy.* 1 p.

iv. 24 May 1771. Same, extending time to 30th inst. *Copy.* 1 p.

v. 31 May 1771. Same, extending time to 10 June, and adding to exceptions in No. ii names of Samuel Jones, Joshua Teague, Samuel Waggoner, Simon Dunn jnr., Abraham Creson, Benjamin Merrill, James Wilkinson snr., Edward Smith, John Bumpass, Joseph Boring, William Rankin, William Robeson, John Winkler, John Wilcox. *Copy.* 1 p.

vi. 9 June 1771. Same, offering reward of £100 and 1000 acres of land for taking dead or alive each of following: Hermon Husbands, James Hunter, Rednap Howell, William Butler. *Copy.* 1 p.

vii. 11 June 1771. Same, extending time for submission to 10 July, repeating exceptions in Nos. ii and v, and adding Jacob Felker and Thomas Person. *Copy.* 1 p. [C.O.5, 315, fos. 7–14d; signed original of covering letter, endorsed Read 15 May 1772, and copies of enclosures, in C.O.5, 302, fos. 115–123d; entry of covering letter in C.O.5, 329, pp. 18–21]

1571

18 October, Charlotte Town, I. of St John

Governor Walter Patterson to Earl of Hillsborough. Mr Fergus lost at sea; I have appointed John Patterson and George Burns to be of Council of Island of St John. Indian corn, oats, barley and potatoes do well. If proprietors exert themselves, this island will be garden of America. *Signed.* 2 pp. *Endorsed*, R, 9 December [C.O.226, 4, fos. 95–96d; entry in C.O.227, 2, pp. 37–39]

1572

18 October, Halifax

President Benjamin Green to Earl of Hillsborough (No. 82). Lord William Campbell sailed for Boston yesterday and I have taken on administration. *Signed.* 1 p. *Endorsed,* R, 22 November. [C.O.217, 48, fos. 76–77d; signed duplicate, endorsed Read 15 May 1772, in C.O.217, 26, fos. 108–109d; entry in C.O.218, 18, pp. 9–10]

1573

20 October, St Augustine

Lieut.-Governor John Moultrie to Earl of Hillsborough (No. 8). Chief Justice Drayton has resigned from Council, leaving only five members in the province, one of whom resides at great distance. *Signed.* 2 pp. *Endorsed,* R, 23 December. *Enclosed:*

i. St Augustine, 15 October 1771. William Drayton to Lieut.-Governor Moultrie, resigning from Council. *Copy.* 1 p.

ii. St Augustine, 20 October 1771. Lieut.-Governor Moultrie to William Drayton, accepting resignation. *Copy.* ½ p. [C.O.5, 552, fos. 68–71d; signed duplicate of covering letter and copies of enclosures, in C.O.5, 545, fos. 63–66d; entry of covering letter in C.O.5, 567, pp. 211–212]

1574

21 October, S. Carolina

* Governor Lord Charles Montagu to Earl of Hillsborough. Disputes in Assembly over Tax Bill continue warm. Public credit low, officers unpaid. I have no house. *Signed.* 2 small pp. *Endorsed,* R, 5 December. [C.O.5, 394, fos. 104–105d; entry in C.O.5, 409, pp. 241–242]

1575

21 October, Burlington

Governor William Franklin to Earl of Hillsborough (No. 35), acknowledging Nos. 31–32. Legislature will meet 20 November. I am concerned that Commissioners of Customs at Boston transmitted Hatton's complaint to Treasury, but pleased that you approve inquiry by Council of New Jersey. *Signed.* 1¼ pp. *Endorsed,* R, 16 December. [C.O.5, 991, fos. 96–97d; entry in C.O.5, 1001, pp. 141–143]

1576

21 October, Burlington

Same to Commissioners for Trade and Plantations, acknowledging letter of 21 June and explaining Act for support of government. There has been no attempt by legislature of New Jersey to give further currency to our present paper credit. I have little hope that Assembly will recede from claim of sole right of appointing agent. *Signed.* 3 pp. *Endorsed,* Recd. 16 December 1771, Read 21 February 1772. [C.O.5, 979, fos. 39–40d]

1577

23 October, Whitehall

John Pownall to Lieut.-Governor John Moultrie, recommending Archibald Neelson who is to make full report on state of settlement under Dr Turnbull. *Entry.* ½ p. [C.O.5, 246, p. 30]

1578

23 October, Savannah

President James Habersham to Earl of Hillsborough (No. 4). The province flourishes, and is at peace with the Indians. I have not called Assembly. I must think proceedings of the last arose from overheated passions of a few men. For some years opposition to government has been promoted throughout H.M.'s dominions on this continent. However, such disputes appear at present to have subsided. Francis Harris, member of Council, colonel of militia and resident in this province for thirty-three years, died about fourteen days ago. Rice crop will be short because of heavy spring and autumn rains, but indigo will make good crops. *Signed.* 3 pp. *Endorsed,* R, 23 December. [C.O.5, 661, fos. 82–83d; entry in C.O.5, 678, pp. 246–249]

1579

23 October, St John's

Address of thanks by merchants, traders and adventurers of St John's, Newfoundland, to Governor John Byron for endeavours in promoting fishery. *Signed,* Robert Bulley and twenty others. 2½ pp. *Endorsed,* R, 3 December 1771. [C.O.194, 30, fos. 80–81d]

1580

24 October, Boston

Governor Thomas Hutchinson to Earl of Hillsborough (No. 14), enclosing proceedings of Assembly relating to intrusions in Eastern Country, with plan of part of River Penobscot. Falls, where Indians petition for township, are between thirty and forty miles from Fort Pownall. There are fine trees for masts, and river is navigable up to Condeskeeg River for largest mast-ship. Settlers are continually moving back into this country. *Signed.* ¾ p. *Endorsed,* R, 22 November 1771. *Enclosed:*

i. Certificate, dated 24 October 1771, that John Cotton is deputy secretary of Massachusetts. *Seal. Signed,* T. Hutchinson. *Countersigned,* Thomas Flucker. ¾ p.

ii. Message of Governor Hutchinson to Council and House of Representatives, 27 September 1770. *Copy,* certified by John Cotton. 2½ pp.

iii. 10–20 November 1770. Proceedings of Council and House of Representatives. *Copy,* certified by John Cotton. 2½ pp.

iv. Message of Governor Hutchinson to Council and Assembly, 30 May 1771. *Copy,* certified as No. ii. 2 pp.

v. 7 June 1771. Proceedings of Council. *Copy,* certified as No. ii. 2 pp.

vi. 14 June 1771. Proceedings of House of Representatives. *Copy,* certified as No. ii. 2½ pp.

vii. 19 June 1771. Message of Governor Hutchinson to House of Representatives. *Copy,* certified as No. ii. 1½ pp.

viii. Plan of part of Penobscot River. 1 large p. [M.P.G.525]

ix. Certificate, as No. i. ¾ p.

x. 23 October 1771. Minutes of Council. Resolved, that assertion in letter signed Junius Americanus in *Boston Gazette and Country Journal* of 21 October 1771, and said to be taken from *Bingley's Journal* of 29 June 1771, that Lieut.-Governor Oliver is recorded in Council's books as a perjured traitor, is false, groundless and malicious. *Copy,* certified by John Cotton. 1 p.

xi. *Massachusetts Gazette and Boston Weekly Newsletter,* 24 October 1771. *Printed.* 4 pp. [C.O.5, 760, fos. 287–307d; entry of covering letter, dated 14 October, in C.O.5, 768, pp. 218–219]

1581

25 October, New Bern

Governor Josiah Martin to Earl of Hillsborough (No. 5). Some of the Spaniards mentioned in No. 3 are still here, having fallen into dispute with Stephen Williams, master of *Hope* which was to have taken them to Cadiz. *Duplicate. Signed.* 3 pp. *Endorsed,* R, 21 February 1772, original not recd. [C.O.5, 315, fos. 15–16d; signed original, endorsed Read 15 May 1772, in C.O.5, 302, fos. 124–126d; entry in C.O.5, 329, pp. 22–25]

1582

26 October, Williamsburg

Governor Earl of Dunmore to Earl of Hillsborough (No. 2 [*sic*]), enclosing following. *Signed.* 1 p. *Endorsed,* R, 16 December. *Enclosed:*

i. Address of congratulation by mayor etc. of Williamsburg to Governor Earl of Dunmore, with answer. *Copy.* 3 pp.

ii. Same, by William and Mary College, with answer. *Copy.* 3½ pp.

iii. Same, by Church of England clergy in Virginia, with answer. *Copy.* 3 pp.

iv. Same, by Council of Virginia, with answer. *Copy*. 2 pp. [C.O.5, 1349, fos. 184–194d; entry of covering letter in C.O.5, 1372, p. 191]

1583

31 October, Quebec

Lieut.-Governor H. T. Cramahé to Earl of Hillsborough (No. 15), acknowledging No. 41, which arrived in time to prevent my sending commissioners to New York to meet those of other colonies concerned in Indian trade. Great difficulty of traders in recovering debts and securing property in upper country can be remedied only at home. I have appointed Henry Kneller Advocate-General to succeed George Suckling, left the province. *Signed*. 2 pp. *Endorsed*, R, 20 December. [C.O.42, 31, fos. 69–70d; entry in C.O.43, 13, pp. 20–21; signed duplicate, endorsed Read 18 December 1771, in C.O.42, 8, fos. 53–54d]

1584

31 October, Savannah

President James Habersham to Earl of Hillsborough (No. 5), reporting affair between some back-settlers and party of Creeks, one of whom was killed. Papers enclosed; Edward Barnard, magistrate at Augusta, ordered to make inquiry. If people were suffered to take private revenge, we should be in no better state than the most savage of mankind. I have asked Mr Galphin to use his influence with the Creeks and also with the settlers to stop such proceedings. Unless straggling parties of Creeks are checked, our peace with the Creeks in general will be interrupted. Our back-settlers encourage them, contrary to law. Military post on Oconee River would stop this and keep settlers in order, if Creeks and Cherokees join in surrendering lands they have offered. Indigo in demand; great quantity made in Carolina which, with Georgia and the two Floridas, could supply not only Great Britain but all Europe. *Signed*. 6 pp. *Endorsed*, R, 23 December. *Enclosed*:

  i. Minutes of Council of Georgia, 29 October 1771, concerning murder and robbery by whites at Occone River; letter from Edward Barnard, 23 October 1771; affidavit sworn by Martin Weatherford, 24 October 1771. *Copy*, certified by Alexander Wylly. 3 large pp.

  ii. Savannah, 29 October 1771. Talk from President James Habersham to headmen and warriors of Creek nation, concerning attack by whites on Creek horse-stealers. Guilty will be punished. Do not let straggling parties go near white settlements. *Copy*. 2 pp. [C.O.5, 661, fos. 84–91d; signed duplicate of covering letter, endorsed Read 15 May 1772, and copies of enclosures, in C.O.5, 651, fos. 155–164d; entry of covering letter in C.O.5, 678, pp. 249–254]

1585

1 November, Admiralty

Lords of Admiralty to Earl of Hillsborough, enclosing papers which relate to insult by Spanish *guardacostas* to H.M. schooner *Sir Edward Hawke*. *Signed*, J. Buller, Lisburne, A. Hervey. 1½ pp. *Endorsed*, R, 1 November. *Enclosed*:

    i. Seven papers in above case. [C.O.5, 119, Pt. 1, fos. 9–25d; entry in C.O.5, 247, pp. 8–22]

1586

1 November, St James's

Earl of Rochford to John Pownall, requesting papers on disagreeable affair in limits of Sir George Rodney's command. *Entry*. ½ p. [C.O.5, 247, p. 8]

1587

1 November, Whitehall

John Pownall to Richard Sutton, sending for Lord Rochford's information copy of letter from Admiralty of this date and papers from Rear-Admiral Rodney relative to insult by Spaniards. *Draft*. 1 p. [C.O.5, 138, fos. 200–201d; entry in C.O.5, 250, p. 1]

1588

1 November, Whitehall

Same to Master of Lloyd's Coffee House. It does not appear that any considerable damage was done by earthquake in Jamaica on 3 September. *Entry*. ½ p. [C.O.5, 250, p. 2]

1589

1 November, Williamsburg

Governor Earl of Dunmore to Earl of Hillsborough (No. 3), enclosing following. On Council's advice, I have dissolved Assembly and issued writs for new one, though averse to it as productive of riot here as in England. *Signed*. 1 p. *Endorsed*, R, 13 December. *Enclosed*:

    i. List of ships cleared outwards, Upper District, James River, 5 April–5 July 1771. *Signed*, Lewis Burwell, Naval Officer. 1 large p.

    ii. Same entered inwards, same period. *Signed*, as No. i. 1 large p.

    iii. Same outwards, 5 July–10 October 1771. *Signed*, as No. i. 1 large p.

    iv. Same inwards, same period. *Signed*, as No. i. 1 large p.

    v. List of ships entered inwards, Accomack, 5 April–5 July 1771. *Signed*, D. Bowman, Naval Officer. 1 large p.

    vi. List of ships entered inwards, Rappahannock River, 25 March–24 June 1771 and 24 June–29 September 1771. *Signed*, Charles Neilson, Naval Officer. 1 large p.

    vii. Same outwards, same periods. *Signed*, as No. vi. 1 large p.

viii. List of ships entered inwards, Accomack, 5 July–10 October 1771. *Signed,* as No. v. 1 large p.

ix. Same outwards, same period. *Signed,* as No. v. 1 large p.

x. List of ships entered inwards, York River, 24 December 1770–24 June 1771. *Signed,* Cary Goosley, deputy Naval Officer. 1 large p.

xi. Same outwards, same period. *Signed,* as No. x. 1 large p.

xii. List of ships entered inwards, and cleared outwards, South Potomack, 5 April–5 July 1771. *Signed,* Richard Lee, Naval Officer. 1 large p.

xiii. Same, inwards and outwards, 5 July–10 October 1771. *Signed,* as No. xii. 1 large p. [C.O.5, 1349, fos. 195–208d; entry of covering letter in C.O.5, 1372, p. 190]

1590

2 November, R.I.

Governor Joseph Wanton to Earl of Hillsborough, acknowledging letter of 19 July. Mr Dudley, Collector of Customs at Newport, in April last boarded a ship in dead of night and was abused by sailors, supposed drunk; for what ensued, see enclosed. No application was made for apprehension of those persons. Justices of Superior Court deny that application was made to them by Customs officers for protection. Customs officers have traduced this colony. *Signed.* 3 small pp. *Endorsed,* R, 7 February. *Enclosed :*

i. Custom-house, Rhode Island, 6 April 1771. Richard Beale, deputy Collector, and John Nicoll, Comptroller, to Governor of Rhode Island. Collector was disabled in attempt to seize *Polly,* George Champlin, master. Order requested to prevent ship's escape. *Copy.* ½ small p.

ii. Newport, 6 April 1771. Governor Wanton's reply to preceding. I have instructed captain of Fort George to stop vessel if attempt be made to carry her out. *Copy.* 1 small p.

iii. Newport, 12 April 1771. Governor Wanton to Charles Dudley. Owners of ship were not concerned in disorder. No appearance of design to attack Custom-house or officers; but in case of need civil authority will be asserted. *Copy.* 1 small p. [C.O.5, 1284, fos. 158–165d; signed duplicate of covering letter, endorsed Read 15 May 1772, and copies of enclosures in C.O.5, 1278, fos. 70–77d; entry of covering letter in C.O.5, 1300, pp. 29–32]

1591

2 November, Pensacola

John Stuart to Earl of Hillsborough (No. 35), reporting congress with Upper Creeks. They deferred cession of lands on River Scambia but granted cession on Coosa River. I am preparing to meet Choctaws at Mobile. Abuses by traders must be restrained. *Signed.* 2 pp. *Endorsed,* R, 21 February 1772. *Enclosed:*

i. Abstract of address of Council of West Florida to Earl of Hillsborough, transmitted by Lieut.-Governor Durnford, 9 July 1770, on need for promised congress with Indians. *Copy.* ¼ p.

ii. Declaration by John Stuart, entered in minutes of Council of West Florida, denying promise of congress. *Copy.* 1¾ pp.

iii. Pensacola, 9 October 1771. Notice given by John Stuart that from 1 January next no person will be permitted to trade or reside in Choctaw and Chickasaw nations without licence of governor of one of the provinces in Southern District. *Copy. Signatory,* William Ogilvy, secretary. 1½ pp. [C.O.5, 73, fos. 15–21d; entry of covering letter, wrongly dated 22 November, in C.O.5, 228, pp. 104–106; signed duplicate of covering letter, endorsed Read 15 May 1772, and copies of enclosures in C.O.323, 27, pp. 157–172]

1592

3 November, Charlotte Town, I. of St John

Governor Walter Patterson to Earl of Hillsborough, asking permission to take stone from Cape Breton. *Duplicate. Signed.* ¾ p. *Endorsed,* R, 9 March 1772, original not recd. [C.O.226, 5, fos. 3–4d; entry in C.O. 227, 2, pp. 40–41]

1593

4 November, Pensacola

John Stuart to Earl of Hillsborough (No. 36). Congress with Upper Creeks ended. Chiefs expressed concern for depredations of Seminolies in neighbourhood of St Mark. Full report to follow. *Signed.* 1 p. *Endorsed,* R, 24 March 1772. *Enclosed:*

i. Pensacola, 4 November 1771. Affidavit, sworn before Attorney-General E. R. Wegg, by Joseph Cornell and John Simpson, interpreters, that they faithfully interpreted at congress with Upper Creeks, and that Emistisiguo said that no promise was made by Governor Johnstone or Superintendent in 1765 of another congress after three years. *Copy.* 1¼ pp. [C.O.5, 73, fos. 40–43d; entry of covering letter in C.O.5, 228, pp. 109–110]

1594

5 November, Boston

Governor Thomas Hutchinson to Earl of Hillsborough (No. 15). Governor and Council are frequently convened as court. In New Hampshire, governor gives his voice with the Council and causes are determined by majority. Am I to acquiesce in majority, although I may differ from it? This part of Council's business is much increased of late. *Signed.* 1¾ pp. *Endorsed,* R, 9 December. [C.O.5, 760, fos. 314–315d; entry in C.O.5, 768, pp. 219–221; signed duplicate, endorsed Read 15 May 1772, in C.O.5, 894, pp. 329–332]

1595

6 November, Whitehall

William Knox to Anthony Todd. Lord Hillsborough expected to arrive from Ireland tomorrow; American packets to be detained. *Entry.* ¼ p. [C.O.5, 250, p. 2]

1596

6 November, New York

* Lieut.-General Thomas Gage to Earl of Hillsborough (No. 66), acknowledging No. 48. It is too late in season for repairs to Castle William. 29th regiment has left New Jersey for St Augustine: Governor Franklin and most of better sort of people regret the troops leaving. Present Assembly of New Jersey is composed of more low people than ever before; better sort wish supplies granted. It must be left to Governor Franklin how to act to obtain arrear due for quartering; demand should be made, or it will be construed as tame acquiescence. Works at Newfoundland were not begun until 12 August and were impeded by reduction of allowance for labour to 6d. a day. Sir W. Johnson expected back from Six Nations. I have reviewed Scots Fusiliers at Philadelphia and found it in good order. *Signed.* 5¼ pp. *Endorsed,* R, 16 December. *Enclosed:*

i. Burlington, 28 October 1771. Extract of letter from Governor Franklin to General Gage. Removal of 29th regiment, however agreeable to Assembly, will be regretted by most considerable [MS: considerate] part of inhabitants. *Copy.* ½ p. [C.O.5, 89, fos. 185–190d; entry of covering letter in C.O.5, 234, pp. 249–252]

1597

6 November, New York

Governor William Tryon to Earl of Hillsborough (No. 8), recommending application of King's College to be erected into a university, to be presented to H.M. by Dr Cooper. *Signed.* 1¾ pp. *Endorsed,* R, 16 December. *Enclosed:*

i. Extract of report of committee appointed to consider ways and means for promoting interest of King's College. *Copy.* 2 pp. [C.O.5, 1102, fos. 317–320d; entry of covering letter in C.O.5, 1138, p. 244; signed duplicate of covering letter, endorsed Read 12 May 1772, and copy of enclosure, in C.O.5, 1075, fos. 201–204d]

1598

6 November, New York

Same to same (No. 9), acknowledging No. 5 and duplicates of preceding papers. Assembly prorogued to first week of December. Copy of letters patent to Frederick Philipse enclosed. The works are begun and silver discovered. *Signed*. 1½ pp. *Endorsed*, R, 16 December. *Enclosed:*

   i. New York, 25 September 1771. Letters patent to Frederick Philipse, granting royal mines of gold and silver in manor of Philipse-burgh, Westchester County, for ninety-nine years, paying one-fifteenth of gross ore or one-twentieth of gold and silver. *Copy*, certified by G. Banyar. 13 pp. [C.O.5, 1102, fos. 321–329d; entry of covering letter in C.O.5, 1138, p. 243; signed duplicate of covering letter, endorsed Read 15 May 1772, with PS. explaining that second copy of enclosure is not sent, in C.O.5, 1075, fos. 205–206d]

1599

7 November

Robert Allen to Lord Rochford. French proposals concerning Canada Reconnoissances are inadmissible. We propose payment in four annual instalments, beginning January next. *Copy*. 4 pp. [C.O.5, 43, fos. 287–288d]

1600

9 November, Whitehall

William Knox to Anthony Todd. American packets not to be detained beyond tonight. *Entry*. ¼ p. [C.O.5, 250, p. 2]

1601

9 November, G.P.O.

Anthony Todd to John Pownall, acknowledging letter of 18 October and enclosing following. *Signed*. 1 small p. *Endorsed*, R, 9th. *Enclosed:*

   i. G.P.O., 6 November 1771. Anthony Todd to Lieut.-Governor William Bull. Postmaster-General has appointed George Roupell deputy Postmaster-General for Southern District of North America. *Copy*. 1½ pp. [C.O.5, 134, fos. 292–295d]

1602

9 November, Williamsburg

Governor Earl of Dunmore to Earl of Hillsborough (No. 4). Mr Blair died 5th inst. I have for present appointed my private secretary, Mr Foy, deputy Auditor. Important that appointment, if to be made by Auditor-General, should be approved by me. *Signed*. PS. Accounts enclosed. 2¼ pp. *Endorsed*, R, 13 January 1772. *Enclosed:*

i. Account of revenue of 2s. per hogshead in Virginia, 25 April–
25 October 1771. *Signed,* Richard Corbin, deputy Receiver-General.
Examined by John Blair, jnr., for John Blair, deputy Auditor, and
by Earl of Dunmore. 1½ pp. [C.O.5, 1350, fos. 3–6d; signed duplicate
of covering letter, endorsed Read 15 May 1772, in C.O.5, 1333, fos.
174–175d; entry of covering letter in C.O.5, 1372, pp. 191–193]

1603

10 November, New Bern

★ Governor Josiah Martin to Earl of Hillsborough (No. 6). Rumour of
boundary line to be settled between North and South Carolina gives
great alarm; it would cut off large, flourishing tract and diminish
governor's little emoluments. Province will never enjoy perfect peace
until Earl Granville's proprietary right is vested in Crown; it is valued
at £60,000. Report here is that Lieut.-Governor Mercer is to be
promoted to new government on the Ohio; Mr Hasell recommended.
Signed. 2½ pp. *Endorsed,* R, 27 March 1772. [C.O.5, 315, fos. 17–18d;
signed duplicate, endorsed Read 29 July 1772, in C.O.5, 302, fos.
127–128d; entry in C.O.5, 329, pp. 26–28]

1604

12 November

Richard Jackson to Commissioners for Trade and Plantations. Act
passed in New York in 1771 to empower Philip Van Cortlandt, heir
of Mary Walton, tenant in tail of estate in New York City, to hold
same in fee simple, is not improper in point of law. *Signed.* 1 p. *Endorsed,*
Recd. 13 November, Read 12 December 1771. [C.O.5, 1075, fos. 172–
173d]

1605

13 November, S. Carolina

Governor Lord Charles Montagu to Earl of Hillsborough (No. 3).
Commons House committed public Treasurers to gaol. Upper House
could not agree to Tax Bill. Assembly dissolved 5th inst. New Assembly
will not meet until I receive H.M.'s instructions. *Signed.* 2½ pp.
Endorsed, R, 23 December. *Enclosed:*

i. 5 November 1771. Warrant by Commons House of Assembly
of South Carolina for committment to gaol of Henry Peronneau
and Benjamin Dart. *Copy,* certified by Roger Pinckney, provost
marshal. *Signatory,* P. Manigault, Speaker. 1½ pp.

ii. 4–5 November 1771. Extract of journals of Commons House. 7 pp.
[C.O.5, 394, fos. 106–114d; entry of covering letter in C.O.5, 409,
pp. 243–244]

1606

14 November, Portsmouth

Governor John Byron to Earl of Hillsborough, notifying arrival this day. *Signed.* 1½ pp. *Endorsed*, R, 16th. [C.O.194, 30, fos. 76–77d; entry in C.O.195, 12, p. 121]

1607

15 November, N.H.

* Governor John Wentworth to Earl of Hillsborough (No. 39). On 26 October, *Resolution*, Richard Keeting, and part of her cargo were seized at Piscataqua for breach of Acts of Trade. Armed men boarded her and seized molasses; reward offered for discovery of rioters. Rest of cargo forcibly taken away on 7 November by unknown men. Jesse Saville, Customs waiter, was rescued from mob on 14 November. Through zeal of magistracy, a riotous attempt was suppressed. Provincial officers and principal merchants disapprove of such trespass. *Signed.* 14 small pp. *Endorsed*, R, 21 February 1772. *Enclosed:*

i. 31 October 1771. Proclamation by Governor Wentworth offering reward of 200 dollars for discovery of principal actors in riot of 26 October. *Copy*, certified by Theodore Atkinson, secretary. 1½ pp. [C.O.5, 937, fos. 104–113d; signed duplicate of covering letter, endorsed Read 15 May 1772, and copy of enclosure in C.O.5, 930, fos. 136–145d; entry of covering letter in C.O.5, 945, pp. 208–215]

1608

16 November, Whitehall

Earl of Hillsborough to Earl of Rochford, sending extract of Governor Tryon's letter of 2nd ult. and other papers on complaint of Daniel Frisby of seizure of his vessel by Spanish *guardacosta*. *Draft.* 1 p. [C.O.5, 138, fos. 202–203d; entry in C.O.5, 250, p. 3]

1609

16 November, Whitehall

Same to Governors of Jamaica, West Florida and South Carolina. Packet-boats between said colonies are not to be detained beyond time limited except in cases of absolute necessity, which are to be reported. *Draft.* 1 p. [C.O.5, 72, fos. 315–316d; entry in C.O.5, 241, p. 393]

1610

16 November, Whitehall

Same to Postmaster-General, sending copy of circular [No. 1609] on detention of mail ships. Governors have no funds to pay demurrage; when necessity arises I will send you report so that you can apply to Treasury. *Draft.* 1 p. [C.O.5, 134, fos. 296–297d; entry in C.O.5, 250, p. 3]

1611

16 November, Whitehall

John Pownall to Anthony Todd, sending copy of Lord Hillsborough's letter to Governor of Grenada concerning Mr Middleton's withholding money due to Post Office. *Draft.* ½ p. [C.O.5, 134, fos. 298–299d; entry in C.O.5, 250, p. 1]

1612

16 November, Whitehall

Same to John Robinson. Earl of Hillsborough is of opinion that Alice Heron, widow of Benjamin Heron, late deputy secretary of North Carolina, should be compensated for his labour in making abstract of land grants. *Draft.* ¾ p. [C.O.5, 145, fos. 10–11d; entry in C.O.5, 250, p. 4]

1613

16 November, Whitehall

Same to same, sending copy of report of Attorney- and Solicitor-General on case of Naval Officer of Rhode Island [No. 1425]. *Draft.* ¾ p. [C.O.5, 145, fos. 8–9d; entry in C.O.5, 250, p. 5]

1614

16 November, Whitehall

Same to same. In reply to letter of 28 September, payment to Governor Bruere may be made from revenue arising to Crown from sales and leases of lands in Bermuda. *Draft.* 1 p. [C.O.5, 145, fos. 6–7d; entry in C.O.5, 250, p. 5]

1615

16 November, Admiralty

Lords of Admiralty to Earl of Hillsborough, enclosing papers relating to case of H.M. schooner *Sir Edward Hawke*. *Signed,* J. Buller, Palmerston, A. Hervey. 1 p. *Endorsed,* R, 16th. *Enclosed:*

i. Three papers in above case. [C.O.5, 119, Pt. 1, fos. 26–36d]

1616

16 November, St Augustine

Lieut.-Governor John Moultrie to Earl of Hillsborough (No. 9), enclosing following. Indigo crop estimated at twenty thousandweight. *Signed.* 1 p. *Endorsed,* R, 4 March 1772. *Enclosed:*

i. Naval officer's list of vessels entering St Augustine, 24 June 1770–29 September 1770. 2 large pp.

ii. Same, 29 September 1770–25 December 1770. 2 large pp.

iii. Same, 25 December 1770–25 March 1771. 2 large pp.

iv. Same, 25 March 1771–24 June 1771. 2 large pp.

v. Naval officer's list of vessels clearing from St Augustine, 24 June 1770–29 September 1770. 2 large pp.

vi. Same, 29 September 1770–25 December 1770. 1½ large pp.

vii. Same, 25 December 1770–25 March 1771. 1 large p.

viii. Same, 25 March 1771–24 June 1771. 1½ large pp. [C.O.5, 552, fos. 74–93d; signed duplicate of covering letter, endorsed Read 15 May 1772, in C.O.5, 545, fos. 67–68d; entry of covering letter in C.O.5, 567, pp. 212–213]

1617

17 November, Spring Gdns., Charing-cross, London

* Major Robert Rogers to Earl of Hillsborough, soliciting pension of 15s. a day and renewal of commission as major. *Signed.* 7 small pp. [C.O.5, 154, fos. 29–32d]

1618

18 November, Quebec

Lieut.-Governor H. T. Cramahé to Earl of Hillsborough (No. 16), enclosing following. Staves, cut on Lake Champlain, are floated over rapids at Chambli, down St Lawrence to Quebec, thence shipped to mother country: memorial enclosed. There is not enough shipping to carry the staves at reasonable rate since import of British spirits ceased, though this year grain trade brought abundance. *Signed.* 3½ pp. *Endorsed*, R, 11 January 1772. *Enclosed:*

i. Quebec, 18 November 1771. Report on manufactures in Quebec. *Signed*, H. T. Cramahé. 2½ pp.

ii. Quebec, 25 October 1771. Memorial of merchants and traders of Quebec to Lieut.-Governor Cramahé, seeking changes in bounty on import into Great Britain of white oak staves and heading. *Copy*, certified by H. T. Cramahé. *Signatories*, Colin Drummond and sixteen others. 4 pp. [C.O.42, 31, fos. 71–77d; entry of covering letter in C.O.43, 13, pp. 22–24; signed duplicate of covering letter, endorsed Read 15 May 1772, and copies of enclosures, in C.O.42, 8, fos. 55–62d]

1619

19 November, Admiralty

Lords of Admiralty to Earl of Hillsborough, enclosing papers relating to case of H.M. schooner *Sir Edward Hawke*. *Signed*, J. Buller, Palmerston, A. Hervey. 2 pp. *Endorsed*, R, 20th. *Enclosed:*

i. Two papers in above case. [C.O.5, 119, Pt. 1, fos. 37–42d; entry in C.O.5, 247, pp. 22–27]

1620

20 November, St James's

Earl of Rochford to Earl of Hillsborough, asking for papers as he is to see Spanish ambassador tomorrow. ½ small p. [C.O.5, 138, fos. 204–205d]

1621

20 November, Whitehall

Earl of Hillsborough to Earl of Rochford, sending further papers respecting *Sir Edward Hawke* schooner. *Draft.* 1¼ pp. [C.O.5, 138, fos. 206–207d; entry in C.O.5, 250, p. 6]

1622

21 November, Whitehall

Same to same, sending extract of letter from governor of Newfoundland and other papers concerning French chaloupes seized for fishing without limits prescribed by treaty. *Draft.* ½ p. [C.O.5, 138, fos. 208–209d; entry, dated 22 November, in C.O.5, 250, p. 9]

1623

22 November, Whitehall

John Pownall to Clerk of Council in Waiting, sending copy of letter from John, Thomas and Samuel Freebody of Rhode Island, and declaration on oath touching complaint that Governor and Company and courts of Rhode Island have treated H.M.'s Order in Council with contempt. *Draft.* 1 p. [C.O.5, 133, fos. 155–156d; entry in C.O.5, 250, p. 8]

1624

22 November, Whitehall

Same to same, sending extract of General Gage's letter concerning Company of Mine Adventurers, applicants for grant of mines on Lake Superior. *Draft.* ¾ p. [C.O.5, 133, fos. 157–158d; entry in C.O.5, 250, p. 7]

1625

22 November, Whitehall

Same to same, sending papers touching complaint of delay in courts of justice in Barbados. *Draft.* ½ p. [C.O.5, 133, fos. 159–160d; entry in C.O.5, 250, p. 7]

1626

25 November, Connecticut

* Church of England Clergy of Connecticut to Earl of Hillsborough, setting forth need for American episcopate. Strength of Dissenters who would oppose appears too inconsiderable to be taken notice of; now is the time. *Signed*, Jeremiah Leaming, secretary. 2 pp. *Endorsed*, R, 4 May 1772. [C.O.5, 1284, fo. 114, 114d; entry in C.O.5, 1300, pp. 134–136]

1627

26 November, London

Edward Mease to [Earl of Hillsborough], enclosing narrative of journey to Natchez and through Choctaw nation. Settlement in so fine a country would be advantageous. *Signed*. 3 small pp. *Enclosed*:

i. Narrative of journey through several parts of the province of West Florida in 1770 and 1771. By Edward Mease. Begins 4 November 1770, ends 2 April 1771. 98 small pp. [C.O.5, 588, pp. 325–434]

1628

[26 November]

Petition of Louis Dumesnil De St Pierre, J.P. for Granville County, South Carolina, to Commissioners for Trade and Plantations. He was promised grant of 40,000 acres of land in Nova Scotia in 1767 to settle French and German Protestants. He and his party had a bad crossing and were forced into Charleston and stayed in South Carolina. He settled at New Bordeaux. Prays for 20,000 acres in Georgia. *Signed*. 2½ pp. *Endorsed*, Recd. 26 November, Read 12 December 1771. [C.O.5, 651, fos. 129–130d]

1629

27 November, Savannah

President James Habersham to Earl of Hillsborough (No. 6). George Galphin reports that headman of Lower Creeks said that Indians were more to blame than whites, and that the Indians who were killed were of Oakfuskee town, some of whom killed two whites at the Ocoonees. Private satisfaction for public injuries is very dangerous: we need to be on more respectable footing in the back-country. I have again written to magistrates at Augusta to exert themselves to get the people who committed late murder. *Signed*. 2¼ pp. *Endorsed*, R, 24 January 1772. [C.O.5, 661, fos. 95–96d; signed duplicate, endorsed Read 15 May 1772, in C.O.5, 651, fos. 165–166d; entry in C.O.5, 678, pp. 255–257]

1630

28 November, Whitehall

Order of Council, referring following to Commissioners for Trade and Plantations. *Seal. Signed.* 1 p. *Endorsed,* Recd. 6 December 1771, Read 30 January 1772. *Enclosed :*

i. Memorial of Henry Remsen and associates to Privy Council, seeking confirmation of title bought from Indians to lands in Albany County, New York, on north and south sides of Mohawk River. Crown grants have deprived them of most valuable land. *Copy.* 1¼ pp.

ii. New York, 1 July 1771. Petition of same to Governor Earl of Dunmore, defining lands and asking for stay of grants there till H.M.'s pleasure be known. *Copy.* 2½ pp. [C.O.5, 1075, fos. 186–191d]

1631

28 November, Boston

Governor Thomas Hutchinson to Earl of Hillsborough (No. 16), enclosing papers on assault on Comptroller of Customs at Falmouth. I hope to secure assailants; J.P.s are charged with great deficiency. Opposition to Acts of Trade increases. Prosecution of persons concerned in late seditious papers is being attempted. General Court prorogued to 22 January. *Signed.* 1½ pp. *Endorsed,* R, 11 January 1772. *Enclosed :*

i. Custom-house, Boston, 26 November 1771. Commissioners of Customs to Governor Hutchinson, enclosing following. Disposition to import in defiance of laws of revenue and trade continues. *Copy,* certified by John Cotton, deputy secretary. *Signatories,* Benjamin Hallowell, jnr., Henry Hulton, William Burch. 1 p.

ii. Boston, 27 November 1771. Representation of Arthur Savage to Governor Hutchinson. On 12 November he was attacked by band of armed, disguised persons, who obtained from him name of an informer.
Mr Savage attended Governor and Council of Massachusetts, and identified certain of his assailants. Sworn to, 27 November 1771, before Governor Hutchinson. Attested by Thomas Flucker, secretary. *Copy,* certified as No. i. 5½ pp.

★ iii. Boston, 19 November 1771. Arthur Savage to Commissioners of Customs, describing assault. *Copy,* certified as No. i. 3½ pp.

iv. Boston, 27 November 1771. Proceedings of Council of Massachusetts on assault on Arthur Savage. *Copy,* certified as No. i. 2 pp.

v. *Massachusetts Gazette and Boston Weekly Newsletter,* 28 November 1771, containing reply by 'Chronus' to *Massachusetts Spy* of 14 November. *Printed.* 4 pp.

vi. New York, 6 November 1771. Governor William Tryon to Governor Hutchinson, proposing settlement of New York–Massachusetts boundary by agreement. *Copy.* 2½ pp.

vii. Boston, 25 and 28 November 1771. Two letters from Governor Hutchinson to Governor Tryon, in reply to preceding. *Copy.* 1½ pp. [C.O.5, 761, fos. 1–20d; signed duplicate of covering letter, endorsed Read 15 May 1772, and copies of first part of No. ii and of Nos. vi-vii, in C.O.5, 894, pp. 333–352; entry of covering letter in C.O.5, 768, pp. 222–223]

1632

29 November, Admiralty

Lords of Admiralty to Earl of Hillsborough, enclosing papers relating to lighthouse at Halifax, Nova Scotia. *Signed,* Sandwich, J. Buller, A. Hervey. 2 pp. *Enclosed :*

i. *Salisbury,* 9 October 1771. Commodore Gambier to Philip Stephens. *Copy.* 2¼ pp.

ii. 31 May 1771. Captain Linzee of *Beaver* sloop to Commodore Gambier. *Copy.* ½ p.

iii. Memorandum by Captain M. Squire. *Copy.* ½ p.

iv. Statement by Robert Arnold, master of *Senegal. Copy.* ½ p.

v. Halifax, 27 September 1771. Minutes of Council of Nova Scotia. *Copy.* 2 pp.

vi. Halifax, 26 September 1771. Governor Lord William Campbell to [Commodore Gambier]. *Copy.* ½ p.

vii. Hertford Street, 20 November 1771. Commodore Gambier to Philip Stephens. *Copy.* 3 pp. [C.O.5, 119, Pt. 1, fos. 43–58d; entry of covering letter in C.O.5, 247, pp. 27–28]

1633

[29 November]

Paper on proposals for payment to holders of Canada Reconnoissances. *French.* 2½ small pp. *Endorsed,* R, 29 November 1771 from M. Langlois. [C.O.5, 43, fos. 291–292d]

1634

[30 November]

Petition of Ursule Prevot, wife of Adrian Pochet de St André, lieutenant of infantry and J.P. in Canada, to Earl of Hillsborough, soliciting royal bounty. *French. Signed.* 2½ pp. *Endorsed,* Read by the King, 30 November. [C.O.5, 114, fos. 94–95d; entry in C.O.43, 13, pp. 19–20]

1635

2 December, Whitehall

* Earl of Hillsborough to Governor Earl of Dunmore (No. 4, separate), explaining difficulties about Virginia's proposed copper halfpence. £1000 would be better than £2500 for first experiment. *Draft.* 4 pp. [C.O.5, 1349, fos. 175–177d; entry in C.O.5, 1375, pp. 160–163]

1636

3 December, Whitehall

Same to Lieut.-Governor Michael Francklin. Return to Nova Scotia to take on government in absence of Lord William Campbell. *Draft.* ¾ p. [C.O.217, 48, fos. 78–79d; entry in C.O.218, 25, p. 99]

1637

3 December, New York

* Governor William Tryon to Earl of Hillsborough (No. 10). Only twenty-two miles of survey of line between New York and Canada so far completed; copy enclosed. I have proposed 1 March for commissioners to proceed: survey will be carried to main branch of Connecticut River. Council advised me to appoint some gentleman to give personal attendance to the matter in room of Mr Benzell, who preferred a trip to Canada. *Signed.* 2¼ pp. *Endorsed*, R, 13 January 1772. *Enclosed :*

> i. Map of part of latitude 45, boundary between New York and Quebec, by Joseph Smith, copied by C. J. Sauthier, 1771. 1 large p. [M.P.G.21] [C.O.5, 1103, fos. 3–5d; entry of covering letter in C.O.5, 1138, pp. 245–246; signed duplicate of covering letter, endorsed Read 15 May 1772, in C.O.5, 1075, fos. 209–210d]

1638

4 December, Whitehall

Earl of Hillsborough to Earl of Rochford. Judges in Massachusetts having hesitated to release Ebenezer Richardson, convicted of murder, without authentic copy of royal pardon, H.M. has consented that a general Newgate pardon pass Great Seal. *Draft.* 1¼ pp. [C.O.5, 138, fos. 210–211d; entry in C.O.5, 250, pp. 9–10]

1639

4 December, Whitehall

* Same to Lieut.-General Thomas Gage (No. 49), acknowledging letters. Batteries at Pensacola to be completed and barracks built as soon as may be. You are to order abandonment of Fort Chartres and reduction of all establishments incident to that post. If you think some temporary establishment should be effected at Kaskaskies or elsewhere in the district, you are to execute whatever plans you judge most effectual until final resolution shall be taken on arrangements finally necessary for that country. It is to be wished that troops there will be withdrawn or, if a number need to be retained, that it will be as small as possible. I have always thought that the inhabitants should be removed to Quebec or other established colony, but there are too many obstacles. You are to consider and report whether permanent establishment should be made there. Garrison at Fort Pitt also to be withdrawn, unless you think it absolutely necessary. Posts on the Lakes to be kept up, at least for the present; necessary repairs there to be executed. Order inhabitants of St Vincent to return from it; if they refuse, report what measures advisable to compel them. It is hoped that affair of insult to one of H.M. schooners off Cartagena will be satisfactorily settled. Duke of Gloucester has recovered from illness at Leghorn. *Draft.* 7¼ pp. [C.O.5, 89, fos. 180–184d; entry in C.O.5, 243, pp. 23–28]

1640

4 December, Whitehall

* Same to Governor William Tryon (No. 6). Jurisdiction in land dispute between New York and New Hampshire was finally decided by Order in Council of 20 July 1764. Final determination of claims of property was suspended, but Board of Trade has reported to Privy Council and necessary instructions will soon be sent. Your demand to governor of St Domingo for reparation approved, but you went too far in demanding punishment of officer responsible. It is not proper to put before your Council matters of general public nature not related to the colony. Report fully method of proceeding on application for grants of land; if there is abuse, it must be stopped. Communicating to Council a letter not containing H.M.'s directions to do so is breach of circular of 2 September 1768. Duke of Gloucester recovered from illness at Leghorn. *Draft.* 5 pp. [C.O.5, 1102, fos. 311–313d; entry in C.O.5, 1141, pp. 193–198]

1641

4 December, Whitehall

Same to Governor Walter Patterson (No. 4), acknowledging letter of 3 September. Ordinances referred to Board of Trade. Mr Wright approved as Surveyor. Plan of Charlotte Town must be left to your discretion. It is impracticable for me to advise you about public buildings: proceed within limits of allowance. *Draft.* 3½ pp. [C.O.226, 4, fos. 90–92d]

1642

4 December, Whitehall

Same to Governor Earl of Dunmore (No. 5), acknowledging letter of 9 July. Measures taken in Virginia for flood relief approved, though clause whereby Treasurer's notes are made tender in payment of taxes may contravene Act of Parliament. Fine on James Anderson remitted.

Papers sent concerning apprentice. Duke of Gloucester recovered from illness at Leghorn. *Draft.* 3 pp. *Enclosed:*

i. Petition of William Dolman to Commissioners for Trade and Plantations, praying for release of apprentice seduced into going to Virginia. 1 p. [C.O.5, 1349, fos. 178–181d; entry of covering letter in C.O.5, 1375, pp. 164–165]

1643

4 December, Whitehall

* Same to Governor Josiah Martin (No. 4), acknowledging No. 1. Your conduct approved. Pursue any lenient measure that may quiet people's minds. Any plan not contradicting Act of Parliament for restraining bills of credit will be favourably considered. Property of Benjamin Merril to be granted to his widow and children. *Draft.* 3¾ pp. [C.O.5, 314, fos. 280–283d; entry in C.O.5, 332, pp. 95–98]

1644

4 December, Whitehall

* Same to Governor Thomas Hutchinson (No. 11), acknowledging Nos. 5–14. Doctrines in address of House of Representatives in answer to your message on your 27th instruction strike at the dependence of colonies on Crown and Parliament. A tax imposed on income of a transient officer of the Crown, not deriving from money granted in the colony, is unjust and arbitrary. It is not the instruction but the King's right to give it that is questioned. Refuse assent to supply bills of such kind. Transmission of copy of royal warrant for pardon of criminals in colonies has been in use for more than fifty years. The judges' objections are not sufficient ground to change procedure. Authenticated copy of general Newgate pardon will, however, be sent as soon as completed. *Entry.* 5½ pp. [C.O.5, 765, pp. 215–220; draft in C.O.5, 760, fos. 308–312d]

1645

4 December, Whitehall

Same to Governor Lord William Campbell (No. 52), hoping for recovery of his health. Governors may not return to England during commission. Duke of Gloucester recovered from illness at Leghorn. *Draft.* 1¼ pp. [C.O.217, 48, fos. 82–83d; entry in C.O.218, 25, pp. 100–101]

1646

4 December, Whitehall

Same to Governor Peter Chester (No. 5), acknowledging Nos. 20–24. Settlement of banks of Mississippi and communication with the Iberville cannot be considered without Mr Durnford's report. More particular state required of grants of lands which have not been cultivated; it would be irregular to re-grant them without legal proof. I agree that exchanges of location of land grants would be bad precedent. *Draft.* 2¼ pp. [C.O.5, 588, pp. 435–438; entry in C.O.5, 619, pp. 86–87]

1647

4 December, Whitehall

Same to Governor William Franklin (No. 33), acknowledging Nos. 33–34. Your refusal to seal writ for new election for Essex County, New Jersey, approved. *Draft.* 1 p. [C.O.5, 991, fos. 94–95d; entry in C.O.5, 1003, p. 51]

1648

4 December, Whitehall

Same to Governor Lord Charles Montagu (No. 47), acknowledging letter of 26 September. Hopes administration will not be entangled with difficulties created by Assembly and that additional instruction will be seen as restoration of constitution. Mr Milligen's memorial referred to Treasury. Duke of Gloucester recovered from disorder. *Draft.* 2 pp. [C.O.5, 394, fos. 102–103d; entry in C.O.5, 408, pp. 71–73]

1649

4 December, Whitehall

Same to Governor Joseph Wanton (No. 22), acknowledging letter of 3 July. Letter and declaration of John, Thomas and Samuel Freebody are now before Privy Council. *Draft.* 1¼ pp. [C.O.5, 1284, fos. 156–157d; entry in C.O.5, 1301, pp. 450–451]

1650

4 December, Whitehall

Same to Lieut.-Governor H. T. Cramahé (No. 42), acknowledging Nos. 12–14. King approves your continuing Quebec–New York boundary as far as Connecticut River. Do not consent to appointment of commissioners to attend congress on any occasion in future. Delay in settlement of affairs of Quebec has been unavoidable. Duke of Gloucester recovered from illness at Leghorn. *Draft.* 3 pp. [C.O.42, 31, fos. 67–68d; entry in C.O.43, 8, pp. 98–100]

1651

4 December, Whitehall

Same to Deputy Governor Robert Eden (No. 22), acknowledging No. 10. I cannot suppose that Maryland will not revive the Inspection law. I see with satisfaction return of confidence between Britain and colonies. *Draft.* 1 p. [C.O.5, 1284, fos. 100–101d; entry in C.O.5, 1301, p. 17]

1652

4 December, Whitehall

Same to Lieut.-Governor John Moultrie (No. 43), acknowledging Nos. 2–5. Your application to Major Mackenzie was justified. Your proposal of occasional presents to Indians deserves attention. Discontinuance of allowance to Provost Marshal was proper. *Draft.* 1½ pp. [C.O.5, 552, fos. 62–63d; entry in C.O.5, 566, pp. 50–51]

1653

4 December, Whitehall

* Same to President James Habersham (No. 39). Your conduct in not calling Assembly approved. H.M. believes that the unwarrantable doctrines of late Assembly are not the sense of people in general and will be discountenanced by every honest man. When new Assembly meets, you will negative their choice of Speaker, and if they dispute the right of such negative you will dissolve them forthwith. *Draft.* 2¼ pp. [C.O.5, 661, fos. 73–74d; entry in C.O.5, 677, pp. 60–62]

1654

4 December, Whitehall

Same to President Benjamin Green, acknowledging letter of 18 October. Lieut.-Governor Francklin has been ordered to return to Nova Scotia. *Draft.* 1 p. [C.O.217, 48, fos. 80–81d; entry in C.O.218, 25, p. 100]

1655

4 December, Whitehall

* Same to Sir William Johnson (No. 17), acknowledging No. 16, and expressing satisfaction at detection of authors of attempt to stir up Indians on the Ohio and at outcome of congress with Six Nations at Johnson Hall. On plan for Indian affairs, nothing can be done until commissioners meeting at New York on 1 December have made recommendations. General Gage has stated need to chastise Kickapoos and Potawatomis. *Draft.* 3¾ pp. [C.O.5, 72, fos. 317–319d; entry in C.O.5, 241, pp. 394–397]

1656

4 December, New York

* Lieut.-General Thomas Gage to Earl of Hillsborough (No. 67). Sir W. Johnson is satisfied that Six Nations are resolved to manifest fidelity to English and bring Western Indians to order. News from Ohio is that eleven villages of Ouabache, Miamis and Lake Michigan Indians will attack Illinois next spring. Ohio tribes resent settlers; speech enclosed. Mr Croghan has given up as Sir W. Johnson's deputy.

Repairs at Castle William will not be completed before midsummer. *Signed.* 2¾ pp. *Endorsed,* R, 13 January 1772. *Enclosed:*

    * i. Speech from Chiefs of Delawares, Munsies and Mohicans, to Governors of Pennsylvania, Maryland and Virginia, protesting at encroachment west of Alleghanies. Meeting desired. Killbuck, speaker. *Copy.* 2½ pp. [C.O.5, 90, fos. 3–6d; entry in C.O.5, 235, pp. 1–3]

1657

4 December, Williamsburg

Governor Earl of Dunmore to Earl of Hillsborough (No. 5), enclosing following. *Signed.* ½ p. *Endorsed,* R, 27 January 1772. *Enclosed:*

    i. List of ships entered inwards, Hampton, 5 April–5 July 1771. *Signed,* Wilson Miles Cary, Naval Officer. 1 large p.

    ii. Same, outwards, same period. 1 large p.

    iii. Same, inwards, 5 July–10 October 1771. 1 large p.

    iv. Same, outwards, same period. *Signed,* as No. i. 1 large p. [C.O.5, 1350, fos. 7–10d; entry of covering letter in C.O.5, 1372, p. 193]

1658

4 December, New York

Governor William Tryon to Earl of Hillsborough (No. 11), enclosing report of seizures since arrival in government. 4 Geo. III c. 15 gives governor one-third of seizures but, taken with 5 Geo. III c. 45, excludes him from share of seizures not made on land. Requests share equal to that of flag officer. *Signed.* 3¾ pp. *Endorsed,* R, 13 January 1772. *Enclosed:*

    * i. Customs House, New York, 29 November 1771. Account of seizures made by ships of war in port of New York: three vessels. Account of seizures made by officers of Customs in the port: two vessels. *Copy. Signatories,* Andrew Elliott, Collector; Lambert Moore, Comptroller. 1 p. [C.O.5, 1103, fos. 6–9d; entry of covering letter in C.O.5, 1138, pp. 246–248; signed duplicate of covering letter, endorsed Read 15 May 1772, and copy of enclosure, in C.O.5, 1075, fos. 207–208d, 211–213d]

1659

4 December, New York

Same to John Pownall, acknowledging letters of 4 and 17 September. *Signed.* ½ p. *Endorsed,* R, 14 January 1772. [C.O.5, 1103, fos. 12–13d]

1660

4 December, Portsmouth, N.H.

★ John Wentworth, Surveyor-General of Woods, to Earl of Hillsborough, acknowledging letter of 3 July. Mr Jackson's reports confirm that pines on both sides of Kennebec River belong to H.M. Proprietors have asked for compensation; copy of their petition enclosed. Complaints of waste are partly justified, so many trees selected for masts proving rotten, and others damaged when sprung. Prosecutions for trespass met with difficulties, particularly from Judge Wells of New York, and have been expensive. *Signed.* 8 pp. *Endorsed,* R, 22 May 1772. *Enclosed:*

i. Extracts from patents of New Plymouth and other Plymouth records relating to lands on Kennebec River. Manuscript copy of pamphlet referred to in letter of 22 October 1770 [*see* No. 682]: one printed copy only could be got at that time, which was sent to Treasury. 27 pp.

ii. Boston, 18 December 1771. Petition of proprietors of Kennebec purchase, Lincoln County, Massachusetts, to Lords of Admiralty. There is no reservation of white pines in their titles. They have preserved pines, but to no advantage to themselves. Agents of contractors damage lands; compensation sought. *Copy. Signatories,* James Bowdoin, James Pitts, Silvester Gardiner, Benjamin Hallowell, committee of proprietors. 3 pp.

iii. Brief state of title of Kennebec proprietors to Kennebec purchase. *Copy.* 13½ pp.

iv. Extract from last Act of Parliament for preserving H.M.'s woods in America. *Copy.* 1 p.

v. Account of expenses in prosecutions against William Dean, Willard Dean and William Dean, jnr., at suit of John Wentworth. *Copy.* 6½ pp. [C.O.5, 73, fos. 109–141d; entry of covering letter in C.O.5, 228, pp. 132–141]

1661

4 December, Buckingham-street, London

Lieut.-Governor Michael Francklin to Earl of Hillsborough, acknowledging letter of 3rd inst. I shall embark for Nova Scotia by first conveyance. *Signed.* ¾ p. *Endorsed,* R, 5th. [C.O.217, 48, fos. 84–85d; entry in C.O.218, 18, p. 10]

1662

5 December, Whitehall

John Pownall to Grey Cooper, sending memorial of Mr Milligen, surgeon to garrisons in South Carolina, for additional salary. *Draft.* ½ p. [C.O.5, 145, fos. 12–13d; entry in C.O.5, 250, p. 10]

1663

5 December, New York

Governor William Tryon to Earl of Hillsborough (No. 12). Assembly prorogued to 7 January. *Signed.* ½ p. *Endorsed,* R, 13 January 1772. [C.O.5, 1103, fos. 10–11d; entry in C.O.5, 1138, p. 248; signed duplicate, endorsed Read 15 May 1772, in C.O.5, 1075, fos. 214–215d]

1664

10 December, Whitehall

John Pownall to Richard Jackson, requesting draft of clause to be put in commissions to governors empowering them to issue commissions for custody of idiots. *Entry.* 1 p. [C.O.324, 18, p. 392]

1665

10 December, New York

* Governor William Tryon to Earl of Hillsborough (No. 13). M. Chartier Lolbiniere presented enclosed claim to seigniories of De Hokard, north of Crown Point, and D'Allanville, south of Crown Point. Almost all of former has been granted away by this province; Council did not esteem his title to latter good. He goes to England to implore H.M.'s attention. Papers expected from Lieut.-Governor Cramahé respecting French claims to lands on Lake Champlain; I hope some principle will be established by H.M. that will finally settle disputes. *Signed.* 3¼ pp. *Endorsed,* R, 11 February 1772. *Enclosed:*

i. Petition of Michel Chartier de Lolbiniere of Canada to Governor Tryon, claiming seigniories, one on Lake Champlain extending to Lake George, the other on east side of Lake Champlain. *Copy,* certified by G. Banyar. 2¼ pp.

ii. New York, 2 December 1771. Minutes of Council of New York, recording consideration of above petition. *Copy,* certified as No. i. 2¼ pp. [C.O.5, 1103, fos. 18–24d; entry of covering letter in C.O.5, 1138, pp. 251–252; duplicate of covering letter, endorsed Read 15 May 1772, in C.O.5, 1075, fos. 216–218d]

1666

11 December, Boston

Governor Thomas Hutchinson to Earl of Hillsborough (No. 17), enclosing following. Council was unanimous in advice to dismiss J.P. concerned in publication. *Signed.* 1 small p. *Endorsed,* R, 20 January 1772. *Enclosed:*

i. Boston, 16 November, 10 December 1771. Minutes of Council of Massachusetts, recording proceedings on *Massachusetts Spy* of 14 November. Joseph Greenleaf, supposed to be concerned in printing it, and not attending according to summons, was dismissed office of J.P. *Copy,* certified by Thomas Flucker, secretary. 3 pp.

ii. Boston, 27 November 1771. Same. *Copy*, of No. 1631iv, certified as No. i. 1½ pp.

iii. *Massachusetts Gazette and Boston Weekly Newsletter*, 5 December 1771, with Supplement. *Printed*. 6 pp.

iv. *Massachusetts Gazette and Boston Weekly Newsletter*, 12 December 1771, with Supplement. *Printed*. 6 pp. [C.O.5, 761, fos. 23–34d; entry of covering letter in C.O.5, 768, p. 224]

1667

12 December, Whitehall

John Pownall to Richard Jackson, sending papers relative to Act passed in West Florida in 1770, sent 30 October last. *Entry*. ½ p. [C.O.5, 600, p. 233]

1668

12 December, New Bern

* Governor Josiah Martin to Earl of Hillsborough (No. 7), enclosing following. Most difficult business is to provide for militia forces. It appears that this can be done only by issue of debenture notes. H.M.'s pardon solicited for persons concerned in destroying General Waddell's ammunition. Pardon of as great extent as H.M. shall see fit may be healing measure. H.M.'s favour solicited to widow and seven children of Benjamin Merrill, executed. Papers enclosed on detention of vessel at Vera Cruz. King Pow of Cattawba nation visited last month; the tribe amounts to 600. *Signed*. 5¼ pp. *Endorsed*, R, 27 March 1772. *Enclosed*:

i. Speech of Governor Martin to Assembly of North Carolina. *Copy*, certified by J. Martin. 2½ pp.

ii. Address of Council of North Carolina to Governor Martin. *Copy*. *Signatory*, James Hassell, president. 2¾ pp.

iii. Reply of Governor Martin to preceding. *Copy*, signed by J. Martin. 1¼ pp.

iv. Address of Assembly of North Carolina to Governor Martin. Prohibition of use of paper money changes inconvenience of want of specie into real distress. *Copy*. *Signatory*, R. Caswell, Speaker. 1¾ pp.

v. Reply of Governor Martin to preceding. *Copy*, signed by J. Martin. ½ p.

vi. 7 December 1771. Petition of Assembly of North Carolina to Governor Martin for pardon for all concerned in late insurrection except Herman Husband, Rednap Howell and William Butler. *Copy*. *Signatory*, R. Caswell, Speaker. By order, J. Green, jnr., clerk. ½ p.

vii. New Bern, 9 December 1771. Reply of Governor Martin to preceding. I will lay your request before H.M. *Copy,* signed by J. Martin. ½ p.

viii. Names of persons concerned in blowing up General Waddell's ammunition: James White, James Ashmore, Joshua Hadley, Robert Davis, Benjamin Coghean, William White, jnr., John White, Robert Carruthers. ½ p.

ix. 11 December 1771. Petition of Assembly of North Carolina to Governor Martin for release of master, crew and effects of *John & Elizabeth,* detained at Vera Cruz. *Copy. Signatories,* as No. vi. 1¼ pp.

x. New Bern, 13 December 1771. Certificate by Governor Martin that James Biggleston is notary and tabellion public for Port Beaufort, North Carolina. *Signed.* 1 p.

xi. Affidavit, sworn 3 December 1771 before John Clitherall, by John Simpson of Pitt County, owner of *John & Elizabeth.* Letter from Benjamin Rose to his wife, referring to detention of ship. Letter, dated 30 July 1770, from Ichabod Simpson to Andrew Black, concerning ship. *Copy,* certified by J. Biggleston. 5 pp.

xii. 13 December 1771. Certificate by John Biggleston that No. xi is true copy. *Seal. Signed.* 1 p. [C.O.5, 315, fos. 19–45d; signed duplicate of covering letter, endorsed Read 29 July 1772, and copies of enclosures, No. x dated 2 February 1772 and No. xii dated 1 February 1772, in C.O.5, 302, fos. 129–156d; entry of covering letter in C.O.5, 329, pp. 29–36]

1669

[12 December]

* Memorial of Governor James Wright to Earl of Hillsborough, setting forth insecurity of settlers in Georgia by reason of lack of force to repel Indian depredations. To regulate Indian trade, the nations or tribes should be formed into districts, each province being allotted district and empowered to grant licences. Total stoppage of trade could be imposed, as the behaviour of the Indians may require, provided all provinces concerned were so instructed. There is a tract of rich land between boundary of Georgia and Broad and Oconee Rivers, which Cherokees wish to cede in payment of debts due to traders, though Creeks also claim it. Settlement thereon, and sale of the land in tracts of not more than 1000 acres, would produce enough money to support two troops of rangers, 50 in each, with officers, for defence and security thereof. *Signed.* 14¾ pp. *Endorsed,* Read 12 December 1771. *Enclosed:*

i. Schedule of papers relative to above memorial, with notes thereon. *Signed.* J. Wright. 3¼ pp.

ii. Chote, Cherokee nation, Upper Hills, 22 February 1771. Deed of sale by warriors and sachems to their traders, in consideration

of debts, of land on Broad River. *Copy. Signatories,* Chote: Oconas-
tato. Toqueh: Villanawau. Island Town: Judd's Friend or Ostenego.
Settico: Villanota. Great Tallico: Kenatita. Chilhoue: Hienttylisky
(?). Chilhoue: Scahylosky. Tenassie: Ugy Yuley. *Witnesses,* John
Godfrey Riegger, John Walker, Richard Field. 1 large p.

iii. Toogoolie, 7 March 1771. Speech of Judd's Friend at a convention
of Overhills Cherokee chiefs, asserting right of Cherokees to dispose
of their land to traders. *Copy,* certified by J. Wright. 1¾ pp.

iv. Chotee, Upper Cherokees, 3 May 1771. Talk by headmen and
warriors of Cherokee nation to Governor Wright, indicating readiness to grant the Great King land from Little River up Savannah
River for sixty miles by sixty miles, in consideration of payment of
debts to traders. *Copy. Signatories,* Occunastota, Wolenawa, Judd's
Friend, Attacullaculla. *Witnesses,* Hugh Hamilton, John Godfrey
Riegger, John Walker, Samuel Benn. 1¾ pp.

v. Savannah, 23 May 1771. Talk by Governor Wright to Ocunnas-
tota, Willanawa, Judd's Friend and Attakullakulla, acknowledging
No. iv. I am going to England and will represent your case to the
Great King. Meanwhile you must try to prevail with Creeks to join
you in surrender of these lands. Your people and the traders must not
mark out the lands till the Great King's answer is given. *Copy.* 2 pp.

* vi. Augusta, 6 June 1771. Philemon Kemp, clerk to Robert Mackay
& Co., to Governor Wright, sending talk, dated Oakehoy, Upper
Creeks, 1 May 1771, from Emistisigo and other chiefs of Upper
Creek Nation to the governor. The chiefs protest at white encroach-
ments. They have heard of cession of land at head of the Oconis by
Cherokees. *Copy,* certified by J. Wright. 6 pp.

vii. 25 June 1771. Governor Wright to Emistesego and Gun Merchant, acknowledging No. vi. Your people have killed upwards of
ten whites since Treaty of Augusta. Cherokees must settle with you
rights to lands they wish to cede in payment of debts. I will inquire
into reported encroachments by whites. *Copy.* 2 pp.

vii. Near Fort Charlotte, 8 June 1771, at meeting of Cherokee Indians
and traders. Speech of Ustonaco or Judd's Friend, the Indian chief
who was in England. Land proposed to be ceded is our's, not Creeks,
they know it well. We hope the Great King will not object. Speech of
Oconnastata: if there is any misunderstanding between us and the
Creeks about the land, I will settle it. Judd's Friend spoke again and
showed King George's talk. Everything is the same here as it was at
Chotee. *Copy,* certified by J. Wright. 3 pp.

* ix. Memorial of principal traders to the Creek and Cherokee
nations, to Governor Wright, explaining circumstances of cession of
land on Savannah River to pay off debts. The lands are claimed by
both nations but occupied by neither, and are too near our settlements to be hunting-grounds. The tract is upwards of three million

acres of good land and, if sold in small tracts for moderate consideration, would produce more than enough to discharge the Indians' debts. Pray that distressful, indeed ruinous, situation of the traders be placed before H.M. *Signed,* George Galphin; James Jackson & Co.; Robert Mackay & Co.; for Martin Campbell & Co., Woodgion; Rae, Whitefield & Co.; Edward Bernard; J(?). Waters; James Grierson; James Spalding & Co.; Edward Keating. 2 large pp. [C.O.5, 651, fos. 90–128d]

1670

13 December, Admiralty

Philip Stephens to John Pownall, notifying arrival of *Carysford* at Cork from Jamaica. *Signed.* ½ p. *Addressed.* [C.O.5, 119, Pt. 1, fos. 59–60d]

1671

13 December

Richard Jackson to Commissioners for Trade and Plantations, reporting on twenty-five Acts passed in Massachusetts in April and July 1771, proper in point of law. *Signed.* 2½ pp. *Endorsed,* Recd. 18 December 1771, Read 27 February 1772. [C.O.5, 894, pp. 325–328]

1672

14 December, New York

Governor William Tryon to Earl of Hillsborough (No. 79), enclosing following and soliciting H.M.'s pardon for James Stewart, James Emmerson, William Brown, Forester Mercer, James Copeland and Herman Cox, convicted of high treason at Hillsborough Superior Court. Troops under General Waddell, upwards of 400 not included in enclosed. *Signed.* PS. This letter part of North Carolina correspondence. 2 pp. *Endorsed,* R, 11 February 1772. *Enclosed:*

    i. Return of army encamped at Hermon Husband's on Sandy Creek, 22 May 1771, by detachments and ranks. Total of rank and file, 1017. Wake detachment and light infantry did not join the army before 20 May. *Signed,* William Tryon. 1 p. [C.O.5, 315, fos. 3–6d; entry of covering letter in C.O.5, 329, pp. 17–18]

1673

14 December, R.I.

Governor Joseph Wanton to Earl of Hillsborough, sending answer of General Assembly of Rhode Island to letter of 19 July. Greatest harmony subsists. *Signed.* 1 small p. *Endorsed,* R, 7 February 1772. [C.O.5, 1284, fos. 166–167d; signed duplicate, endorsed Read 15 May 1772, in C.O.5, 1278, fos. 78–79d; entry in C.O.5, 1300, p. 32]

1674

16 December, Williamsburg

Governor Earl of Dunmore to Earl of Hillsborough (No. 6), enclosing following. House of Burgesses meets 6 February. *Signed.* ½ p. *Endorsed,* R, 29 February. *Enclosed:*

    i. Account of quitrents in Virginia, 1770. *Signed,* Richard Corbin, deputy Receiver-General. Examined by Edward Foy, deputy Auditor, and Earl of Dunmore. 3½ pp. [C.O.5, 1350, fos. 13–16d; entry of covering letter in C.O.5, 1372, p. 194]

1675

16 December, Denmark-st., Soho, London

Rev. J. J. Majendie to John Pownall, sending papers concerning Mr Martel. Scheme of new French colony in North America (he to be pastor) having miscarried, he is object worthy of commiseration. *Signed.* 1½ small pp. *Endorsed,* Read 18 December 1771. [C.O.217, 26, fos. 97–98d]

1676

18 December, Whitehall

Commissioners for Trade and Plantations to the King, recommending for approval four private Acts passed in Virginia in 1769–1770 concerning lands of Lewellen Jones, David Garland, Charles Carter, Francis Eppes. *Entry. Signatories,* Hillsborough, Soame Jenyns, William Fitzherbert, Greville. 2½ pp. [C.O.5, 1369, pp. 242–244; draft in C.O.5, 1336, fos. 208–209d]

1677

18 December, Whitehall

Same to same, recommending confirmation of Act passed in South Carolina in 1765 to promote Act to incorporate Winyaw Society. *Draft. Signatories,* Hillsborough, Soame Jenyns, W. Fitzherbert, Greville. 1 p. [C.O.5, 381, fos. 373–374d; entry in C.O.5, 404, pp. 455–456]

1678

18 December, Whitehall

Same to same, recommending grant of 5000 acres of land in South Carolina to Louis Dumesnil de St Pierre. *Draft. Signatories,* as preceding. 3½ pp. [C.O.5, 381, fos. 375–376d; entry in C.O.5, 404, pp. 457–460]

1679

18 December, Whitehall

Same to same, recommending confirmation of Act passed in New York in 1771 to empower Philip Cortlandt to hold an estate in fee simple. *Entry. Signatories,* as preceding. 1½ pp. [C.O.5, 1131, pp. 456–457; draft in C.O.5, 1080, pp. 475–478]

1680

18 December, Whitehall

John Pownall to Richard Jackson, sending papers on claim of Assembly of New Jersey to right of ordering writ for new election on resignation by Representative, for report on legality thereof. *Entry.* 1 p. [C.O.5, 999, p. 252]

1681

18 December, Whitehall

William Knox to William De Brahm, transmitting following, so that he may prepare justification of his conduct. *Draft.* ¾ p. *Enclosed:*

    i. Heads of complaint against William De Brahm, Surveyor of East Florida and Surveyor of Southern District of America. *Copy.* 5½ pp. [C.O.5, 72, fos. 320–325d; entry of covering letter in C.O.5, 241, p. 398]

1682

18 December, Admiralty

Lords of Admiralty to Earl of Hillsborough, enclosing papers concerning conduct of Spanish *guardacostas. Signed,* J. Buller, C. J. Fox, A. Hervey. 1 p. *Endorsed,* R, 19th. *Enclosed:*

    i. Six papers on above subject. [C.O.5, 119, Pt. 1, fos. 61–75d; entry of covering letter and of five enclosures in C.O.5, 247, pp. 29–37]

1683

18 December

Richard Jackson to Commissioners for Trade and Plantations, reporting twenty-one Acts passed in Nova Scotia in 1771 proper in point of law. It is submitted whether it may not be advisable to recommend disallowance of Act of 1771 additional to Act relating to wills etc. *Signed.* 3¼ large pp. *Endorsed,* Recd. 18 December 1771, Read 5 February 1772. [C.O.217, 26, fos. 101–103d]

1684

20 December, Whitehall

Earl of Hillsborough to Earl of Rochford, sending further paper on insult stated to have been offered to H.M.'s flag at Cartagena in case of *Hawke* schooner. *Draft.* ½ p. [C.O.5, 138, fos. 212–213d; entry in C.O.5, 250, p. 11]

1685

20 December, Admiralty

Lords of Admiralty to Earl of Hillsborough, enclosing papers relating to conduct of logwood cutters in Bay of Honduras. *Signed,* J. Buller, C. J. Fox, A. Hervey. 1 p. *Endorsed,* R, 21st. *Enclosed:*

    i. Thirty-three papers on above subject. [C.O.5, 119, Pt. 1, fos. 78–143d; entry of covering letter and list of enclosures in C.O.5, 247, pp. 38–39]

1686

20 December, Whitehall

John Pownall to John Robinson, sending extract of letter from General Melville with views on disposal of King's lands in Bequia. *Draft.* ½ p. [C.O.5, 145, fos. 24–25d; entry in C.O.5, 250, p. 12]

1687

20 December, Treasury

John Robinson to John Pownall, enclosing following, for Lord Hillsborough to instruct Governor of Newfoundland to support Customs officers. *Signed.* 1 p. *Endorsed,* R, 21st. *Enclosed:*

    i. London, 5 December 1771. Memorial of Alexander Dun, Collector of Customs at Newfoundland, to Lords of Treasury. Trading people allege government has no right to appoint Customs officers there. Governor Byron has not fully supported the officers. Unless his fees are secured, memorialist will be unable to execute office. *Copy.* 4¼ pp.

    ii. St John's, 28 July 1770. Order by Governor John Byron regulating fees to be charged by Customs officers at St John's; and letter, dated 19 September, from him to Comptroller of Customs authorizing same fees as at Halifax. *Copy.* 5 pp. [C.O.5, 145, fos. 14–23d; entry of covering letter in C.O.5, 247, pp. 37–38]

1688

20 December, Admiralty

Philip Stephens to John Pownall, sending originals of papers mentioned in Board's letter of this date. Return requested. *Signed.* 1 small p. *Endorsed,* R, 21st. [C.O.5, 119, Pt. 1, fos. 76–77d]

1689

24 December, London

* Thomas and John Penn to Earl of Hillsborough, acknowledging letter of 19 July. Customs officers are assisted by government of Pennsylvania. Matter has not been truly or impartially represented to you. *Signed.* 3 small pp. [C.O.5, 1284, fos. 25–26d; entry in C.O.5, 1300, pp. 366–368]

1690

26 December, New Bern

* Governor Josiah Martin to Earl of Hillsborough (No. 8). Assembly dissolved 23rd inst. I have assented to Act for raising £60,000 proclamation money, the only expedient they would adopt. Instruction regarding boundary with South Carolina received; Assembly refused to defray charge. No opening last session to procure amendments in laws proposed by Commissioners for Trade and Plantations in letter of 12 December 1770. After action with insurgents, 6409 men took oaths to government; 7 or 800 stand of arms collected from them, mostly unserviceable. *Signed.* 4 pp. *Endorsed,* R, 27 March 1772. *Enclosed :*

i. 21 December 1771. Address of Assembly of North Carolina to Governor Martin, protesting at boundary with South Carolina. *Copy. Signatory,* R. Caswell, Speaker. By order, J. Green, jnr., clerk. 2 pp. [C.O.5, 315, fos. 46–49d; signed duplicate of covering letter, endorsed Read 29 July 1772, and copy of enclosure, in C.O.5, 302, fos. 157–161d; entry of covering letter in C.O.5, 329, pp. 36–41]

1691

26 December, Burlington

Governor William Franklin to Commissioners for Trade and Plantations. Assembly of New Jersey agreed to appointing of agent by votes of Council and Assembly, to which I concurred. *Signed.* 1 p. *Endorsed,* Recd. 20 February, Read 21 February 1772. [C.O.5, 979, fos. 41–42d]

1692

26 December, Montreal

Joseph Fleury, Seigneur de Dechambault, to Governor Guy Carleton, enclosing following. *French. Signed.* 4 pp. *Endorsed,* R, 26 March 1772. Read by the King. *Enclosed :*

i. Montreal, 24 October 1765. Agreement for use of house in Montreal by troops. *French. Copy. Signatories,* Dechambault, John Carden. 1 small p.

ii. Memorial of Joseph Fleury to Earl of Hillsborough, praying for recovery of house in Michilimackinac and damages. *French*. 3 pp. *Endorsed*, Read by the King.

iii. Montreal, 26 December 1771. Memorial of same to the King, concerning use of houses in Montreal and Michilimackinac by troops. *French*. *Signed*. 6¼ pp. *Endorsed*, Read by the King. [C.O.42, 31, fos. 80–88d]

1693

27 December, St James's

Order of King in Council, approving Act passed in Virginia in 1769 to dock entail of lands of David Garland. Like Order in respect of three other private Acts passed 1767–1770. *Copy*. 1½ pp. *Endorsed*, Recd. 12 December, Read 21 December 1772. [C.O.5, 1334, fos. 28–29d]

1694

27 December, St James's

Same, approving Act passed in New York in 1770 to enable Philip Van Cortlandt to hold house in fee simple. *Copy*. 1 p. *Endorsed*, Recd. 12 December, Read 21 December 1772. [C.O.5, 1076, fos. 212–213d]

1695

27 December, Burlington

Governor William Franklin to Earl of Hillsborough (No. 36). Assembly have provided for arrears due for troops, disallowing two articles on General Gage's account but allowing all that was usual. Colony is to raise £15,000 a year till 1783 to extinguish debt from late war of £200,000 currency, and think they should be exempt from supporting troops. Appointment of agent was carried with difficulty. *Signed*. 3 pp. *Endorsed*, R, 21 February 1772. *Enclosed*:

i. 21 November 1771. Governor Franklin's speech to Assembly of New Jersey. *Printed*. 1 p.

ii. 25 November 1771. Address of Representatives of New Jersey to Governor Franklin regretting disallowance of Acts. *Printed*. 1 p.

iii. 7 December 1771. Governor Franklin's message to Assembly on provision for troops. With Assembly's reply of 16 December 1771. *Copy*. 3½ pp.

iv. 18 December 1771. Governor Franklin's message to Assembly on same subject. With Assembly's reply of 20 December 1771. *Copy*. 3½ pp.

v. 21 December 1771. Governor Franklin's speech to Assembly at closing of session. *Copy*. 1¼ pp. [C.O.5, 991, fos. 100–109d; entry of covering letter in C.O.5, 1001, pp. 144–147]

1696

27 December, Berners-Street, London

* Governor James Wright to Commissioners for Trade and Plantations, arguing against grants of large tracts of land in the back parts of Georgia, and elsewhere. Such settlements, out of reach of law and government, would be too independent and become province within province. Coastal lands should be well-peopled and settlement gradually extended. My ideas are not chimerical, I know something of the situation and state of things in America. *Signed.* 2¾ pp. *Endorsed,* Recd. 2 January, Read 28 March 1772. [C.O.5, 651, fos. 153–154d]

1697

28 December, Mobile

* Governor Peter Chester to Earl of Hillsborough (no number, duplicate numbered 39), reporting meeting with Creeks. We asked for cession of land on River Escambia but they evaded the request by saying property of their lands was in common. They agreed to marking of old boundary line next May. Superintendent thinks they will grant the land on Escambia. Minutes of congress sent by this packet. Between 1500 and 1600 Chickasaws and Choctaws have arrived here, more expected. No. 4 and Mr Pownall's of 4 September acknowledged. *Signed.* 4 pp. *Endorsed,* R, 4 March 1772. [C.O.5, 589, pp. 13–18; signed duplicate, endorsed Read 15 May 1772, in C.O.5, 578, pp. 351–356; entry in C.O.5, 621, pp. 121–125]

1698

28 December, St Augustine

Lieut.-Governor John Moultrie to Earl of Hillsborough (No. 10). Dr Turnbull has resigned from Council; William Owen appointed until H.M.'s pleasure be known. There are only five members of Council appointed by H.M., including myself, now in East Florida. Frederick G. Mulcaster and Arthur Gordon recommended to be of the Council. *Signed.* 2 pp. *Endorsed,* R, 13 April. [C.O.5, 552, fos. 103–104d; signed duplicate, endorsed Read 15 May 1772, in C.O.5, 545, fos. 69–70d; entry in C.O.5, 567, pp. 217–218]

1699

29 December, Mobile

John Stuart to Earl of Hillsborough (No. 37), acknowledging letter of 3 July and leave to go to northern province on account of health. *Signed.* 1½ small pp. *Endorsed,* R, 4 March 1772. [C.O.5, 73, fos. 22–23d; entry in C.O.5, 228, p. 107]

1700

29 December, Mobile

Same to same (No. 38), acknowledging No. 22. About 1500 Choctaws and Chickasaws are here. Creek determination upon lands on Scambia expected. *Signed.* 2 small pp. *Endorsed*, R, 4 March 1772. *Enclosed:*

★ i. Pensacola, 29 October–2 November 1771. Report of congress of chiefs and warriors of Upper Creek nation, held by John Stuart. Present: Governor Chester; Brig.-General Haldimand; Lieut.-Governor Durnford; Charles Stuart; members of Council of West Florida; Captain Carkett of H.M.S. *Lowestoft;* Major Dickson and officers of 16th Regiment; Emistisiguo, great medal chief; Noethlocko or the Second Man, Tepoy or the Fighter, and Beaver Tooth King, small medal chiefs; with other ruling chiefs and principal warriors of sixteen towns of Alibamous, Abikas and Tallipousses; Joseph Cornell, John Simpson, interpreters. With treaty confirming former cession of land and granting further cession on Coosa River. *Copy*, certified by William Ogilvy. 24 pp. [C.O.5, 73, fos. 24–37d; entry of covering letter in C.O.5, 228, pp. 108–109]

1701

30 December, Savannah

President James Habersham to Earl of Hillsborough (No. 7). Settler named Carey at Queensborough has been murdered by a Creek. Talk received from Lower Creeks saying that Indian killed at Oconee River did not steal horses. They know I have no coercive power to oblige them to compliance with treaty. I have hinted to them that trade may be stopped: to do so would need unanimous consent of Virginia and all governments south, and the stop would have to include Cherokees, Chickasaws and Choctaws. Creeks want to keep trade open, for they cannot now subsist without supplies from English. Our commerce with Great Britain would soon increase if we were secure from insults of any Indian neighbours. I shall not call Assembly, unless for utmost necessity, until I know H.M.'s pleasure. *Signed.* 2½ pp. *Endorsed*, R, 24 February 1772. *Enclosed:*

i. Minutes of Council of Georgia, 9 December 1771, recording talk from headmen of Creeks, 2 November 1771; George Galphin's letter to the Indians, 2 December 1771; and President Habersham's talk to headmen of Creeks, 9 December 1771, demanding that the murderer, Sugley, be killed. *Copy*, certified by Alexander Wylly. 6 pp. [C.O.5, 661, fos. 97–102d; signed duplicate of covering letter, endorsed Read 15 May 1772, and copy of enclosure in C.O.5, 651, fos. 167–171d; entry of covering letter in C.O.5, 678, pp. 258–261]

1702

[?*1771*]

Letter from Lieutenant P. Sinclair, 15th regiment, further soliciting claim to occupy house in Detroit. Contractors for vessels on the Lakes have not fulfilled one article of their contract. *Signed*. 1 p. [C.O.5, 89, fos. 178–179d]

1703

[?1771]

Paper by holders of Canada Reconnoissances to [?Lord Rochford], accusing French of bad faith. 4 small pp. [C.O.5, 43, fos. 293–294d]

1704

[?1771]

Part of paper on subject of Canada Reconnoissances. Care must be taken in lottery to take place in March. 1 small p. [C.O.5, 43, fos. 295–296d]

1705

[?1771]

Explanation of procedure under treaty signed at London 29 March last for liquidating Canada paper. *Draft*. 1½ pp. [C.O.5, 43, fos. 308–309d]

1706

[?1771]

Memorial of holders of Canada Reconnoissances to Lord Weymouth, applying again for assistance in dealing with the French. 2½ pp. [C.O.5, 43, fos. 312–313d]

1707

[?1771]

Case of holders of Reconnoissances given in exchange for Canada paper. 3½ large pp. [C.O.5, 43, fos. 324–325d]

1708

[?1771]

Draft of part of convention between England and France for liquidation of Canada paper money. 1½ pp. [C.O.5, 43, fos. 334–335d]

The following undated petitions, addressed mainly to the King and the Earl of Hillsborough, appear to belong to the period of Hillsborough's tenure of office as Secretary of State for the American Department.

1709

Memorial of Isaac Levy to Committee of Council for Plantation Affairs, showing that he was unlawfully dispossessed of islands of Ossaba and Sapalo off coast of Georgia in 1759 and setting forth terms on which he would take as compensation lease of coalmine in Cape Breton Island. 3 pp. [C.O.5, 114, fos. 9–10d]

1710

Memorial of proprietors of land in East Florida to Earl of Hillsborough, requesting appointment of one of H.M.'s sloops to St Augustine. *Copy.* 1½ pp. *Annexed:*

i. Note that *Bonetta* sloop, ten guns, eighty men, and a schooner, eight guns, thirty men, are stationed on East Florida coast. ½ small p. [C.O.5, 114, fos. 11–14d]

1711

Memorial of linen manufacturers of Great Britain and Ireland to Commissioners of Treasury, seeking legislation to stop frauds in entry of foreign linen and to continue and extend bounty on export of British linens. 1½ pp. [C.O.5, 114, fos. 15–16d; another copy at fo. 17]

1712

Memorial of John Metcalfe, late salt master at Fort Pitt, to Earl of Hillsborough, with complaints against Captain Ecuyer, and requesting relief. 3 pp. *Enclosed:*

i. Account of John Metcalfe's damages. 1½ pp. [C.O.5, 114, fos. 19–22d]

1713

Memorial of Peter Taylor, on behalf on William Collins, Clerk of Crown and Common Pleas in East Florida, to Earl of Hillsborough, complaining of no salary being attached to his offices. *Signed.* 1¼ pp. [C.O.5, 114, fos. 44–45d]

1714

Petition of John Wright, formerly private in 43rd regiment, to Earl of Hillsborough, soliciting royal bounty. 1 p. [C.O.5, 114, fos. 46–47d]

1715

Memorial of George Campbell to Earl of Hillsborough, soliciting government of Michilimackinac, now vacant. *Signed.* 1 p. [C.O.5, 114, fo. 48]

1716

Memorial of merchants trading to Canada to Earl of Hillsborough, recommending George Campbell to be Governor of Michilimackinac. *Signed,* Edward Bridger and twenty-four others. 1 p. [C.O.5, 114, fos. 49–50d]

1717

Memorial of Jonathan Hoare of Nova Scotia, late an officer in H.M.'s service, to Earl of Hillsborough, soliciting employment. *Signed.* 2¼ pp. [C.O.5, 114, fos. 52–53d]

1718

Petition of Elizabeth Tolver, formerly of Guadeloupe, now of Dublin, to the King, seeking reward for her service in discovering plot to massacre the British during the occupation of Guadeloupe. *Signed.* 1 p. *Enclosed:*

    i. Dublin, 2 December 1768. Declaration by Major William Butler and six other officers of 63rd and 65th regiments that facts in above petition are true. Statement by Simon Fraser, A.D.C., that the petition was laid before Lord Lieutenant of Ireland and £30 ordered to defray petitioner's expenses. *Copy.* ¾ p. [C.O.5, 114, fos. 54–55d]

1719

Petition of Lieutenant Patrick Sinclair, 15th regiment, late commander of H.M.'s vessels on Lakes Erie, Superior [MS: Sinclair], Huron and Michigan, to Earl of Hillsborough, soliciting vacant post of superintendent of navigation, arms etc. on the Lakes. 2 pp. *Endorsed,* From Colonel Mackey. *Enclosed:*

    i. Unsigned statement of need for supervisor to check private contractors who man and victual the vessels on the Lakes. 1 small p. [C.O.5, 114, fos. 56–59d]

1720

Petition of William Moor, minister in Halifax, on behalf of himself and other dissenting ministers in Nova Scotia, to the King, soliciting contribution to support of ministry. *Signed.* 2½ pp. *Enclosed:*

    i. *Case of the Protestant Dissenters in Nova Scotia.* Printed. 3½ pp. [C.O.5, 114, fos. 60–63d]

1721

Memorial of John Christopher Roberts, Secretary, Register etc. of Quebec, to Earl of Hillsborough, complaining of non-payment of certain fees assigned to his office. 3 pp. *Enclosed:*

i. Quebec, 28 October 1768. Extract from Public Register, by Boisseau, greffier. *French.* Certified by George Allsopp, Deputy Clerk of Enrolments. *Copy.* 1 p.

ii. Quebec, 24 October 1768. Extract from same by same. *French.* Certified, as No. i. *Copy.* 1 p.

iii. Opinion by Charles Yorke in favour of claims of Secretary of Quebec. *Signed.* Case certified truly stated, by John Pownall. 1¼ pp. [C.O.5, 114, fos. 72–80d, with copy of No. iii]

1722

Petition of John Hunt to Earl of Hillsborough, soliciting appointment as missionary on Island of St John. *Signed.* 2 small pp. [C.O.5, 114, fos. 81–82d]

1723

Memorial of Lady Moore, widow of Sir Henry Moore, Bt., late Governor of New York, on behalf of herself and children, to the King, soliciting some recognition of expenses Governor Moore was at and which his death prevented being made by land grants. 1½ pp. [C.O.5, 114, fos. 83–84d]

1724

Petition of H.M.'s Messengers in Ordinary to Earl of Hillsborough, for increase of salary. 2½ pp. [C.O.5, 114, fos. 85–86d]

1725

Case of Nicholas Darby, merchant, who first began to establish a fishery on coast of Labrador in 1765; with complaints against Lieutenant Samuel Davis. 2½ pp. *Enclosed:*

i. H.M.S. *Otter*, Spithead, 19 October 1770. Certificate by William Williams, formerly commanding officer on coast of Labrador, that Lieutenant Davis illegally took Nicholas Darby's oil. *Copy.* ½ p. [C.O.5, 114, fos. 87–89d]

1726

Petition of Anne Underwood, daughter of the late Sir John Stuart, one of the Knights of Nova Scotia, to the King, seeking permission for her husband John, to resign his place as land waiter in the Customs to another gentleman whereby he would receive a small present. *Copy.* 2 pp. [C.O.5, 114, fos. 96–97d]

1727

3 April, Tom's Coffee House, Cornhill, London

Committee of Proprietors of British Canada paper to Earl of Hillsborough, enclosing the following. ¼ small p. *Enclosed :*

    i. Memorial of holders of reconnoissances given in exchange for Canada paper, to Viscount Weymouth, seeking assistance in obtaining payment. 2 pp. [C.O.5, 114, fos. 98–101d]

1728

Petition of John Cramond, late of Norfolk, Virginia, to Earl of Hillsborough, soliciting appointment to command one of the small vessels to be stationed on North American coasts to prevent smuggling. ½ p. [C.O.5, 114, fo. 106]

1729

11 Nov., Lincoln's Inn Sq., London

Edward Montagu to [? Earl of Hillsborough], declining to act in the way suggested. *Signed.* 1 small p. *Endorsed,* Mr Montagu, Remonstrance. [C.O.5, 114, fos. 109–110d]

1730

Petition of Robert Wills and William Ray, merchants of Belfast, to Earl of Hillsborough, soliciting an order to government of South Carolina for payment of bounty in respect of poor Protestants transported to that colony in 1767. 2½ pp. [C.O.5, 114, fos. 111–112d]

1731

Petition of Nathaniel Jones, barrister-at-law, formerly Chief Justice of the Jerseys, to Earl of Hillsborough, asking for redress for wrongs done to him in 1760. 1 p. [C.O.5, 114, fos. 118–119d]

1732

Memorial of Moses Franks to the King, on behalf of sufferers by Indian depredations in North America, for confirmation of grants of Indian lands. 2¼ pp. [C.O.5, 114, fos. 120–121d]

1733

Memorial of Captain Joseph Smith Speer to Earl of Hillsborough, soliciting royal bounty in recognition of his services in collecting plans and charts. 1 p. [C.O.5, 114, fos. 122–123d]

1734

Petition of John Shattock, of the Narrangansett nation, on behalf of himself and the whole of that nation, to the King, soliciting order to government of Rhode Island restoring lands unlawfully sold and forbidding purchase of such lands for the future. *Signed*(?). [C.O.5, 114, fos. 124–125d]

1735

Petition of Colonel John Bradstreet to Earl of Hillsborough, soliciting recognition of his services in the expedition against Fort Frontenac and as deputy Q.M.G. in North America. 1 p. [C.O.5, 114, fos. 126–127d]

1736

Petition of inhabitants of Massachusetts in London to the King, protesting at non-summoning of the General Court of that province. 2½ pp. [C.O.5, 114, fos. 128–129d]

1737

Memorial of George Middleton, formerly captain in Scottish troops of the States General, to Earl of Hillsborough, soliciting appointment in North America. *Signed*(?). 2¼ small pp. [C.O.5, 114, fos. 134–135d]

1738

Memorial of William Gerard de Brahm, Surveyor of Southern District of North America, to Lords of Treasury, seeking payment of £700 17s. *Signed*. 1 p. *Endorsed*, Approved by Commissioners for Trade and Plantations of the memorial being presented to Lords of Treasury. [C.O.5, 114, fos. 139–140d]

1739

Petition of Lieut.-Colonel Ralph Walsh, 31st regiment, to the King, soliciting appointment as Governor of Pensacola, vacant by death of Governor Elliott. ¾ p. [C.O.5, 114, fos. 141–142d]

1740

Memorial of Major Joseph Gorham, formerly commandant of H.M.'s rangers in North America and one of the Council in Nova Scotia, to the King, soliciting appointment to one of the vacant American governments or some other recognition. 3 pp. [C.O.5, 114, fos. 143–144d]

1741

Memorial of Robert Farmar, late major, 34th regiment, to Earl of Hillsborough, soliciting the government of West Florida, vacant by death of Governor Elliott. 1½ pp. [C.O.5, 114, fos. 145–146d]

1742

Case of George Clarke, Secretary of New York, for restoration of office of Register, granted separately by Governor Moore to John French in 1766. 3 pp. *Enclosed*:

i. 10 April 1761. Letters patent granting office of Secretary of New York to George Clarke. *Copy.* 1½ pp.

ii. 6 December 1689. Letters patent appointing Matthew Clarkson Secretary of New York. *Copy.* 1¼ pp. [C.O.5, 114, fos. 149–154d]

1743

Memorial of Lieutenant James Douglas, Royal Regiment, to Viscount Barrington, soliciting recognition of his services since 1745. 1 p. [C.O.5, 114, fos. 175–176d]

1744

Petition of Thomas Walter Yonge, Waggon-Master-General of Great Britain, to the King, praying for grant of 20,000 acres of land in Cape Breton Island. ¾ p. [C.O.5, 114, fos. 179–180d; another copy at fos. 181–182d]

1745

Memorial of Jacques Arnold of Strasbourg, brother of Abraham Arnold, sugar-refiner of Jamaica, who died 25 May 1766, concerning inheritance of property. *French.* 1½ pp. [C.O.5, 114, fos. 183–184d]

1746

Memorial of Lieutenant Philip Pittman, 15th regiment, to Earl of Hillsborough, soliciting appointment as Lieut.-Governor of Tobago. 1¼ pp. [C.O.5, 114, fos. 185–186d]

1747

Petition of Elizabeth Tolver, late of Guadeloupe, to Earl of Hillsborough, soliciting royal bounty for her services in discovering a conspiracy against the British during the occupation of Guadeloupe. *Signed.* 2¾ pp. [C.O.5, 114, fos. 191–192d]

1748

Memorial of Allan Auld, of London, merchant, and James Lawrie, settler in Bay of Honduras, to Earl of Hillsborough, requesting appointment of a person in a ministerial character to uphold the rights of settlers against the Spaniards. *Signed.* 2 pp. [C.O.5, 114, fos. 195–196d]

1749

Petition of inhabitants of Bay of Honduras to Earl of Hillsborough, requesting appointment of Captain James Lawrie to be Governor or Superintendent there. *Signed,* James Lawrie and nineteen others. 2½ pp. [C.O.5, 114, fos. 197–198d]

1750

Memorial of Allan Auld of London, merchant, and James Lawrie, settler in Bay of Honduras, to Earl of Hillsborough, seeking redress for molestations by Spaniards. *Signed.* 2½ pp. *Annexed:*

i. Laws and regulations for government of H.M.'s subjects in Bay of Honduras, presented by Sir William Burnaby, c-in-c. Jamaica Squadron, approved by the inhabitants, and confirmed by Sir W. Burnaby in 1765. *Printed.* 4 pp. [C.O.5, 114, fos. 199–202d]

1751

Memorial of merchants trading to West Florida to Earl of Hillsborough, notifying defenceless state of that province. *Signed*, George Johnstone and twenty-five others. 3 pp. [C.O.5, 114, fos. 203–204d]

1752

Memorial of Lieutenant Adolphus Benzell, Royal Regiment, to the King, for recognition of his services since 1755. 1 p. [C.O.5, 114, fos. 221–222d]

1753

Memorial of Lady Catherina Maria Moore, widow of Sir John Henry Moore, Bt., former governor of New York, to the King, soliciting royal bounty for herself and children. 2¾ pp. [C.O.5, 114, fos. 264–265d]

1754

Memorial of Michael Scott, barrister-at-law, formerly Attorney-General of Grenada, to Earl of Hillsborough, soliciting the office of Chief Justice of Grenada. 2¼ pp. [C.O.5, 114, fos. 266–267d]

Registers etc.

1755

Lists of South Carolina land grants, 31 October 1769–12 April 1771: part of a volume covering 1768–1773. [C.O.5, 399, fos. 40–67]

1756

Lists of same, 4 May 1771–1 October 1771. [C.O.324, 54, fos. 176–180d]

1757

West Florida. Land grants, 1769–1770: eighty-five printed forms completed, with some blanks. [C.O.5, 606]

1758

West Florida. Register of mortgages, conveyances, manumissions, 1768–1772, with index. [C.O.5, 605]

1759

West Florida. Register of letters of attorney, bonds, bills of sale, manumissions, beginning 8 November 1771: part of a volume covering 1771–1779. [C.O.5, 613]

1760

West Florida. Register of mortgages, with index: part of a volume covering 1770–1779. [C.O.5, 612]

1761

North America. Entries of army commissions, stating name, rank, regiment of officer, and date of commission. [For 1770–1771: C.O.324, 42, pp. 164–319]

INDEX

NOTE ON THE INDEX

References are to entry-numbers *not* to pages.

Board Letters

Signers of letters from the Board of Admiralty, the Board of Ordnance and the Board of Trade (Commissioners for Trade and Plantations) have *not* been indexed.

Addresses

Most letters bear the name of the Government office or provincial capital in which they were written, e.g. Whitehall, Treasury, New York, Boston. These have *not* been indexed. Addresses of letters written from less common places, e.g. Alamance, Cussiters, Dartmouth, *have* been indexed.

Indians

Indians were mentioned by correspondents sometimes as 'Indians'; sometimes under their national names, e.g. 'Cherokees'; and sometimes by geographical location e.g. 'Western Indians'. References in the index may occur under: (i) the national name; (ii) 'Indians' generally; (iii) 'Indians, Northern', 'Indians, Southern', 'Indians, Western'; (iv) the colony particularly concerned, e.g. 'West Florida, Indians'. In the case of the Creek Indians, references occur under 'Creeks', 'Creeks, Lower', 'Creeks, Upper'.

INDEX

Abery, Alexander, Inspector of R. Thames, report by, 1486ii.

Abikas, Upper Creeks, 1700i.

Accomack, Va., Naval Officer's returns for, 1589v, 1589viii-ix.

Adams, Samuel, 349ii, 1175.

Adamson, Robert, soldier, 14th regt., affidavit of, 709ix.

Addicott, John, soldier, 29th regt., affidavit of, 709lxviii.

Admiralty Courts in America (see also Vice-Admiralty): not competent to try cases of murder on high seas, 567; objections to, 440; proceedings, 213.

Admiralty, Board of (see also under Stephens, P.).
letters from, 285, 319, 502, 557, 594, 595, 874, 910, 941, 1131, 1322, 1547, 1552, 1585, 1615, 1619, 1632, 1682, 1685.
letters to, 15, 91, 103, 207, 294, 307–309, 341, 474, 626–628, 670, 843–845, 881, 883, 901, 936, 937, 1110, 1144,
petitions to, 874i, 1660ii,
pirate sent to, 3,
plans of lands e. and w. of Mississippi in office of, 398,
secretary, see Stephens, P.,
survey of N.S. by, 1515.

Advocate-General, of England, see Marriott, J.

Aeolus, H.M.S., 1541ii.

Africa, merchants trading to, petitions of, 375, 479.

Aiken, James, of Mooretown, N.Y., affidavit of, 1047liv.

Ainslie, Thomas, Collector of Customs, Quebec: dispute with Governor Carleton, 457, 457i, 457vii, 457xi, 457xiii, 457xvi; letters from, 457xiv, 457xvii, 666; letter to, 457x; memorial of, 1068.

Aitkin, John, in Quebec, 290i.

Alabama R., 1525, Indian disturbances on, 1121ii.

Alabamas (Alibamous), Upper Creeks, 1700i.

Alamance (Alamansee) N.C.: Battle of, 1435; accounts of, 1226, 1310i, 1326, 1326i, 1433, 1434; casualties at, 1434; letters dated at, 1226, 1433i-ii; plan of, 1434i-ii.

Alatchaway Indians, see Latchaway.

Albany, N.Y.: affidavits sworn at, 783i, 1047xliv-xlviii; C. of E. at, 1440xii.

Albany County, N.Y.: Indian title to land in, 1630i; land grants in 1093xiv, 1093xvii; riot in, 710xiv.

Alexander, Giles, of Boston, petition of, 932i.

Alexander, Moses, col. in N.C. militia, 1434iv.

aliens, 317, 433, and see naturalization.

Alleghany (Allegane) Mts., lands to w. of (see also under Stanwix, Treaty of; Va., land grants; Walpole, T.); disposal of, 545; land grants in, 554i, 674, 674i, 674iii-iv, 694, 694i; settlement of, 400; white encroachments on, 1656.

Allen, Robert, negotiator on behalf of proprietors of Canada Reconnoissances, 1422: letters from, 944, 1001, 1083, 1156, 1176, 1177, 1599; letter to, 1083i.

All Saints parish, Craven Co., S.C., 737, 803.

Allsopp, George, deputy clerk of Council of Quebec: documents certified by, 221ii, 246i, 290, 453i, 457ii-v, 457ix-x, 564i, 665i, 904i, 1123i, 1554i, 1559i, 1721i-ii, letters from, 457iv, 457x; letter to, 457v.

Americans, remain subjects of England, 438.

Amherst, Lieut.-Gen. Sir Jefrey, 892, petition of, 363i, 388.

Amherst, Fort, I. of St John, letter dated from, 1497.

Amit R., W. Fla., 1336i: map of, mentioned, 1535; report on, 1535; town proposed on, 1535.

Anderson, Andrew, petitions for land in N.Y., 1093ii.

Anderson, James, fine on, in Va., remitted, 1347, 1642.

Andrew, negro servant of O. Wendell, witness in Boston trials, 735ii, 774i.

Andrews, Rev. William, of Schenectady, N.Y., 1440xiii.

Anna Teresa, packet, 757.

Annapolis, Md., printer at, 447i.

Annapolis Royal, N.S., 331i, fortifications: dismantling of, 538, 543, 654; plan of, 331ii.

Anson Co., N.C., disaffection in, 257.

Antelope, H.M.S., 883i.

Antigua, ordnance in, 79; settler from, in Ga., see Mackinnan, C.W.

Apalachicola, limit of Creek line, 134i.

Appleton, John, witness in Boston trial, 774i.

463

[Mississippi River and Valley]
398i, 1052, 1200,
Choctaws claim land on, 134, do not, 1536i,
entrance to, ship fails to find, 415, French on, 618,
fur-trade, 481i: cannot be guaranteed to G.B., 542; illicit, see *Florida Packet,*
Indians of, 1033: attitude of, to forts, 706; British and Spanish agents for, contrasted, 762; deputy needed for, 763, 977, 989, 1121i, 1200, and see Thomas, J.; small tribes, 1535, 1536i; trade, 618,
lands to e. and w. of, plans of, mentioned, 398,
mines, 1043,
navigability, 53, 618, 1092, 1545i,
smuggling, 1200, see *Florida Packet,*
Spanish troops and settlements on and near, 374, 417i, 618, 623, 923, 1044,
survey of, 754, 850,
trade of, 618, 706.
Mississippi River, Lower (see also under Bute; Manchac; Miss. R.; Iberville; Natchez): British troops on, needed, 1336, 1336i, 1535; Indians, 134ii, 393, and see Thomas, J.; land grants on, 1336, 1336i-ii, 1525viii, 1535; map of, mentioned, 1535; settlement, 482i, 1325, 1646, and see Natchez; survey of, needed, 1336i, and see under W. Fla.
Mississippi River, Upper (see also under Chartres; Illinois; Kaskaskia; Miss. R.): French troops on, 399; fur-trade, 434i, 706; Spanish commander, attentive to Indians, 1441.
Missouri, River, trade, 618, fur-trade, 434i.
Mitchell, Jacob, in N.C., 1434iv.
Mitchell, William, of James R., Va., memorial of, 1316i.
Mobile, W. Fla.,
Act erecting county of, disallowed, 877, 1257, 1284, 1314,
barracks, 70, 476,
Customs officer, see Blackwell, J.,
fort, old, ruinous, 70, 476, 570, 570v, 1042,
Fort Charlotte, 1349: plans of, 1349 xiii; reports on, 1349vi-viii,
garrison at, 531,
Indians at, 531: commissioners for, see Henderson, Westrop; congress, 1525, 1525x, 1591, 1697, 1700; depredations, 498,
inhabitants of, address by, 312viii,
lands at, held by French and Indian title, 333,
letters dated at, 550iii, 756ii-iii, 756 viii, 763ii, 763iv, 1032i, 1389, 1525ix, 1536ii, 1697, 1699, 1700,
minister at, see Gordon,
road to Pensacola from, 216,
Treaty of (1765), with Choctaws,

134i.
Mobile Bay, British troops at, 216, 487i; new town on, needed, 70, plan of, 487ii.
Mobile River, British post on, cost of proposed, 216i; Choctaw boundary, 134.
Mobiliens, Indians, desert to Spaniards, 1336i.
Moelle River, 904.
Mohawk River, 1047xiii, 1630i.
Mohicans, agent, see Gracraft, R.; complain of white encroachment, 1656i.
Molineaux, William, leader in non-importation, Boston, 56ii.
Monberaut, Montault de, former deputy for Indian affairs, W. Fla. (1764–65), complaint of, 550, 550i-iii, 551, 756, 756i-xiv.
Monk's Corner, S.C., 389.
Monmouth Co., N.J., riots in, 303, 303i, 467.
Monsell, Capt. William, 29th regt., 709 lxxii.
Montagu, Lord Charles, Governor of South Carolina: arrives in S.C., 1528, 1528i-ii; going to S.C., 717, 736, 821, 1026, 1088, 1189, 1203; instruction, additional to, 236i, 268i, 1250i; letters from, 733, 794, 1528, 1574, 1605; letters to, 717, 736, 1145, 1640.
Montagu, Edward, agent of Va., letter from, 1729; letter to, 903; petition of, 51, 108.
Montagu, John, Earl of Sandwich: Lord Commnr. for Admiralty, for letters signed by, see under Admiralty, Lords; Postmaster-General, letter to, 376, and see under P.M.G.
Montagu, Rear-Admiral [John], 1107.
Montague, General, of Windsor, 1521i.
Montagu Fort, Bahamas, plan of, 570iii; report on, 570iv.
Montgomerie, Archibald, Earl of Eglinton, petition of, for land in N.Y., 455i.
Montgomery, Hugh, soldier, 29th regt., trial of, 925i.
Montreal, 457xvii, 506; letters dated at, 541, 690, 1692, 1692i, 1692iii.
Montressor, Capt. John, engineer, 1091 iv: estimates by, 1266ii-iii; repairs to C. William by, 596; plans by, 570i-iii, 923i; reports by, 923ii-iv.
Moodie, Thomas, deputy Secretary of Ga., gaoled, 1018, 1018ii.
Mooers, Edmund, petition of, 600iii.
Moore, Sir Henry, late govr. of N.Y., 5, 11, 352, 516i, 1440, 1723, 1753; letter from, 1126i.
Moore, Lady, widow of above, memorials of, 1723, 1753.
Moore, James, col. in N.C. militia, 1434iv.
Moor, Jacob, soldier, 14th regt., affidavit of, 709xliii.
Moore, Lambert, Comptroller of Customs, N.Y., report by, 1658i.

under masts; N.C.; pines; pitch; tar; turpentine.

Neale, Christopher, capt. in N.C. militia, 1434iv.

Ned, negro of J. Hatton, 1393xi-xii.

Needham, see Hindley & Needham.

Neelson, Archibald, to enquire into Greek settlement, E. Fla., 1577.

Neil, Arthur, of Tower of London, report by, 69.

Neil, Arthur, appointed Cllr. of W. Fla., 175, 237.

Neilson, Charles, Naval Officer, Rappahannock, returns by, 1589vi-vii.

Neisser, George, of New York, 1440xvi.

Nelson, William, President of Council, acting Governor of Virginia, 1029, 1119, 1456: addresses to, 1395ii-iii; assumes govt., 668, 668i-ii; documents signed by, 705i-ii; letters from, 668, 674, 693, 694, 705, 730, 825, 848, 849, 863, 864, 963–965, 1015, 1077–1079, 1133, 1227, 1248, 1249, 1286, 1316, 1347, 1395, 1417, 1424, 1468; letters to, 822, 900, 988, 1315, 1445, 1505; memorial to, 1316i; speech of, 1395i.

Neothlocko or Second Man, small medal chief, Upper Creeks, 793ii, 1700i.

Nepesiquet, N.S., land grant at, 869i.

Ness, John, ensign, 14th regt., 709x, 709xiii; affidavit of, 709vii.

Neufville, John, non-importer, S.C., 779.

New Bern (Newbern), N.C.: govr.'s palace at, 390; grand jury, 1119ii; school at, Act concerning, disallowed, 699, 827, 828, 1293.

New Bordeaux, S.C., 1628.

Newbury, N.Y., 1047lv.

New England: Eastern, 385, 1089, and see Mass., Eastern; manufactures, 1523; ships of, at Magdalen I., 1540; survey of, 1523.

New Fane township, N.Y., 932i.

Newfoundland: Act of Parliament (10 & 11 William III) respecting, 340; British troops in, 892, and see under St John's; Customs officers, see Dun, fees in, 368i, 1687ii, and see under St John's; Customs officers, see Dun, A., govt.'s right to appoint, questioned, 1687i; engineers at, 1160; fishery (see also under fishery; France), 319, 368, 368i, 884i, 1131, 1138, French, 240i, 323, 323i, 340, 732, 732i, 884ii; Governor, see Byron, J., instructions to, 319, 1131, 1144; Naval Officer, fees of, 368i, needed, 480, post of, solicited, 1196iii; R.N. ships for, 881, 941i; shore-establishments, growth of, 240; traders etc., memorials of, 368i, 480iv.

Newgate pardon, for use in Mass., 1460, 1638, 1644.

New Hampshire,
Acts: reports on, 509, 875, 1103; sent to England, 697, 1523; for dividing province into counties, 135, 509, 522, 664, 801, 814, 833, 1523; to

restrain usury, 509, 523, 801, 814,
agriculture, encouragement of, an impediment to manufacture, 1523,
Assembly: minutes and journals, 697, 1523, 1523iv; petition of, against Revenue Acts, 255, 466; proceedings of, 135, 1523,
bills of credit, 1007, 1306, circulate in Mass., 1037,
boundary with N.Y., 1047, 1047xxiii, 1093: disorders on, 1350, 1549; disputed, 516i, 783, 1047, 1047i-l, 1640, and see Conn. R., lands to w. of; map of, 1047xxix,
bounds of, defined (1742), 1047viii, (1750), 1047xiv, (1764), 1047x,
building contractors in, 773,
coins, foreign, rating of, stopped, 316, 367, 386, 397, 456i, 800, 814, 1523,
Council: appointments to, 255, 636, 711, 731, 814; judicial functions of, 1594; proceedings of, on lands w. of Conn. R., 135, 1465i,
counties, Act for dividing province into, 509, 522, 664, 801, 833,
Crown Point claimed by, 516i,
Governor, see Wentworth, J.: custody of idiots by, 9, 39, 606, 961; decline of power in trade matters, 1523; judicial functions, 1594,
idiots, custody of, 9, 39, 606, 961,
judicature, system of, altered, 509,
land grants, w. of Conn. R., 1047xxv, 1047xxvii, 1283, and see Conn. R., lands to w. of,
loyalty of, 605,
magistrates, suppress riot, 1607,
manufacturers, 135, 1523,
Mass. boycotts trade with, 689,
militia, 1523,
Naval Officer, decline of authority of, 1523; deputy, see Russell, E.,
non-importation, no association for, 135,
quitrents, 1523,
roads, many made, 1523,
Secretary, see Atkinson, T.,
survey of, 1523,
Surveyor of White Pines, see Ruggles,
usury, Act to restrain, 509, 523, 801, 814,
wilderness, settlement of, 1523.

New Hampshire Gazette, cutting from, 218ii.

New Jersey,
Acts: reports on, 508, 789, 1109, 1318; sent to England, 95, 919; for dividing Bergen Common, disallowed, 95, 211, 249, 381, 404; for duty on slaves imported, 789; for emitting bills of credit, disallowed, 95, 250, 381, 404, 632; for enlarging Assembly, 795; for choosing representatives to Assembly, 508, 527; for regulating practice of law, disallowed, 508, 519, 798, 812; for recovery of debts, disallowed, 303, 1318, 1327,

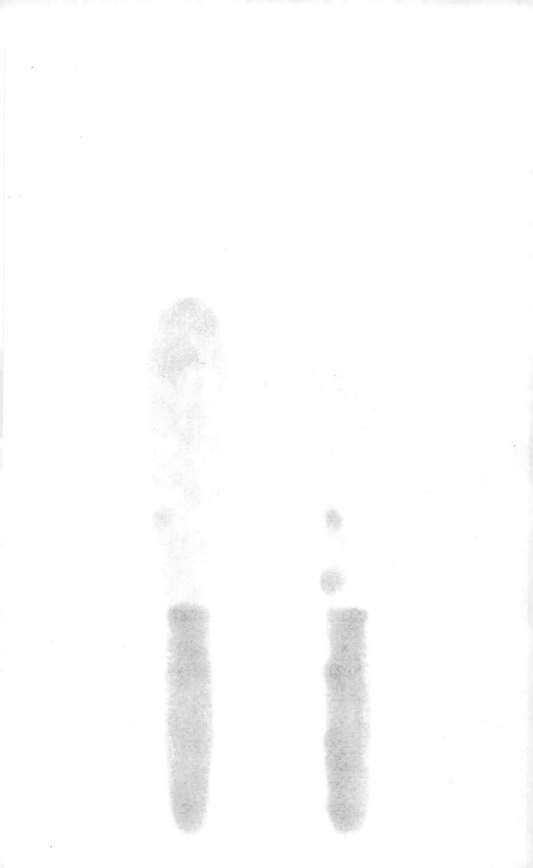

DATE DUE	